A TASTE OF FREEDOM

A TASTE OF FREEDOM

The ICU in Rural South Africa 1924–1930

HELEN BRADFORD

Yale University Press · New Haven and London 1987

Designed by Faith Glasgow
Set in Linotron Bembo and printed in Great Britain by The Bath Press, Avon

Library of Congress Cataloguing-in-Publication Data

Bradford, Helen.
  A taste of freedom.

  Bibliography: p.
  Includes index.
  1. I.C.U. (South Africa)—History. 2. Trade-unions,
Black—South Africa—History. I. Title.
HD8801.A5I1634 1987   331.88′0968   87-10451
ISBN 0-300-03873-9

To all those who worked the land
but reaped bitter harvest,
especially   Charles Kumalo
             Leonard Mdingi
             Rose Mthimunye
        and Elijah Ngcobo

CONTENTS

List of Illustrations   ix
List of Abbreviations   x
Glossary   xi
Preface   xii

1. INTRODUCTION   1
    Formation of the ICU   2
    Years of Flux: the mid-1920s   8
    Remaking the Past   13

2. MASTERS AND SERVANTS: *The South African
    Countryside, 1920–1930*   21
        Commercial Agriculture: The 'Squeezing' of
            Farmers   23
        The 'Squeezing' of Blacks on Farms   34
        Ideologies and Cultures   41
        Resistance and Repression   49
        The Dynamics of Dispossession   55
        Conclusion   59

3. EDUCATED AND CIVILIZED AGITATORS: *The Social
    Origins and Character of ICU Leadership, 1924–1929*   63
        Downward Class Mobility   67
        Downward Identification: Politics, Ideology and
            Struggle   74
        Upward Identification: Salaried Positions in
            the ICU   81

4. ORGANIZATION AND IDEOLOGY, 1926–1928   88
    Traditionalists, Chiefs and the ICU   95
    The Land Question: 'Derived' and 'Inherent'
        Solutions   104
    Organization in Rural Hinterlands   107
    Socialism and Nationalism   113
    Liberalism and Farm Workers   119
    Separatist Christianity and Garveyism   123
    Tactics   127
    Embryonic Organs of Popular Power   138
    Conclusion   143

5. RESISTANCE, REPRESSION AND REFORM: *The ICU
    in the Transvaal, 1926–1929*   145
    Land and Liberation: the Eastern Transvaal,
        1926–1928   148
    Wages, Workers and Whites: the Western,
        Central and Northern Transvaal, 1927–1929   161
    Conclusion   182

6. LYNCH LAW AND LABOURERS: *The ICU
    in Umvoti, 1927–1928*   186
    uMgungundlovana: Agrarian Struggles
        from the Late Nineteenth Century   188
    The 'I SEE YOU' in Greytown   195
    Friction between Farmers and State   204

7. PIGS, AMERICANS AND THE MILLENNIUM: *The ICU
    in the Transkeian Territories, 1927–1932*   213
    Ama Melika Ayeza   214
    The ICU in Pondoland   218
    Lightning, Pigs and Witchcraft   224
    Millenarianism in Eastern Pondoland and
        Southern Natal   228
    The ICU in the Broader Transkeian Territories   240

8. CONCLUSION   246
        Sprawling across the South African Stage   247
        Imperfectly Drilled   256
        Patterns of Participation, Opposition and
            Struggle in the Countryside   259
        No Easy Struggle for Freedom   272

Notes   279
Bibliography   339
Index   355

LIST OF ILLUSTRATIONS

1. ICU Branches in existence at some time between 1919 and 1925   7

2. ICU Branches in existence at some time between 1926 and 1930   14

3. Combined index of producers' prices of agricultural (excluding pastoral) products   28

4. Total area under cultivation (including fallow land) on white farms   28

5. Price of unrefined wool   30

6. Number of white-owned woolled sheep on farms   30

7. Map of the Transvaal   147

8. Map of the Transkeian Territories   216

9. Map of Natal   251

ABBREVIATIONS

AME	African Methodist Episcopal Church
ANC	African National Congress
CNC	Chief Native Commissioner
CP	Communist Party of South Africa
ICU	Industrial and Commercial Workers' Union of Africa
ICU *yase* Natal	Industrial and Commercial Workers' Union of Natal
ICWU	Industrial and Commercial Coloured and Native Workers' (Amalgamated) Union of Africa
IICU	Independent Industrial and Commercial Workers' Union of Africa
NAU	Natal Agricultural Union
SAAU	South African Agricultural Union
TAU	Transvaal Agricultural Union
TNC	Transvaal Native Congress

GLOSSARY

abaphakathi	people-in-the-middle
Amalaita gangs	urban African gangs of 'social bandits', consisting largely of the unemployed and domestic servants
Ama Melika ayeza	the Americans are coming
AmaRespectables	members of the 'respectable' African elite
baas	master
igoso	leader of a dance association, transformed into a 'general' in 'faction fights'
imithi	medicines
impundulu	the lightning bird amongst the Mpondo
induna	headman/foreman
ingom'ebusuku	a musical style popular amongst Zulu-speaking migrants
izemtiti	pass-exempted Africans
Keaubona	'I SEE YOU' in Sotho
lobola	bridewealth amongst Zulu-speakers
'Madoda Azibozo'	'Eight-Men-in-One' – the nickname given to Alexander Jabavu
ratlahoboros	an onomatopoeic word referring to gun-toting 'Boers'
'Sisiyu'	the name by which some Mpondo knew the ICU
tshokobezi badge	the traditional Zulu war symbol, consisting of ox or cow tails bound around the head
ukuthakatha	the use of witchcraft or sorcery for the destruction of life or goods
uMgungundlovana	Greytown
utshwala	a grain-based beer of low alcoholic content
Vuka Afrika	Awake Africa

PREFACE

At the time of writing, civil war rages through South Africa. In a period of acute economic crisis, the white minority regime and monopoly capital are under more concerted attack than ever before in this century. Student uprisings, mass strikes and armed attacks by cadres of the African National Congress in the towns and cities of this country have captured world-wide attention.

Yet the extent to which the struggle has advanced in the South African countryside has received much less recognition. In the words of one Jonas, a black rural lawyer:

> People think that it is those in the urban areas who are so advanced, that they have the most access to ANC literature, but I'll tell you, it spreads first in these rural areas, before it ever reaches the cities. The cities are the last place to get the things we see regularly. I always try to explain to my friends from Joburg and Durban that they don't realize how much politically conscious in that direction the people are in the rural areas. It makes sense, anyway, because if there was to be an infiltration, who would be the first to give an ANC cadre water? It will be the people in the bush. Who will be the first to give him shelter? It will be the people in the bush. And that's why so many of them have been arrested in this area. There are many, many of these cadres who come into the country and then stay in the bush first, for a long, long time, to look at the situation.[1]

But Jonas ridiculed the idea that ANC guerillas were being delayed by the need to educate illiterate blacks about the iniquities of apartheid. He thought the foundations of their anger had been laid much earlier: by dire poverty on farms, urban influx control, and forced resettlement of millions of Africans to teeming slums in Bantustans.

> I'm satisfied that the rural people are very highly politically conscious, and they don't need anybody from the outside to tell

them what their problems are. Because they live through this whole thing, they are politicized by their living conditions, by removals. It's a lie to say that they need someone to instigate them – they don't. I think all they need, maybe, is political marshalling of their anger. If that is marshalled it can take only one direction, and that is of resistance.[2]

Sixty years ago, the rural poor were 'marshalled' by leaders of the Industrial and Commercial Workers' Union of Africa (ICU). By tapping grassroots anger in the countryside, they created one of the most radical movements ever seen in South Africa. They also demonstrated that rural struggles have a proud place in the long history of black resistance to exploitation and oppression. Today, when this lesson is in danger of being forgotten, it is useful to recall the urgings of ICU leaders: that the creation of a politics for the future is partially dependent upon the recovery of the conflicts of the past.[3]

Resurrecting protest movements of the rural under-classes is, however, a demanding as well as a valuable exercise in apartheid South Africa. Although interviews are the most important new source used in this book, white academics can perhaps be forgiven for their reluctance to mine the memories of blacks in the countryside. Many state officials know only too well that history has political implications, and permits to enter racially segregated areas are not easily obtained from Location Superintendents, Bantustan authorities, or the Security Police. Moreover, if prior clearance has not been granted, it can be even harder to persuade the elderly and vulnerable that talking about the past is neither the first nor the last step on the road to jail.[4] It is difficult to exaggerate, or to dismiss as groundless, the fear and self-censorship that generally operate when an unknown white person questions illiterate blacks about a political movement.

In July 1980, for example, my research assistant Vusi Nkumane and I arrived unannounced at a hut in a Bantustan. We were met by Elijah Ngcobo, who had acquired considerable wariness during his eighty-odd years in South Africa. His suspicions were confirmed when we casually mentioned the ICU, and at this point he refused to continue the discussion. Ultimately, however, he agreed to talk about his life as a farm labourer. In a second interview, he was sufficiently confident to describe vividly the experiences of others in the ICU.

Unfortunately, these untranscribed tapes were amongst a batch which the Security Police 'lost' after confiscating them during a raid. So in December 1981, we anxiously returned to Ngcobo, ascertained that he had not been troubled by the police in the interim, and asked if we could continue to question him. This time Ngcobo freely agreed, although he continued to deny vigorously that he himself had ever brought the Union's famed red membership ticket. Finally, at the start of our fifth interview, Elijah Ngcobo declared he 'suddenly remembered in the night' that he had been an ICU member, and began at last to talk frankly of his personal experiences in the Union.

There were many others whose 'ignorance' of ICU-inspired protest could not be shaken, or whose testimonies were subject to other weaknesses of oral history. Not only are human memories fallible, but when they are those of illiterate blacks, dates are usually the first casualty. Furthermore, much has happened since the days of the ICU, and there are occasions when new values or organizations are imposed on the old. Thus confusion between the ICU and the African National Congress is common, and some interviews have to be treated extremely gingerly because informants are speaking about a movement which sold them green or white membership cards. Similarly, there is sometimes a tendency to envisage the fate of Union activists in terms of those of latter-day organizers. According to one old man, A.W.G. Champion was imprisoned on Robben Island. In his mind, an ICU official had joined the ranks of South Africa's most famous jailed black leaders such as Nelson Mandela.

Yet no historical sources are free of bias. None can be used safely without applying such elementary rules as checking for internal consistency and external confirmation. And in these respects, much of the testimony of blacks who lived through the 1920s is as reliable as the words of whites now enshrined in archives or publications. Almost inevitably, the latter are crusted over with racial and class prejudices; almost invariably, they ignore or partially distort the resistance of the rural poor drawn from a subject race. At the very least, allowing the African rank-and-file to speak for themselves provides an essential counterbalance to information derived from the depositories of the dominant classes.

In this book, however, people and documents often 'talk' only in translation. Afrikaans has been deliberately retained in some instances: unlike English, it is a language as familiar to many rural blacks as to their white masters. But most vernacular testimonies appear solely in their English form. An effort, however, has been made to retain dialect, and to let words bear witness to their origins in a racist, multilingual society. Hence I have not bowdlerized offensive terms like 'kaffir': to do so would whitewash social relations which were considerably more distasteful. Although I have conformed to current popular usage by employing 'blacks' to refer to 'Africans',

'Indians' or 'coloureds', I have retained conventional South African terms for those who suffer from racial discrimination. Finally, instead of littering this book with *sics*, I have corrected glaring spelling, punctuation or grammatical errors only where they detract from the sense of a citation. Hence the vast majority of direct quotations are mediated by translation alone. At best, they are in the speaker's or writer's own words (partly because their meaning is sometimes delightfully ambiguous). More importantly, these expressions have their own nuances which help recapture the past, and reinforce the recognition that people's experiences were shaped by their own historical times.

The same might be said of this book, which started as a Ph.D. thesis at the University of the Witwatersrand. Here it was supervised by Charles van Onselen, Director of the African Studies Institute and its attached Oral History Project. Far and away my greatest debt is due to him. He undertook – with boundless energy, insight and intellectual vitality – to convert a misanthropic ex-mathematician into a social historian. If he did not succeed, his constant stimulation and support nonetheless powerfully shaped this work, as did his own considerable skills as an historian and writer.

Maureen Swan also shouldered the burden of teaching me these arts. She provided thought-provoking comments on almost every section of this book, as did Peter Delius, Shula Marks and Stanley Trapido. William Beinart and Baruch Hirson similarly helped me refine many arguments and awkward formulations, and were munificent with their own sources. So, too, were Tim Clynick, Tim Couzens and Rob Morrell. Jeremy Krikler obtained last-minute details; Ian Phimister kindly chased up references in a Cape newspaper; and Phillip Stickler ably drew the maps. In addition, my thanks go to my mother and to Sandi Prosalendis, who were respectively involved in mendacious and madcap attempts to secure ICU-related photographs.

Much assistance was provided by the staff of the African Studies Institute. Of those who worked for its Oral History Project, I must single out Vusi Nkumane. He initiated me into the trials of conducting interviews in rural South Africa, translated and transcribed these and other source materials and remained ever ready to help with queries about Nguni expressions. In Natal, Jacob Dhlomo and Charles Kumalo were authoritative informants, who exercised their enviable persuasive powers to convince others to talk. In Pondoland, interviewing was almost painless, thanks to the generous support of Annie Mgetyana and Leonard Mdingi.

For funding, I am grateful to the University of the Witwatersrand, which administered the Vice-Chancellor's Research Award, and to the   Human   Sciences   Research   Council.   For   their hospitality during my sojourns in Pietermaritzburg, my thanks go to Rob Morrell's parents. Much credit is due to Irene Yiangou, who transformed dog-eared thesis chapters into immaculate copy with remarkable equanimity.

Although – or because – many people found this study either irritating or unreadable, they were of enormous assistance in ensuring its completion. Raymond Suttner was particularly concerned about the accuracy of my political 'line': his attempts to improve it sometimes left indelible marks on this book. Colin Bundy knows how much his personal support has meant to me – the value of his editorial eye was outweighed only by his assumption of an inordinate amount of domestic labour. By displaying no interest whatsoever in the ICU, Helen Mathews and Liz McGregor helped maintain my sanity. My debt is equally great to Lynn Maseko. Indeed, I held her responsible for the original thesis, and, as a less ambiguous accolade, am deeply grateful for her comradeship over the years.

1. INTRODUCTION

If the struggle for freedom by South African blacks is no easy one, then this is doubly true of those living in the countryside. They are notoriously difficult to organize, and in this respect at least, little has changed over the last sixty years. Then as today, many were grouped in tiny clusters, and separated by vast distances and wretched poverty from others even within the same district. In the reserves, the lives of women in particular were narrowly circumscribed by their season-bound struggles to wrest a living from the soil. On farms, large numbers of blacks were 'pre-industrial' in outlook; most were unskilled and easily replaceable; and almost all were inexperienced in modern forms of organization. Living on the private property of white masters, they were also subject to a host of sanctions inhibiting protest. Oppressed and far-flung, isolated and illiterate, the rural poor have for generations been given contemptuous nicknames by urban black sophisticates, and have been largely neglected by political movements.

Yet for a brief period in the 1920s, the winds of change were apparent. At a theoretical level, this was most clearly evident within the Communist Party of South Africa (CP). Founded four years after the Russian Revolution − which continued to send shock waves through the white dominant classes as proof that both capital and minority regimes could be overthrown − the Party originally dismissed African peasant-workers as submissive and backward. By 1925, however, at a conference attended by black delegates who were also leaders of the ICU, it was resolved that the land and peasant questions were of the utmost importance. Having made some progress in rural organization over the following three years, the Communist Party Executive Committee then explicitly stated the reasons for its focus on the countryside:

> South Africa is a black country, the majority of its population is black and so is the majority of the workers and peasants. The bulk

of the South African population is the black peasantry, whose land has been expropriated by the white minority. Seven eighths of the land is owned by the whites. Hence the national question in South Africa, which is based upon the agrarian question, lies at the foundation of the revolution in South Africa. The black peasantry constitutes the basic moving force of the revolution in alliance with and under the leadership of the working class.[1]

In practice, it was the ICU that demonstrated the validity of some of these observations. Infused with the traditions and demands of ordinary Africans, the movement spread like wildfire through the countryside. During 1927–28, branches mushroomed in the smallest of villages, and illiterate rural blacks formed the bulk of its estimated 150,000 to 250,000-strong membership. Faced with strikes, refusals to work, cattle-maiming and other more generalized forms of defiance, angry white farmers invoked state intervention on the grounds that this was not trade unionism but 'general upheaval'.[2] Undeniably, the ICU in its heyday mobilized rural Africans in a way which no South African movement has accomplished before or since.

It did so, however, only after years of organizing urban African and 'coloured' workers. In the later 1920s, the Union was in fact a fundamentally different creature from either the pre-1924 or the post-1930 versions. It was in its most overtly nationalist phase – due partly to an influx of schooled intellectuals as organizers. Its supporters were primarily Africans – who constituted not only the most oppressed group within the broader black populace, but also the vast majority of blacks living in the countryside. And it was operating in a very distinctive context. Thus the organizational shift to the countryside in the mid-1920s was but one of an intertwined set of discontinuities. The ICU's racial character, class composition and ideological orientation had radically altered since 1919, when a tiny trade union was formed amongst primarily 'coloured' dock workers in the southernmost city of Africa.

Formation of the ICU

Immediately after the First World War, black protest hitherto unprecedented in scope and intensity swept through South Africa.[3] Sparked by soaring inflation, it assumed forms ranging from riots and boycotts to strikes and anti-pass campaigns. Erupting in almost every major town as well as in numerous rural areas, this resistance incorporated tens of thousands of unskilled African workers. It also fuelled the emergence of trade unions, and contributed to a realignment of forces on the black political scene.

The President of the then South African Native National Congress, opposing any division between nationalist and class organizations, rejected a suggestion that workers be organized independently of his movement. But H. Selby Msimang, a leading Congressman who had headed a Bloemfontein struggle for wages of four shillings and sixpence a day, nonetheless took the initiative in calling a conference of established and aspirant working-class leaders. The thirty-odd African and 'coloured' activists who attended this July 1920 Bloemfontein gathering were drawn almost exclusively from the Orange Free State, Basutoland and the Cape. Included in their number was a twenty-four year old Nyasalander, Clements Kadalie. As Secretary of the Industrial and Commercial Union (ICU), he had been organizing 'coloured' and African dock workers in Cape Town for over a year.[4]

Those present aimed high: at no less than the creation of 'one great union of skilled and unskilled workers of South Africa, south of the Zambesi'. As their first objective they sought the promotion of the 'social, moral and intellectual interests' of members, as well as obtaining for them 'reasonable conditions of labour', and settling their differences with employers by 'conciliatory means'. Their moderation was however belied by the minimum wages they recommended: eight shillings for an eight-hour day for urban unskilled labourers, and for farm workers four shillings and sixpence (as well as an unheard-of sixpence an hour for overtime). In addition, the abolition of passes and the system of recruited labour was demanded by the newly formed Industrial and Commercial Coloured and Native Workers' (Amalgamated) Union of Africa (ICWU). Indeed, one far-sighted delegate suggested they organize in the reserves to prevent chiefs from collaborating with mine owners in extruding migrant contract workers. Finally, two prominent aims were:

(b) To promote and regulate the condition of work in the farms and to promote the general and material welfare of the members engaged in agricultural pursuits and to help them to obtain a living wage and reasonable contracts and to do all possible to afford members evicted from farms protection.
(c) To see that all females in industries and domestic services are protected by the organization, by encouraging them to enrol in all branches of the Union and to help them obtain a living wage.[5]

At first glance, this focus on two of the most oppressed sectors of the black labour force seems surprisingly radical. This was, after all, a time when females could not join the National Congress, and when 'women and suspected natives' could be excluded from meetings of the Transvaal Native Congress. However, the rights of women were vigorously promoted by the formidable Charlotte Maxeke, President of Congress's auxiliary female organization as well as the only woman present. Her arguments had resonance at the conference: its representatives were about to compete with rivals for members, in a year when black families were struggling to make ends meet, and in a city which had long been a centre of militant female resistance to passes. Thus, doubtless in the hope of mobilizing a marginalized grouping that was clearly becoming a political force in its own right, the delegates resolved

> That the time has come to admit women in the Workers' Union as full members, and that they should be allowed to receive all the same rights as male members, and there should be female representatives in our Conference. Further, that women workers receive equal pay, men and women, for the same work done, and that all members of the Conference should do all they can to get women to join the Workers' Union of the different towns.[6]

The motives for singling out agricultural labourers were much less obscure. Amongst all sectors of the black populace in the 1920s, farm labour was far and away the most important working-class occupation. Furthermore, some 85 per cent of the African population lived in the countryside, and fully proletarianized African urban dwellers were well outnumbered by migrant mine workers and their families. In this peripheral economy, overwhelmingly oriented towards primary industries, rural blacks were in fact a fairly obvious organizational target.[7]

This was certainly so for delegates from the Free State, where nearly 80 per cent of Africans lived on farms. Within weeks of the conference, two ICWU representatives were making their presence felt in the district of Kroonstad. Provided with both cover and mobility by their jobs (as insurance agent and seller of patent medicines), they traversed farms urging strikes for higher wages. By the end of 1920, the district was seething with rumours of pending unrest, and at least one black refused to hire himself out to a white agriculturist on the grounds that all farms would ultimately belong to Africans.[8]

Elsewhere, however, activists understandably preferred to concentrate on the urban constituencies with which they were familiar. Kadalie, having lost to Msimang in the battle for control of the ICWU, retired disgruntled to his dock workers. By threatening a repeat of their unsuccessful 1919 strike, he finally obtained better wages for them. He also pondered anew how to fulfil his overweening personal ambition: to become the African equivalent of the leader of a black American mass movement, the great Marcus Garvey.[9] Similarly, Samuel Masabalala returned from the 1920 conference to Port Elizabeth, where he continued to agitate for a general strike for better wages for town labourers. When he was imprisoned on a trumped-up charge in October 1920, a three-thousand-strong crowd gathered to demand his release. Twenty-four were killed, and a further eight were shot that same night as township residents went on the rampage, attempting to destroy the petrol storage depot and power station.[10]

Despite organizers' focus on the towns, such dramatic urban conflicts reverberated in the countryside. The ICU's first dock strike, called in co-operation with white unions in response to spiralling food prices, involved a refusal to handle export produce. Farmers' reactions were given additional edge by signs that the white labour movement was eagerly absorbing lessons from the Russian Revolution. Claiming somewhat hysterically that they were being subordinated to Bolsheviks, agriculturists argued that they in turn should cut off food supplies to the 'Red Flag people', and that the commando system should be revived. Events in Port Elizabeth elicited even greater alarm. Arguing that their status as the ruling race was being undermined, the Annual Conference of the South African Agricultural Union urged the Prime Minister to prevent any further such outbreaks through 'most drastic steps supported by suitable increased forces'.[11]

This alarm amongst white farmers was not entirely unfounded. News travelled quickly along channels of rural communication, especially as the migrant labour system served as a highly efficient conduit. A month after the bloody confrontation in Port Elizabeth, black agricultural labourers some five hundred miles away in the Free State had heard of the riot, and were consequently so defiant that several farmers were threatened with murder on Christmas Day. Also spreading the news were vernacular pamphlets, hidden in the merchandise which rural storekeepers received from their coastal suppliers. According to one perturbed white:

> At many wholesale stores, in Port Elizabeth and elsewhere, this packing of goods for the up-country trade is done almost entirely by native 'store-boys', who doubtless take the opportunity thus offered to transmit this poisonous stuff to the country districts, in the belief that fellow 'store-boys' will unpack the goods, and, finding the pamphlets, will act as local distributing agents. Much of this stuff is said to be of a violently racial and revolutionary character . . .[12]

Besides contributing to the development of this innovative informal organizational structure, the pent-up militancy in Port Elizabeth also precipitated further changes in the newly-formed ICWU. Pressurized from below, courted by Kadalie, and antagonized by Msimang's moderation in handling wage negotiations during his imprisonment, Masabalala began to reconsider where his allegiances lay. By the end of 1921, Kadalie had partially achieved his dream of heading an expanded ICU, incorporating the prized ICWU branch at Port Elizabeth as well as a couple of others in the Cape. Retaining almost word for word the aims hammered out at the original 1920 unity conference, this new version of the 'one great union' also brazenly kept as its full title 'The Industrial and Commercial Workers' Union of Africa'.[13]

As the ICU slowly expanded through South Africa, it gradually began to direct some organizational effort at farm labourers. By 1922, Western Province leaders were making efforts to contact workers on outlying estates. The following year, an ICU deputation appealed to a Cabinet minister to ban the common western Cape practice of paying farm workers in wine, and Kadalie informed him of labourers' appalling conditions in the Karoo. By 1925, the Union had both expanded beyond the Cape and become sufficiently prestigious for self-appointed agents to emerge. Thus one 'Jan Calf' began holding meetings on Free State farms in this year, claiming he was the ICU Secretary for Wepener. Unfortunately, not only did his wary rural audiences think he was mad and chase him away, but the state also apparently agreed and confined him to a mental hospital.[14]

Of rather more concern to landlords was ICU-linked protest in Bloemfontein, where black discontent had been mounting over both wages and police raids on beer brewers. In April 1925, a one-day stay-away by nearly 23,000 township residents flared up into a riot. Police property was destroyed; men waving red flags strode through the streets declaring 'This is our day'; and five blacks were shot dead. Almost simultaneously, anxious Bloemfontein land-owners discovered ICU members on their holdings. At a time when wool prices were falling, at least one farmers' association immediately decided to set maximum rates of pay for sheep-shearers. In the light of Union demands for a minimum farm-labour wage of four pounds a month, it also tried to persuade all other local agricultural bodies to set a uniform maximum wage of one pound a month.[15]

Even one pound a month was, however, high by standards elsewhere. Organizers' growing awareness of rural poverty was indicated in a 1925 change in the constitution, in which enrolment fees for men and women in the countryside fell from two shillings to one, and weekly subscription rates from sixpence to threepence. This was probably prompted by the abysmally low wages in the eastern Cape, at that time the heartland of the Union's rural support.

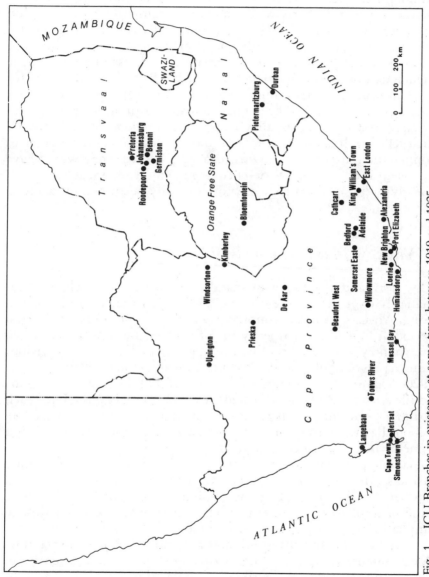

Fig. 1. ICU Branches in existence at some time between 1919 and 1925

Amongst the branches here drawing many and sometimes most of their members from the farms were Adelaide, Bedford, Cathcart, King William's Town, Port Elizabeth and Somerset East.[16]

But branches in which rural support bulked large were atypical. Although the ICU had by 1925 radiated outwards through South Africa, it was still a fairly weak body based primarily in the cities. Of just over two dozen branches, over two-thirds were in the Cape. Of its thirty thousand alleged adherents, three-quarters were said to be urban and 'detribalized'. Of its perhaps ten thousand paid-up male members, only about 1,700 were claimed to be farm workers. As for its significance, the Commissioner of Police wrote dismissively that although 'agitators' had been busy in towns arguing for the equality of black and white races, they had 'not been taken too seriously by their fellows. It is noteworthy that these pseudo-enlightened natives confine their attention to towns, probably because they would have got very little sympathy or encouragement from kraal natives.'[17] Clearly, white authorities were not especially perturbed by the ICU at this stage.

Years of Flux: The mid-1920s

This early and somewhat off-hand assessment was to change dramatically over the next few years, due partly to radical reshaping of South Africa's political economy. 1924–29 was not only the longest period of unbroken prosperity for fifty years, but also a time when the country's political profile was transformed. Following vicious state repression of the 1922 white miners' strike, as well as the 1920–22 depression and post-war weakening of the imperial grip, the South African Party was ousted in the 1924 elections. The 'Pact' coalition – an alliance between the Nationalist and South African Labour Parties – triumphantly replaced a government closely tied to mine owners and British interests.[18]

As the political home of many 'poor whites' and struggling farmers, the Nationalist Party was also an ardent advocate of Afrikaner nationalism. Together with its junior partner, it lost little time in implementing new projects. There was a marked shift in emphasis: from the fostering of mining and other links with the Empire, to the nurturing of national industrial and agricultural development, as well as a 'South Africanist' ideological orientation. Given, too, that the 1922 strike had escalated into the Rand Revolt, aid to manufacturing was combined with a welter of measures designed to transform white wage-earners and lumpenproletarians into active supporters of capitalist relations. Their struggles were increasingly institutionalized through the registration of white trade unions under the 1925 Industrial Conciliation Act. From 1925, the newly-established Wage Board set minimum 'civilized' wages in selected sweated industries. Partly at the expense of thousands of black jobs, the 'poor white' problem was tackled by promoting white employment. In addition, in 1928 the Labour Party secured partial fulfilment of a cherished project: restrictions on the entry of Mozambican labourers who constituted nearly half the African workforce on the gold mines.[19]

As this suggests, economic concessions to white wage-earners were entwined with changes in modes of utilizing and dominating African workers. Thus, although secondary industry remained a sector in which the proportion of white employees was relatively high, it was also one ever hungrier for semi-skilled black labourers. Furthermore, the Pact government's fostering of manufacturing went hand-in-hand with far-reaching developments in ways of ruling the African populace. Segregation was nothing new: it has been aptly characterized as a policy which emerged much earlier to cope with the strains of capitalist industrialization.[20] But the Pact regime sought to take it to its logical conclusion, by extending and rigidifying territorial, political, economic and ideological separation between Africans and whites. 'Gentlemen', stated the confident Minister of Native Affairs to two liberals remonstrating against his government's policy, 'there is one road for the white and another for the black and they never meet. Segregation.'[21]

This elaboration of segregationist measures had a profound impact on the development of the ICU. For one thing, intensification of racial oppression, combined with comprehensive restructuring of class relations, helped to precipitate farm tenants into the Union. For another, a significant shift occurred in the composition of leaders, who in the early 1920s were drawn mainly from poorly educated, full-time wage-earners. From about 1925, faced with ever cruder signposts redirecting them from the high road to the low, large numbers of middle-class Africans began to support the Union. Under their guidance, the movement was transformed from a Cape-based trade union, to a mass movement fighting against white supremacy.[22]

But increasingly militant political stances adopted from 1925 concealed considerable internal disintegration and decay. Constitutionally, ultimate control of the Union was vested in the Annual Conference, to which each branch could send up to four delegates. This body elected the National Council, which in 1926 consisted of thirteen paid officials (the National, General, Provincial and Financial Secretaries), together with six unpaid officers (the President, Vice-Presidents and Trustees). It was here – and especially in the sub-committees of paid leaders – that power was concentrated. From 1924 the Council had control over all funds derived from members' contributions; it had the authority to rescind any branch resolution; and it had the right to appoint or expel any official. This included Branch Secretaries, theoretically elected by a nine- to eleven-person Branch Executive, itself voted in annually by members. Indeed, the National Council's power extended right down to shop stewards, who, supposedly appointed by Branch Executives on a commission basis, had the duty of enrolling members and collecting their dues.[23]

Even on paper, this was not the most democratic of structures, particularly given the limited powers of those on the lower rungs of the hierarchy to hold to account their superiors. To make matters worse, both spirit and letter of the constitution were repeatedly violated. From at least the later 1920s, Annual Conferences were frequently drunken jamborees, at which a list of candidates for the National Council was rubberstamped; branch delegates were unable to raise local problems due to monopolization of meetings by their seniors.[24] Many major policy decisions, such as the making and breaking of alliances with other organizations, were taken by a tiny clique within the National Council, without the knowledge or consent of other officials, let alone the rank-and-file. Furthermore, organizers appointed from above, while sometimes chosen on the basis of their political credentials, often fulfilled less stringent criteria such as membership of kinship, servicemen's or old boys' networks. They rapidly became an independent force: dominating members, establishing personal fiefdoms, and regarding peculation as a per-quisite of the job. Supporters scattered through the countryside were almost powerless to control such men, especially when they were peripatetic District, Provincial or National Secretaries. Not that those clustered in the cities were much more successful: when Durban seamstress Bertha Mkhize recalled the man who was Natal Provincial Secretary from 1925, she stated simply that 'Mr Cham-pion wanted you to do as he thinks. If you don't do as he thinks, he quarrels with you.' Since usurpation of collective powers by authoritarian individual Secretaries existed at every level, such quarrels were endemic in the ICU.[25]

Matters were somewhat better at a branch level, where less mobile officials were perforce more sensitive to the need to create some sense of popular control. Although most Branch Secretaries appear to have been appointed from on high, the election of their Executives was fairly common. Often 'half-educated or raw natives', these men and women included road workers, as well as a domestic servant, a railway labourer and a water-cart driver. But, at least in the cities, there were also instances when the 'election' of a committee of more prominent members of the community was simply announced, or when Branch Executives were completely non-existent. Moreover, especially when the class backgrounds of Secretaries differed from those of the members of their committees, the latter often exercised little control over their nominal subordinates. 'We regarded them as our bosses', stated Charles Kumalo, a shop assistant elected to the Estcourt Executive in Natal due largely to his prowess as a soccer player. Understandably, he stood in awe of the educational and political skills of the ex-teachers who monopolized the paid positions.[26]

Above these 'bosses', however, stood even greater ones, who were none too chary about hiring and firing branch leaders. Indeed, on one occasion a Provincial Secretary summarily appointed an entirely new Branch Executive, having dissolved the old one on the grounds that its members were of 'pliable wig' and wavered as the wind blew them. Since senior officials were hardly innocent of swinging between militancy and subservience – itself often an effect of being black and oppressed in South Africa – such despotic intervention was not always appreciated. In 1925, Kadalie and the corpulent Senior Vice-President Alexander Jabavu (otherwise known as *Madoda Azibozo* or 'Eight-Men-in-One'), visited the Bedford branch. Unbeknown to them, they were blamed for the dismissal of a popular Branch Secretary, ousted by the Eastern Cape Provincial Secretary James Dippa. A mob of women carrying stones in their shawls surrounded the ICU office, bent on vengeance. *Madoda Azibozo* hastily counselled discretion as the better part of valour, and the two fled for their car without addressing a meeting.[27]

Perhaps the fate of what was the strongest rural branch in the Cape best illustrates the debilitating effect of undemocratic practices. When the Adelaide office was first opened in January 1925, farm workers flocked to buy their red membership cards because 'they were convinced that through this organization they would become free men'.[28] Within weeks, however, rank-and-file confidence was shaken by conflict between the elected Branch Executive and the discredited Dippa. Although the latter's opportunism was repeatedly reported to head office, and despite the fact that he was clearly embezzling ICU funds, it was only when he brashly sued the Union for his salary arrears that he was temporarily suspended in late 1926. This was too late, however, for many Adelaide members. They had in addition to cope with farmers' persecution, and, given Dippa's use of ICU money to buy his own farm, the plight of the evicted was particularly unenviable.[29]

The Adelaide débâcle was but one breaker in several waves that crashed against the Union in 1925–6. Disillusioned with corrupt entrenched leaders who failed to fulfil promises, many supporters were drifting away, while most ICU strongholds in the Cape were defunct or dying. At head office in Johannesburg, this atrophy was manifested in acute financial difficulties. In July 1926, cash trickles from branches totalled a paltry forty-five pounds, a mere one-seventh of headquarters' overdraft. Frantically warning his lieutenants that the ICU was 'sinking into the depth of the sea', Kadalie also sternly warned Champion that 'it behoves us as captains of this mighty ship to take steps to prevent the pending disaster'.[30]

The solution attempted was to redirect this leaking vessel into the barely charted rural areas of the three northern provinces. Since these were also the halcyon days of fraternization with the Communists, the Party's growing stress on organizing the peasantry may well have encouraged this decision. Furthermore, the changing nature of ICU leadership almost certainly helped to foster perceptions of the countryside as a site for rallying blacks against the forces of proletarianization affecting privileged and poverty-stricken alike. While many of the urban wage-earning leaders of the earlier 1920s lacked time, mobility and often inclination for rural mobilization, petty bourgeois Africans moving into paid positions were far better placed, not least in that many were already involved in struggles on the land. But undoubtedly the major attraction of the countryside outside the Cape was its almost pristine character. Understandably, coping with disillusioned members was far less attractive than embarking on massive expansion into unexplored rural villages.[31]

Thus, between October 1926 and January 1927, the Free State Provincial Secretary opened nine branches in small towns, while his Transvaal counterpart outdid him with fourteen. Heading the most prosperous urban branch in the ICU, A.W.G. Champion was apparently more reluctant to leave the comforts of Durban for the rigours of rural organization. Nonetheless, when he became Acting National Secretary while Kadalie was absent overseas, his own replacement in Natal opened twenty-one largely village offices between May and July 1927. In financial terms the wisdom of this move was soon apparent: during the final eight months of 1927, Natal enrolment and subscription fees reached the incredible sum of about ten thousand pounds. Simultaneously a snowballing process occurred, in which ever more paid organizers were recruited and dispatched to the lucrative countryside. By the end of the year, over one hundred branches existed, some seventy of them having been established since the doldrums of mid-1926. Most existed in villages where the total urban African population was less than 1,500 people, and perhaps 70 per cent of the Union's membership was drawn from these small towns and their rural hinterlands. Indeed, the ICU's 1928 Economic and Political Programme explicitly recognized that rural blacks were providing the bulk of support, and therefore devoted unprecedented attention to farm workers and 'landless peasants'.[32]

As the ICU shifted its organizational weight from its urban to its rural leg, so its impact on both dominant and subordinate classes changed markedly. Even in far-afield Britain, the august *Times* noted that when 'the movement was confined to the towns comparatively little notice was taken of it. With its spread among farm labourers it caused a great stir.'[33] Or in less restrained terms: as rural membership soared, so protest exploded, landlords panicked, and the ICU reached the zenith of its power and influence. Above all other phases in the Union's history, this was the period which determined its reputation as a movement for national liberation. This was the arena in which the ICU had the greatest impact. And these were the conflicts which assured the Union a lasting place in the history of the struggle for freedom in South Africa.

Remaking The Past

Perhaps more contentiously, these rural upheavals demand a re-writing of some of that history. At the crudest level, they cogently demonstrate the flaws of an urban-oriented approach which is insensitive to the strength, traditions or distinctive features of resistance amongst South Africa's rural poor.[34] They also starkly expose the defects of narrow institutional accounts of popular protests. Many of these are so blind to pressures from below that they see little further than head office decisions and alliances, or so short-sighted that they effectively identify movements with their appointed functionaries.[35] At the very least, ICU-inspired struggles in the countryside point to the significance of local branch dynamics, and to the importance of examining the dialectical relationship between leaders and the led.

This is well illustrated by analysing an argument favoured by numerous radical historians of the Union. Allegedly, a major ideological turning-point occurred in 1926. At the end of the year, an *affaire* with white liberals expedited a divorce from the Communists. Thereafter, supposedly, followed a sharp lurch to the right, manifested in leadership's repudiation of strikes and inability to rise to the militancy of the masses.[36]

While the reactionary responses of some head office bureaucrats to spontaneous protest is indisputable, these were prevalent before 1926, and cannot simply be attributed to the effects of the expulsion of three Party members from the National Council. Moreover, the purge was motivated primarily by CP demands for more democratic

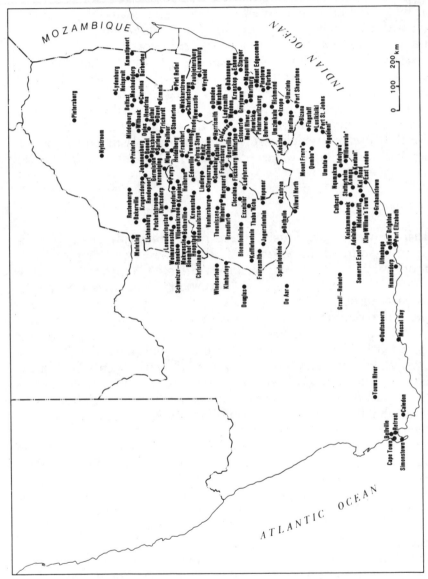

Fig. 2. ICU Branches in existence at some time between 1926 and 1930

control over dictatorial and larcenous officials, including Kadalie himself. The great man's notorious outburst at the time – that 'strikes were wicked, useless and obsolete' – was but an aspect of his skilful manipulation of conservatives who objected to a white-dominated movement calling for greater ICU pugnacity. It was not a long-lasting repudiation of the strike weapon by the entire Union leadership. Leaving aside the numerous calls for work stoppages by lower-level organizers, the National Secretary himself did not consider as binding declarations of tactical incompatibility with political enemies. About a month before the fateful National Council meeting, Kadalie met the paramount chief of western Pondoland. To the latter's dismay, he declared his intention of organizing a 'heavy strike' on the mines, as well as of visiting the Transkei to persuade chiefs and migrants to stop contracting for mine labour at existing wages. A month after the purge, he proudly related the tale of the 1919 dock strike to a Transvaal gathering of farm labourers, and boasted (misleadingly) that it had led to increased wages. Clearly, the content of the National Secretary's discourse depended heavily upon the nature of the audience addressed.[37]

Branch organizers, often drawn from less prestigious sectors of the middle strata, and subject to immediate grass-roots sanctions ranging from rejection of the Union to physical violence, were much more likely than senior officials to act as 'organic intellectuals' of their constituencies. Those based in tiny villages also tended to be more sensitive to the need to mobilize blacks in the countryside. As a Free State Branch Secretary caustically argued at one Annual Conference, 'ICU secretaries wasted time in big towns – eating puddings and the like – instead of going to the rural areas and organize the real workers of the country.'[38] Downward rather than upward identification was further encouraged by minor officials' own grievances against their superiors, who often either ignored burning branch issues, or failed to consult those lower down the hierarchy. Thus 'revolutionary speeches' given by Branch Secretaries to farm labourers in 1927 were attributed to disaffection over the National Council-engineered rift with the CP. In early 1928, even Party leaders recognized the emergence of youthful rural ICU activists, 'honest and sincere working class fighters', who were challenging the 'yellow', 'Pooh-Bah' reformists heading the Union.[39]

In the context of the broader history of black protest in South Africa, this contemporary recognition of leadership differences contains a liberating thrust. Implicitly, it challenges the straitjacketing of struggles within extremely schematic categories. 'Petty bourgeois' is one such confining concept: partly for political reasons, it has frequently been applied to leaders of mass movements in a simplistic, derogatory sense. It has sometimes been employed as an all-embracing explanation for organizational and ideological shortcomings of popular alliances. Indeed, it has not infrequently been wielded as a warning: that the rank-and-file will be haunted by the privileged backgrounds of those who commit class suicide.[40]

The social character of leaders of struggles of the oppressed is, of course, important. This is especially true when the practices and discourses of activists are influenced less by pressures from below than by their own class origins: a scenario all too likely when an undemocratic organization mobilizes the scattered rural poor. Nonetheless, throughout the capitalizing world, the fiercest battles waged by the under-classes in the countryside have more frequently than not been led by organizers deriving from other social groups. Furthermore, the very history of the ICU demonstrates the fallacy of attributing evil incarnate largely to petty bourgeois officials. The Union won mass support only when it changed from a constitutionalist trade union headed mainly by wage-earners to a militant nationalist movement led by men like Champion, 'the immediate future leader of the rising Native Middle Class'.[41]

Nor is 'petty bourgeois' simply an inaccurate characterization of a leadership whose class composition changed over time and varied according to organizational level. By stamping a rigid, bourgeois identity on Union officials, the term also obscures the extent to which they were drawn from a racially oppressed grouping, which was both fractured and extremely susceptible to proletarianization. Hence it masks the fact that blacks who headed the positions of relative privilege open to them in South Africa (from large-scale traders through to cane farmers and lawyers) tended to hold themselves aloof from the Union. If anything, they became Congress leaders, whom the ICU by the mid-1920s characterized as 'the upper stratum of native bourgeoism' or as 'good boys' still tied to the apron strings of white liberals.[42] By contrast, most ICU organizers of the later 1920s were drawn from sections of the lower middle classes which shared the interests of, were ideologically linked to, and were being precipitated into the under-classes. To paraphrase Sartre: the typical rural ICU leader of the later 1920s was a 'petit bourgeois intellectual, no doubt about it. But not every petit bourgeois intellectual [was a rural ICU leader]. The heuristic inadequacy of contemporary Marxism is contained in these two sentences.'[43]

Rather more words are needed to demonstrate a similar dialectic between the concrete and the conceptual in the sphere of white agriculture. On the one hand, promises of land were the single most important factor allowing ICU organizers to take the countryside by storm. Indeed, the struggles they influenced were at least as much against proletarianization as for better working conditions. There were also persistent cleavages between landlords and the state over methods of containing the Union. Thus ICU-inspired rural conflicts implicitly undermine two theses: that South African agriculture was capitalist by the 1920s;[44] and that these capitalist farmers were able to assert the primacy of their interests, within the post-1924 state, over other sectors of the dominant classes.[45]

If, on the other hand, the theoretical tools used to construct such claims are sharpened rather than abandoned, Union-related struggles can be dissected much more delicately. Since the driving motive of capitalism is production for private profit – and it is predicated upon the free sale of labour-power through the wage-form to capital – ICU activists justifiably failed to perceive capitalism in the countryside.[46] In the 1920s, the great bulk of white farmers were capitalizing, not capitalists, while most labourers were being proletarianized, not proletarians. Furthermore, during this era of contested transformation of both agriculture and the state, contradiction was the order of the day. Black tenants could and did demand both land and wages; white farmers could and did both obtain and forfeit political vantage-grounds. In the 1920s, there were neither single years that marked decisive turning-points, nor even unambiguous trajectories of struggle.

In short: the very course of ICU campaigns forcibly demonstrates the limitations of accounts which impose a rigid uniformity on extremely fluid and varied social forces. At the best of times, marching class armies up the hill and down again is an inappropriate way of writing history. It is singularly unhelpful when exploring kaleidoscopic conflicts: where the rank-and-file constantly changes the orders of officers, opposing companies apparently advance or retreat at random, and the boundaries of battalions are so mutable that soldiers can barely be distinguished from civilians.

The battlefield – the actual terrain of struggle – imposes some order on this chaos. So this book begins by examining broad patterns of accumulation, dispossession and dissension on farms, which were being transformed into 'the yawning crack which empties forth human beings'.[47] In fighting against proletarianization, both white masters and black servants were locked in bitter combats which powerfully shaped their responses to the ICU. The extremely precarious position of most white landlords, combined with 'progressive' farmers' conflict-ridden relationship to the state, fuelled ferocious attacks on the Union and its members from above. From below, accelerating changes in rural political economies were already thrusting black tenants into overt opposition. Far from invariably acting as the moving force behind the resistance it evoked, the ICU often merely channelled protest which was already coalescing in other localized institutions.[48]

But organizers did give both focus and form to farm labourers' struggles. The very fact that they were being extruded from the petty bourgeoisie was a crucial feature which enabled the Union, in contrast to Congress, to mesh together the class and nationalist aspirations of tens of thousands of rural blacks. Of course, many organizers' aims continued to be affected by their educated backgrounds; of course, their practices were influenced by their newly acquired salaried positions which finally firmly situated them within the middle strata. But to remain at this level of abstraction is inadequate: whether upward or downward identification occurred at a particular moment was far more closely related to the flux and exigencies of concrete struggle.

Above all, social conflict is waged through organization and ideology. These key facets of the Union were shaped partly by activists' own social origins, which had familiarized them with a cluster of thoroughly modern nationalist ideas and modes of operating. These in turn largely limited their appeal to a very particular constituency amongst the rural poor. Nonetheless, organic leaders must also learn how to follow, and in Natal in particular, 'traditionalists' fundamentally conditioned officials' styles and idioms of mobilization.[49] Indeed, as the illiterate under-classes both spread the message and imposed their views on educated activists, so there were radical changes in the content of ICU ideas on the land question. Finally, organization and ideology were also shaped from above. Without soberly assessing the repressive and reformist armoury of landlords and officials – and exploring the evasive tactics evolved by organizers – it is counter-productive to engage in glib condemnations of activists' 'moderation'.

It would also be unprofitable to continue to pursue these arguments at such levels of generality. While part of this book is an attempt to write history broad enough to answer some of the major political and organizational questions about the rural ICU, there are well-defined limits to discussing the Union's overarching ideology. Although the ICU in its heyday is perhaps correctly remembered as a movement which was national in scope, it encompassed an extraordinary diversity of conflicts and causes, all integrally shaped by local political economies. To explore some of the protean struggles into which leadership's organizational efforts were translated, it is necessary to descend from the heights of the nation to the plains of the region.

The Transvaal is one area of focus, partly because almost the entire gamut of rural ICU-inspired conflicts was represented in this province alone. These ranged from millenarian hopes for instantaneous freedom, to defiance by chiefs of white officialdom; and from 'insolence' by tenants on white farms, to wage demands by fully proletarianized labourers. But the interest of the Transvaal lies also in the ways in which it was atypical. Strategies for reshaping the movement from above were particularly concerted, largely because this province contained the nerve-centres of the ICU and white officialdom, as well as those of both mining and industrial capital. Thus it was here, as landlords began to suffer from an acute seasonal labour shortage, that a trend apparent elsewhere reached its culmination. This was the creation, against the interests of Union members and in the face of bitter opposition from struggling agriculturists, of contradictory alliances between white liberals, 'progressive' farmers, and ICU organizers.

At the other end of the spectrum were the violent skirmishes between landlords and leaders in the Natal district of Umvoti. Events here, although much more dramatic, were symptomatic of those occurring in numerous other Midland regions. Linked to a boom in wattle and sheep, rapidly accelerating dispossession of African tenants helped ignite an explosion when the ICU arrived promising land for all. Unable to secure the desired backing from the state to crush the protest that erupted on farms, white landlords took the law into their own hands. In so doing, they symbolized the fairly widespread tendency for farmers to outstrip the state in attempting to contain ICU struggles on the land.

Applying to a completely different set of actors, the same pattern of leaders being overtaken by the led was evident within the ICU itself. Especially when Union-inspired conflicts reverberated in geographically remote areas, the movement was profoundly shaped from below. Indeed, there were numerous occasions when the ICU was 'captured' by constituencies, and the nature of resistance drew less on Union ideas than on the resources of the rural poor.

One such struggle involved reserve-based traditionalists, who in the main did not easily find a home in the ICU. But in Pondoland in particular, and the Transkeian Territories in general, Union activists won mass support by totally altering their message. Millenarianism. was always a substrand in ICU ideology, as was the recognition that white rulers would be overthrown only by violence. In Pondoland these themes surfaced as dominant ones, expressed in terms of a heady imbroglio of ideas bubbling up from below. Understandably, little is known about this facet of ICU rural organization. It was not, after all, the norm for leaders to prophesy the coming of American Negroes in planes to exterminate whites, and to promise that blacks who killed pigs and bought ICU tickets would fly off to a country free of all suffering.

After these more detailed and regionally specific perspectives, the conclusion returns to a wider terrain. Perhaps ironically, it does so partly by stressing that parochial consciousness was the norm at a time when the rural poor had no shared conception of the South African political economy. The significance of village-pump politics was particularly evident in the various offshoots of the Union that survived for some thirty years, and in the relatively spontaneous conflicts that erupted under the auspices of these fragmented bodies. Possibly the most striking were the beer boycotts launched by traditionalists in Durban, and transformed by village and farm women in broader Natal. These stood in stark contrast to the Union's generally dismal record amongst females. They also highlighted the fact that the migrant labour system, combined with the trend of moving from rural areas via peri-urban settlements to towns, prevented the maintenance of a rigid barrier between city and countryside.

But while this book sweeps across both urban areas and other periods – and provides a close-up view of certain local conflicts – its essential focus is the ICU's relationship to struggles in the South African countryside in the 1920s. So it is a national vision that informs the delineation of general patterns of participation, protest and repression. And it is the rural dimension that is explored in depicting the various strengths, weaknesses and legacies of the Union. Indeed, there were persistent criticisms of organizing in this arena at all. 'If only . . .we could keep the ICU from touching the country districts',[50] wrote Ethelreda Lewis despairingly in 1928 to Winifred Holtby, another prominent liberal attempting to transform the Union into a moderate trade union organizing urban labourers alone. Lewis's motives were suspect, but she did at least stress to Kadalie that the price many farm tenants paid for joining the ICU was eviction.

This was only too true. Indeed, this book is in part a history of an ill-fated rural movement which did not halt capitalization of the countryside, did not rid South Africa of its racist state, and invited retribution on the heads of those who supported it. But it is also an account which attempts to grant the experiences and aspirations of rural blacks validity within their own historical time, recognizes their determination to resist intolerable conditions, and stresses the strength of their desires for a new heaven and a new earth. If the ICU fell far short of this goal, it nonetheless represented a high-water mark in the long struggle against exploitation and oppression in the countryside.

2. MASTERS AND SERVANTS:
The South African Countryside, 1920–1930

In 1926, an Orange Free State ICU organizer met a shabby, twenty-year old labour tenant from Vrede travelling by train to Durban. Horrified by his life history, the official wrote up the man's responses to his questions for readers of the Union's newspaper, *The Workers' Herald*.

I don't know what terms were made on the contract by my father. We make our livelihood from the yearly crops of a 4-acre plot of mealies and kaffir corn. On a bad year one bag of mealies is credited to us every time when we have finished the one already given. We get meat only when a cow or sheep has died, and this does not often happen unless during great thunderstorms. We get no milk at all. We get only the watery part of the sour milk. We use this in eating our dry and half-cooked mealie-meal pap.

We have a very short time to do our pap-cooking. My parents and five of my sisters and seven of us are all farm hands and we all get no pay for services. We serve only to have a right of settling on the farm. We start work from early sunrise until sunset daily excepting Sundays when we have a whole day's rest . . . My father receives a *parsela* (present) remuneration of three pounds after some years of real back-strained farm work, evidently on a good year when the *baas* realises that the yields of the crops have made for him big dividends.

It is a crime for any one of us to pick up and eat any of the fruit in the garden. He (the *baas*) buys no clothes for us. He allows us two months in the year to go and seek work for money, so that we can buy ourselves something to wear. He is totally against our attending any church services. We do so by sneaking away to some neighbouring farm where the farmer is not so much concerned whether natives hold services or not . . .

My father has only two lean horses. All his stock of cattle have dwindled away. They did not graze on the same pasture lands with those of the *baas*. They were fenced round a very small lot of very barren ground, there to expect manna from heaven or die of hunger . . . We are allowed to possess not more than four oxen. And even if we may be in a position to possess some, they plough the farmers' fields, and when they are outspanned they are separated from those of the *baas* and driven to their barren pasture ground. My father does not buy any more oxen for the reason already stated. We are not allowed to possess any sheep at all. The horses are so lean that they are useless as beasts of burden. We only expect to see them die at any moment.[1]

In a microcosm, the unknown labour tenant and his *baas* of the occasional big dividends represented those in the vanguard of rural support and opposition to the ICU in the period 1926–29. Underlying this pattern of participation were the twin trends of African proletarianization and white capitalization. Yet it is clear from the above account that the tenant did not relate to his landlord as worker to capitalist. It was equally clear to contemporary white farmers that although the world was being turned into a 'ghastly machine which works for profit', they themselves were 'groping about rather aimlessly in a miserable backwater of transition'.[2]

In the 1920s, an outstanding feature of South African agriculture was the stunted nature of its emergent relations and forces of production. Although blacks living on farms were being proletarianized, their struggles often still centred around their status as tenants rather than labourers. It was for this reason that rural ICU branches were frequently 'permeated with a sort of insurgent peasant spirit; and the leading problem in the view of thoughtful natives is not wages – but land'.[3] Similarly, accumulation in the countryside was a grinding, precarious and extraordinarily uneven process, dependent in the main on non-capitalist relations of exploitation. So while nascent capital was evident, it was largely capital which, unable to purchase the worker's labour-power at a price covering costs of subsistence, 'enmeshes him in a veritable net of usurious extortion, binds him to itself by kulak methods, and as a result robs him not only of the surplus-value, but of an enormous part of his wages too'.[4] It was precisely because surplus labour was primarily extorted through robbery rather than created through the wage-form that the ICU could not operate as an economistic trade union in the countryside. It was precisely, too, because it was organizing in areas ravaged by primitive accumulation rather than reshaped by capitalism, that the Union inspired rural struggles sufficiently radical to be termed peasants' revolts.[5]

Commercial Agriculture: The 'Squeezing' of Farmers

In the words of Free State ex-labour tenant Motshubelwe Moloko, 'It was our land from time immemorial, we were the indigenous people of the land . . .we stayed there until the *ratlahoboros* took our land'. Absolutely central to rural class differentiation along racially defined lines was this land seizure by conquering white *ratlahoboros*. Dispossession was legalized by what Africans termed 'looting law', the most notorious of which was the 1913 Natives Land Act. This almost entirely prohibited Africans from buying ground outside the 7 per cent of South Africa set aside as reserves; it outlawed black 'squatting' and sharecropping on Free State farms; and it banned Africans from entering into new cash or kind tenancies elsewhere in the country.[6]

Over the following years, the process of separating blacks from the land accelerated, largely because a good 40 per cent of the growing white populace tried to avoid sliding into the under-classes by acquiring farms. Ongoing injections of state aid into white land settlement, combined with developments in disease control and water supply, helped to appease their hunger for ground. After the First World War, even land companies began to reflect the shift in balance from rentier to productive landlords, and sold millions of morgen to farmers. And by the later 1920s, so much Crown land had been allotted to 'poor white' settlement that very little suitable for agriculture was left. In all, between 1918 and 1928, the number of white-occupied farms rose by 23 per cent to reach some 94,000 holdings.[7]

Actual ownership rather than mere possession of land was also becoming ever more crucial for whites. As capitalizing landlords continued to evict from their holdings poorer white tenants with no legal title, so the number of owner-occupied farms rose steadily to reach about 67 per cent of the total in 1930. The exorbitant cost of these purchases was exacerbated by the fact that land prices far exceeded productive values. While this disparity originated during the nineteenth century, when ground was acquired for its mineral or speculative value, it continued in the twentieth century as demand for this finite resource soared. During the two decades after 1910, the price of grazing land increased at about 10 per cent a year, while that of good arable soil rose even more quickly at some 16–22 per cent per annum. Thus prime land costing thirty shillings per morgen in 1908 was selling for ten pounds per morgen twenty years later, while a ranch bought for four hundred pounds in 1910 was sold with few improvements for five thousand pounds in 1928. By this time, the average value of land of a northern Free State maize

farm was £7,854, representing fully two-thirds of the total investment in the holding.[8]

Rocketing land values had two major consequences. First,
operating in tandem with the subdivision of holdings amongst
families, they contributed to the rapid decline in the sizes of farms.
Average areas fell by some 66 per cent over the first thirty years of
the twentieth century, by which time over 80 per cent of holdings
were less than one thousand morgen. In Natal the mean was 514,
while even smaller estates were the norm in some intensively worked
arable districts. Secondly, rising values were both cause and effect of
the backwardness of much of South African agriculture. On the one
hand, since land prices were increasing at a rate which vastly
exceeded that of farming profits, many wealthier agriculturists
fuelled inflation by investing receipts in land speculation rather than
farm improvements. On the other hand, neither option was available
to many poorer whites. Indeed, the draining away of funds into
ground meant that

> Many a farmer is crippled at the very commencement of his
> activities . . . All his available capital, and perhaps all he could
> borrow, is locked up in land, so that fencing, dam-making, boring
> for water and improvement of stock becomes impossible. In a
> frantic endeavour to keep his head above water he allows his farm
> to become overstocked . . .and ends up frequently in the
> bankruptcy court.[9]

Seemingly endless natural disasters reinforced the threat of insol-
vency and dispossession. Drought, disease and a myriad pests
periodically winnowed out landlords who had already survived poor
soils and a fickle climate. 'Every year large quantities of grain are
sown, and every seven years or so large crops are reaped', wrote
farmer Leonard Flemming. Amongst the evils he dwelt on were hail,
late or early frosts, potclay, woolly aphis, borers, cut-worms, lice,
locusts, and weeds. Heading his list of scourges, however, was
drought, of which he satirically remarked that farmers' dams were
impaired when rain occasionally fell and wet them inside.[10]

Shortage and unreliability of rainfall were indeed the primary
ecological constraints. In the mid-1920s, a mere 15 per cent of the
country's largely arid or semi-arid surface was considered potentially
arable, while only about 5 per cent of white farm land was actually
cultivated. Moreover, while drought was the norm not the exception, between 1925 and 1928 the rainfall over large parts of the
country was less than for any previously recorded four-year period.
During these years, entire regions experienced one of the worst
droughts in living memory. Stock worth tens of millions of pounds

was destroyed, and huge tracts of productive land were transformed into barren wastes.[11]

Drought losses were perhaps worst in the central Cape. Entire districts were abandoned to the heat and the dust, as despairing farmers sold their holdings for a song, or simply quit after chalking on the door: 'There is no longer a God. God has forgotten us.' Although the first victims were poorer pastoralists, even wealthy men slid into penury: one estate worth thirty-two thousand pounds produced the risible income of twenty-three pounds in 1927. Simultaneously, thousands of 'coloured' and African herdsmen were rendered superfluous as land-owners tried to minimize drought losses by fencing their farms. Some of the blacks who subsequently poured into towns were inspired by militant ICU speeches. In Graaff-Reinet in 1927, hundreds of destitute Africans refused to pay poll tax, at least one on the grounds that he had been so advised by Kadalie. But in the main, neither these depressed village communities nor farm workers clinging to employment seem to have been particularly enthusiastic about the Union's rhetoric or its prayer meetings for rain.[12]

Social as well as natural tribulations afflicted farmers, situated as they were in a peripheral country where the uneven development of capitalism heavily weighted the terms of exchange against them. Apart from the fact that South Africans were paying some three times as much for implements as their competitors on the world market, from the mid-1920s agricultural prices were falling faster than those for industrial commodities. Furthermore, the very trajectory of capitalist development drastically limited the home market. 'All my early years of farming, whatever you produced, it was a surplus', recalled a Natal landlord. 'We had surpluses of everything: there was too much meat, too much milk, too much butter . . .' All too often, mercantile capital aggravated the problem of realizing profits from produce, by acting as a leech draining away farmers' life-blood. Country traders in particular battened on smaller agriculturists who, by pledging their produce in return for credit, were easy victims of numberless abuses. In the early 1920s, a good one-third of the difference between producers' and retail prices was siphoned into the pockets of middlemen, who understandably found unequal exchange in the countryside to be a profitable sphere of activity.[13]

But deteriorating terms of trade must also be situated in the context of the capitalist world market. From 1925–6, falling farm-product prices contributed to world-wide agricultural depression, as farmers were subordinated to metropolitan industrialists demanding cheaper raw materials, and to huge mercantile concerns engaged in cut-throat competition to supply them. In South Africa, the problem was exacerbated because it coincided with the country's transition from net importer to net exporter of farm products. Representing almost half the total value produced, these agricultural exports ineluctably betrayed their origins in an extremely backward agrarian economy. Reflecting the fact that this was a phase of primitive accumulation, South African farming techniques were generally so predatory and antiquated that they caused staggering declines in soil fertility. The land was often so poor that it would have been left virgin elsewhere, while levels of mechanization were so low that in 1926 only 1 per cent of farms possessed a tractor. Finally, work was extorted primarily from an unwilling labour-force deeming itself to be under duress. Consequently, both labour productivity and crop yields per morgen were usually amongst the lowest in the world. Since these were key determinants of costs of production, it was frequently impossible to sell South African produce at a profit in the international market.[14]

Maize, for example, was far and away the most important cash crop in South Africa, and according to state officials its average yield per morgen was the worst in the world in the mid-1920s. The international price was determined largely by Argentinian production, and when this country produced bumper crops (as in 1927), South African mealies could be sold at less than their cost of production. Since by this time the export price was an important influence on that reigning locally, South African maize in fact yielded little or no profit in the later 1920s. But this was characteristic of a period when capitalist farmers described themselves as manufacturers selling under cost. Only in woolled sheep – which required about one tenth of the labour needed in maize and offered biannual returns – could pastoralists obtain profit rates of some 5 per cent. The key cattle industry was on the verge of collapse, while 'progressive' agriculturists calculated their rates of profits in almost all other sectors as usually less than 3 per cent. In 1926–7, farmers averaged a meagre annual income of one hundred and sixty pounds, which was not only abysmally low compared to the earnings of urban capitalists, but also considerably less than the pay of many white wage earners. As capitalizing landlords continually wailed, better livings were afforded by gambling on horses.[15]

Low incomes and low profit margins; high land prices and high rates of crop and stock failure; falling prices and slow turnovers: this is the context in which farmers' chronic indebtedness must be situated. According to the Governor of the Reserve Bank in 1926, merchants' provision of short-term loans left landlords 'manacled hand and foot by the chains of debt'.[16] More significantly, mortgaging of holdings affected even those who had inherited their

land, or who were wealthier men with access to banks. For tens of
thousands of farmers, this was the only way to buy out co-heirs, to
recover from disastrous seasons, or to ward off creditors clamouring
for payment. As a country banker expressed it,

> Several bills are lying past due in the bank, and further renewal has
> been refused; or unsecured overdraft facilities, granted
> temporarily, have been abused and are now withdrawn; vendue
> accounts with different auctioneers are long overdue; the year's
> credit with two or three storekeepers has been exceeded; and from
> every side legal proceedings . . .are being threatened. The only
> way of escape from the pending catastrophe is by means of
> consolidating all the debts.[17]

Especially in the years of generalized capitalist prosperity from
1924 to 1929, obtaining loans by mortgaging land was usually
extraordinarily easy. By 1930, registered bonds on farms had
escalated to a total of ninety-one million pounds, representing fully
36 per cent of total farm values and an average indebtedness of nearly
one thousand pounds per holding. The great bulk of these loans were
granted by private bodies and individuals, with the latter sometimes
lending on fourth, fifth or even sixth bonds on the same property.
The vast majority too were seen as lucrative investments rather than
as loans to be redeemed by amortization. But if mortgagees were
well-satisfied with rates of interest ranging from 6 per cent to the
usurious double figures of many individuals, it was common
knowledge that amongst many struggling farmers, 'die "intres" vreet
soos vuur' (the 'interest' consumes like fire).[18]

So long as payments were regular and land prices continued to
rise, mortgagors were fairly secure. But in times of countrywide
economic slumps, many mortgagees would abruptly give three to
six month's notice for repayment of the entire loan, and seize
possession of the farms of defaulters. Landlords ruined in this way
were often forced to flee to the towns, where they formed a large
proportion of the 'poor white' population. In the decade after 1922,
this rose by 150 per cent to reach about one-sixth of the entire white
populace.[19]

Thus, by partially separating farmers from ownership of their
primary means of production, mortgage debt had a considerable
impact on the process of class formation in South Africa. Furthermore, the threat of foreclosure was a central factor in the
commercialization of the countryside. By the later 1920s, there were
probably few regions where the majority of farms were not bonded,
and there were certainly districts where this applied to 90 per cent of
all estates. Precisely because most farmers did not have unqualified

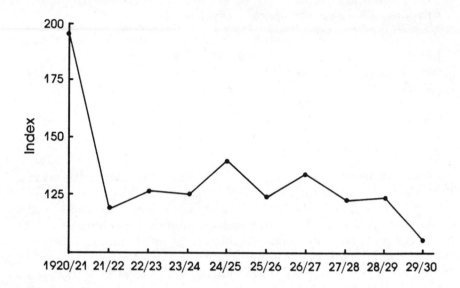

Fig. 3. Combined index of producers' prices of agricultural (excluding pastoral) products

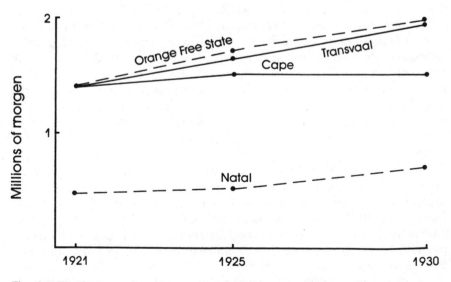

Fig. 4. Total area under cultivation (including fallow land) on white farms
From: *Union Statistics for Fifty Years* (Pretoria 1960)

access to their major means of production, they were forced to produce commodities, forced to try to cover interest payments, and forced to invest money in production with the aim of increasing it.[20]

This did not, however, signify their development into full-blown capitalists. Apart from the continued existence of a significant though diminishing sector oriented solely towards subsistence, most farmers in the 1920s were driven by the need to maximize cash, not profits. Indeed, the great majority kept almost no records at all, and were utterly unable to calculate net returns from their enterprises. For them, the limit of exploitation was set not by agricultural rates of profit – let alone average rates ruling in the economy as a whole – but by the far lower costs of simple reproduction.[21]

Thus it was as capitalizing landlords stalked by the spectre of dispossession that many farmers struggled on through yearly rounds of overwork and underconsumption, bought ground priced way above its productive value, and sold produce at the prohibitively low prices set by mercantile capital. Indeed, since landlords were desperate to recoup losses suffered during the post-war years of drought and depression, many also displayed non-capitalist responses to falling prices. In order to try to maintain income levels, they reacted by expanding rather than contracting production. Thus despite falling agricultural prices between 1925 and 1930, land under cultivation increased both per farm, and also by a total of nearly 20 per cent in the three northern provinces. Similarly, although wool prices were in the main tending downwards over the same period, the attraction of this sector in a generally depressed economy was manifested in a massive 38 per cent increase in the number of white-owned woolled sheep.[22]

Partly because wildly fluctuating yields characterized rural production in this era, prices were not of course always declining. Farmers certainly reacted feverishly to any slight increases in cash returns from a particular product. The key price rises here were of sugar from 1926, maize in 1926–7, wattle bark in 1927, and wool in 1927–8, although there were also occasions when the open sesame was apparently provided by crops ranging from cotton to peanuts. But all too often the improved returns were ephemeral, largely because farmers rushed into the sector, glutted the market, and helped precipitate plummeting prices.[23]

There was, however, a small minority who appeared to have discovered the correct password. In the later 1920s, 'successful' farmers constituted perhaps 10 per cent of the total number.[24] They were concentrated in the Transvaal highveld, the Midlands and coastal belt of Natal, the eastern Orange Free State, and the south-western and eastern Cape. Agribusiness had a small but

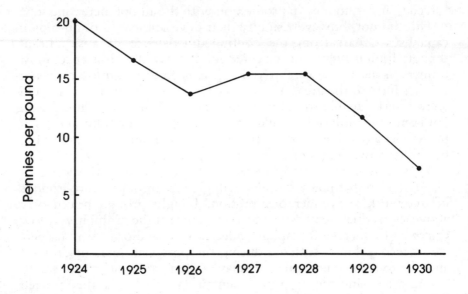

Fig. 5.   Price of unrefined wool

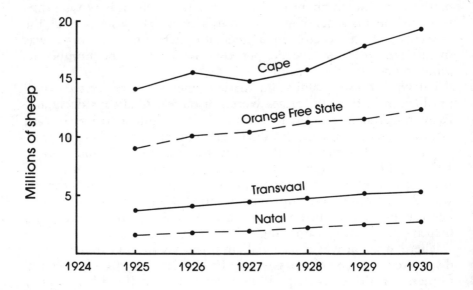

Fig. 6.   Number of white-owned woolled sheep on farms
From: *Union Statistics for Fifty Years* (Pretoria, 1960)

significant presence, often in the form of vast multifaceted companies running plantations. So too did 'cheque book' farmers, whose estates were primarily items of conspicuous consumption. But numerically and socially most important were the 'progressive' landlords. Many were previously or simultaneously lawyers, merchants or businessmen who, in taking up agriculture (often on land acquired through the calling up of mortgages), were encouraging the seepage into the countryside of capitalist modes of operation. These were the men who dominated farmers' associations, to the point where muttered complaints were heard about the 'farmer-commercialists' heading the Cape Agricultural Union. These too were the men who frequently locked into positions of power in villages, as leading lights on school committees, shooting associations, church bodies and political parties. Thus mayors and town councillors could be key figures in agricultural associations, lending a personal touch to the structural dependency of small municipalities on the well-being of their rural hinterlands, and to the urban origins of much of the wealth of 'progressive' farmers.[25]

Such men had usually escaped the clutches of village traders and usurers. They sometimes rented rather than bought land in order to leave funds free for productive investment, and generally kept meticulous records detailing profits. It was from within this grouping that was drawn the bulk of those committed to revolutionizing agrarian relations and forces of production. It was also this constituency that tended to support ideological organs crystallizing out a capitalist ethos, as well as the political representative of larger capital, the South African Party.[26] Even after the ousting of this government, the state, as an institution which condensed within itself broader social contradictions, continued to reflect the presence of 'progressive' farmers within the body politic. Indeed, rural capitalization was actively promoted by some of its branches, notably the Department of Agriculture.[27]

Yet the Minister of Agriculture – unlike the Administrator of the Transvaal, who carped about 'a hothouse growth of industries' at the expense of farming – heartily endorsed the Pact government's primary commitment to the development of a sturdy manufacturing base. Perhaps recalling how he had led 'poor whites' and struggling farmers into rebellion against South African support of Britain in the First World War, General Kemp spoke in 1929 to a Transvaal gathering in Bethal, where some of the most developed capitalists in the country farmed. Here he lauded the achievement of establishing secondary industries in a country where imperialists siphoned out profits from primary sectors. 'It would be foolish', he argued, 'to say that the Afrikander should remain on the farm, while the wealth of the country falls into the hands of people who have previously monopolized the commerce of the country.'[28] It would be equally foolish, he might have added, to expect import-substitution industrialization to occur in the absence of an expansion of exports. Not surprisingly, much of the increased state aid for agriculture in this period was directed into enhancing export potential.[29] As the body responsible for regulating both the rising national debt and the balance of payments in a time of rapidly increasing imports, the state understandably attempted to make South African produce more competitive internationally.

While 'progressive' farmers were undoubtedly assisted by such aid, under the Pact regime they largely considered themselves as victims not victors. Aside from the fact that the political party with which they had closest ties was out of power, their organizational linkages with state apparatuses were extremely weak. In the context of sharp reminders from officialdom that farmers' associations were extremely unrepresentative, those bodies found their requests to comment on draft legislation affecting agriculture repeatedly ignored. So too were their more generalized recommendations. In 1927 the Transvaal Agricultural Union (TAU) had twenty-seven of its thirty-two resolutions rejected, while the Natal Agricultural Union (NAU) fared little better with a score of forty-three lost out of fifty-three. Various advisory committees and produce boards were state- rather than farmer-controlled, which resulted in leading capitalists either resigning in frustration or terming them a farce. The resuscitation of the Farmers' Party in the later 1920s was but the organized expression of complaints by 'progressives' that Parliament ignored agriculturists and gave them inadequate aid; that almost all state bodies were permeated with party politics; and that the Pact government was nothing more nor less than the farmers' enemy.[30]

The material basis for these grievances lay in the numerous instances when the interests of capitalist agriculturists were blatantly overridden in favour of broader Pact policy. Organized farming displayed considerable unease over the widening of the industrial-agricultural price gap implicit in the 1925 Wage Act, and outright opposition when the ICU won from the state the right to have the Act applied to Africans. Furthermore, while support for industrial protection had been given in the hope that this would increase the home market, disillusion could rapidly set in when sectional interests were threatened. Thus, extraordinarily heavy rail and customs duties on power paraffin until the end of the decade severely hampered the use of tractors, and were perceived as hamstringing better-off agriculturists in order to foster potential industries. Antagonism was also aroused by the subordination of wealthier to poorer farmers.

Capitalist agriculturists, who often already had direct links to wholesalers and the mines, frequently opposed marketing schemes forcing them to sell to a state-controlled monopoly. Moreover, intense dissatisfaction was expressed over the paltriness of the maximum loan (two thousand pounds) set by the Land Bank. This institution was in fact starved of funds at a time when state revenues were steadily rising, and its average loan in 1927 was the meagre sum of three hundred and fifty pounds.[31]

At least one contemporary economist confirmed that the Pact government's agrarian policies were directed less at nurturing capitalists than at saving small strugglers. The latter did not in fact fare much better at the hands of the Land Bank: since credit was extended only if wealthier landlords stood security, new or intensified aid available through loan or drought relief schemes did little to relieve the plight of the poor. Furthermore, in the face of concerted opposition from a broad spectrum of capitalist and white wage-earning elements, the state rapidly backed off from its commitment to curtail middleman profits by enforcing the marketing of all maize through co-operatives. Nonetheless, numerous state projects were initiated to stem the flow of fully proletarianized whites off farms.[32] Since the haemorrhage of 'poor whites' into towns was regarded as a serious threat to social stability, this policy had widespread support amongst the dominant classes. In the telling words of mine magnate Sir Abe Bailey addressing a Cape agricultural show in 1927, a stable populace wedded to the land was the 'best antidote to Bolshevik poison'. The success of agriculture, he argued, was not a farmers' question 'but a national question. The Government must assist those farmers who have been knocked out . . . Better assist them, and not create more permanent unemployed and unemployables known as "the poor whites".'[33]

In stark contrast to their struggling compatriots, 'progressive' farmers rarely succeeded in having their particular interests accepted as a 'national question'. Far from being a powerful social force able to convert other sectors of the dominant classes to general political principles, agricultural capitalists were but an emergent and still tiny minority in a backward countryside. Moreover, landlords' political and economic weakness had considerable impact on the course of ICU-inspired rural conflicts. At a time when most farmers were battling for survival, and were utterly dependent on unfree labour locked into a coercive system of controls, they perceived themselves as having insufficient purchase on public authorities to secure the enforcement or extension of state-imposed restraints. Claiming that it was useless to expect a weak government to deal adequately with the ICU challenge, landlords therefore tended to develop their own solutions, which rapidly extended to taking the law into their own hands. Undeniably, the success of their strategy was influenced by long experience of doing precisely that on their own holdings.

The 'Squeezing' of Blacks on Farms

'The African question is the land question':[34] this 1923 declaration by a white liberal neatly captures the major reason for black tenants' presence on white farms. The only ground to which Africans had relatively assured claims was located in the reserves, the vast majority of which were overstocked, overpopulated, and sometimes well on their way to being transformed into rural slums. Furthermore, where conditions were less desperate, tenure was less secure. Thus as farms spread over the surface of South Africa during the early twentieth century, so choice sections of the reserves were expropriated for white agriculturists. In addition, when the 1926 Natives Land Amendment Bill was introduced to fulfil the overdue promise of enlarging areas open to African occupation, it lopped off some 2.5 million morgen from estimates made a decade earlier, because this was now considered land suitable for white occupation.[35]

When the Native Affairs Commission toured the country that same year to ascertain African views on the Bill, it discovered that demands for more ground were nationwide. Land hunger was an absolutely central feature of black rural consciousness in this period. The material base of precolonial polities had after all lain in access to ground; moreover, South African capitalism rested on a wage system which did not cover familial subsistence. Small wonder that many Africans rejected the Bill's solution of buying farms, and wanted no less than the return of ground originally expropriated. Thus the summarized representations of blacks in Estcourt were: 'Great question is land, as Natives have to roam from farm to farm . . . Natives don't understand buying land, consider country theirs.'[36] Indeed they did. As an ex-Free State labour tenant expressed it, 'A black man's roots go very deep into the soil of his own land.' Or, in the words of Natal Congressman John Dube, Africans' greatest grievance was their landlessness, and 'the black ox has nowhere to feed, and the white ox seems to have all the pasture'.[37]

Such feeling ran especially high in Natal. Here African population densities were far greater than anywhere else in the country except the Transkeian Territories, and even the passage of the Land Bill would have provided on average only minute sub-subsistence plots far smaller than those promised in the Cape and Transvaal. Land hunger here had long acquired cultural expression, in forms such as songs bewailing the fate of those forced to leave ancestral homes where their forefathers lay buried. One such Zulu-composed lament was *iLand Act:*

> We are children of Africa
> We cry for our land
> Zulu, Xhosa, Sotho
> Zulu, Xhosa, Sotho unite
> We are mad over the Land Act
> A terrible law that allows sojourners
> To deny us our land
> Crying that we the people
> Should pay to get our land back
> We cry for the children of our fathers
> Who roam around the world without a home
> Even in the land of their forefathers.[38]

In regions where elements of precolonial social relations had been conserved, lamentations about landlessness had particularly great popular resonance. In Natal, due both to settler manipulation and to African defence of indigenous institutions, particularist identities, bearing strong traces of the past, were given powerful support in economic, civil and political society. These identities were integrally connected to land, as was signified most crudely by the fact that only the subjects of chiefs could live in reserves, while only those with access to ground could easily maintain customs such as the giving of cattle in bridewealth. Here, then, the struggle for land was much more than a struggle against proletarianization. It was also an attempt to maintain an entire complex of social relationships which provided continuity with the mighty Zulu kingdom. Indeed, the extent to which the burden of the past was still felt in the present was manifested in early 1927, when a deputation of chiefs and headmen pleaded for the return of the 'lost lands' of northern Natal, seized by the Boers from Cetshwayo in 1884–5.[39]

Thus, for multifarious reasons, gaining access to relatively fertile farm ground was the alpha and the omega, the prime and often the sole reason for black tenants' submission to white landlords. They did so in a variety of guises. Since Parliamentary edicts did not necessarily change patterns of appropriation, hundreds of thousands of blacks paying cash rent were alive, well, and occasionally thriving in the 1920s. They were concentrated in the Transvaal and Natal, and situated primarily on the property of land companies. Other options also existed: in Natal in 1927, there were some 95,000 Africans hiring ground from absentee white land-owners, an estimated 90,000 'squatters' on white-occupied farms, and about 46,000 rent-paying tenants on Crown land. The profoundly unprofitable nature of South African agriculture, combined with the resistance of blacks to proletarianization, therefore meant that tenants paying cash rent still composed a hefty one-fifth of Natal's rural population, and probably at least as high a proportion in the Transvaal.[40]

Sharecroppers, too, continued to put a plough to the ground in many arable districts in all provinces. Landlords involved in this system were mainly struggling farmers absolutely dependent on their tenants' means of production, or wealthy (often absentee) land-owners for whom sharecropping offered better returns than taking full control of productive processes. In 1927, a prominent agriculturist claimed that 80 per cent of farming in the northern Free State, and 90 per cent in the western Transvaal, was performed on a sharecropping basis.[41] Although this was probably an exaggeration, there were almost certainly entire districts where some 75 per cent of maize was produced by black peasants.[42] For them, ploughing on the halves offered unparalleled opportunities for accumulation, and they fought desperately to retain their relatively privileged niches. But by the 1920s, half-shares had often been replaced by derde deel, despite the fact that 'people protested. They protested because the spans of oxen were theirs, labour was also theirs, but a white farmer got two bags and they only got one bag each.'[43]

But if the balance of power was swinging against sharecroppers, it had already decisively swung against other Africans who worked on farms. These included wage-labourers, found amongst some land-lords all of the time and most landlords some of the time. By 1925, larger capitalist agriculturists were being serviced by nearly three hundred labour recruiters, many of whom concentrated on signing up 'mine rejects' and adolescents on six- to twelve-month contracts. For those unable to afford the higher wage bills and capitation fees associated with recruited workers, an alternative was available. This was to rely entirely on labourers hired from reserves, neighbouring states, African-owned farms, adjacent towns, or nearby holdings where tenants were currently unemployed. These were precisely the sources whence derived seasonal labourers, who washed like spring tides through farms for harvesting or shearing.[44]

Unfortunately, such workers were extremely unreliable and much more expensive in cash terms than resident blacks. Moreover, casual wage-labourers tended to avoid farms without tenants, whose absence deprived them of congenial sleeping accommodation and suggested that the landlord was overly harsh. So for the great majority of farmers in the region east of the central Cape, labour tenants were a necessary evil. Although their contracts with land-lords were subject to infinite variations, the common denominator lay in the fact that black families, in return for the work of at least one member of the homestead, resided on the farm, cultivated a patch of ground and obtained grazing for stock. These were relationships that revolved primarily around use- not exchange-values: as an authoritative government commission expressed it in 1925, agriculture was 'not yet generally on a cash basis, or even on a wage basis.'[45]

This was partly due to the resistance of labour tenants. To the chagrin of 'progressive' farmers, many stubbornly refused to accept cash in exchange for patches of arable land, while some fought struggles underpinned by such explicit statements as 'We do not want wages, we want ground.' Labour tenants' most basic concern was to obtain sufficient to eat – and although their plots were often of poor quality and seldom adequate for subsistence needs, they nonetheless usually furnished the bulk of food during good seasons. Moreover, these provisions were cheaper than those sold by traders or landlords, and better than the virtually inedible mealie meal so frequently palmed off as rations on working members of the family.[46]

In arable districts, ploughing and planting this land was increas-ingly dependent on landlords' equipment. This was not an unmixed blessing: it frequently meant that the work was performed too early or too late in the season to ensure good crops. However, cultivation and harvesting were largely the tasks of women, which fuelled male antagonism to farmers' calling on the labour of black females. This in itself was often overdetermined by patriarchal possessiveness: in the words of a Transvaal tenant, 'I must work for the *baas*, but not my wife . . . I buy a woman to work for me.'[47]

'Buying' wives to work for husbands generally had as its precon-dition access to some ten to twenty head of cattle. It was this passage of stock against females that was the usual way of setting in motion the cycle that transformed male workers into homestead heads supported by their families. The exchange also lay at the heart of male control over the productive and reproductive capacities of women and their children, and was prerequisite for increasing the labour-power attached to a homestead. Furthermore, cattle were vital as draught animals, and as producers of milk, meat, fuel, hides and calves. As stores of wealth and items of trade, they were also keys to political authority and social differentiation. For all these reasons, obtaining pastures was far and away the most important reason for surrender to tenancy by homestead heads. Many were those who refused to decrease their cattle in exchange for greater cash wages, or who asked for trek passes rather than obeying orders to reduce their large stock. Other animals were also valued: horses for transport, as well as sheep, goats, pigs and hens for their cash-producing potential. But prime importance was attached to herds, because 'cattle beget children' and 'a man is no man unless he has a cow'.[48] Typically, the negotiation of labour tenant contracts centred around cattle and children, with landlords grudgingly trading off grazing for the first in exchange for sufficient labour from the second.[49]

As this suggests, fathers as well as farmers were involved in the extraction of labour from homestead members. Generally, a contract binding on all subordinates was made with the patriarch alone. As well as supervising conduct and work, he controlled familial remu-neration, often including the cash wages of working household members. German Skhosana, who refused to work for his Transvaal landlord on the grounds that the contract bound only the homestead head, tasted the bitterness of those who saw fathers transformed into foremen. He was whipped by the farmer until 'it looked as if I had been burnt with a hot iron . . . My father's response broke my heart because he was unsympathetic. That really broke my heart.'[50]

Partly due to the antagonism of such youths, the alliance between black elders and white masters was a contradictory one which was not always consummated. To reap its benefits, homestead heads often had to apply new sanctions such as disinheriting children who refused to labour. Similarly, white landlords tried to enlist the powers of the law to legitimate their ugly partnership with black elders. Farmers' attraction to the system was understandable: not only could they harness patriarchal authority to replace one deserting family member with another, but they could also obtain the services of the entire household at a cost far less than paying the equivalent number of wage-workers.[51]

Although drawing on black family labour was a site of intense struggle, by the 1920s children ten years old or younger were regularly being employed in tasks such as herding and seasonal labour. Women were being called up for domestic work in the farmer's house, as well as for weeding, hoeing and reaping. But the brunt of labour generally fell on the shoulders of youths, who theoretically worked from sunrise to sunset. Theoretically too, their annual periods of service ranged from those imposed by the *somaar* system (whereby tenants simply had to be available at the whim of their landlords); to a quasi-feudal contract involving working between two and four days a week throughout the year; to the more capitalist arrangement of labouring for a continuous three, six, or twelve months out of twelve. But in practice, the irregularity of agricultural work cycles meant that in certain seasons blacks could be forced into back-breaking days stretching from 2 a.m. to 9 p.m. Thus the employer of Free State tenant Phillip Masike was nick-named 'Kick the blankets' due to his custom of harshly arousing workers at about one o'clock in the morning. Furthermore, as struggling landlords farmed more intensively, so work-loads showed a steady upward trend on both a daily and a yearly basis. Spiralling land prices also intensified drives to appropriate more labour, and to substitute *môre-kom* for the *somaar* system. The connection was not lost on some African intellectuals: as primary gave way to secondary resistance, so mortgage debt was incorporated into their labour theory of value. According to a ICU organizer speaking to a gathering of Free State tenants – who were increasingly being forced to work most of the year – the province was white-owned because Africans were 'paying the bond on the farms and the farmers are looking on . . . These are not their farms. We have worked and paid for them.'[52]

They undoubtedly laboured hardest for 'progressive' agriculturists, who showed a distinct predilection for extracting from tenants every ounce of their physical strength, as well as every minute of their waking lives. Such whites themselves complained about the added work entailed in trying to produce profitably, using methods more advanced than those characteristic of landlords who plundered the soil or left stock to fend for themselves. According to capitalist mixed farmer Marthinus Raath of Witzieshoek in the Free State,

> no sooner have you finished harvesting than it is time to make hay . . . and then it is time for the mealies and then it is time to begin to plough; and when you have finished ploughing for the mealies, then it is time to cut the oats and so it continues endlessly . . .we work 13 months in the year.[53]

But it was black youths, not white landlords, who performed most of the arduous manual drudgery. And it was black youths whose bodies were relentlessly swallowed up in these Sisyphean tasks, and then rejected once their physical strength was broken. 'Hey! Farm work killed us', exclaimed Retsishe Mapaila when reflecting back on his years as a Transvaal tenant in this period. 'We are no longer people as we are now.'[54]

Farm work undermined black bodies all the more because remuneration almost invariably failed to cover the costs of subsistence. Cash was by this time a necessity, both for state-imposed levies and also often for food. But in vast regions of the country – including most of the Transvaal, northern Natal, and much of the northern

Free State – monetary payment of labour tenants was highly unusual. 'Hawu? Be paid? He, be paid? There was no payment. We were farm workers', bluntly stated Esther Sibanyoni, an eastern Transvaal labour tenant in the 1920s.[55] Apart from selling crops and stock (which remained a significant source of cash or at least 'good fors' from stores),[56] and aside from toiling as a wage labourer on neighbouring farms during free periods, the only other option was urban work. For most Transvaal farm tenants, as well as for many in the northern regions of the Free State and Natal, the Witwatersrand metropolis served as a magnet, and numerous men 'took "joyini" bound for Johannesburg'. But males also used 'to foot it' or entrain for other labour centres or even nearby villages.[57] Here for some months each year, they would work in mines, factories, the tertiary sector or whites' houses. To a much lesser degree, women too would move briefly to towns to work 'for a paying white man', or, especially when industrial enterprises were located in the countryside, to make money from beer-brewing or prostitution. The establishment of such personal linkages between town and countryside supplemented those centring around weekend mingling at beer drinks, brothels, churches and concerts, and were crucial in the transmission to farms of urban ideas and forms of political mobilization. Certainly white masters were acutely aware of the extent to which labour in towns raised worker consciousness on farms. Thus refusal of passes to leave holdings was based not only upon fear of desertion, but also upon knowledge that many who returned demanded Saturdays off or higher wages.[58]

Farmers' outrage at such demands to be treated as urban workers were of course conditioned by their own precarious position in comparison to employers in cities. Indeed, most remained on the land only by ruthlessly driving down tenants' remuneration, and ceaselessly hunting for increased inputs of black-owned labour-power, means of production and produce. In so doing, they subjected resident workers to relationships which violated almost every norm of capitalist exploitation. In the eyes of many Africans, as well as those of a significant number of white magistrates and liberals, labour tenancy approximated slavery, forced labour or serfdom. In the words of an eastern Transvaal victim,

> it was slavery because we were not master of a single thing, not even of ourselves. A native on a farm has rights to nothing; he is not master of himself, he is not master of his wife or of his children; he is master of nothing.[59]

Undeniably, labour tenants were not owners of labour-power which each temporarily sold to an employer for a specific purpose.

Aside from the fate of those whose services were bartered away above their heads, it was common practice for landlords arbitrarily to extend the period of contracts; to demand summarily the labour of uncontracted wives or children; to 'lend' labour tenants to neighbours; and to tie families indefinitely to farms via debt peonage, passes or retention of tax receipts. Unquestionably, too, homestead heads were not owners of their means of production. Innumerable landlords used tenants' oxen and implements, seized their prize stock (often as fines for fictitious offences), gelded their male animals, appropriated the cream produced by their cows, and commonly descended to robbing them even of the dung excreted by their cattle. Not even tenants' so-called remuneration was free from farmers' grasping fingers. Many indefinitely withheld cash wages and demanded monetary payment for use of pastures. Some reappropriated virgin ground as soon as it had been adequately cleared by tenants. Others contributed endless teams of wild oxen as 'aid' in servants' ploughing. Furthermore, numerous masters used tenants' arable plots to plant their own winter crops, to provide their own winter fodder, or to increase their own harvests by evicting the servants before reaping. Themselves subordinated to external forces demanding their pound of flesh, innumerable farmers survived by demanding from labour tenants 'flesh, blood, bones and all'.[60]

Ideologies and Cultures[61]

Virulent racism buttressed masters in such relationships with servants. Like most white employers, landlords reduced their labourers to 'boys'. But unlike 'organic intellectuals' of manufacturing capital (who were increasingly representing Africans as children on the lowest rungs of an evolutionary hierarchy ordered by class and race),[62] many struggling white farmers subordinated ideas of boyhood to those of eternal barbarism. Utterly dependent on forms of appropriation in which labourers were members of a subject race, and fearing a fate in which they were reduced to competing with blacks on the urban labour-market, landlords verging on 'poor whiteism' often drew on much older notions of conquest, civilization and savagery to differentiate themselves from the heathen 'kaffirs'. In the run-up to the 'Black Peril' election of 1924, one Nationalist Party ideologue appealed to this constituency by claiming that whites were fleeing the countryside, *'voorgedrewe deur die aanstormende assegaau-lose hordes van naturelle'* (driven out by the insurgent, though now unarmed hordes of natives), only to find in the cities similar 'black hordes' suffocating white civilization.[63] Or in the almost offhand words of a Transvaal farmer,

> The two races are bound to come into collision. It will be a question of the survival of the fittest . . . Why delay the process of extermination? Our interests come before the black man's. If it means killing the black man in the last resort we must do it.[64]

From here, it was an easy step down towards relegating Africans to non-human worlds. This was partly an overdetermined expression of non-capitalist relations: where labourers remain attached to the land, they are frequently treated by dominant groups as no more than an inorganic condition of production.[65] Thus many white masters contemptuously gave their workers names of beasts, commodities or months of the year, such as 'Bobbejaan' ('Baboon'), 'Sixpence' or 'September'. In addition, numerous farmers had no hesitation in calling their labourers 'louse-brained anthropoids' with 'animal instincts'. They were equally prone to refer to their holdings as being 'stocked with natives', who either needed 'thinning out' or had to be 'broken in'. Small wonder that one of the most heartfelt grievances of farm labourers was that 'Boers have never treated a black man like a human being.'[66]

Because tenants dwelt as well as worked on white landlords' domains, masters had numerous opportunities to dehumanize their private as well as labouring lives. In the interests of enhancing productivity and suppressing conflict, many strove to contain external ideological influences and forms of organization. Thus they often banned attendance at social gatherings, denied children schooling and forbade visitors entry to their property. Their rulings were fiercely contested, and blacks certainly surreptitiously reappropriated certain rights. But it was particularly difficult for Africans to batter down defences erected around the colonizers' culture, since this was perceived as integral to white superiority. Thus Jacob Motha recalled that if a black wore smart clothes on the Transvaal farm where he was a labour tenant, 'you would be shot dead! A kaffir wearing clothes? – No! No! No!' Similarly, ex-labour tenant Lucas Nandela remembered that Africans wearing ties on Sundays on his Free State farm ran the risk of being assaulted by landlords, who cursed: '*Jy reken jy is 'n wit mens, jou verdomde ding*' (You think you are a white person, you damned thing). And if a black was so daring as to

> approach a Boer's home being elegantly dressed, the children would say, '*Ma, daar kom 'n mens aan.*' Once you are nearer and they notice that you are a black, they would then say, '*O! Nee, Ma, is nie 'n mens nie, is 'n kaffer.*'[67]

Yet the realities of extracting work from 'kaffirs' forced landlords to recognize the contradictions in a philosophy that denied their labourers humanity. Indeed, especially amongst wealthier farmers, harsh racism was sometimes tempered by their adoption of some of the benevolence of familial figures of authority. Often this was little more than enlightened self-interest, as when farmers paid labourers' poll taxes to avoid losing them to jails, or supplied generous rations to minimize theft. Alternatively, masters might provide 'good' servants with economic assistance: perhaps free dipping, or selling tenants' produce through the farmers' own channels which offered better prices.

If such aid flowed less from land-owners' generosity than from their need to retain labour, reduce friction and justify exploitation, there were nonetheless agriculturists who had 'a real affection and concern for their people.'[68] Indeed, the very intimacy of farm life, combined with the master-servant relationship itself, helped nurture a stunted approximation of the ethic of paternalism. There were mistresses who acted as tenants' midwives, named children, ran night-schools, and even baked cakes for special occasions. And there were certainly blacks who responded to this ideology of mutual obligations with loyal service. Recalling his days as a Natal labour tenant, Moses Majola angrily rejected a suggestion that hungry men might steal. Black parents, he claimed, would send their children to 'go to the missus, and we would ask what we could eat with our porridge. Sometimes she gave us milk; she gave us fat or sugar . . . [Whites] gave us what we wanted.' In so doing, they clearly linked individual Africans to their families in ways which inhibited the development of tenant protest and independence.[69]

Such forms of social control were not, however, widespread. For one thing, they were too expensive. In the words of a capitalist agriculturist who had already allowed his tenants a school and a church, and was contemplating laying out a football field, 'A large percentage of the farmers . . .are pioneers, and they have no time really to think of any frills.'[70] For another, blacks who were enmeshed in paternalistic relationships with landlords were primarily those whose racial, class or cultural attributes decreased the distance between them and white masters. They included skilled, acculturated workers and 'coloured' foremen, as well as those whom farmers proudly described as their 'very good educated boys' or as their exemplary '*ryk volk*' (rich people). Thus is was to mourn the death of an outstanding sharecropper, and to give sympathy to his privileged and competent labouring son, that a Lindley landlord and his family attended the funeral of Ndie Makume's grandfather, all 'crying as if a white man had died'.[71]

Although labour tenants rarely achieved such closeness with masters, some did try to turn the doctrine of reciprocal duties into a weapon for survival. In this they often met with opposition from 'progressive' farmers, who complained about black females running to the 'missus' for everything. Indeed, as the devolution of the mutual obligations of paternalism onto women and children suggests, the ethic was losing appeal amongst labour tenants and landlords alike. As widening class and racial gaps encouraged the development of an Africanist consciousness, so farmers became aware that resident workers were less dependent and co-operative than in the past. Overt hatred was in fact being expressed for tenants who enjoyed favours from whites, or who called on landlords to settle internal disputes. Furthermore, indebted farmers were themselves abandoning or commercializing many customary rights. Thus the replacement of black by white patriarchs in numerous spheres also involved the introduction of the cash-nexus. By the 1920s, many youths were having to pay in money for medicines, food and grazing for cattle.[72]

In the broader society too, paternalism was losing ground as it was subsumed within an ideology more capitalist in orientation. The rise of twentieth-century 'economic liberalism' was integrally related to problems of capital accumulation experienced by all sectors of the emergent national bourgeoisie. Many of its proponents identified three central needs relating to African workers: to use them more economically; to enhance their efficiency; and to raise their purchasing power. The first was a function of the almost universal shortage of black industrial workers in 1925, combined with the shrill protests of mining capital from 1927 over the pending Mozambican Convention, and a perennial shortage of seasonal farm labour which had reached crisis proportions in the Transvaal by 1929. The second was related to fears of increased industrial wage bills for whites, and to efforts to break into world markets on competitive terms. Given the difficulties presented by the latter, the third concern derived from the desire to expand the black market. One strongly mooted solution to all these problems was that of enhanced productivity by better-paid African workers. Indeed, this killed even more birds with one stone: whenever black-white conflicts intensified, higher pay was vigorously promoted as a means of defusing militancy.[73]

'Progressive' farmers were themselves increasingly subscribing to some of these ideas. In part, this was a consequence of changes in the labour processes on their farms. Liberalism's emphasis on the skilled individual had considerable resonance for those in the vanguard of adopting implements such as tractors, where 'an intelligent native replaces a horde of malcontent labourers'. The constant battle to dispose of surpluses also caused organized agriculture to display tentative interest in the notion of blacks as high-wage consumers rather than as mere cheap 'boys'. Often linked to this were calls for better pay to encourage greater intensity and continuity of farm labour. As '*Ryk*' wrote to *The Farmer's Weekly*, if landlords considered Africans from an economic rather than political standpoint, they would establish a proper system of cash wages to enhance efficiency and increase the home market.[74]

This thesis was expressed even more forcibly by the Secretary for Agriculture. Stating in 1925 that Africans were expensive not cheap labourers, he claimed that their inefficiency led to enormous losses in terms of decreased and inferior production. Therefore, in an extraordinarily convoluted argument which nevertheless displayed the linkages between liberalism, industry and the volatile white underclasses:

> The native should be raised in the scale of civilization in order that he might give a greater return, not only in quantity but also in quality of output . . . It was to the advantage of the white man that the native be raised. More intelligent labour would increase production from a given area or per unit, while increased production would lessen the cost thereof and the cost of living. A reduction in the cost of living would promote the establishment of manufacturing industries, and thereby give an opportunity of employment to a larger white population. This opportunity would react on agricultural and pastoral production, and the latter would react on the manufacturing industires.[75]

As their resistance to exchanging land for cash already testified, labour tenants usually attached very different meanings to being 'raised in the scale of civilization'. Black rural subcultures nurtured oppositional as well as alternative values to those of either white liberals or racists – as was made starkly evident to a Natal farmer unable to persuade a trusted tenant to become an *induna* for fear of the reaction of his fellows. As tightly knit communities, labour tenants were well placed to exert such pressures. Living perhaps a mile from the farmhouse, and generally separated by much greater distances from other Africans, the four to six homesteads on an average farm were bound together by geographical isolation alone. Furthermore, they sometimes worked together in groups related by blood and marriage; they frequently shared political and cultural traditions; and they always had in common subjugation to their landlord. Since much farm labour was performed in isolation, the work-place was often less important than the home in engendering solidarity. Here women played a key role, not only in establishing mutual aid networks indispensable to survival when impoverishment was the norm, but also in maintaining older customs revolving around the socialization of children and collective labour on plots. Since their traditional work-cum-beer parties frequently involved blacks from neighbouring estates, these helped both decrease tenants' isolation, and also situated them within broader cultural configurations linked to the past.[76]

In a much wider sense, the land question was central in breathing new life into practices and ideas originating in earlier days. In districts where large blocks of ground were controlled by Africans, or where black polities had prior claim to farms now partitioned amongst whites, particular patches of soil were often considered as belonging to the subjects of specific chiefs. In the context of acute land hunger, this in turn could direct struggles for ground inwards, to the point where fierce battles arose involving tenants and reserve-dwellers alike. Indeed, new youth groups developed in some regions to co-ordinate such conflicts. thus, as the power of chiefs declined in the almost entirely absentee-owned district of Weenen, Natal, so that of the *igoso* rose. Transformed from leaders of dance associations to 'generals' elected by youths, these war leaders controlled their own territories, exercised more authority over young men than did black or white officialdom, and would lead their armed detachments to weddings and beer drinks where 'faction fights' often erupted.[77]

Particularist loyalties were also sustained by contact with the reserves. In addition to socializing with herbalists and seasonal workers, many tenants were involved in cattle-loaning relationships with dwellers in locations, while some went so far as to maintain huts in these areas. Moreover, both rural and urban work situations frequently reinforced the importance of traditions focused around a common territory, culture and descent. In part, this was due to the deliberate reinforcement of class with ethnic antagonisms by employers and the state. Men in supervisory positions – such as '*baas*-boys' on farms – were thus often drawn from alien language-groups. In part, too, it was due to African initiatives in establishing migration patterns and defensive associations. As a mine worker during the First World War, Jason Jingoes did not mix much with non-Basotho men 'because I was afraid of them, not knowing their language. Each group kept pretty much to itself.' Similarly, the significance of ethnic divisions on farms was borne home to Naboth Mokgatle when, as a teenager hired to pick oranges in the Transvaal in 1925, he had difficulty in carrying a heavy ladder. Most of the other workers were 'from other tribes and lack sympathy for me'. It was only aid from two friends – 'my tribal men' – that enabled him to conceal his weakness from his employer.[78]

But if ethnic antagonisms could inhibit the emergence of unity amongst workers, ethnic solidarities could underpin resistance by sections of the labour force. Sometimes this was due to the positing of alternative norms. In the Transvaal, farmers bemoaned the existence of initiation schools, claiming that 95 per cent of youths were either swept off by their parents or themselves deserted in defiance of white masters. Far more disruptive countrywide were the beer drinks that formed the cornerstone of male farm workers' social lives. Held over the weekends – and especially prevalent when labourers were needed most for harvesting of summer crops – these were key arenas for the dissemination of news. In so far as they were also centres of disaffection and could induce two-day long hangovers, they also symbolized farmers' inability to impose on their labourers a friction-free industrial work rhythm.[79]

More overt protest sometimes drew heavily on particularist cultures, especially when workers were hired from areas effectively under African control. In 1928, a Natal sugar estate had recruited nearly half of its 120-strong labour force from Weenen, by then an ICU stronghold. Following a delay in the payment of their wages, almost all the members of the Weenen gang gathered at the office to demand their pay. After the manager had refused their request, the men retreated to their barracks singing a war song. Armed with sticks, they continued to dance and sing in a manner highly suggestive of a detachment led by an *igoso*. One of their number addressed them, urging the killing of their master, and arguing that whites 'came from England to this country and say this country is theirs whereas it belongs to the Natives'. At sunrise the following day, having sung in Zulu 'the man who touches us will touch war', the armed group crowded round the office. But an *induna* had informed on them, and the presence of the police was sufficient to force them back to work.[80]

Yet such instances of ethnic attributes informing resistance occurred to a much lesser extent amongst labour tenants. Situational evocation of particularist loyalties remained common: according to a resigned Transvaal chief, in good times farm-dwellers would say,

'I have nothing to do with the native laws, I am living here on the farm of my master, and he is the only one I obey.' But then, when bad times come and they have to leave the farms . . .they will say, 'I am a Makwena' or whatever it is, and they say, 'We want our rights.'[81]

Nonetheless, lack of land, leisure and autonomy all undermined practices and values which identified farm-dwellers as members of particular chiefdoms. Compared to location residents, tenants tended to resort less to chiefs' courts, to hold fewer ritual killings or large dances, and to display smaller kinship networks, less polygyny and greater individualism. They also generally had greater aspirations for assimilation into a modern world. While many Transvaal labour tenants quietly differentiated themselves from reserve-dwellers through their desires for the white man's food and clothing, a Cape resident worker overtly declared: 'I am a person from European country, I do not know anything about the country of the Xhosa.'[82] Small wonder that in a period when the policy of 'retribalization' was on the ascendancy as a means of segregating black from white, officialdom expressed considerable anxiety about the 'detribalization' apparent on farms.[83]

They were particularly concerned about the control over tenants by the two-thousand-odd chiefs and headmen on the state's payroll. White agriculturists themselves helped undermine the authority of this older political elite. Chiefs who lived on farms were often being reduced to ordinary labourers, while those with other landed bases were frequently refused permission to visit followers. The state, too, was tardy in the implementation of its *volte-face* in policy: from crushing traditional leaders as vanguards of resistance, to incorporating them as forces of control. Thus in the mid 1920s, almost no chiefs were recognized in the Free State, while only those in the reserves obtained salaries in the Transvaal.[84]

Furthermore, numerous farm labourers had either left locations or were reluctant to return precisely because of chiefly tyranny. Amongst these state-appointees were men who demanded compulsory labour tributes, imposed a multitude of levies, or accumulated land at the expense of followers. Their emergence as a distinct stratum of exploiters was supported by many white capitalists, who gave bribes of capitation fees to chiefs who extruded migrant labourers. Naboth Mokgatle experienced the hardships of those subject to black political authorities who collaborated with employers. In an attempt to escape life as a farm worker, Mokgatle sought a pass from his chief who had contracted to supply youths to a tobacco factory. Mokgatle refused to work there – and the man likewise refused to issue him with a pass. Undoubtedly, the transformations wrought in the roles of such chiefs fuelled popular support for movements led from outside the ranks of the traditional elite. As a Natal ICU member exclaimed when his chief publicly berated followers for supporting the Union, 'We who live on private lands are the sufferers . . . You should have kept away from our meeting. We are suffering, and you have nowhere to put us.'[85]

Another manifestation of decreasing allegiance to traditionalist leaders and values was growing acceptance of Christianity. Earlier in the twentieth century, the stronghold of this new religion on farms had been found amongst the wealthier peasants and acculturated blacks often employed in skilled or supervisory positions. But from the 1920s, there was a remarkable shift in the class composition of converts and the nature of churches to which they belonged. In 1921, while some 32 per cent of rural Africans defined themselves as Christians, only about 50,000 of the 1.3 million converts were members of separatist churches. Fifteen years later, adherents of these Zionist and Ethiopian bodies had increased by nearly 1,500 per cent, standing at over a million Africans. The vast majority of these converts were situated in the countryside, and the great bulk of them were members of the rural poor. Above all, the appeal of these independent churches lay in their proto-nationalism, and in their pledges to lead blacks literally and figuratively to the promised land.[86]

Tenants' very membership of independent churches was almost invariably an act of defiance. Quick to recognize their politicizing role, farmers often forbade entry to separatist ministers or evicted lay preachers from their holdings. However, many blacks tenaciously clung to bodies preaching such revolutionary messages as Africa for the Africans, as well as freedom from serfdom and black ownership of all land. In addition, independent churches allowed farm workers a taste of black-controlled collective activity which could override even ethnic divisions. In 1927, an African minister in an orthodox mission church anxiously warned his Transvaal landlord of separatist activities in the district:

> The Natives inclusive the Cape boys, Basothos, Zulus and all the other tribes at all Prayer Meetings pray to God for deliverance from the present yoke of oppression, they pray for the old conditions under President Kruger where they received land to plough and payment in cattle or horses. At present he stated that the Native has not anything left and that he is only working for a few shillings on which it is impossible to maintain a family . . .unless such freedom as under the old Boer Republic was secured a rising of the Natives would take place . . .they would prefer death rather than the present treatment . . .they do not trust *one* European Missioner nor the white man in gene-ral . . .the present conditions would be driven to a conclusion very soon.[87]

Resistance and Repression

But the norm amongst farm labourers was not overt collective resistance but subterranean individualistic protest. Thus, a work stoppage amongst labour tenants, let alone a rising, was almost unthinkable for western Transvaal ex-sharecropper Kas Maine. In his dismissive words, *'Hoe sal jy kan "strike" maak en jy is binnekant 'n man se huis, "strike" binnekant man se huis, jy kan mos nie so doen nie'* (how can you strike when you are inside a man's house, strike inside a man's house, you just can't do that). Not that the only restraint was that imposed by living on the white man's property: the quasi-jail conditions on many holdings themselves inhibited open confrontations. 'You had to escape. We moved by escaping', recalled Esther Sibanyoni, powerfully evoking the clandestine nature of one of the most common forms of protest. Many deserters also had to evade familial warders, especially when they were youths opposing a system so imbricated with reshaped kinship structures that those who contributed most to the homestead's security had little control over its property or their own lives. July Lusiba, having fled from an eastern Transvaal holding because he was not paid, was recalled by his relatives. He fiercely argued that he was not obliged to work against his will, since he did not 'have a field of my own like my father . . . They said, but, I was his child, and so I was held responsible. I said I was his child but I was not a tenant.' For Lusiba, such cogent class logic outweighed any considerations of clan, and he quickly absconded again to the towns.[88]

If desertion was an act aimed less at threatening farmers than escaping intolerable conditions, not so the anarchic violence endemic in the underpoliced countryside. Hatred for masters and their property could explode in such vengeful acts as poking hooked wire up oxen to damage their entrails, driving needles into the brains of sheep, or poisoning landlords by mixing arsenite of soda, used for dipping, into their tea. Very often, such protest was both retaliatory and drawing on popular traditions of justice. Sheep were stolen because rations were inadequate; wheat stacks were fired due to unfair dismissals; fences were cut because tenants' cattle had inadequate grazing; prize stock was poisoned because labourers had been murdered; farmers were boycotted because they were notorious for harshness; and agriculturists were killed for withholding wages.[89]

Covert and spontaneous though many such crimes of protest were, they were nonetheless capable of being incorporated into a broader movement fighting against violations of customary rights. They could also be stunningly effective: there were farmers forced to leave districts because the black intelligence network starved them of labour. Furthermore, pocketbooks were frequently badly hit. In the eastern Transvaal, a labourer who declared he was 'not going to allow any white man to beat him', responded to a thrashing by setting fire to a barn and causing damage of over two thousand pounds.[90] In East Griqualand, malicious poisoning of stock cost pastoralists some six thousand pounds over a couple of years in the later 1920s, while at least one farmer sold out because he was unable to stand the losses incurred through stock theft. Countrywide, 147,000 beasts were reported stolen in 1927, and although rustling was not necessarily an act of protest, it frequently involved the rejection of relations of exploitation that denied blacks their subsistence. For Kas Maine's wife, stealing was just 'another way of making ends meet'. Jantjie the Jacobsdal sheep-thief took matters much further by becoming a social bandit. Revelling in white commandos' vain pursuits of him, Jantjie sent farmers taunting messages, via their black herdsmen, that he was ever in their midst, and would sometimes mockingly laugh from the bushes when whites discovered his meat sizzling on the coals.[91]

Resident workers in particular were generally in the vanguard of protest. Because they were tenants as well as labourers, their resistance was qualitatively different from that of hired hands. As a leading agriculturist complained, the labour tenant '*het 'n soort van gevoel wat die huur kaffer nie het nie; hy het die gevoel dat hy net soveel reg op die plaas het as die eienaar*' (has a sort of feeling which the hired kaffir has not; he has the feeling that he has just as much right to the farm as the owner').[92] Sometimes this challenge to white ownership was legitimated by translating precapitalist norms of ownership into a new context, and arguing that all land belonged to the government rather than to private individuals. Much more widespread was the belief that blacks had prior right to the ground. Thus labour tenants were notorious for mutilating stock, stealing wood, or letting their cattle roam all over the farm, because 'this was our land from the beginning'. July Lusiba had already participated in the collective theft of crops when his landlord shifted to poorer plots tenants who regarded the entire holding as their own. After his first desertion, he was inspired to new heights. In attempting to resolve the contradiction between being a labourer and not yet a tenant, he one night 'hoisted my white flags marking the boundaries of my own declared farm'. He triumphantly recalled his landlord's shock in the morning on seeing the flying flags, and deserted that same day when his master grimly went off to report him.[93]

Labour tenants were equally infamous for being inefficient, uncooperative and deliberately destructive workers. Farmers complained angrily that these servants were often reluctant to leave their own crops and tend to those of their masters. Labour tenants tried, they claimed, to dawdle to work and to knock off early, and intentionally wasted about one-quarter of the time supposedly spent working. 'They call it themselves "forced labour", and they are very difficult to get on with . . .these men do not obey their masters, and that is why we are against it, and it upsets all your other labour', complained one 'progressive' farmer.[94] Or as another expressed it, he would not have a tenant on his Free State farm if he could obtain sufficient hired labour. 'They are useless scavengers and very expensive . . . They flog our oxen and cows at milking, and if you tell them to stop it you get cheek or "Pay me and let me go".'[95]

At first glance, there was a web of coercive legislation which masters could invoke to suppress such protest. Under the Natal Masters and Servants Act, first-offender labour tenants could be sentenced to a month's imprisonment for refusal to labour, for carelessly performed work, or for absence from the holding without permission. Two month's imprisonment on spare diet awaited those who damaged their masters' property or insulted their persons. In addition, pass laws, vagrancy legislation and regulations relating to the dipping and movement of cattle harshly discriminated between black and white. (Often the former were subjected to criminal sanctions for offences for which the latter paid no or only civil penalties.) Such legal class instruments were made even sharper by pressures which undermined the autonomy of courts from white landlords. According to one rural magistrate, the popularity of men like himself depended largely on the severity shown in sentencing blacks, 'and if his sense of justice is not sufficiently developed it may easily be swamped by a desire to be well spoken of by the farmers'.[96] Understandably, at least one labour tenant regarded the magistrate as having been bribed by his master,[97] and many abrogated rights of complaint because subsequent victimization – including being charged for desertion – generally left them in an even worse state.

The experiences of Natal labour tenant Mtateni Ndwandwe in Ngotshe well illustrate the blacks' vulnerability before these interlocking mechanisms of control. Having contracted to work for six months in 1926, he was forced to labour for an unbroken sixteen months without pay. After his cattle were confiscated when he took a week off to recover from an injury incurred during work, he deserted, and was sentenced to two and a half months' imprisonment. For refusing to work on his return to the farm until his stock was restored, he spent sixteen days in the estate's lock-up, most of which time he was obliged to break up cotton cake with handcuffs on his hands. Immediately upon release he fled, was captured, handcuffed and locked up again, and was ultimately dragged back to court on a charge of desertion. The complacent magistrate expressed doubt about Ndwandwe's allegations, and, despite discharging him on the grounds that his arrest had been illegal, was little impressed by the black tenant's declaration that 'I did not complain to the police as I thought [my master] was acting under Government authority.'[98]

Yet Ndwandwe's acquittal also points to the existence of differences between masters and magistrates on the issue of suppressing protest. Landlords complained endlessly about the ineffectiveness of the state. Many claimed bitterly that courts were biased towards Africans and the pass laws were a farce; that the police were useless and assistance from the Native Affairs Department was a myth; and that it was impossible to farm successfully under existing legislation.[99] Perhaps the conflicts are best captured by examining opposing attitudes to stock theft. Pastoralists' own solutions ranged from herding labourers into closed compounds from sunset to sunrise, to branding cattle thieves on the forehead, and from sentencing first offenders to ten years, to giving farmers the legal right to shoot them. Not surprisingly, the Deputy Commissioner of Police in the eastern Cape aroused a furore in 1925, when he declared that stock theft occurred because some landlords underpaid, underfed and mistreated their labourers.[100]

Clearly, the interests and outlooks of social forces deeply opposed to the primitive nature of South African agriculture, and committed to economic upliftment as a way of defusing conflict, were crystallized out in some state apparatuses. Although 'progressive' farmers went some way along this road, neither they nor their struggling compatriots tended to go as far as officials in certain state departments. Landlords' frustration with the Native Affairs Department, for example, was well-founded. Privately, many Native Commissioners urged better treatment of farm labourers. Publicly in their role as magistrates, some refused to convict tenants subject to contracts perceived as reducing blacks to serfdom. Indeed, when addressing the annual conference of the SAAU in 1928, the Secretary for Native Affairs even urged relaxation of the pass laws tying blacks to farms. Although purges of personnel and reordering of lines of authority were transforming this Department in a more repressive direction, the elections of 1924 clearly did not instantaneously reshape an apparatus previously infused with certain 'liberal' tenets of large-scale capital.[101]

Nor did the advent of the Pact regime give farmers undisputed purchase on the legislature. More than a decade after Union, relations between masters and servants were still regulated by a chaotic, provincially differentiated thicket of legislation, much of it formulated years earlier in response to completely different relations of production. When the judiciary stuck to the letter of such laws, the results for agriculturists could be disastrous. In the early 1920s, a series of Supreme Court decisions imposed grave limitations on landlords' ability to use the Masters and Servants Acts against their tenants. While a 1926 Amendment patched up some of the worst fissures in Natal and the Transvaal, gaping holes remained, partly because agricultural interests had been subordinated to those of urban capitalists and white wage-earners. In some districts, this in itself allowed black resistance to labour obligations to gain momentum. Even before the advent of the ICU, numerous youths realized they could not be convicted for breaking contracts made by homestead heads, and simply refused to enter service.[102]

Such resistance was another wedge widening the gap between farmers and the state. By destroying, stealing, forging, loaning and selling the unsophisticated documents supposedly maintaining them as a cheap and servile labour force, Africans fuelled white complaints that passes were not worth the paper on which they were written. Indeed, when blacks on one Transvaal farm had studied how their master 'twists his hand when signing', their foreman could produce permits 'more beautiful' than the originals. Moreover, in Natal by the 1920s, labour tenant resistance to carrying identification passes had won them de facto freedom from the practices of using these permits to enforce contracts, check desertion, peg wages and control movement. Since, however, labour agreements made without the endorsement of passes were still technically illegal, many landlords were helpless when attempting to charge farm workers defended by ICU lawyers with having broken their contracts.[103]

In trying to use the state's repressive armoury to discipline workers, masters were also disadvantaged by their very location in the countryside. Charging blacks in court involved repeated absences from farms, as well as travelling many miles to police camps and magistrates. Furthermore, the expense was often prohibitive. Statistics confirm farmers' claims that courts were used only in the last resorts; even assuming that African farm labourers constituted all of the 20,752 Masters and Servants prosecutions in 1926, this meant that less than 5 per cent of regular workers were so charged. In addition, many other forms of rural resistance were extraordinarily difficult to attribute to individuals. Given, too, the critical and ever worsening countrywide shortage of constables throughout the 1920s, as well as they ability of communities to make life unbearable for police informers, many crimes of protest simply went unpunished by the state.[104]

The limitations of state intervention in rural conflict gave a final twist to landlords' role as masters, in so far as farmers deliberately assumed some of the powers of the repressive apparatuses. This was apparent in their appropriation of the functions of magistrates and chiefs in settling disputes amongst labourers. It was evident too in their establishing themselves as law-makers in order to rectify shortfalls in existing legislation. In the Free State, where the courts had undermined a regulation forcing blacks to obtain a 'special' pass to move off the farm, farmer Marthinus Raath bluntly informed his tenants: '*my wet is dat as jul van die plaas afgaan dan moet jul 'n pas dra; ek het niks die land se wette te doen nie*' (my law is that if you move off the farm then you must carry a pass; I have nothing to do with the laws of the land). And to enforce a will that had nothing to do with the laws of the land, farmers concentrated in their hands the means of exercising physical violence.[105]

Thus fists, whips and guns were central in maintaining master-servant relationships on farms. Undeniably, the ability to exercise control by injuring black bodies was for white masters one of the advantages of employing African labour. According to one farmer, while you could 'boot, biff or sjambok the "bally nigger" if he does not do everything expected of him, you cannot treat the white labourer in the same way'. Indeed you could not: African nicknames for landlords such as 'Ra-Sjambok' or, more ominously, 'killer of other men', give some indication of the sheer barbarism that went unchecked on isolated holdings. Labourers were murdered for refusing to say 'good day, *baas*', and were shot for demanding withheld wages. They were killed by being hung upside down on a tree and thrashed to a pulp, or by being tied to galloping horses which dragged their mutilated bodies long after life had expired.[106] It was a brutal and bloody world that black farm labourers inhabited in the 1920s. It was made all the more so by the less physically obtrusive but equally violent course of capitalist penetration.

The Dynamics of Dispossession

Amongst 'progressive' farmers, abolition of labour tenancy had by this time been grafted on to earlier calls for suppression of 'kaffir farming'. This was more than a response to the difficulties of controlling recalcitrant resident workers in the absence of adequate support from the state. It was also a way of tackling a whole complex of farming interests through one institution. Labour tenants, after all, exacerbated the problems of soaring land values by holding ground out of the sphere of production. They increased the difficulty of selling produce at a profit, both because they were paid predominantly in kind and because they hindered increases in productivity. They acted as a brake on the development of productive forces by constantly migrating (and deserting) to towns, and they undermined the estates' viability with their scrub stock and primitive methods of cultivation. Numerous wealthier landlords tackled some of these difficulties by buying 'labour farms', so that tenants lived separately from the holdings on which production occurred. But by the mid-1920s, leading members of the Executives of provincial Farmers' Unions had agreed on a far more radical solution. They were almost unanimous that labour tenancy was a disgraceful form of 'partial slavery'. Such men and women should, they argued, be replaced by blacks trained in agriculture, paid entirely in cash, and working at least eleven months out of twelve. Completely within the paradigm of classical liberalism, they argued that only such 'free labour' would produce efficient and economic farm workers.[107]

Understandably, the solution of paying farm labourers entirely in cash did not have mass appeal. Confronted with statistics referring to the high rental values of tenants' land, most farmers replied from their own logic that 'money is still more expensive'.[108] But if bourgeois methods of accountancy were used to allocate cash values to the various items of tenants' remuneration, then in most types of arable farming labour tenants constituted at least 25 per cent of running expenses.[109] It was a cost exceeded only by that of interest – and as cultivation increased and farm sizes diminished, it was an expense that became even more real to the mass of farmers. In maize districts, where holdings were smaller, farming more intensive and land values higher than average, by the end of the decade even tenants' patches of arable ground were being valued in commodity terms by agriculturists. Far more widespread dismay was expressed over the fact that countrywide, land worth eighteen million pounds was being 'wasted' on tenants' grazing. Gone were the days when labour tenants were considered to be working for nothing: they were increasingly being generally recognized as prohibitively expensive.[110]

Thus, in a process which was uneven but inexorable, farmers were limiting the size and quality of arable plots and pastures. In the Cape by the end of the decade, labour tenancy had effectively ceased to exist in all but a few eastern districts. In the Free State in the thirty years after Union, the size of the pasturage permitted dropped by an estimated 40 to 50 per cent. Innumerable tenants were shifted to less fertile plots, while the spread of fencing and paddocking allowed masters to confine servants' beasts to inadequate, overgrazed camps. Small stock was the first to suffer: between 1923 and 1929, the number of tenant-owned woolled sheep fell by nearly 70,000. Although in absolute numbers African-owned cattle dropped in the Cape alone, by the end of the decade it was only the exceptional farmer who was not setting tighter limits on the number allowed.[111] Many were the tenants leaving farms in arable districts because 'the contract was "sour". Because when your livestock multiplied the Boers would say you must reduce them.'[112] Many too were the youths encouraged to desert, because elders could no longer provide bridewealth to hold juniors to farms.

Wealthier and non-labouring tenants were among the first victims of these restrictions. In 1927, it was reported that evictions of Natal 'squatters' were common, as Crown land was alienated to settlers and as estates became too small to contain tenants ever less able to pay rising rents. Moreover, it had become fairly common in Natal and elsewhere to cheat sharecroppers out of the entire harvest by evicting them before reaping. Such ill-gotten gains – combined with the fact that these were years of intensified state assistance and easy mortgage credit – allowed agriculturists to invest in more sophisticated implements which decreased their reliance on blacks' ploughing equipment. In particular, there was a marked shift from one-furrow to two-share ploughs. Vernacular names for various versions of those two implements – the 'pick-me-up' versus the 'flying best man' – neatly symbolize the extent to which this allowed farmers to plough greater acreages more quickly with less dependence on sharecroppers.[113]

Labour tenants also suffered badly in this drive to rid farms of surplus blacks, especially since remaining residents could be driven harder to make good their loss. They were rejected or left as a result of stock limitations; due to desertion by a child; or because the land allotted to them could more profitably be used for wattle, sugar or sheep. Indeed, so common was the fate of eviction that labour tenants were termed 'grasshoppers of the field',[114] often given no more than three days' notice to jump from one farm to another together with their families and their stock. By the later 1920s, analogies were being drawn with the creation of a 'poor white' problem in Elizabethan England during the transition to capitalist wool farming. According to a journalist reporting on his travels through the Free State in 1928,

> Day after day one overtakes or meets dismal processions of labour-tenants in search of a new home, mere starveling scarecrows . . .with household goods dear at two pounds a family, trapesing in search of a home through country valued at five to six pounds an acre, where sheep are a gilt-edged investment.[115]

Their plight was given political dimensions by the Land Amendment Bill. As well as enlarging the area open to African purchase, this turned the screws on tenants. Carefully catering for the needs of small agriculturists, it allowed all farmers to retain five labour tenant families. Reinforcing the general drive to extract as much work from as few homesteads as possible, it defined labour tenants as those who, together with twelve- to eighteen-year old dependents, worked at least six months each year on a white-occupied farm. All other black residents who did not conform to this definition, or who exceeded the set limit, were subject to prohibitive licence fees. In essence, the state was attempting to eliminate the sharecropping and 'squatting' peasantry; to increase the labour appropriated from resident workers; to make farmers for whom this supply was still inadequate obtain hired hands from the reserves; and to augment the flow of migrant labour to other sectors of the economy.[116]

Protagonists of the Bill ardently promoted the onslaught on tenants. At that time a Free State sharecropper, Voetganger Manapa sourly remembered a meeting of 'Boers' addressed by the Prime Minister at Dover. According to him, General Hertzog focused on the fact that black peasants were the economic equals of white farmers, and declared:

> the day they are awakened in their minds you won't have people to drive your horses . . .you should finish their livestock and leave them with nothing. They shouldn't go on killing the land. They should work for you and come to beg for mealie meal if they starve.

Like numerous other wealthier peasants, Manapa dated the end of sharecropping, as well as relentless reduction in stock, to the very year that Hertzog appeared to encourage landlords in these actions. Associating as he did sharecropping landlords with Jews, he defined the Pact period as one in which 'Afrikaners came into the Parliament and ousted the Jews', and 'these little Boers started Hertzog's "law"'.[117]

Although 'Hertzog's law' has been interpreted as yet another sign that the Pact government favoured agricultural capital, 'progressive' farmers facing competition from better-paying employers were in fact demanding additional measures to ensure they benefitted from the wage labourers expected to emerge phoenix-like from the ashes of the peasantry. However, no success was achieved in efforts to expand the areas from which mine recruiters were banned. Mouthing liberal platitudes about Africans' right to sell their labour in the best market, the Secretary for Native Affairs simply responded that the government opposed any recommendation restricting the supply of mine labourers. Nor did organized agriculture make any headway with suggestions which strikingly prefigured policies implemented decades later in apartheid South Africa. Thus the NAU's call for a state-run labour bureaux system was brushed aside, as was the TAU's claim that white prosperity depended on complete urban segregation, and on gradual repatriation to the countryside of all male Africans apart from those accommodated in compounds.[118]

Similarly, landlords were not in the main delighted that less land than promised a decade earlier was being added to the reserves. On the contrary, they were infuriated by the offer of any additional land at all. Unlike mine owners, agriculturists had little interest in enlarging these hinterlands of migrant workers. For them, the unreliability of wage labour proved only that it was insufficiently proletarianized. At Free State farmers' meetings, there were hostile questions as to whether the Bill was in white or black interests.[119] The NAU, which had already resolved that not another acre of land should be given to Africans, called a special conference in 1927 for its Executive to justify public support for the Bill's land provisions. Many angry members were not mollified by their President's explanation that land was to be given to prevent blacks seizing the vote, and that 'The ICU was a warning to them to put their house in order.'[120] The path of reform was a perilous one, and if it entailed giving Africans ground at the expense of farmers, then there were many who preferred to tread more repressive roads. Temporarily, they had their way: the Bill was not in fact enacted for another nine years.

Thus, in the 1920s, blacks frequently experienced the shedding of a surplus population from the farms in terms of being abruptly dumped on the roadside, 'knowing not whither to go'.[121] Population statistics drily point to the ultimate choices they made. Countrywide between 1926 and 1936, the number of Africans on white-owned farms rose more slowly than the general population increase, while the reverse was true of black-owned farms and towns. The most striking shifts occurred in Natal. Here the proportion of Africans on holdings owned or occupied by non-Africans remained almost static in absolute terms, and fell dramatically from 41 to 26 per cent of the province's total African population. Simultaneously, numbers in the reserves increased by almost one-quarter; on African-owned holdings they doubled; and in towns they more than trebled.[122] Primitive accumulation in the countryside was clearly more than the infliction of untold misery on black tenants by separating them from land and stock. It was more, too, than a process whereby soil was incorporated into nascent capital. It was also a precondition for rapid industrial development, in so far as masses of Africans were suddenly severed from their means of subsistence and thrown onto the labour-market as vulnerable proletarians.

Conclusion

If agrarian transformations helped precipitate workers into the cities, then urban growth facilitated the emergence of capitalists in the countryside. But the terms of exchange were always heavily tilted against landlords. While the development of capital in towns provided many 'progressive' farmers with not only their initial wealth but also greater markets, these were rarely large or profitable enough to sustain accumulation from agriculture alone. Although the ease with which mortgage credit could be obtained encouraged commercialization of the countryside, it also contributed to class differentiation and to the exodus of 'poor whites' from the land. Despite the fact that many struggling landlords supported a government promoting manufacturing, white jobs and the maintenance of settlers in the countryside, this particular trajectory of development widened the gap between 'progressive' farmers and the state. And while some capitalist agriculturists were assuming the ideological colouring of the rising national bourgeoisie, liberalism ill-suited a grouping whose vulnerability induced a tendency to 'squeeze' rather than 'uplift' their labourers.

'Progressive' farmers did, however, draw on liberal ideas to posit the abolition of tenancy as the key to tackling an entire nexus of problems. Their commitment to this solution was not simply verbal: there was a growing tendency amongst capitalist farmers to replace all resident blacks with wage-labourers.[123] For this grouping at least, older relations of exploitation were being transformed into fetters on further capital accumulation. By contrast, amongst the mass of small farmers faced with rocketing land prices, decreased farm sizes and greater indebtedness, it was the threat of dispossession not the lure of capitalization that forced them to turn on their tenants.

Proletarianization thus hung like the sword of Damocles over the bulk of white masters and black servants alike, infusing their struggles with considerable hatred and despair. By the end of the decade, state officials were anxiously commenting that the labour tenant system, having worked well for decades, was causing considerable trouble due to cutbacks in land. 'Hence the questions of the amount of remuneration for farm labour, and of the quantity and quality of labour supplied have come to the fore.'[124] Only too well did black tenants know this. Their tortuous transition from peasants to proletarians involved dispossession, extension of work periods, intrusion of the cash-nexus, and loosening of bonds with chiefdoms. And their sense of being subject to rapidly deteriorating conditions was expressed by a Natal African from Ixopo: 'In the olden days the farmers allowed the natives to live comfortably, but it is now suddenly that they have adopted a different attitude and we feel it.'[125]

There were other key developments in the 1920s, as downward transmission of farmers' pressures contributed to capitalization of the countryside. Firstly, some 50,000 whites were added to the landed

populace between 1918 and 1931, after which year the trend was reversed and figures began to fall. Since the accommodation of this peak population occurred partly through the spread of white-occupied farms over the face of South Africa, tens of thousands of blacks were for the first time either brought into the orbit of tenancy or threatened with dispossession. Secondly, landlords' ability to make economic concessions diminished as the transition from a net importing to an exporting country of agricultural produce necess-itated greater involvement in a generally depressed world market. As one farmer expressed it in 1927, 'It will be impossible for the maize grower to compete with the Argentine in the maize markets of the world if he has to pay higher wages'.[126] Thirdly, as sharecroppers, 'squatters' and labour tenants were thrust ever closer in class terms to hired hands, so the desertion of farm youths to towns came to constitute one of the most important migrational movements of the era. Fourthly, from the late 1920s it was evident that in terms of agricultural production as well as stock and implement ownership, farm tenants were on average poorer than reserve-dwellers. Thus it was in this decade that a major turning-point occurred. From being the eagerly sought-after site of a prosperous peasantry in the early twentieth century, white holdings were by the 1920s predominantly the work-places of a poverty-stricken tenantry, and by the 1950s regarded by many reserve-dwellers as 'something to which one may be driven by calamity'.[127]

In resisting this fundamental transformation, tenants testified to the fact that it is frequently the process of proletarianization rather than its end result that produces the most militant explosions.[128] Their protest was rooted in subcultures, the oppositional character of which was being consolidated by work in towns as well as by separatist churches. And despite its generally individualistic and clandestine nature, it was often extremely effective. Nonetheless, tenants' resources were few, their divisions many and their enemy strong. Eviction was the most important weapon held by landlords – and insecurity of tenure exacerbated class, ethnic and familial differences inhibiting the emergence of overt, collective protest. Furthermore, even trajectories of struggle were at issue in this time of transition. If land-hunger remained of widespread importance, cash wages were also being thrust to the fore in the very process of transformation into workers.

However, immediately prior to the ICU's rural activities, news of the Land Amendment Bill sharply raised both tenants' levels of struggle and their consciousness of themselves as rural cultivators. Paradoxically, while 'Hertzog's law' was sometimes understood as confirming the alliance between landlords and the state, those who

recognized a disjuncture between the two forces could place a very
different interpretation on the news as it filtered down to farms.
Thus in early 1927, rumours of the mooted 50 per cent increase in
area open to African occupation precipitated a flurry of strikes in the
Natal Midlands, based upon the belief that farms were to be
expropriated from landlords and granted to labourers. Months
before the ICU formally appeared in Weenen, the wealthy farmer
representing the district announced in Parliament that

> practically the whole of my natives are on strike. I asked the reason
> why and they said – We have been informed that the Prime
> Minister is passing legislation which is going to take all these farms
> which the white men own and hand them over to us, so why
> should we work.[129]

Why indeed – especially when underlying tensions were coming to
a head and the ICU arrived with a similar message. Ndie Makume's
recollections of the Pact period capture the coalescence of some of
these strands, as well as the extent to which this was a time which
sharply broke with the past. For him, 'It was between 1926 and 1927
when the world changed for us.' Hertzog's laws, he claimed, were
responsible for the fall in maize prices and the end of sharecropping;
they also encouraged Boers to reduce tenants' plots, limit their stock,
and force Africans to work for nothing. But he recalled that these
were also the years when there came people asking: 'Man! Tell us
where your grandfathers were settled? And you would tell them, and
complain to them that the whites came and drove your people away.'
In short, these years were for him simultaneously 'the time when
General Hertzog was already standing on top of the black man's
head', and 'the time . . .when those men came, those who said they
were going to liberate people . . .Kadalie'.[130]

Although these liberators were Africans who can all too easily be
dismissed as 'petty bourgeois', contemporary white landlords were
far more perturbed by the nature of the class alliance being forged.
According to the TAU President in 1927, farmers with families
scattered on lonely holdings dared not be complacent 'while an
uneducated, semi-civilized, largely irresponsible and, under certain
conditions, highly inflammable native population is being incited to
class hatred, sedition and law breaking by agitators, no matter how
highly educated and civilized these agitators may be'.[131] From
exploring just how inflammable the black rural poor was, we can
now turn to examine why the match was lit by these 'educated and
civilized agitators'.

3. EDUCATED AND CIVILIZED AGITATORS:

The Social Origins and Character of ICU Leadership, 1924–1930

'Nothing but social contradiction in action': there are few more apt characterizations of the petty bourgeoisie.[1] On the one hand, members of this grouping resemble capitalists: they either own small-scale property or exercise a managerial role over the exploited and oppressed. On the other hand, they resemble the working class in performing either manual or mental labour. Small wonder that they are notorious for simultaneously condensing conflicting interests and wavering between the bourgeoisie and the proletariat.

But in specific times and places, elements within the broader middle classes can identify with the downtrodden. Thus in racist societies where capitalism is not full-grown, colour and class combine to encourage the weak intermediate strata to act as men of the people rather than as minions of the powerful. And where racial oppression is compounded by downward social mobility in more developed capitalist countries, the political consequences are potentially explosive. 'In view of their impending transfer into the proletariat', even the traditionally most conservative sector of the petty bourgeoisie, the self-employed, can become revolutionary. Moreover, many more groupings within the wider oppressed middle strata may 'desert their own standpoint to place themselves at that of the proletariat', and thus 'defend not their present, but their future interests'.[2] In the backward countryside of peripheral South Africa, ICU organizers undoubtedly never subordinated themselves to the underdeveloped working class. But because they were being precipitated into the labouring poor, they certainly partially transcended some of the contradictions of their backgrounds.

To begin at the beginning: with the elitist origins of most Union officials of the later 1920s. In a society where some 66 per cent of Africans were non-Christian, about 75 per cent were labourers or rural cultivators, nearly 90 per cent were illiterate, and almost 100 per cent had no direct voice in Parliament, ICU leaders of this period were predominantly Christian, educated men, drawn from the middle strata and including amongst themselves a sprinkling of voters. In many and probably most cases, they were the children of the privileged. Some obtained their preferential access to resources through being related to precolonial ruling groups. More frequently, they were the sons of professionals such as ministers or teachers. To a significant degree, they were also drawn from a rural elite: from relatively wealthy families based on freehold property, mission reserves, locations and farms.[3]

Before directing their offspring onto paths of privilege, parents named them in ways symbolizing acceptance of the cultural superiority of their white rulers. While the overwhelming majority of Union leaders had English (often Biblical) names, some – like Cecil Rhodes Mama and Conan Doyle Modiakgotla – bore even more overt signs of their origins in households which approved of the civilizing mission of the imperialists. Acquiring an identity as a child of God, a reader of books and a citizen of the Empire was an integral part of the childhood of numerous ICU organizers. So too was emulating the lifestyles of wealthier whites, with some leaders having fathers 'who insisted upon us living and behaving as respective (sic) Europeans'.[4]

Becoming a member of the black 'AmaRespectables' was, however, increasingly difficult. Nearly all ICU leaders were born after the 1886 discovery that potentially immense profits lay concealed beneath the ground of the Witwatersrand. Many were in fact conceived after the turn of the century, and they often derided their Congress rivals as the 'Old Brigade'. This use of youthfulness as a political metaphor aptly symbolized the radical changes in black middle-class lives over one generation. As monopoly capital seized hold of the gold mines, so economic and political dominance abruptly shifted from white merchants and rentier landlords, to 'Randlords', manufacturers and commercial farmers. In the process, a vast African labour force was coerced into being on a scale that left little room for 'black Englishmen'. And as the policy of segregation began to permeate all the fissures of South African society, so future ICU leaders found it ever harder to follow in their fathers' footsteps.[5]

This is well illustrated in the case of Gilbert Coka, a Union activist who was born the son of relatively prosperous Vryheid 'squatters' in 1910. Two years later, their white landlord demanded the labour services of Gilbert's elder brother, and to safeguard their children's education his parents reluctantly left for town. Here their fortunes rapidly deteriorated, as the wages earned by Gilbert's father became increasingly less adequate for the family's survival. Moreover, like many other ICU organizers, Gilbert was a junior son, his life chances subordinated to those of his elder siblings. By the time he was ready for secondary school his penurious father could no longer scrape together the required ten to twenty pounds per annum. Hence Gilbert spent part of 1923 herding cattle, and it was only after teaching for a year, and experiencing the indignities of life as a domestic servant, that he clambered into Standard Seven.[6]

Coka's desperate struggle to obtain secondary education was related to the fact that school, rather than church, was by then the dominant institution consolidating the black *AmaRespectables*. Education – especially higher education – was of the essence in escaping from the ranks of labourers and poor peasants into those of the salariat and successful self-employed. It was a prerequisite for evading politically coercive measures such as the obligation to carry passes and exclusion from Parliament. And it was the key to identifying culturally with the white dominant classes against the black under-classes. Precisely because it condensed so many meanings, 'education' was a central ideological symbol around which the middle classes coalesced, and through which they differentiated themselves from the masses. Thus from the heights of Gilbert Coka's Standard Six schooling, his girlfriends of the mid-1920s looked very small: 'as most of them were but indifferently educated, I looked down upon them as country louts'.[7]

As their insistence on the insignia of 'education' or 'civilization' suggests, numerous other organizers held similar views. Not only had the great majority of them passed through the lower reaches of school, but many had also bridged the financial chasm separating primary from secondary education. Indeed, a significant number had actually graduated as teachers. Moreover, despite head office complaints about the poor English of Branch Secretaries, this force-feeding on mission school diet was not restricted to senior officials. While minor leaders did tend to be less educated, six of the ten branch organizers whose scholastic careers are known had qualified as teachers. In a country where only about one hundred Africans could boast the same, five had actually passed Standard Eight. Since only 702 Africans were in secondary school in 1924, paid Union activists of the later 1920s were in fact intellectual giants.[8]

For this they paid an ideological as well as a monetary price. Immersion in the religion of white missionaries involved listening to sermons such as that given to students at Lovedale, the premier Cape school, on the Eighth Commandment, in which pupils were gravely informed of the sanctity of property and the sinfulness of Communism. Furthermore, the very form of secular tuition taught students to revere individual achievement, to bow to authority, and to value the lifestyle of their conquerors. Similarly, its content was directed at teaching pupils to equate civilization with colonial expansion and barbarism with tribal Africa. English was thus far and away the most important subject, while history examinations in Natal crudely emphasized the fact of conquest with questions like: 'What took place on December 16, 1838?' In ways which ranged from teaching the secrets that distinguish mental from manual labour to encouraging the singing of *Rule Britannia*, mission schools devoted much effort to nurturing a middle class with the appropriate ideological orientation. Their success was partially reflected in the fact that some 25 per cent of Africans enlisting for overseas duty in the First World War were drawn from the educated elite, mainly from the teaching profession. Amongst the numerous future ICU organizers who demonstrated loyalty to the Empire in this way was the well-schooled Jason Jingoes, who joined up partly because 'I, as a member of the British Commonwealth, felt deeply involved.'[9]

Yet for various reasons, mission schools did not once and for all imbue Union officials with liberal, constitutionalist ideas. First, unlike many older Congress leaders, most ICU organizers were taught at a time when schools were being wrenched into line with segregationist South Africa. Increasingly mission education of the 1910s and 1920s was directed at preparing pupils for lives of obedient subordination rather than equal opportunity. As such, it was often bitterly resented. Secondly, the theory that schools inculcated moderate methods of protest is belied even by student resistance. Thus Champion displayed an early rebellious streak, and was expelled for organizing pupils against the missionaries' disciplinary regime. Many more future ICU activists were probably affected by the 1920 conflict at their *alma mater*, Lovedale. After refusing to eat the cheaper bread foisted on them as a cost-cutting exercise, about three hundred students hoisted the Red Flag and marched on the school. Here they gutted the grain store, wrecked the electric power house, smashed all church windows and stoned the principal. At a time when alliances were already being forged between the educated and the illiterate, this display of militancy symbolized the limits to missionaries' endeavours to reconcile the schooled to their lot.[10]

Indeed, the generalized post-war upsurge of resistance forced the dominant classes to recognize that much more was needed for this exercise than education alone. Both mining and commercial establishments hastily provided funds for new bodies such as the Johannesburg Bantu Men's Social Centre (where the petty bourgeoisie would hopefully while away leisure hours in respectable activities), as well as the personnel for novel institutions like Joint Councils (which provided an arena for educated blacks to voice their grievances). These private initiatives backed by white liberals had some success: certainly they attracted as members men like Champion, H. Selby Msimang and Alexander Jabavu. Moreover, the state supplemented these attempts to divorce the middle from the dangerous classes. Thus, in addition to the creation of various political safety-valves like Native Advisory Boards, draft legislation in the early 1920s proffered to 'more advanced natives' better housing, urban freehold rights and lighter pass laws.[11]

But these were the solutions of larger capital, and they were strongly opposed by the constituencies that the Nationalist and Labour Parties were trying to mobilize. As black resistance subsided during the post-war economic slump – and as the Rand Revolt drove home the lesson of widespread white opposition to African advancement – so the costs of consolidating a black middle class were re-evaluated. The South African Party itself abandoned the above-mentioned draft bills, and replaced them with the 1923 Natives Urban Areas Act. In this draconian law, dividing the black populace was less important than impelling all Africans to 'minister to the needs of the White man'.[12] When the Pact coalition came to power, it intensified the assault on the economic base, the political rights and the ideological role of the African middle classes. Their hopes shattered, ICU organizers were quick to perceive the implications of these measures. In addressing an Orange Free State meeting in 1926, Keable 'Mote claimed angrily that the Government wanted to make them all slaves to get cheap labour.[13].

Downward Class Mobility

For fringe members of the middle strata, this threat of being reduced to workers was very real. For many Union officials with access to plots in mission reserves, locations or African-owned farms, it was already almost impossible to survive off the land alone. As the 1927 Natal Provincial Secretary Sam Dunn knew full well, even a hundred-acre allotment of cane land was unworkable without substantial monetary backing obtainable only by labouring in town. Champion too found that neither inheriting an interest in his father's holdings nor possessing a small mission reserve plot saved him from the urban wage-earning market. Furthermore, although numerous (mostly Natal-based) organizers continued to straddle town and countryside, the 'civilized labour policy' edged them closer to dispossession by undermining the practice of channelling urban incomes into rural areas. The 'gradual but certain elimination of the

Native landowner' identified by officialdom in the early 1920s was clearly apparent by 1926, when African-owned holdings were less in area than ten years previously, and Champion was about to sell his landed inheritance.[14]

Equally vulnerable to proletarianization were other small-scale producers and property owners. Like Doyle Modiakgotla, a building contractor with no fixed job when he became an ICU Provincial Secretary, African artisans were often losing their independent livelihoods. By the late 1920s, fewer than 60 per cent of mission-trained craftsmen were self-employed. Amongst those hardest hit were shoemakers, who were competing not only with mechanizing factories and 'poor whites' but also with British manufacturers who were dumping cheap boots for the African market in South Africa. Due largely to pressure from this last quarter, one white employer gave notice in 1927 that his factory was closing, because conditions were worse than ever before. Almost certainly, the numerous educated bootmakers and cobblers who entered Union branch structures at this time would have agreed. Indeed, those practising this craft were prominent amongst blacks being forced down the class ladder into the ranks of deskilled labourers. Partly to avoid the higher wages enforced in the industry by the Pact government, whites were converting desperate African cobblers into their semi-proletarianized outworkers. Apparently in this position was the boot repairer Joseph Bhengu of Empangeni, Zululand, who was being 'housed and supported by Europeans' at the same time as he addressed ICU meetings in 1927.[15]

Other members of the black self-employed hardly fared much better. 'I am not making a living, I am making only a little bit of a living', exclaimed a butcher in 1931, doubtless expressing the feelings of his fellow tradesmen involved as ICU activists.[16] Selling services could be even less remunerative: by the time he became Bloemfontein Branch Secretary, James Mogaecho had been reduced to combining his flamboyant comic acting in 'Dem Darkies' with the mundane duties of a clerk. The fact that in 1921 less than 0.2 per cent of the African male population were traders, hawkers or artisans indicates the lack of profit in such occupations. In part, this was a consequence of dependence on penurious consumers; in part, it was due to rigid state-imposed restrictions. Especially in small towns, municipal authorities tended to be extremely sensitive to the interests of the white petty bourgeoisie and to farmers' fears of a labour shortage. Thus Peter Malepe, Branch Chairman in the Free State village of Parys from 1927, was allowed to hawk wood in the location, but was forbidden to run an eating-house. African traders were in fact prohibited in the Free State, and here as elsewhere burdensome licence fees, exorbitant rents and a myriad petty restrictions stifled most other forms of accumulation.[17]

Largely because the probability of being extruded as a wage-earner was considerably greater than that of emerging as a capitalist, many who had scrambled into self-employment were willing to articulate worker demands. Not that they ceased in the struggle to differentiate themselves from ordinary blacks. Almost certainly, most Kroonstad ICU Women's Section leaders were distinguished from those forced into the labour-market by possession of a house, and hence ability to draw rent from lodgers. In fighting against increased municipal rates, they were defending their middle-class status. Yet so precarious was their position that a mere sixpenny monthly increment precipitated them into militant protest. And so close were they to the working class that the demand for higher wages was a central focus of their struggle.[18]

Separate women's sections of the Union also existed in Natal and the eastern Transvaal, while elsewhere as well there were female delegates to conferences and female branch activists. But black women, subordinated to men in almost every sphere of life, were hardly obvious leadership material for a male-dominated protest movement. Hence they were always in a tiny minority amongst officials, and it appears to have been mainly middle-class women – like the Natal nurse Miss. C. Ntombela – who most easily broke through the constraints inhibiting female participation in leadership. At least some of these women appear to have attained their positions through relationships with male organizers. As one ex-ICU member recalled, the minimum duty of the wife of an official was to join the Union, to avoid arousing supporters' suspicions.[19]

Like women, humble craftsmen such as cobblers were generally confined to the lower leadership levels within the ICU. The same fate met even James Ngcobo, a self-proclaimed 'bricklayer and carpenter by trade and an architect by profession'.[20] White-collar aspirations or no, in the eyes of many senior officials such people were firmly situated on the inferior side of the mental/manual divide that traversed even the educated stratum itself. Moreover, for those who were simultaneously small-scale producers and activists, restriction to local levels of organization was imposed by the very nature of their daily lives.

Differences in ICU salaries reinforced the social gap between such rooted branch leaders and itinerant senior officials. As early as 1924, the inability of the latter to live the life of the poorly remunerated or unpaid former was epitomized in Kadalie's visit to Upington in the Cape. Here he was not only expected to stay with the penurious 'coloured' Branch Secretary and his large family in a tiny house in the township, but also to share their cheap food and unhygienic water. Rejecting such a dramatic reduction in his living standards, Kadalie spent two hungry days haunting the post office, sending off telegrams to headquarters appealing for ready cash, and drinking only from the municipal tap. Whether members witnessed such elitist behaviour is unclear, but certainly Kadalie's meeting here was exceptionally poorly attended.[21]

By the later 1920s, most paid officials had additional reasons for considering themselves superior to either self-employed branch activists or ordinary blacks. Although many had previously been foremen or mine compound clerks, the great bulk were drawn from prestigious white-collar jobs in non-productive sectors of the economy. Thus the majority of Branch Secretaries had been teachers, while other occupations represented at this and higher levels included interpreters, bank clerks and book-keepers. In functional terms, the very nature of these jobs could place their occupants in an antagonistic position to the masses. Albert Nzula, one of the many state employees who subsequently became ICU organizers, had translated magisterial pronouncements to those convicted under the pass laws. Keable 'Mote, a teacher, had helped instill the inferiority of manual to mental labour. And James Dippa, one of the numerous Union leaders who had been mine compound clerks, had participated in waking workers at 4a.m. and sjambokking them into line. Undeniably, the education of these activists had often been used to assist the subordination of Africans to white employers, white authority and white culture.[22]

Nonetheless, the structural antagonism between such black employees and their white masters must also be acknowledged. Here the issue of pay was of the essence: most white-collar employees received pittances which barely acknowledged the role they played for capital and the state. As Congressman John Dube stated sourly,

It does not matter how much a Native has improved or qualified himself, he is only 'A Kaffir'; that is the ordinary white man's view, 'He is only "A Kaffir" and ought to get a Kaffir's wage'.[23]

Indeed, the pay of many at the lower levels of the salariat – such as most mine clerks and teachers – was often less than that of skilled black mine workers. Moreover, even those who earned more than labourers often experienced greater impoverishment, either because they had no other source of income or because they were frantically trying to maintain 'civilized' standards. Hence indigence was a major impulse behind the post-war surge of white-collar organization. This was especially noticeable in the teaching profession, into the ranks of which many reluctantly entered, and from which they escaped with relief. Yet the various African teachers' unions had little success in alleviating the 'lean and hungry look' of black school staff. Throughout the 1920s, the great bulk of them irregularly received two to five pounds a month. (Since over 70 per cent of Natal and Free State teachers were unqualified, large numbers were concentrated at the lower end of this scale.) Small wonder that many instructors in the countryside were critically dependent on income derived from land and stock, and whole-heartedly shared workers' grievances about the terms on which they sold their labour-power. Like poverty-stricken rural teachers elsewhere, their life experiences were so similar to those of uneducated labourers that they could well be metaphorically termed 'the proletarians of the learned class'.[24]

The migratory existence of many white-collar employees also paralleled that of ordinary workers. Badly paid posts – generally without leave, pensions, tenure or increments – hardly fulfilled the aspirations of educated Africans. Hence Champion (interpreter-cum-policeman-cum-salesman-cum-clerk) held no fewer than eight jobs over twelve years before becoming a labour organizer. Similarly, Jason Jingoes spent eight years drifting around as a teacher and clerk before substituting these dead-end careers for an ICU position. Understandably, the Union's four pounds a month Branch Secretaryship was attractive to such disillusioned wage-earners, some of whom were entering the labour-market every three months.[25]

In part, this constant movement was a consequence of devaluation of middle strata skills and status. Between 1918 and 1926, as the white new petty bourgeoisie increased by a massive 44 per cent, so their black counterparts were forced to ever lower levels in the hierarchy of control. Kadalie's only South African experience as a clerk terminated abruptly when whites refused to work under him. And while teachers evaded competition from racist whites, they could not escape intensified surveillance by the state. As discriminatory syllabi were enforced from the early 1920s, and as white inspectors tightened their hold over black staff, so resentful teachers became increasingly aware that their autonomy was being eroded. They were also being rendered more vulnerable to extrusion: two Estcourt branch organizers were ex-teachers ignominiously dismissed for violating the state's rigid sexual code of behaviour.[26]

Those cast out from white-collar employment in this way found it difficult to claw their way up. During the First World War, it was reported that openings 'for merely book-learned Native men and women are few. The tendency to close all clerical occupations to Natives makes teaching almost the only non-manual vocation open to them.'[27] By 1921, less than 1 per cent of African males could find work as professionals, interpreters, clerks or shop assistants. After the advent of the Pact government, even the teaching conduit began to prove incapable of absorbing mission school graduates. Better-paid staff were being replaced by unqualified instructors clamouring for employment, while some state functionaries anxiously intoned that jobs for educated Africans were 'everywhere deplorably limited'. But at a time when absorbing 'poor whites' was a national priority, most sectors of the dominant classes were only too happy to dispense with the services of black intellectuals who produced no profits.[28]

Schooled, productive wage-earners were not necessarily any more successful, as mission-trained printer Henry Tyamzashe knew full well. In 1921, having been fired because he was black, he wrote to Lovedale pointedly asking why he had been educated. According to him, lack of finance inhibited self-employment, while legislative colour bars – and racist white trade unions – blocked entry to skilled work. 'It is useless to send our children to school to learn trades when work, the means of livelihood, is denied them', he wrote bitterly. And in a statement that encapsulated a key difference between Congressmen and Union leaders of the future, he insisted: 'The Native question cannot be solved apart from the economic.'[29]

Although Tyamzashe had found employment as a foreman in an Indian-owned Johannesburg printing firm by 1925, the ascendancy of social forces represented by the Pact government accelerated the process pushing him out of the petty bourgeoisie. As a black sweated employee, he suffered instant dismissal when the state enforced the payment of wage rates demanded by the white Typographical Union. Fortunately, as an ICU member, the enraged Tyamzashe could appeal for assistance. Presaging its role as a magnet for educated blacks being squeezed out of their jobs, the Union's first success in the industrial heart of South Africa was securing back pay for this aspirant businessman. Within months, Tyamzashe had exchanged his unemployed status for that of sub-editor of *The Workers' Herald*.[30]

Thus it was as victims of rapidly encroaching proletarianization that numerous educated blacks entered the Union as leaders. Some were men without jobs: primary schools bulging at the seams were extruding literate Africans at a pace too fast for segregationist South Africa. Others were self-employed blacks who had been reduced to skilled labour for others, white-collar employees whose intellectual functions had been downgraded or petty bourgeois elements clinging to the margins of independence. Most were frustrated and poorly remunerated; almost all were members of a growing 'army of starveling "intellectuals"', people whose lot was 'in no wise more enviable than that of the "ordinary" wage-worker'.[31]

Indeed, many ICU Secretaryships became the province of blacks whose experiences were often indistinguishable from those of typical labourers. Some had been underground miners, experiencing to the full the horrors of compound life and vicious white overseers. Others had been domestic servants: Jason Jingoes had spent long hours scrubbing for whites who subsequently accused him of theft to avoid paying his wages. At least one organizer, Joseph Malaza, had previously been a farm labourer. Appropriately enough, he was District Secretary for Bethal, and captured the attention of brutally exploited workers here by relating how his master nearly thrashed him to death in his youth.[32]

Nor was all this proletarian experience concentrated in the past. Like the educated and pass-exempted Thomas Mbeki who became Transvaal Provincial Secretary, numerous leaders joined the ICU as ordinary labourers. This was especially true of foreign-born blacks, often unable to speak the vernacular and hence totally redundant as mediators between white capitalists and black workers. West Indian-born J.G. Gumbs was a chemist reduced to a dock rigger during his long presidency of the Union. Similarly Kadalie, despite his white-collar posts in northern colonies, was for years after his 1918 move to South Africa compelled to work as a packer, messenger and parcel 'boy'.[33]

Of course, it was possible to fall further than the law-abiding working class. Stealing from whites was a favourite way of closing the gap between petty bourgeois incomes and expenses, and could in addition be a challenge to white values and white law. Provincial Secretaries Alex Maduna and Sam Dunn both had such thefts in their backgrounds. So too did Simon Elias, apparently an independent legal agent before he became a Free State organizer. In 1907, after years spent working for a pittance from a Bloemfontein commercial firm, Elias was instantly sacked when he asked for a rise. He decided then and there that 'I could not work for a White man unless he considered I was a human being.' But the following eighteen years of self-employment were hard ones, and in 1910 Elias spent a month in jail for theft. Five years later, his repertoire had expanded to housebreaking and theft, for which he earned three months' hard labour or a fifteen-pound fine. Apparently, the sentences neither served as deterrents nor taught him discretion: in 1925, he spent three months in prison for stealing from the ICU.[34]

But as leaders' rogue pasts permeated the ICU's present, the movement gained as much ideologically as it lost in hard cash.

According to one commentator, Union-led protest was particularly provocative because organizers

> were not drawn from the 'respectable classes'. They had come straight from the ranks of the workers themselves, and they had a ruggedness and militancy that men accustomed to making obeisances before authority found outrageous.[35]

Of course, the more significant point was that activists had risen from the rank-and-file only after they had lost their commissions in the *corps d'élite*. As volatile youths in an increasingly oppressive society, Union officials had acquired skills and knowledge grooming them for jobs beyond the wildest dreams of most ordinary blacks. But when turned out into a hostile world, most had been demoted, degraded, or dumped on the economic scrap-yard inhabited by the labouring poor. It was precisely this actual or imminent transfer from one class to another that underlay organizers' impassioned yet sophisticated defence of the interests of their futures.

Downward Identification: Politics, Ideology and Struggle

Yet ICU leaders did not quit the *AmaRespectables* for the masses simply because this was the logic of their own narrowly defined class trajectories. The growing economic gulf separating them from upper-middle-class blacks and the white bourgeoisie was reflected and reinforced in many more subtle ways. Politically, culturally, socially and ideologically, marginal members of the intermediate strata were being flung into the milieu of the common people. And it was partly for these reasons that Kadalie had considerable success when he set out to recruit 'intelligent leadership' for his movement from 1925.[36]

Correctly, he claimed that the African intellectuals who responded had decided they had no other channel through which to voice their grievances. After the First World War, white liberals proved at best weak sponsors and at worst potent enemies of the *AmaRespectables*. By 1920, middle-class Africans who had witnessed the passage of repressive legislation and the brutal crushing of black protest were in no mood for uncritical reliance on these 'friends of the natives'. Four years later, a clear breach in liberal hegemony was evident as all major organizations with black voters, including the ICU, backed the Pact coalition. But the limitations inherent in supporting yet another sector of the ruling groups soon became apparent. As the disillusioned Kadalie subsequently argued: instead of redistributing goods previously reserved for big finance amongst all South Africans, the Pact government had given the black child stones.[37]

One of the major threats posed by the legislature was a Bill to strip some sixteen thousand educated, propertied and wealthier Cape Africans of the vote. The following year, the 1927 Native Administration Act powerfully reinforced the alliance between capitalists and chiefs, and attested to the political irrelevance of educated blacks to white rulers. Union activists were stung by the impending removal of a voting right which many had yet to attain, and also scathingly denounced the compensation offered. They rejected the whites who would represent Africans in Parliament as 'dummies', and saw no place for themselves amongst the chiefs and the 'good boys' who would staff the proposed Native Council.[38] To an even greater degree than their upper stratum compatriots, lower-middle-class blacks were being thrust closer to the masses on the issue of substantial exclusion from both existing and proposed forms of westernized political representation.

The same was true with regard to passes. As it was, exemption was not granted to such modest men as hawkers, ministers in most independent churches, or unqualified teachers in the Free State. Furthermore, even the privileged *izemtiti* (pass-exempted Africans) remained subject to police harassment to produce their certificates, which were applicable only in the province of issue. Thus at least one exempted African found himself once again subject to the full battery of pass legislation when transferred as an ICU organizer from Natal to the Transvaal. To make matters worse: from the mid-1920s the state began to whittle away the ranks of the *izemtiti*, an action which the South African Agricultural Union had long been demanding. Both Kadalie's and 'Mote's applications for exemption were rejected, and like so many other ICU officials they were continually harassed under the pass laws. Furthermore, the existing thicket of municipal regulations became almost impenetrable under the Urban Areas Act. By the mid-1920s in the repressive inland provinces, local controls affecting even provincially exempted blacks often included visitors' passes, residential passes, stand permits, seeking-work passes, employment registration certificates, work-on-own-behalf certificates and entertainment permits. Clearly, it was becoming ever more difficult for urbanized lower-middle-class blacks to identify with the sentiments of the elitist Native Farmers' Association of the eastern Cape: that 'the better class Natives travel freely, unmolested and without passes, while the lower class are required to carry a pass when moving in places where they are unknown'.[39]

It was also becoming ever more possible for members of the intermediate strata to acquire proto-nationalist world-views in reaction to the heightened racial oppression and class suppression that structured their daily lives. Both white state functionaries and upper–middle-class Africans anxiously commented on the rise of 'race consciousness', and claimed that contempt for whites was especially evident in country villages where blacks were so harshly treated by white employers. Thus Champion, having absorbed some ICU ideas at the meetings he attended as a spy for the Chamber of Mines, explained to his reluctant wife why he had decided to become a Union leader:

> I feel the call that I should leave . . .my big salary and suffer with the people that I have been kraaling and marshalling for the capitalists, some of whom I will never meet, in order to ameliorate my nation's conditions.[40]

Separatist churches were often of great significance in consolidating such commitment to an African nation. Orthodox Christianity, in which obedience to God was inextricably tied to subordination to whites, was increasingly unacceptable to lower-middle-class blacks of this period. Hence fringe members of the petty bourgeoisie were drawn into the popular groundswell of anti-white feeling manifested in the burgeoning of Ethiopian churches. Most ICU activists-cum-ministers emerged from these bodies, and very many Union officials belonged to them. And although numerous leaders descended no further than the respectable African Methodist Episcopal Church (AME), this class-bound body was singularly vocal in its nationalism. According to a leading white minister in 1926, its message of 'Africa for the Kaffir' made it the *'gevaarlikste seksie naas die Mohammedane'* (most dangerous sect after the Muslims).[41] As if exposing Union activists to such pernicious doctrines was not enough, the AME also provided them with invaluable organizational skills. This was especially important for women, blocked off as they were from most associations other than the Congress Women's League. Undoubtedly, Mabel Klassen's experience as an AME official contributed to her development as a 'fearless lady organizer'.[42]

At ICU branch levels, leaders were often drawn from less sophisticated Ethiopian churches. This fed into the Union's millenarian undertones, and also helped to infuse numerous separatist churches with ICU overtones. Thus the enterprising Lucas Sethabela of Lindley, Orange Free State, had for years been trying to sue the Brethern Mission Church for expelling him as their preacher. His ultimate solution was to win ICU chairmanship, to establish the Union Brethern Mission Church, and to continue his quarrel, 'for he trust the money of the ICU'. Such opportunism aside, separatist ministers were generally valuable assets on Branch Executives. This was markedly so in rural organization: thanks to their past experience of clandestine work on farms, preacher-activists often successfully penetrated these bastions of white reaction.[43]

External ideological inputs were, however, crucial in transforming rejection of white religion into a broader nationalist outlook. As servicemen, numerous organizers had been exposed to world-wide anti-colonial struggles and to less racially discriminatory societies. The profound transformation which this frequently wrought in their world views was expressed by Jingoes, who claimed those who returned 'were different from the other people at home. Our behaviour, as we showed the South Africans, was . . .more like what was expected among them of a white man.' When potential leaders leave and later re-enter backward and cramped regions, the impact of their more advanced ideas and practices has often been crucial in accelerating change:

> An *élite* consisting of some of the most active, energetic, enterprising and disciplined members of the society [goes] abroad and assimilates the culture and historical experiences of the most advanced countries of the West, without however losing the most essential characteristics of its own nationality, that is to say without breaking its sentimental and historical links with its own people. Having thus performed its intellectual apprenticeship it returns to its own country and compels the people to an enforced awakening, skipping historical stages in the process.[44]

Yet activists who never departed the shores of South Africa could also appropriate and transmit ideas highly suitable for a forced march to modernization. The rise of Afrikaner nationalism had a magnetic effect: innumerable officials adapted for themselves the inflammable ideas used by their oppressors to fight British imperialism. Furthermore, leaders eagerly read about anti-colonial struggles in India, and there was obvious use to which they could put the declarations by eminent world statesmen about the rights of oppressed nations to self-determination. Not surprisingly, such tenets were prominent within the ICU's discourse. As the Orange Free State Provincial Secretary Keable 'Mote told a village audience: 'I am going to speak about the spirit of the age, which is that every nationality in the world is struggling for political freedom.'[45]

Perhaps so: but it was the struggle of Africans in particular that most concerned Union organizers. Hence Garveyism had considerable appeal, not least due to its association with the ideas of American liberators and 'Africa for the Africans'. The class character of its nationalism also touched a chord amongst many fringe members of the middle classes. Indeed, the ICU's first business venture was '"The Black Man" Company', founded in 1920 in co-operation with the Universal Negro Improvement Association. In addition to the

establishment of co-operative stores, this body sought the organization of workers 'throughout the African Continent, by means of
establishing a Branch . . .of the Company in various centres deemed
necessary by the Directors'. Even after the break with the Garveyists
in 1921, some ICU officials continued to be deeply influenced by
their ideology, and to flirt with notions of trade unionism as a wing
of a black economic self-help movement.[46]

Yet if many lower-middle-class blacks were attracted by bourgeois nationalist ideas, there were also those who were influenced by
organized socialism. This was particularly true of educated
employees who were intimately acquainted with exploitation.
Amongst such individuals was Herbert Msane, a wage-earner on the
mines for a decade before becoming a Branch Secretary in Greytown, Natal. During mass protest on the Rand in 1918, he wrote a
vivid pamphlet betokening his membership of the socialist Industrial
Workers of Africa. Drawing on rural idioms to denounce white
capitalists, he forcefully told blacks to 'forget all distinctions of
nationalities', because 'you are oppressed and milked and you are the
cows they live on . . .Native Workers! Unite! Workers! Unite!'[47]

Another veteran of the Industrial Workers of Africa was the
teacher William Thibedi, who in the mid-1920s was a Communist
Party member as well as an ICU shop-steward. After it resolved in
1924 to concentrate on the black proletariat, the Party had a
significant impact on the development of the Union's intellectuals.
The first ICU branch in the Transvaal was in fact established by
white Communists and their African recruits, including Thomas
Mbeki. By 1926, five members of the Union's National Council
were Party members, and the resolution barring dual membership
that same year did not eradicate socialist influences. Tactically and
theoretically, those who had contact with the CP were frequently
more sophisticated than other organizers, and the Party certainly
concentrated some educated minds on the possibility of joining in
struggle with black workers and peasants.[48]

Of much greater import in facilitating this alliance were diffuse
pressures from below. Class barriers were difficult to maintain in
segregated, overcrowded townships, especially when petty bourgeois blacks were losing their footing on their privileged rungs.
Thus numerous unemployed mission-trained craftsmen allegedly
lived 'riotous degraded lives, associating with the lowest class, and
even with criminals'.[49] In the countryside too, the bonds of
community, culture and racial oppression could reinforce tendencies
to downward identification by the lower middle classes. As the sole
teacher in a ramshackle rural school, Coka for the first time lived in a
hut and subsisted on mealie-meal. Through daily visits to pupils'

homesteads, he gained an intimate knowledge of the tribulations of migrant labourers' families. Most isolated, penurious rural teachers were in fact compelled to live near and with the people, not least to maintain school attendance, and to win the support of local notables who generally had considerable influence over their lives. For Union leaders like Jacob Nhlapo, who taught for two years at a Reitz farm school in the Free State before becoming Branch Secretary there, the links thus forged were crucial in ICU penetration of the countryside.[50]

Ethnically-orientated cultural events also helped integrate petty bourgeois blacks into rural communities. Even when middle-class Africans were drawn from families which had disassociated themselves from chiefdoms, they generally grew up speaking the language of a particular ethnic group, participating in some of its political and cultural practices, and often acquiring a pantheon of heroes who had resisted white conquest. In new situations, pressures from below could rapidly induce them to invoke these attributes in order to elide class differences. Coka, clumsily participating in 'ancient traditions of which I knew little', quickly realized that this was the high road to popularity for 'a townboy, a teacher, and an educated young man'.[51]

Such fraternization could itself lead schooled blacks to articulate the hardships of those whose lives they shared. Kadalie claimed it was his exposure as a mine clerk to 'the systematic torture of the African people in Southern Rhodesia that kindled the spirit of revolt in me'. His subsequent emergence as a popular spokesman and disseminator of ideas derived from the wider world was in fact symptomatic of a much broader trend. Especially in the intellectual wastes of the countryside, the few available literate blacks were invariably nudged into central positions in communities. A male teacher, on the farms and villages where his work so often took him, was 'in many cases the only decently educated person'. Understandably, illiterate Africans saw him as much more than an instructor: they sought him out for 'advice in their own difficulties'; he frequently occupied 'a position of authority and respect'; and he was perceived as being capable of interpreting the white man's civilization. As in other countries, the professional and political roles of rural teachers were so closely intertwined that it was relatively easy for them to become activists challenging oppressors on their own terms. Similarly, humble literate cobblers were prominent as grass-roots leaders in movements in capitalizing Europe as well as in the ICU in South Africa. Thus it was partly as archetypal ideologists of ordinary rural people (and partly because Union officials arriving in a village tended to gravitate towards middle-class men), that petty bourgeois blacks almost certainly predominated in elected positions on branch committees in the countryside.[52]

Many such spokesmen for the labouring poor had already served an apprenticeship in localized struggles. In addition to those Union activists who had headed some of the post-war wage and anti-pass campaigns, there were many who had played a leading role in small-scale collective resistance. Their constituencies ranged from scholars and servicemen to peasants, pass-bearing women, and workers. Before becoming an ICU official, compound foreman Jim London was sacked for articulating the grievances of black workers before a Wage Board hearing. Abel Ngcobo, who had won mass support in a Natal mission reserve in his battles against land restrictions and for democratic elections, continued the struggle after his appointment as a Union organizer. Likewise, in the early 1920s, Josiah Moshoko had been Secretary of the Harrismith Vigilance Committee, which campaigned against passes for women. Within weeks of the first ICU meeting here, Moshoko was again fighting the same issue – this time as a Union Branch Secretary. Clearly, ICU-led resistance was often but an extension of existing conflicts, considerably broadened by the injection of resources and leadership on a national scale.[53]

This was especially true in the countryside. Here the introduction of militant schooled activists from the outside – and the transformation of middle-class villagers into full-time Union officials – had weighty implications. It provided the opportunity for the rural poor to escape circumscribed worlds, which prepared them well for individualistic defiance but provided little training for more sophisticated, unified protests. Moreover, there was virtually no other way in which the consciousness and struggles of ordinary blacks could be refined and directed onto a higher plane. The new social groups tortuously emerging in the countryside did not spontaneously throw up intellectuals with advanced skills and innovative ideas. Without the mediation of schools and churches, labour tenants on farms and the semi-proletarianized in reserves did not automatically generate thinking and organizing elements providing a wider social and political awareness. Consequently, most larger-scale struggles on the land in twentieth-century South Africa have been dependent on leaders who were deeply influenced by social forces other than the rural under-classes. Here as elsewhere, almost 'every organic development of the peasant masses, up to a certain point', has been linked to and contingent upon shifts amongst this self-same category of intellectuals.[54]

Hence, in the later 1920s, it was of considerable significance that marginalized middle-class blacks had already been impelled into motion. Nor did future ICU leaders have to travel far before reaching the masses. As educated, racially oppressed men and women, they were often erstwhile ideologists of the labouring poor, and generally derived from social groupings being eroded by the forces of proletarianization. It was precisely this complex of factors that enabled them so easily to identify with rural blacks on the four key issues of the day: racial discrimination, landlessness, low wages and passes. The difference this made to the class content of the nationalism propagated by the two major political bodies of the time was succinctly expressed by Charles Kumalo:

> The ICU fought for freedom. Those of Congress also fought for freedom but didn't talk about money. The ICU was concerned with wages . . .[and helping the evicted] back onto the farms . . .and claimed that in freedom people would be liberated and not be stopped for passes.[55]

Upward Identification: Salaried Positions In The ICU

But the ICU message was a contradictory one, and these were not the only claims made about the nature of freedom. Indeed, organizers' paid positions at last gave them opportunities to scramble back into the middle classes, and provided a material base for upward identification. By monopolizing the tasks of conception and control within the Union, officials increasingly and ironically developed skills and obligations distancing them from the under-classes. In larger branches this gap often widened, in so far as many activists delegated more menial work to a plethora of hired clerks, chauffeurs, and even general factotums acting as cooks-cum-servants-cum-errand-'boys'. Furthermore, where leaders retained or obtained through their ICU work a stake in property, their interests could rapidly collide with those of their members. Thus Johannes Mogorosi, the Kroonstad Branch Chairman who simultaneously ran an eating-house and rented three stands in the location, was noticeably wary about risking his investment by prolonging ICU protest over municipal rates. Operating on a far grander scale, Champion augmented his landed interests by soliciting thousands of pounds from workers – and diverting thousands more from general Union funds – to finance an extensive network of urban enterprises. Between 1925 and 1928, these included the *Vuka Afrika* Company (an eating-house-cum-general dealer managed by Champion's wife); the Natal Boot and Shoe Repairing Hospital; Star Tailors; a newspaper, *Udibi lwase Afrika*; the African Workers' Club; and a clothing factory, the African Workers' Co-operative Society. As a man prominent in the black businessmen's organization, the United National Association of Commerce and Industry Ltd, Champion also manifested his growing shift from the salaried to the propertied petty bourgeoisie in ever more explicit denunciations of Communism. He disagreed with it, he declared in 1929, because it was a system under which wealthy men's possessions were distributed amongst the poor. Prone to such delightfully unambiguous statements and practices, Champion was the very model of an upwardly mobile petty bourgeois leader.[56]

As such, he was also the subject of rueful admiration amongst some ICU officials. According to one, 'Champion was a wise man, for he did not use his money for drink and women but banked it, though it was stolen money.'[57] Nor was he alone in attempting to neutralize certain contradictions in order to mobilize the proletariat in the cause of the propertied. In Durban, a few other organizers fervently promoted a scheme whereby ordinary blacks bought one-pound shares in the African Workers' Co-operative Society: 'the ONLY Co-operative in South Africa for the BLACKMAN'. Allegedly, black labourers were thereby giving employment 'to your own people in your own Factory and Stores', and taking 'the greatest possible step towards the economic emancipation of the African Workers'.[58] Similarly, Tyamzashe abandoned trade unionist principles to argue that 'The vast Army of Members of the ICU have one great power in common . . .their spending Power.' As articulated in *The Workers' Herald* in 1927, his aim was the creation of a six-million shilling fund, enough to start one thousand ventures, of three hundred pounds each, in such fields as carpentry, shoemaking, wholesale stores and even banking. The ICU, he stated sternly, advised 'an industrial policy that will make the Native scratch for himself'.[59]

Encouraging the African labourer to 'scratch for himself' – or more accurately, to scratch for his leaders – was hardly the most worker-orientated programme. Other undercurrents of bourgeois nationalism were also apparent as the Union attempted to encompass the interests of black non-labourers. Speaking at De Aar in the Karoo, Kadalie promised his audience that if they united they could become farmers selling to their own racial group. Elsewhere, activists boasted that the Union's millions of pounds would be used to buy farms and businesses for Africans. Even segregation was occasionally supported on the grounds that it would allow blacks to build up their own industries. More frequently, organizers disassociated themselves from state policy, but continued to fight legal and verbal battles on behalf of the middle strata. Thus in small country towns, some attention was paid to the struggle of privileged rural cultivators to remain outside the working class. Access to land was crucial here, and there were regular denunciations of laws preventing Africans from renting, buying or obtaining mortgages on farms. In addition, especially in the northern Free State and south-western Transvaal, leaders sometimes supported sharecroppers by 'fighting for the halves'.[60]

Some were also striving to defend the sectional interests of the 'educated' as opposed to the 'raw native'. Perhaps the worst instances of special pleading were occasioned by the pass system, with a number of officials arguing that passes were utterly inappropriate for 'civilized' blacks, but fit for the 'riff-raff', the loafers, the savages, and undesirable women. Such resurgence of narrow social prejudices – and convergence with strands of liberal ideology – was encouraged by the various bodies and individuals trying to detach the middle strata from the masses. Although their vigour had increased since the ICU rose to prominence, their hold on organizers fluctuated according to the exigencies of struggle. But Champion for one remained loyal to the Bantu Men's Social Centre throughout his period in the Union, while lesser organizers were often also elected representatives on Advisory Boards. In addition, more than two-thirds of the delegates to one 1927 ICU conference were members of Congress, whose constitutionalist programme of equal rights for all civilized men accorded fully with classical liberal tenets.[61]

Although it was rare for organizers to advance the interests of the *AmaRespectables* alone, it was common to mobilize around issues which were a particular affront to the dignity of the middle strata. Thus Champion's victory against the humiliating dipping system in Durban – whereby all Africans entering the city were deloused to prevent typhus – was initiated by him because 'there was no respect for civilized natives. There was steam, and you had to go and have a bath with other boys, of different nationalities.'[62] The obverse side to this distaste for mixing with the unwashed masses from alien ethnic groups was a seemingly pathetic desire for support from sympathetic whites. While the best-known example was Kadalie's flirtation with white liberals, lesser organizers too tried to win from individuals recognition of humanity denied by the dominant race. This motive probably fuelled their desperate attempts to secure white dignitaries on Union platforms, and perhaps even influenced their efforts to establish cordial relations with white policemen. Certainly, some leaders invited constables to meetings, seated them on the very tables from which they spoke, and ended by leading three cheers for these uniformed agents of the state. Indeed, as an ICU member in Durban, Detective Sergeant R. Arnold attended Branch Executive meetings as Champion's personal friend and was an influential figure in policy decisions.[63]

Such overtures to official and civilian white opponents were not the most desirable tactics for a protest movement. Arnold, for example, deliberately fomented divisions within the Union, and was probably the state's most important asset in an organization already riddled with government informers. Similarly, white reactionaries who decided to seize the proffered hand of friendship were frequently successful in considerably diminishing the impact of the ICU. Their statements at meetings usually involved promises of protection against Union intimidation, insistence that wage increases be accompanied by greater productivity, or simply blunt assertions – like those made by a Zululand sugar planter – that blacks could not evade their labour contracts.[64] Their mere presence, combined with the moderating effect this often had on Union officials, could make audiences uneasy. At Ventersburg in the Free State, the first ICU meeting was opened by the Location Superintendent and attended by the Mayor, the Deputy Mayor, the Justice of the Peace, the Sergeant of Police and about forty other whites. As if this implicit unity between black leaders and white masters was not enough, a Union speaker promised to follow in the footsteps of 'our White fathers', and appealed to officials to help the ICU 'educate the misguided natives'. Local blacks were quick to perceive just how misguided they were. Only a few dozen farm labourers enrolled: most were understandably loath to support an elitist organization that wooed their own oppressors.[65]

At this meeting, as at many others where the presence of whites transformed the exercise into an assertion of equality, organizers displayed their mastery of the colonizer's tongue by haranguing their audience in high-flown English. In part, this was a laudable attempt to forge a nation broader than that defined by particularist loyalties. As Kadalie proclaimed, he was 'interested in the cause of the natives not the cause of Zulus, Fingoes or Xhosas'.[66] More mundanely, numerous activists were unable to speak a language familiar to the community they addressed. But more ominously, shunning the vernacular and the values it enshrined often represented an assertion of superiority: of western over indigenous cultures; of the capitalist present over the precolonial past; and of the black middle classes over the masses. In clinging to language as a symbol of civilization, it was not simply English that many leaders tried to speak and write – but ornate English, polysyllabic English, English that required at least a secondary school education to comprehend. Understandably, this increased popular dependency on educated brokers. A Transvaal gathering had every justification for its angry response to a leader who addressed them in bombastic English in the absence of an interpreter.[67]

Insistence on English was but one of the numerous factors that inhibited participation at village meetings, and tended to increase the distance between leaders and the led. Surrounded by crowds of other blacks as well as by white farmers and officials, it was extremely difficult for uneducated members of the labouring poor to question these superior speakers. Often the latter not only arrived in expensive Buicks and Chryslers, but also loomed above audiences on platforms, brandished written material and orated through a translator. Generally well-dressed, they frequently evidenced a preference for the white man's style of living. There could have been few rural Africans in Kranskop who owned – as did Branch Secretary James Ngcobo – three suits, three ties, and the entire gamut of equipment deemed necessary by motor-cycle fanatics. Similarly, the nickname 'white man' given to Champion by Natal blacks added popular credence to the latter's claim that 'I and my family have long adopted European standards of life and we cannot now subsist on the wage paid to labourers.'[68] Indeed they could not, for these relatively luxurious lifestyles were of course being financed by members' contributions. Peculation aside, even Branch Secretaries were paid about one-third more than the average African mine worker. As for Kadalie, his fiercely defended 1927 salary of thirty pounds a month was at least sixty times that of many farm labourers. According to one CP member, overpayment of organizers contributed more to the ICU's demise than almost any other factor.[69]

Yet the condemnations of hindsight fail to capture the complexity of ICU leaders' activities in the countryside. Undoubtedly, officials receiving relatively high salaries (which were on occasion channelled into property), and dominating the masses as they performed their intellectual labour, could display many of the least appealing characteristics of the Janus-like middle classes. Undeniably, they sometimes appeared as 'civilized' sell-outs, or bourgeois nationalists, or elitist wiseacres. Yet the reasons for their conduct extended well beyond their past or contemporary social situations. After all, the overall composition of a movement, and the circumstances in which it is operating, are ultimately far more significant determinants of leaders' practices and discourses.

Thus, many organizers were manipulators as well as manipulated, as they trod the thorny path between winning black support and warding off white repression. There were, for example, spin-offs from amicable relations with policemen, not least in the form of information and protection from rabid racists.[70] In addition, the search for white sympathizers was in part an attempt to secure allies, whose ambiguous position was thoroughly appreciated. As one speaker noted of two liberals persuaded onto the ICU's platform,

when we Bantu hunted the elephant we used to use tame, decoy elephants, so that the wild ones said – 'You see, those creatures are not so dangerous. They have some of our own kind with them.'[71]

While liberals hardly proved to be 'tame elephants', there were indeed occasions when their support proved valuable in thwarting attacks made by 'the wild ones'.

The very intensity of opposition to the Union was also a pointer to its non-elitist character. In general during the later 1920s, the weight of under-class membership was so great that strands of bourgeois nationalism were generally subordinate within the broader ICU message. They were articulated largely by senior officials, and by no means fooled the *AmaRespectables*. Making virtue of necessity in 1928, the conservative Senior Vice-President Madoda Azibozo claimed:

> If the ICU was for intellectuals it would be like many other past native organizations, it would soon be defunct. The ICU is for the raw natives . . .the educated natives are a burden to us because they do not want to join us.[72]

While many upper-middle-class blacks knew full well that their interests did not lie with the Union, many 'raw natives' felt differently about the intellectuals who did assume leadership posts. Indeed, organizers' rerouting of ICU funds into their personal (and very partial) participation in the culture of the *AmaRespectables* and the white bourgeoisie often enhanced their initial impact in the countryside. As a CP member perceptively described the Union's effect on farm labourers:

> the speaker often rouses his audience to a high pitch of enthusiasm. He speaks the white man's language and wears good clothes; he reads the white man's books and quotes against him; . . .he carries the war into the enemy's camp. Speaking English with difficulty or not at all, illiterate, clad in a blanket or the cast-off clothes of Europeans, timid, afraid to answer back when he is cuffed or beaten, the native worker looks on and applauds. He identifies himself with his leader. The leader knows what is best and will deliver him out of Egypt.[73]

If this illusion was unfortunate, it was not out of joint with its time. Dominated social groups do not spontaneously question class hierarchies or demand democracy. Like many other lessons in struggles against the powerful or privileged, these are ones that have to be painfully learned. Internalizing their own class and racial inferiorities, and knowing full well that adopting elements of white lifestyle was itself an act of resistance, many rural blacks revered officials precisely because they had all the trappings of leaders. In the context of racism so brutal that it often reduced Africans to animals, self-styled black 'swells' were in fact powerfully asserting the humanity of all non-traditionalists who suffered under racial oppression. And in the context of popular political cultures bearing strong traces of the past, notions of leadership by chiefs were easily projected onto men who, however different, retained the advantage of belonging overtly to a higher social group. The dictum that movements tend to get the activists they deserve is no mere cliché: there are very real styles to which aspirant leaders must conform if they are to secure a mass following.[74]

Clearly, exploring paid organizers' origins in the lower levels of the intermediate strata, and their objective membership of the middle classes, is necessary but not sufficient for analysing their practices. Their background encouraged activists to identify with ordinary blacks on the crucial issues of the day. Their paid positions helped to distance them from members in some respects, and contributed to an ideological undercurrent in which sectional interests were stressed. But the picture remains partial unless other dimensions are added: the consciousness of the rural poor, the constraints of dependency, and the concrete forms of organization and ideology through which struggles in the countryside were waged. For the purposes of exposition, ICU leaders have been analysed separately from white masters and black servants in the countryside. For the purposes of historical understanding, these social forces must be reunited in their complex interactions. Briefly, they were inextricably bound together, fundamentally shaping the terms on which were fought mutually antagonistic struggles against proletarianization, as well as contradictory battles over the right to rule South Africa.

4. ORGANIZATION AND IDEOLOGY, 1926–1928[1]

'By trade or occupation a Native Agitator':[2] the courts could find no better way of classifying the nature of the work performed by an ICU activist. Despite the fact that the agitator thesis was part of settler mythology, it had here a solid foundation in the mass gatherings that formed the major thrust of the ICU's organizational drive. Unbeknown to whites, these meetings also symbolized the history of the Union: the transitory attraction of thousands on the basis of stirring speeches, followed by dispersal into isolated units without any lasting organizational legacy. In the long term, it proved counter-productive to rely so heavily on an inherently undemocratic and ultimately wearisome technique. But in the short term, the cause of organizing the weak to confront the strong was well served by aggressive and spectacular Union gatherings. The power of subordinated groups derives principally from their unity, and it was above all in huge ICU crowds that this was temporarily experienced.

Extensive preparation was important if meetings were to succeed in the countryside. A Transvaal organizer learnt this the hard way, after tacking a poster to a tree appealing to 'oppressed black toilers' to attend a gathering the following day. Since the local township housed less than eighty adults, this short notice resulted in the meeting attracting half a dozen 'toilers' and almost as many detectives. To avoid such fiascos, verbal communication was of the essence. Often the word was spread to the rural areas by urban location residents, especially those who regularly travelled between town and countryside. Moreover, before alien organizers arrived, the Union sometimes delegated the spadework to agents already in the village, who proved invaluable if they were respected men rooted in local political structures. Youths too were often employed to distribute fiery handbills, while telephone poles and stores were sometimes placarded with racy posters declaring in the vernacular: 'Awake, awake, awake and stand up for your rights!'[3]

Invariably, the biggest meetings were held on Sundays, since this was the only day full-time labourers could break from the grind of work. This immediately exacerbated conflicts with mission churches, whose services sometimes had to be cancelled because communicants preferred to flock to Union gatherings. While ICU organizers were none too distressed by this, they could not afford to alienate separatist bodies. Combined with the fact that itinerant higher officials were not always available on Sundays, this meant that gatherings were often held on Saturdays and weekdays in addition – or sometimes even daily in periods of popular upsurge.

Obtaining a suitable venue was also fraught with difficulties. 'Mote was obliged to address one meeting from the side of the road, and continual police warnings about disruption of traffic doubtless diluted the force of his message. Bad weather could dramatically decrease attendance at open-air gatherings, and organizers' desperation to obtain indoor venues can be judged from a Natal Branch Secretary's appeal for the use of the white farmers' Agricultural Hall for meetings.[4] At best, modest separatist churches were made available to the Union. In the main, officials had to content themselves with soccer fields and commonages, as well as with general assembly points like bus stops.

One advantage of outdoor venues was their ability to accommodate the thousands of blacks who could surge into town. For the under-classes, there was enormous attraction in having their suppressed longings and particularized grievances transformed into public aspirations and universal woes. Many farm labourers walked twenty miles to hear speakers; others rode in on bicycles, carts or horses. Indeed, the number of tethered horses was sometimes so great that meetings took on the military overtones of laagers, and Free State municipal authorities used this as an excuse to ban gatherings. Predictably, the presence of thousands of alien Africans in the heartland of their domain outraged most whites, who were quick to perceive that isolated servants were being welded together into a unified body.[5]

Generally, the crowd included a small but significant number of women and children. In this important respect, Union gatherings were more representative than those in most chiefdoms, and the ICU message could be disseminated through channels other than those controlled by adult males. Since oppressed men are not necessarily political animals, members of the dominant sex could be more attracted by the added festivity given to the occasion by the presence of women. Thus Elijah Ngcobo, a farm worker living on an African-owned holding in Bulwer, claimed to have attended meetings not to have his consciousness raised, but to 'observe and propose love to girls'.[6]

If 'girls' were present in sufficient numbers for Ngcobo's purposes in Bulwer, female participation in broader Union activities was in general extremely limited. The political mobilization of women was profoundly affected by the inequities of the sexual division of labour, combined with unequal access to resources as basic as money or a horse. Thus Linah Mhlongo, who in the 1920s not only worked for both rural and urban whites but also shouldered the burden of domestic labour, had little recollection of ICU activities in Vryheid. Instead, she railed against male leisure-time activities:

> A woman had no time . . . Women worked harder than men . . . We worked, we bred children, everything done by a woman. You worked even when pregnant. You couldn't rest.

Nor could you engage in many other activities. Most African women were discriminated against in access to the means of production; they were largely excluded from black political and juridical processes; they were assigned an inferior position in cultural affairs; and they were perpetual minors within male-dominated households. Indeed, the effectiveness of marriage in subjugating Zulu-speaking females who donned wifely garb was expressed in a proverb: 'akuqhalaqhala lahlul' isidwaba' – no defiant woman ever defeated a leather skirt. Small wonder that one Natal reserve-dweller obediently acquiesced when forbidden by her menfolk to attend ICU gatherings.[7]

Most male Union organizers failed to address the fact that females often experienced the cheap labour system and racist state through these mediating structures of patriarchy. On the contrary: despite the constitutional commitment to equality, women were marginalized throughout the existence of the ICU. Kadalie's patronizing attitude in 1919 – when he promised that if enough 'girls' joined they could form a separate branch – was given concrete expression in later years in the formation of Women's Sections of the Union. Furthermore, most male leaders overtly and repeatedly expressed their sense of sexual superiority. All too frequently, women were regarded as workers whose wages should be less than half those of their male equivalents; as wives who should divorce their husbands if the latter were not ICU members; as persons whose domestic skills should be utilized in providing male organizers with entertainment and food; as child-minders who should not attend ICU meetings with crying babies; and as inferior beings whose aspirations could be dismissed.[8]

Admittedly, there were some notable occasions when females forced organizers to take their concerns seriously, or when males transcended such sexism. In late 1926, Mbeki stated that he found it disquieting that the Union had failed to draw female workers into its ranks. He stressed that in other countries such labourers were in the vanguard of the proletariat, and were 'indispensable in the huge struggle for the abolition of the capitalist monkey tricks of enslavement'. But if this was true, it was not a sentiment that moved many overburdened female workers, let alone the vast majority of black women who fell outside the boundaries of this class category. Although female membership increased from some 1,500 in 1924 to Kadalie's wild estimate of 12,000 in 1927 (allegedly mainly farm and domestic servants), women still constituted less than 15 per cent of those who bought red tickets during this period.[9]

Consequently, most Union gatherings were attended largely by men, who profoundly shaped their form as well as their content. In particular, they drove home to many Union activists the necessity of providing an eloquent speaker. Persuasive oratory was an important component of political power in most chiefdoms, and rural black males tended to be acutely sensitive to gradations in speaking skills. Thus they often ignored meetings convened by relatively inept local orators, and would converge on the town only when men like Kadalie were present.

Above all others, it was he who could draw and sway the crowds. Tall and impressive, he was a magnetic personality and a charismatic demagogue. As Lucas Nqandela recalled of ICU days when he was a labour tenant, 'We would all flock to Kroonstad anxious to hear Kadalie insulting the whites and promising us liberation from their oppression.' Similarly, ex-resident worker Lucas Nhlabathi claimed that Africans would travel all the way from farms to Standerton in the Transvaal to listen to him.

> He would really speak for us . . . [Kadalie and Mbeki] would stand on top of a cart and boom their voices across to the people. The Boers would be dead silent also listening. He would say, 'This country belongs to the black people.'[10]

Partly by silencing and swearing at white farmers, Kadalie rapidly acquired an image of a man transcending normal class, racial and even national boundaries. Thanks perhaps to his public speaking lessons at the Efficiency Institute in 1920, he also had an extraordinary ability to voice the emotions of the moment, and to give a performance which showmen might envy. Indeed, the National Secretary may well have fostered the widespread notion that the ICU had supernatural powers. According to a man who was then a Zululand teacher, many unsophisticated Africans supported Kadalie because they wanted access to his magical herbs, which supposedly allowed him to 'take newspapers, fold them nicely, and start talking his things, and the paper changed to money!' Apart from outdoing

the white man's Lord who only changed water into wine, Kadalie
sometimes employed his marvellous sense of the dramatic in symbolically stripping away the trappings of western civilization and
thereby reasserting his place with ordinary people. As he strode up
and down on a table, wagon or cart, he would on occasion build up to
his climax by successively tearing off his coat, waistcoat, collar, and
finally his tie. The illiterate poor, who communicated primarily
through voices and gestures, symbols and rituals, could not have
missed the social meaning of this charade.[11]

Flamboyant and theatrical, Kadalie was a supreme egoist who
eagerly nurtured the personality cult that swiftly enveloped him. By
exploiting popular perceptions that he was the 'Great Chief' – and by
taking advantage of an organizational structure that was both fluid and
undemocratic – he exacerbated the tendency for the ICU to be treated
as synonymous with himself. But he was also a man of boundless
energy, whose whirlwind speaking tours established a direct rapport
between the leader and the led in almost every village in the country.
As an archetypal populist agitator rather than an organizer, he was
unsurpassed within the ICU, and his ability to inspire audiences fell
little short of genius.[12]

The big, forceful A.W.G. Champion also usually enjoyed joyous
welcomes. 'Oh, speak, dense forest . . .Hurrah; speak, dense forest',
shouted Durban crowds, using his praise name *Mahlathi Mnyama*, or
'Black Forest'. Just as the Nkandla woodlands had once sheltered Zulu
warriors, so this Union official was now thought to provide a refuge
for the troubled. As the rather more combative 'Lion of the North',
the dynamic Thomas Mbeki would sometimes address vociferously
cheering crowds for up to six hours. Clearly, oratory was seen as a
vehicle of political success not only by audiences rooted in older
cultures, but also by activists whose professions had so often consisted
of manipulating language. Thus 'Mote on occasion told his listeners
how other great speakers had achieved state power, or impatiently
dismissed interpreters for being insufficiently fiery.[13]

Undeniably, considerable pageantry infused the presentation of the
ICU's message, to the point where the Union could well be accused of
conducting its struggle through popular theatre. In the short run, this
approach evidenced every sign of success. After all,

> for most people most of the time, and for the overwhelming
> majority of persons raised in verbo-motor cultures all of the time,
> the most profound expressions of the meanings they find in life are
> surely made in highly charged forms of patterned action.[14]

Hence unlike the earlier, poorly attended meetings of the Industrial
Workers of Africa (which were unattractive partly because they lacked

entertainment), well-organized Union gatherings drew crowds numbering in the thousands. Unlike many dull and moderate Congress speeches, inflammatory ICU orations combined with colourful demonstrations were thoroughly appreciated by the masses. And unlike the assemblies of most other political bodies at the time, ICU meetings were in themselves sufficient to elicit soaring membership and fantastic financial returns. After a successful performance in the countryside, organizers would be mobbed as they touted red membership cards to all and sundry. Literate bystanders would be frantically roped in to deal with the crush, and containers ranging from pails to sugar sacks would often overflow with coins. In Barberton, the mountain of money collected after one meeting had to be trundled to the bank by four people using a wheelbarrow. Over a week in late 1927, Natal branches sent the Durban Provincial Office so many coins that two tedious days were spent counting them up as nearly one thousand pounds.[15]

Close to twelve thousand pounds was transferred to head office over the year 1927, and this was by no means the total collected. Much of this enormous sum was derived from enrolment fees. Cards in the countryside were widely considered as one-off investments: rather than pay the steep weekly subscription of threepence, many rural blacks acquired new tickets at particularly inspiring meetings. At a Free State gathering in the late 1920s, many Africans amongst the thousands of farm workers present were clutching two, three or even four membership cards. Thus the rural poor, unwilling or unable to abide by new-fangled rules about financing a modern organization, were partially responsible for the ICU's focus on public meetings. And since they sought a return on their investment, they also deeply conditioned the wild rhetoric whereby leaders sought to capture imaginations ever anew.[16]

A diffuse African nationalism lay at the heart of the ICU's ideology. All over the countryside, organizers would cry out that blacks wanted freedom in the land of their forefathers. 'We say farewell to you who do not want to join the ICU, for we are marching forward to meet Africa . . .*VUKA AFRIKA! BUYA AFRIKA!*' exclaimed a Transvaal official in *The Workers' Herald*. Or, as Kadalie declaimed at one meeting, whites were 'robbers and damn thieves' and the country must belong 'to the people and the workers'. On occasion, a total reversal of the social order was promised: 'Dirty Jim' would be boss, while Mr Whiteman carried a pass and white madams struggled home under bundles of washing. Sometimes the Garveyist slogan 'Africa for the Africans' was promoted: activists demanded the expulsion of whites and made audiences chant aloud, 'Africa shall be restored to us even if it be by blood.' Most commonly, however, they insisted on either approximate or complete economic, political and social equality with their oppressors. As Kadalie bluntly told one gathering: 'what is good enough for the white man is good enough for you'.[17]

If this could be interpreted in crude, material terms, so could the factors underpinning the rise of the ICU's ideology. Modern nationalism, after all, is a potent mass force only in societies already transfigured by the 'dual revolution': by the violent processes whereby capitalism has become economically and politically dominant.[18] But it could certainly grip particular groupings in a country where these transformations were well under way. Partly because millions of migrants had been brutally and sometimes permanently uprooted from the land, age-old localized communities were disintegrating as they were incorporated into a new order. Moreover, the inhabitants of South Africa were being clumsily sutured together by transport and postal services, printing and literacy. Indeed, it was the very advance of technology that enabled the Union to exist as a national organization.

More importantly, South Africa's 'dual revolution' was occurring in a grotesquely uneven fashion. On the one hand, there was a miniscule, urban white bourgeoisie emulating metropolitan lifestyles, and about one in ten adult South Africans were enfranchized. On the other hand, the vast majority of the population were poverty-stricken blacks in the countryside, semi-proletarianized and voteless. Furthermore, their struggles moved fairly easily onto the political terrain, since in securing their subordination, 'the state was everything, civil society was primordial and gelatinous'.[19] In all, the ICU's nationalist ideology, like so many others, was a manifestation of enormous underlying fault-lines. There were disjunctures between development and underdevelopment, between the powerful and the powerless, between society and the state, and between 'the fact of not having and the awareness of this intolerable absence'.[20]

Yet this consciousness emerged at a specific time, and the ICU's nationalism assumed a particular form. It was articulated by restless, educated young men, whose own lives had been distorted by the impact of uneven development, and who reacted by turning to the masses. The people listened – and promptly infused these 'derived' ideas with their own oral traditions and daily experiences. Hence the Union's message was ultimately created through the assimilation and transformation of a wide range of beliefs.

Significantly, the main thrust of this protest ideology was the liberation of the African labouring poor from white domination. Its impact was so great that it was almost a 'popular religion'. For a brief period, and for many blacks, the ICU was a major intellectual force.

It was well on the way to creating a hegemonic ideology, which informed 'with its spirit all taste, morality, customs, religious and political principles and all social relations, particularly in their intellectual and moral connotations'.[21]

The processes which this involved were much more than preaching to the masses. Union offices alone helped integrate numerous activists into the bleak world of rural blacks. Throughout the week, these rooms were generally packed with people, desperate for support against white masters or officialdom. In Estcourt, where three correspondence clerks kept the office open for fourteen hours a day, the flood of complainants was overwhelming. Charles Kumalo recalled that crowds would be waiting outside the building in the morning, and that 'they cried of suffering and poverty and disease'. Similarly, office work initiated Gilbert Coka into the full horror of the lives of Vryheid labour tenants, and he discovered that 'there was terrorism right under my nose'. Unquestionably, the rank-and-file helped radicalize organizers. Undeniably too, by educating the educators, they contributed to an ideology with considerable popular resonance.[22]

Traditionalists, Chiefs and the ICU

Equality with whites was not an aspiration that appealed to all blacks. Hundreds of thousands of Africans were more concerned about reproducing older social relationships, especially those centring around the chiefdom and the homestead economy. For traditionalists, attachment to the land provided the material base for a completely different ideology of resistance: one which rejected white-imposed political, economic and cultural norms, and which strove to defend the integrity of non–capitalist political economies.[23] Because their narrow worlds had been both conserved and irrevocably changed by colonial and capitalist penetration, such 'backward-looking' struggles were deeply ambiguous. They could mesh all too well with segregationist policies of 'retribalizing' blacks in stagnant reserves. Or they might 'express exactly the opposite of traditionalism: a refusal to accept capitalist legality', and a complete denial of legitimacy to the new social forces disrupting their lives. In this sense, it was possible for resistance imbued with older but reworked symbols and traditions to resemble 'the most radical of class conflicts', and represent 'a more "advanced" and "modern" attitude than European-style trade unionism'.[24]

In either case, the ICU could meet with considerable ideological resistance from traditionalists (who were mainly reserve-dwellers, but also included blacks on farms or migrants in cities). At his first meeting in Weenen, a Natal stronghold of traditionalism, the aptly named Alphabet Caluza painted utopian and doubtless modern pictures of a future South Africa. A significant proportion of his audience simply refused to join. As an elderly woman sternly informed him, 'she had been told nothing. She had come, she said, to learn how the land of Dingane and Mpande might be reclaimed from the white men, but instead she had been told many things that mattered naught.'[25]

Many were also opposed to the ICU's efforts to harness as broad an alliance as possible behind its programme. Organizationally, membership was open to anyone. Ideologically, 'African' sometimes assumed the wider meaning of all those committed to the black man's cause. Thus the term 'coloured' was on occasion denounced for splitting the African race, while a white sympathizer could be praised as a 'black European'. But such nationalism was too broad for many in a society where the privileges of colour frequently compounded those of class. In Natal, it was commonly believed that the 'coloured' Sam Dunn should not be a leader, allegedly because his pro-white stance exacerbated his original sin of being half-white. As for full-blooded whites, one Free State audience could barely be controlled when informed that their oppressors were allowed to join the ICU. Certainly for Lucas Nqandela, this was the end. Although initially a Union enthusiast, his suspicions were aroused the day he saw farmers attending a meeting clutching red cards. He decided then and there that Kadalie was collaborating with the 'Boers', and that their joint and only aim was to extract money from blacks.[26]

Not surprisingly, ethnicity was another sensitive issue. After all, it was hard to improve the South African prescription for people to seize hold of parochial identities for political purposes. Take a tract of land containing a multiplicity of heterogeneous precapitalist societies, in which production is deeply integrated with territory, kinship, language and political authority. Let the boundaries of the country as a whole and the reserves in particular be 'jerry-built by imperialism'. Add mine magnates and traditionalist blacks striving, with uneven success, to preserve older social formations. And then insert petty bourgeois nationalist politicians, striving to 'stitch together alliances and rally constituencies'.[27]

Understandably, this exercise sometimes fell apart at the seams. As an unknown man from Nyasaland, Kadalie himself was initially rejected as the head of the ICWU, on the grounds that he could not speak the tongues of Shaka, Moshoeshoe or Hintsa. In later days he did not even allow Afrikaans to be written, which resulted in certain 'coloureds' refusing to join because they could read neither the constitution nor *The Workers' Herald*. Such insensitivity to language, which as a prime symbol of ethnic identity carried with it a host of values and associations, clearly undermined the value of ICU propaganda. In Natal, unsold *Heralds* piled up because 'the Zulus do not care for the paper when there is no Zulu'. Nor did some blacks care for a movement led by men from a different ethnic group, or from the new elite, rather than the old. Even in the Free State, there were complaints from commoners that certain officials were unfit to be treasurers because they were not of royal blood. Indeed, in more traditionalist regions, numerous ordinary Africans refused to join unless the Union was first sanctioned by indigenous political authorities.[28]

As state functionaries, but also as links to the past and sometimes still leaders of the present, chiefs were in an ambivalent structural position. Acting in unholy alliance, numerous 'progressive' farmers, white officials and upper-middle-class Africans attempted to win them over into an anti-ICU bloc. Threatening chiefs with dismissal was not the least of their weapons: in Kranskop, landlords and the magistrate applied to the Defence Force for arms to combat Union meetings held by members of the older political elite. The language of persuasion was only slightly less crude, and involved reworking traditionalist objections to the Union. The ICU, it was argued, aimed at undermining 'tribal' loyalties and authorities, and at uniting all workers together under leaders with distinctly 'Bolshevist' leanings. And if neither this nor exposure of the corruption of Union activists proved sufficient, there was always the ploy of bribing chiefs themselves. After the state had provided him with a long-desired trip to Cape Town, a stay in a hotel, and even entertainment, an important Natal chief self-righteously announced to a committee of white Parliamentarians that ICU leaders were thieves. Once they had reached such states of compliance, black authorities could be turned inwards on their own commoners. Thus one Natal chief berated his followers at a Union meeting also attended by the magistrate and police: 'you people have, without my knowledge and consent, joined this new movement, which I do not approve of, and which has caused a considerable amount of trouble to my people and their landlords.'[29]

Prime target in all these manoeuvres was Solomon ka Dinizulu, grandson of Cetshwayo, who was the last independent Zulu monarch. Amongst commoners in Natal, Solomon retained enormous prestige, both as a living link to the Zulu kingdom and as the traditional guarantor of the nation's welfare. Furthermore, expressing loyalty to him was a way of articulating antagonism to the state, which, by refusing to recognize Solomon's claims to the paramountcy, made him a symbol of the oppression of all Zulu-speaking blacks. Crowned with the political and ideological hegemony which his forebears had established, and wearing the mantle of estrangement from whites, Solomon ka Dinizulu could attract crowds of thousands when travelling around the countryside. Even cane-cutters simply downed their tools to attend on their 'king who was not a king'.[30]

By the later 1920s, some highly capitalized sugar planters were wedded to a strategy which would undercut Solomon's popular appeal in one sphere, yet boost it in another. Together with members of the black upper middle classes, they had cogent reasons for imploring the state to recognise the Zulu monarch. As a segregationist sugar farmer expressed it, the choice facing the country was the creation of a race-proud 'Bantu Nation . . .or a Black Proletariat using all the recognized methods for the complete overthrow of whites on the basis of class'.[31] To ensure that Zulu-speakers chose old-fashioned colour above modish class, members of this coalition urged the refurbishing and utilization of Solomon's traditional powers.

As the ICU rose to prominence, so the value and necessity of such tactics became more apparent. Thus *Inkatha ka Zulu*, created by the Zulu elite to help Solomon win state recognition, was lauded by officialdom as 'the most promising counterblast' to the Union. Unfortunately, the under-classes seemed much more reluctant to contribute to the cause of their king. The ICU's progress was accompanied by a dramatic reduction in payments to *Inkatha's* treasury, thereby jeopardizing the financial status of the heavily indebted royal family. Doubtless, Solomon also saw the Union as a threat to his own scheme of raising money to protect Zululand from white encroachment, and he was certainly piqued by the failure of the ICU to honour him adequately.[32]

His disgruntlement provided sufficient leverage for his coterie of supporters. The first shot was fired in an August 1927 edition of a newspaper edited by John Dube, himself Solomon's long-standing friend, and a fierce political opponent of the ICU. In this forum, the head of the Zulu royal family denounced the militancy, corruption and non-Zulu nature of the Union, and ordered chiefs to 'Kill this thing in all your tribes.'[33] The second round occurred within days, at the instigation of sugar baron William Campbell. He assembled fully a thousand black workers at the Natal Sugar Estates, and asked his two associates, Dube and Solomon, to make suitable speeches.

His careful preparations were almost ruined, since the self-designated king arrived – but refused to speak. Maintaining ambiguous relations with the powerful and the people lay at the heart of Solomon's strategy for survival. Nonetheless, his silent presence was probably more effective than Dube's anti-ICU commination. When three ICU activists gatecrashed the gathering, workers passively watched them trudge away after being ordered off the property. Within months, Africans in this area were demanding the return of their membership fees, and a delighted Campbell was suggesting a scheme whereby whites paid off the mounting debts of the heir to the throne. In the disapproving words of the Secretary for Native Affairs, the proposal was 'nothing more nor less than an attempt to get Solomon under the thumb of the employers of labour and to use him against the ICU.' Although officials might later have rued their quashing of this plan, at the time Solomon appeared to need no additional direction to play his part in social control.[34]

While the Zulu royal family's public antagonism was a grievous blow to the Union, so too was the fact that hostile or neutral chiefs were probably in the majority in South Africa at large. 'I would like to know, my fellow countrymen, why chiefs are not joining the ICU', asked a Transvaal activist in late 1927. The answer lay in the fact that many of these men were opposed both to the changing of the political guard and to the threat posed by the Union to white rulers from whom their authority ultimately derived. By this time, these traditional leaders were primarily 'chiefs by the state', not 'chiefs by the people'. Those who had embraced their position as government functionaries could and did inform on organizers, call for their arrest, and do their utmost to block ICU expansion.[35]

Yet the alliances constantly being created and dissolved in the countryside were tangled ones. If, for many anti-ICU groupings, chiefs were pawns in a high-stake political game, traditional authorities themselves preferred a more independent role. Indeed, they could vigorously pursue the Union in attempts to fulfil sectional interests denied them by racial oppression. In both the Transvaal and Basutoland, certain chiefs displayed great interest in supplying the ICU in its proposed scheme of selling grain and stock cheaply to members. Chief Mtamo of Kranskop aimed even higher than these frustrated agriculturists: he hoped the gifts purveyed to him by the Branch Secretary would ultimately extend to a car.[36]

Clearly, the ICU was also a contender in the battle for the allegiance of indigenous authorities. The activities of a Cape Branch Secretary – who in 1926 was traipsing through outlying country areas visiting chiefs and headmen – were by no means unusual. Many rural organizers actively wooed these older leaders, not least because they recognized that strikes could be defeated by 'scabs' delivered by chiefs. And although they readily denounced those who opposed them for being in league with white mine owners and officials, they were forced in the countryside to recognize the hold of these men on popular consciousness. Consequently, in addition to proffering material inducements, they struggled 'to assimilate and to conquer "ideologically" the traditional intellectuals' of the countryside.[37]

They also tried to incorporate or neutralize certain ideas and objections being thrust upon them from below. All nationalist leaders face the self-same dilemma: that of having to mobilize parochial people, and then creating of them an 'imagined political community', self-conscious of its identity and difference from alien oppressors. And almost all nationalist movements resolve the problem by turning to the cultural and political past. By gazing backwards, they 'summon up what energy they can from the particular "inheritance" they are stuck with, in order to leap forward'.[38]

ICU leaders, unfortunately, were 'stuck with' ethnicity. In Natal in particular, the ruins of South Africa's most powerful precolonial kingdom haunted the present. Furthermore, in order to detach commoners from inimical chiefs, organizers were virtually compelled to demonstrate that Solomon and his royalist supporters held no monopoly over defining the interests of Zulu-speakers. They did so by side-stepping the putative king and his father, and instead linking themselves to the proud tradition of independent monarchs of the kingdom.

Natal, then, was the one province where village gatherings were frequently addressed in the vernacular, and where ICU intellectuals eagerly drew on (or invented) older traditions to construct their political base. Sam Dunn in particular needed to be enveloped in the glories of dead generations: apart from being 'coloured', he was also the son of a chief who had opposed the royalist cause. So he proudly preferred to orate in Zulu rather than English, and went as far back in the royal line as possible in casting his appeals to this ethnic group. Indeed, he acquired as his nickname the phrase he repeatedly used to apostrophize audiences: *Zulu kwa Malandela*, meaning 'Zulus, descendants of the founder of our nation'.[39]

At a time when the rural poor also conceived of themselves in terms of lineages, chiefdoms and clans, even more parochial loyalties could be invoked. Thus the people of Vryheid were hailed as 'the famous Abaqulusi, who are never conquered'. Historical myth though this was, harking back to past militant Qulusi support for the Zulu kingdom nonetheless fostered the confidence and continuity needed for present protest. But the ambiguous ethnic variable could also be deployed in an accurate as well as successful fashion: to expose new contradictions between white employers and black workers. When one organizer asked whether any farm labourers in his audience earned enough to pay *lobola* (bridewealth), he got a resounding response: 'None!'[40]

Leaders also appropriated a well-worn theme in the appeals of Zulu-speaking chiefs for more land. The latter had repeatedly alleged that white rulers had broken a promise to Cetshwayo by a British imperialist: 'as sure as the sun rose in the east and set in the west, this country belonged to the Natives, and not to the Europeans'. While ICU restatements of this pledge possibly referred to the whole of South Africa rather than just Zululand, there were certainly occasions when politicized Zulu ethnicity surged to the fore. Champion, who at the time was a member of the Zulu society, was about eighty years old before he wanted to 'forget this Zuluism and try to teach myself Africanism'. Even before the formation of the ICU *yase* Natal in May 1928, he hovered close to conceiving nationalism in terms of Zulu-speakers alone. Indeed, he undoubtedly agreed with a Zulu-speaking Free State official, who announced that when the ICU restored the country to blacks, 'The Zulus will be the head of the Natives in South Africa.'[41]

Such ethnic arrogance was, however, rare outside Natal, and perhaps a few districts in the Cape which were allegedly run by appeals to 'tribal jealousies'. In the main, organizers in other provinces restricted themselves to using the symbols of the past to call the present into question. A favourite stratagem was to incorporate references to forefathers, thereby invoking a host of associations with indigenous religions and with Africans' prior right to the country. 'Here lie the bones of your forefathers and no other nation. This is the land of our forefathers', was a Transvaal labour tenant's recollection of a speech by Kadalie. Precolonial heroes sometimes bulked even larger than contemporary sympathetic chiefs, as when blacks were urged to abandon the god of the white man for that of Moshoeshoe, Moroka, Cetshwayo, and – to complete the glorious roll-call – Kadalie. Finally, folktales, proverbs and vernacular nicknames were used to defend tactics, to analyse grievances and to ridicule whites. Thus the Prime Minister, with his 'Native Bills' and his assertions that 'the European is fully determined that South Africa shall be governed by the white man', was derisively labelled *Tsalitoro* – the Dreamer.[42]

Besides speeches, other practices and institutions were used to indicate a certain flexibility to traditionalist concerns. Organizationally, grass-roots pressure for leaders with prestige in precolonial societies could be accommodated on branch committees. In the Transvaal, a diviner was elected to one Executive, while a chief allegedly braved official wrath by becoming Chairman of another. The National Council was also fairly carefully balanced to appease ethnic sensibilities: in 1927, each of the major black racial and language groups was represented, and three-quarters of its members were Africans. Furthermore, antagonism to whites – which was by no means exclusive to traditionalists – was partly diffused by genuine commitment to black leadership. With the exception of Kadalie, the entire 1927 National Council opposed the appointment of white officials. So too did the great bulk of delegates to the conference held at the end of the year, soon after Kadalie returned from his overseas machniations with European trade unionists. The National Secretary alienated them by arguing that many knew less about the ICU than his erstwhile British secretary, later to be claimed as one of his 'White Sweethearts'. Delegates responded with contemptuous remarks, rich in meaning in a society where skin-colour symbolized so much: 'Kadalie, you went out black; have you returned white?'[43]

Yet their heated opposition cannot simply be attributed to racism. Many organizers were already battling to alter the perceptions of members whose 'common sense' led them to reject white members. But in a nationalist movement, non-racialism does not necessarily extend to embracing white officials. Indeed, incorporating white leaders could actively undermine this principle, and ICU activists were justifiably suspicious that they would be manipulated by men enjoying most of the privileges and skills of the oppressors. Furthermore, white officials could – and from mid-1928, in the form of Advisor 'Wee Willie Winkie' Ballinger, did – fundamentally alter the nature of the movement in the eyes of the rank-and-file. The impact of the ICU in the countryside was powerfully conditioned by the fact that it was led by blacks, and organizers were rightly wary of moves to dilute its nationalist character.[44]

They were also politically acute in allowing the cultural arena to become one where the contradictions between traditional and modern nationalists were resolved in a non-antagonistic fashion. Thus leaders sometimes attempted to attract large audiences by laying on beer, or even a slaughtered ox. Alternatively, the rank-and-file imposed their own norms on organizers in order to incorporate them into a more familiar world. Some did this by perceiving ICU officials as 'chiefs', and by giving them (and occasionally their cars) nicknames which made them less alien. Others subtly indicated a preference for a change of attire. In the Free State, Zulu-speakers presented District Secretary Robert Dumah with a splendid cloak made of leopard and other wild animal skins, as a sign of their appreciation 'of his conspicuous spirit of a warrior'. Similarly, Mbeki was indirectly pressurized in Swaziland, where to his surprise he was offered not western food but beer and meat. He conformed magnificently to the spirit of the occasion: 'When he spoke the warriors of Swaziland remembered the olden days when they were ruled by Africans.'[45]

Elsewhere, some audiences not only recalled but also acted as warriors of yore. When thousands of Africans flooded into Vryheid for the first meeting, they drew on age-set and regimental traditions to co-ordinate their entry.

Old Zulu War veterans, ringed men from the farms . . . young men from the farms, middle-aged men from the mines, workers from the town, were all marching, column upon column, towards the venue of assembly.

Such processions in martial formation readily evoked memories of the Zulu kingdom, and speeches that day predictably referred to the conquest of Cetshwayo.[46]

Yet while leaders mentioned a past king, they focused on dispossession from white farms. Above all, it was the ICU's solutions to the land question that helped neutralize many traditionalist objections to its activities. According to ex-Free State resident worker Phillip Masike, Kadalie told them that 'We would live like our forefathers used to do. The land would be ours and we wouldn't be ruled by the Boers any longer.' Or in the more dismissive words of Trifinah Mdhlalose of Vryheid, traditionalist labour tenants like her father paid with a cow to join the ICU, because they thought the country would indeed be restored to blacks. 'They lived in the past glory of their ancestors . . . They believed that they would achieve their goal of getting the land.'[47]

Amongst chiefs, too, agrarian issues bulked high in determining whether they would throw in their lot with the Union. For some, there were certainly other compelling reasons, such as long-standing disputes with white officialdom, or pressures from their followers below. But one major factor was often the accelerating pace of proletarianization. Most chiefs who supported the ICU appear to have been men whose people were either scattered over white farms, mission reserves or Crown land, or were being inexorably squeezed out of grossly overcrowded reserves or African-owned farms. Unable to prevent the transformation of their followers (and sometimes themselves) into workers only tenuously attached to land, many such men were desperately seeking new ways to regain independent powers. 'Redemption has come and that is the ICU', exclaimed the aged chief Hoyi Ngomane at a Transvaal meeting. Such sentiments were typical amongst indigenous authorities who, like Ngomane, had recently been forced by whites to abandon ancestral grounds, and who believed the Union would lead them to the promised land.[48]

The Land Question: 'Derived' and 'Inherent' Solutions

There were, however, two very different routes to this goal. At almost every meeting attended by whites, ICU officials who spoke on this burning issue did no more than promise ground to the man who waited for redistribution through the capitalist market. As Champion paternalistically expressed it when addressing a rural Natal audience in 1927, 'Pay your red money and let us fight for you . . .come to the ICU and we will buy farms for you.' Understandably, rumours swept through Natal that Africans would receive farms if they paid two shillings and sixpence. Organizers here and elsewhere sometimes nervously responded by escalating the price for a holding. Thus, according to a Transvaal activist in mid-1927: 'The ICU people of this district are working hard donating money so that by August they should have their own land . . . Run to the office of the ICU and produce your own money and buy a piece of ground.'[49]

Yet there was a far more radical approach to the agrarian question. The 'inherent', traditional belief of many ordinary rural blacks was that the land belonged to them, and that the expropriators should be expropriated. Primarily in a belt stretching from the southern Natal Midlands to the eastern Transvaal, the ICU was commonly associated with this position. Elijah Ngcobo's wife remembered of Union leaders only that they had said: 'White people are nothing. We are the people who know about the land. The land is ours.' Much more frequently, however, a 'derived' element modified these inherent Africanist notions that all whites were alien *ratlahoboros*, and that indigenous people were the only true heirs to the country. Like Elijah Ngcobo himself, many who actually went to meetings returned with the belief that it was ICU members in particular who could repossess white farms, and that they could do so precisely because they had joined a powerful organization. Ngcobo's testimony captures the heart of what was regarded as the Union's message in many areas of Natal in 1927:

> The ICU said the white people no longer had land, the land had been taken over by them . . . They said people were then entitled to take over their fields and take their stock, and said we should take whatever we wanted . . .the card was going to scare the white man away when you produced it. He would not dare oppose you, whatever you did on the farms, so long as you had the ICU membership card.[50]

As these incendiary ideas were transmitted through the extended chains of rural communication, they became the property of the rural poor to a far greater extent than that of Union activists. The red cards themselves encouraged this, with their vernacular injunctions to members to take their share of the work of spreading the message and recruiting support. So too did the situation of intense insecurity of tenure on farms, which meant that many individuals projected their own longings onto ICU liberators who had miraculously arrived. Thus, tidings that so accurately reflected the popular mood, and were both important and flexible enough to encompass a host of aspirations, spread fast and furiously through the countryside. Long before the first Vryheid ICU meeting was held, rumours had swept the district that the Union would force 'Boers' to disgorge their farms, and that it heralded armed conflict against whites. Similarly, almost before the first official ICU meeting had been held in rural Natal, an exhilarated tenant returned from Durban and refused to work off a debt. According to an outraged 'Country JP', who claimed knowledge of several similar incidents, this man

> told my native he had joined a people called ICU, and they have told me 'I must not work for my landlord and I do not require to pay rent, and I am to plough as much ground as will feed my family. I have a ticket here and can go out in the streets of Durban any time of the night.'[51]

Whether or not Durban organizers ever said anything of the sort, there was patently enormous potential for conflict between 'inherent' and 'derived' solutions to the land question. This was well illustrated in a pathetic vignette from Melmoth, Zululand, which in the 1920s was a scene of mass evictions of 'squatters' and labour tenants. As entire chiefdoms were effectively eliminated, so ordinary blacks were won over by ICU-linked rumours that 'there is no need to buy land since natives cannot be ejected from farms, and as all the land will be given back to the Natives'.[52] This popular version of the Union's message was, after all, only a small shift away from the age-old belief that all ground in the district belonged to Solomon.

But there was an unbridgeable chasm between the Union's official policy of buying and selling property on the market, and the consciousness of many traditionalists. Both black and white local authorities made this unhappy discovery when they tried to use a pliant and 'modern' Union activist as a weapon against these land-hungry peasants. They eagerly set up and attended an ICU meeting held by this lone organizer, who urged commoners to finance the purchase of a farm for their chief. But his words fell on stony ground. 'Many said that the ICU man had been bribed by the White man, and they said they wanted to hear what Kadalie had to say.' Like peasants the world over, these men simply repudiated an unpalatable message from their immediate superiors, and looked to their 'Great Chief' for justice.[53]

Their faith was touching – and not entirely misplaced. Kadalie never seriously or consistently advocated that blacks could not be evicted; indeed, as Champion sarcastically declared, he was not even particularly concerned about purchasing land. Yet like so many other Union officials, he could not always afford to repudiate ordinary people and lesser leaders as they joyously formulated answers to the agrarian question. In 1928, for instance, in front of white authorities, he addressed a gathering in Estcourt. The district had for months been a hotbed of rumours about land redistribution, which Kadalie cautiously confirmed: 'It would not be long before the Native took over the farms of the whiteman.' Impelled, probably unwillingly, to add his weight to an ideology of popular protest that had emerged primarily from below, Kadalie was perhaps acutely aware at this moment of the dangers of letting 'inherent' ideas loose on the world. Nationalist mobilization had unleashed the enormous 'energies contained in customary social structures' – and 'once these well-springs have been tapped there is no real guarantee that the great forces released will be "controllable"'.[54]

Initially, rural activists appear to have attempted to curb their constituencies only when they were within earshot of whites. Thus it was at village meetings that a Natal Branch Secretary, Nathaniel Mcunu, held firmly to his policy that moderation must rule at gatherings attended 'by our opponents "ABELUNGU" [white people]', and meekly offered votes of thanks to white policemen present. In less exposed forums, Mcunu was an ardent Africanist, an admirer of Bambatha's rebellion, and a fierce opponent of land expropriation by whites. It rapidly came to the ears of farmers here that the ICU was telling Africans to cut down fences and plough where they liked. Without ever seeing a Union official, the semi-educated Nokwala Mthembu heard a variation of these tidings well suited to the modernizing aspirations of rural cultivators on the Ixopo mission station where she lived.

> They said they had come to cut down fences on the farms. The fields which the white people took away from us would be given back to us. We would plough them with tractors. The roads that were closed would be opened and used. They instructed us to plough the fields of which we had been deprived. If you had built your house, they said you should not leave. Stay there, we have come to put the land right.[55]

If and when Union leaders made such promises, they almost invariably did so in the countryside proper. This was an obvious arena for being both able and obliged to articulate ideas which had often been absorbed into folk wisdom even before officials arrived. Certainly, activists at rural venues tended to display greater sensitivity to the world-views of ordinary blacks. In part this was because they were often shop stewards from local communities, and were effectively free of Union discipline in making whatever claims would sell their red tickets. In part, too, it was the liberating effect of the absence of a phalanx of policemen and white farmers. Finally, it tended to be easier for ordinary blacks to impress their own concerns upon speakers. Not only did rural audiences usually number in the tens rather than the thousands, but also the actual or quasi-illegality of many rural meetings made leaders far more dependent on listeners. Evading detection involved more than abandoning the insignia of superiority such as English speeches and elevated platforms. It also meant according the hopes and fears of ordinary blacks sufficient consideration to minimize the possibility of betrayal.

Thus it was in a reserve, not a village, that the claim was made:

> if they do not join the ICU they will find that the day will come, when they will be ruled by the boot of the white man, and the Government would sell the location under them to some big company, who would plant the whole location with either wattles, cotton or other crops.[56]

Similarly, it was at a chief's homestead on an African-owned farm that Kadalie fully indulged himself in swearing which had resonance for rural blacks. In many African vernaculars, the word for 'pig' is also a strong term of verbal abuse, and the National Secretary certainly regarded swine as an appropriate metaphor for white settlers. 'If you want to see what a Boer is like, you must get a pig', he declaimed to the gathering on this Transvaal farm. 'After scrubbing it, you must fetch a Boer; you will see that these people are pigs.' According to Israel Mathuloe (who may have been recalling popular aspirations rather than Kadalie's words), the great man also promised here that his Union would strip the 'pigs' of their farms.[57]

Patently, there was a dialectical relationship between what leaders said and where they said it. The message articulated at rural meetings could differ fundamentally from that proclaimed in the towns. So too did the problems and pressures faced by organizers. Hence exploring the ICU's position on the land question – and assessing its rural impact – involves delving more deeply into its activities in the countryside proper.

Organization in Rural Hinterlands

In trying to breach the walls of white-owned farms, ICU leaders were sometimes risking their lives. Western Cape officials could count themselves lucky in merely being threatened with prosecution for trespass: in all other provinces, certain agriculturists freely proclaimed their intention of shooting Union leaders. In the Transvaal, at least one organizer visiting a tenant had a narrow escape from a highly suspicious farmer, while Elijah Ngcobo laconically claimed that no Bulwer official would have dared to enter a farm, because whites would have shot him dead. Even those using kinship or their jobs as a pretext had a difficult time if discovered; one unfortunate Ethiopian minister was brutally treated for his supposed ICU connections. As early as 1923, a Union deputation had in fact requested a Cabinet Minister 'to find a solution to break open the close doors of entering into the farms.'[58]

But if the doors were 'close', they were not locked, and ICU activists enjoyed a considerable degree of success in squeezing through. To do so their first and foremost need was transport, and Union funds were often expended to assure officials of mobility. In Estcourt, the three senior organizers devoted their weekdays to pedalling through the countryside on ICU bicycles, holding meetings in the reserves and 'preaching the ICU gospel' on farms. Those whose branches were more popular – or who had better access to head office funds – could travel in greater style. Riding in cars or on motorbikes, they sometimes harangued even stragglers on the road as they made periodic forays into the property of white masters.[59]

There were various reasons for visiting farms. Trifinah Mdhlalose recalled ICU activists (probably shop stewards) going from hut to hut on her Vryheid farm, being paid in kind for the tickets they sold on the strength of promises of an end to evictions and the return of the country to blacks. In Estcourt, one Union agent found the best way to sell red tickets was to make more concrete the meaning of restoration of land. Concentrating entirely on members of his Hlubi chiefdom (who were all scattered on white-owned holdings), he claimed the ICU would eject whites from ground confiscated from their rebel chief Langalibalele more than fifty years earlier.[60]

Organizers also traversed farms to discuss pressing grievances or impending court cases. Fairly frequently, too, they held meetings, which were sometimes requested by tenants themselves. On a Free State farm, an ICU leader was summoned and introduced to the assembled group of resident blacks by one of their number, who thereby played his part in the shaping of the Union from below. Alternatively, officials themselves convened a gathering on a specific holding, drawing an audience from adjacent farms. According to Charles Kumalo, in Estcourt they even held Saturday night concerts, at half the price of their urban counterparts. These one-shilling, night-long events on farms were better, he claimed, due to the absence of a curfew and because activists offered beer to get more patrons.[61]

Beer drinks, together with other social gatherings, were in fact of some significance in organization in the countryside. Since they were generally open to the public, they provided leaders with excellent cover as well as with an in-built audience. Furthermore, they allowed labourers to come together to discuss the Union. When complaining of the ICU, a Transvaal agriculturist noted that on his farm during weekends, 'natives talked politics, drank beer, and held church simultaneously'.[62] Clearly, the cultural space carved out by tenants was perceived as providing an uncomfortably large number of opportunities for sedition to spread.

Africans also talked Union politics in other rural arenas to which they had greater claim. Mission reserves were an important home-base for several organizers, especially in Natal. Here officials utilized well-established social networks in the ICU's cause, and often locked into older struggles over the conditions of tenure on these plots. It is probable too that the farms on which numerous branch activists lived were mainly black-owned, which meant that the land issue had long been infused with political overtones. At least some leaders living on such holdings used their homes as Union offices, thereby evading municipal harassment of both themselves and those who came to lay complaints.[63]

Finally, Union gatherings were regularly convened in areas controlled by indigenous authorities who were prepared to exploit the ambiguities of their situations. If all 'colonial politics is the politics of the tightrope', this was particularly evident to chiefs. But just as Solomon's silent opposition had greatly diminished the ICU's impact on sugar estates, so lesser chiefs' covert support considerably enhanced its leverage in other rural arenas. In Estcourt, numerous black traditional leaders publicly proclaimed their antipathy to the Union – but privately granted permission for meetings to be held in their reserves. Although the chiefs themselves cannily remained absent, their headmen were present (and risked much less since they were not usually paid by the state). Commoners also flocked to the gatherings: their chiefs had 'said people should go so that they should be free'. And since the meetings were held beneath the trees where court cases were heard, they easily passed as part of the normal political processes of a chiefdom.[64]

Chiefs who gave more overt support by attending, addressing or even calling ICU meetings were influential allies. Their powers of persuasion – or coercion – were impressive: a Natal chief, Kopolo, actually fined his subjects for not attending his land-buying, pro-ICU assemblies. Mtamo of Kranskop had a much lighter touch, in accordance with the popular legitimacy he had acquired. He headed a group based mainly in a drought-stricken location, which was unable to absorb inflowing evictees from farms. According to a disapproving policeman, he gave white authorities no assistance in arresting his followers, attended almost all beer drinks in the reserve, and was regarded as a commoner. Nonetheless, his authority as a chief was immediately evident when Branch Secretary James Ngcobo asked him to call the first meeting in Kranskop. Mtamo promptly put into operation the hierarchical lines of communication running from him down to the lowliest homestead head, and notified some one thousand widely scattered commoners of the Sunday gathering in his reserve. Besides providing Ngcobo with a large audience and credibility, this also meant that surveillance was partially foiled. Landlords, blissfully unaware of the summons their labourers had received, became suspicious only when crowds of blacks streamed past their holdings claiming to be headed for church.[65]

In comparison to meetings in villages, those in the countryside proper sometimes had the disadvantage of being convened in venues which excluded women. Although this had tactical value in so far as court places or meeting spaces outside a chief's homestead were common assembly points for adult men, it also contributed to low female participation in the Union. Furthermore, even when women were admitted, age inequalities could be even more pronounced than in the urban areas. Thus at an assembly in a Natal reserve in 1928, only older males among the thirty men and twenty-nine women present attempted to question the speakers.[66]

Officialdom, however, was concerned not about the less representative nature of many rural gatherings, but about the fact that they were occurring at all. While differences existed within the white body politic over the appropriate response to the ICU's organization in villages, there was near unanimity that the reserves were out of bounds. Moulding a 'Bantu Nation' unquestionably necessitated the exclusion from this Nation's home-base of any movement propagating ideas about class. So chiefs like Mtamo and Kopolo were sacked. In the Transkeian Territories, the pass system, the police and the courts were used to charge, imprison and deport activists unable to prove 'citizenship' of the region. Zulu-speaking Bertha Mkhize was thus arrested in the border village of Bizana, where whites claimed 'they did not require Natal Wisdom amongst the Pondos'. Nor did settlers appreciate ICU intellectuals operating amongst blacks in South Africa's external labour reservoirs. So Union leaders were either debarred or deported from Basutoland, Southern Rhodesia and South West Africa. Finally in October 1927, a measure was introduced for South African regions less well barricaded behind legislation. On the grounds that chiefs' authority was being undermined by the ICU, the government prohibited meetings of more than ten people in the reserves and mission locations, unless permission had first been granted by the white magistrate as well as by the black chief or headman.[67]

The ICU responded in various ways to this unequivocal message to leave rural non-workers alone. The worst scenario occurred when it was caught between the pincers of state repression and traditionalist suspicion. In this case, if organizers firmly adhered to the Union's relatively sophisticated ideas and tactics, they generally failed to have much impact. Indeed some activists, lacking either the resources or the inclination for illegal work amongst 'backward' reserve-dwellers, simply renounced the attempt. Thus numerous unhealthy, relatively inaccessible and strongly traditionalist locations in the northern Transvaal appear to have been completely omitted from the ICU's sphere of operations.

While an alternative to abandonment was whistle-stop illegal tours through the reserves, both stratagems contributed to the burgeoning of branches run largely or completely by men only peripherally connected to the Union. These could be sanctioned by accredited organizers, as were those established in Basutoland after 'Mote's rushed visit to the region. They could also be repudiated, as were the 'fictitious agencies . . .throughout the whole of Zululand' complained of by a Natal Branch Secretary.[68] At best, such branches were run by ICU members or shop stewards. At worst, they were headed by self-appointed agents hoping to cash in on the Union's prestige. And in either case, the ICU's mode of operating was usually totally transformed. Meetings and offices had to be hidden from the eyes of whites – and sometimes from those of hostile chiefs as well. Activists were deriving many of their ideas from their constituencies rather than Union headquarters, and were forced to focus largely on concerns close to the hearts of rural cultivators. Frequently, these were either peasant or local political issues. 'All the Natives with their red tickets say I am nothing', expostulated a chief in a Natal reserve, where his opponents had expanded their long-standing conflict with him by identifying with the ICU. Indeed, Union members here had reinterpreted the ICU's message to incorporate local traditions and trajectories of struggle, and were far more concerned about their corrupt chief's imposition of 'lover's fees' than any broader ICU ideology.[69]

Somewhat more standard activities in the reserves occurred when the Union exploited the fact that the state was not a monolithic bloc. Thanks to a Supreme Court verdict overturning the original ruling, Union meetings in locations were effectively unbanned for about four months from mid-1928. Furthermore, grass-roots resistance could intensify contradictions within the local state to the point where ordinary blacks won the day. For instance, in the winter of 1928, an ICU gathering in a Natal reserve was technically legal, although it had not been approved by black political authorities. Unusually, a white policeman was present, and he noted that most present disapproved of the chief's angry order for the audience to disperse. Requesting his African subordinate 'to keep cool and say nothing', the white man opted for allowing organizers to state one of the Union's most typical themes: that unity was strength, and all must therefore join the ICU.[70]

There were many other instances where commoners disassociated themselves from the older elite's antagonism to the Union. Ngcobo recalled being summoned to his chief's homestead, and being informed by him and his headmen that they had received no instructions from officialdom confirming the ICU's claims about land. Some ordinary blacks responded by reaffirming the ICU's message, and three days later a group of dissidents – mainly young married men – held their own meeting. Amongst them was Ngcobo, who remembered they decided that their chief had misunderstood the Union. They resolved to go to white farmers' plantations to cut firewood for themselves: a fairly mild action in a district where, according to Ngcobo, many 'went to plunder the white men's fields and claimed that they had taken over their farms'.[71]

Clearly, the anti-ICU position of most African political authorities did not in itself determine the allegiances of many rural blacks. This was especially true of those based outside the reserves. Even Solomon ka Dinizulu was defied on a massive scale: Natal membership figures peaked at some 88,000.[72] Weighed and found wanting partly due to their inability to provide land, traditional leaders were being deserted for new men promising farms for the price of a ticket.

Significantly, however, there were well-defined limits to the ability or willingness of organizers to accommodate traditionalists. Despite certain ideological concessions, and despite efforts to woo chiefs and penetrate the reserves, the Union did not in the main focus on winning over this constituency. With the important exception of Natal – where particularist loyalties were strongest, where activists took these seriously, and where the bulk of membership was situated – Union intellectuals were not overly anxious to lard their speeches with ingredients derived from the past. On the contrary: an excess of elements such as ethnicity was perceived as positively dangerous. Many organizers were far too aware that these older cultural inheritances could divide members, fragment the Union and provide a regional base for opportunistic leaders. For sound nationalist reasons, the dominant line in the ICU was that 'Africanism and Christianity should replace tribalism.'[73]

Similarly, although wages never dislodged land as a mobilizing issue, at village meetings officials repeatedly insisted on the importance of higher pay. For many of them, proletarianization was an irreversible fact of life – and a potentially acceptable one at that. Thus, arguments that wages were too low to maintain the homestead economy were generally few and far between. Much more commonly, rural blacks were assured that better pay would allow men to be dressed in suits and be termed 'Mister' rather than 'kaffir'; it would enable women to adorn themselves in crêpe de chine and acquire fat chins like the whites; and it would permit families to live in electrified houses eating puddings like the mine magnates in Parktown. As 'Mote expressed it at a Free State meeting, he was shocked to find that men were naked under their overcoats, and that women were swathed in woollen blankets. If they fought for three pounds a month, he argued, he could come to their village and 'find a lady who I can take as a sweetheart wearing silks, as I don't want to share her blanket'.[74]

If this would alienate blanketed men and women, so be it. ICU officials were in the main contesting the unevenness of South Africa's 'dual revolution', not progress itself. They certainly glanced at their cultural heritages – and briefly let loose 'inherent' ideas about land that were perhaps the fastest short-cut through South African history imaginable. Yet struggles infused with these older peasant and parochial beliefs also seriously threatened modern nationalist development. Understandably, these educated men preferred to concentrate on the safer and much more accessible constituency of the *abaphakathi*: 'the people in the middle', who were self-consciously suspended between or in transition from the old to the new. In remoulding and being shaped by the experiences and traditions of this grouping, activists drew heavily on the western ideologies of socialism, liberalism and Christianity.

Socialism and Nationalism

Like Tom Nairn, one might say that 'of all the weird mixtures and alliances engendered by . . . the direct transference of advanced ideas or techniques into under-developed lands', the most important may have been the displacement of socialism into peripheral countries. Yet while the worldwide diffusion of this ideology was significant, so too was the way it tended to be assimilated in backward zones.

It was bound to become part of their great compensatory drive to catch up – an ideology of development or industrialization, rather than one of post-capitalist society. In this position within the world economy, it has of course become a subordinate ally of nationalism.[75]

In South Africa in the later 1920s, it was perhaps debatable whether socialism was even a minor ally of the ICU's nationalism. But notwithstanding the party political break, Communists continued to provide the Union with organizational and ideological inputs, and some senior ICU officials still considered themselves socialists. Although a more accurate label might have been social democrats – given their tendency to contrast the lawless militancy of Communist 'Political Murderers' to their own struggle 'to constitutionally overthrow capitalism' – certain Party precepts did retain considerable force.[76] In particular, the notion that equality between black and white would be achieved only if all workers fought together for socialism received an added boost from September 1927. Seeking to clip the wings of the ICU's nationalism – and to prevent outraged farmers from taking the law into their own hands – the state used the newly passed Native Administration Act against several organizers advocating so-called hostility between black and white. As the heavy artillery in the battle to set the ideological limits of dissent, the Act carried penalties of up to a year's imprisonment, and gave activists considerable incentive to focus on class rather than racial contradictions.

Thus numerous leaders publicly insisted that capitalists were the common enemy of both black and white workers, and pointedly referred to the ICU's white membership. Whites of socialist persuasion were invited to share platforms: a student, John Wainer, addressed rousing meetings in the Free State with Kadalie. Since the two were shot at as they drove to Bloemfontein, it was providential that the idealistic Wainer had already given his life to 'Socialism and Sociology'. Although Kadalie had no such grounding in academic Marxism, he could use the Union's constitutional preamble to repudiate accusations that his movement sought racial warfare. So when trying to establish closer relations with the white Trade Union Congress in 1927, he bluntly referred to this dramatic declaration of intent. It had been written when the CP was regarded as an ally, and was hardly likely to appease the fears of white wage-earners:

Whereas the interests of the workers and those of the employers are opposed to each other, the former living by selling their labour, receiving for it only part of the wealth they produce; and the latter living by exploiting the labour of the workers; depriving the workers of a part of the product of their labour in the form of profit, no peace can be between the two classes, a struggle must always obtain about the division of the products of human labour, until the workers through their industrial organisations take from the capitalist class the means of production, to be owned and controlled by the workers for the benefit of all, instead of for the profit of a few. Under such a system he who does not work, neither shall he eat. The basis of remuneration shall be the principle from every man according to his abilities, to every man according to his needs. This is the goal for which the ICU strives along with all other organised workers throughout the world.[77]

It was in the Free State, where proletarianization was furthest advanced in both town and countryside, that activists really took such ideas to heart. Prior to the CP purge, small town audiences were told that the aim of the Union was to obtain a government like that of 'Holy Russia', 'a communist Government . . . elected by and representative of the masses of the people, whites and blacks'.[78] References to the great and glorious Russia were more muted after 1926, but village organizers continued to call for the nationalization of means of production, and to denounce bloodsucking capitalists who used passes, taxes and the recruiting system to reduce workers to slaves. The ICU, they cried, aimed for economic revolution, so that the wealth of the country would be shared by the working class which produced it. In mid-1927, Free State municipalities were thrown into a panic by a flamboyant red poster advertizing the start of a great Free State campaign in Kroonstad. 'Now is the time to consolidate and strengthen the LABOUR MOVEMENT in preparation for the next SOCIALIST COMMONWEALTH', it proclaimed. 'WORKERS OF THE WORLD UNITE, YOU HAVE NOTHING TO LOSE BUT YOUR CHAINS.'[79]

The stirring meeting which this advertized was attended by about four thousand Africans, who subsequently poured out onto the streets under a banner declaring that capitalism, low wages and high municipal rates were the enemies of the workers. Moreover, at least one Free State audience passed a resolution 'to fight the capitalist classes, with a view to the final abolition of the capitalist system and the emancipation of the proletariat from the oppression of capitalist exploitation'. Such statements were always intended in a colour-blind sense. To the annoyance of Congressmen, capitalists were black as well as white. And to the approval of Communists, proletarians were white as well as black.[80]

Yet declarations like this were not the norm, even amongst Union intellectuals with socialist inclinations. Many officials were themselves suspicious of closer relations with racist white unions, and the great bulk had at their fingertips the ability to invoke racial prejudice to malign political opponents. And unlike white Communists who argued that the interests of black, white and yellow slaves were identical, ICU organizers were forced by their own life experiences to take cognisance of the differences. Mbeki had raised the issue with the British CP in 1926: 'owing to the fact the foundation of South Africa is based on colour discrimination and racial animosity stumbling blocks in advocating our pure class policy we were to contend with'. Within the South African CP, leading black members stressed the same point: the problem with fighting undiluted class warfare was that the bulk of the African labouring population was less concerned about exploitation by capitalists than racial oppression by all whites.[81]

One solution was to back away from proletarian purity. Some ICU leaders did this by projecting working-class unity into the future: as a Transvaal Branch Secretary declaimed in 1928,

> The white workers of South Africa were very foolish as they only believed in the colour of their skins, but the time would come when they would not have a strike of colour in South Africa, but a strike of the combined workers, and they would then demand that a working man should be Premier.

Others reversed this relationship between political and economic struggles, and argued that the ruling capitalists and land-owners would only give way when white and black workers were political equals. Clearly, for many ICU activists the struggle against capital could not but be linked with – and was generally subordinated to – the struggle for national liberation.[82]

The ICU had given notice of this even at the height of its fraternization with the CP, with clarion calls like 'African proletarians unite, you have nothing to lose but slavery, and a fruitful and wealthy Africa to win.' In this later period, socialist traditions were often further reworked as they were incorporated into a nationalist ideology. For example, May Day processions were held, but in protest against the pass laws. Chains had to be broken, otherwise Africans would remain landless in the country of their forefathers. Karl Marx was invoked – to argue that every economic question was also a political question, and that if the ICU copied the 'futile "non-political" attitude of our white contemporaries', it would be 'leaving the political machines to the unchallenged control of our class enemies'. Finally, in the Union's ideology as in reality, the bosses who enriched themselves were almost invariably whites, and the workers who were exploited were generally Africans. Thus leaders stressed it was blacks who built houses, roads and railways; blacks who dug out gold and slaved on farms; and blacks who had to regain their country.[83]

It was also, in a further deviation from CP policy, blacks who had to struggle for the right to enter the petty (and occasionally the *haute*) bourgeoisie. While any organization that caters for the antagonistic interests of different classes is likely to become a site of struggle, many middle strata concerns were by no means opposed by the masses. At a time, therefore, when an important reason for leaving farms was to obtain schooling for offspring, the demand for free education for all blacks was widely accepted. Moreover, Union leaders could evoke wild enthusiasm from village audiences by suggesting that blacks should replace whites as chauffeurs or even as Location Superintendents. Indeed, for many an ICU audience, the unacceptable face of South African capitalism was its whiteness, not its physiognomy. This was partly because memories of past autonomy were still fresh enough to be translated into a new context. As Moses Kotane aptly expressed it, he was bewildered when he entered the CP as a worker in 1928, because he

> did not know what a proletarian was, or why it should be good to be a proletarian. We were told that a proletarian had nothing but his labour power. Coming from an independent people, I could not see how someone who had nothing was worthy of respect. I had worked for white farmers, and I could never understand anyone remaining satisfied to spend his whole life working for such people. In fact I despised them for lacking pride and ambition. To me a man had to be independent and self-sufficient; a man who worked for others appeared to me like a beggar, with no dignity.[84]

It was largely due to the prevalence of such sentiments that it took time for the ICU to be wracked with conflict over the upwardly mobile ambitions of many organizers. As the worst offender, Champion had his dubious transactions publicly exposed in 1926. Yet Durban membership continued to soar, reaching some 45,000 in December 1927. Four months later, when head office suspended Champion for fraud, Durban labourers fervently supported their leader and gave Kadalie one of the worst thrashings of his life. While their ardour was due partly to their perceptions of Champion as a man who fought valiantly for the rights of workers, there were also many who saw Champion's enterprises as benefitting themselves as well as their owner. This was true even of the clothing factory, where Bertha Mkhize worked. It was a period when tailoring here was dominated by non-Africans, and when white trade unionists were attempting to block black entrance into the textile industry on the grounds of their 'dirtiness'. Mkhize recalled that Albert Batty, the ICU's white founding father, touted for orders in Durban's commercial centre, and returned with yards of material. 'We did the work and he sent it back to West Street and – (clapping hands) – they never knew it was the Africans that did this work so they bought it!'[85]

Undeniably, being black and often semi-proletarianized in a racist society fundamentally conditioned Africans' ideas of the direction their struggle should take. It also contributed to a situation where very few ICU organizers proffered pure socialism to the masses. In a country where economic exploitation was predicated upon racial oppression, some did, however, anticipate and perhaps transcend crucial developments in the CP's policy. From the late 1920s up to the present, the South African Communist Party's strategy has been shaped by that adopted in 1928: to struggle for 'an independent native South African republic as a stage towards a workers' and peasants' republic, with full equal rights for all races, black, coloured and white'.[86] Some years earlier, Kadalie had expressed similar sentiments:

> We are aiming at the building up in Africa of a National Labour Organisation of the aboriginals, through which we shall break the walls of white autocracy. We must prevent the exploitation of our people on the mines and on the farms, and obtain increased wages for them. We shall not rest there. We will open the gates of the Houses of legislation, now under the control of the white oligarchy, and from this step we shall claim equality of purpose with the white workers of the world to overthrow the capitalist system of government and usher in a co-operative Commonwealth one, a system of Government which is not foreign to the aboriginal of Africa.[87]

Despite its romantic Africanism, and despite its flawed 'stage-ist' conception of radical transformation, Kadalie's declared strategy contained two key insights. It insisted on the centrality of the African proletariat, and it emphasized unity with 'workers of the world'. Since the material conditions for the realization of this vision hardly existed, it is not surprising that Kadalie's perceptions found only fitful and unsustained expression in the Union's tactics. Nonetheless, from the conflict-ridden relationship between international socialism and African nationalism, there had emerged a seminal political perspective. It was so far in advance of its times that it continues to resonate today.

Liberalism and Farm Workers

In the 1920s in the countryside, the proletariat that existed was so rudimentary and weak that socialism never stood a chance. Instead, activists grappled with the grim reality of violent primitive accumulation. They tried to grip both horns of the dilemma: to expand upon the common-sense ideas of both the most backward and the most developed social groups on the land. Outside the earshot of whites, they and their land-hungry supporters urged a radical recreation of the past, by turning the world upside-down. Instead of expropriation of the many by the few, there should be expropriation of the minority by the majority. At most village meetings and ICU conferences, however, leaders propogated beliefs underpinned by a very different conception of the class that would lead the transformation of the countryside. In essence, they recognized the revolutionary role of the bourgeoisie in sweeping away primitive techniques, personal dependence and poverty. But they wanted to telescope this process, so that black farm labourers, then and there, finally saw the progressive face of capitalism.

Thus it was the very immaturity of capitalist development in the countryside that underlay ideological convergence between Union officials on the one hand and 'progressive' farmers on the other. Like more advanced landlords, ICU activists perceived on farms a system of slavery which reduced human beings to the status of property or beasts of burden. Many were shocked by the prevailing poverty, and horrified by the lawlessness reigning on white holdings. Farm labourers, they claimed, were invariably underpaid and overworked; they could be driven handcuffed in front of a horse just for asking for coffee; and they were 'fed on mealiepap and shot like pigs'. Of particular concern was the issue of evictions, not least because the existence of this sanction inhibited support for the Union. Leaders regularly pointed to the illegality of instantaneous notice, and frequently promised that the ICU would put an end to farmers' crude practice of saying, '*Vat jou goed en trek Ferreira*' (Take your goods and leave Ferreira).[88]

The Union's public position on rural labourers was thus informed by a major tenet of economic liberalism. This was that workers should meet farmers as equals in the market-place, free to sell their own labour-power, for a limited period of time, for wages. Even the rituals legitimating the master-servant relationship were rejected: 'Don't greet your masters with your hat in hand, that's complete nonsense, look him in the eye when you talk to him.' More significantly, Charles Kumalo recalled Kadalie telling them that farm workers should 'work normally like all other people. They should be employed permanently and be paid normal wages . . . A person should be free to leave a job whenever he wanted to.' It was this commitment to the 'normalization' of farm labour that inspired repeated ICU calls for these workers to be included under the 1925 Wage Act (which applied to many other blacks). Similarly, although organizers could be tempted to downgrade the value of labour-power of rural Africans, a common demand in 1927 was for farm and all other workers to receive eight shillings a day, precisely the minimum wages for whites urged by the Labour Party. Poverty-stricken tenants did not have to be fully proletarianized for this fantastic wage to have enormous appeal. Even Tolo Manoto, at that time a sharecropper after years as an ordinary worker and labour tenant, qualified his claim that he 'never understood the movement clearly and what was good about it'. While he never joined Kadalie's supporters, 'on the question of increasing wages, we understood and agreed with him'.[89]

The ideologues of more advanced sectors of rural and urban capital might well have echoed Manoto's disapproval of the ICU – and his agreement with leaders on certain fundamental issues. When an ICU Vice-President claimed the rate of evictions was such that they threatened human life and property, he was voicing the fears of many owners of the means of production. Organizers denouncing the illegal and unjust practices of farmers were doing precisely the same as certain white officials and liberals trying to curb the spread of the Union. In condemning farm workers' wretched living conditions and exhausting hours, leaders were well within the paradigm of those who advocated better treatment to expand the home market and enhance efficiency. Indeed, some activists even argued for higher wages in precisely the same terms as liberals. In the Free State, a favourite claim was that:

> Their organization was of as much advantage to 'Mr. White Man', as to the Black man, for the White man's trade and business would be doubled as a consequence of the higher wages paid to Natives by reason of the greater buying capacity of the higher-paid Native, and yet Mr. White man expelled them from their farms.[90]

At times, however, ICU leaders completely left their followers behind as they converged with 'progressive' landlords and their spokesmen. Activists did so partly because they were not under the control of the weak, fragmented under-classes, and so were able to express freely their own prejudices, aspirations or political judge-ments. Hence a handful of conservative Union officials also appro-priated the less appealing strand of economic liberalism: if wages rose, then productivity must also be increased. As Henderson Binda sternly advised one audience in the language of their oppressors: *'Hulle kan nie 'n goeie salaris vir slegte werk verwag nie. Spreker is seker dat as hulle goeie werk, beter werk lewer, sal die baas ook gewillig wees om meer te betaal'* (They cannot expect a good salary for bad work. The speaker is certain that if they perform good work, better work, the master will also be willing to pay more). When Champion sought representation at the South African Agricultural Union's Annual Conference in 1927, he did not even bother to attempt such a compromise between landlords and labourers. In a letter drafted by Batty, he simply claimed that the aims of the two bodies were similar, since 'the ICU would welcome . . . "a uniform maximum (*sic*) wage for labourers for the different farming operations"'.[91]

He also claimed that the ICU would welcome a uniform system of contracts, thereby pointing to another key area of congruence between leaders and landlords. Despite being deeply angered by the violation of verbal agreements, illiterate tenants – and especially their children – generally regarded a written contract, backed by penal sanctions, as *''n slag yster om vir ons te vang'* (a death trap to catch us). Struggling landlords accustomed to illegal practices had much the same attitude to involving the state in their affairs. However, most ICU officials, deeply committed to exploiting the gap between landlords and the law, and aware that tenants had no hope of enforcing verbal agreements in the white man's court, favoured formal contracts. So too did many state functionaries, white liberals and 'progressive' farmers, although they had a very different view of the role of the law. Since they correctly recognized that the juridico-legal apparatus served primarily the interests of white masters, they saw several advantages in uniform, written contracts which closely defined tenants' obligations and possessions. For them, these increased the ability of the courts to punish recalcitrant labourers, smoothed the path of capital accumulation by containing conflict at acceptable levels, enhanced the class unity of white agriculturists, and were thus a strong weapon in crushing ICU-inspired protest.[92]

Hence a bizarre scenario was played out in the countryside. On the one hand, 'progressive' farmers attempted to 'teach [the native] the sacredness of a contract' by inflicting an enforceable agreement on tenants and poorer landlords alike. On the other hand, ICU activists tried to 'teach the rank and file to ask their masters to make written contracts'. Completely opposing aims and analyses had produced the same solution to the problem of making labour agreements accord with the increasingly capitalist face of South African agriculture.[93]

Very similar patterns can be discerned as opposing groups struggled to make the South African state conform to the western norm. Just as capitalists and the under-classes had acquired certain common interests in the course of the unfinished transformation of the countryside, so white liberals and black people were drawn together by the incomplete nature of the bourgeois democratic revolution. Furthermore, just as Union activists sometimes allied with landlords against labour tenants, so leaders sometimes united with liberals against ICU members. Indeed, they could do so in ways which were even more unsavoury than the Union's most outlandish interventions in the countryside.[94]

For all this, the extent of agreement between ICU organizers and either larger capitalists or liberals should not be exaggerated. For one thing, the seemingly liberal symbols which studded the Union's broader message – British justice, fair play, fair wages, constitutional action, and even Queen Victoria – had usually kept their form but changed their content. As they were detached from their bourgeois matrix and incorporated into a language of resistance, they had in fact been transformed. Farmers wedded to an ideology of naked *baasskap*, and a repressive state headed by Afrikaner nationalists, were accused of gross violations of the principles of British justice and liberty to all races. The black man was hailed as 'bona fide citizen of the Empire' to encourage him to fight for the right to vote. Liberalism's attention to individual rights was employed to insist that blacks must be paid enough 'to live like people – like the white people, must be treated not as children but as men and women in the land of their forefathers, and must be regarded as human beings instead of 'a profit-giving tool for the exploiter'. Finally, the language of liberalism was invoked for protection: never were claims to constitutionalism more vehement than when leaders were threatened with violence, attempting to negotiate with farmers, or trying to win white allies both within and outside South Africa.[95]

Apart from this tactical use of symbols, the 'liberalism' that infused ICU speeches was frequently radically different from that propagated by members of the 'master race'. Numerous leaders urged the abolition of passes for all, while white liberals hoped instead for the elimination of minor instances of discrimination against the elite. Many called for equal political rights, while 'friends of the natives' reckoned that only about 1 per cent of Africans were fit to exercise the vote. Large numbers demanded black workers be treated as if they were white, when the very existence of mining and farming was predicated upon an ultra-cheap African labour force enmeshed in extra-economic controls. Finally, activists often called for freedom of speech, of assembly and of organization, when white domination and capital accumulation depended upon the maintenance of a rightless and disorganized black populace.[96]

Hence it is too easy to characterize these ICU demands as being those of democratized liberalism. In an international perspective this was undoubtedly so. But in South Africa, the transformation of classical liberalism into liberal democracy occurred in a stunted and warped fashion, with the 'Cape tradition' emerging in the 1920s as liberal segregationism, touting separate political institutions for separate, racially-defined 'nations'. The ICU was blazing a very different trail as it sought to extend and deepen political freedom.[97]

Similarly, the Union was not 'merely' fighting for bourgeois objectives. In all societies where the labouring poor are politically rightless, it is imperative that they struggle

> for those freedoms – freedom of the press, organization and assembly, universal suffrage, local self-government – which a timid bourgeoisie, in spite of the bourgeois nature of these demands, can do without, but without which the workers can never win their emancipation.[98]

Even more pertinently: in the 1920s, South Africa's bourgeois democratic revolution *could not* be extended downwards to incorporate the entire populace. It was not a question of timidity: it was a matter of life and death. When the ICU rallied the black under-classes under a banner inscribed with liberal, bourgeois demands, it was challenging the entire system of racial domination, and thereby the very viability of capitalism itself.[99]

Separatist Christianity and Garveyism

Ideas and symbols which were western but not white were as attractive to Union intellectuals as those derived from the ideologies of socialism and liberalism. Separatist Christianity in particular had a powerful presence in the ICU's message – an appropriate reflection of the gradual replacement of the chiefdom by the church as the growth point for national consciousness and political opposition. Many leaders were acutely aware of the extent to which the Christianity of white missionaries propped up the existing social order. As the ICU's President exclaimed at the 1925 Annual Conference, 'For Christ's sake tell the Europeans to keep their white Jesus and let you have your own land which they took from you.' Arguing that whites used their churches to keep blacks in slavery, numerous organizers also urged members to transfer their allegiance to Ethiopian bodies.[100]

In a broader sense, Christianity was often used as a vehicle through which class and racial antagonisms were expressed. Although it was a contradictory ideology which internalized the master-servant relationships that prevailed at its birth, its radical elements could be most effectively exploited. Thus the positing of heavenly Lords above those on earth had profound implications for the oppressed: as one ICU activist asserted, 'God did not want them to carry passes.' Moreover, even armed struggle could be suggested through Biblical symbolism. Speaking in a Free State village, 'Mote promised that

> I shall not cease in my fight, nor shall my sword slip in my hand, until I have built a new Jerusalem for my people. Like John at Patmos, I see a New City and a new life for my people.[101]

As this suggests, the messianic traditions of Christianity fed into the millenarian undertones common in ICU speeches. Leaders often reeled off biblical quotations proving that the Union was a divine institution and that God Himself was with them. So too was His Son: the role of the Christ of the black people was often attributed to National and Provincial Secretaries, who were selling holy tickets and preaching the new religion of the ICU. Even the Holy Spirit could be enlisted: when Kadalie explained the meaning of the Union's initials in East London in 1927, he sweepingly claimed that I stood for God the Father, C for God the Son, and U for God the Holy Ghost. Having established this intimate relationship with the Holy Trinity, organizers found it easy to argue that success was inevitable because God was shepherding their Union. He was leading supporters to a new heaven and a new earth – or, in the language of Exodus, He was conducting the enslaved children of Israel to the promised land. Fortunately, He had adapted Himself to the modernized needs of his flock. Simon Elias informed an audience that he could see, 'far away on the horizon, Jehovah coming to lead you to the land of Canaan, . . . where you will each drive your own motor-car and dress your womenfolk in fugi silk and crêpe de chine'.[102] Occasionally, too, He was assigned a date for His intervention. Probably influenced by Watch Tower beliefs, one District Secretary would confidently tell meetings that 'We know we are going to be the next rulers according to the bible', or that 'The dominion of the Gentiles ceased in 1914, and on May 29, 1928, Armageddon would occur. The ICU would prepare the natives to meet this climax in the proper way.'[103]

As well as informing the ICU's ideology, separatist churches also influenced certain methods of organization. In a mediated form, this was evident in the Union's annual conferences, its Sunday collections and its auction concerts. More significantly, it was apparent in the styles of oratory favoured by leaders, such as their use of call-and-response to focus attention and evoke solidarity: 'Do you work?' –

'Yes!' – 'Do you eat?' – 'No!' Like black ministers too, many Union officials resorted to fiery 'roaring' and emotional appeals to win applause or deafening cheers; and to have caused women to weep was reckoned as the pinnacle of achievement. The Union was complementing not competing with independent churches, and many supporters undoubtedly expected these new preachers to afford a similar emotional release. Indeed, some rural leaders went so far as to term their gatherings 'revival meetings', while a white contemporary scornfully dismissed them as 'emissaries of the hot-gospeller type'.[104]

Quasi-religious fervour was also invoked by the very form of ICU meetings, in which a nationalist prayer often preceded the centrally important 'sermon'. Hymns too were commonly used, and were even given new lyrics praising the Union. Songs had enormous significance in uniting illiterate blacks: those in which oppositional values were embedded allowed even the timid to raise a cry of protest in a manner perceived as legitimate. A popular favourite was the Xhosa hymn *'Nkosi Sikelel' iAfrika'* ('God bless Africa'). Despite its melancholy cadences and focus on supernatural deliverance, this was generally lustily sung by ICU audiences as an expression of pride in Africa and commitment to the cause of freedom. Moreover, in the best musical traditions of its members – and since the ANC had recently adopted the refrain as its anthem – the Union creatively appropriated *'Nkosi Sikelel' iAfrika'*. By adding two final lines (and an additional verse in the eastern Cape), the ICU could lay claim to its very own national paean. So in the 1920s, the song which has now come 'to symbolize more than any other piece of expressive culture the struggle for African unity and liberation in South Africa',[105] reverberated through the countryside in this form:

> God bless Africa
> May her fame increase
> Hear our prayers
> God, bless us.
>
> Descend, Spirit
> Descend, Spirit
> Descend Holy Spirit
> Let the ICU
> Fill the world.[106]

Yet useful as religion was amongst the pious *abaphakathi*, it had its limitations amongst those who were already sloughing off belief in God. Often the political purposes it served were performed equally well by other means. Thus in the sphere of music, the lesson of resistance was sometimes taught by familiarizing audiences with *The Red Flag*, that desperate yet defiant anthem of the British labour movement. Also popular amongst the African elite and ICU leadership was '*Vukani Mawethu*' ('Awake my People'), an exhortatory freedom song that resurfaced in South Africa's 1976 uprisings. And in the broader arena of culture and ideology, organizers made much of another complex of notions which could define them as modern nationalists: those associated with the leading blacks in the world, Americans.[107]

Although ICU officials operated primarily with concepts of a South African state and nation, Garveyism fuelled a Pan-Africanist substrand within their ideology. Thus both *The Workers' Herald* and the Union's notepaper were emblazoned with '*VUKA AFRIKA*', written in white letters across a black continent, itself proudly placed in the centre of the globe. Similarly, when Mbeki told rural Transvaal blacks of 'the rise and fall of nations starting with the Romans right up to the Republic of America', he urged that Africa in its entirety 'should rise up with strength'. Some organizers publicly proclaimed that the 'ICU of Africa' would expand far beyond the continent's southernmost tip. And in the vivid words of a Union pamphlet advertizing all-night auction concerts in Durban, 'The time has come when the African Workers should make their voice heard through the AFRICAN CONTINENT.'[108]

It was, however, American blacks rather than African workers who were meeting this challenge through the most inspiring of Garveyist promises – that four hundred million blacks would fight to the death to free Africa of its colonial masters. In South Africa by the mid-1920s, the belief that American liberators were arriving had permeated to the remotest rural districts. Moreover, great impetus had been given to subcultures in which oppositional significance was attached to all things American. Many ICU activists were quick to capitalize on both these developments, by claiming either personal knowledge or adopting accoutrements of their transatlantic exemplar. President Gumbs, a Garveyist whom ICU officials themselves accepted as a descendent of American blacks, addressed a Free State meeting, stressing his origins and claiming that 'we' would reclaim Africa. Kadalie had no qualms about announcing that he had travelled in the States, and while his 'American accent' may have been a figment of a reporter's imagination, such impressions were encouraged by the very English that officials spoke. Indeed, at least one organizer was advertized as speaking 'in Negro dialect'.[109]

There were other ways in which organizers indicated Afro-American leanings, and hence distanced themselves from conservative Eurocentric black politicians. *The Workers' Herald* extolled the deeds of Negro novelists and boxers, and one activist promised that the Union would form tennis and football teams to play in Jamaica and America. Others called for members to emulate the achievements of their United States comrades, who, they claimed, were bankers not slaves. Furthermore, the ICU's red membership cards, red flag and green badges fortuitously fitted into the red, green and black colour scheme adopted by the Garveyists as the colours of the Negro race. Enterprising organizers could easily extend the metaphor: in Bulwer, officials ostentatiously adopted a black uniform complete with a black cap and red scarf, and surrounded the ICU office with four flags, alternately red and green. Almost certainly, their style was dictated by the fact that they were operating on the peripheries of a Garveyist movement, and knew full well how widespread was the popular cry: '*Ama Melika ayeza*' – 'the Americans are coming'.[110]

Elsewhere, too, various versions of Garveyism had been internalized so rapidly that the Union's organizational practices buckled under the weight of the impatient rural poor. A Natal school inspector was hastily summoned to act as an unpaid leader, because officials

> couldn't cope with the amount of pressure that there was, people came from long distances to get a card to be a member of the ICU. They regarded it with a lot of importance. They must have a card to show when an angel came from America. If you didn't possess that card to show to that angel you were lost. So they wouldn't leave, they'd press us to write out that ticket or card to identify them with the ICU.[111]

From Christianity, Garveyism and the Union, to red tickets for American angels: the marriage of 'derived' and 'inherent' ideas produced many such fabulous offspring.

Tactics

Although numerous ICU activists were only too happy to foster fantasies which were simultaneously lucrative, there were many who engaged with reality as they tried to alleviate the plight of rural Africans. Not that it was easy to find appropriate ways of furthering the struggles of the most depressed and scattered sector of the black populace. Nor, given the unevenness of capitalist development and consciousness, was it possible to settle on a single plan of action. Hence the ICU advocated tactics ranging from petitions, legal battles and passive resistance, through to work stoppages, land seizures and bloody warfare.

Interestingly enough, the countryside had been sufficiently transformed for some leaders and landlords to be influenced by patterns of conflict in the more advanced urban areas. As Free State officials, 'Mote and Elias drew on their experiences during the aftermath of the 1925 stay-away in Bloemfontein. Here they had been involved in negotiations, in threatening strikes, and in partially successful efforts to enforce higher pay through a Wage Board determination. Most farmers, however, were less inclined than urban employers to believe reformers who urged: 'Invite the Wages Board to come down and the ICU is done.' It was only in Frankfort, the increasingly capitalized heart of the maize triangle, that landlords concurred that concessions were the best way of institutionalizing struggle.[112]

After a couple of militant gatherings here, Elias wrote to the Town Council threatening 'catastrophe' if farmers did not discuss labour conditions with the Union. Whilst obdurately insisting that such a meeting did not entail recognition – and frantically appealing to the central state to crush agitation – councillors embarked on the sophisticated strategy of trying to reshape the ICU before it had a popular following. In June 1927, together with six farming representatives, they met an ICU deputation consisting of 'Mote, Elias and ten black supporters. The lesson of including the rank-and-file had been well learnt by the Union in Bloemfontein, where a negotiating team consisting entirely of leaders had justifiably feared having 'daggers across our own house' after they bowed to employers' demands.[113]

Pertinently stating that tenants feared being shot if they complained in person about withheld crops and poor wages, 'Mote wanted to negotiate better conditions with the farmers' association in October. Elias's requests were for permission to reside in the township, and to open an ICU branch. Both were then smartly caught in the classic contradiction: for their demands to be met, it was necessary that neither their form nor their content posed a fundamental challenge to the existing order. Moreover, they were presumably acting without a mandate from below – and their ten black supporters scarcely represented an obdurate rural proletariat breathing down their necks. Pressurized, too, by the hostility emanating from whites, as well as by the knowledge that farmers were threatening to shoot them, both hastily began to compromise. Elias nervously denied that the ICU advocated written contracts: a retraction that probably decreased his appeal for these 'progressive' agriculturists. More shrewdly, 'Mote repudiated demands for eight shillings a day for farm labourers, and claimed they wanted only three shillings and sixpence. Both adopted the ideological vocabulary of those confronting them, and promised constitutional action under white guidance. When 'Mote also condemned Communism later that day, the CP bluntly accused him of 'crawling flat on his stomach in the presence of the exploiter'.[114]

There was some truth in this charge, although it took into account neither the constraints of negotiations nor the tactic of adopting deferential masks. But back in the world where they were subject to pressures from below as much as from above, the old defiance reasserted itself. Elias, correctly assessing that he would in any event receive his lodger's permit, refused to pledge either to abide by municipal regulations or to approach the Council only through the Native Advisory Board. Within three weeks, he and other ICU activists held a rabble-rousing meeting appealing for all blacks to join before October. They also indicated the sanctions they could apply if negotiations failed. In the words of one official inspired by the quasi-syndicalist beliefs common in the Union, 'When we say: "Down your spades, outspan the wagons, stop ploughing", you must do so and the battle is over.' When 'Mote asked whether those present accepted the threat of eviction – and another leader excitedly promised that township supporters would feed them for two years – over a thousand Africans rose in a body and shouted: 'We accept!'[115]

Neither the strike nor the October meeting ever materialized. Before the arrival of the Union's white advisor, William Ballinger, other attempts to negotiate with farmers also failed. In part, this was because the ICU lacked the organized grass-roots backing required to force recognition from reluctant landlords. Indeed, negotiations were rarely achieved even when the ICU was operating amongst cohesive village communities or gangs of workers, and scattered farm workers tenuously linked by their red cards formed an incomparably worse base. In part, too, it was due to racial prejudices so strong that farmers perceived merely talking to African trade unionists as a concession of equality. Thus the Executive of the Natal Agricultural Union initially agreed to invite Champion to their Anti-ICU conference, but retracted in horror upon discovering that his name belied his racial origins. Finally, proposed talks could founder when 'progressive' farmers were overridden by their undercapitalized compatriots. Thus in mid-1927, the Executives of the Modder Rivier and Bloemfontein District Farmers' Associations arranged a fearsome reception for ICU leaders to explain their aims. Those invited to a police-station meeting of the Bloemfontein Association included delegates from the Town Council, the Chamber of Commerce, the CID and the Department of Defence, while those consulted about it included the military Chief-of-Staff and the Cabinet. But careful preparations for this show of force were sabotaged when Bloemfontein farmers arrived in town. Like ordinary landlords in the Modder Rivier Association, they clearly believed the ICU's aim was the non-negotiable one of 'challeng[ing] the supremacy of the White over the Black'. After a summary discussion, Union representatives were abruptly refused entrance.[116]

This outlaw status, combined with the need to maintain membership's interest, fuelled much militant rhetoric. 'If we unite we shall be able to give those employers who are robbers a good beating. The ICU believes in strikes if the Capitalist does not give you justice', urged one Transvaal leader. Like inexperienced organizers of fledgling working classes elsewhere, ICU activists often assumed that a general strike would paralyse society, and some proposed mass work stoppages against landlessness, or against Hertzog's four 'Native Bills'. In such cases, it was perhaps fortunate that the Union never had the organizational muscle to translate words into action. An absence from work-places, even on a vast scale, is not the same as an assault on the state, and 'as a political weapon, strikes are nearly always profoundly ineffectual'.[117]

Given its heterogeneous base, however, the Union could not confine itself to typical working-class tactics. Some leaders called for action appropriate to almost all African males: refusal to carry or pay for either passes or tax receipts. Others – more cynical about the effects of passive resistance in a harshly repressive society – infused their speeches with the language of bloodshed. Apart from references to Field Marshal Kadalie drilling his forces for a countrywide pass-burning, there were numerous dark threats about a forthcoming 'very big smash up'. As in a speech by Elias to a crowd in Parys in 1927, this was often mingled with contradictory calls for other forms of action.

If you have to buy your freedom with bloodshed, then let it be so. (Applause) . . . You have seen how Swanepoel employs five natives to plough all his lands, and then he sells the crops for two thousand or two million pounds, paying his boys twenty-four pounds for the labour. We are out to crush that sort of white man by means of the law . . . if they won't pay you proper wages we shall tell you to cease work, and stop at home . . . You are so strong that you can stop all work, all trains, in fact all Africa.[118]

Especially when they were riding the crest of a popular upsurge, activists could suggest concrete, illegal action even at urban meetings. Thus there were those who urged that municipal rates should not be paid, that workers must stop labouring immediately in order to win eight shillings a day, or that passes should be burnt almost instantaneously. Sometimes organizers participated in the action they advocated: one official challenged petty segregation by marching with members into a hotel to demand dinner. More frequently, they engaged in opportunistic demagogy. In Natal in 1928, two leaders arrogantly headed off demands for the land they had promised by attempting to whip up support for direct action. They urged wary rural blacks to burn their tax receipts and passes, and, armed with assegais, to raze the court house to the ground. Predictably, both were arrested before a less exposed farm meeting allowed them to assess the level of support for their plans.[119]

More commonly too, activists made bombastic promises of imminent freedom while remaining within the bounds of legality. In so doing, they made much use of rhetorical questions to suggest protest indirectly. They also repeatedly postponed the day of reckoning: a typical theme was that 'it is not far off when we will have our country back again, it may be a few months yet'.[120] Allegedly, at a signal from the ICU passes would be abolished; by next year poll tax would be gone; within two years a general strike would be called. To the future was left the time when fences would be felled and farms would belong to blacks. And to a day known only to the National Council was left the time of 'bloody revolution'. For the moment, blacks must unite in the ICU, and wait.[121]

Given the diverse and divided constituencies that the Union was trying to mobilize against the privileged and powerful, this stress on solidarity was unexceptionable. Given, too, that leaders were ardent and inexperienced young activists – impatient for a future where their talents would be recognized, and judged by their ICU peers in terms of the number of tickets they sold – their promises of imminent freedom were understandable. But why was there this apparent disjuncture between their extravagant predictions and their failure to prepare the masses for great deeds? Why this 'death-defying "overcoming of obstacles" in fantasy', and a simultaneous 'reckless disregard of all the actual circumstances' of struggle?[122] Why were they fuelling the flames of spontaneous protest, but not employing disciplined organization to transform this into a conflagration?

The answer lay mainly in the enormous difficulties of incorporating the unsophisticated rural poor into a network of structures linked to branches in villages. In addition, these objective problems were perceived in a particular way by educated men opposing extremely coercive employers and the state. Union leaders were, after all, operating in the shadow of the post-war era of *'platskiet politiek'*, and of the bloody ICU confrontations in urban areas. These had instilled a very real and justifiable fear of imprisonment and death for those who overstepped permissible boundaries. ('Mote, for example, told audiences that he 'did not half run when they started shooting' in Bloemfontein in 1925). Such considerations doubtless informed the prevalent belief that organizing the rural poor involved no more than uniting them, peacefully, under an umbrella body.

Since peasant commandos could not defeat modern troops, officials could legitimately warn over-eager audiences to

> put down your sticks, your knobkerries and your shields . . . Don't fight the white man or they will only wipe you out . . . We have not the strength to force the question, so we must ask nicely, and this can be done by you all joining the ICU and then our voice will be heard.[123]

Yet there were also many occasions when activists' perceptions of political realities were informed less by their breadth of vision than by their own narrow interests. Publicly, Kadalie had bragged that not even a bayonet in his chest would stop his struggle for workers' rights. Privately, he was remarkably reluctant to test the legality of a ruling banning him from Natal in 1926. The exasperated Champion eventually travelled to Johannesburg, bought him his rail ticket, and 'made Mr. Kadalie sit with me as a parcel, to hide his identity'.[124]

This was an ironic reversal of roles for the National Secretary, who preferred to consign members to the fate of passively sitting as parcels. Indeed, most leaders tended to see themselves as active and sophisticated men, mediating between white employers and their silent servants. And they could be extremely disparaging about struggles which depended less on their skills than on members' traditions of resistance. As Kadalie informed a Natal audience, 'Do not hit the white people with your sticks, that is only for savages. People with brains fight with statistics, so fight, my people, with statistics.' Mathematical combat was hardly an arena in which the rank-and-file could be expected to take the initiative, and promoting such tactics helped both entrench the position of leadership and foster the belief that the Union was run by officials not members. Using a medley of metaphors, activists deliberately reinforced this image: the ICU was a star guiding blacks from bondage; it was Noah's ark; it was a cure for members bitten by snakes. In all, it was an organization whose leaders had been trained to 'schoolmaster the workers from above', and who saw and solved the daily problems of blacks.[125]

In addition to activists' educated origins and middle-class positions, the material base for such paternalism lay in the fact that ICU offices – not members' work-places or residences – were the primary sites where attempts were made to alleviate grievances. If deputations or correspondence had no effect – and many were the farmers who contemptuously tore up 'cheeky' letters – then the impasse was often resolved by referring complaints to legal authorities. 'We had a lawyer in Durban, we had a lawyer in Pietermaritzburg, we had a lawyer in Ladysmith, we had a lawyer in Dundee, we had a lawyer in Vryheid, we had a lawyer in Stanger, we had a lawyer in every big town', commented Champion proudly of the hallmark of Union tactics, especially in Natal.[126] Precisely because the courts did provide some redress, leaders were not obliged to intensify and broaden their work in order to inspire mass resistance.

In short: activists' social backgrounds, strongly reinforced by their daily activities within a Union with its own traditions of struggle, conspired against any further organizational innovations. In the narrow space open for manoeuvre in the countryside, they were deliverers of the people, not revolutionaries committed to self-emancipation of the rural poor. Moreover, there was an intimate relationship, not a disjuncture, between their focus on resplendent goals and their omission of the means to attain them. Since the rank-and-file was barely involved in any institutionalized structures, leaders understandably could not perceive any social force that would realize their dreams. Consequently, many retreated into utopian visions of freedom in the future. Likewise, as long as their fantastic claims were believed, there was little incentive to abandon heady oratory for the hard grind of grass-roots work. Clearly, once officials had begun to sway between ideological crowing and organizational cowering, there was a self-perpetuating dynamic to their oscillation.

Of course, this rhythm could easily be disrupted by the vigorous responses of both the upper and under-classes to leadership's grandiloquence. But since these reactions often threatened activists' positions as pace-makers of a viable movement – as well as their personal safeties – they tended to induce a dilution of rhetoric, not a strengthening of structures. Thus many organizers speedily moved from bluster to caution as soon as their oratory was taken seriously. Like 'Mote and Elias, they frequently tried to defuse rural protest by asserting their own superior skills:

> You mustn't make trouble with your masters and mistresses, you have too little brain, and don't understand or know how to negotiate; through your gossip we are being placed in the wrong light, and then we are called agitators, no, you must keep quiet and do your work.[127]

Yet while crude clashes in the countryside were hardly the forte of most ICU officials, they performed much better in the more refined arena of the court-house. This was not an unmixed blessing: by undercutting certain ideological and organizational options, the Union's focus on litigation had a number of adverse effects. Every case helped to entrench the Union's role as an intermediary, and, by increasing the legal expertise of leaders, to enhance their social distance from members. Moreover, as activists became ever more dependent on anti–Communist, liberal lawyers like Cecil Cowley of Durban, so 'law and order' were insidiously pushed to the fore. Sceptical members would be manoeuvred into support of the legal system, and audiences would be assured – with breathtaking sincerity – that 'natives lost cases not because the white man was unjust, but because the native failed to present his case in the right way'. The legal weapon was increasingly seen as the only one available in the struggle against farmers, and the chimerical day of collective defiance was repeatedly postponed until the latest test case had been concluded.[128]

To make matters worse, the costs of lawsuits were astronomical. Country branches in Natal blithely accumulated monthly legal bills of over two hundred pounds, while Cowley alone extorted well over three thousand pounds during the last five months of 1927. Funds poured out on an endless stream of individual cases, many quite unrelated to any progressive economic or political cause. In Estcourt, for example, one case defended was that of a foreman, whose ill-gotten wealth in the form of four racehorses was derived from theft of railway property. While it was unclear whether a commission from Cowley did in fact underpin Champion's unrepentant legalism, there is little doubt that some organizers were little more than touts for lawyers.[129]

As such, they often had little to show for their efforts to wrest victories from a code sanctioning the exploitation and oppression of black labourers. Over a period of three months in a Natal district, the ICU lost every one of its twenty confrontations with farmers. Even triumphs could rapidly be nullified by changes in the law. And to the extent that the Union subordinated mass struggles to battles in court, its tactics were perfectly acceptable to both magistrates and some 'progressive' agriculturists. Thus Zululand planters were only shocked into joint repressive action with their Natal compatriots when they were read the ICU's constitutional preamble – and promptly concluded it was a 'Third International communistic body masquerading under the cloak of a trade union'. Prior to this, secure in the knowledge that their recruited labour was tightly controlled by written contracts, they had been content with a Union that confined its action to legal matters.[130]

But the law was neither an instrument of white rulers nor even an adequate reflection of capitalist interests. Certainly it restricted as well as endorsed the class power of farmers: there was a marked difference between the extra-legal coercion often exercised on farms, and the very real rights of the labouring poor – such as that to wages – enshrined in the law. Similarly, the judiciary enjoyed a contradictory relationship to both white landlords and the broader state, with the Supreme Court in particular constituting a liberal strong-hold within a state undergoing reconstruction. As the only potentially powerful and minimally receptive state institutions to which the ICU had access, the courts were a justifiable site of struggle.[131]

They were also an arena where important advances were made. In Natal, there were significant Supreme Court rulings: they eroded the pass laws, determined that workers had to receive a month's wages in lieu of notice, and established that tenants under order of eviction were allowed to remain on farms until they had reaped their crops. In the magistrates' courts there were further triumphs. These ranged from the protection of tenants' property against rapacious landlords, to raising the price of an illegal eviction to a sum equal to farmers' average annual income. By exploiting procedural law and technicalities, lawyers did indeed make a difference in courts structurally biased against the rural poor.[132]

According to one magistrate, the ICU's legal victories also appeared 'to have terrified the farmers all over Natal'. Both here and in the Free State, there was a flurry of activity as landlords called for self-imposed levies to protect their fellows, often snared by unknown provisions of laws passed seventy years earlier. In a society characterized by a deep gulf between powerful whites and voteless blacks, passions were easily aroused by these unprecedented legal challenges. This was reflected not least in virulent reactions to lawyers who acted for the Union. At best, their practices were boycotted; at worst, they were ostracized and had to elude mobs bent on tarring and feathering them as traitors. Breaking white ranks to support a black movement was not an offence that members of the master race easily condoned.[133]

Nor did they appreciate defensive legal action which helped the ICU breach the barriers erected around it by the white oligarchy. Many activists were repeatedly persecuted under a myriad laws. Apart from the use of pass legislation to restrict officials to a province or even a district, the jungle of residential and other controls was often so dense as to severely inhibit organization. In both the Transvaal and the Free State, dozens of leaders were refused permission to live in urban locations, or prohibited from remaining in the area for longer than three hours. In addition, innumerable meetings were simply totally forbidden. A common response was outright defiance – and of those who were subsequently prosecuted, many were acquitted on legal technicalities. Thus Jason Jingoes was charged more than forty times and, thanks to lawyers and the expertise derived from them, was convicted only thrice. Furthermore, at least one local authority conceded the right to organize, recognizing that court battles could otherwise publicly force rulers to give in to the ruled.[134]

So far as members were concerned, legal victories were of enormous importance in attracting support. Litigation had been a real solution to many forms of social conflict in earlier days. In a new context, where the courts of the white man were costly and those of the chief often corrupt, 'every Native now begins to have the fullest confidence in [the ICU] which promises powerful monetary assistance in bringing up their complaints in the courts of justice'.[135] Indeed, it was only after the Union had proved that legal battles could lighten the burdens of the exploited and oppressed that Natal membership began to soar. In the countryside, tenants fervently hailed the chance to reap their crops before eviction. And the relief afforded blacks in towns is palpable in the words of Bertha Mkhize:

> Before the ICU . . . a white man would just come and kick you for no reason . . . And if you are working for a European, when he doesn't want you anymore, he'll say 'Go away' and spoil your pass . . . Now the ICU fought against that. That was one of the reasons I joined the ICU. Fought against that very much, and they had a lawyer, Cowley and Cowley of Durban, and he fought! Eh, that man did fight for the African people. And always the white man lost the case and had to pay.[136]

The white man did not always lose, of course, but Mkhize's testimony bears witness to the extent of grass-roots support for the ICU's court battles. To argue that legalistic leaders never rose to the challenge of popular militancy is to romanticize the willingness of the labouring poor to storm the barricades. The commitment of subordinated groups to law and order should never be under-estimated. Not only are the norms of the dominant classes often internalized, but 'indiscipline' can also be contrary to under-class codes of behaviour. Nor do illegal protests necessarily further struggles more than constitutional actions. Simply in order to fight, achieving and defending specific legal rights is a key tactic whereby movements acquire 'first a soil to stand on, air, light and space'.[137]

So although Union activists never went much further than winning this space, this in itself was a victory for many rural blacks. After all, what alternative option was open to a desperate old man who travelled all the way from a Transvaal farm to the Johannesburg ICU office, to state that his missing son had been viciously thrashed, locked up and presumably murdered by his landlord? Small wonder that many brutally oppressed farm labourers were only too relieved to leave confrontation with farmers to these masterful organizers and their lawyers. Indeed, the extent to which the Union's appeal lay precisely in its role as an intermediary was indicated by popular reinterpretations of its name. It became the 'I SEE YOU' – in Sotho, the *Keaubona* – because 'I see you sees our suffering'. Or in the words of Jason Jingoes:

> Although its initials stood for a fancy title, to us Bantu it meant basically: when you ill-treat the African people, I See You; if you kick them off the pavements and say they must go together with the cars and the ox-carts, I See You; I See You when you do not protect the Bantu; when an African woman with a child on her back is knocked down by the cars in the street, I See You; I See You when you kick my brother, *I See You.*[138]

In the long run, members could demand more than simply 'seeing'. At one meeting in Johannesburg, disillusionment with constitutional efforts to abolish pass laws took the form of support for physical attacks on pass offices. Significantly, however, it was only after legal tactics had been found wanting that the rank-and-file proposed such a militant programme. Initially, even legal defeats could be turned to account. When Kadalie was convicted for defying the ban on his entry into Natal, a crowd of workers carried him shoulder-high from the court to the ICU office, lustily singing '*Nkosi Sikelel' iAfrika*', and hailing him as a martyr.[139]

In the rural areas, too, the bonds of submission and respect were markedly weakened as labourers became aware that white authority could be overtly and successfully challenged. Moreover, legal tactics turned not only the court-house but also the countryside into a site of struggle. In Dunn's reserve in Natal, a vicious conflict dragged on for over a decade, fuelled by Champion's legal triumphs over 'coloured' landlords illicitly evicting African tenants. Over a period measured in months rather than years, precisely the same occurred on many white farms. Here ratification of blacks' rights to stay temporarily on holdings gave an enormous boost to struggles to remain permanently on the land. It achieved this effect partly by driving home what courts did – and did not – sanction, thereby enabling the rural poor both to utilize and to take heed of the law in their larger battles. These were valuable lessons, if absorbed, since 'the first condition for the success of such [an illicit] struggle is scrupulous regard for legality, and all revolutionary bragging and outbursts of passion lead inevitably to defeat'.[140]

As usual, however, many ingenious blacks in the countryside learnt a somewhat different lesson from that of struggling to legalize their actions. Frequently, their contradictory desires for legality and freedom were resolved in rumours that the ICU itself was a sovereign law-maker. In the courts, this was manifested when an

African claimed he could not be charged, because he was a Union member. (More poignantly, a farm labourer being prosecuted under the Masters and Servants Act held in front of him an upside down ICU pamphlet.) And on white holdings, many blacks took direct action because they believed the Union's 'law' allowed them to seize farms.[141]

Manifestly, the ICU's legal focus, combined with the Land Amendment Bill, contributed in unforeseen ways to the eruption of rural protest. Far from detracting from concrete struggles, in the short term it both enhanced grass-roots confidence and significantly broadened the terrain of struggle. In addition, victories in court cogently demonstrated that the ICU was not simply a 'centralized body to express the views of workers', as District Secretary Robert Dumah declared. It was not merely a leading force in political and ideological spheres, creating a new sense of reality for innumerable blacks. Through the courts, the ICU was also legally enforcing its discipline on those who virulently opposed it. So there was some substance to the other prong of Dumah's argument: that in the ICU, 'the natives had their own government'. Although the Union was infinitely more vulnerable, and rested on a completely different class base, it did indeed bear a faint resemblance to the state, itself defined as 'hegemony protected by the armour of coercion'.[142]

Embryonic Organs of Popular Power

The ICU was constituting itself as a rudimentary but nonetheless alternative power centre in wide-ranging spheres of social and state activities. On occasion, the authority of farmers and officialdom was directly appropriated, as when Transvaal organizers issued fake passes to allow members to attend meetings. In the main, however, the services provided by the Union did not overtly challenge the dominant classes. 'Parallel dual power is the necessary prehistory of a confrontational dual power', and often the ICU was doing no more than bridging the gap between disintegrating traditionalist and racist capitalist worlds. But especially when infused with the creativity of members, even superficially moderate activities could point the way to the development of innovative, popular institutions. Fragmentary and partial though they were, these attempts to broaden the conflict to various arenas of society were nonetheless significant.[143]

Thus, in addition to its meetings and office work, the ICU promoted alternative political and cultural practices to those through which whites shaped the ideas of blacks, particularly those of the middle strata. It did so naturally in the course of its work: some Free

State branches became foci of opposition to Advisory Boards, and the entire country was deluged with ICU newspapers, pamphlets, booklets and even calendars. But there were also deliberate attempts to establish or support institutions with longer-term effects. By 1926, the Durban branch was running a night school with 150 pupils and four teachers, to all of whom Champion would periodically lecture. The following year, this had blossomed into the ICU Educational League, and there were also evening classes on the Rand where English was taught four times a week. Although these were but drops in the ocean in creating an independent educational system, the Union had much greater impact on the related sphere of religion. Here innumerable Ethiopian churches acquired ICU connections, which doubtless reinforced the efforts of these bodies to contest the 'spontaneous' consent of blacks to white domination.[144]

The fact that force played a major role in securing this consent had not escaped the notice of the Union. From 1928, there were attempts to create militias in a couple of urban centres. Durban's 'Unity League', whose supporters were frequently armed with sticks and clubs, tried to protect the organization from attacks by white civilians. Often clad in imposing red tunics and jodhpurs, its recruits also directed their coercive powers at the under-classes. As well as vigorously ascertaining whether or not Africans had bought their red tickets, they also administered popular justice.[145]

So, too, did other Union activists throughout the country. In tiny Makwassie in the western Transvaal, the ICU was perceived as a substitute for chiefs, and leaders were frequently approached to settle civil disputes amongst supporters. For them, the Union was an ideal alternative to both the inaccessible courts of the older elite and the expensive, intimidatory ones of the white magistrate. Organizers had to devote much time to hearing these cases, and in the process a judicial system evolved which bore traces of its mixed parentage. After the plaintiff had laid a charge, the Branch Committee would summon the defendant, allow both to present their evidence, intervene in the general discussion, and finally pass judgement which expressed the general consensus. As a form of justice which was both participatory and democratic, it clearly harked back to certain judicial norms of precolonial days. But the nature of many cases heard, and the powers at the disposal of the 'judges', often arose within the context of capitalism. Desperate women, no longer able to rely on older sanctions protecting wives, regularly resorted to the ICU 'court' in domestic conflicts over maintenance. Union officials took a progressive if hard line; they not only threatened errant husbands with loss of their membership, but also sternly informed them, 'You pay up the money, or we'll go and spoil your work.'[146]

In addition to duplicating in a transformed way some of the repressive and ideological functions of the state, the ICU provided other more mundane services unobtainable from either rulers or employers. For one thing, it responded to demands for a lost-property-cum-policing bureau. 'For any lost article like a pass, poll tax receipt, rail ticket, article of clothing, and the like, the ICU was consulted, and the lost article was very often traced.' For another, it was often popularly perceived as an agency providing either bridewealth or cash loans – which it certainly was for some organizers. Furthermore, the Union theoretically provided social security benefits. Constitutionally, branches were empowered to impose levies on members to provide death benefits, as well as to make pension, sickness, unemployment and – from 1928 – strike benefit payments. Thus at least one branch attempted to provide struggling unemployed members with thirty shillings a month, while the entire National Council attended and paid for the funeral of an ardent ICU supporter on the mines.[147]

At no stage, however, do these payments appear to have been made on a systematic basis. Despite eager demands for death benefits in particular, penurious ICU members were generally unwilling to pay additional levies. Moreover, there was opposition from certain venal or bureaucratic senior officials, unwilling either to declare strikes official or to concede burial expenses to ordinary claimants. Although branches might dip into their own treasuries, these could be almost empty if activists had adhered to the constitution, and retained only such funds as were raised through commercial or social activities.[148]

This last factor did, however, give additional impetus to the trend of converting ICU premises into worlds in themselves. Somewhat ostentatiously, Bloemfontein leaders applied for thirty-three sites in the township, to accommodate offices, clubs, an entertainment hall, an employees' residence and a recreation ground. Although this branch was grudgingly granted only two plots, numerous Union premises elsewhere did extend to living-quarters, social centres, libraries and tea-rooms. Unfortunately, the Union's eating establishments were subject to precisely the same constraints as other petty bourgeois enterprises. Café after café proved a failure, and by early 1928 there were only a handful of Free State and Natal branches with cash on hand from entrepreneurial activities and entertainment.[149]

Yet if these activities generally proved financial failures, they were nonetheless significant in both organizational and political terms. The thirty-four pounds raised by the Bloemfontein branch from one concert was earmarked for sending an activist to Free State villages, while the attendance of delegates at conferences often depended on prior fund-raising concerts.[150] Moreover, although ICU dances and bazaars hardly constituted resistance in themselves, they laid an invaluable foundation for united opposition. Consciousness is not altered solely or even largely by imbibing the words of leaders, but rather by active participation in the creation of new values. In a dehumanizing environment largely lacking in venues for legal entertainment, the ICU's cultural events fostered cohesion, afforded collective enjoyment, and reaffirmed blacks' right to shape the world for themselves.

This was true even of Union premises, despite their generally squalid surrounds. Both members and officials often embellished the rooms to foster both class and racial pride in their movement. At the office itself, functional equipment such as typewriters and telephones (and sometimes shutters to protect inmates from stones), could be supplemented with stylish furnishings. Outside was frequently a signboard advertizing forthcoming meetings, and a pole on which fluttered the red flag, with its Union emblem. As financial ventures, clubs and cafés called for even more effort. On the walls of the Workers' Hall in Johannesburg were painted a lifelike black miner, and a shackled African Samson ominously toppling white pillars. Even the doors and windows were emblazoned with brightly coloured slogans such as 'Workers of the world, unite!' At the tea-room next door, the walls were studded with pictures of famous blacks like Marcus Garvey. Meals were eaten to the rousing strains of gramophone recordings of songs such as *The Red Flag* (and possibly also to those of the polished ICU group, Makatshwa's Choir). Both aurally and visually, the overall image was one of an organization committed to the cause of black labour in particular and black nationalism in general.[151]

Elsewhere, this could be a nationalism with a very different class orientation. In 1925–6 in Durban, illiterate labourers would hardly have abandoned vibrant shebeens to flock to the African Workers' Club. Not only was this expensive: it was also the embodiment of elitist forms of enjoyment. While a couple of people on the platform engaged in piano-playing, comic songs and dance routines, about 150 mainly lower-middle-class men and women would sit (and sleep) sedately in their chairs, periodically partaking of lemonade, tea and cake. Even when this was replaced by nightly ballroom dancing to the strains of gramophone records, the middle strata preserved their social distance by opting for avant-garde dances not known to the general populace. The aim, as Champion expressed it, was to run concerts indistinguishable from those of whites.[152]

Yet as the ICU began to attract a mass following, so it generally began to direct itself to the much wider constituency of the 'new

African'. These were men and women willing to pay one shilling to two shillings and sixpence for cultural events which materialized not only desires for equality, but also pride in racial identity. Since the concert and dance format was common to both middle and working classes, both could be attracted to a Cape 'grand concert' with refreshments served by 'African beauties'. A much neater meshing of class-based cultural preferences occurred in Johannesburg, where Makatshwa's Choir, accompanied by one of the most elite swing orchestras of the era, performed Zulu working-class *ingom'ebusuku* – 'night music'. As a syncretic style, *ingom'ebusuku* simultaneously defined migrants as non-traditional townsmen, while still drawing on familiar religious and rural ethnic traditions. New songs in this style thus represented the deployment 'of "traditional" African culture for purposes of positive self-identification and unity in a modern political context' – and Union supporters were not slow to exploit this.[153] *Ingom'ebusuku* informed much of the repertoire of choirs that sang at the Workers' Hall, as well as numerous songs promoting the ICU written by a Bloemfontein composer.[154]

Paradoxically, the incorporation of older musical forms was probably more pronounced in cities crammed with migrants than in villages, where audiences were almost certainly mainly urban dwellers. In these small towns, expressive forms used to define blacks as fully capable of taking their place in a modern world included brass bands, their players sometimes dressed in smart military uniforms. In Estcourt, the office was equipped with an organ, purchased from ICU funds and vigorously played by an organizer to the delight of Saturday night audiences. Also popular at these events were jazz vocals, sung by choirs of domestic labourers. As a musical style associated with black America and accepted by a wide range of classes, jazz was able both to bridge social differences and to help forge an up-to-date African cultural identity.[155] So too were songs drawing on Pan-Africanist themes. Kadalie was much taken by the 'great chorus' sung by an ICU choir in Durban:

> O Africa awaken,
> The morning is at hand,
> No more art thou forsaken,
> From far thy children cry
> That Africa be free.

As for Champion, he hoped that this song would one day be remembered 'as the universal song for Africa's liberation'.[156]

Conclusion

Yet for all the ICU's seminal importance in placing the liberation of the rural poor on the agenda in South Africa, it had severe limitations. Although many a leader had begun to participate 'in practical life, as constructor, organizer, "permanent persuader" and not just a simple orator',[157] the vast majority of blacks perceived activists only in their roles as eloquent men who momentarily aroused passions. The stubborn reality of the countryside – and the perceptions of both officials and followers of their tasks – had blocked a full-scale transition from agitation to organization. Hence the ICU acted largely as a voice for the oppressed, not a force for freedom. Indeed, it recklessly squandered almost the only asset it possessed – numbers. Arithmetical collectivities of sympathizers, each buying a red card before dispersing to scattered homes, were very different from disciplined, active participants in combined struggle.

Nonetheless, the ICU's strengths were as remarkable as its weaknesses. Its ideology was no arbitrary flight of fancy: it was deeply rooted in the uneven and incomplete nature of South Africa's 'dual revolution'. As such, it had both an historical and psychological validity. It could '"organise" human masses, and create the terrain on which men move, acquire consciousness of their position, struggle'.[158] But the ICU's message was no rationalistic reflection of objective structures either, since activists were constantly in touch with people's experiences and interpretations of these underlying forces. And they learnt as well as taught: from traditionalists with their radical beliefs about land; from the *abaphakathi* familiar with separatist Christianity and Garveyism; from white intellectuals propagating socialism, and from landlords adhering to economic liberalism. Hence they created a flexible nationalist ideology – so flexible, indeed, that it was often a higgledy-piggledy jumble of 'inherent' and 'derived' ideas. But it also contained some valuable political insights, and certainly converted tens of thousands of rural Africans to visions of radically altered lives in a transfigured social order.

It did so partly because the ICU's message both encompassed and was materialized in an extraordinary range of spheres. These included the work-place and petty bourgeois enterprises, modern and traditionalist politics, religion and education, justice and entertainment, and even the intimate domain of the family. Given that the Union was trying to unite the scattered, illiterate rural poor in a struggle for national liberation, this extensive sweep across civil and political society was in itself enormously important. It meant that people who did not attend a single meeting were nonetheless exposed to the 'I SEE YOU'. It also meant that the Union went some way towards challenging the multiple foundations of racist, capitalist South Africa, and to positing in their place new values, new relationships and new institutions.

The extent to which it did this in particular regions, and the particular ideological strands that were pushed to the fore, depended on the dialectical relationships established between organizers, constituencies and the dominant classes. These in turn were shaped by local political economies, local cultures and local traditions of resistance. Even more importantly, the characteristics of the Union in a parochial world depended on the speed at which structures and struggles were being transformed. In exploring the conflicts that erupted in the countryside, the national characteristics of the ICU's organization and ideology form only a backdrop. Having set this in place, it is necessary to move forward onto a smaller but more clearly delineated regional stage.

5. RESISTANCE, REPRESSION AND REFORM:
The ICU in the Transvaal, 1926–1929

In 1925, a Heidelberg labour tenant Jacob Ntshona wrote a pitiful letter to the Prime Minister:

> Mr. Hatang has employed me and therefore we made an agreement . . . of Six months and after when we have made it . . . the Commissioner and Mr. Hatang agreed together that I must work for 12 Months instead of Six with all my instruments and my family . . . and after that they have expelled me from the farm and they took all my victuals and therefore I am asking from you Sir if that thing is the right law or not.[1]

Ntshona's plight left officialdom quite unmoved. Like many rural Transvaal Africans at this time, he was caught up in a process which had the full support of the state: the 'squeezing' of black tenants to facilitate the development of commercial agriculture. Between 1921 and 1930, in an uneven but relentless process, white-owned land under cultivation in this province soared by a staggering 40 per cent, while the number of white-owned woolled sheep increased by over two million between 1923 and 1930. Simultaneously for many rural blacks, the 1920s was a decade of accelerating dispossession, increasing labour obligations and growing destitution. Large numbers of 'squatters' and labour tenants were ruthlessly evicted in this period, because 'the white farmer is making more use than he did originally of his farm and the farm is becoming too small for himself, his children and the natives'.[2] Of the Africans who remained, many had their stock and land holdings severely limited. In addition, longer periods of service were being imposed. Between 1917 and 1930 in the Ermelo and Carolina districts, the average period for which labour tenants had to work rose from three to six months. Yet another means whereby more labour was extracted was by forcing 'squatters' and non-productive members of labour tenant families to toil on farms. Undoubtedly, the press-ganging of Ntshona's entire household into service was common practice in the period 1918–30, when the number of regular African farm labourers in the Transvaal increased by some 65 per cent to reach over 150,000 men and women.[3]

A region where proletarianization and capitalization had long been in evidence was the eastern highveld, largely coincident with the districts of Bethal, Carolina, Ermelo, Heidelberg, Standerton and Wakkerstroom. Almost all land here had been appropriated by settlers decades previously, and in the absence of reserves, the vast bulk of rural blacks lived on white-owned farms. As valuable, intensively worked, 'highly developed white man's country', this region was unquestionably the prime Transvaal farming area, where nascent capital was clearly apparent. Furthermore, by the second decade of the twentieth century, black tenants here tended to have 'largely freed themselves from the constraints of tribal rule'; to have 'reached a higher stage of civilisation', and to be 'richer and more prosperous than their compatriots of the low veld'.[4] This privileged status was however being undermined in the later 1920s, when there was a significant increase in production – centring around maize and sheep – and a veritable onslaught against tenants. Many were the Africans who experienced a sudden 'great change' in their conditions, and who had similar tales to that of one man who fled from his Standerton farm to town in 1930. He did so

> because my master did not allow me to own my cattle – he told me to sell all the cattle except one cow; I had some horses also, but he told me to keep one steed. I had to work on the farm with my wife and children from morning till evening and I was not paid, so I decided to leave the farm for Alexandra.[5]

While the development of commercial farming in the mainly middleveld districts of Middelburg, Piet Retief and Volksrust lagged behind that of the highveld, similar pressures were evident here. Moreover in both areas, dispossession was not in the main accompanied by the payment of cash wages to labour tenants, or by the large-scale replacement of the latter by hired workers. Apart from the numerous capitalist farmers in Bethal – who tended to recruit labourers and pay them money – most eastern Transvaal landlords reacted as crudely to labour tenants' demands for cash as did a Piet Retief agriculturist. 'You people', he exclaimed, 'you shit on my farm, you rear stock on my farm, and you till my land, so you are not going to be paid, you bloody fools.'[6]

In the eastern lowveld districts of Barberton, Lydenburg, Nelspruit and Pilgrims Rest, as well as in some areas of the middleveld, capitalist penetration occurred much more abruptly. In the early twentieth century, land dispossession and commercial farming were

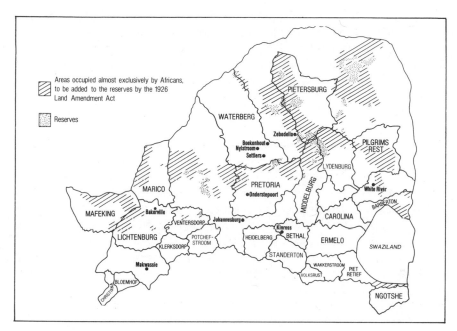

Fig. 7. Map of the Transvaal

far less extensive here than in the rest of the eastern Transvaal. This rapidly changed as white settlers began to pour into the region after the First World War, often converting land used merely for winter grazing into productive farms. Consequently, the cost to blacks of hiring land soared: in Middelburg, Africans living in one congested reserve were by 1925 paying 400 to 500 per cent more than a few years earlier. 'Squatters', many of them grouped under chiefs who shared their fate, were either evicted in their thousands or for the first time reduced to labour tenants. Resident workers too were expelled, particularly by capitalizing fruit, tobacco and cotton farmers. With their much more sharply delineated seasonal labour requirements, many of these landlords found it more profitable to employ hired or recruited labour on their Barberton, Nelspruit or White River estates. In all, blacks, ranging from relatively wealthy chiefs on state-owned land to reserve-dwellers who had previously found loopholes in laws confining them to their locations, suddenly found proletarianization staring them in the face.[7]

Many of those faced with overnight changes in their conditions of tenure beat a retreat to neighbouring reserves. But they had grave difficulties in obtaining ground there: according to a Lydenburg chief, 'there was no room in the locations for natives who had been chased off private farms'. Furthermore, poverty was the norm in these unhealthy regions spurned by white landlords. By 1927 in a White River reserve, the constant flow of farm-evictees, combined with the continuation of a two-year-long drought, had brought numerous Africans to the verge of starvation. Predictably, land hunger was acute in this region, and White River farmers nervously commented on 'general Native restlessness locally'.[8]

So too did landlords in other areas of the Transvaal. During the early and mid-1920s, state officials were bombarded with anxious reports, claiming that 'the farm labourer and squatters . . . are showing signs of discontent with the conditions under which they are serving'; that *'die naturelle [word] oorals opstandig'* (the natives are becoming rebellious everywhere), and even that *'die kaffers wil . . . die wit mense vermoor'* (the kaffirs want to . . . murder the white people) and thereafter appropriate their farms.[9] While this reflected landlords' nightmares more than daytime reality, there were indeed instances of fairly threatening collective action. In Waterberg in the north-west, Crown land allocated to a settler had to be abandoned to 'squatters', who defeated all efforts either to evict them or to force them to work. In Middelburg, newly arrived settlers in the lowveld had to combat arson of their wheat stacks and veld, theft of their crops and equipment, slaughter of their animals, overt take-overs of their land, and work resistance extending to strikes by those tenants who remained. And in the early 1920s, the Transvaal Native Congress (TNC) attracted considerable support in the northern and eastern Transvaal countryside by focusing on rural grievances. Under its influence, groups of labour tenants in Standerton and its environs struck for cash payment, demanded the abolition of passes and threatened to kill their employers. Some claimed that the Congress membership card entitled them to plough where they pleased, and gave them the right to live rent-free on farms which they claimed as their own. Although their protest was rapidly crushed, similar strands of popular thinking were rearticulated by the ICU, which considerably intensified prevalent rural discontent and resistance.[10]

Land and Liberation: the Eastern Transvaal, 1926–1928

The ICU's Transvaal activities were heralded by the establishment of branches on the Witwatersrand from late 1924. After two years, the movement began to have an impact in the rural areas. Most village branches were established in the eastern and south-eastern districts from late 1926, and in the northern, western and south-western Transvaal about a year later. At a conservative estimate, some 23,000 Transvaal Africans were members during 1927. Over the longer time-span of the later 1920s, many more thousands either joined or supported an organization which proclaimed itself in this province as the 'ICU comet . . . to guide the oppressed toiling masses of Africa.'[11]

The path of the comet was not, however, an easy one, as was exemplified by the harassment of Barberton organizers. After a month's work in this township, in August 1927 Branch Secretary Donald Labase had his lodger's permit revoked, his registration as a daily labourer cancelled, and a pass defining him as self-employed refused. Only six days were granted him to seek work; on the seventh he was charged for being in the area without the requisite permission. Almost simultaneously, the Union was denied the right to rent an office in town, and a local newspaper smugly announced that the branch had been checkmated. The pronouncement was premature: some six months later, the Lydenburg Branch Secretary Abdul Mahomed managed to hold a Barberton meeting, at which he declared that blacks must 'fight the Government and get our freedom and expel the white man from our land'. For this speech, he was not only fined fifteen pounds under the Native Administration Act, but also deported back to Zanzibar. Clearly, some municipalities barred few holds in their determination to rid themselves of the ICU canker.[12]

The prevalence of such repressive measures in the inland provinces made organization harder than in Natal and the Cape, where the iron fist was more frequently covered with a velvet glove. It was also in the context of such restrictions that economically and politically privileged leaders demonstrated their value. In Middelburg, the local authorities were unable summarily to eject Mbeki from the township because he had certain rights as a pass-exempted African. Although they forbade him to organize and twice took him to court on petty charges, neither line of attack proved successful. Nor was it possible to dislodge the second Branch Chairman, a trader as well as an elected member of the Native Advisory Board. But activists who were simultaneously employees, or who had little political standing, were far easier prey. The first Middelburg Branch Chairman, a lowly municipal wage-earner, was instantaneously sacked and ordered to leave the location. Proceedings against the first Branch Secretary Theo Ramonti, a teacher living on a Wesleyan church stand, were more protracted but equally efficacious. After informing the Education Department of Ramonti's seditious activities, and threatening the Wesleyans with loss of their site, the municipality refused Ramonti a residential permit. Having twice been prosecuted for being in the township without the appropriate pass, the disheartened Ramonti left Middelburg in October 1926. Clearly, the largely petty bourgeois composition of the ICU leadership was on occasion due mainly to pressures from above, and could in fact further the cause of organization. Furthermore, while some Transvaal activists may have been opportunistic in taking up Union positions, most undeniably required considerable dedication to cope with the victimization to which they were subjected.[13]

In addition to persecuting officials, local whites frequently did all in their power to minimize popular participation. Preventing the establishment of an office was one tactic: in Middelburg, the women's branch of one farmers' union tried to persuade the owner of the Union's premises to terminate the lease. And if gatherings could not be effectively prohibited, then terrorizing supporters was a common method of hindering organization. In Volksrust and Wakkerstroom, where ICU members were predominantly labour tenants, landlords adopted a policy of

> ejecting them from their farms and [of] prosecuting any man or woman they discovered to be a member of the Union. Members were so prosecuted that they were afraid even to enter the Organization's offices . . . [Masters refused] to issue 'special passes' to the workers to attend meetings. Workers ventured to go without passes. At Wakkerstroom the Police adopted a similar attitude by organising special patrols on Sundays for carrying out their duties under the pass laws. Huge sums were collected by the court in fines.[14]

Opposition to the Union was by no means the prerogative of whites. Certain black political leaders – ranging from chiefs to Advisory Board members – boycotted, disrupted or requested the banning of ICU meetings. So too did numerous Congressmen, deeply worried by the ICU's popular appeal and its ideological leanings. From 1924 they were pointedly delineating the differences between the organizations, and claiming that Congress sought to establish financiers within the nation it was building, while the Union was opposed to all capitalists and discouraged African ownership. At the TNC Annual Conference in 1925, the President dramatically declared that 'Jesus Christ was betrayed by Judas Iscariot precisely in the same manner that the ICU had betrayed the Congress'. Such ill-feeling was equally apparent in rural towns where the two movements competed for membership. Indeed, Union activists often initiated organization in the eastern districts by exposing collaboration between white authorities and black 'good boys', by denouncing the opposition of 'a queer bunch of intellectuals', or by popularizing slogans such as 'Hands off, Old Leadership'.[15]

Yet if the Union was detested from the first by many officials and upper-middle-class Africans, the same was not true of the black rural poor. In the eastern Transvaal – the heartland of ICU support – audiences could forcefully demonstrate their antagonism to those who tried to break up their meetings. At a large gathering in Kinross in mid-1927, one white and two black constables stormed in to demand 'specials'. Since landlords were responding to the Union by refusing such permits, almost the entire crowd was self-consciously passless, and many were only too willing to extend their passive into active resistance. One policeman was attacked, and when his fellows tried to beat up the assailant, they too became victims of the angry throng. Before the severely injured white man began shooting, the Bethal Secretary Joseph Malaza fortunately managed to calm his audience. He was subsequently elated about the victories achieved: no one was charged for assaulting the white constable, and no one was arrested for being without 'specials'. The lessons he drew were the obvious ones. Since the government could not jail everyone, all members of all Union branches should engage in similar resistance so that passes would be abolished by the end of the year.[16]

Similar attacks on the police occurred elsewhere. In Barberton, there was an attempt to rescue those arrested under the pass laws by storming their captors. In Nelspruit in early 1928, when a gathering was prohibited so late that people were already streaming into town, mass passive resistance erupted. When uniformed agents of the state arrived to disperse the milling crowd, they found that black leadership had been stiffened by the presence of fewer than twenty-seven chiefs and twenty-four headmen. Futhermore,

> the chiefs with their regiments came forward and 9,000 people sang *Nkosi Sikelel' iAfrika*, and they demanded that they should all be arrested . . . the police spoke among themselves wanting to know where they were going to put all these people and it was said that they should all go; there were three cheers and they left for the Location, and the man of the people spoke . . .[17]

It was by no means unusual for eastern Transvaal low- and middleveld chiefs to regard ICU organizers as 'men of the people'. Indigenous authorities' support for Congress had been steadily waning, due. largely to this body's inability to solve the land question. When the 'I SEE YOU' arrived, promising farms and freedom at a time when these were burning issues for commoners and chiefs alike, many members of the older political elite threw their support behind this new movement. On a single day in early 1927, nearly two thousand ordinary blacks were shepherded into the ICU by a Barberton man, Diniso Nkosi, who was probably a Swazi chief's councillor. Nkosi also appeared at the Union's Annual Conference as the representative of nine 'chiefs and princesses', who had told him: 'If you find that Kadalie was a black man, then you can address our compliments and sympathy to him. If you found that he was not a black man, then keep quiet and come back to us.'[18] Their exclusivist nationalism was understandable. Nkosi gave a pitiful account of the plight of men of his region, who were being forcibly removed to a hilly wilderness where there was neither adequate pasture nor water, and where large game damaged crops and devoured grazing. 'I am prepared to fight for my freedom', he declared; 'I am . . . ready to die at any moment rather than prolong this misery.'[19]

Others of even higher rank shared his sentiments. Numerous Swazi chiefs, who were in a particularly invidious position because no reserve had been demarcated for them, enthusiastically attended meetings with hundreds of followers. Indeed, the ICU soon included amongst its eastern Transvaal organizers Norman Nxumalo, the uncle of King Sobhuza of Swaziland, and close friend of leading Congressmen. Doubtless impressed by this blatant shift of allegiance by a member of the royal family, many chiefs on both sides of the border bought red tickets, together with thousands of their Swazi followers.[20]

So far as non-Swazi black authorities were concerned, their support for the Union was integrally related to their political and economic insecurity on Crown, company or white farmers' land. In Pilgrims Rest, chief Chaane was based on a mine-owned holding, and allowed ICU activists to hold meetings on property that, lamentably, was not his own. In Piet Retief, where three of five chiefs and thirteen of twenty-four headmen were ICU members, all but one lived on privately owned land, and hence received neither recognition nor a salary from the state. In the context of railway developments which were transforming winter grazing into valuable land, and the 1927 wattle boom which almost instantaneously changed black-occupied farms into tenantless plantations, both Swazi and Zulu-speaking authorities here responded with fervour when organizers visited holdings to enrol members.[21]

In a province where even a patient in a Pretoria leper hospital was calling meetings of inmates on behalf of the ICU, the Union's message was, as usual, given new twists by the rank-and-file. According to July Lusiba, his labour tenant father bought a ticket in Nelspruit because he believed 'they would live better after taking over the farm from the white man . . . When the top leaders came you had to show him this card, after which he would leave the farm to you.' On a mine-owned holding in Pilgrims Rest (where no ICU branch existed), chief Pitas Mogane bought a red card after men selling them addressed a meeting there, saying 'that war was coming. So we should raise those tickets during the war.' How this would help was unclear: all that was certain was that some of the Union's power had rubbed off onto their cards.[22]

Yet such notions were not merely projections of popular longings onto the ICU. They had substantial support from the amalgam of 'inherent' and 'derived' ideas being propagated by Union organizers. Kadalie himself boasted in Middelburg about the expensive farm which his movement had bought, and some credibility was lent to his lie when local activists desperately tried to buy land for Barberton members. Moreover, Mbeki publicly proclaimed that 'It is high time for us to make war with the white races.' Impatient with the ICU's own good time, some Nelspruit leaders swore that there would be freedom by Christmas 1927. In a region where the very existence of black rural cultivators was being suddenly and fundamentally threatened, leaders as well as members could be swept away on the current of hopes for land and liberation.[23]

Perhaps the meshing of 'common-sense' and 'derived' ideas is best illustrated by exploring organization in the single district of Middelburg. Thanks to its fertile southern highveld – and to the distribution of the defeated Ndebele across this area as tenants some forty years earlier – it was an important maize, tobacco and sheep region. As such, familiar trends were manifested here in the form of evictions, longer contracts, limitations on stock, and mounting discontent amongst tenants. In the bitter words of ex-resident worker Esther Sibanyoni, Middelburg landlords 'sat on your marrow'. Or as her daughter Rose Mthimunye expressed it, their miserable life dragged 'on and on and on and on until the arrival of Mbeki'.[24]

In some respects, the harassment of ICU activists and supporters in this district actually furthered the cause of organization. Ex-labour tenant Jacob Motha recalled that Mbeki used to come to their rescue when police demanded passes, telling the constables 'to set us free and rather lock him up and they would eventually set us free . . . That made him popular and people would say that he was a true liberator.' Rural blacks not only stated this but also demonstrated their commitment by flocking to join. In a town where less than two hundred adult males lived in the urban location, the ICU rapidly became known here as a farm labourers' movement, and a landlord soon claimed that it was impossible to fill labour complements without including ICU members.[25]

Since the ICU seems to have made little impact on the northern bushveld reserves in Middelburg, tenants almost certainly formed most of the throng of blacks who attended a township meeting addressed by Mbeki in July 1926. This was followed by a colourful demonstration: the crowd marched in a four-deep column up the long hill to the town office, which to the accompaniment of thunderous cheers was opened by two landless chiefs, Bashele and Mahlangu. From there, the procession wound its way through the streets to a huge gathering in the heart of the white urban area. The symbolic meaning of this trek from township to town was underlined by almost continuous singing of *'Nkosi Sikelel' iAfrika'*, while the very composition of the cavalcade indicated the breadth of the black alliance appropriating the whites' physical domain. As an ICU activist with a sharp eye for social and gender distinctions expressed it, the column was led by the two chiefs, 'decorated' at its head by women, healthily studded with 'intellectuals', and 'composed of 75 per cent of the true proletariate'. After a highly successful meeting, the singing procession strode back to the location, where 'the Red Flag was the final demonstration of the day, and after three cheers for the success of the work the crowd dispersed filled with new vigour, yea'.[26]

The exuberance apparent at this demonstration was also channelled into an extraordinarily popular campaign: to win the right for blacks to walk on pavements. Petty though this may have seemed, it was a topical issue and a practical struggle, one which rural blacks could probably win. It also harked back to a tale which innumerable audiences were told: that their great Union was born because Kadalie was pushed off a sidewalk by a white man. Furthermore, Congress had recently been fighting similar pavement battles in the Transvaal. Above all, it was a manifestation of 'derived' political education at its best:

> It is not enough *to explain* to the workers that they are politically oppressed (any more than it is *to explain* to them that their interests are antagonistic to the interests of the employers). Agitation must be conducted with regard to every concrete example of this oppression . . . [which] affects the most diverse classes of society . . . [which] manifests itself in the most varied spheres of life and activity – vocational, civic, personal, family, religious, scientific, etc. etc.[27]

Significantly, although exclusion from the sidewalks affected all blacks, the ICU's adoption of this issue had the potential of increasing class as well as national consciousness. The Middelburg branch of the Native Teachers' Association had for years been demanding that exempted blacks be allowed to tread the hallowed ground preserved for whites. When Mbeki led his campaign, however, he gave substance to his speeches that all blacks were 'on the same footing as Europeans', by directing not only the petty bourgeoisie but also the poor onto the sidewalks. The protests made a lasting impression on both Motha and Mthimunye: according to the latter,

> They began to be free. They were given little red cards. So they began to be free. They began to be free to move on pavements, away from the streets of the cars. They were made to walk on pavements, walking side by side with the whites and rubbing shoulders with them . . . Mbeki and co. brought us to this position for we used not to mix . . . – You did not walk on the pavement [before?] – No! Awi-i-i-i-! Walk side by side with the *baas*! Oh no, you were not even allowed to sit on a chair.[28]

Interestingly enough, Mthimunye added that 'it was only America that made us sit'. Perhaps encouraged by meetings held in the countryside proper – such as that on a neighbouring mission station – or perhaps entirely through their own initiative, rural Africans expanded on the ICU's message so that it more closely reflected their own traditions and aspirations. For one thing, Mbeki was assimilated as an American liberator. He was nicknamed '*Amelika*', and perceived as an invincible hero who was addressed as 'Sir' by whites. For another, although neither Mthimunye nor Sibanyoni attended an ICU meeting, both heard from their menfolk that Kadalie and Mbeki 'came to free months [of toil] from us', and both believed that it was through the Union that 'people started getting leave to rest at home'. Understandably, the orthodox ICU commitment to 'normalization' of farm labour was not particularly attractive in a region where households were smouldering with resentment at being transformed from 'squatters' to labour tenants, where women were antagonistic to being called up for domestic work, and men opposed the extension of their contracts from three to six or even twelve months. Predictably too, some resident workers appear to have developed their own version of their fate if evicted for ICU membership. Despite Kadalie's explicit statement that such victimization should be reported to the Branch Secretary, who would ensure that tenants won their rights from the state, numerous landlords apparently knew the secret hopes of evictees. As Motha expressed it, 'they would give you a trek pass and tell you to go to Kadalie for a farm'.[29]

Other forms of protest in Middelburg – such as leaving white churches, demanding higher wages, and generalized 'cheekiness' – were characteristic of the eastern Transvaal as a whole. Typically, ICU-influenced defiance was diffuse and multi-faceted, inspired both by organizers' injunctions and by members' reinterpretations thereof. In Barberton in 1927, the Native Commissioner complained that local Africans 'who are ignorant and unsophisticated take the teachings of the ICU to mean that they must not carry passes, pay taxes, dog licences or dipping fees'. In Lydenburg, a landlord who had previously paid all his labour tenants' taxes – and doubtless kept the receipts to immobilize workers on his farm – was partially forced to forgo this practice, because the ICU 'frightened them that he wanted to make them slaves'. And throughout the region, the major form of ICU-inspired protest was 'insolence'. As used by white masters, the term referred to most of the economic, political and ideological challenges to their authority that fervent responses to the 'I SEE YOU' entailed. Thus 'insubordination' included activities such as defying farmers to attend vibrant Sunday gatherings, appealing to the organization for support in conflicts with masters, assaulting policemen trying to stop the progress of the passless to meetings, and jubilation over legal victories. In addition, most instances in this period of individualized types of resistance were immediately attributed by landlords to the ICU. As one Wakkerstroom farmer expressed it, as a result of Union activities, farm workers *'wil nou werk net soos hul wil en jy mag niks sê of meneer het baie meer to sê en gereed is om aanranding te pleeg'* (now want to work just as they will and you cannot say anything or 'the gentleman' has much more to say and is ready to assault you).[30]

Yet despite landlords' assertions that the Union bore sole responsibility for intensified resistance, the ICU almost invariably merely influenced protest. Without an organizational infrastructure extending beyond meetings, offices and lawyers, leaders' effect on continuing struggles in the countryside could be very marginal. Indeed, resistance tended to erupt only when their speeches had resonance for blacks enmeshed in very particular circumstances. Furthermore, Africans' own traditions of struggle and patterns of association could totally transform the nature of opposition suggested by activists.

An extreme example of this occurred in Bethal, a district notorious for employers' ill-treatment of recruited labourers. Even other landlords claimed that workers here existed 'in a state of almost semi-slavery . . . exploited to the utmost by the majority of employers'.[31] Deaths from disease and gruesome assaults were not uncommon, and Bethal farmers and their foremen were regularly charged with culpable homicide throughout the 1920s. Amongst those who acquired blood on their hands was Sam Gafenowitz, well-known as one of the most 'progressive' farmers in Kinross. As almost the biggest maize producer in this region, he employed two or three hundred recruited workers in his operations. According to his ex-manager in late 1926, he was also 'about the limit'. In this

year he had already been charged for withholding wages, inves-
tigated for engaging Africans under spurious contracts, accused of
regaining through his store all the cash actually paid, and denounced
for viciously giving one labourer an almost incredible 109 strokes.[32]

In circumstances as wretched as these, it was not only local
Ndebele labour tenants who from 1926 vigorously supported the
Union. Two workers recruited from Basutoland, 'Isaac Rand' and
'Jacob', also absorbed elements of the *Keaubona's* message. In
mid-1927 on Gafenowitz's farm, they 'made a speech to the natives
telling them that they were as good as the white man, had all the
rights and privileges of white men and should not be afraid of the
master'. Although the strike by all workers the next day was
crushed, and while both Isaac and Jacob were convicted for inciting
the stoppage, the former returned to the farm after serving his
sentence. Here he remained a leading figure in a series of more
individualized kinds of defiance, including desertions and throwing
stones at the farmhouse. Yet Gafenowitz let the matter rest: Bethal
landlords were becoming increasingly unable to obtain or retain
labour, and Gafenowitz himself had recently been struck off the roll
of those permitted access to Rhodesian recruits. Thus, on the
grounds that he desperately needed labour as the maize season got
underway, the owner of Mizpah Estate retained the services of 'Isaac
Rand'.[33]

But in January 1928, he was unable to ignore a new upsurge of
protest. According to a press report, a second strike was mooted on
Mizpah Estate as a direct result of a Kinross ICU meeting attended
by about eight thousand Africans. 'The natives were there instructed
not to resume their labours on the farms, but to strike unless they
were being paid 7s.6d. to 8s. per day.' But this injunction could be
interpreted in very different ways by Mizpah's workers, recruited
from different areas, having very varied experiences of proletarianization, and having diverse ethnic affiliations overlaid by class antagonisms. Or as the newspaper expressed it more crudely: 'The
Basotho on this farm wanted to strike, but could not get the support
of the other natives . . . and they were therefore incensed both
against the natives of the other tribes and the white men.'[34]

This was a somewhat simplistic account of events on an estate
where both ethnic and class tensions had reached a new crescendo.
The forty-odd labourers recruited from Basutoland had formed a
cohesive group of vigilantes. Just before the Union meeting, they
had embarked on a series of assaults on white and Zulu-speaking
foremen who beat up fellow Sothos. Two days after the strike call, a
series of 'faction fights' broke out both near the farmhouse and in the
compound, with the Basotho gang shouting that 'they were going to

kill all the whites as well as the blacks who were helping the whites'. After a sleepless night expecting precisely this fate, Gafenowitz and his armed white overseers collected together a group of loyalist Zulu-speaking wage-earners, and a bloody fracas occurred. Led by Isaac – who was allegedly calling for their master to be killed – the Sotho labourers successively rushed upon and retreated before the crowd opposing them. Their cause was, however, a lost one. Gafenowitz himself killed two of them and badly injured a third, and that afternoon all the workers from Basutoland were marched to Bethal by two constables.[35]

The incidents on Mizpah Estate suggest little more than knowledge amongst some of its workers of the ICU's call for equality and perhaps its proposed strike action. But Bethal landlords held a very different view. Most thoroughly approved of Gafenowitz's acquittal on a charge of culpable homicide, partly on the grounds that any one of them could have suffered the same fate due to the 'recent attitude of the natives'. The armed clash also fuelled their assertions that their difficulties in controlling labourers increased daily due to ICU activities, and that the organization was 'a source of grave anxiety to the farmers'.[36]

In general, landlords' fears about the Union were quite out of proportion to the actual danger posed. Indeed, the problem was precisely that the ICU became a focus for generalized disquiet: it was a period when labourers had every right to be restless, when many farmers were battling to keep their heads above water, and when 'progressive' agriculturists were largely alienated from the state. Like so many other movements which have mercilessly exposed society's 'quarrel with itself', and have violated norms about the place of the under-classes, it heralded

> the inception of troubling times – especially for those sections of the population who have an overwhelming commitment to the continuation of the *status quo*. 'Troubling times', when social anxiety is widespread but fails to find an organised public or political expression, give rise to the displacement of social anxiety on to convenient scapegoat groups. This is the origin of the 'moral panic' – a spiral in which the social groups who perceive their world and position as threatened, identify a 'responsible enemy', and emerge as the vociferous guardians of traditional values.[37]

Thus the term 'ICU' condensed a whole nexus of disturbing tensions and images: of the '*vrotsige kaffer*' (rotten kaffir) who had killed a farmer; of American Negroes promising black liberation; of 'educated, yet foul-smelling blacks' who were breaking down class and racial barriers; and of 'detribalization', Communism and the collapse of white supremacy. Some public media legitimated and escalated farmers' fears with sensationalist reports. As the official newspaper of the Nationalist Party, *Ons Vaderland* took horrified delight in reporting that Africans at an ICU meeting had discussed the sharing out of white women once the men had been killed, and in announcing that an eastern Transvaal Branch Secretary was being charged for assaulting a white female. In addition to linking the Union to the social evil of sex across the colour bar, it printed ominous letters such as that from a Middelburg farmer. According to him, Kadalie had long been stirring up blacks 'to revolution', and neither urban dwellers nor the Government realized '*hoe dreigend die gevaar vir die plattelandse bewoners word nie*' (how threatening the danger for rural inhabitants is becoming).[38]

In the context of this 'moral panic', numerous farmers' associations were not satisfied with merely evicting or boycotting all ICU members and marking 'ICU' on their passes or tax receipts. They also edged towards more violent or military responses. Hence the White River Farmers' Association was treated to an address by an ex-intelligence member of the Indian Army, who told them to stamp out sedition by calling out the police for every instance of insubordination, and to try to force the state to adopt a more repressive policy towards the Union. Furthermore, the fear that resistance would develop into rebellion haunted numerous white masters. Many already had strong folk or personal memories of 'treacherous' surprise attacks by nineteenth-century chiefdoms – such as the slaying of Piet Retief by Dingane's forces. As a Wakkerstroom landlord regularly shouted to his tenants about ninety years later: 'Hey men, we shall never forget Dingane, from our present generation to coming generations, we shall never forget Dingane.' Now many a rural community had found new

> folk-devils to people its nightmare; the nightmare of a society which, in some fundamental way, had lost its sway and authority over its [under-classes], which had failed to win their hearts, minds and consent, a society teetering towards 'anarchy', secreting, at its heart, . . . an 'Enemy'.[39]

Hence a mood approximating collective hysteria could sweep through a region, with ICU meetings representing covert declarations of war. In a poorer area north of Lydenburg, where some settlers already feared blacks would force them out of the country, an eight-hundred-strong gathering caused considerable alarm. Almost instantaneously, arms and ammunition were sold out; families fled to town, and a defence committee was temporarily established. In areas bordering on Swaziland, reactions were even more extreme. In Carolina, a *Blanke Beskermings Bond* (White Protection League) was formed in response to the Union, while in the south-eastern corner of Piet Retief, some whites were so panic-stricken that they temporarily fled the district.[40]

Although this last incident occurred in a district where farmers already feared that the ICU was about to incite rebellion, it had its origins in protest peripherally influenced by the Union in the neighbouring Natal region of Ngotshe. In January 1928, two groups of about forty workers from adjacent estates here had deserted in order to inform the magistrate that they were 'absolutely miserable; highly dissatisfied; treatment disgraceful'. This news was rapidly transmitted – and doubtless exaggerated – to one Dingley, an excitable manager of a Piet Retief estate. In early March, a week after Swaziland authorities had made public their concern about Union 'agitation' in their country, and on the same day that Piet Retief landlords held another anti-ICU meeting, Dingley was allegedly warned by four trusted servants to flee with all other whites to avoid being massacred by the Swazi. At this point, rumours snowballed amongst both black and white, as each group found scapegoats onto which to project its anxieties. Dingley and other white wage-earners on their estate, Onverwacht, interpreted whistle blasts by herders as a signal for the Swazi attack; they took preparations for a war dance as irrefutable evidence of impending hostilities, and believed that the (mainly Swazi) workers in the compound had all 'freely discussed the way in which they would do away with the Whites'. A suggestion that all whites should sleep with rifles next to their beds did little to defuse their alarm: within forty-eight hours, all Onverwacht whites had decamped to Ngotshe.[41]

Ironically, this in turn greatly perturbed the blacks they left behind on their Piet Retief estate. The following day, 155 Onverwacht labourers struck, and were 'roaming about the area in gangs of one hundred'. Officialdom rapidly intervened to secure their return to work, and the Secretary for Native Affairs wearily dismissed the flurry of associated reports on the grounds that they emanated from 'a very agitated population'. While his impatience was understandable, the fact that both districts were seething with rumours was nonetheless significant. Responsiveness to hearsay is after all related to the extent to which this supports specific ideologies and interests. Furthermore, the efflorescence of rumours is often the first sign that underlying tensions are becoming more acute, and certainly action taken on their basis is true in its consequences, if false in its premises.[42]

To the growing concern of many eastern Transvaal ICU organizers, precisely the same was true of the upsurge of protest amongst the rural poor. Fearful for their own safety, and incapable of offering much aid to the evicted – let alone of fulfilling earlier wild promises – many activists were by late 1927 toning down their speeches. They were also attempting to defuse expectations which, sometimes for reasons beyond their control, had been projected onto a movement which *was* able to offer some support to unorganized and brutally subordinated Africans. Perhaps this growing moderation is best epitomized by an address given at Standerton in December 1927 by the Bethal District Secretary. An ex-farm labourer who six months previously had advocated mass resistance to abolish the pass laws, Malaza was now much more cautious. Stressing that the Union was a pure trade union that sought only to redress grievances by constitutional means, he asked each member to pay five shillings to fight the pass laws legally. He also warned them that the Union was not as of the days of yore:

> Some of you have been misled by speakers who said that the ICU had great power, even over the white man, and then you go away and spread this false doctrine from worker to worker on the farms . . . Some of his audience had perhaps come here with the expectation that they would be declared free today, that they would get eight pounds a month, and also other things . . . But the red card . . . certainly does not mean that the native is free of obligations to his master. No, the ICU recognises that the white man is the father of the native . . . Therefore they ask that the white man must lead them.[43]

It did not need the final touch of leading three cheers for the five whites present for Malaza to have made a speech of which liberals would have been proud. At least officially, the heady nationalist days of land and liberation were being slowly phased out. From 1928, the ICU in the Transvaal was increasingly focused on wages, workers and whites.

Wages, Workers and Whites: the Western, Central and Northern Transvaal, 1927–1929

From mid-1926, hoping to influence top ICU leaders, Johannesburg novelist Ethelreda Lewis busied herself assembling a small number of mainly lower-middle-class whites. Based largely in cities, they were an eclectic group. Their political outlooks ranged from passionate anti-Communism to paternalistic humanitarianism, and from social democracy to a desire 'to remove the Color Bar to give the Native a chance and *get Cheaper Labour*'.[44] They were united, however, by their admiration for moderate sections of the British labour movement, and by their acceptance of Lewis's premise that it was better for white South Africans to sanction suitably-led African trade unionism than to concentrate merely on winning over upper-middle-class blacks. Above all, their aim was to transform the ICU into a constitutionalist, non–political trade union, which concentrated on urban workers, negotiated over wages and was recognized under the Industrial Conciliation Act.

At head office, their influence was felt almost immediately. It was manifested in lectures at the Workers' Hall on such topics as 'Social Advancement', in the donation of books carefully selected to stress 'co-operation between capital and labour', and in the purge of the Communists. Members of this tiny grouping managed to extend their impact through their links to like-minded intellectuals and labour organizers in more advanced capitalist countries. This greatly facilitated several achievements, including the ICU's affiliation to the social democratic International Federation of Trade Unions in 1927, and the shepherding of Kadalie during his European tour 'from one decent group to another so as to keep him safe from the wrong groups', as well as the rewriting of the Union's constitution and excision of its preamble by a British trade unionist. Although the network of liberals within and outside South Africa only managed to 'keep Kadalie on the rails' sporadically, and then generally only in the presence of ICU officials rather than mass audiences, the change in the National Secretary on his return to South Africa in November 1927 nonetheless startled organizers. Their 'Great Chief' had come back convinced that Union activists were backward, and that the ICU needed not only its new constitution based on the most modern model that the metropole could offer, but also a British advisor to transform it into a pure trade union. In his words, he felt like 'the Biblical Moses, who had gone to Mount Sinai, returning with the new commandments to the children of Israel below'.[45]

The children of Israel, however, were not all that easily persuaded. In particular, many minor officials were unimpressed by the Special Congress called in December to ratify the new commandments. As Orange Free State Branch Secretary John Mancoe expostulated: 'What was the good of revising the constitution when people had no homes? He was sitting on fire at Winburg because the people demanded something practical.' Champion too was annoyed by Kadalie's dismissal of the importance of the land question, and deeply disturbed to discover that reorganization entailed removal of financial powers from Provincial Secretaries, as well as drastic reductions in legal expenditures and salaried organizers in Natal.

While there were other factors behind the splintering off of this province from the parent ICU in mid-1928, the almost impossible task of restructuring the movement into an economistic trade union run by honest officials was central.[46]

In the Transvaal, however, Kadalie had somewhat greater success in getting key officials to toe the new line. Apart from District Secretary Malaza, branch organizer Jason Jingoes of the western Transvaal was temporarily quite happy to accept that the ICU was 'built purely and solely upon British Trade Union principles'. So were two of Kadalie's inexperienced henchmen, including his personal secretary Abe Phoofolo. Between them they carved up the domain previously serviced by the fiery Mbeki, who had been dismissed on Kadalie's return on the grounds of drunkenness. Finally, 'Mote too was transferred to the Transvaal in early 1928, following an acrimonious conflict with Kadalie about his allegedly overly defiant attitudes in Kroonstad. This ex-firebrand, doubtless aware that his reputation for fast living on ICU funds could result in his suffering the same fate as Mbeki, was remarkably subdued during his 1928 career as Provincial Secretary for the south-western Transvaal. Although certain radical notions were periodically propounded, his generally lack-lustre reformism was exemplified in a speech at Christiana in late 1928:

> The natives had passed the monkey stage with the tail, and had to live up to evolution and receive good living wages . . . They must join the ICU and also beg their employers for better conditions. This should be attained not by force but by constitutional lines . . . They wanted a living wage of 3s. 6d. a day, gradually rising to 8s. a day.[47]

In part, the fairly limited impact of the Union in the northern and western Transvaal countryside must be attributed to this cautious trade unionist approach. It was hardly tailored to meet the aspirations of Africans who were primarily traditionalists in the reserves or sharecroppers and labour tenants on farms. Predictably, members here appear to have been mainly urban blacks. Thus, despite a huge turn-out at the first meeting in Bloemhof in late 1928, only about two hundred people joined after hearing a speech by 'Mote where 'the dignity of labour was preached to a very high pitch' and 'the natives were told to obey their masters and work if they were to get an increase in wages'. In part too, the relative lack of interest in the Union by farm residents was due to conditions specific to this area. Both the western and northern Transvaal were generally far poorer and more backward than the east, and were not in the main subject to similar spurts of agricultural development. On the contrary: in the later 1920s, drought, disease and locusts took a heavy toll, resulting in dramatic reductions of production in some districts. Indeed, following the worst and most prolonged drought on record in the northern Transvaal, poorer farmers were begging for food from Africans in 1927, while many blacks were surviving on prickly pears. Both the northern Transvaal and the drought-stricken central Cape bore out the thesis that while impending tribulations often stimulate protest, actual pauperization tends to inhibit it.[48]

Membership in these regions was also restricted because the ICU was steadily less able to pay full-time Branch Secretaries. Thus although a thriving branch existed at Makwassie where Jingoes was based, the same was far from true of surrounding villages which were only sporadically visited by peripatetic activists. This problem was exacerbated insofar as the ICU's reputation as a movement which mismanaged funds had preceded it – and in towns which were already Congress or Communist Party strongholds, political opponents hammered this issue home. It was partly for this reason that by September 1928, the Pietersburg branch had only twenty-five members after a full two months of organizing there. Similarly in Potchefstroom, where almost all the township residents were Communist supporters, the ICU's first meeting gained it precisely three members, as listeners heatedly accused leaders of 'getting rich' on the high enrolment and subscription fees.[49]

Yet although landlords in this region tended to be relatively unaffected by the Union, there were nevertheless incidents which aroused considerable ire. Certainly some farmers evicted resident workers with ICU connections, and the action of the Klerksdorp municipality in demanding registration certificates of newly arrived women was regarded as an additional burden for such tenants to bear. There were also isolated instances of political resistance. According to Israel Mathuloe, Kadalie – having slipped his liberal bonds when he addressed blacks on an African-owned farm in Ventersdorp district – inspired blacks there to throw away their passes. Furthermore, as elsewhere, farmers tended to attribute labour difficulties to the Union, and to be extremely perturbed by legal challenges. Jingoes recalled how antagonistic landlords were to a court victory which he achieved for a prosperous tenant. Not only were they so shocked as to declare 'it was unthinkable that a White's integrity should be called into question by a kaffir', but they also poured out of court grimly eyeing Jingoes as the source of their alleged increase in labour trouble since the arrival of the ICU.[50]

They undoubtedly had far fewer problems than their diamond-digging compatriots. In the Lichtenburg district, the recent discovery of rich, alluvial, diamondiferous farms like Grasfontein had proved a godsend for landlords from the depressed western and northern Transvaal. Since many were justifiably convinced that prospecting was no more of a gamble than agriculture, by 1927 there were an estimated 80,000 whites and over 100,000 blacks crammed into the sixty-three square miles covered by the diggings. But while this was an abrupt urbanization of the countryside, it was also ruralization of a giant slum. About half the whites had been or were still agriculturists, and farmer–diggers were often accompanied by their black tenants. Hence the seasonal rhythms and experiences of the land interpenetrated with those of this primitive industry. As ex-sharecropper Kas Maine expressed it, '*as ons klaar geploeg het dan werk ons sommer op die diggery . . . Toe werk ek weer klaar plaas, toe gaat ek weer terug . . . So gaan dit aan, die plaas se mense het net so gewerk*' (When we had finished ploughing, then we worked on the diggings . . . Then I finished work on the farm, then I went back again . . . So it continued, farm people worked just like that).[51]

Many other blacks renewed their rural links more frequently, with weekend visits to Mafeking and its adjacent reserve. Both areas had ICU branches, whose activists appointed men to enrol inhabitants of the diggings as members. By early 1928, branches had been established in the heart of the diamond fields, and several meetings had been addressed by 'Mote and Doyle Modiakgotla. In May that year, when Kadalie himself visited the diggings, workers were increasingly agitated about wages.[52]

This was not simply because their cost of living was extraordinarily high on these waterless and isolated wastes. As angry Grasfontein men asserted, it was also because a government supposedly supporting 'poor whites' had capitulated to large capitalist concerns. Soaring alluvial diamond production played havoc with the rigidly regulated market whereby major mining companies normally controlled the value of this luxury commodity. In response, new legislation was passed, drastically tightening the conditions under which men could obtain permission to work claims. The squeeze this put on diggers was exacerbated as the price of diamonds fell precipitously in mid-1928, by which time harvests in the south-western and northern Transvaal were known to be poor – sometimes as little as 20 per cent of the average. Hence marginalized employers, most of whom were probably living on less than five pounds a month, decided that black wages should be savagely reduced – by a third or even a half – to twelve shillings a week.[53]

Africans were informed of this decision on Friday 15 June, and conflicts escalated pell-mell the following week. On Monday, 5,000 were out on strike demanding fifteen shillings a week. On Tuesday,

20,000 had stopped work; on Wednesday, all labour on the diggings had been suspended and an estimated 35,000 blacks were on strike. Although senior ICU officials like 'Mote had from the first day pleaded for men 'to resume work pending the result of a conference', their listeners remained unmoved. As one man argued with sound class logic, 'The price of diamonds has got nothing to do with us – we want our money.' Police flooded onto the fields; diggers went into laager and formed commandos; and Africans roamed through the diggings armed with pick handles and sticks.[54]

Since this was at that time the second largest strike in South African history, officialdom was not slow to intervene. Three days into the stoppage, representatives of several central state departments arrived to instil in 'poor whites' a very different approach to class struggle. They bluntly stated that sixteen shillings a week was a minimum acceptable wage; that the mines were short of labour and paid far better; that employers should negotiate with employees, and that control of the strike should be left to the police, not to white vigilantes. Representatives of the latter heatedly responded that diggers should be free to make their own individual arrangements with labourers, and that they absolutely refused to meet ICU leaders. The extent of their hostility towards the Union – which diggers firmly believed was responsible for the strike – was made clear when a Grasfontein man informed these officials that if he and his compatriots found where 'Mote or Kadalie were hiding, they would give them 'a free grave on the diggings'.[55]

Yet although the stoppage was known to whites as the 'Kadalie strike', it was the black rank-and-file who were forcing senior officials to bend to their will. When Kadalie, Modiakgotla and 'Mote braved diggers' wrath by publicly appearing on the fields that same eventful Wednesday, they had totally shifted their position. Head office, they now declared, had decided to support the strike, and four organizers would come to the diggings that very night. Not that this was necessary: minor activists appear to have been only too anxious to decrease the gap between themselves and ordinary workers. 'Daardie ICU, dis hulle wat "strike" gemaak het' (That ICU, it was they who caused the strike), argued Kas Maine, when speaking of the pickets organized by these nameless leaders. In his disapproving words,

> they would stop you from working. They get hold of you, there at the claim, they tell you you must get out, you must not work, because the man does not want to pay. That was the time of the ICU.[56]

More accurately, that was the time when ordinary blacks, with some input from lesser ICU activists, brought the diggings to a halt and even spread the stoppage to farm workers on an adjacent holding. Their astounding achievement also forced the diggers to compromise. By Friday, most whites were prepared to pay fifteen shillings a week; by Monday, life was back to normal on the fields. Workers, however, were probably less satisfied than 'Mote with this conclusion to their struggle: while the original demand of the strikers had been attained, conditions on the diggings were still such as to cause simmering unrest. Certainly the Lichtenburg Branch Secretary almost immediately interviewed state officials to obtain an assurance that whites who defrauded blacks of their wages would be deprived of their diggers' certificates. When he addressed a mass meeting two weeks later, he also injected a broader political note into a review of the strike. It was caused, he claimed, not only by the fall in wages, but also by the brutality of police who were employed by a state that had betrayed workers' interests. 'Now let us say, "Away with this Government, away with this obnoxious pass system and let us obtain freedom."'[57]

His clarion call jarred with his proud announcement that a Scottish gentleman was about to come to South Africa to organize the ICU. William Ballinger, whose lack of experience in trade unionism was apparently outweighed by his anti-Communism, in fact arrived within days, as the embodiment of liberal hopes that they would at last conclusively drive 'a wedge between the native and the Moscow agitator'. His timing was unfortunate: the Union was in the midst of one of its periodic collapses, almost identical in causation, if worse in severity, to that of mid-1926. A couple of weeks before Ballinger's arrival, leading officials including Modiakgotla and 'Mote had publicly issued a manifesto calling for 'Clean Administration', and were privately proclaiming that 'Kadalie must go'. Most organizers' salaries had not been paid for months, and no money was coming in from any quarter. Yet despite the scene of chaos that greeted Ballinger as he arrived at head office to find the furniture being attached to pay creditors, his white supporters grimly soldiered on. They not only paid his fare to South Africa, but also embarked on frantic fund-raising to keep Ballinger 'independent of native resources'.[58]

'Wee Willie Winkie' did his best to repay his backers. His presence alone elicited much more overt support for the Union from persons financed by, employed by or otherwise connected to the Chamber of Mines, the Joint Councils, the churches, and 'Native Administration'. Thus, within a week of his arrival, an ICU patron who was the Chamber of Mines accountant had arranged for Ballinger to meet a representative of the body that controlled the commanding heights of South Africa's economy. The General Manager of the Chamber of

Mines was 'quite reassured and pleased with Mr. Ballinger and his intention' – as were the Secretaries of both Native Affairs and Labour. Within months, the Prime Minister himself was assuring hostile delegates at the Free State Nationalist Party Congress that 'far from there being any reason for expelling Mr. Ballinger, he was, perhaps, to be welcomed. They should not be antagonistic to native aspirations to secure reasonable wages.' Officialdom had in fact agreed to admit Ballinger to the country – albeit on a three-month extendable permit to placate white public opinion – immediately upon learning from Scotland Yard that his chief duty would be to counteract Communism amongst African workers. As CP member Eddie Roux caustically expressed it, the government would have been foolish not to accept 'a down-with-the-Reds constitutional-socialist', at a time when 'white political overseers of the "kaffirs" are becoming as necessary as labour recruiters'.[59]

Ballinger certainly quickly took to his job as an overseer. He introduced a stamp system to curtail peculation, as well as Johannesburg educational classes with a 'splendid curriculum' including such subjects as hygiene. Carefully censored films were shown every Monday by the cleric who had diverted the attention of black miners from the 1922 Rand Revolt with Charlie Chaplin movies, and lectures were given by university academics on such relevant topics as 'The Border Ballads'. In addition, Ballinger made a heavy-handed attempt to change the composition of ICU leadership. Shocked by the drinking, drug-taking and womanizing he perceived at head office, and distressed by ICU officials who 'constantly stir[red] up trouble in the country districts', he tried to sack many of the worst offenders. He also attempted to employ 'sane' upper-middle-class conservatives, and even hoped to persuade white trade unionists to supervise ICU branch activists. And for almost a year, he promoted the policy advocated by his white patrons: '"conciliation", "No Strikes" and "Industrial Action only"'.[60]

If this was a programme that offered little to blacks in the countryside, there was another rural constituency for which it could have much greater appeal. Provided they were under sufficient pressure – such as a shortage of labourers who were not ICU members – even poorer farmers could suddenly see the Union in a new light. This was well demonstrated at Volksrust, where evictions of ICU supporters had climaxed in March 1928, and where members were 'more concerned with the land question than anything else'. The Union, however, retained its mass base, primarily because District Secretary Lot Mazibuko – acting upon a recent Annual Conference decision to acquire farms for such victims – announced he had found a seller of a holding. Moreover, reaping season was

impending, so maize farmers were about to reach the most vulnerable point in their annual production cycle. To make matters worse:
certain agriculturists who had recklessly evicted all ICU members
were unable to obtain harvest hands. Because the cost of recruited
workers was too high, and 'since all natives seemed to be members
of the ICU', in desperation four of them actually applied to the
Union office for labourers, and accepted owners of red tickets under
written contracts of service. This unprecedented concession encouraged Mazibuko in his next step. Again abiding by a decision taken at
the 1928 Conference, he wrote to the Volksrust District Farmers'
Union in June, asking for a conference to discuss landlords' previous
hostility as well as the issue of wages.[61]

Signs were not lacking that 'progressive' farmers would be
amenable to this suggestion. The original anti-ICU resolutions
drafted by the Executive had been relatively liberal, in stating that
efficient service would command fair remuneration, and in appealing
for all employers to treat their African employees with justice.
Furthermore, the chairman had noted a great improvement in ICU
leaders after the passage of the Native Administration Act. In
addition, some wealthier agriculturists were beginning to invest in
tractors, which increased their need for a disciplined labour force. In
all, when Ballinger arrived to enhance the convergence between
self-consciously capitalizing farmers and ICU leaders, the Executive
agreed in September 1928 to receive a Union deputation.[62]

It was an amicable meeting, in which Ballinger, Kadalie and
Mazibuko agreed with these landlords that they had common
interests. In a district where 70 to 90 per cent of farm workers were
labour tenants working six months for nothing, and where
Mazibuko perceived the major abuse to be violation of contracts by
landlords demanding additional labour, the ICU recommendations
were none too startling. Mazibuko advocated that hired hands
should be paid two pounds and ten shillings a month. Resident
workers, he argued, should be under written contracts allowing
them three to six morgen to cultivate and sufficient cattle to plough
this patch, and in return would give six months free labour. Such
demands did not require a single change in the practices of capitalist
farmers on the Executive such as the 'potato king, W. Gillespie.[63]

Gillespie was also one of the two prominent landlords who,
immediately after the conference, offered to accommodate evicted
ICU members on their holdings. The scheme he outlined to
Ballinger was a transparent attempt to use a Union leader to
discipline these Africans on his newly acquired Natal 'labour farm',
and incidentally to save himself the cost of a white overseer. But his
proposal threw the Advisor and his white friends into a turmoil: they

feared they could not find an organizer who was 'a really first-class man who could supervise it personally'. Hence, for reasons which would have shamed almost any black ICU leader, Ballinger was still stalling on the issue when he returned to Volksrust in October.[64]

Here, however, he was to have one of his first experiences of being treated by struggling landlords as a 'White Kaffir'. Although he had been invited by the Executive to address their District Union on the ICU's aims, rank-and-file farmers bluntly excluded him from their meeting. They then heatedly quoted ICU speeches from newspaper clippings, expressed great indignation at the action of the Executive in recognizing the ICU, and unanimously resolved to ask the government to deport Ballinger. Members of the Executive valiantly continued to argue that it was a great mistake for farmers not to take Mazibuko 'into their confidence'. Repression, they claimed, would only encourage the large secret meetings being held where Africans were told that whites wanted to block their every effort at progress. Moreover, the ICU demands were reasonable ones, 'being adopted by most progressive farmers who realise what an asset the native is to South Africa', and in any event 'the ICU disciplined men who would not work'.[65]

Such divergent responses to the Union amongst landlords were often intimately linked to emerging class differences. On the one hand, there were those whose precarious position and absolute dependence on cheap labour predisposed them to repressive tactics. Although they could be backed into a corner – as were the four Volksrust farmers unable to afford recruited workers – in general they discerned neither the necessity nor the advantage of broader reforms. On the other hand, in areas where the ICU had sufficient grass-roots support to threaten production itself, economically advanced farmers could propose innovative ways of responding to the Union. As relatively wealthy and well-developed capitalist landlords, men on the Volksrust Executive believed they could both preserve and enhance their class power by incorporationist tactics. They noted that leaders of black workers could become foremen of white employers, performing the classic function of the 'management of discontent'. They saw that by exposing grievances, labourers' organizations could forewarn farmers about potentially disruptive economic or political struggles. And they recognized that unions could be allies in their own efforts to shift profit-making onto a higher plane, where accumulation increasingly depended on greater productivity, not primitive 'squeezing'. In all, they were well positioned to perceive that in its current phase, the ICU would probably strengthen, not weaken, capitalist relations of production in the countryside.

But even when landlords were under pressure from below, the course of pure class logic never ran smooth. It was repeatedly reinforced or disturbed by political and ideological factors, as well as by concrete conflicts. Thus Gillespie was sufficiently shaken by the arguments of ordinary landlords to withdraw his offer to accommodate ICU members on his 'labour farm'. Likewise, rank-and-file farmers' contempt for their Executive's reasoning was undoubtedly due partly to their abhorrence of the ICU's nationalist aims, and probably affected by confrontations culminating only days before.[66]

At Onderstepoort Laboratory on the outskirts of Pretoria, there had occurred what was perhaps the apogee of worker-oriented, ICU-influenced protest amongst Transvaal farm labourers. Like many non-tenants, these men were housed in a compound subsequently declared unfit for human habitation, and, due largely to pressure from local landlords, were paid as though they were untrained, casual hands. But unlike most others, these employees tending the animals used for experimentation did 'practically skilled work', and some had worked there for years on end as monthy-paid labourers. These factors were significant in shaping their protest, which began in mid-1928 when the approximately one hundred ICU members amongst them decided to demand higher wages. Having had bitter experience of the victimization of a previous deputation, the six elected representatives asked two Pretoria ICU officials to be present at their initial meeting with the Director of Veterinary Research.[67]

After the interview had been granted, the affair became embroiled in a much larger conflict. Opposing tactics of reform and repression were also traversing the state. The Department of Labour in particular was pressing for action which would create an entirely new terrain of struggle for black workers. It had for years been urging not only that the ICU should be officially recognized, but also that it should be registered under the Industrial Conciliation Act. Indeed, notwithstanding the exclusion of 'pass-bearing natives' from the compass of that law, the Secretary for Labour had quietly granted the Union provisional registration in 1924.[68]

In pressing for this to be formalized, the Department's officials had aims as crude and explicit as those of Volksrust's 'progressive' farmers. They wanted to emasculate the ICU, to turn black trade unions into weapons of social control, and to facilitate industrial development. In addition to arguing that unregulated conditions undermined industrial standards, they stressed that since the organization of black workers could not be prevented, it was necessary to guide these bodies into suitable channels, where they made reasonable demands in a constitutional fashion. Through registration, stated the Secretary of Labour in late 1927, 'an important check would be administered to the ICU – the political would be replaced by the purely industrial aspect'. There was a good deal of truth in this, as Labour Department officials knew full well from observing the domestication of white workers' struggles as their organizations were registered under the Act. World-wide, too, outlawed unions have understandably seen radical political changes as a prerequisite for their very survival. Yet their horizons often dramatically shrank once they were granted legal standing, and encircled by bureaucratic restraints.[69]

But defensive rather than formative action was the overwhelming preference of most state officials. Like the great bulk of their white constituency, they leant towards forcibly suppressing contradictions, not risking their explosion on an exposed arena. Thus most Cabinet ministers, including the Prime Minister, agreed with the Secretary for Native Affairs that trade unionism was in advance of the 'native mentality' and that 'the time was not ripe' for recognition, let alone registration. In particular, the Minister of Agriculture held extremely strong views on the issue, and ordered that no one in his Department was to allow the ICU to represent black grievances.[70]

Whether he did this before or after the first Onderstepoort interview is unclear, but he had certainly done so by mid-September when the same deputation attempted a second meeting. This time, the Director of Veterinary Research refused to negotiate with ICU leaders Abe Phoofolo and Ishmael Moroe, and fired the workers' representatives when they in turn refused to negotiate without the ICU. As an indication of the level of organization and solidarity here, some seventy farm workers then handed in a month's notice. This was followed in early October by a three-day strike of these labourers, over the dismissal of their representatives and the non-recognition of the ICU. On the third day, Union organizers arrived at Onderstepoort, closely followed by 'several motor cars . . . with Government officials, viz: Native Affairs, Secretary for Agriculture, Chief of Police and a large number of Constables who were armed with clubs, etc.' Kadalie, who was denied access to the Director, was also forbidden to address the workers unless he persuaded them to end the strike. This he refused to do, and the labourers were forced back to work while ICU leaders were hustled off the property.[71]

But having been exposed to a veritable 'school of war' during their first strike, some blacks were still prepared to continue the battle. Two days later, after a meeting in the compound, they embarked on a second stay-away. They also displayed feelings of hope and confidence typical in wildcat strikes, which temporarily overturn relations of power and production. 'Kadalie was bringing food in his motor car for all who did not go to work', promised pickets.

Somewhat more realistically, they warned disbelievers attempting to leave for work that 'who goes past here will die'.[72]

Once again, however, the police descended, and the strikers were obliged to undertake a forced march to Pretoria's prison. The following day the magistrate, having delivered himself of the opinions that 'a servant is not a free man', and that the ICU had no right to interfere 'between farmers and their labourers', fined seventy-one of the seventy-five under the Masters and Servants Act. These workers were also all instantly sacked: a rash decision which Laboratory officials quickly tried to rescind by confining some of the most valued strikers in the compound. Yet up to the last, these Onderstepoort employees evidenced a high degree of class awareness. If they did not know it already, their struggle had certainly taught them that unity was their only defence against capital backed by the forces of law and order. The four leading pickets – at least one of whom had been on the original deputation and had worked there for six years – simply stated that 'if they wanted them back they should bring back all the other natives dismissed'. It was a brave demonstration of solidarity, since the strikers were all still unemployed and homeless when the ICU's Pretoria branch held a grand dance on their behalf some two months later.[73]

For other social groupings, the Onderstepoort affair had consequences as momentous. For one thing, it formed part of the backdrop to a Cabinet crisis. Just over a week after General Kemp refused to see an ICU deputation about the fate of the Laboratory labourers, a Labour Party minister met a Union delegation to discuss the grievances of Johannesburg black post office employees. In order to remove Walter Madeley – who had not only flouted Cabinet policy on recognizing the ICU but was also under increasing attack, due partly to his policy of paying all Africans in his department eight shillings a day – Hertzog was forced to resign temporarily to reshuffle his ministers. For Kadalie at least, this was 'one of my major achievements on the political stage of South Africa'.[74]

Perhaps so – but it was also linked to his undoing. The ICU's white patrons had been outraged by Union leaders' support for the Onderstepoort strike. Hertzog received from them a flurry of letters, stressing that whites had repeatedly told Kadalie – and had won Ballinger's agreement – that the Union should not meddle with farm labourers. Within a week of the second Onderstepoort stoppage, Lewis pointedly wrote to Kadalie threatening to cut off the ICU's money supply if he would not meet his Advisor half-way. Since he presumably showed no signs of doing this, the Gordian knot was cut at the end of October: Kadalie was suspended for drunkenness. He immediately took his revenge with a fiery speech at Lichtenburg. He vigorously attacked the pass system, declared he would like to contest that seat in the forthcoming elections, and proclaimed to applause that he had come 'to preach the doctrine of a greater South Africa – not a doctrine of supremacy of one race over the other, but for a South Africa where Kadalie's children and General Hertzog's children were equal'.[75]

This speech proved the last straw for white liberals. Although it is unclear whether Kadalie was actually sacked by Ballinger as he claimed, he was certainly arrested for trespassing in the ICU office. He resigned; rescinded his resignation and tried to whip up support behind the slogan 'BALLINGER MUST GO'; accepted the post of Transvaal Provincial Secretary when it became clear that he could not oust his Advisor; and finally, in February 1929, again resigned from the movement he had founded ten years previously. He took with him most of the more experienced, militant and popular officials – who might have had their own disagreements with Kadalie, but were even more opposed to being treated as 'schoolboys' by their new white *baas*. By mid-March, they were fervently promoting the Independent ICU (IICU), which was advertized as a body which would revert to the old defiance that had characterized the ICU before it became a 'Good–Boy organization' run by the Chamber of Mines and the Joint Councils.[76]

The IICU appears to have had little impact in the Transvaal, and Kadalie was wise in almost immediately transferring its headquarters to East London, where he was relatively unknown. Although the energetic Mbeki might have made some progress as IICU Transvaal Provincial Secretary, by September 1929 he was languishing in jail, having been charged by the Independents for embezzlement. In all, the IICU meeting held in the Zebedelia location in the northern Transvaal in August 1929 was possibly typical. The Independents had by this time launched a land settlement scheme which, before it collapsed, allegedly attracted thousands of new members 'who may otherwise not have been interested in the trade Union movement'. The forty Zebedelia men who attended the gathering were not, however, impressed either by IICU urgings to fight for higher wages, or by claims that if they each donated one pound, the Union would pay off the balance on any farm they were purchasing, and give them ten years to pay back this interest-free loan. A representative of the 'Zebedelia Tribe' simply responded that they were coping quite adequately with buying land and needed no help – a point driven home when not one man bought an IICU ticket.[77]

The ICU faced a similar uphill battle in attempting to combat popular disillusionment and disinterest. Many eastern Transvaal branches had by this time either seceded or virtually collapsed. For instance, by late 1928 the Middelburg Branch Secretary – who undoubtedly had not been paid for months – had absconded without the knowledge of the Branch Executive. He had closed the office and, in eloquent testimony to the depths of his indignation and impoverishment, had even sold the Union's typewriter. The cash book showed a large income, all spent, as had been the sixty-two pounds collected to buy a farm. Worst of all, members refused to pay their dues and demanded that the office be reopened, 'not with money they were going to pay; but with money that they have already subscribed'.[78]

Ironically, although 1929 was a year in which the ICU steadily lost black rural support and generally failed to inspire protest, it was also the year in which it made its greatest impact on the Transvaal Agricultural Union (TAU). The origins of this lay in events in the Springbok Flats in the southern part of the Waterberg district. In stark contrast to much of the rest of the western and northern Transvaal, the development of capitalist and commercial agriculture here in the 1920s was dramatic. In large part, this was due to the extension of transport facilities to an area where the fertile black soil was probably the richest in the country, and where the major crop, maize, could be produced at a considerable profit. Settlers came pouring in; land companies sold off huge tracts; and thousands of acres which two decades previously had been tenanted only by springbok (and Africans) were put to the plough. By the late 1920s, local farmers' associations were being termed some of the most 'progressive' in the country. The Springbok Flats Association itself was chaired by John Duff, an ex-Labour Party leader who had been involved in white wage-earner struggles the previous decade, and who had then become a leading capitalist maize farmer. The South Waterberg Association – the most powerful in the district – displayed the characteristic 'progressive' traits of having a significant number of members who were not simply farmers but also lawyers, hoteliers, or other urban businessmen. And the Waterberg District Farmers' Union, to which were affiliated some twenty bodies (including Town Councils and Chambers of Commerce), was probably the strongest of its kind in South Africa.[79]

By mid-1928 the ICU had an informal presence in this region, known as one where Africans were relatively wealthy stock-owners. Its influence spread partly because South Waterberg blacks lived up to their reputation of being 'detribalized' to the point where many read the white man's newspapers. Thus they rapidly heard of Kadalie's acquittal under the Native Administration Act for a speech threatening an ICU campaign to burn passes. At least one labour tenant promptly informed his master that blacks no longer needed to carry these permits: '*Hul voorman het die saak gewin teen die witmense, hulle is nou veilig*' (Their leader had won the case against the white people, they are now safe).[80]

At both the 1927 and 1928 TAU Annual Congresses, Waterberg farmers had adopted a moderate position on the ICU. Although the resolution passed at the latter event in September was that Ballinger's permit should not be renewed, Duff had shrewdly argued that landlords did not yet know whether Ballinger was doing good work or bad. Within weeks, Waterberg agriculturists were to discover the answer for themselves. They learnt that a white man was amongst the speakers addressing large gatherings in the southern reserves bordering the districts of Waterberg and Pretoria, and that organizers were urging blacks to join the ICU and demand higher wages. This had immediate implications for 'progressive' maize farmers like Duff, Major Doyle and A. Manson in the Settlers area of Springbok Flats, since these locations normally supplied much of the seasonal labour for the ploughing which had just begun. Unfortunately for them, large numbers of these reserve-dwellers both joined the Union and took its message to heart. In early October, Springbok Flats landlords were confronted with children, adolescents and young men all insisting on a wage increase of some ten to fifteen shillings a month.[81]

In their determination not to give in to the ICU, many wealthier farmers promptly bought labour-saving machinery. By January 1929 there were in fact forty tractors in the Settlers area – compared to two, four years previously – and almost every second farmer here had access to one. This was a tribute not only to the ICU, but also to the work of men like Doyle and Duff in the Farmers' Party, which was about to win considerable decreases in the cost of power paraffin. Producers of peanuts, the second most important crop in the southern Flats, had a somewhat greater problem, since machinery to replace the women who reaped this labour-intensive crop was extremely expensive. However, in February anxious groundnut producers held a meeting, hoping to form a co-operative to import an American mechanical picker, and thereby to minimize dependence on 'screeching hooligans', who, 'at any moment . . . might demand two shillings and sixpence a bag for picking, or they might strike and leave the nut crop to rot'.[82]

Their nervousness was understandable: by this time there was considerable ICU activity in the area, and a branch had been opened at Nylstroom to cope with the demands of a membership which reputedly stood at five hundred. In February, a large Union meeting decided to formulate wage demands to present to Waterberg's

Kas Maine, sharecropper in Bloemhof in the 1920s

Elijah Ngcobo, who lived on an African-owned holding and worked on a Bulwer farm in the 1920s

Esther Sibanyoni and her daughter Rose Mthimunyc, labour tenants in Middelburg in the 1920s

Clements Kadalie (seated) and
A. G. W. Champion in 1927

William Ballinger

A two-hundred-strong crowd of Weenen women on their first march on the
canteen: a photograph which the ICU *yase* Natal published under the title *Amakosikaze
akwa Nobamba eyocita utshwala* – 'Women of Weenen going to spill beer'

farming and commercial community. By mid-1929, Nylstroom organizers claimed a paid-up membership of 1,200, and landlords were complaining bitterly about insubordination, theft, and, in one case, about an African who insolently grazed his cattle on a farmer's holding and assaulted the owner who tried to prevent this. So far as blacks were concerned, this was undoubtedly justifiable retaliation against incoming 'usurpers', who either turned off 'squatters' or forced them into labour tenancy, and who drastically limited the possibility of hiring extra land as pasture. But for whites such as the Commandant of the Waterberg Commando, it was clear that 'Never before had the farmers of Waterberg been confronted with such a menace as the ICU.'[83]

In the view of the Waterberg District Farmers' Union, however, the 'menace' should be controlled by incorporationist methods. At the Annual Congress in May, there was almost unanimous agreement to accede to a request from the ICU's headquarters that a deputation be received to discuss working conditions. Although farmers legitimated this concession on the grounds that it was necessary 'to see that the organization progressed on right lines', a far more pressing economic problem underlay their decision. This was, as Ballinger well knew, an increasingly critical shortage of labourers in both the quantity and the quality desired.[84]

The absolute shortage of seasonal labour was due largely to the recent restrictions on the entry of Mozambican migrants to South Africa. The mines were consequently casting their internal nets ever wider, and waiving requirements for contracts at least nine months long. From mid-1929, Waterberg Africans eagerly responded, mainly because their crops were at best only 10 per cent of the norm. Hence every train to Johannesburg was packed not only with large numbers of reserve-dwellers, but also with tenants who had previously devoted their six- to nine-month 'free period' to working for wages on adjacent farms. Since most of them were sufficiently educated to write their own passes, which the police then endorsed, landlords' worst nightmares had materialized by mid-year when the maize was due to be reaped. For the first time in living memory on the Springbok Flats, almost no casual labour besides that of black school children was available.[85]

If this concentrated wealthier landlords' minds on the benefits of paying wages competitive with the mines, the very nature of farming in the south increased their need for a skilled, stable work-force. While Springbok Flats soil was extremely fertile, it was also exceptionally heavy ground needing careful preparation before it yielded its riches. Given, too, the irregularity of rainfall in the region, it was essential either to plough as quickly as possible in summer, taking care not to lose too much moisture, or to resort to winter ploughing, as 'progressive' landlords were doing. This meant, as the local Boekenhout Farmers' Association expressed it when approving of negotiations with the ICU, that the plough driver had to be able 'to drive a team and not merely flog the hind oxen. A ploughman must understand a plough and be able to adjust the levers and plough a reasonable daily area without supervision or assistance.' It meant, too, that 'progressive' farmers who had abandoned oxen for tractors went considerably further than Boekenhout landlords in demanding regular trained labourers, who neither deserted before ploughing nor regarded Monday as a holiday. Doyle was one of those who regarded labour tenants as inefficient quasi-slaves, who should be replaced by proficient wage-workers labouring throughout the year. As the President of the District Union, he was to discover how close he was to Ballinger on this point, when the twenty-member Executive met the ICU delegation in Nylstroom at the end of June.[86]

Ballinger, who included in his four-strong team the relatively experienced negotiators Mazibuko and Moroe, immediately started by stating that power farming would soon replace manual labour, and that it was impossible to get Africans skilled enough to handle machinery. 'However, if the farmers want to work with the ICU, native labour will so improve that qualified workers will emerge, who could indeed do that sort of work.' After complaining about the oppressive nature of the pass system, he concluded by stating that landlords were divided between the reasonable 'progressive' farmers, and the backward men who relied on the evil system of unpaid labour tenancy.[87]

Mazibuko, who had greater sympathy for and knowledge of the aspirations of labour tenants to land and cattle, adopted a rather different position. He argued that written contracts – which the ICU wished to be drawn up between masters and servants in the presence of organizers and the magistrate – should explicitly grant tenants time to work their own land even in busy seasons. Immediately Duff interjected to say that labour tenancy should be abolished and that the 'native' should work for a wage. It was then left to the head official Joe Kokozela to accede to this, by recommending three pounds a month, a house, and good food for a male adult with a small family, with five pounds if there were more than two children. Finally, he stated that the ICU aimed 'to educate the natives and to teach them to be obedient, and above all, to make a man realise that he must give a good day's work for a good day's wage'. Small wonder that Duff emerged saying that the proceedings had been satisfactory, and that the ICU delegates were intelligent men.[88]

It is highly unlikely that the Executive ever received a mandate from rank-and-file northern Waterberg farmers for these initial negotiations. The northern sector was a region in which newly settled 'poor whites' predominated, and also one which by mid-1929 was covered by a pall of depression, due both to the drought and to the collapse of the tobacco market. In all probability the two 'backward farmers' who arrived at this Nylstroom meeting, armed with revolvers to shoot the African ICU officials and a sjambok to whip Ballinger, derived from this area. Furthermore, although authorization had been obtained from the South Waterberg Farmers' Association, complications arose when this body received its report-back. Leading the opposition was the TAU President, A. Manson, who heatedly argued that the time was not ripe for the recognition of a black trade union. Although this was a view he had held for some time, recent Waterberg events possibly confirmed his hostility to the Union. A week earlier, African cultivators in the southern locations, where there were numerous ICU supporters, had demanded higher prices for the maize they sold. It was not only rural storekeepers heavily dependent on this trade who were displeased. Southern Waterberg landlords, whose harvests had already been delayed for weeks because they were unable to obtain labour from these traditional recruiting grounds, must also have been angered by this allegedly ICU-inspired protest.[89]

Nonetheless, Duff won the day by vehemently insisting that farmers were driving Africans to Communism at a time of an acute labour shortage, and Settlers landlords agreed to the principle of conferences with blacks. Similarly, although Boekenhout farmers resolved that their representatives should not, at such meetings, express personal views 'on important questions such as that squatter labour should, or should not, be abolished', they too approved of negotiations with the ICU. They also passed a series of resolutions which, in slightly amended form, were those submitted by the District Union to the TAU's Annual Congress in September. These were that 'recognition of the ICU by the Transvaal Agricultural Union be discussed', using the following guidelines:

> This congress approves in principle of the organisation of native employees and the meeting of representatives of organisations of employers and employees . . . This congress has no objection to written contracts . . . Up to now the objection has come from the natives . . . this congress considers that before wages can be raised greater efficiency and permanency of work must be demanded. This congress considers that some system of tests for skilled labourers might be organised under the supervision of the union and the ICU and natives fulfilling such tests should be given

certificates as skilled agricultural labourers. This congress thoroughly appreciates that the more young natives can be kept from drifting into the towns the better.[90]

It would be hard to invent a better example of the way in which changing conditions of production – combined with acute labour shortages and visible grass-roots support for the ICU – were throwing up economically liberal responses to the organization of the black under-classes.

But if one or more variables in this equation was absent, diametrically opposed solutions could be proposed. Waterberg landlords were given an unwelcome reminder of this when they sent their resolutions to what was advertized as the most momentous meeting in the history of the TAU. A committee, largely staffed by 'progressive' farmers who believed Kadalie had made Africans exceptionally 'troublesome', deigned to include the Waterberg proposals on the agenda. The possibility of the TAU accepting even rigidly controlled reformist initiatives was further diminished when Ballinger and his General Secretary sent a telegram to the Congress. While this urged support for the rejected resolutions (and indeed Ballinger had already been drawn into discussions on better training of farm workers and the issuing of efficiency certificates), it also expressed considerably more militant sentiments than those heard in Nylstroom. It stated that the conditions of farm labourers were deplorable; that the trek pass was an instrument of oppression; that the ICU favoured smallholdings for peasants with security of tenure, and that 'Refusal to negotiate will justify extremist tactics and policy of boycott.'[91]

If the crowing of Ons Vaderland was to be believed, party political and ethnic differences between landlords produced divergent responses to this telegram and to the broader issue of recognition of the ICU. 'On the one side', it declared, there were 'the people favouring equality (in this case mostly the English SAP farmers of the Springbok Flats), and on the other side the men who support segregation between white and black'. More accurately, some farmers who had become leading capitalists had done so through the harsh repression of rural labour, and through bitter struggles under the banner of Afrikaner nationalism. The cement of history united them in opposition to many English-speaking members of the same class, who had often acquired their capital in different ways, and who had rallied to the cause of the Farmers' or South African Party. Five months earlier, members of the South Waterberg Farmers' Association had been taunted by Nationalists for complaining that Afrikaans dominated at local schools, and for being non-bilingual men who were sometimes of Russian origin (which carried both political and anti-semitic overtones). Less than three months after the Nationalists had been returned to Parliament with an increased majority after a bitterly fought 'Black Peril' election, it was not surprising that the anti-Afrikaans, anti-Nationalist, *'nie 100% boere'* (not 100% farmers) of the Springbok Flats made little headway at a congress of an Agricultural Union which was becoming increasingly sycophantic towards the government.[92]

The arguments at the Congress in favour of recognizing the ICU were in fact typical of those of liberals advocating economic concessions to defuse political struggle, reformers seeking new ways to neutralize contradictions, and capitalists trying to facilitate accumulation by altering the character of their labour force. Doyle, who had just returned from a conference of the International Labour Organization where Kadalie had made a great impact two years earlier, was clearly shaken by the changing balance of power between colonizers and the colonized. He read statements by black representatives stressing that hatred for whites would persist as long as discrimination existed. He argued that Africans had the right to a fair day's pay for a fair day's work, and that whites could not continue to dominate without providing justice and fair play. His assertions that the great issue facing them was to assist the ICU to organize 'on the right lines . . . [so] that they would be assured of a supply of efficient labour' were extended by a Marico farmer, who insisted that Ballinger had done much to make the ICU a constitutional movement. Another Waterberg man stressed that continued repression would result only in revolt; Duff claimed that the ICU was a force controlling workers, and rode his hobby-horse about Africans preferring cash wages to a share of the harvest. But not even an additional point made by the same Marico farmer – that 'poor whites' stood a better chance if Africans acquired a little greater consuming power – swayed those present. Most delegates solidly supported a leading Nationalist, H. Abercrombie, who drew on pre-election rhetoric in an impassioned speech about dark clouds gathering on the horizon, as he denounced the ICU as a seditious organization undermining white civilization. 'We do not want the Kadalie type of native who came with Communism in the one hand and organisation in the other', he declaimed to rounds of applause. His declaration that whites from Europe knew nothing of the 'kaffir question', and that 'we object to interlopers who come here to teach us our business', won him another ovation. Other delegates chimed in with claims that Ballinger had made matters even worse than Kadalie; that 'natives' could do all the organizing they wished once they were segregated; and that to discuss trade unionism with

Africans would be to grant them equal status. A motion of censure of the Waterberg landlords was rapidly passed, while the TAU's final resolution on the ICU was that 'This congress considers that the natives are not ripe for trade union principles.'[93]

Despite its blustering telegram, the ICU was in no position to respond with 'extremist tactics'. Instead, despite innumerable unity conferences, it continued steadily to fragment. For a time head office organizers lived off money dribbling in from white supporters. For a time too, several branches survived by cutting their links with headquarters, and clinging to their funds, 'as in the past Kadalie had eaten our moneys, we must keep them ourselves'.[94] But it was increasingly evident that the process of disintegration was irreversible.

For Ethelreda Lewis, this was explicable in terms of it having been impossible to find a born leader who stayed sober. Ballinger was rather more perceptive about some of the reasons for the ICU's collapse in the Transvaal. By the early 1930s, he had decided that in a country where the most elementary trade union activity (such as the Onderstepoort strike) immediately brought African political disabilities to the fore, 'native trade unionism cannot restrict itself to mere "economism"'. Indeed, he condemned white liberals who sought this end as sentimentalists who failed to realize that there was a racial problem in Africa.[95] In effect, he came close to the recognition that there was an ineluctable tendency for narrowly defined, moderate trade unions in South Africa to collapse, as inappropriate vehicles to realize African aspirations for economic freedom, let alone political liberation.

Conclusion

To assert that this tendency existed is not to concede the validity of the TAU resolution that Africans were not 'ripe' for trade unionism. This revealed more about landlords' racism – and their own unreadiness to open the Pandora's Box of reform – than about rural blacks' responses to the ICU. The strikes at the Lichtenburg diggings and the Onderstepoort Laboratory, as well as the wage demands in areas such as Waterberg, made it clear that many Africans were excellent recruits to a movement striving for better working conditions. This was particularly true of more proletarianized blacks, labouring together in relatively large groups for cash. At Onderstepoort for example, the relatively stable, large group of workers, completely separated from the land and housed together in a compound, were well placed to respond to the Union by organizing around wages, negotiating with the Director, and ultimately striking.

Yet there remains a grain of truth in the TAU resolution, as was most evident in the eastern Transvaal. It was not that semi-proletarianized blacks were 'unripe' for trade unionism: the Bethal District Secretary was well aware that many hoped the ICU would obtain for them eight pounds a month. Rather, it was that capitalism had not advanced sufficiently to develop an under-class 'which by education, tradition and habit looks upon the conditions of that mode of production as self-evident laws of Nature'.[96] So the rural poor were able to think the unthinkable, and pursue much more than limited improvements in their labouring conditions. Some desired an end to passes, taxes, dipping, police harassment and white-dominated churches. But many more went beyond the confines of specific instances of racial oppression. They wanted land; they expected war, and they longed for the 'I SEE YOU' to bring 'freedom'. Accelerating dispossession, combined with the mere arrival in villages of confident men denouncing whites and offering legal support, provided a fertile soil for such faith to flourish. As ex-Standerton labour tenant Lucas Nhlabathi expressed it, 'Man, we thought we were getting our country back through Kadalie.'[97]

If most hoped rather than organized for deliverance, the growth of black awareness that liberation was an attainable objective still proved sufficient to induce vicious repression. Evictions, police raids, imprisonment, and generalized harassment of organizers were not least among the factors contributing to the demise of the ICU. Furthermore, if white fears of armed rebellion were largely groundless, the 'moral panics' that erupted nonetheless bore testimony to the depth of hostility between black and white. There were indeed farm labourers who longed to kill landlords, and Sam Gafenowitz could well argue that he was defending his life when he shot the two workers during the riot on his estate.

For various reasons, more reformist tactics were also used to contain the Union. An incorporationist approach could certainly suit the political and economic needs of well-developed capitalist farmers, who already subscribed to some of the beliefs of liberalism. But it was only after Ballinger and his supporters had wrought sufficient changes that they were prepared to risk making concessions. Furthermore, their minds had to be concentrated by strong popular support for the ICU in their region. In addition, in districts ranging from Bethal and Volksrust to Pretoria and Waterberg, quantitative or qualitative shortages of labour were of key significance. For farmers producing perishable products and bound by the rhythms of nature, seasonal deficits of labourers could become intolerable. Similarly, amongst those practising more scientific farming or requiring changed labour processes for ecological reasons, skilled workers could become a necessity. Again and again, it was white masters' requirements, either for better-trained labourers or for seasonal servants in larger numbers, that limited their ability to victimize defiant blacks, and helped persuade two major 'progressive' associations to come to the negotiating table.

Shortages of farm labour were, however, related to another factor that induced relatively liberal responses from the dominant classes. This was the ongoing industrial revolution in the heart of the Transvaal, the Witwatersrand. The support given by the Director of Native Labour for registration of the Union was underlain by the need to protect capital accumulation in the mines and industries here. Similarly, the qualified approval of the Chamber of Mines for the reshaping of the ICU under Ballinger was linked to capital's abiding concern to minimize the politicization of blacks labouring in the hub of South Africa.

The fact that Johannesburg was the biggest city in the country further facilitated liberal intervention in ICU affairs, insofar as it was one of the few centres with a white middle class large enough for the appeals of reformist intellectuals to have some resonance. Moreover, Ethelreda Lewis's interest in the Union was deeply affected by 'Goldburg', since she loathed the city as the prime South African exemplar of the 'Machine Age' and 'Slimes' that were destroying the morals of Africans best left in their 'natural' state in the countryside. 'It is a wicked spot like Johannesburg which cries out for an organisation like the ICU', she wrote to Holtby in 1928. 'And the ICU work will purify itself and justify itself when it co-operates closely with *social betterment* in the towns, for natives.'[98]

Reformist initiatives did not, of course, necessarily further the ICU's cause in the Transvaal. In the main, the influence of white liberals was profoundly destructive. It helped to depoliticize leaders, diminish the attraction of the movement to many members of the rural poor and decrease the militancy of numerous struggles. In the worst instances, it facilitated an alliance between Union leaders and 'progressive' farmers against black labourers, who needed to be made more efficient, obedient, and to be stripped of their land.

Yet as the 1929 TAU Congress demonstrated, it was only a minority of even 'progressive' farmers who favoured such sophisticated tactics. And while Transvaal landlords were constrained by factors which made their reactions to the Union less brutal than in many other regions, many compensated by fantasizing about exceeding the repression exercised by their fellows elsewhere. Nowhere was this clearer than in their responses to events in the Natal

Midlands district of Umvoti. As one eastern Transvaal farmer expressed it, if the ICU were to conduct itself in the same way in his region, '*ons sal hulle nie brand, maar doodskiet!*' (we will not burn [their offices] but shoot them dead!).[99] He was, however, perhaps misreading the anger and aims of Umvoti landlords. If the ICU was partly a folk-devil in the Transvaal, it was a far more real threat in Natal, and if Umvoti whites failed to lynch at least one organizer, it was not for want of trying.

6. LYNCH LAW AND LABOURERS:
The ICU in Umvoti, 1927–1928

'Not since the days of the native rebellion of 20 odd years ago has Greytown reached such an emotional pitch', wrote an excited reporter of events in this town on 1 March 1928. Zabuloni Gwaza – the man who had introduced the ICU into Greytown – had been flung into jail on suspicion of desecrating the white cemetery. Hoping to '[lynch] the brute limb from limb', incensed whites armed with shot-guns twice stormed the prison, and grappled with the police outside the very doors of Gwaza's cell. At noon, as bells tolled, businesses closed, and both black and white poured into town, an impassioned anti-ICU meeting was attended by crowds of farmers. Shortly thereafter, hundreds of Africans successfully forestalled a raid on the Union office. But in the same afternoon, about seventy whites surged past the police guarding the office, smashed up the interior, and made a huge bonfire of all documents and furniture. Then members of the mob, roaring off in their cars towards Umvoti's thornveld, 'started to drive the Natives towards the Hills'. Several black/white clashes erupted, and the ICU Branch Secretary was hounded down and thrashed in a mealie field. Finally, at about 8 p.m., as police reinforcements streamed in to patrol the district with their machine-guns, eight cars packed with Greytown men pulled up outside the ICU office in the neighbouring village of Kranskop. Here they triumphantly fired all the contents, and scoured a nearby farm for the ICU Secretary. Clearly, Umvoti whites had every intention of preventing rural protest from once again exploding outwards from Greytown into an armed rebellion.[1]

Such vicious action against the Union by white vigilantes was hardly unprecedented. In the Orange Free State in 1927–28, state officials frequently had great difficulty in controlling volatile white civilians. In Jagersfontein and Reitz, farmers' and miners' attempts to break up Union gatherings were prevented only by timely intervention by the police, magistrates and, in Jagersfontein, the mine manager. In Parys, the magistrate anxiously warned the Secretary for Native Affairs that whites, especially agriculturists, were overtly declaring that they themselves would deal with the ICU if the authorities continued to do nothing. In Heilbron, a landlord actually murdered an African for being a Union member. As the Officer in Command of the district had warned, if ICU activities *'nie van Regeringswee gestop word nie ek my nie verantwoordelik stel vir wat mense in hierdie Kommando in hulle woede mag doen'* (are not stopped by the Government I shall not hold myself responsible for what people in this Commando may do in their fury). And in Kroonstad, Mmaseabi Mafumane laconically alleged that 'school children who were found by whites in possession of those badges were shot to death. That was when we stopped our children going to school.'[2]

Perhaps the speed with which Free State men leapt for their firearms was greatest in Memel. In early 1928, after 'Mote and the Branch Secretary from the neighbouring village of Vrede had addressed a meeting here in defiance of local authorities, rumours of an impending rising spread so rapidly that they galvanized into action landlords in adjacent districts. Being closer at hand, Vrede farmers were even more concerned. An agriculturist who was also an officer in the Rifle Association was approached by numerous whites for arms and ammunition, while the mayor had fifteen rifles deposited in his office by landlords preparing for the next ICU meeting. On the day for which this was advertized – which happily coincided with a religious gathering which invariably drew town and countryside together – about one hundred fully armed farmers descended on the tiny village. Their secular aims ranged from forcibly preventing the Union meeting, to 'wip[ing] out that pest of a location'. In all probability, 'Mote and the Branch Secretary were only too relieved that they had already been charged for the first gathering, and had been granted bail only on the condition that they remained well outside the boundaries of Memel.[3]

In these two years, however, it was apparently only in Natal that whites other than the police violently confronted Union activists or supporters on a scale large enough to perturb officialdom. In Estcourt, some German settlers were so angered on learning that the ICU was promising to remove whites from land originally inhabited by members of Langalibalele's polity, that they conducted an armed demonstration outside the homestead of his grandson, the unrecognized paramount chief of the Hlubi. And in Bergville in late 1927, thirty Natal Carbineers abandoned their temporary camp outside the township for a midnight raid on the Union office. They broke down the door, assaulted the sleeping Branch and Assistant Secretaries, burnt all the documents, and allegedly stole nearly one hundred pounds. Despite the apparently genuine desire of the Minister of

Justice to prosecute these members of the Defence Force, the affair was quickly forgotten. Indeed, the Bergville Farmers' Association put pressure on local newspapers to prevent news of the attack being made public, on the grounds that no fresh impetus should be given to the reputedly dying local branch.[4]

But it was in Umvoti that there occurred the most concerted anti-ICU attacks, inspired by the belief that 'if the Government will not take steps to stop the ICU we must ourselves'. In part, the intensity of conflict here was a consequence of recent agrarian developments in a region which had long been a crucible of capitalist development in the Natal countryside. In part, too, it was a result of abiding memories of Bambatha's rebellion of 1906. Many whites were still angry and many blacks still proud when they recalled that four white policemen had been killed by men of this small Zondi chiefdom as they swept through the thornveld shouting the war-cry of the Zulu royal family. If the disturbances of 1927–28 were somewhat different, the echoes of 1906 were nonetheless ever present.[5]

uMgungundlovana:[6] Agrarian Struggle From The Late Nineteenth Century

From the mid-nineteenth century, Umvoti County had been considered the most important, prosperous and favoured rural region within Natal. The district itself consisted of hilly grassland, descending towards the north and north-west into dry thornveld, and rising elsewhere into well-watered middle- and highveld. As the process of white conquest proceeded, so Umvoti's prime land was appropriated from the indigenous population first by Dutch and German Trekkers, then by British commercial farmers, and finally by absentee rentier landlords. For the vastly greater number of blacks, officialdom demarcated the small Umvoti reserve in the east, consisting of precipitous bushveld so infertile that it comprised some of the worst land in Natal. In 1927, an ICU activist was doing no more than giving voice to 'inherent' ideas when he claimed: 'Greytown is one portion of Umvoti county which is very fertile, it is also rich agriculturally, and all whites living in this area are comfortable. It is a place which should have been solely inhabited by blacks.'[7]

Yet Africans gave up neither their land nor their labour without a struggle. Although by the late nineteenth century whites had established private property rights over some 80 per cent of Umvoti, many farmers had been reluctantly forced to accept cash rather than labour rent from an incipient black peasantry on their holdings. Moreover, despite landlords' efforts to charge exorbitant rents, there were definite limits to battening on blacks in this way. It was as 'oppressed and sque[e]zed' cash tenants that members of Bambatha's chiefdom were precipitated into rebellion in 1906 by the imposition of a poll tax. For numerous whites, this served as a bloody reminder that rack-renting was not the solution to making a living from the land. Nor, however, was the use of local black labour in agricultural production. Frustrated by the refusal of reserve-dwellers to work on their farms, and exasperated by the recalcitrance of labour tenants in the performance of their contracts, capitalizing white land-owners took the path already pioneered by Natal's sugar farmers. Between the 1880s and the 1910s, many of them turned to cheap, vulnerable, indentured Indian workers. This in turn facilitated a permanent and profitable shift in the source from which the bulk of agricultural revenue was derived. The well-watered middleveld was all that a wattle farmer could desire, and while Africans were 'unable to stand such work as wattle stripping . . . the coolie is perfectly adapted'.[8]

Unfortunately for the viability of commercial wattle plantations, the importation of indentured Indian labour was forbidden from 1911. Combined with the fact that rising land values and shrinking holdings meant that ground was increasingly valued for cultivation, this induced a renewed attempt to proletarianize local blacks. Cash rent tenants – who comprised a substantial one-third of Umvoti's black farm population in 1916 – were slowly ground down to become labour tenants. Africans in the nearby reserves – which were already so congested that land-hunger often fuelled 'faction fights' – were by this time sufficiently desperate to be providing some 40 per cent of farmers' labour requirements, at a wage of about one shilling a day. Finally, labour tenants themselves were the victims of a concerted 'squeeze'.[9]

Reflecting the class differentiation amongst white landlords, this pressure on resident workers took two major forms. Wattle companies and wealthier farmers tended to base large pools of black labour on separate Weenen or Umvoti thornveld holdings in the north-west, in the heart of which lay Bambatha's territory. At best, stock could be farmed in this region. At worst, the holdings were like Lonsdale, which consisted mainly of cacti and wild rubber growing on hilly, stony land. It could, in the opinion of local landlords, be used only as a 'labour farm', since it was 'absolutely unsuitable for ordinary farming'. African men living in such agricultural disaster areas often had to work even in the six months they were not contracted to landlords, and did so either in the towns or as farm labourers paying off advances of food. Yet these 'labour farms' also had their advantages, particularly in allowing the development of a community life amongst the hundreds of blacks they frequently accommodated. Moreover, because whites interfered less in the management of these sweetveld holdings, many Africans were able to accumulate large herds of stock, and to practise unhindered customs rooted in precolonial days.[10]

Tenants living and working on the same farm as less substantial landlords tended to be present in far smaller numbers (perhaps averaging five homesteads per holding), under much tighter control and considerably worse off materially. Whereas twenty years previously a homestead could obtain some ninety acres of land and the right to run an unlimited number of cattle, by the 1920s arable plots had generally been restricted to a meagre one to two acres, and cattle to ten head per household. Furthermore, most homesteads were dependent on landlords for both short- and long-term survival. Oxen needed to plough their own plots were borrowed from farmers, while food for subsistence as well as cattle for bridewealth were regularly obtained by working extra months for landlords. As ex-Umvoti labour tenant Jacob Dhlomo expressed it, in each of their six contracted months men toiled for 'Nothing! Only ten shillings', while in their six 'free' months they worked for *lobola* and 'for mealie bags'. Moses Majola similarly stressed the extent to which labour extraction was bound up with the rhythm of production on these sub-subsistence plots. The food they produced, he said,

> would be enough for one year, and then another year it wouldn't, and then we had to borrow food from the farmer . . . and therefore we couldn't be paid, we had to work for those bags which we took . . . so all the money which your son was supposed to get was taken.[11]

It was hardly surprising that smaller agriculturists of this period preferred to pay in mealie bags rather than cash. From the outbreak of the First World War, bank managers' eulogies about Umvoti farmers were replaced by criticisms that most holdings were heavily bonded, while the bulk of landlords were indebted and patently undeserving of their reputation of being amongst the most 'progressive' farmers in Natal. By the mid-1920s, it was widely recognized that the 250 per cent increase in land prices over the past decade was totally disproportionate to the productive value of farms. The vital wattle industry had been in the doldrums for several years, and the district was badly overstocked with scrub cattle. Banks, ever quick to discern a poor investment, accelerated the downward spiral by aiming 'at having all weak advances eliminated without delay'.[12] Between 1919 and 1926, loans to Umvoti residents by the Standard Bank declined precipitously from over one hundred and fifty thousand to less than forty thousand pounds, while overdrafts secured by farm property shrank from seventeen thousand pounds to zero. Moreover, wealthier farmers' attempts to balance on their urban leg was being badly impaired, as was underlined by the liquidation in 1925 of both the Umvoti Trading Company and the local co-operative wattle extract concern. Luckless Umvoti landlords were not only suffering from having to compete with more developed capitalist farmers on a highly unstable world market: they were also sinking beneath the weight of exorbitant land costs and rapacious bankers.[13]

The fate of Daniel Havemann well illustrates the extent to which white farmers as well as black tenants were being 'squeezed'. By the 1910s, Daniel together with his numerous sons was making a good living on the estate Umvotipoort appropriated by his German Voortrekker father sixty years previously. 'Daniel was a rich white man', recalled Jumaima Dladla, whose brothers worked on the Rand during the teens to pay off cash rent to Havemann. 'He had lots of cattle and sheep . . . Thousands . . . There were Indians as well . . . Daniel had a big shop. He was a rich man.' Indeed he was: in 1923 he was estimated to be worth twelve thousand pounds. Yet the post-war slump and rising land values were steadily taking their toll. By 1920, at least three of his sons had left to farm in Zululand. Five years later, one Umvoti-based son, Paul Havemann, was declared insolvent, having abandoned all efforts to pay his creditors from wattle bark proceeds. The Standard Bank, despairing of securing repayment from Paul's only assets of stock, wagons and furniture, turned the screws on his father, who had guaranteed the thousands of pounds worth of liabilities incurred by his offspring. Thus Daniel, by now heavily indebted and mortgaged up to the hilt, was in 1926 forced to surrender two farms, including the ancestral Umvotipoort.[14]

While Daniel may have been exceptionally unlucky in having so many children come of age in this period, his son's disastrous career was similar to that of many younger men. If they owned land, it was generally so overburdened with debt that their interest payments were the equivalent of rent to their creditors. If they did not – thereby forming part of the 20 per cent of Umvoti agriculturists who leased their land or farmed on the shares – it was very difficult to obtain loans. In both cases, it was extremely hard to survive the tortuously slow turnover period of money invested in wattle, which should ideally be stripped only after eight years. It was also impossible to afford the good stock and well-managed plantations that were the only hope of minimal profits in these years, or to have cash on hand for the migrant workers and 'labour farms' that were the only solution to farming wattle on a worthwhile scale. Small

wonder that the 1920–22 depression precipitated a crop of insol-
vencies amongst insubstantial farmers like James Martens, and that
in the post-war years a growing number of Umvoti whites were on
the verge of being shaken off the land.[15]

In the context of this very real threat of proletarianization, the
relative profitability of wool noticeably changed landlords'
previously jaundiced attitude to sheep farming. A far more important development, however, was the boom in wattle bark prices. This
in itself was related to rapid expansion and changes in the labour
processes of the British leather industry. In their tanning operations,
manufacturers were increasingly using extract derived from wattle
bark (over which South Africa held a monopoly on world markets),
rather than that obtained from quebracho (which took a century to
mature and was grown mainly in Argentina, where the state was
increasingly reluctant to grant land for plantations). Thus in 1926,
for the first time in years, stick bark prices reached a profitable level.
In 1927, spiralling prices meant that every acre under mature wattle
was worth some thirty pounds, double its value only a couple of
years previously. In one fell swoop, wattle cultivation was
momentarily transformed from an industry surviving only due to
the demand for mine props, into one which was more profitable than
any other branch of farming in South Africa, and which provided
more foreign exchange than sugar.[16]

On the three hundred or so white-occupied farms in Umvoti,
landlords feverishly seized these opportunities to recoup their losses.
Between 1923 and 1930, the number of white-owned woolled sheep
in the district rose by over 90 per cent. As one neighbouring Estcourt
farmer wryly observed, 'the yearly wool cheque puts new heart into
Bank Managers if it does nothing else'. Much more heartening to the
latter was the transformation of hillsides into plantations. At a
conservative estimate, land under cultivation in the region rose by
one-third between 1926 and 1930, due almost entirely to the planting
of some 12,000 morgen with wattle. But according to the elated
President of the Umvoti Agricultural Society, the increase between
1927 and 1928 alone was one of 75 per cent.[17]

Since the average Umvoti farm was only about 660 morgen in
size, and since the additional land required for sheep was even greater
than needed for wattle, massive restructuring of land-usage patterns
was clearly required. Above all else, this involved evictions. As
Natal's Chief Native Commissioner (CNC) succinctly expressed it,
farmers' widespread tendency 'to put more and more land under . . .
wattle and other slow maturing crops and to embark on extensive
ranching operations renders the presence of labour tenants superfluous; indeed, every acre of land they occupy is of more value to the

farmer than their labour'.[18] Corporate capital flooded into the district, buying up wattle land and ejecting all resident blacks. Simultaneously, some companies and wealthier landlords either sold their 'labour farms' – because 'the wattle farmer is already finding it more economical to employ only paid labour in place of labour tenants' – or evicted all black dwellers in order to use these holdings exclusively for their own stock. Finally, both large and small farmers rid themselves of all 'superfluous' Africans on their own estates, which in particular meant those paying cash rent or owning large herds of cattle. If they did not leave quickly enough, whites seized their stock and sued them in court. Moreover, hardly had these homesteads been thrown off the farm before their land – including family graves – was put to the plough or to pasture. In the late 1920s in Umvoti, as happened elsewhere during the process of primitive accumulation, 'sheep ate men', trees replaced tenants, and human beings were completely subordinated to the pursuit of profit.[19]

If evictions were one side of the coin in the development of capitalist agriculture, the increased use of wage labour was the other. While smaller maize and wattle growers drew heavily on the neighbouring reserves and on the 'free' time of tenants on 'labour farms', corporate capital and large planters recruited more tightly controlled 'thirty day ticket' labour from Pondoland and Basutoland. As state officials recognized, this gave blacks toiling on wattle plantations many of the characteristics of industrial workers. Not only were relatively large numbers of labourers employed – a five-hundred morgen plantation could easily retain forty workers throughout the year – but they were also often utilizing sophisticated equipment ranging from tractors to turbines. In addition, by the 1920s most farmers were succeeding where their fathers had failed. Through piece-wages and the task system, they were slowly but surely imposing an industrial rhythm and their own time-discipline on African workers.[20]

It was precisely because the task system cruelly intensified labour that local Africans had long resisted it. Wattle work, for instance, included the tiring activities of ploughing land, thinning plantations, felling trees, stripping them of bark and hauling lumber. But especially in times of depressed prices, it was necessary to squeeze out even more labour per hour if money was to be made. As one farmer expressed it, stripping had to be done cheaply if the industry was to survive: 'If you put a native on he cuts 200 lb. a day and you get very little. But if he goes faster and you watch him you will get 2,000 lb.' Of course, supervision was superfluous if piece-wages turned farm workers into their own foremen – which in effect transformed wattle labour into an unequal contest between landlords and their workers' bodies. Indeed, even white officialdom recognized that the tasks were way beyond the strength of youths; that women loathed the heavy labour involved in thinning plantations; and that labourers whose main diet was mealie meal were being physically undermined by the primitive conditions in the industry.[21]

Undeniably, the wattle boom aggravated the existing miserable conditions by both intensifying labour and increasing demands on the remaining tenant homesteads. First, men had to plough hundreds of morgen in an extremely short period of time. 'I drove a tractor', recalled Jacob Dhlomo of his pressurized existence ploughing and planting maize and wattle in this period. 'The fields we ploughed were very large. On that farm, I really suffered. I felt that I was a real farm labourer.' Secondly, farmers apparently compelled homesteads to supply more female labour. While the number of regular male labourers increased by only 10 per cent between 1925 and 1930, the number of regular females increased by 68 per cent. Although women had long been forced to weed and reap maize, they now may well have been weeding plantations and helping their menfolk complete their stripping tasks. Thirdly, because farmers were frantically trying to cash in on the boom, they demanded that labourers strip trees left for years during the slump, as well as immature wattles in overgrown, bag-worm infested plantations. Furthermore, they insisted that workers strip way past summer, despite the fact that the trees became increasingly 'bark-bound' as the winter approached. Since stripping such wattles simultaneously increased the work-load and decreased the yield, for many tasked labourers this meant that at the end of a day more exhausting than usual, their pay was either docked completely or cut by about half.[22]

The way in which farm labourers responded to these agrarian developments of the later 1920s was shaped by their own traditions and experiences. Significantly, their lives and aspirations were still deeply structured by institutions and values rooted in precolonial days. Even tenants who had lived on white holdings for decades continued to perceive themselves as members of chiefdoms, and land-hunger was still a fundamental feature of black rural consciousness. Indeed, at least amongst the Cunu in the thornveld, farm workers defined land according to the section of their chiefdom to which it belonged. 'Although the farm belonged to whites, the "phantom districts" into which the farms were incorporated "belonged" to the labourers.'[23]

Yet the struggles of rural blacks were also suffused with beliefs that derived from their incorporation into a capitalist society ruled by white racists. Ironically, it was the very success of cash rent tenants in delaying their transformation into farm labourers – combined with the inability of a peasantry to establish itself outside the mission reserves – that accelerated their absorption into the urban workforce. From at least the 1880s, blacks' experiences in towns fed into the demands they made of farmers for higher wages. Similarly, their exposure to Christianity nurtured a challenge to white cultural hegemony through separatist churches.[24] And their assimilation into a world far wider than the confines of a chiefdom increased the attraction of pan-Zulu or proto-nationalist ideologies. It was precisely the Greytown ICU's ability to articulate these various strands in rural consciousness – capitalist and non-capitalist, precolonial and colonial, ethnic and nationalist – that facilitated its enormous success in Umvoti.

The 'I SEE YOU' in Greytown

When Acting Natal Provincial Secretary Sam Dunn discovered that many Umvoti Africans were being almost instantaneously evicted and had nowhere to go because the reserves were 'full to over-flowing', he piously declared that if the ICU had not existed to defuse popular anger, 'the country would undoubtedly have been faced with a similar crisis to that of 1906'. However, Zabuloni Gwaza, the thirty-five year old Branch Secretary who arrived in Greytown in April 1927, was far more willing to exploit the crisis situation that awaited him. Born in Kranskop, he was well aware of both local concerns and rural traditions. Together with his assistant Ignatius Makanya, he proclaimed a harsh Africanist message. According to them, 'a fire had been set burning which would have the desired effect of driving the white from the country, which really belongs to the native, and thus ridding the natives of the burdens and hardships imposed by white control'. The class content with which activists imbued these burdens was well calculated to appeal to the resident labourers who formed over half of Umvoti's black population: they 'preached the doctrine of taking away farms and freeing the tenants from their obligations to supply labour'. Moreover, they spoke both literally and figuratively in the language of Zulu nationalism. When Jacob Dhlomo explained why ICU leaders called for Africans to join separatist rather than mission churches, and proclaimed their disbelief in the God of the white man, he stated simply: 'They wanted us to be Zulu-like.'[25]

In this quest for 'Zulu-ness' Gwaza also sought to assimilate to the Union's message older traditions, particularly those of primary resistance. Cetshwayo's grave lay some forty miles away from the Mpanza valley, where Bambatha's men had ambushed the whites.

The burning of their king's last resting-place in 1906 by white troops had embittered many Zulu-speakers. Combined with current anger over the desecration of the burial grounds of evicted tenants, this possibly contributed to Gwaza's act of revenge in mid-1927. Symbolically – and somewhat drunkenly – he smashed the glass protecting a wreath on the graves of the police killed in the rebellion. Probably too, this was partly inspired by the fact that he was on his way to a wedding on a thornveld farm, which not only adjoined the holding where Bambatha once lived, but was also the very estate on which the constabulary had camped hours before the ambush occurred. There could have been few better opportunities offered to ICU activists to mesh political radicalism and popular culture. Before conforming to local norms by abandoning their white man's liquor and repairing to drink beer, Gwaza and Makanya stood within the *induna*'s cattle byre. In their role as ICU organizers, they spoke about legally enforced ejectments to the surrounding circle of men. These included Bambatha's nephew, and Gwaza made a concerted effort to use his graveyard exploits to instil defiance: 'you white farmers servants better tell your masters . . . I have broken the glass on the Europeans' grave . . .'[26]

Whether or not they obeyed this injunction, white farmers' servants joyfully welcomed an organization which forcefully articulated their hopes, while simultaneously appealing to the symbols of politicized Zulu ethnicity. Furthermore, the Union's ability to reverse the devastating changes which they faced seemed confirmed by its Greytown legal victories, as well as by its powerful presence in the country at large. Thus as evictions soared and farm work intensified, exultant Africans flocked to support the 'I SEE YOU'. One of the first meetings on Greytown's race track drew four to five thousand people, and within weeks the roads every Sunday were crowded with blacks streaming to the gatherings. By early June 1927, organizers claimed to have sold an astounding ten thousand red tickets to a population that included only some 1,500 urban Africans. Material possessions further proclaimed the popularity of the branch. A plot worth nearly five hundred pounds was bought in the name of the African Workers' Club, and organizers were stylishly taken to farm meetings in a large ICU car manned by a full-time chauffeur.[27]

Partly as a result of these rural recruitment drives, Umvoti membership peaked in early 1928 at an alleged sixteen thousand people: over 80 per cent of the enumerated adult population of the district. But hundreds of ordinary blacks, including migrants returning from the cities, also contributed to these huge figures by becoming self-appointed propagandists. In so doing, they chose – and changed – those elements of the Union's message most relevant to themselves. Despair over the destruction of the old order was being converted into hope in the imminence of the new, and in the process the Union's tidings once again assumed distinctly millenarian overtones. Some claimed that Africans who joined the ICU would get eight shillings a day. Others 'rejoiced when they heard about the ICU' because they believed 'weapons were to be bought to rise against the whites . . . They thought they would get more cattle and pastures.' Jumaima Dladla was one of those who hoped the 'I SEE YOU' would put an end to tenancy, to white-owned property, and thereby to racial oppression itself. 'What I heard was that when labour tenancy was abolished, the country would belong to Africans.'[28]

While there were already signs in the neighbouring districts of Weenen and Estcourt that direct action was being taken to abolish labour tenancy, the first stoppages in Umvoti occurred only in early May. This was precisely the time at which tenants were reaping their bumper crops. For the first time in years, even in the thorns, harvests seemed large enough to cover subsistence needs. Freed of the spectre of starvation, tenants who had worked off their six months had no need to bond themselves to farmers for mealie bags. Moreover, not only was the ICU providing the ideological cohesion necessary to transform reluctance to work into resistance, but this was also the high point of the rural blacks' social year. Thus, as about 90 per cent of Umvoti farmers moved into the period of peak demand for seasonal labour, so they were confronted by an 'absolute refusal to work'.[29]

Although this was a form of action typical of semi-proletarianized blacks, many of the stoppages in this period also reflected the degree to which agrarian capitalism had developed. The ICU's wage demands had enormous resonance amongst Umvoti's poverty-stricken, increasingly proletarianized workforce. Indeed, there is every indication that Gwaza paid little if any attention to the issue of pay, and that it was farm workers themselves who made this element of the national ICU's ideology their own.[30] Undoubtedly, the attraction of 'eight shillings a day' was accentuated by its linking of payment to *time* – and implicitly to an eight-hour day – rather than to physically exhausting tasks. May, after all, was the month in which wattle labourers were being forced into more arduous work for ever-decreasing wages, and in which farmers' extraordinarily good maize crop boded ill for the physical well-being of tasked workers. It was also the month of final tax demands, which, by devouring some 20 per cent of the average homestead's annual income, sharply focused attention on the need for higher pay. When in addition wage demands began erupting in adjacent districts, the scene was set for what William Deane, a leading wattle planter and the Umvoti Member of Parliament, termed paralysis of work on the farms. On 19 May, this alarmed South African Party MP announced:

> The farmers in my district have only a limited time in which to strip wattle bark. The natives are demanding this 1s. an hour, and the wattle growers cannot pay such an unreasonable demand . . . the crops are ready to be reaped, but the natives refuse to do so unless they receive 8s. a day.[31]

They were still so refusing by mid-June: clearly the stoppages continued for weeks, spreading by contagion from farm to farm.

Were these strikes supported by labourers from all social groups? The work-force, after all, was fragmented into 'contract' tenant youths, 'free' tenant youths, tenant women and children, hired hands from nearby reserves, and recruited workers from Pondoland and Basutoland. Certainly in the eyes of employers and the state, temporary migrants from far afield did not display much class solidarity. Wealthier farmers and companies were in fact recruiting these labourers – under rigid contracts – in ever increasing numbers in 1927–8. (Furthermore, the magistrate noted that it was 'locals', not 'foreigners', who participated in another aspect of ICU-influenced protest: the refusal to pay poll taxes.)[32]

Did hired hands from nearby reserves join the strikes? Although Dhlomo claimed that chiefs were 'too law-abiding by then' to support the Union, the ICU had from the start been holding large gatherings in neighbouring locations. In a region where appointments of new black political authorities after Bambatha's rebellion had left many commoners intensely hostile to their supposed rulers, the opposition of loyalist chiefs did not necessarily have much effect. Moreover, there were popular men like Njengabantu, who had been temporarily deposed in 1904 partly for 'insulting' the magistrate by voicing his people's grievances. By the 1920s, he was bitterly antagonistic to white missionaries, to officialdom's interference with his traditional powers, and to state policies which had resulted in acute land shortage. Thus Deane warned Umvoti whites that they had much to fear from malcontent chiefs, and by mid-1928 the majority of Njengabantu's Bomvu people, most of whom lived in the Umvoti reserve, were ICU members. Since landlords were heavily dependent on seasonal labour from this and other locations, it is possible that hired hands did indeed contribute to the 'paralysis' of work on farms.[33]

Unquestionably, however, it was labour tenants who were in the vanguard of this form of protest. As happened so often, the fact that they related to farmers not only as proletarians but also as peasants actually enhanced their militancy. For one thing, their bumper harvests increased their ability and inclination to resist demands on their labour-power. For another, they sorely resented being paid less for more work than hired hands, and desperately needed higher wages to compensate for the 'squeezing' suffered over the years. In all likelihood too, many were already under threat of eviction, and hence had little to lose.

Their pugnacity was all the greater because the bonds of community reinforced those of class. The solidarity which this helped generate was particularly evident on 'labour farms'. Here there already existed networks of co-operative relationships to co-ordinate management of the holdings. In addition, tenants' greater control over resources – as well as their physical distance from their landlords – considerably enhanced their bargaining-power. Given, too, that evictions were most extensive in this region, and that these affected tenants with a long reputation for rebelliousness, it is not surprising that participation in ICU-related protest appears to have been especially pronounced amongst blacks here. As a prominent anti-ICU landlord expressed it, the thornveld of Weenen and Umvoti had historically 'always been the storm centres' of 'Native trouble'.[34]

This 'trouble' was also stamped with the traits of an *abaphakathi* social grouping. While the very fact that labour tenants were striking for higher wages indicated the extent to which they had been proletarianized, land-hunger and objection to labour dues also fuelled these demonstrations. When the CNC rushed to Greytown with police to crush the stoppages, he made little or no mention of demands for better pay. Instead, he sternly ordered chiefs to instruct their people that farmers would not be dispossessed of their holdings, and that tenants would not be freed of their labour obligations. As the fantastic nature of tenants' claims for a 2,000 per cent increase itself suggests, many blacks were fighting as much against proletarianization as for wages equal to those of whites. Indeed, they sometimes neatly articulated their dual objectives: an outraged Weenen landlord declared his 'labour farm' people were 'on strike for a minimum of 8/- a day and in addition claim his farm as their destined property'.[35]

Yet despite the significance of the emergence of rural struggles which had the form (if not the content) of urban working-class conflicts, the importance of the strikes should not be over-estimated. Not only were those involved unable to disrupt production significantly,[36] but also far more limited types of protest tended to prevail. As ever, whites' major complaint in this period was rather of 'insolence'. In part, this referred to the Union's attack on ideological bonds that, in the guise of religion, bound black oppressed to white oppressors. In 1927, black membership of the farmer-dominated Nederduitsche Gereformeerde Kerk fell significantly, allegedly due to '*die Kadalie gees wat 'n baie nadelige uitwerking het op die jong volk veral op Kerklik gebied*' (the Kadalie spirit which has a very detrimental effect on young people especially where the Church is concerned). In part, too, it referred to the challenge to the political authority of the state implicit in the steady decline of poll tax payments. Although this was attributed solely to the ICU, the Union was once again merely locking into a spontaneous struggle against the sudden imposition of a heavy new burden in 1926. The demand for poll tax had precipitated the Bambatha rebellion, and twenty years later a one-pound levy remained almost intolerable for men paid ten shillings a month. Finally, both officials and landlords were infuriated by the intensification on farms of muted, evasive, but nonetheless damaging informal protest. In Kranskop, this included groups of labourers reclaiming the use of old footpaths on white farms, and deliberately leaving gates open so that stock grazed on ripe maize. In Umvoti itself, reassertion of customary rights and resistance to farmers was reflected in soaring convictions under the Masters and Servants Act. According to the magistrate, the 31 per cent increase in criminal cases in Umvoti between 1926 and 1927 was due to the ICU, which 'stirred up the native farm tenants and caused considerable restlessness and alarm – and during the first half of the year assaults on Europeans were of frequent occurrence'.[37]

He forebore to mention that violence made up the very fabric of Umvoti rural society, and suffused with its spirit all relations between landlords and labourers. Most Umvoti farmers regarded the law and the police as totally inadequate to their purpose of controlling and exploiting their workers. In 1925 their Agricultural Society had proposed confronting constables because of 'the unsatisfactory method in which delinquents are followed up . . . depositions are made for crime committed, and the deposition is just thrown in the Pigeon-hole and forgotten'. Consequently, many masters preferred to rely on their own brute force to discipline servants who had not accepted the right of white farmers ruthlessly to abuse them. Thus, in an economy in which black labour-power came cheap, black bodies were the site on which white farmers exercised their power. And in a world in which black males were constantly struggling against their definition as 'boys', white men consolidated their superiority by savagely beating both them and their women. Some of the most vivid memories of those who worked on Umvoti farms in the 1920s centred around the brutal, bodily violence to which they were subjected. For the smallest offences, they were threatened with guns, beaten with sticks and thrashed with horsewhips by whites ideologically committed to the notion that they were dealing with a race of savages.[38]

The presence of the ICU in this raw, dehumanizing world heightened farm workers' confidence and sharpened their sense of justice. Not that labourers involved in the rash of assaults on white landlords were necessarily ICU members. There is no known association between the Union and the farm worker Muziwake Cele who, when two Kranskop whites struck him with a stick, grabbed his testicles and subjected him to racist taunts, responded by calling them 'two bloody fucking hells' and almost felled them to the ground. Yet the ICU had undoubtedly influenced the consciousness of two Cunu men who retaliated against Louis Nourse on his Umvoti thornveld stock farm. Nourse was attempting to extend the working time and to discipline the private lives of his unmarried male tenants, by forcing them to sleep in his nearby 'Kaffir house' rather than in their own homes. Having disobeyed his order, the twenty-three year old Nkanyama Magutshwa and the twenty-year old Vimbindlu Zakwe arrived for work fifteen minutes after sunrise. After being abused and struck by Nourse, Zakwe declared 'there is no law to stop us going out at night', and both demanded to be charged in court rather than beaten. When the indignant farmer attacked them, both retaliated with their fighting-sticks. They forced the injured Nourse to back out of the fight, ignored his order that they return to work, and illegally left the farm for the ICU office. From here they were hastily dispatched to the police station to lay a charge of assault – only to find that Nourse had preceded them. Their brief moment of victory was over, and their confidence in the courts was presumably shaken the following day when they were sentenced to six months' hard labour.[39]

This incident was characteristic of much of the initial ICU-related protest on farms, in its individualistic nature, in its connection to proletarianization, and in suggesting workers' faith in the law. Magutshwa and Zakwe were also fairly typical participants. Predictably, young males appear to have taken a leading role. Not only did they bear the brunt of landlords' exactions, but they were also more aware of urban conditions, and less restricted by dependents than elders or women. And certainly Cunu men were prominent in ICU activities. While Cunu people constituted almost half of Umvoti's farm tenants, those who were evicted or 'squeezed' were in a desperate position because the Cunu had not been allocated a ward in the Umvoti reserve. Moreover they lived primarily in the thornveld, and were deeply enmeshed in relationships with the Cunu in

Weenen. This was precisely the area where ICU-influenced strikes had been extremely widespread, and where there had emerged gangs of semi-proletarianized youths notorious for their 'faction fights'. By the mid-1930s at the latest, there was an *igoso* based on Nourse's farm, and by this time Cunu men from Umvoti had for years been participating in group clashes in Weenen. Thus the use of fighting-sticks by Magutshwa and Zakwe probably testified to familiarity not only with herdboys' recreational activities, but also with youthful subcultures focused around 'faction fights'. Furthermore, apart from sometimes apparently permeating the dynamic of dispute between landlords and labourers, these emergent subcultures undermined the control exercised over youths by their elders. Thus young males, whose growing economic independence was reinforced by consider-able social and political autonomy, were not necessarily mindful of the anti-ICU warnings of homestead heads or Umvoti chiefs.[40]

Of course, women were not immersed in these militaristic, male-dominated practices to anything like the same extent. Their involvement in farm protest – and in 1927 fully one-quarter of Masters and Servants cases were against black females – was often reinforced by traditions quite distinct from those of youths. In particular, actions such as refusal to work were frequently informed by popular beliefs that women's places were in their menfolks' homes not farmers' houses. Such patriarchal values were probably being vigorously asserted in this period of increased demands on female labour, and this alone was likely to have affected women's resistance more than ICU precepts. Certainly, male Umvoti organizers conformed with ease to the prevalent view that politics and protest were the prerogatives of men. Thus, although a small minority of women always attended urban meetings, Jumaima Dladla claimed little knowledge of the Union. 'I stayed at home. Men might know that'; red tickets were issued 'to men and not to us women'.[41]

But members or not, women and children were deeply affected by farmers' response to the ICU's challenge. Apart from violence, landlords utilized their single most powerful weapon against tenant dissidence: their control of the land, and their right to evict black residents. Here Umvoti landlords – and indeed Natal farmers in general – acted as a class. In early June 1927, the Natal Agricultural Union (NAU) sent to all affiliated associations a set of draft resolutions:

1)   That the members of this Association solemnly bind them-selves to turn all natives off their property who remain or become members of the ICU.

2) That any native who refuses to work be turned off at a month's notice.

3) That kraal heads have complete control of and contract for unmarried inmates of their kraal.

4) That the mere fact of a native residing on privately owned lands be accepted as sufficient proof of his having contracted with the proprietor of such lands.

5) That when decisions of Magistrates have to be reviewed in native cases, Judges of the Native High Courts, who understand such cases, should review such judgements and not Judges of the Supreme Court.

6) That proprietors should bind themselves not to take on natives rejected from other farmers for refusal to work, theft or for other crimes.[42]

These resolutions could hardly have meshed better with landlords' broader struggles: to clear 'surplus' Africans from their land; to secure legal backing for alliances forged between white farmers and black patriarchs, and to subject every tenant to the constraints of the Masters and Servants Act. Significantly, these repressive tactics were also based on the assumption that alternative sources of labour were available. Unlike the Transvaal, Natal contained reserves which not only constituted an unprecedented 30 per cent of its land area, but also accommodated a reliable reserve army of agricultural labour. Until the late 1930s, mine recruiting was actually banned in over half Natal's magisterial districts, including Umvoti. As an influential government commission noted at this time, 'Natal Province has always been very jealous of its Native labour supply and, supported by powerful backing, it has achieved considerable success.'[43]

Unfortunately, Umvoti was one of the minority of Natal districts in which the average farmer was not particularly close to a reserve. This, combined with the recognition that at least some labour tenants were required, led to a minor modification when a well-attended meeting of the Umvoti Agricultural Society discussed the proposals in the last week of June. They were unanimously passed – with the exception of the first recommendation. Here it was decided that only 'active' ICU members would be evicted.[44]

The extent of 'activity' was, however, immediately revealed. Landlords blithely bypassed the suggestion that at least a month's notice was required, and vigorously attempted to clear their estates of dissident blacks before 30 June, the end of the agricultural year. As happened elsewhere in Natal to those suspected of ICU activities, Umvoti farmers 'spied them out, felling their huts to the ground . . . and throwing them on to the roads, confiscating their stock if they did not leave quickly enough'. Needless to say, black tenants were extremely vulnerable to this heavy-handed response. 'Whoa-a-a! Then horror befell us. We suffered . . . Ha! Then the heat was on', remembered Jacob Mchunu of ICU-related evictions in Estcourt. From the end of June 1927, homeless blacks thronged the streets of Greytown, and inundated the ICU office with pleas for the promised farms. They were to be bitterly disappointed. Although Champion made fairly concerted efforts to buy local farms, he was frustrated both by the Union's lack of funds and by the state's rejection of all ICU applications to purchase holdings. Although Makanya led a large deputation of evicted men to the magistrate to plead for accommod-ation, he was brusquely told that farms belonged to the whites and that refuge should be sought in the reserves. And although local blacks began to collect money to buy the thornveld holding of a sympathetic Indian who had provisionally accommodated some evictees, they were fully aware that this farm, Lonsdale, was totally inadequate. Thus it was that the 'Wandering Natives in Greytown' were largely left to roam through the veld with their emaciated stock, as they frantically appealed to chiefs for land in the congested reserve, or tried to conceal the reason for their eviction from suspicious landlords.[45]

It was in this context that the ICU actually increased its membership by becoming associated with claims that landlords had no right to evict their tenants. According to Moses Majola, Union activists said that

> when the white man evicted you, you shouldn't leave, but you should come to us and join. We shall give you the law which pro-hibits the white man from evicting you . . . [People] believed that the ICU would persuade the white man to let them stay on the farms.

Indeed people did, with their belief reinforced by the fact that refusing to leave the property claimed by the white man was an age-old form of resistance, and one highly appropriate to existing conditions. Hence from about mid-1927, tenants either returned to the farms from which they had been ejected, or simply ignored their notices and refused to quit. As the CNC expressed it in mid-1928, resident blacks 'have adopted an attitude of passive resistance . . . and are placing every possible difficulty in the way of the authorities'. As he also pointed out, it was not only ICU rallying cries that spurred on this action, but also dissension within the ranks of the ruling classes themselves.[46]

Friction between Farmers and State

Umvoti farmers and their ideologues had long since realized that they needed to mobilize a broad anti-ICU alliance. Using the institutions that had shape their own social power – the rifle associations, the churches, the press and political parties – they vigorously disseminated the view that the Union threatened both white domination and capitalism itself. It sought black rule, they argued, and its activities could culminate in an African uprising like Bambatha's rebellion. Moreover, since the Union was a socialist organization, the African uprising might well be followed by a Bolshevik revolution. For this reason, they demanded that the state should immediately weigh in on the side of farmers. Indeed, one of the first responses of Umvoti whites to the ICU was the holding of a joint Nationalist-South African Party meeting, to request the Prime Minister to pass a comprehensive Anti-Sedition Act.[47]

Now the South African state was certainly committed to defending three basic principles: that white supremacy should be maintained; that private property was sacrosanct; and that workers could not repudiate their contracts. When the ICU or rural blacks in Umvoti undermined any of these cardinal tenets, then officialdom responded swiftly and forcibly. Thus all primarily repressive forms of state apparatus – the police, the courts, the prisons, the 'Native Administration' and the legislature – were enlisted to intimidate and punish protesters and organizers. In addition, an attempt was made to engage the Union at an ideological level by ordering chiefs to counter ICU propaganda.

Yet for all this, since antagonistic views to those of many farmers were inscribed within the very structures of the state, Umvoti agriculturists attempting to suppress ICU-related protests were frequently frustrated by the authorities. To their intense annoyance, a leading official in the Department of Health blandly declared that the Umvoti unrest reflected the inadequacies of farm workers' diet. Furthermore, the government refused the NAU's request to proscribe the Union. Finally, as Greytown landlords attempted to counter the ICU's legal challenges, they angrily discovered that they could rely upon neither the local nor the Supreme Courts.[48]

From the start, farmers had been outraged by the Union's partial success in transforming the law from a weapon against servants to an instrument of their defence. Their fury at being publicly arraigned – on charges ranging from impounding cattle to withholding wages – was captured by a Greytown lawyer, who claimed that the ICU 'winning cases in the courts created by ourselves is injustice'. But when tenants commenced refusing to quit farms, landlords' exasperation with the legal system reached new heights. Such was the level of black militancy that individual agriculturists found their guns insufficient to enforce their eviction notices, and were driven to enlist the law and the police on their side. They obtained some satisfaction:

about 160 ejectment orders were granted against black homesteads in 1927. Nonetheless, white farmers' already tenuous faith in the law was steadily eroded as the Supreme Court repeatedly overturned local rulings, and as ICU lawyers successfully argued that numerous evictions were illegal. Above all, landlords were incensed by the apparent inability of the state to respond adequately to tenants who obdurately returned to farms even after having been subjected to police-enforced ejectments.[49]

Up to this point, apart from the fall-off in tax payments, there were few signs that blacks were heeding Gwaza's claim that they no longer need respect the magistrate.[50] Nor did his desecration of the police graves inspire attacks on living white officials. In part, this was because the white state, as manifested most concretely in the magistrate, had acquired a degree of moral hegemony which landlords were far from attaining. Moreover, for at least some farm labourers, the ICU's successful manoeuvres in the space between landlords and the law reinforced the belief that the oppressed could win rights from their oppressors without challenging the state.

However, the ability of a racist court to secure black acquiescence in the white man's rule was both partial and unstable. Besides being able to draw on alternative traditions of justice, rural blacks' ideas about the legitimacy of the state and the possibility of opposing it were forged in the process of struggle. When the ICU and certain tenants proved they could compel even the forces of law and order to retreat, increasing numbers of blacks defied their ejectment orders, and concretely demonstrated their contempt for the courts and police.

So too did Magcitshimane Mcunu, a thirty-two year old Cunu who was almost certainly an ICU member. In October 1927 Mcunu, who had returned to his farm after an ejectment order had been enforced against him, was charged with trespass in a test case before crowds of blacks and whites. For technical reasons, the magistrate was compelled to discharge him, and the triumphant Mcunu turned the packed courtroom into a political arena. On being dismissed and ordered to salute in the customary ritual of obeisance,

A big commotion was caused and the Induna Native Constable Makayana again called upon accused to salute the Court and the accused remarked in a loud insolent manner '*Angi kuleki Inkosi*' (I am not saluting the 'chief') and made for the exit at the back of the Court Room and the Induna native Sergeant Magidi pulled him back and made him salute which accused did by pressing his elbow against his ribs and lifting his hand, his fingers only showing just above his chin.[51]

Gestures have subversive power – and Mcunu's three-month sentence for open contempt of the white man's court did little to pacify local farmers. All around them, black resistance seemed to be spreading unchecked while the state was in disarray. In Estcourt, white police were refusing to execute ejectment orders. In Mooi River, resistance to evictions had culminated in a series of bloody confrontations between constables and crowds of Africans. And in Umvoti itself, an outbreak of midnight stock-maiming extended the scope of tenants' challenge to landlords' property. To make matters worse, wattle bark prices began to plummet from November 1927, and the following year farmers lost their cherished contract to supply timber to the mines. The summer rains failed – and by early 1928 agriculturists were fully aware that they were entering the worst drought for some thirty years. And like predators swooping in for the kill, banks intensified their pressure on farmers, a number of whom had already been sued by storekeepers in the course of 1927. By early 1928, fears about the looming economic crisis were subordinated only to fury about the apparent helplessness of the state to check tenant resistance.[52]

It was in this context that Zabuloni Gwaza detonated an explosion. Dismissed from the ICU in August 1927 for 'misconduct', Gwaza's plans to form an opposition movement for those who did not want to work for whites were foiled by his imprisonment until February 1928 for desecrating the police graves. Four days after his release, two Voortrekker graves were wrecked. On 29 February, of leap year 1928, over one hundred headstones were toppled in Greytown's white cemetery. By breaking taboos surrounding death, these acts not only enraged white citizens, but also had the appeal of natural justice for blacks. Moreover, the placing at the cemetery of two cow tails – one black, one white – was interpreted by whites as a Zulu symbol of war, while for blacks it undoubtedly evoked memories of the *tshokobezi* badges worn by those who fought in Bambatha's rebellion.[53]

On the morning of 1 March, Gwaza was roughly thrown into jail as the prime suspect. This time, embittered Umvoti whites were not prepared to rely on officialdom to punish adequately the man who had pioneered the ICU. They embarked on five days of mayhem, itself infused with the diverse military traditions of fighting for British imperialism, Boer autonomy, or simply white supremacy.[54] Apart from the attempt to lynch Gwaza and the successful wrecking of the Greytown and Kranskop offices, they made two spirited bids to attack the Pietermaritzburg ICU Hall; they had extensive contact with the whites who burnt the Weenen office; they were probably linked to the effort to destroy the Estcourt office; they would have destroyed the Dalton office had it existed; and in general they did all in their power to annihilate the ICU's presence in their vicinity.[55]

From the outset, officialdom's response to this virulent counter-attack was shaped by fear of African retaliation. From 1927, enough Natal ICU organizers had been declaring that 'something is going to happen in May' to cause unease amongst senior state functionaries. When Sam Dunn, bitterly antagonistic to the Union after being sacked and charged for peculation in 1927, informed the CNC in early 1928 that an ICU rebellion was indeed in the offing, some credence was given to this tale. According to him, on a fixed day in the harvest month of May 1928, this most traditional of months for rural uprisings, an

> ultimatum was to be given to the European section of the community among the conditions of which were that Natives were to get a fixed minimum wage for their labour and that certain lands to which they deemed they had a right were to be returned to them forthwith. A period of two days was to be given for the acceptance or rejection of the terms and if they were not agreed to then the Natives were to strike work and proceed forcibly or otherwise to appropriate European property. This, it was anticipated, would lead to reprisals on the part of Europeans and the first reprisals were to be the signal for the full plot to be given effect to. The Natives, working individually but according to plan, were to massacre the whites respectively marked for them, so that none should escape. Arsenals, barracks and police posts also were to be seized by planned combinations of individual Natives . . . the coloured people were to be used only up to a certain point but that in the final catastrophe they were to share the fate of the whites.[56]

Although white officials took this information with a pinch of salt, they were sufficiently perturbed to recommend censorship over ICU mail. They also sent out mobile squadrons patrolling Weenen, Estcourt and the thornveld region of Umvoti in February; they called for a series of police reports on 'Native Unrest' in Natal in the same month; and they appointed a secret agent communicating with the Defence Force in code. When Umvoti whites took the law into their own hands in early March, state functionaries were partially convinced that this could be read by ICU supporters as the new signal for 'the full plot to be given effect to'. So in the context of a telegram from the Minister of Defence to the Prime Minister – that unless the Greytown mob was controlled, 'native reprisals by members ICU may result firing cane wattles etcetera' – white authorities actively protected the Union and overtly clashed with the raiders.[57]

Once it became apparent that no such black revolt was in the offing, however, vigorous attempts were made to heal the breach between local whites and officialdom. A handful of those involved in the raids were charged and received trifling fines. Senior state functionaries scathingly overrode ICU objections to the nominal sentences, while the magistrate who sentenced the men aggressively argued:

> farmers cannot get Natives who fail to fulfil their contracts moved off their land . . . the aggrieved parties are the whites; they have applied to the Law for a remedy and the law has failed utterly to help them. If they . . . adopt primitive measures for redress can anyone blame them?[58]

It was not only farmers with tenants who favoured primitive measures. The leader of the Greytown raiders was, for example, the twenty-eight year old hothead Cyril Browning, who bought slaughter stock for the butchery owned by his wealthy father. But this in itself meant he was well-placed to know and sympathize with the tribulations of poorer pastoralists in the thornveld. Indeed, the motley nature of those involved in the raids – urban English businessmen sped off with struggling Afrikaner farmers and a German messenger of the court – testified to the tightly knit nature of white Umvoti society. A complex skein of bonds based on kinship and marriage, as well as on economic and legal relationships, cross-cut political and cultural affiliations, and linked town to countryside. Above all, the interests and institutions of the master race welded white Umvoti together in almost unanimous antagonism to the ICU. One of the largest meetings ever held amongst Greytown whites was that in early March 1928 to launch the Anti-ICU: a succinctly titled society pledged to support white supremacy.[59]

Yet for all this appearance of a united white community, the great bulk of those charged for their involvement in the raids appear to have been poorer whites, partially or completely proletarianized.[60] Often they were stragglers at the hind end of large families, now either farming with their kin on the shares or occupying badly paid jobs in town. Many if not most of them lived on thornveld farms near the Mpanza valley, a hotbed of ICU activity. Here they were engaged either in pastoralism or in doomed attempts to participate in the wattle boom by planting these trees on totally unsuitable ground. A significant proportion of them were well known to the Standard Bank as 'weak names'; indeed, at least four had in the recent past been declared insolvent. Amongst them was Paul Havemann, who by this time was based on a Kranskop holding with the inauspicious name of Klipnek. Another raider who personified many of these trends was James Martens, who lived on a subsection of a farm adjoining that where Bambatha had lived. Like others in the 'Greytown mob' taken to court by the ICU, he had been successfully prosecuted for withholding wages. The poverty of such men was made abjectly clear during their trials: one-third of the Greytown whites fined five pounds each for the Kranskop raid had to pay in ten-shilling instalments. Small wonder that these raiders were violently opposed to the idea of Africans obtaining equal opportunities. As farmers whose only chance of survival was a rapid response to the sheep or wattle booms, many were understandably outraged when faced with refusals to work, refusals to quit, or demands for eight shillings a day. For these marginalized men, ICU-related resistance deeply threatened their class as well as their racial identities.[61]

The presence of this incipient and actual class differentiation amongst Umvoti whites explains more than the pattern of participation in the raids. It also helps to account for the ideology used to channel – and limit – the actions of poorer whites. To a large extent, those who organized the Anti-ICU meetings, as well as those who led the lynching and arson, were relatively well-off businessmen and farmers. Especially prominent amongst them were English South African Party men, enormously antagonistic to the Pact government. Although many of them were convinced that 'eight shillings a day' Walter Madeley was ultimately responsible for the strikes, they were also doubtless alarmed by their growing political alienation from white wage-earners, as well as from Afrikaner farmers sliding into penury.[62] Joined by local Nationalist Party leaders – who, as wealthy farmers, appear to have been equally uneasy about socialism – they drummed into their poorer compatriots that the ICU was 'the Communist part of the Labour Party backed up by Russia'.[63] By thus linking the hated ICU to the Labour Party and to socialism, dual objects were attained: rioters clashed with the Union as members of the white oligarchy, and the development of working-class consciousness amongst an objectively differentiated community was obstructed.

Of more immediate concern to social forces operating on a national scale was the need to inculcate the notion that whites could not take the law into their own hands. Institutions ranging from the press through to political parties and upper echelons of the state were all involved in this process. Apart from the ideological work which this entailed – such as the comparison of the 'Greytown lynch mob' and their Anti-ICU organization to the Ku Klux Klan – the ability of the repressive state apparatuses to protect private property was enhanced. Thus magistrates were informed by the Minister of Justice of the most appropriate legal tools to employ to secure evictions, while constables were sternly informed by the Chief of Police of the necessity of implementing ejectment orders. In this way, landlords' major grievances about state inaction vis-à-vis tenants resisting removal was partially removed.[64]

But the apparent success of the June 1928 evictions was due not only to the greater efficiency of the state, but also to the devastating drought. As stock died, homesteads went hungry and men streamed

off the land to seek work, tenants found it more difficult to resist the
more effective reprisals. Furthermore, the ICU was offering them
little or no support. Branch organizers were locked in conflict with
senior officials: apart from complaining that headquarters had bun-
gled the buying of land in Umvoti, local activists understandably felt
that their sacrifices during the raids far exceeded those of their
superiors. James Ngcobo's bravery had in fact won him grudging
admiration from the constables who informed him that the arrival of
the 'Greytown Commando' was imminent. He had calmly cleared
the Kranskop office of valuables, and waited there alone until the last
minute, declaring that 'if he was going to die, he preferred to die on
the premises'. Kadalie, by contrast, had left members to defend the
Pietermaritzburg Hall, as he scuttled away after the first police
warning. Not surprisingly, Umvoti organizers were therefore
antagonistic to senior officials, who refused to appear in the district,
yet ordered them to return to a place where the chances were high
that each would again become a 'pillar that was stripped . . . until he
remained a beam without bark'. Understandably too, when neither
regional activists nor Champion put in promised appearances at the
first ICU meeting held after the raids, the Greytown Branch
Executive passed a vote of no confidence in both Kadalie and
Champion.[65]

This distancing of local organizers from the leaders of both the
ICU and the ICU *yase* Natal did not, however, improve their
standing with landlords. Outwardly, the latter had largely conformed to the modes of containment now favoured by the state and the
NAU. They were promoting written contracts, pressing for tighter
control over the Union by magistrates, and advocating greater
adherence to 'the tribal system of governing the natives'. Yet
ongoing statements about defending their rights with rifles were by
no means empty threats. At the above-mentioned meeting in June
1928, Anti-ICU members ominously circled the office in their cars.
Only sixteen Africans braved entry, and after these faithful few had
discussed fund-raising for the erection of protective netting around
their building, James Martens addressed them, saying:

> he had given all ICU boys on his farm notice to quit, and if they
> had not left by Saturday he intended to burn their huts. This
> attitude, he explained, was one that all the farmers had decided to
> adopt towards the ICU natives.[66]

Even this did not completely cow Umvoti blacks. Three months
later, at least one thousand Africans attended the first and apparently
only Greytown meeting of the ICU *yase* Natal, called to discuss the
position of blacks on farms. Yet they could not have been much

impressed by assurances that 'if the Native Workers in Greytown obey and behave themselves like a people, the white masters will always listen to their grievances'. The consciousness of many Umvoti blacks had long transcended such beliefs, and from then on they appear to have decided to go it alone. The legacy of the Union was not completely eradicated; it reappeared not least in the 1930s in opposition to white churches by 'ICY (*sic*) agitators'. But a boycott of the municipal beer hall – in full swing in Greytown months before similar protests swept through Natal under Union auspices in 1929 – seems to have been organized entirely by local people, drawing on traditional ideas about how *utshwala* should be brewed. Similarly, the assaults on farmers, opposition to labour dues and even land takeovers during the next few years appear to have been spontaneous, endemic forms of resistance, bearing no trace of ICU organizational involvement or inspiration.[67]

While the Union was defeated in Umvoti and other farming districts partly due to heavy-handed repression, 'lynch law' was considerably less pronounced in the reserves. Here the absence of the powerful sanction of eviction was compounded by the invisibility of many ICU leaders. Thus in Pondoland, where typical 'derived' patterns of Union organization and ideology were submerged beneath popular spontaneity and traditionalist folklore, officialdom was often confounded. If it was relatively easy to identify activists who harangued village gatherings or petitioned magistrates, it was comparatively hard to do so when their tactics were determined by the belief that whites were enemies who would soon be incinerated. If it was feasible to eject labour tenants who refused to work, it was more problematic to prevent traditionalists from slaughtering their own pigs. And if it was possible to harness the courts to instil the idea of private property, it was impossible to imprison the Mpondo who merely dreamed of the day when American blacks would drop balls of fire and bring freedom. Whites could in fact do little but wait, nervously speculating how soon culturally expressed violence against oppression would explode into armed struggle to attain a new heaven and a new earth.

7. PIGS, AMERICANS AND THE MILLENNIUM:
The ICU in the Transkeian Territories, 1927–1932

Hope, so the old adage runs, springs eternal in the human breast. Hope for an apocalyptic transformation of the existing world into a perfect one is rather more restricted. Typically, movements inspired by such longings arise amongst the poor and oppressed faced with abrupt and disastrous changes in their traditional ways of life. Usually, they occur amongst those who are inexperienced in struggle, or who cannot rely on their own resources in setting a disordered world to rights. Consequently, as a millenarian movement coalesces around a belief in total, imminent salvation, its followers do not normally anticipate long and bitter conflicts to achieve their utopia. Instead, they perceive 'a bad world which must soon end, to be followed by the Day of Change which would initiate the good world, where those who had been at the bottom would be at the top'. And they expect the metamorphosis

> to make itself, by divine revelation, by an announcement from on high, by a miracle – they expect it to happen somehow. The part of the people before the change is to gather together, to prepare itself, to watch the signs of coming doom, to listen to the prophets who predict the coming of the great day, and perhaps to undertake certain ritual measures against the moment of decision and change.[1]

Although millenarian movements have frequently been associated with the disruptions caused by capitalist penetration and the imposition of colonial rule, these upheavals were slow to manifest themselves in Pondoland. 'Why should we work?', asked Mpondo peasants at the turn of the twentieth century, a scant half-dozen years after their territory had been annexed. 'Is not the country ours, and have we not lots of land and many women and children to cultivate it? We prefer to remain as we are.'[2] In comparison to most other reserves, peasant production peaked late; labour dribbled out very slowly, and large-scale rural decline was evident only in the 1930s.

Culturally too, the Mpondo were a byword for conservatism, and by this time less than 5 per cent of the population were Christians. As one leading segregationist ideologue expressed it, 'in Pondoland the disintegration of native life is by no means so alarming as in other parts of South Africa.'[3]

Nonetheless, the pace of transformation was accelerating in the 1920s. Shortage of arable plots was becoming apparent. At the end of the decade the Chief Magistrate of the Territories commented with surprise that in some districts, 'even in Pondoland', 'fresh lands cannot be found'. Although cattle numbers continued to grow through the twenties, they did so at a declining rate which by the early 1930s had become negative. Migrancy was rapidly increasing. In 1926 it was estimated that, just as in the reserves as a whole, at least half the men over eighteen would be working away from home during the course of the year. Cultural innovation too was evident, not least in the growth of 'numberless Native sects and free-lance "preachers"'. Finally, the gap between commoners and black rulers was widening. Although popular demands had previously been voiced largely through chiefs, the ICU represented the first mass movement where members of the new elite articulated the aspirations of ordinary Mpondo people.[4]

They did so in a highly unusual way. To a greater extent than in most other reserves in South Africa, the ICU here was 'captured' by its constituency. Apparently, the 'inherent' ideas of traditionalist cultivators bulked larger in the Union's message than the more typical nationalist notions of educated men.[5] More accurately: at the heart of the ICU's tidings lay not age-old, parochial custom, but a proto-nationalist, 'derived' belief that had already been absorbed into popular consciousness. As 'common-sense' was Garveyized and Garveyism was domesticated during the 1920s, so traditionalists and literate men could unite around a stirring idea with cross-class appeal: *'Ama Melika ayeza'* – the Americans are coming.

Ama Melika Ayeza

Partly because Afro-Americans appeared further advanced in their struggle against racial oppression, the black middle strata in South Africa had long been extraordinarily receptive to their influence. After the First World War, the prestige of these heroes was boosted, as indebted European powers ceded to America economic and military dominance. In the African hinterlands of imperialism, the changing of the guard was readily translated into enhanced powers for Afro-Americans. This trend was energetically encouraged by the

Garveyist movement, with its widely advertized shipping line, its plans for a flying squadron, and its promises to free Africa of colonial masters. In 1920, even the staid Natal Native Congress had succumbed to the fashion of producing black 'American' Garveyists on political platforms. Declaring in Durban that 'he was one of the Negro organizers who had been sent to South Africa on behalf of the Negroes', one speaker reaffirmed to his thousand-strong audience that Africa would be liberated, and that Americans had their own fleets and ammunition.[6]

Such widespread and unequivocal statements had a powerful hold on the imagination of ordinary blacks. Five days after the 1921 massacre of the Israelites at Bulhoek – whose intransigence was partly inspired by hope of American military aid – the West African James Aggrey spoke in Umtata to a gathering of 1,500 men. Although one of his prime aims was to counter the influence of Garveyism, he was ironically perceived by many eager Transkeians as

> the herald of an invading band of Negroes – they thought all Americans were Negroes – who would drive the whites of South Africa into the sea. Men came to the meeting in Umtata on horseback with empty sacks for saddle-cloths. He will order the merchants to sell their goods cheaply – he may even compel them to give their goods away for nothing! . . . The empty grain bags under the saddles were to carry away these easily gotten possessions.

It was not only commoners who held such expectations but also a petty chief. He sullenly stated that Aggrey had not said what was anticipated, namely, 'The American Government'.[7]

Despite Aggrey, the insidious diffusion of the hope of '*Ama Melika ayeza*' continued. It was spread partly by reports of Garveyist activities in the press, especially those in the coveted newspaper of the American-based Universal Negro Improvement Association. Although this was probably most widely read by dissident members of the middle strata, it also reached literate mine workers as well as blacks in rural Natal and Pondoland. Separatist churches too helped infuse popular consciousness with the American dream – and some were harbingers of Transkeian millenarian movements. In 1925, an Ethiopian deacon in the Pondoland district of Bizana was urging blacks not to pay taxes,

> as all white people are to be turned away from this Country by the american negroes. Thats why they see flying machines flies up and down it is because these machines are carrying Gold and Silver and all British treasures away from this Country.[8]

Above all, however, the cry '*Ama Melika ayeza*' was spread by word of mouth down a human chain which extended far beyond South

African borders, and which encompassed the length and breadth of this southernmost country in Africa. Thus it was not only a Transkeian mine clerk member of the ICU who 'waited everyday for those Americans to come to free South Africa'. The same dream animated Africans ranging from Cape teachers to Ciskeian prisoners, and from Durban dock workers to labour tenants in the eastern Transvaal. Their common vision contained the political judgement that violence was necessary for liberation, and that help would come from the capitalist future rather than the precolonial past. Thus the deliverers were westernized blacks, not ancestors; their weapons were the latest in military technology, not assegais; and their material wealth lay in the white man's goods, not cattle. As was stated in 1927 by the principal of a Pondoland teacher-training college, Emfundisweni:

> unsophisticated natives in these parts . . . regard the voice of America as that of a mighty race of black people overseas, dreaded by all European nations . . . [They] manufacture for their own purposes engines, locomotives, ships, motor cars, aeroplanes, and mighty weapons of war . . . today the word America (*iMelika*) is a household word symbolic of nothing else but Bantu National freedom and liberty.[9]

Fig. 8.   Map of the Transkeian Territories

By this time, a Garveyist, Wellington Buthelezi, had already been organizing around these beliefs in the Transkeian Territories. During 1925 and 1926, when he operated mainly in East Griqualand, he gave an intellectual gloss to the myth of American liberators by neatly twisting the War Debt quarrel between imperialist powers. He claimed that King George had promised Africa to American Negroes in return for their war service, but that Hertzog was refusing to hand over the country. Afro-Americans were therefore coming in ships and planes to liberate South Africa, and would destroy in the process all whites and non-Wellingtonites. As a modernized herbalist – with a battery to give patients electric shocks – he also capitalized on his proven talents as a magician. He acquired a crystal into which his followers would gaze, whereupon 'they would see numbers of aeroplanes and motor cars filled with negro troops sailing in the sky, awaiting the call to land'.[10]

It was aeroplanes that most enthralled audiences in these inland regions. Apart from being sufficiently novel to attract crowds of blacks and whites whenever they landed in the Transkei, they occupied a special place in Africans' conceptions of their oppressors. While some believed aircraft were the means whereby whites communicated with God, many others saw them as the supreme symbol of settlers' military dominance. ICU organizers themselves, well aware of the aerial bombings used to crush both black and white resistance in the early 1920s, repeatedly focused on these instruments of terror. As Kadalie once expressed it, 'The way to liberty passes through Gaol, thorns, aeroplanes, big flying machines and Great Government authorities.' Small wonder that there was enormous appeal in the idea of having 'big flying machines' filled with black deliverers.[11]

Especially before Buthelezi was deported from the Transkei in March 1927, his movement's stark Africanism had a distinct bias towards a particular social stratum. The brave new world had sharp modern contours: Africans would fill positions ranging from traders and factory owners to lawyers and policemen, and would receive goods such as wagons, houses and free clothing. In the meantime, Wellingtonites were told to focus on combating white cultural domination, by detaching Africans from the religion and education of their oppressors and incorporating them into Ethiopian churches and 'American' schools. Understandably, the support-base for such a movement was primarily disaffected 'school people'. Most of Wellington's thousands of adherents were semi-educated Christians, increasingly unable either to cling to the margins of rural commodity producers, or to clamber into the ranks of the petty bourgeoisie. As an East Griqualand policeman stated, 'it is not the uncivilized native who is keen on joining this organization but the half educated dressed native'. In most regions, supporters were in fact drawn predominantly from Hlubi and Mfengu communities, long in the vanguard of black struggles to gain economic and cultural niches in a modern world.[12]

Yet there were strange contradictions amongst *Ama Melika* believers in the Transkei in the later 1920s. In Pondoland, those who longed for the Americans to arrive were drawn from the most traditionalist locations, and were often led by illiterate Mpondo men. Furthermore, when pig-killing became the mark of a true convert in 1927, the slaughter of swine was concentrated in Pondoland and southern Natal. Much of this region was not directly penetrated by the Wellingtonites, and even the existence of Buthelezi was unknown to most people in eastern Pondoland. Instead, they called their millennial, hog-killing movement by the name of the ICU. This was no coincidence: activists here might have abandoned the orthodox ideology of their organization, but not the very name of the Union that employed them.[13]

The ICU in Pondoland

Ideas associated with the ICU were constantly percolating back to Pondoland through the migrant labour system. Although the Union's formal presence was limited on the mines where most Mpondo men worked, some quickly learnt that this was an attractive body to join. One Sunday in 1927, the superintendent of a Witwatersrand location was horrified to find his domain invaded by about two thousand (mainly Mpondo) miners, who had come to enrol in the Union and attend its meeting. Hastily, he disillusioned them of the belief that red tickets conferred the right to enter the township freely. He did not, however, realize that even more subversive popular ideas were making their presence felt in capital's heartland. Thus one Mpondo traditionalist from Lusikisiki bought a ticket on the mines from ICU activists who 'said that the Americans were coming and the people working on the mines were going to be released from labour'.[14]

In Natal, too, Mpondo migrants could discover fairly easily that the ICU was linked to Americans and apocalypses. While few on the wattle plantations and sugar fields appear to have supported the Union, it was difficult for blacks to avoid the quasi-Garveyist ideas circulating in this province when organization was at its peak. Some accredited officials were being hailed as American blacks come to deliver Africans from slavery. Others were selling cards to great throngs of people who believed the arrival of American angels was imminent – or who thought the 'red ticket of promise' was a panacea for all ills, including leprosy. Indeed, in a region where self-appointed activists flourished, 'the raw, untutored Zulu' was being told in 1927

> that a new and powerful race of people is to come shortly out of the sea, and an end will then be made of all tyranny and wrong. Those possessing the red ticket will be safe from all violence, while those who have it not will be lost. [15]

More orthodox ideas about the Union were already being disseminated in Pondoland by struggling members of the middle strata. The ICU 'came by papers here, by correspondents', claimed James Mvunelo, who augmented a meagre salary as head of a Lusikisiki school by distributing *The Workers' Herald* for Johannesburg officials. However, literature alone was clearly unsatisfactory for many educated blacks, and from 1926 letters began to pour into head office demanding the Union's presence in Pondoland. One missive came from the executive of a self-styled 'civilized' Mpondo association based at Emfundisweni. Referring to their own network of branches throughout Pondoland, the authors pleaded for the ICU to extend beyond workers, and to mobilize the entire community in rural backwaters. They detailed the injustices of the court system, where the poor lost cases about rape because they were unable to afford lawyers. They denounced the spread of commercialism and the abrogation of custom. Not only were women arrested for chopping down trees for firewood, but homesteads also had to pay money for an arable plot, cash for a house site, and on top of that money for tax. 'We call upon you, Kadalie', they cried, 'to be near us and to change these commercial laws to customary laws.' Their letter could hardly have stated more clearly their opposition to transformations wrought in political, economic and judicial spheres by incorporation into a capitalist and colonial world. While the authors were based at a college which symbolized the cultural forces undermining traditionalist society, they clearly shared with the broader community antagonism to the commoditization of social relations in ways which utterly disrupted relations between men, women, justice and nature. [16]

They also shared bitterness over the new taxes. In 1925, in an effort to foster secondary industrialization, the price of cotton blankets rose some 300 per cent as a result of a dramatic increase in customs duties. Especially amongst poorer groups, blankets were an almost indispensable item of everyday clothing, and the price increase allegedly thrust more men into migrancy. Furthermore, as

Umvoti blacks knew full well, direct taxation soared from mid-1926 as the segregationist principle that blacks should finance their own 'development' was applied countrywide. Instead of 14s. 6d. a year, homestead heads with one wife had to pay 30s. Instead of being absolutely free of tax obligations, young men not yet heads of families had to pay 20s. poll tax. And instead of collecting about seven thousand pounds per annum in tax, the Bizana magistrate estimated he would accumulate sixteen thousand pounds in 1926–7. Plunder of the peasantry on this scale was both economically crippling and morally outrageous. The poll tax alone was the equivalent of take-home pay for a month's work on the cane fields, and the average traditionalist household in a western Pondoland district only spent around three to four pounds in cash a year. Doubtless, too, the Mpondo found this tax on male heads as extraordinary as did the Zulu, amongst whom it passed into the proverb – 'It is incomprehensible, it is the poll tax'.[17]

The change in the tax structure was also linked to the imposition of the long-rejected 'Bunga' system of indirect rule on eastern Pondoland. By the mid-1920s, these ineffective advisory bodies had spread to all other Transkeian regions, and were widely disliked by ordinary blacks. For one thing, the councils were regarded as 'a taxing machine from which they consider they do not derive sufficient benefit'. For another, they administered the hated stock-dipping and agricultural programmes – projects which in eastern Pondoland had already aroused suspicion of collaboration between the paramount and whites to the detriment of rank-and-file Mpondo peasants. Finally, there was deep-rooted opposition to them as puppet political bodies. Undoubtedly this generalized antagonism underlay the concerted efforts of the eastern Mpondo elite to obtain less white control and greater popular participation in their councils. But having been compromised by their desire to exercise more influence over the spending of the greatly increased taxes, they found their demands and deputations ignored. In July 1927, despite a telegram expressing 'hottest possible protest', the Bunga system was unilaterally imposed. In the short term, the boorishness with which it was introduced angered the very groups it was meant to placate, and white traders commented anxiously on the sullen suspicion with which many blacks regarded these new councils.[18]

Economic conditions were, however, far more important in fuelling discontent amongst commoners. The preceding year's drought had necessitated large imports of maize, and while some doubtless coped by falling further into debt, there were widespread shortages of food in eastern Pondoland by early 1927. The mood of deep unease was well captured in a July letter to a Johannesburg newspaper from a Bizana teacher, W. Damoyi:

A pall of ignorance hangs over our heads here in Pondoland, that is why you hear nothing from us when we die. It is unbelievably hot, the last time we had rain was in April. The cattle are suffering, we don't know what is wrong. When harvest time comes there are places where nothing is reaped because of this drought. Illness is also taking its toll.

If anything, the plight of most homesteads worsened over the next few months. Ploughing usually began after the September rains on the coast, and around November inland, and migrants often made a point of returning for this season. But a semi-circular belt stretching from coastal Pondoland through southern Natal to East Griqualand experienced an exceptionally hot, dry spring and summer. As if fears of having to buy grain for the second year running were not enough, the new taxes had to be paid by the end of September. Although some sold their cattle to obtain cash, low prices and traders' disinterest inhibited this response. Sheep were not shorn until later in spring, and many stores gave 'good fors' rather than money for grain. As a Lusikisiki headman tartly told the magistrate in early October when reprimanded for failing to report ICU activities: 'Money is scarce. Shops don't buy our stock or goods. We ask that the issue of writs [for taxes] be delayed.'[19]

It was thus an abnormally disturbed region – pulsating with economic distress, political chagrin and ideological turbulence – that the ICU entered in mid-1927. By September, when East Griqualand organization was already under way, orthodox Union tactics were making their mark in Pondoland, with the Port St. Johns Branch Secretary demanding workmen's compensation from local firms. A month later, Champion was trying to reopen the Flagstaff office, the collapse of which was probably related to state and settler attempts to stamp out ICU activities in this reservoir of mine labour. He was also responding to importunate demands for the Union's presence by sending Natal organizers as emissaries to Pondoland and East Griqualand. Between 1927 and 1928, one such accredited official 'marshalled 5,000 men in Pondoland for the ICU cause'.[20]

To accomplish this feat through normal ICU methods of mobilization, however, was not easy. As 'aliens' from Natal, leaders could, if discovered, be forced to leave the Transkei. One such victim was Enoch Mdletye, a Transkeian teacher who worked as a District Secretary in Natal during 1927. But in October of that year, his career as Assistant Branch Secretary in an East Griqualand village abruptly ended before the doors of the office were opened. On the grounds that he no longer paid tax in the Territories, he was told he had abrogated automatic rights of entry to the Transkei. Given thirty hours to leave, and rearrested and deported when he tried to return after paying his tax, Mdletye was understandably more cautious when sent to Bizana as an ICU official. During 1928–9 when he proselytized there about the coming of Americans, he also firmly staked out his claim to Transkeian rights by settling in a location with his family.[21]

Like Mdletye, some ICU leaders caught up in the millennial fervour were experienced officials, but many more appear to have been appointed on the shop-steward system so favoured in Natal. Those attracted to and accepted for these jobs were mainly literate, Zulu-speaking men. As such, they were able to hide themelves from the eyes of white officials by merging with the ongoing influx into Pondoland of 'progressive' Nguni-speaking immigrants from more congested regions, including southern Natal. Many settled in tents or applied to headmen for sites, which were generally used as ICU offices. Since the various shop-stewards were often completely independent of one another, these Union 'branches' could be dotted around the various locations in a district. Furthermore, as mere shop-stewards, these men were under few organizational constraints as they rode the currents of rural thinking, sometimes making a considerable profit by quadrupling the prices of the batches of tickets they had been given to sell. Such unorthodox approaches to mass mobilization were not always appreciated by senior officials. In August 1927, the Transkeian Provincial Secretary complained of extravagant language by 'ill-formed Branches, whose Officers are not well versed with our Objects'.[22]

However, ICU agents from Natal had much greater credibility within their constituencies. Their literacy alone was of central importance, and they were also remembered as 'respectable' men who 'did not fear whites'. These were no small advantages in a society where the place of diviners as innovators was being ceded to blacks with status in the white man's terms. They were also Zulu-speakers, and as such associated with a polity which had inflicted military defeat on the Mpondo in the past, and with a region where the flourishing of the ICU again demonstrated pre-eminence. Moreover, many were probably much more familiar with the Union's version of Garveyist ideas than were Mpondo migrants to Natal. Finally, most were strangers, operating in a world permeated with beliefs about the superiority of foreigners in controlling supernatural forces, and infused with hopes for the coming of alien Americans.[23]

They were not, however, too strange. For one thing, their temporary settlement in Pondoland locations helped to deflect the distrust that peasants often project onto those who do not share their lives. For another, they frequently headed a network of local agents, many of whom were ordinary illiterate men, acting as runners issuing tickets and as speakers at meetings.[24] Even more significantly, ICU agents generally took cognisance of the fact that the chieftaincy was still a major focus for commoners, and a key institution in the creation of a community out of scattered homesteads.

They achieved considerable success in wooing these representatives of the older political elite. Bertie Mgetyana, then an illiterate youth in a poor traditionalist family locked into migrancy, recalled that numerous commoners in Bizana first heard of the ICU when they were called to their respective 'great places' and told: 'there are people who are coming who are going to preach about the ICU. We must go and listen to their preachings.' Apart from preparing the way for the Union, numerous headmen and chiefs became ICU members, and allowed meetings to be held at their 'great places'. While the paths of chiefs and commoners were beginning to diverge, and while this in itself conditioned the rise of the ICU, it was still possible for outgoing and incoming political leaders to unite in articulating popular opinion.[25]

In cultural terms, this fusion of the old with the new in Union organization was personified by Reverend Filbert Mdodana. Born in Zululand, Mdodana had been trained in America as a Baptist minister, but later seceded from the mission body to form his own Regular Christian Baptist Church. By 1927, he was an imposing middle-aged herbalist-cum-minister, whose religious circuit stretched from Harding in Natal to Fingoland, and included congregations in Bizana, Lusikisiki, Flagstaff and East Griqualand. His American-influenced pentecostal church attracted considerable interest, because 'he was the first person who shouted in the river, conducting a service in the river'. This ritualistic casting out of evil in preparation for salvation also involved the keeping of certain taboos: in Harding, Mdodana's adherents refused to eat pork. Sub-preachers may well have introduced this innovation, since they generally had some latitude in deciding how best to incorporate local beliefs. Another sub-minister was Lenze Nomsuka, who proselytized at chief Nobulongwe's 'great place' in Flagstaff. Having been educated to Standard Five, Nomsuka was greatly trusted by the chief, partly because he was one of the few literate men available.[26]

By contrast, Mdodana's good relationships with Mpondo ruling authorities rested on his medical and magical skills. In general, herbalists' power over life and death accorded them high social status in a society largely lacking in alternative medical treatment. In particular, Mdodana's miraculous cures evoked profound admiration from both headmen and commoners. According to Lenze Nom-suka's nephew, 'whenever there was something wrong, they used to say, go to Reverend Mdodana, he will just lay on hands and prepare medicine and that person would be cured'. His *imithi* were often magical charms: he even provided roots which, when chewed, guaranteed invisibility. Furthermore, he had specialized in an arena that was a focus of ritual amongst the Mpondo. Each spring, many peasants would call on the services of a lightning doctor to protect their homesteads during Pondoland's vicious electric storms. With his roots and charmed wooden pegs, Mdodana was celebrated for his skills in warding off lightning.[27]

This, then, was an influential ICU organizer in eastern Pondoland: both an American-trained separatist minister familiar with apocalyptic Biblical prophecies, and an itinerant herbalist catering for the magico-medical needs of the traditionalist Mpondo. He was a charismatic leader whose very past enabled him to win acceptance for new ways of relating to heavenly powers, and new means of obtaining protection from evil. These novel solutions were, however, rooted in the world of Mpondo folklore, and took full account of that fact that ideas about bewitchment and sorcery 'permeate[d] the whole of life'.[28]

Lightning, Pigs and Witchcraft

Many if not most ICU organizers believed in the existence of witches (who possessed mystical familiars through which they damaged life or property), as well as in sorcerers (who used real medicines to do the same). Numerous leaders further resembled the rural poor in accepting that supernatural powers could be harnessed. As an ex-East London Branch Secretary impatiently explained to a white anthropologist, '*Impundulu*' – the lightning bird – 'is a thing which exists . . . It has been trapped by herbalists, with medicines.' It could not only be ensnared: many credited that it could also be used to combat white military technology. In the volatile days following the Bloemfontein riots of 1925, Simon Elias more than once threatened that, 'if we strike and the white people shoot us, we will go to our forefathers' graves and throw up ground which will make the lightning come and kill the white people'.[29]

Amongst Zulu-speakers, there had evolved an elaborate magico-religious system surrounding lightning. The reddish lightning bird – sometimes perceived as a ball of fire – was held to have been sent to strike homes by the Lord-of-the-Sky, by witches, or by lightning doctors themselves. As this dazzling force descended, it was thought to be attracted to all white objects. Hence it was necessary to chase away or conceal all white animals during electric storms. It was also essential to use anti-lightning charms, the main components of which were chosen for their similarity to the lightning birds. In the 1920s, key ingredients were red vegetable or mineral substances. Significantly, pig fat played no role whatsoever in these protective medicines. Indeed, it was almost certainly taboo, being thought so dangerous that it overpowered any other nostrum.[30]

Amongst the southern Nguni, by contrast, lard was often the poor person's amulet. In Pondoland, the lightning doctor frequently asked his clients to slaughter a hog, and incorporated its fat into his charms. Traditionalists who could not afford medicines would also use pig fat to heal incisions and to guard against *ukuthakatha* (witchcraft and sorcery). Since it was common Mpondo belief that it was 'that European, the Government, who *ukuthakatha*',[31] Bizana peasants prudently smeared their insteps with lard prior to appearances before the magistrate.[32]

The assumed potency of pig fat was linked to its origins as the offal of animals closely associated with pollution and death.[33] Hogs were natural vehicles for beliefs about degradation and decay. As creatures unsuited to hot, dry climates, they often wallowed in their own excrement to keep damp. As omniverous scavengers, they lived largely on natural and bodily waste, which meant their flesh was composed mainly of oily fat. Thanks to their predilection for faeces, the vast majority of Transkeian pigs in the 1920s were vectors of tapeworm, which gave hogs measles and pork-eaters parasitic diseases. As if this were not enough to induce the status of being despised animals in all Nguni societies, hogs shared with hens the dubious distinction of being domestic animals introduced to South Africa by whites.[34]

Various taboos reflected and reinforced the unease with which pigs were regarded. Together with hens, they were the only edible creatures allocated to the care of Mpondo women. In the sphere of consumption, too, pigs were allocated an inferior place. Although most Transkeians ate pork by the 1920s, it was believed to infect Mpondo people temporarily with ritual impurity. Most Zulu-speakers spurned the 'smelly' flesh of this animal, and prohibitions were even stronger amongst social groups already obsessed with purification and danger. Thus Zulu Zionists, supported by Biblical precedent in the conviction that hogs conveyed pollution and demons, had a tendency to predict cataclysmic disaster for sinful pork-eaters and pig-owners.[35]

So too, on occasion, did other prophets. Between the 1880s and 1910s – arguably the period of most dramatic change in southern Africa – there occurred at least six outbreaks of hog-slaughtering in Pondoland and Natal. Almost invariably, these were associated with disruption of the natural or social order by alien forces potentially bearing death in their wake. Some killings were informed by beliefs that hogs could transmit mortal disease to people or animals. But since the great majority of deaths were in any event attributed to witchcraft or sorcery, other eruptions of hog-slaughtering were explicitly inspired by fears that pigs were bewitching people. In times of upheaval, despised, wandering creatures living off the most powerful ingredients for sorcery were almost overdetermined as vectors of *ukuthakatha*.[36]

During Bambatha's rebellion, for instance, a wave of swine-slaughtering swept through western Pondoland, inspired by the conviction that a leading Zulu figure in the revolt had bewitched a hog. This white boar would fly down the coast 'uttering cries, to which if any domestic pigs responded the inhabitants of the kraal would all fall down dead, thus . . . exterminat[ing] all not in sympathy with the rebellion'. Amongst the northern Nguni, the stock-killing associated with this revolt was also linked to the politicization of magic. Dinizulu, who as the Zulu monarch was reputedly able to control natural forces, was thought to have ordered Africans to destroy all pigs, white fowl, white goats and all tools made by settlers. Those who complied had little difficulty in understanding that objects marked for destruction by lightning were being extended from white animals to whites themselves, as well as to the goods they had introduced. In Natal, the usual explanation for obeying Dinizulu's command was that those who refused would be killed by lightning. In Zululand, it was argued that lightning was attracted to pigs and lard, and that provided blacks rid themselves of these items, only tax-collectors would be struck.[37]

Twenty years later, the ICU message to Mpondo peasants bore a striking resemblance to these rumours circulating in Zululand. This was not immediately apparent: numerous reasons could be adduced for once again displacing tensions onto hogs in a time of distress. Thus pigs' responsibility for disease was one explanation given by an ICU agent based close to the Natal border of East Griqualand, where the first outbreak of slaughtering occurred in 1927. In August that same year, hog-killing swept through a Wellingtonite stronghold deeper in the heart of East Griqualand. The magistrate had done no more than order a census of pigs – but this helped fuel a belief that Wellington was sending an enormous hog to threaten ordinary pigs and their owners. Finally, in the same month, ICU activists in Flagstaff were ordering the destruction of pigs, and declaring that 'disobedience of this order will bring its punishment when the fleet of air ships from America arrives to drive the white man into the sea'.[38]

But from then on, as homesteads scrabbled for cash to meet taxes, and employed men like Mdodana to protect themselves against lightning, the messages of various prophets began to cohere. Working amongst a much less sophisticated constituency than Wellington, with his cars and troops, ICU shop-stewards linked older technologies to the new by politicizing the powers of the lightning bird. Yet this ambivalent heavenly force was regarded as dangerous, even when harnessed by airborne Americans for social good. Predictably, in defining the destructiveness of their extraordinarily powerful lightning bird, Zulu-speaking ICU organizers operated within the logic of 'inherent' ideas in Natal. Thus their balls of fire were attracted to white stock, and if blacks wished to escape being burnt to death like settlers, they had to kill their white animals.[39] Moreover, just like the lightning supposedly commanded by Dinizulu in Zululand in 1905, the ICU's heavenly flames sought out not only hogs but also lard.

Significantly, then, it was not just traditional scapegoats that had to be destroyed: it was also traditional charms. Indeed, it was precisely because pigs were fatty that they had to be eliminated. In Mount Ayliff, an East Griqualand village close to Pondoland, the magistrate announced in September that ICU agents in his and adjacent districts were urging blacks to 'kill their pigs, otherwise these will be struck by something from above, which will convert the fat into paraffin and then burn the owners and their huts'. The following month, Union activists were causing considerable turmoil in Lusikisiki. Alexander Soji, who was then a forest guard, recalled that the ICU 'sent people to Pondoland to say that a big war was coming . . . they must kill their pigs for everything would get burnt by the Americans and the pigs' fat would make all the huts burn down.' Or as James Mvunelo firmly stated,

> when the Americans came, all the people who had pigs would be destroyed by the fat of pigs. Fire would break out and then the whole vicinity would be destroyed. That's why pigs had to be got rid of. Because of their fat.

Thus, apparently for the first time in the history of swine-slaughter in southern Nguni regions, lard had to be destroyed as well.[40]

There was, of course, an inherent appeal in the notion that blanket-bombing with sheets of flame would ignite fatty animals. Moreover, lard was already connected to fire because it was used to make candles, while the combustible properties of paraffin were only too well known. Leonard Mdingi, then a child in a poor traditionalist family, remembered having to stop using paraffin and start buying manufactured candles during the time of the ICU. Certainly the dominant articulated rationale behind ordering and accepting the destruction of lard was its association with inflammability.[41]

Yet symbolic acts often have underlying meanings – and one strand feeding into the ICU's taboo appears to have been the role of pig fat in combating lightning in Pondoland. Threatened with fire from the sky dropped by American magicians, the natural response of many poor Mpondo peasants was to rush to lard for protection. Not only was this ineffective in the eyes of Zulu-speaking organizers, but it also undermined their efforts to tout tickets as charms. As has happened worldwide, a movement positing new ways of responding to danger made a swingeing attack on traditional solutions.[42] Modern medicine-men were replacing the old, and the changing of the guard simultaneously required that existing talismans be brought into discredit.

But they were medicine-men in more senses than one, since lard was also linked to witchcraft. Furthermore, informants recalled being told that 'this aeroplane could not fly where there were pigs or their fat', and that the Americans had said, 'we won't work well if the lard is there'. According to Mdingi, the Americans were going to help the Mpondo 'regain their freedom . . . by magic, not by fighting. And that is why pigs had to be destroyed.'[43] Even more pertinently, ICU leaders and their supporters took for granted the existence of intimate linkages between wizardry, settlers and swine. Whites, after all, would be expected to combat Americans waging war with their own witchcraft. Pigs were notorious vectors of bewitchment amongst the Mpondo, while their fat was regarded as perilously potent by most Zulu-speakers. Highly schematically: the ICU message and its acceptance appear to have been structured by beliefs that hogs and lard could be used by white witches at war to render the magic of American liberators ineffective. As such, pigs and their fat had to be eliminated, so that black Americans could confront white South Africans on terms which allowed their planes to fly, their flames to fall, and the Mpondo to regain their freedom.

Millenarianism in Eastern Pondoland and Southern Natal

By mid-spring, 'Americans' exhorting hog-slaughter to escape destruction by lightning were operating far beyond the confines of recognized movements, and pig-killing was reported from almost every district in the Transkeian Territories. Although there are hints that the ICU had more than a hand in this in several districts, its activities in late 1927 were concentrated in eastern Pondoland. By

November, the tidings had also spread to adjacent Natal locations occupied by the Amaci chiefdom of Mpondo origin. Here disgruntled Union leaders, ejected from their recently opened Harding office, gave further substance to the rumours by announcing that the catclysm would occur on Christmas Day. (The date was a favourite one for apocalyptic liberation: it was associated with the return of migrant men and the leanest period of the agricultural year, as well as with carousing, off-guard whites.) On 25 December, they declared, either fire from heaven or lightning would kill all whites, all blacks without ICU tickets, and all Africans who had not destroyed pigs, lard and white fowl. Moreover, 'shortly an Aeroplane would appear and as soon as it did it would become necessary for all natives to stand with their ICU tickets in their hands'.[44]

As summer set in, Mdodana became suspected of being the prime agent behind these rumours; he was also receiving letters in Bizana addressed to him as the ICU Branch Secretary. By this time, too, he had been barred from Flagstaff, where his sub-minister Lenze Nomsuka had turned chief Nobulongwe's 'great place' into a '*Sisiyu*' recruitment centre. In mid–December, Mdodana and Nomsuka fetched membership cards from Durban and returned to their base at a Bizana homestead to hold a meeting. Preaching a message almost identical to that propagated in Harding, they enrolled two hundred men and women drawn from all over eastern Pondoland and East Griqualand. Presumably, too, they were partially responsible for the eighty pounds or so deposited in the Durban ICU office from Pondoland during the latter half of 1927.[45]

By this stage, there was considerable uniformity in the Union's millennial tidings. As a white missionary expressed it, many Mpondo people believed

> that flocks of aeroplanes will come over from America, destroying all white people. They will fly low over the country, and native kraals where ICU tickets were not exhibited by the people will be blotted out by fire from heaven . . . Numbers of pigs and white fowls have been killed by order of the ICU people.

He failed to mention that those who displayed their red tickets to the planes thought they would be flown away to a country purged of all evil. 'Even children would just wave this card to the aeroplane and be picked up . . . All suffering would come to an end', recalled Bertie Mgetyana. An uneducated Mpondo man then working in Harding was horrified when asked if he wouldn't be burnt if he stood next to someone who had no ticket. 'No! No! I would be protected by my ticket. I would simply show the red side of it. I would fly away on the aeroplane . . . to that country. The stubborn ones would be burnt to death.' The dominant belief was that the whole country, together with whites and faithless blacks, would be incinerated, while ticket-holders would fly away to a new land 'where they would be governed well' and 'the ICU would inherit the earth'. But the contours of the new world were left extremely vague. Unlike many Wellingtonites, the rural Mpondo poor did not long for white capitalism to be refashioned in black. They completely rejected the existing order; they yearned for the destruction of the evil ones; and they infused their dreams of a new heaven and earth with a medley of incoherent hopes.[46]

Yet as the very appearance of Americans and plane tickets suggests, there were elements of the ICU's message which were rooted in a capitalist society. Although more orthodox 'derived' ideas were often swamped in the millennial fervour, activists did articulate opposition to institutions locking blacks into badly-paid jobs, and into a commoditized society on unfavourable terms. Some emphasized the ICU's wage demand of eight shillings a day. (Even in the largest commercial centre of the region, Port St. Johns, this was rapidly transformed into the belief that labourers would inst-antaneously obtain this wage once all pigs and white cattle were destroyed.) Others attacked storekeepers, who as recruiters and creditors entrenched dependence on migrant labour, and as buyers and sellers had tilted the terms of trade against the Mpondo. Around Lusikisiki, blacks were told to disregard debts to traders because the American invasion was imminent, while in Bizana they were informed that all stores would be replaced by 'new shops of the good ICU'.[47]

Uneducated Africans were also presented with the middle strata's cultural escape routes from an oppressive society. Since many of Mdodana's sub-ministers were transformed into ICU agents, the influences of separatist religion were soon apparent. According to Leonard Mdingi, Mdodana reinforced the appeal of his Baptist sect in Bizana by claiming that American liberators would applaud those who joined his church. Mdingi also recalled organizers like Mdletye addressing meetings 'sort of dressed like Zions', in long white gowns. Mdodana himself went even further along the road of institutionalizing the links between the Union and world-views alternative to those of missionaries. In 1928, an African Industrial and Commercial Academy was advertized in Bizana, to be run by 'Rev. Mdodana, MA, BD, DD'.[48]

If a Lusikisiki minister thus had some justification for complaining that the ICU had 'damaged most of our schools and churches', offficialdom had reason for concern about threats posed to white political rule. In addition to promising that the ICU would change legislation so that Africans were no longer oppressed, activists proffered help to those who fell foul of the law while waiting for the existing government to be destroyed. As well as offering assistance at Bizana trials, organizers here provided bail for anyone who already had a red ticket, or was prepared to buy one on release, or whose relatives paid for one and brought it to prison. Understandably, blacks began to feel that miracles were being worked before their eyes: 'there were absolutely no people in gaol because the ICU people protected them'.[49]

Above all, ICU activists took up the issue of taxation. Their focus was fitting: the rapid decline in political and economic fortunes associated with the imposition of this burden was possibly the single most important factor facilitating the emergence of a millenarian movement in Pondoland during this period. Almost without fail, agents urged blacks to refuse to pay. While some added the rider that taxes had been refunded in East Griqualand, or that the Americans would abolish the system, others bluntly advocated the destruction of tax receipts. Their exhortations were well received. In both Mount Ayliff and Flagstaff there was a pronounced decline in payments during September; once the deadline had passed, resistance became more militant. In Lusikisiki and Harding there were groups who refused to pay; in Flagstaff some burnt their receipts. In one location in Bizana, 'people tore up their poll tax receipts and said they don't care for these old things, this new government of ICU is going to tell us what to do'.[50]

But even ferment over taxes was subordinate to excitement about pigs, planes and Americans. An extremely broad movement coalesced around these images. Amongst those who slaughtered pigs and bought plane tickets were chiefs, headmen, separatist ministers, large sections of congregations in both Ethiopian and mission churches, and 'school people'. Undeniably, however, it was the traditionalist rural poor and migrant labourers who 'were the backbone of the ICU here, because they were the people who were thirsty for liberation'.[51] As with so many millennial dreams in Africa, the attraction was greatest for struggling cultivators being dragged into a capitalizing and racially oppressive world at an accelerating pace. Furthermore, like so many other such movements, readiness for deliverance had to be demonstrated with certain actions. Rooted in two worlds, the ICU insisted that salvation depended upon both the mass slaughter of animals – a practice 'traditionally' associated with millennial liberation – and the buying of trade union membership cards – the modern way of fighting for freedom. And it was precisely those whose situation pulled them both backwards towards the past and forwards towards the future who responded on a mass scale.[52]

Their willingness to move partially into modernity was well illustrated by the substitutes developed for lard in the spheres of healing and witchcraft. Since the Mpondo were in any event constantly searching for better *imithi* and had by this time eagerly embraced patent medicines, many simply bought Vaseline to replace pig fat as soothing lotion. Similarly, incorporation into a colonial world – where whites had forbidden the practice of divining – had already helped shift the search for solutions to wizardry away from those proffered by traditional witch-finders. As the Bizana magistrate commented in 1926, the power of diviners had considerably decreased in his district, although faith in herbalists remained profound. In a society where the success of sorcerers and witches was 'constantly on the minds of people', many were only too willing to believe that tickets sold by new medicine-men were more effective talismans than lard.[53]

Yet the ICU message was not accepted in its entirety. Innovations must have some resonance amongst audiences if they are to be socially approved – and certain notions introduced by literate, Zulu-speaking men were partially or totally rejected. Thus while the idea of sheets of flame did win mass allegiance, there were still those who preferred to think in older terms of danger borne by extraordinary beasts. Before the concept of heavenly fire was incorporated into popular consciousness in Lusikisiki, some traditionalists imagined all households with pigs would be burnt by an animal. This creature was 'coming from the seas and going along the Umzimvubu river with some writing on the side and it was eating mealies'. Even less acceptable was the Zulu belief that pigs were so dangerous and unclean that those entering the millennium with new charms could not eat them. In Pondoland, rural cultivators already short of food generally feasted on their slain swine. And although 'Sisiyu' agents in Harding flogged children for stealing abandoned pork, in Pondoland they appear to have been forced to temper their taboos.[54]

ICU orders to destroy economically and socially valuable white animals aroused much greater opposition. Some killed white fowl, which were in any case insignificant women's animals, grouped together with pigs. But the Mpondo had no tradition of concealing white stock during storms: the greatest tribute paid to the idea that whiteness attracted lightning was to ban contact with milk. Thus in Harding amongst the Amaci, ICU urgings to kill white fowl were first translated into the belief that pigs would set fire to hens of all colours, which would then fly around setting huts alight. Many then logically concluded there was no point in killing fowl, since people would be safe provided there were no hogs. Similarly, in Lusikisiki, an old man recalled that 'When they said you must kill white cattle people refused, and that was the end of it.' Making the best of this recalcitrance, some ICU agents insisted that cows should be symbolically mutilated by nipping off their tail hairs.[55]

Pigs, however, were another matter. 'Inherent' Mpondo beliefs about these animals already associated them with evil, witchcraft and death. Moreover, as creatures bred almost exclusively for consumption, they certainly tempted the fates in the hot and hungry months of late 1927. If they were not actually dying in temperatures of over 100°F, many of them must have been particularly unpleasant household guests. In addition, pressures to slaughter invariably increased in periods when there was little food for people and even less for pigs. Hogs were sources of high-quality protein and fat, as well as scavengers which, when hungry, menaced the scarce food resources of humans and stock. And as arable lands edged closer to huts, they caused considerable friction between pig-owners and plot-holders. Hence pigs were not only evocative, subtle symbols in the summer of 1927: whether as foragers or as food-stores, they were also material comestibles.[56]

Both then and today, the '*Sisiyu*' in Pondoland is linked above all to hog-killing. 'Wherever I went I found pork, to whatever kraal', claimed Mvunelo of Lusikisiki, whence it was reported by a headman in early October that 'people have finished all their pigs'. In Harding, the killing was extensive, though confined almost entirely to locations occupied by the Amaci. In Flagstaff, 'no one had a pig left' in Nobulongwe's location. In Bizana, the census listed a fall of 7,500 pigs between 1927 and 1928: according to Mgetyana, pigs would have been eradicated from the district if some had not been hidden in the forest.[57]

For those who slaughtered their swine, disposal could be problematic. Some burnt the pork, since homesteads with several hogs found it impossible to consume all the meat before it putrefied. Others threw it far from their huts; yet others drove the pigs away and abandoned them. For Mpondo believers, the task of distancing themselves from lard also involved some effort. Although it could be sold by those quick off the mark, there was generally such a glut that it was thrown into forests, cast into rivers, dumped in furrows, buried in pails, or simply left lying in huge piles in the veld alongside the smashed calabashes that had contained it.[58]

Since the actual killing of pigs was the task of men – and was often performed by homestead heads like Mdingi's father – the scale of destruction provides a crude index of the extent to which males adhered to millennial beliefs. But women were more ambiguously placed with regard to the wholesale extermination of almost the only edible animal they partially controlled. Undoubtedly, those who enjoyed a degree of economic security – and whose migrant or peasant menfolk were at home – could be in the van of those urging slaughter. According to Esther Hlangabezo, then a married woman living in a traditionalist homestead, 'The women would hear the news of the aeroplane, and then ask their husbands if they could kill their pigs, and the men would agree.' But it is possible that in Pondoland, as elsewhere in the Transkeian Territories, 'pigs look[ed] after widows' and were sold by Christians to pay school or church fees. Certainly one Mpondo woman, reluctant to destroy some of the few assets she possessed, walked miles to hand over a sow and its litter to her mission church minister.[59]

There were others, too, who concluded that as long as swine were physically removed from their own homesteads, they could remain within the spirit of the ICU message without liquidating valuable resources. Selling pigs was one option: while white storekeepers displayed scant interest in buying these diseased animals, there was some trading amongst the Mpondo themselves. In Harding, some successfully managed to exchange hogs for cash, and in Pondoland many tried, often in vain. Alternatively, distant sties were built for swine which continued to be fed: an option that was probably favoured largely by 'school people'. Others killed fat pigs but accorded surreptitious care to lean ones. They could hedge their bets while doing this: according to Hlangabezo, believers trying to retain their hogs would 'tie a rope round the pigs' legs and fasten them amongst the trees in the forest, so that the aeroplane should burn just that particular spot'.[60]

The generalized poverty to which such efforts bear witness was equally apparent in the sphere of obtaining tickets for the plane. Yet while red cards costing two to five shillings each were beyond the reach of many Mpondo peasants, thousands were sufficiently motivated to scrape together the requisite funds. Hope for the millennium certainly fuelled enthusiasm: 'anyone who did not have this paper would not be picked up by the aeroplane'. Nor, however, would they escape incineration, and a very real element of terror was injected into the frantic rush for the new talismans. Men – and often women and children – all had to have their own tickets, and an abiding popular memory of ICU offices is one of endless queues. This helps explain why, in terms of money transmitted to headquarters, the fifth most important branch in South Africa in 1927 was based in the tiny village of Harding. Between November and December alone, over two thousand membership cards were sold, many of them to people from Pondoland. In addition to being sometimes cheaper, Harding tickets were frequently required because Pondoland agents would often run out of stock completely in a matter of days. Thus Bizana neighbours combined to send Mgetyana's ex-miner brother on the forty-odd mile round-trip to Harding, armed with a list of names so that cards could be correctly issued. He returned with saddle-bags so full that they barely closed. In Mgetyana's words, 'This thing was big. Even those who were sceptical at first ended up believing in the ICU . . . Everyone was saying, "I bought it! I have it!"'[61]

According to the logic of commodity-exchange, the tickets were of course entirely appropriate for entering aeroplanes. They were also, however, acceptable as protection against fire from the sky. For one thing, it was commonly believed that the cards were brought to ICU offices by planes. The impression was fostered by at least some organizers, who doubtless realized the importance of suggesting that the new charms were being provided by the pilots-cum-medicine-men in command of the heavenly flames. For another, blood could substitute for fat in protective *imithi*. Kadalie himself had claimed that ICU tickets were symbols of blood in the black struggle for freedom – and in all Nguni societies, red was widely understood to represent the life-giving and transformative essence of blood. Mpondo ICU members were often acutely aware that it was the *red* side of a red and white ticket that had to be displayed to the planes. In a world where red was a colour mediating between the quick and the dead, and white was a hue associated with lightning, the correct use of this new form of protection was clearly a matter of considerable importance.[62]

The new *impundulu* was not the only alien force before which cards could replace lard. Illiterate men regarded the cards with awe: 'These ICU tickets were beautiful, beautiful . . . They were two-tone – red on one side and white on the other. There was some writing on them . . . If you had this paper you had everything.' A trade union ticket inscribed in the arcane code of English, bearing the owner's name, was readily invested with protective properties against a whole range of threats posed by modern forces. Consequently, refusing to pay tax was not necessarily a sign of the acquisition of political consciousness appropriate to resisting the white state, since ICU cards in themselves were often believed to provide protection against imprisonment. When confronted by the magistrate and police, numerous defaulters in both Bizana and Lusikisiki confidently whipped out their red tickets. From lard on feet to cards in hand: such was one result of the activities of ICU leaders amongst a peasantry searching for new protection against *ukuthakatha*.[63]

Many, however, were looking for more than organizers offered, and were only too willing to embroider on a message of hope and destruction. Thus the forests became commonly accepted as a refuge for those without tickets, who would run for their lives when hearing the sound of aeroplane engines. Card-holders by contrast were filled with excitement, and on at least one occasion congregated to await the arrival of the American planes. Under the leadership of a Lusikisiki headman, believers selected a flat strip of ground and on the chosen day poured in on horseback, clutching their tickets. But in the mid-afternoon, they were informed that the Americans were not after all arriving that day, and that until recalled they must keep their cards and kill all pigs. Enthusiasm was not necessarily blunted by such disappointments, and it was probably after Christmas, the day of liberation, that ICU members in Bizana marched into a shop with a box. When the white trader was unable to lift it, they jubilantly spread the news that he had been defeated by a case containing 'the wonders of the Americans who would be coming over'.[64]

Within the limits of popular opinion, local propagandists had a fairly free hand in suggesting such embellishments. A favourite way of enhancing the might of airborne liberators was to grant them control over additional powers drawn from the realm of the Lord-of-the-Sky. Falling stars were said to be the work of the Americans and were called *Ikhwezi Lesiyu* – 'The Star of the ICU'. Perhaps inspired by an eclipse of the moon in late 1927, or by older millenarian prophecies, some believed that on the great day the sun would rise only to its noon position. Thereafter it would fall back to the east, all would be dark, and blacks would have to drive home their cattle and wait.[65] Union activists themselves were sometimes attributed with up-to-date aerial powers, although these could be infused with rustic overtones. In February 1928, a black stranger arrived in Harding from Bizana, claiming to be an American on a plane trip and the head of the ICU in South Africa. After a few days he departed, watched by a youth with an enviably untrammelled imagination. Under oath, the latter swore that a 'yellowish thing', rattling like tins and flapping its wings, had settled in front of them like a stork. 'Two persons showed their faces through a hole and the stranger went up to them and returned with a letter.' The lad then hastened off with this missive to his chief, and excitedly informed him that an aeroplane had flown the American away.[66]

But perhaps even greater ingenuity was displayed by the stranger, who was a good example of an 'ICU leader' thrown up in the wake of a popular and profitable movement. He was a poor, illiterate middle-aged man, who tried to enhance his credibility amongst Africans by speaking only English (which was bad) and scribbling letters (which were meaningless). On the grounds that local officials were overcharging and illegitimately selling tickets to children, he spent his time in Harding recalling red cards with promises of refunds. Alarmed branch organizers decided that a man dressed in rags could not be all he claimed, but were able to do little to stop his ingenious method of acquiring red tickets. Other 'agents' may have resorted to more desperate measures, and might have cashed in on the common ICU practice of handing out slips when cards had run out. Thus the minority Mpondo tradition that there were white tickets cheaper than red cards, or that ICU cards were blue, perhaps relates to such self-appointed activists. Similarly, over and above the tendency to project wondrous characteristics onto men who were often claiming to be Americans, it may have been the extravagance of freelance agents that fostered beliefs that some organizers were Griquas, or Indian-Africans, or yellow strangers riding white horses.[67]

Such rumours were inevitable in a period of great fear and exultation, when innumerable prophets were spreading the news. 'You will die if you do not buy the ticket!' preached a minister in the independent African Native Church, thereby ensuring that his entire congregation equipped themselves with cards. The tidings were also spread through songs, and some traditionalists translated salvation from above into more familiar kinship terms: 'ICU – o father, ICU – o father'. At school concerts in Bizana, children sang more sophisticated nationalist lyrics about ICU agents. One song was composed by the self-same Damoyi whose words had previously captured Pondoland's winter of discontent, and whose stanza now celebrated a political spring:

> Son of Kadalie, you Kadalie, o Kadalie.
> See the hero, the son of Kadalie, you Kadalie,
> You, young man, you have come to unite
> Flocks that spurn each other, Shangaans and Coloureds,
> Son of a black man in the land of our ancestors.[68]

But while many 'school people' were ardent supporters both of more orthodox ICU ideas and of pig-killing, there were also those who distanced themselves from the movement in its millenarian form. Hog-slaughter won little support from 'the educated and semi-educated' in Harding, nor from a Christian community clustered around a Pondoland mission station. Such groups often overlapped with wealthier stock-owners and market-oriented crop-producers, from which strata virulent opponents like Xoko were drawn. As a homestead head, Xoko forbade his wife and brothers to buy tickets, and would stubbornly sit out the sound of plane engines while these luckless believers fled to the forest. As he firmly told his family, the magistrate had not approved of the movement, and since ICU activists were not mine owners, their talk of higher wages was nonsense.[69]

Political conservatism and western rationality similarly fuelled the opposition of salaried members of the petty bourgeoisie, whose jobs generally bound them into dependence on the state, and whose escape from migrancy was related to integration into colonial culture. Soji, for instance, 'told the people they were stupid' to think Americans could see the small ICU tickets from their planes. As a prison warder married to a teacher, Pato's father objected to the fact that the ICU was 'against the law'. This in itself was an important consideration for chiefs towards the top of the hierarchy of black state functionaries, especially as the ICU threatened their own authority as well. Thus a Union agent was thrashed at the 'great place' of the paramount for acting as a 'new Nonquase'. And in October 1927, the regent sent his secretary to address a meeting of Lusikisiki headmen convened by the magistrate. These men had all failed to inform on the ICU, and the secretary sternly told them that the organization was simply a money-making concern; that the taxes it opposed were for popular benefit, and that it was a movement challenging the government.[70]

Settlers were far more concerned that the Union was against them personally. As in the hog-slaughtering before Bambatha's rebellion, many whites construed the killings as the precursor of a rebellion in which they were next in line. In Harding, panic-stricken farmers rushed to buy ammunition and insurance as swine were butchered in their district. Although this was an extremely crude reaction to blacks' attempts to invoke magic far more potent than guns, it was based on the well-founded assumption that hostility to whites was somehow being expressed through a pogrom of pigs.[71]

Slaughtering swine was not, of course, illegal. Combined with the forms of organization and ideology associated with the 'Sisiyu' in Pondoland, this made it difficult for the state to act quickly enough to crush the movement. However, in addition to bolstering the forces of internal opposition, officials could wield their own powers as soon as the law was actually broken. Thus those who had destroyed tax receipts or refused to pay were promptly brought to book. According to Mgetyana, police

> used to ask people to produce their poll tax receipts and if they produced the red tickets they would be arrested, and told that the ICU was never a government . . . So people started throwing the tickets away and started looking for money to pay poll tax.

Tickets were even less help to organizers who became too prominent. In January 1928, Mdodana was expelled from Bizana, and spent the rest of the year being continually harassed as he ducked in and out of eastern Pondoland. While state action was generally too tardy and clumsy to stop the spread of the movement, it could at least increase the price of supporting it.[72]

The collapse of the ICU in its millenarian form was in fact more closely related to the internal problems of any such movement. Not that rural patience or ingenuity should be underestimated: localized groupings could straggle on for years, changing in character to accommodate non-fulfilment of prophecies.[73] In Bizana, for instance, hope lived on through 1928, doubtless boosted by heavenly intervention on Christmas Day in the form of glorious rains. Nonetheless, the drought was broken far too late: maize harvests throughout Pondoland were considerably worse than the meagre ones of the year before. As bad times worsened, so anxiety deepened, and faith was not enhanced when the treasurer decamped with ICU funds. Educated blacks began to gather support as they disrupted the meetings of the remaining agents, who were themselves confronting acute financial difficulties through being unable to attract new members. After the initial surge of ticket-buying, Union leaders faced precisely the same problem in convincing sceptics as did the Wellingtonite Edward Maqolo: 'The Americans was said to be coming to Africa and people will not join the Movement as they don't see the Americans.' When the short-lived village office in Bizana collapsed in early 1929 because Mdodana was unable to pay the rent, he and Mdletye made overnight departures to avoid the storm of protest. An old man sadly recalled that the message conveyed by the vacant office was driven home by the police: 'Yaa, we are going to get you, where are those ICUs of yours who were so powerful?' But there was little need for state functionaries to fuel the flames. The district was already seething with accusations that '*Sisuyu*' leaders were little more than thieves, traitors and tax-collectors.[74]

Such condemnations have considerable force. They can be amplified with criticisms that activists subordinated themselves to peasant spontaneity, and completely failed to provide effective tactics or ideologies for channelling the existing ferment. Yet such rationalist, retrospective strictures fail to come to terms with the extent to which millenarianism was in the air in Pondoland. If ICU agents had not faithfully articulated popular aspirations and drawn heavily on folklore, they would not have united and swept into motion thousands of illiterate traditionalists. 'The new middle-class intelligentsia of nationalism had to invite the masses into history; and the invitation-card had to be written in a language they understood.'[75]

In the broader Transkeian Territories, Union leaders were to learn as forcibly that

> there was no other way of doing it. Mobilization had to be in terms of what was there; and the whole point of the dilemma was that there was nothing there – none of the economic and political institutions of modernity now so needed. All that there *was* was the people and peculiarities of the region: its inherited *ethnos*, speech folklore, skin-colour and so on. Nationalism works through *differentiae* like those because it has to . . . People are what it has to go on: in the archetypal situation of the really poor or 'under-developed' territory, it may be more or less all that nationalists have going for them.[76]

The ICU in the Broader Transkeian Territories

It is no easy task to disentangle the plethora of ICUs operating in the Territories from 1928. The parent Union opened an Umtata branch, touched down at Tsolo and Qumbu, allegedly had the sanction of the paramount chief of western Pondoland, reputedly ran three large branches in Pondoland, and certainly asserted control over the running of Mdodana's Bizana branch. The Transkeian ICU seceded in about March 1928, and fly-by-night organizers Louis Faro and Elias Mabodla opened or revitalized branches in Mount Frere, Qumbu, Ngqeleni and Port St Johns, and possibly in Tabankulu, Lusikisiki and Mount Fletcher. The ICU *yase* Natal seceded in May 1928, and Champion continued to send emissaries to Pondoland. The Independent ICU was formed in March 1929, whereafter it held meetings and sometimes opened branches in Kentani, Nqamakwe, Willowvale, Idutywa, Elliotdale, Lady Frere and Umtata, as well as in several Ciskeian locations. Finally, splintering reached its absurd conclusion with Mabodla's formation in 1931 of an Elliotdale branch of the 'IICU of the Transkei'.[77]

In previously unorganized country towns, the impact of the Union could be enormous. In the East Griqualand village of Mount Frere, a schoolboy, Oscar Mpetha, helped in the offices of the Transkeian ICU. Many years later, he claimed almost everyone in the town was caught up in the movement. He recalled one victory with glee:

> There were curfew bells at 9 o'clock in Mount Frere. And one day a big meeting was called, on Sunday, and all people were invited to defy that curfew, and walk in the street at 7.30. Women and even children were involved in marching in the street. They would

take nearly half of the street, take one long side, march down the street, then up again, down again, singing '*Hamba* ICU', which means 'Go Forward ICU'. *Hamba* ICU, we march, *hamba, hamba, hamba* ICU. It was after 11 when we stopped. The curfew bells were immediately stopped.[78]

Yet, as Mpetha also remembered, the Wellingtonites held firm sway over Mount Frere's rural areas. The fate of most if not all Transkeian and parent ICU branches suggests that organizers who adhered to an ideology rooted in the aspirations of workers and the middle strata could not move much beyond the confines of dissident 'school' communities and small towns. Unless activists treated the reserves as more than a labour reservoir for white capital, unless they respected the specificities of rural consciousness and modes of organizing, and unless they incorporated folklore and made concessions to millennial longings, they did not attract mass peasant support. On the contrary, they met with indifference or antagonism. ICU orators, calling for rural blacks to strike like their urban comrades, could be asked 'how they were to go on strike and with what object as they were not in anyone's employ'. Alternatively, abstract calls for unity and support for urban struggles could be interrupted mid-stream with questions as to whether those who combined would still be prosecuted for not destroying noxious weeds.[79]

Perhaps the limitations of the Union's orthodox, 'derived' ideas were demonstrated most graphically in Pondoland. Although millennial fervour can sometimes be harnessed by more sophisticated radical movements, no non-millenarian ICU operating here appears to have performed this task or attracted mass support. There was an enormous gap between officials fighting for limited ends and audiences seeking a new heaven and earth, as was evidenced in the reception of four organizers in Lusikisiki in May 1928. One of them immediately stated that 'the ICU were not out to tell people to kill their pigs and not to pay their taxes and such things'. Instead, it was out to tell them about non-racialism, wages, the opening of shops, and burial benefits so that the dead would not be eaten by birds. The audience was not impressed. People were suspicious about claims that the chief approved, and hostile to white membership. They asked whether ICU blessings would be provided free, and queried: 'Did you ever see the body of a non-ICU being eaten by birds?' Only four Africans bought tickets, and police commented that it was clear that the Mpondo of Lusikisiki disapproved of the movement.[80]

Activists who were prepared to let 'inherent' ideas bulk large in their message could, however, make some headway. It was for this reason that the IICU was partially successful in the southern Transkeian Territories. In particular, Kentani became a Union stronghold. It was a densely populated region, increasingly characterized by land shortages and poor harvests, and extruding ever more migrant labourers whose wages were vital in relieving chronic indebtedness. Nonetheless, there were signs that the ardently traditionalist rural poor and migrant workers did not perceive themselves primarily as proletarians. During the depression of the early 1920s, the district was simmering with migrant-propagated rumours that Americans were coming to help blacks kill all whites. Some years later, a petition from the 'Gaikas and Gcalekas of Kentani' gave support to the state's segregationist policy, provided it protected rural resources, returned migrants from urban slums, and accorded respect to both chief and custom. Amongst those favouring the preservation of the age-old institutions of the Xhosa was Dorrington Mqayi, himself related to Kentani's ruling elite, and a member of the IICU's East London strike committee.[81]

The strike itself broke out in January 1930, and involved thousands of workers demanding higher wages. Both before and after it erupted, IICU officials made concerted efforts to attract Kentani members on a ticket of higher pay for local workers and rural backing for the East London struggle. Nonetheless, as Elias Mabodla traversed Kentani trying to collect funds for the defence of the imprisoned strike committee, his message dramatically altered to accommodate those *resisting* proletarianization. It became militantly Africanist, and it appears to have been this that enabled him to claim two thousand members by March, including 'a good many of the red natives'. He stated that he could make all whites leave the country; he urged blacks not to migrate to the mines; he exhorted non-payment of taxes; he helped peasants obtain better prices for wool; he promised one thousand bags of mealies to relieve starvation, and he dwelt on the looming legislative threat of a five-pound tax on non-labourers. He also bolstered his authority by claiming he was a successor of Ntsikana, a prophet favoured by IICU propagandists who wished to tap the springs of Xhosa nationalism whilst remaining within a separatist Christian tradition. Ntsikana, he argued, urged blacks to take the Bibles but not the money of the whites: 'we took the money as well and so they perished you'.[82]

The East London strikers were, however, 'perished' because their demands for more money remained unmet. Embittered by the complete failure of the strike, a wave of East London IICU leaders departed for the Transkeian hinterlands in mid-1930, swearing to organize the locations to prevent future scabbing and to force whites to increase wages. But, like Mabodla, they rapidly discovered that an undiluted focus on the grievances of workers would not win over the 'natives wearing red blankets' who formed the bulk of their audiences. Organizers like Mqayi thus increasingly associated themselves with symbols rooted in a precolonial past, and with a 'red' historical tradition of resistance to the colonialists. In Kentani itself, officials appear to have been swept away by grass-roots desires to return to a way of life that existed before large-scale proletarianization and significant white incursion. By mid-year, over five thousand members were claimed, and by November, Nguni mythology was being coupled to the promise of a life of plenty in the rural areas. After a lean year in the lands and deepening depression in the cities, a talking crow was prophesying good rains and good harvests. It was so persuasive that some Johannesburg workers sought to return home, doubtless influenced by the fact that the speaking crow of Kentani was also saying, 'there is a great War coming . . . It tells the Amaxhosas to join the IICU and that there will come bloodshed next year.' Rumours flourishing in Gcalekaland advanced the date to the anniversary of the battle of Blood River, and a significant number of blacks left East London before 16 December because they believed that 'a fire will drop from the heavens at East London and kill all the people'. By this time, experiences in rural locations were diffusing into IICU organization in East London itself. Within weeks, officials here were calling for the employment of witchcraft against whites, and were predicting that 'something serious is coming'. 'You must now claim for the blood of chief Hintsa', they urged, referring to the Xhosa king killed by whites during colonial warfare a century earlier.[83]

Pressures from the rural poor could clearly submerge 'derived' nationalist ideas beneath notions of great wars, witchcraft, heavenly fire and talking crows. As in Pondoland, articulating such ideas enabled the Union briefly to ride the groundswell of a mass movement. As also in Pondoland, the failure of predictions to materialize – and suspicion about the personal gains of prophets – could damage credibility beyond repair. By mid-1932, the IICU had splintered into numerous fragments, and was reportedly dead in the Transkei.[84]

This was not entirely true. Both the ICU in Pondoland and the IICU in the southern Transkei burnt themselves out in a matter of years by using the current idioms of traditionalist culture to mobilize a mass base. As the Wellingtonites knew full well, appealing to a narrower constituency – a dissident 'school' community – could have longer-lasting results. This was particularly evident when localized movements drew on ICU ideas but forged their own directions. In concluding this discussion of Union activities in the Transkeian

Territories, it is perhaps fitting to end with a Mfengu movement which incorporated an astounding array of influences, including some derived from the ICU, the Transkeian ICU and the IICU.

When the ubiquitous Mabodla arrived fresh from Kentani to open an IICU office in Nqamakwe in mid-1930, he linked up with a three-hundred-strong '*Ama Melika*' movement firmly rooted in a disaffected, semi-educated peasantry. This alliance was headed by ex-Wellingtonite Edward Maqolo; it included ex-ICU and Transkeian ICU members; it was still associated with an 'American' school, and it had recently branched out into all-night religious services infused with apocalyptic prophecies. Within two years, its support base had swollen to 1,800 men, women and children, many of whom were proud owners of IICU membership cards. With considerable encouragement from an IICU activist, the leaders of this movement were also increasingly devoting their intellectual energies to the analysis of dreams which foretold the redemption of Africa.[85]

Thus one gathering was treated to a long exposition of a dream about the white man and his *impundulu*, which was threatening to 'eat up the Bantu', while black mushrooms were singing 'Arise! O! Native and take your position!' Another meeting was devoted to analysing a dream about a man hitting a cow suckling from its heifer – which was interpreted as 'It is the white man who sucks from the native and these are the Americans who strike the cow.' But perhaps the dream which most aptly condensed the various political and ideological influences impinging on this movement was one about trains without engines, running to Maqolo's house, accompanied by three guards who predicted the arrival of the Americans. Supporters solemnly 'solved' this dream: the guards represented Garvey, Kad-alie and a local activist, while the trains were their respective organizations, 'all tied up and united at Maqolo's'. Indeed they were – and people less desperate than Mpondo peasants could afford to wait for the predicted arrival of a locomotive from over the seas. In 1934, 'the beating of drums of the Maqolo movement' still echoed through Nqamakwe locations.[86]

Dreams, Americans and *impundulu* in Fingoland; visions, crows and heavenly fire in Gcalekaland; balls of fire, Americans and pigs in Pondoland: in the Transkeian Territories in this period, the language through which hopes and fears were expressed clearly partially transcended class and regional boundaries. The various symbols were also symptoms of very real differences between the trajectories of struggle of traditionalists and modern nationalists. Most Transkeians in this period were not seeking equality with whites, incorporation into a national Parliament, non-racialism or burial

benefits. They were attracted instead to militant Africanist programmes, which – if they were to gain a mass following – had to be
couched in the idioms of popular culture and to offer support to
those resisting proletarianization. Above all, they had to cater for
longings for a 'great war' which would completely eradicate white
South Africans from the face of the earth. It was racial oppression
more than class exploitation that moved Transkeian peasants to
action in this period, and their prime concern was to find ways of
defeating a mighty white enemy. Powerless as they were, the black
rural poor turned to airborne Americans, precolonial military heroes
and magico–witchcraft beliefs. That their movements were doomed
to failure should not obscure their radical essence. They contained
the realization that warfare would precede liberation. And they were
based on the belief that the new heaven and earth would be shorn of
racists and ruled by blacks.

8. CONCLUSION

'The ICU', commented an observer in 1930, 'sprawls across the South African stage, like a pantomime dragon whose imperfectly drilled front and rear sections fail to mimic convincingly the unified control of life.'[1] The metaphor was apposite not only for the death throes of the Union, but also for most of its existence. It was a fluid, contradictory movement more than a disciplined, uniform organization. It articulated a multiplicity of ideas about the past, present and future; it embraced a host of causes, and it encompassed an extraordinary range of struggles.

Its motley character was exacerbated by the sharp shifts it underwent in the course of its brief history. In 1919, in the context of an upsurge of working-class protest, the ICU was formed as a trade union. In the mid-1920s, as racial oppression intensified and the process of proletarianization accelerated, it was transformed into a nationalist movement. Hundreds of lower-middle-class blacks under economic, political and ideological attack were thrust into alliance with tens of thousands of rural Africans undergoing dispossession. For a couple of years, the ICU channelled and intensified the protests of extremely disparate social groups. But by the end of the decade, the Union had splintered into numerous, uncoordinated segments.

Although these displayed no 'unified control', they could nonetheless evidence signs of life. As in the Transkei, these offshoots sometimes displayed greater animation than the parent body, precisely because they were more strongly influenced from below. Instead of stumbling across the whole stage, 'rear sections' could pick their way more sure-footedly across a smaller arena. And instead of vainly trying to redirect the entire dragon, tightly-knit audiences could successfully intervene to determine the direction of separate parts. Far from being insignificant bit-players following the star turn, these fragments often demonstrated the power – ephemeral though it was – of subordinating the national, the organized and the leaders to the local, the spontaneous and the led.

Sprawling across the South African Stage

This was certainly evident in the resistance against municipal beer monopolies fuelled by the ICU *yase* Natal in 1929. These were not merely amongst the most violent protests in the history of the Union. Nor were they simply one of the rare occasions when male organizers publicly gave pride of place to females: 'Right from Weenen to Newcastle women fought well, but they could not succeed because their men were in collusion with the Government.'[2] They were also campaigns in which the combatants drew particularly heavily on their own resources and gender-differentiated histories. In large part, the singularly bellicose nature of the beer protests was due to their infusion with experiences of sexual oppression on the one hand, and traditionalist forms of struggle on the other.

Their genesis lay in the convergence of interests of three distinct groups in Durban. After the ICU *yase* Natal seceded in May 1928, it deliberately recruited female beer-sellers in an attempt to combat waning finances and membership. According to persistent rumours, these 'shebeen queens' were the moving spirit behind subsequent protests against canteens which competed with their trade. However, Champion and his petty bourgeois cohorts also longed for legal entry into the harbour city's lucrative *utshwala* market, currently dominated by black women and the white local authority. In the context of new legislation which tightened municipalities' monopoly grip over brewing, as well as the erection of another beer hall, Champion began to co-ordinate resistance. But the campaign only took off when it attracted the support of migrant dock workers, themselves increasingly aware of the role of canteens in buttressing African exploitation and oppression. In June 1929, they fiercely articulated their antagonism to the channelling of municipal *utshwala* receipts into compounds 'full of bad laws', and added their weight to a boycott supported by the ICU *yase* Natal.[3]

Determined members of the Union's Women's Auxiliary, together with many of Durban's male migrant workers, then 'acted as Secret Agents throughout Natal'.[4] They disseminated ideas and tactics that had crystallized out in the Durban boycott, and a rash of demonstrations promptly erupted in nine towns dotting the countryside.[5] Typically, women marched through streets, chanted war songs, raided beer halls, assaulted male drinkers, and behaved in 'a riotous manner, dancing, shouting and striking their sticks on the ground'.[6] Almost everywhere, they vigorously reasserted ICU *yase* Natal-derived demands for closure of the canteens and legalization of domestic brewing.

The relatively coherent thrust and unified ideology of geographically separate protests was, however, undermined by key transformations of the campaign as it was transmitted from city to countryside. From being a project supported largely by urban male migrants, it became one sustained mainly by female non-workers from farms, villages and their fringes. From being an incarnation of the exploitation of labour by capital, the canteen became a symbol of the oppression of women by men. And from being resistance in which there was high-profile ICU *yase* Natal activity, it became protest in which Union activists were almost invisible.

Nonetheless, the ICU undoubtedly influenced the course of the women's demonstrations. In addition to Durban-derived effects on their timing and trajectories, the prior existence of ICU village branches critically affected the boycotts. For one thing, the experiences of earlier confrontation and organization were resuscitated: not least in the form of support given to the women by black policemen who covertly approved of the Union. For another, thousands of tenant homesteads had been evicted from farms for associating themselves with the 'I SEE YOU' or the struggles it inspired. Spurned by landlords and frequently unable to settle in the overcrowded reserves, these evictees poured into towns in such numbers that the slum areas were often totally overburdened. Since urban jobs for women were extremely limited, many of these destitute females from the farms were forced into a grim struggle for survival – and brewing was certainly one way of making ends meet.

In addition, considerable antagonism to the Union existed among male tenants driven into villages or peri-urban areas. A year before the boycott erupted in Dundee, the ICU Branch Secretary was almost murdered by infuriated men ejected from farms for associating with the organization. According to the doleful Secretary, 'they wanted their money . . .they said we were in league with the Dutch farmers'.[7] Such hostility was so prevalent in northern Natal that the ICU *yase* Natal was unable either to persuade any extant branches to join it in secession, or to establish any new branches in the area thereafter. Hence in the countryside, differential sexual incorporation into the ICU in its heyday – and equally pronounced gender disparities in the extent to which hard-earned pennies had been lost through the purchase of red cards – may well have contributed to male reluctance to associate themselves with any campaign linked to the ICU *yase* Natal.[8]

For females, however, the anti-canteen protests struck a deep chord. The beer halls undermined the two key gender-specific activities of brewing and prostitution, and induced especially vicious enforcement of beer restrictions contained in the 1928 Liquor Act. In a year when the depression was beginning to bite, money for *utshwala* also cut into funds for food and endangered the retention of housing. These were no mean considerations for women whose lives were structured primarily around the home and domestic labour – and whose own earnings could be legally appropriated by their menfolk. At a time when numerous females were being marginalized in familial conflicts over resources, and when incomes were habitually inadequate to household subsistence, many women were only too willing to join a political struggle over the direction in which male wages flowed. To add insult to injury, moreover, municipal monopolies barred females and were the foci of an aggressively masculine subculture. After carousing in venues that consolidated their identities as dominant males, men were, so demonstrators complained, 'coming home drunk and ill-treating them'.[9] Both subjectively and objectively, beer halls clearly symbolized and intensified the oppression of African women.

Less obvious, perhaps, were the gender-related dimensions of other pressures impelling females into the protests. Estcourt women, for example, raised a familiar cry at the start of their campaign: 'Their landlords had compelled them to reduce their farm stock and they were poverty-stricken. They wanted the canteen closed.'[10] But livestock limitations were not neutral in their effects on sexual or class inequalities, and such females were frequently referring to the holdings of women and the poor. While men owned almost all cattle, increasing numbers of females had gained rights of disposal over goats, whose breeding capacity was such that families could survive off them during the absence of male migrant workers. Goats, however, were regarded by white landlords as destructive animals, and by black tenants as poor men's cattle, so their chances of survival were slim as farmers applied pressure on male homestead heads to reduce their holdings. The Estcourt women were justifiably bitter: between 1927 and 1930 in this district, the number of African-owned cattle remained almost static, while the number of non-Angora goats fell by 22 per cent.

Yet it was often social factors conducive to female assertiveness, rather than a more parlous economic plight, that distinguished demonstrators from their law-abiding sisters. Thus women accustomed to fighting their own battles in a patriarchal world were often disproportionately represented in the leadership of the boycotts. They included wives in effective control of their households for most of the year, as well as unmarried females living with lovers and paying the price for defying a morality which defined women in terms of their husbands. Such spokeswomen were quick to give verbal content to their assumption of 'male' roles as household

heads, breadwinners and contesters of convention. As one demon-
strator defiantly informed a white magistrate: 'We are now the
men.'[11]

Her assertion was an apt slogan for protests in which ever more
females usurped male identities, male practices and male violence. In
Durban during the early stages of the boycott, members of the
Women's Auxiliary were armed with sjamboks as they marched in
processions headed by a brass band. Later, astonished male
organizers described an Auxiliary leader who fought white vigilantes
as 'the woman in the man who stood before the forces . . .in military
attire' and released many men from 'the jaws of the lion'. In the
countryside, militancy tended to be expressed in a more traditional,
segregated fashion, partly reflecting the fact that gender relations
here had been less thoroughly transformed by capitalist inroads. In
Dundee, the females independently mustered in marching formation, paraded in threes, chanted war songs and brandished their
weapons. While they were clearly influenced by men's 'faction
fights', they were also forging a new and forbidden identity, from
which they were proscribed both as women and as members of a
conquered nation. Weenen women went even further by adopting
male accoutrements redolent of anti-colonial warfare. Some wore
men's loin-cloths during their second raid on the canteen; most
flaunted *tshokobezi* badges and feathers, and all were armed with
staves. Indeed, Charles Kumalo recalled that in Estcourt the female
leaders came mainly from the farms, 'because they knew how to
fight with sticks . . . They also chose people who knew how to sing
praises. As it was clear that people wanted war. They sang battle
songs when they went to attack.'[12]

Initially, male officialdom's response to these bellicose demonstrations was shot through with the chivalrous considerations that
normally masked female oppression. But from the end of 1929,
magistrates all over the countryside began to abandon their paternalism, and to impose ever harsher jail sentences without the option
of fines. Imprisonment for clashes with male drinkers or the police
was an unmitigated disaster for mothers with small children, and it
rapidly brought the women's shows of force to an end. It was also a
major factor in terminating protests in which females had vividly
demonstrated that they suffered under gender as well as racial
oppression. In so doing, they had utterly transformed the initial ICU
yase Natal campaign.

Durban male migrants did not lag far behind in this sphere. Like
the women, they infused their boycott with the economic, political
and cultural specificities peculiar to their own situations and histories. In particular, they drew on a wealth of martial traditions,

Fig. 9.   Map of Natal

ranging from those of precolonial regimental organization to those of Scottish military bands and the Native Labour Contingent of the First World War. If belligerent cultural expressions for women involved appropriating black male modes of behaviour, for men it could entail incorporating the traditions of both primary resistance and imperialist warfare.[13]

In early 1930 when the Durban beer boycott was still at its height, this was epitomized by a Saturday night concert at the ICU Workers' Hall. When invited to it, Margery Perham was somewhat stunned to see several thousand African men crammed into the downstairs section of the warehouse. Many had been or were still members of *Amalaita* gangs – themselves seminal in fostering a virile belligerence directed against white oppressors – and most were domestic servants fresh from the countryside. All were naked but for their loin-cloths and metal ornaments, triumphantly asserting their identities as the subjects of chiefs rather than the servants of madams. Successive teams of men – some trained in *ngoma* dancing by Union leaders drawn from the heart of traditionalist Natal – would rush forward out of the great throng squatting on the rickety floor. According to Perham, each crash of their feet

> was accompanied by the pounding of hundreds of sticks, and a simultaneous shout so that the rhythm was deafening. One team

did a dance founded on the British Tommy . . . They marched in ranks, formed fours, saluted, bringing their hands down with a resounding smack on their bare thighs, carrying their sticks like rifles, whistling famous half-remembered tunes of the war . . . But their own war-dance was the best of all. There were about three hundred dancers, all wearing white fur rings around knees, ankles and wrists, and carrying sticks festooned with white feathers. The joints of their arms were bound with gold and silver wire; some wore baldrics of leopard or catskin or embroidery of white and scarlet beads . . . Now they advanced, singing with sticks levelled at me like spears. Champion shouted the translation in my ear:

> Who has taken our country from us?
> Who has taken it?
> Come out! Let us fight!
> The land was ours. Now it is taken.
> We have no more freedom left in it.
> Come out and fight!
> The land is ours, now it is taken.
> Fight! Fight!
> Shame on the man who is burned in his hut!
> Come out and fight![14]

Ideologically, such reworking of older rural traditions linked struggles of the present to warlike tactics of the past, and fuelled the militancy of male migrants during the boycott. Organizationally, the culmination of this traditionalist bias was reached some months later. In an effort to transform his fluctuating support base into one which actually contributed to ICU *yase* Natal funds, Champion once again turned to the countryside. In addition to successfully summoning some twenty chiefs to Durban, he at last secured an interview in September 1930 with Solomon ka Dinizulu.[15]

Although Solomon had possibly been playing a double game with his anti-ICU mentors for some time,[16] it was only when his defiant struggle for the paramountcy had placed intolerable strains on his relations with officialdom that he openly met Union officials. The encounter was almost farcical: it involved little more than Solomon appearing at the ICU Hall, which was packed with an audience for 'Dem Darkies', and advocating *rapprochement* with the Natal Native Congress. Immediately afterwards the adroit Champion advertized an ICU *yase* Natal banquet for all members to see their 'king'. But the claimant to the throne backed off – and lay in bed while Champion, together with three thousand supporters, nearly smashed down the door to secure his appearance. Solomon hastily departed the political maelstrom of Durban, though not without first accepting ten pounds from Champion and the loan of the ICU car. Oscillating to the end, Solomon's ambiguous relationships with the state and the ICU were not only integral to his struggle to become 'King of this country', but also indices of his essential powerlessness.[17]

Not that white officialdom could afford to regard with equanimity a liaison between these two African leaders. On the contrary: the spectre of the ICU *yase* Natal being approved by the most important traditionalist representative of Zulu-speakers was for them insufferable. Paradoxically, this was partly because by looking to the past – to primary resistance, to abundant land, to the absence of whites and to an African king – this ICU offshoot was potentially more dangerous than movements which sought the full incorporation of blacks into a modern world. In the minds of white state functionaries, trade unions organizing black workers could – just – be contained and controlled. But this was not true of the ICU *yase* Natal in 1930, where meetings included praise songs for warlike Zulu 'chiefs' ranging from Shaka to Champion; where six-thousand-strong audiences took up the cry: *'Humu! Humu! Ematsheni!'* ('Zulu regiments disperse! The beer halls!'); where migrants invoked war through cultural practices; and, most importantly, where support could be claimed from the son of the king-designate who had reputedly masterminded Bambatha's rebellion. The solution was to smash this febrile syncretism. Solomon's stipend was halved and he was severely reprimanded for associating with Champion. And under the provisions of the newly amended Riotous Assemblies Act, the leader of the ICU *yase* Natal was himself effectively banished from Natal for three years from September 1930.[18]

In reverse, then, the state was applying the same principles as had guided its opposition to ICU organization of reserve-dwellers. Here the fear was not that the dissemination of ideas about class and nation would make 'retribalization' impossible, but that adherence to traditionalist ideologies would make an already militant labour force unmanageable. At all costs, the old and the new had to be kept apart. 'Common-sense' rural traditions were not to be reworked in the towns in subversive ways, nor were sophisticated urbanites to reshape popular world-views in the countryside. And in Durban – by this time the Union's centre of gravity in Natal – state repression was largely adequate to this task. By the end of the year in the harbour city, both the beer boycott and the ICU *yase* Natal were well on the way to extinction.

As usual, however, the state was less successful outside the major urban centres. In the late 1930s, ICU *yase* Natal leaders were still active in the rural regions. One such man was Nkonke Vilikazi, who in 1938 addressed reserve-dwellers at beer gatherings near Bergville. Against the background of the state's attempt to transform the role of locations in South Africa's political economy,[19] the theme of his speeches was that 'There is no law to enable the white man to erect contour drains, there is no law to enable whiteman to erect fences and take away your grazing, there is no law compelling you to eradicate weeds.' At a time when blacks were being relentlessly but illegally stripped of their remaining rights of control over land, cross-fertilization between traditionalists and modern nationalists was clearly still possible.[20]

By this time, however, many ICU *yase* Natal leaders were more active in the African National Congress than in their original organization. Thus it was as ANC rather than ICU representatives that Vilikazi and Champion harangued a Bergville meeting on the same issue a month later. Unfortunately, Union leaders' increasingly cordial relationship with Congress did little to infuse the older movement with any of the earlier energy and creativity of the 'I SEE YOU'. Like most black political organizations, it was generally in the doldrums for years after the fragmentation of the Union. In 1947, ANC membership peaked for that decade at just over five thousand people, and it was only some time later that Congress achieved the ICU's ability to mesh together class and nationalist aspirations in a way which had mass appeal. Given this dearth of countryside movements able to articulate popular grievances, it was not surprising that localized Union branches straggled on in all four provinces during the 1930s; some even continued into the 1940s.[21]

Perhaps one of the most interesting was the ironically entitled 'United ICU', headed in Pretoria by one Robert Malatji. In 1942, he dispatched an organizer to establish a branch in Lydenburg, a Transvaal district notorious for harsh state measures against tenants, and even more famous for farm residents' successful resistance.[22] Amongst the various rural issues tackled by the Union was the plight of some seven hundred 'squatter' households, threatened with eviction when their farm, Kalkfontein, changed hands from a rentier to a productive landlord.[23] Their defensive struggle was particularly significant, not least as a harbinger of those waged in subsequent decades by victims of the government's policy of resettlement.

Malatji held his first meeting with Kalkfontein's black residents in 1946, three years after they had first begun to tussle with their new landlord. In August 1947, he sent to the area one S. Mabilu, an ICU activist who had known the tenants since childhood. These organizational efforts were very belated: in the same month, the inhabitants of over eighty huts were roughly thrown off the farm by a bailiff by a bailiff and seventy-five armed policemen. But the resilient community could draw on its own resources in responding with defiance. Within weeks, all those evicted had returned, although chief Masha was conspicuous by his absence.

The next two years were characterized by a flurry of court cases and police raids, as well as by increasing ICU membership amongst these Kalkfontein tenants, who persistently re-infiltrated the farm after being ejected by constables. Finally, in mid-1949, a year after the Nationalists had been returned to power on an apartheid ticket, the entire community was dumped on barren, state-owned land some forty miles away. Here large households – often comprising four or five women, their children and a male homestead head – were squeezed into tents and abandoned without food. Not surprisingly, they ignored Masha who had approved of their resettlement, and within days all had decamped to the Sekhukhuneland location, where conditions were marginally better.

Despite being forbidden to do so, Malatji and Mabilu then held a meeting in this reserve. They deplored the fact that the new arrivals could not obtain land in the overcrowded location, and that all were forbidden to cut either grass or wood. They also urged the ex-Kalkfontein 'squatters' to return to their ancestral homes. In familiar language, they promised that 'This card of the ICU's is your freedom.' In an equally time-honoured tradition, they exhorted those present to 'organize under the ICU, and then, if you are evicted, you can come to us'. They then put it to the vote that those from Kalkfontein should return. The result, according to Malatji, was that the three chiefs who had opposed the meeting 'were voted out', sixty-two men bought red tickets, and the ICU's membership in the region was boosted to over seven hundred.

A less auspicious consequence was that Malatji was almost immediately charged for inciting men to return to the farm. Apparently, this brought to an end ICU involvement in resistance to these early forced removals. It did not, however, eliminate Malatji's Union with its claimed membership of some four thousand at the end of 1951. At this stage, Malatji was based in Pretoria; he called himself President and General Secretary of the Industrial and Commercial Workers' Union of Africa, and asserted that his movement could trace its origins back to the ICU which started in January 1919.[24]

While this might have been a statement that Kadalie would have disputed, it was also one made after his death. His IICU had struggled on in East London after the 1930 strike, facetiously known as the 'Independent' 'Independent' ICU after secessions occurred in the early 1930s. By this time Kadalie was being met with overt hostility at many meetings, with the few who bothered to attend sometimes remarking that he 'was again asking for money and he has not explained the money he stole'. Given his need to regain attention with spectacular promises, white officialdom's claims about his activities during the Second World War are dismayingly credible. Allegedly, Kadalie was masterminding the activities of agents in the rural areas of the district of King William's Town, where, provided they were paid a monthly fee, these men handed out certificates protecting blacks if the Japanese invaded. Somewhat more characteristic behaviour was evident in 1947, when, following the victimization of a shop steward at an East London textile mill, Kadalie was the moving spirit behind a strike of some one hundred workers who were members of his Union. Clearly, the contradictions which had manifested themselves throughout the ICU's history were still present within this tiny fragment.[25]

Imperfectly Drilled

Abbreviated though these accounts of a handful of Union offshoots are, they highlight some of the major motifs visible many years earlier during the parent ICU's heyday. The inexorable tendency towards secessions was not simply a matter of theft, personal differences between activists, or even extraordinarily swift growth which stretched the movement way beyond its limited organizational capacities. Underlying the fragmentation was the parochial nature of politics in a country which was not even twenty years old as a nation state, and which was still experiencing a transition to capitalism in the countryside. Precisely because South Africa's 'dual revolution' was so far from completion, the ICU's nationalist project was fatally undermined.

Undoubtedly, it enjoyed some of the preconditions for momentary success. As lower-middle-class blacks were forcibly exposed to the maladies of uneven development, so they sought an antidote in mobilizing the poor and oppressed. The social background of most senior ICU leaders had familiarized them with a nexus of broad nationalist ideas, and they tended to conceive of their organization and aims in terms of South Africa at large. Since the class content of their diffuse African nationalism had immediate popular appeal, they could and did draw thousands to their meetings.

Nonetheless, their objectives as well as their ability to achieve them were adulterated in the very act of mobilizing 'real men, formed in specific historical relations, with specific feelings, outlooks, fragmentary conceptions of the world'.[26] Although activists were trying to unite the masses across ethnic, regional, racial and class boundaries, this was a time when the mental horizons of many rural Africans barely stretched beyond considerations of clan in a parochial community. The illiterate under-classes had not internalized the existence of a South African political economy; they had not coalesced into clear-cut 'popular classes' at a national level. Rural experiences were diverse, regionally specific and deeply affected by dissimilar precolonial pasts. Each district, let alone each province, had a balance of social forces peculiar to it alone. And even within the same locality, many blacks had different experiences of proletarianization, varied class backgrounds, diverse ethnic affiliations and gender-distinctive histories. Small wonder that if a Zulu-speaking male labour tenant could temporarily unite with a Mpondo peasant woman under an umbrella organization, their divergent aspirations could rapidly pull both them and their Union apart. Nor was it surprising that the ICU's nationalist campaign in the countryside was a disorganized venture: not the least of the reasons lay with the unsophisticated 'real men' whom it recruited.

The 'imperfectly drilled' appearance of the Union was also a consequence of the parochial nature of grievances. Although generalized hardships arose from the legislative interventions and social engineering of the national state, particular pressures were often of greater concern to the ICU's disparate constituencies. Impending economic distress due to drought was a recurrent but regionalized tribulation amongst cultivators shackled by the dictates of nature. For many farm tenants, accelerated dispossession due to spurts of agricultural development was the most significant factor in the abrupt deterioration of their lot. As in so many rural movements, collective ICU-related struggles usually erupted not because people were informed that they were exploited and oppressed, but because their awareness of concrete poverty and persecution was sharpened by sudden discontinuities in their immediate, idiosyncratic worlds.

Consequently, unless activists engaged with the specificities of stubbornly localized trajectories of struggle, generally they lost all appeal. Leaders had to learn how to follow: a task easier for rooted lower-level officials than for their peripatetic superiors, and simpler for those who penetrated the countryside proper. But as the under-classes pushed parochial idioms and issues into branch organizers' discourse, so they frequently displaced the broader nationalist content of the ICU's message. They could also partially 'capture' the Union as they projected their own very particular longings onto the movements and expanded on its message so that it better reflected their own concerns. If leaders were swept along with the

the tide, then patterns of protest could be shaped less by the ICU than by the 'inherent' ideas and organizational traditions of the rural poor.

There were, of course, drawbacks when ICU leaders conceded too much to the led. There were pitfalls in emphasizing folklore – when, for example, this contributed to a millenarian movement of Mpondo bent on killing their pigs. There were dangers in unleashing 'inherent' solutions to the agrarian question – when this fuelled beliefs that the ICU had already reappropriated the land. And there were perils in incorporating ethnic traditions – when this inhibited broader unity, and was uncomfortably close to the 'retribalization' constantly advocated as a method of containing the ICU.

Yet the Union also achieved some spectacular successes in reworking the 'common-sense' tactics and traditions of a host of social groups. When leaders harnessed the older lines of communication running from sympathetic chiefs down to humble commoners, ICU meetings benefitted from being hidden from the eyes of authority. Both sacred symbols and secular swing bands were employed to express new political meanings and resolve modern contradictions. Furthermore, although ideological elements such as liberalism or ethnicity were certainly ambiguous, it was politically crucial that these should not be ceded entirely to alternative leaders of the people. More significantly, the progressive potential of such elements was sometimes realized. By expanding on liberal interpellations, democracy was placed more firmly on the agenda. And by reworking narrower ethnic traditions, a potent anti-colonial and anti-capitalist content was often lent to resistance.

At its best, then, the ICU achieved the ideal aim of both ideological and organizational struggle: to bring spontaneity

> into line with modern theory – but in a living and historically effective manner. The leaders themselves spoke of the 'spontaneity' of the movement, and rightly so. This assertion was a stimulus, a tonic, an element of unification in depth; above all it denied that the movement was arbitrary, a cooked-up venture, and stressed its historical necessity. It gave the masses a 'theoretical' consciousness of being creators of *historical* and institutional *values*, of being founders of a State. This unity between 'spontaneity' and 'conscious leadership' or 'discipline' is precisely the real political action of the subaltern classes, in so far as this is mass politics and not merely an adventure by groups claiming to represent the masses.[27]

Although the ICU was plagued by the opposite problem – of 'adventures' by ordinary demonstrators claiming Union approval –

its activities were rarely completely shaped from below. In general, 'inherent' notions and traditions of resistance were interpenetrated with 'derived' organizational forms and ideas. Even in Pondoland, shop stewards tried to mobilize members against key institutions of an oppressive and exploitative society. In most other areas characterized by popular upsurges (such as the eastern Transvaal and Natal), officials made even greater efforts to marry direction and education with spontaneity and millenarianism. While their nationalism was elementary and extremely flexible, it normally included the novel creed that the African poor should unite to win their political freedom. Although the concrete assistance proffered by activists was very rudimentary, supporters eagerly grasped at their legal aid and letters to farmers. On a local level, leaders typically succeeded in imposing some overarching ideological cohesion and organizational infrastructure on those they led.

That the ICU as a whole had a more amorphous appearance was a product of the unevenness of popular consciousness and parochial pressures. In the South African countryside of the 1920s, a mass black opposition movement could not but assume a disjointed form. Yet the wonder was not that the Union appeared as a patchwork creature in a tragicomedy with a decentralized plot. The wonder was rather that inexperienced rural audiences for the first time participated in creating a movement which, however inchoate, propagated a message so relevant that it briefly resembled a popular religion, and which inspired struggles so intense that they momentarily dominated the South African stage.

Patterns of Participation, Opposition and Struggle in the Countryside

It is hazardous to generalize about patterns of participation in a movement which was so deeply affected by the terrain it traversed. Without doubt, the typical rural supporter was an African male labour tenant. And the typical rural opponent was a white male farmer. But wider issues of race, gender and class are more difficult to explore on a countrywide basis. In large part, this is because struggles were strongly influenced by regional political economies, and these have not been charted for South Africa at large.

Thus, while Africans constituted the great bulk of those who bought red tickets in the countryside in the later 1920s, it is harder to discern the rural dimensions of 'coloured' membership in this same period. It is probable that the urban bias of the early 1920s continued, and that the Africanization of leadership following the expulsion of 'coloured' Communists in 1926 inhibited the mobilization of this sector of farm workers in the Cape. Certainly one Johannes de Villiers wrote to *The Workers' Herald* in 1927 from this province, stressing that he noticed prejudice in the Union's paper towards his racial group. His argument that 'coloured' agricultural labourers were as exploited as their African counterparts, and that 'it is very expedient that they should unify themselves under the banner of the ICU', reinforces the impression that activists in declining Cape branches were not particularly exerting themselves in creating this alliance.[28]

While the formation of such an alliance was at least a feasible task, the barriers segregating black from white were almost insuperable. In contrast to the fairly sizeable group of fifteen thousand 'coloured' members claimed in early 1928, there were merely 250 whites. Apparently, they were mainly students, social democrats and wage-earners in the towns. The sprinkling of rural white members in the Free State and Transvaal may have been mostly 'respectable men', as ICU leaders proudly proclaimed. But many may also have harboured the ulterior motive of undermining organization in the countryside.[29]

The relative publicity accorded to white supporters by the Union was not bestowed upon the handful of Indian members. Despite the ICU's fairly warm relations with the Trade Union Congress in India, in South Africa the National Council's only Indian representative was also the only official, apart from Kadalie, who displayed any interest in mobilizing members of this group. There is no indication that their concerns were shared by organizers in Natal, where Indians were overwhelmingly concentrated. Nor, for that matter, are there signs that the Indian poor were particularly attracted to a movement which, especially after the formation of the ICU *yase* Natal, was strongly infused with the sentiments of politicized Zulu ethnicity. Divisions amongst blacks were extremely stark in Natal in the 1920s. Prior trade union organization amongst Indians (such as it was) had not extended to Africans, and it was almost unprecedented for the two groups to share political platforms. Some Indian merchants certainly courted Union leaders (in a transparent attempt to gain more customers), while yet other Indian property owners in Natal villages rented their premises or land to the movement. But the ICU almost completely failed to bridge the profound cultural differences between the Indian and African rural under-classes.[30]

Although the Union paid considerably more attention to mobilizing African women, most females had no contact with its urban-based Women's Sections. And although 'Mote later ruefully regarded females as 'the real fighters',[31] rural women were generally

conspicuous by their absence from the ICU's struggles and structures. In part, this was because they experienced capitalism, the state
and the family – as well as popular organizations – through the prism
of patriarchy. Given the Union's numerous exclusively male meetings in the countryside, together with the barriers preventing females
from visiting villages, the great majority of rural women did not
even have direct contact with ICU activists and ideas. Like the labour
tenant Esther Sibanyoni and the reserve-dweller Ernestina Mekgwe,
they merely 'heard about them from the menfolk'. Moreover, most
females in the countryside were apparently either unwilling or
unable to further rework an attenuated ICU message for the purpose
of protest. On a rare occasion when they did – in the anti-canteen
demonstrations – they spontaneously invested the Union campaign
with antagonism to their subordination as a sex.[32]

Since rural African women were notoriously the most traditionalist sector of all blacks,[33] there were also cultural and class
dimensions to their under-representation in the Union. Like their
male counterparts, they were often fighting on very different
battlegrounds from ICU officials. At least in the villages, accredited
leaders aimed their message primarily at those who had to some
extent broken away from older social relations and ideologies. And
in the country as a whole, traditionalists did not flock to the Union in
sufficient numbers to divert it from its modernizing road.

In some areas, however, defenders of the older order were able to
remake the ICU largely in their own image. In Natal, the eastern
Transvaal and the Transkeian Territories, accredited organizers sold
tickets to traditionalists on a significant scale. This feat was achieved
mainly because local, lesser leaders – and perhaps ordinary blacks to
an even greater extent – partially or totally transformed the Union's
orthodox ideology. The ways in which they did this varied
considerably: from promising land or politicizing ethnicity, through
to predicting the imminence of a 'great war'. But the essence of their
message was the same: in a rapidly changing and increasingly
capitalist dispensation, the 'I SEE YOU' would support traditionalists in their struggle to defend a non-assimilated, non-
proletarian identity.

The bulk of rural ICU supporters, however, derived from the
uneducated *abaphakathi*. Like most petty bourgeois Union members,
many of these 'people in the middle' had already embraced ideologies
distancing them from traditionalists. Indeed, the ICU attracted not
only numerous members of independent churches, but also a sizeable
contingent of those belonging to white-run bodies or based on
mission land. Not surprisingly, almost every mission church in
South Africa was enormously antagonistic to the Union (although

some modified their position once Ballinger arrived). In Natal, Catholic priests went so far as to establish a Catholic African Union to combat the ICU, and to refuse the sacrament to all known holders of red tickets. Elsewhere, too, the power of mission churches in the sphere of social control was demonstrated when Africans threatened with excommunication promptly abandoned the Union. Landlords were quick to pick up such cues. By 1928 in the Free State, farmers previously antagonistic to preachers proselytizing amongst their servants were welcoming white ministers from a church which flaunted its credentials as a 'bulwark against the ICU'.[34]

Such attempts to shore up the breaches in farm defences did not necessarily counter tenants' cogent economic reasons for supporting the Union. In all three northernmost provinces, even privileged sharecroppers attended ICU meetings and bought red tickets. Amongst them were Africans under intense pressure to reduce their stock and toil as labour tenants, as well as those who were being defrauded of their rightful portions of harvests. Indeed, Champion claimed that it was men who ploughed on the halves who benefitted most from the Natal Supreme Court's decision that all tenants had to be given reasonable notice, and be allowed to reap their crops. Landlords in this province, he asserted, were evicting peasants before mid-year and appropriating their entire harvests. But after the Union's legal victory,

> many natives took away their crops and left nothing to the farmer as his share . . .the native tenants, peasants, collected all the crops – if it was 100 bags, 100 bags, and left nothing to the farmer and the farmers started to hate my Union . . .[35]

Yet the ICU rarely if ever emphasized the fight for the halves: in all probability, sharecropper support never bulked large enough to make this a significant issue. Most privileged rural entrepreneurs had in fact every reason for a considered and cautious response to the Union. When Kas Maine explained why he never enrolled in the movement – 'I was looking too much after my farming' – he was probably expressing the feelings of many other sharecroppers in the south-western Transvaal and northern Free State. At a time when the pall of agricultural depression was being lifted by the opening of a highly lucrative competitive market on the diamond diggings, the ICU may understandably have seemed a waste of time. In addition, Maine stressed that he 'was a man of the farms and as such didn't want to quarrel with the whites. The whites would fight you if they found you in possession of [a membership card].' Pressed further on the issue, he exclaimed:

You know, I stay very clear of such things . . . Look, the law, if
that is the law, you follow the law. Don't stand and argue . . .
[White people] are just like a river . . .you've got nothing in your
hand with which to stem them.[36]

Others also had political and ideological reservations about the
Union. Jameson Molete, the educated son of a relatively wealthy
sharecropper, expressed his superiority over the labouring poor and
their leaders in a way reminiscent of many upper-middle-class
blacks. He did not join the Union, he said, because 'it was for the
workers . . . Do you know that [Kadalie] was not educated? If you
could hear him talking English, he was just forcing it.' Ndie
Makume was equally dismissive about the ICU, and apparently did
not see a red ticket as a solution to being severely 'squeezed' as a
sharecropper. 'If a person expressed dissatisfaction [about this],
where could he go?' he asked pointedly. 'It was better for a person to
keep quiet rather than to talk.' Indeed it was, if one was trying to
maintain an illegal relationship with landlords who were extremely
likely to be hostile to the Union. If such men of the farms were also
enmeshed with patriarchs of holdings in an ethic of mutual obligations, they had yet another incentive to hold their tongues. ICU
leaders recognized – and derided – the way in which some tenants'
commitment to the maintenance of stunted paternalistic relations
inhibited their support for the Union. As one activist caustically
proclaimed, 'you men who are concerned with Boers' coffee because
you like it, we say farewell to you'.[37]

There was a similar parting of the ways between the Union and
many 'squatters', who had much the same reasons as sharecroppers
for refusing to risk their livelihoods at a time when their presence
was increasingly redundant. But although few were sufficiently
enamoured with the ICU to withhold their rent forthwith, some
were prepared to do so if they believed the law provided additional
protection. Thus in the province where the Union boasted a lawyer
in every village, an Estcourt 'squatter' was emboldened to turn
arcane differences between legal codes to his advantage. When the
state-owned land on which he had been living was granted to a
settler in 1927, this 'ICU convert' scorned an order from his new
master to leave. Instead, he obdurately claimed the right to graze his
stock where he pleased, insisted on ploughing his old fields, and
declined to pay the tripled dipping fees which his landlord then
imposed in a desperate effort to drive him off the holding. Like a
significant number of other 'squatters' in Natal, this tenant successfully and licitly thwarted eviction attempts for months. To the ire of
many poorer landlords short of time and money, civil law was their

only remedy. And to the anger of the Estcourt magistrate accustomed to the summary criminal code, the police were apparently so wary of prosecution by the Union that they refused to execute his *ultra vires* ejectment orders.[38]

A much finer legal mesh, however, had been designed to entrap farm workers in general and recruited labourers in particular. Partly because the latter were bound by tight contracts – regulated by a law with far fewer loopholes than the Masters and Servants Act – the ICU generally fared poorly amongst them. On occasion, some of these harshly exploited workers articulated opposition to their employers in terms similar to those used by the Union. But it was much more common for well-developed capitalist farmers to comment smugly on the lack of ICU-related 'trouble' amongst their migrant labourers.[39]

They forebore to mention that they were reaping the benefits of many of the far-reaching controls which made the mines so difficult to penetrate. In addition to labouring under legal constraints similar to those affecting black miners, recruited farm workers were also often confined to compounds, which made it difficult for activists to gain access to them. Moreover, they were often temporary aliens in the district. As such, they were less likely to develop long-term, deep-seated grievances, and could be indifferent to ICU leaders who imbued their message with local ethnic traditions and concerns. Finally, and possibly most significantly, they were not attached to the land at their place of work. If their conditions were miserable, they were generally not rapidly deteriorating, and hence one major impulse for spontaneous opposition was absent.

Most casual workers, too, were neither pushed into protest by farmers' sudden impositions, nor pulled into resistance by the bonds of solidarity which united resident workers. Under very specific circumstances – such as the acute labour shortage in the Transvaal – some capitalized on their scarcity value by demanding higher wages. But the ICU was generally unable to exploit any independent upsurge and direct it against landlords. As a prominent politician declared when strikes in his Natal district were at their peak:

> Why did [the ICU] ignore the natives in the locations where there was at present no trouble? Boys did not come out of the locations demanding 8s. a day; they knew it would be absurd. But the farm labour tenants were doing so.[40]

While his contention was not entirely true even for his own region, it was correct in pointing to the national norm. In ICU days, just as before, it was labour tenants who were in the vanguard of protest.

These male resident workers, who almost certainly provided the bulk of membership in the later 1920s, were drawn from very specific regions. ICU branches with the strongest farm-worker support were largely situated in the eastern Cape, central and northern Natal, the eastern and northern Free State, and the eastern Transvaal. These were precisely the regions either where 'progressive' farmers were concentrated, or where radical rural transformations were in progress as farms previously unoccupied by whites were put to productive use. They were also generally districts where landlords concentrated on arable farming or forestry – especially maize and wattle – or were rapidly increasing their flocks of sheep. Hence these were usually the areas where the 'squeeze' on labour tenants was greatest, and where existing black rural ferment temporarily found expression in ICU-influenced protest. This was especially true of Natal: evictions were particularly concerted there; land-hunger was extremely acute; relatively vibrant social structures in fairly large adjacent reserves supported visions of an alternative future; and the ICU made the greatest concessions to politicized ethnicity.

There was a second characteristic that many of these male supporters shared. Analysts of rural protest have frequently emphasized that it is 'middle peasants' who are initially most militant, and that their poorer fellows often join them only when external support proves that the power of landlords and the state can indeed be successfully challenged.[41] Some have stressed, too, that possession of plots provides a degree of independence from farmers – and that when arable and pastoral production are combined, the measure of communal regulation of life which this entails feeds into the ability to organize collectively.[42] The patterns of participation detected here lend some support to such suggestions. In northern Natal, it was frequently those with 'large herds of cattle and flocks of goats' who rushed to ICU offices when evicted.[43] In Umvoti, Africans on 'labour' or sweetveld farms appear to have been most defiant, and tenants' bumper harvests undoubtedly contributed to their ability to challenge white masters. In the Transvaal, protest was concentrated in the east, where African resident workers were more prosperous than usual. And in the Free State, the Union made little headway amongst tenants in the poorer south, where pastoralism predominated and farm-dwellers often had no arable plots.

Apparently, then, it was not simply the fact of being 'squeezed' that thrust numerous male resident workers into the ICU. Instead, their particular circumstances both enabled and inclined them to resist the abrupt denial of privileges which, while less than those granted to most sharecroppers and 'squatters', still kept them out of the ranks of the stockless and landless. In essence, their situation bore a striking resemblance to that of the bulk of Union organizers. Both groups were losing their footing on the rungs of class ladders – and it was their joint efforts to regain at least the *status quo ante* that fostered their alliance.

The point bears emphasis. As the process of proletarianization accelerated in the 1920s, so two pivotal social groupings, destined for a better future, were being dumped in economic dead ends. As casualties of downward social mobility, lower-middle-class black intellectuals provided the initiatory impulse indispensable for a rural mass movement. But if they acted as the pistons, it was the victims of primitive accumulation who served as the steam. Moreover, it was precisely because both groups were still caught in the throes of proletarianization that their struggles had a particularly militant and violent edge. As a rural movement, the ICU emerged when it did, and acquired its characteristic features, as a byproduct of Africans' forced march into the working class.

But the ICU was also profoundly shaped by a further similarity between its labour tenant supporters and their Union mentors: both groups consisted largely of relatively young males. Very often, it was mainly youths (who performed most of the labour) who enrolled; it was young men who claimed ICU sanction as they refused to work. It was twenty-eight year old labour tenants like Lucas Nqandela who were told at meetings to buy tickets for their parents as well; it was resident workers' sons who, as the prospects of following in their fathers' footsteps faded, longed for the ICU's farms. Simultaneously, it was 'older and more responsible natives' who repeatedly called for the spread of the Union to be prevented, and it was elders who at gatherings reprimanded organizers young enough to be their children. At a Transvaal Agricultural Union conference, 'progressive' farmers were urged to intensify their efforts to harness these contradictions within homesteads. 'It was the young native that joined up', they were told, 'and not the older generation of natives, who were obedient and law-abiding, and it was to the older native that they must look.'[44]

If landlords could look with hope to the 'older native', ICU leaders were often acutely aware of their cross-class affinity with the youth. As one Union activist stressed when railing against the appalling conditions of labour tenants, 'It may be that our fathers and forebears submitted to that kind of living, but we, representing the younger generation, are now rebelling against it.' Leaders and labourers chafed against the moderation of their elders, whether these were represented by fathers who allied with farmers, or by Congressmen who united with conservatives. And by combining in the ICU as the rising generation, they exemplified a larger phenomenon: a current of urgency and militancy flowing through black political struggles in South Africa, generated by the energy and impatience of the self-consciously young.[45]

Despite the vanguard role of youthful labourers, ICU-influenced protest by tenants did not necessarily look towards a working-class future. There were large numbers – almost certainly a majority – who were fighting a rearguard battle, and whose resistance was determined primarily by their experiences and aspirations as rural cultivators. When such men repudiated their labour obligations or resisted eviction, their actions bore only a superficial similarity to the strikes and sit-ins of fully proletarianized workers. As many silently demonstrated when stubbornly refusing to work without even bothering to make any demands, these labour tenants were fighting for much greater changes than limited reforms in their working conditions.

Those who longed for a return to the past engaged in multifarious forms of protest. Some ingenuously reappropriated the prerogative of living and moving freely on the land, claiming that the farms and the footpaths that traversed them were theirs by traditional right. Others had a touching faith in the boundless, quasi-magical powers of the Union. Thus many a man bought his red ticket and then simply repudiated his labour obligations, 'stating that the ICU would soon free him. Others passed through farm-lands and defied landlords to stop them.' Like peasants the world over, they regarded the body representing them as 'an unlimited governmental power that protects them against the other classes and sends them rain and sunshine from above'.[46]

Of course, there were also those whose transitional situation encouraged the adoption of Union demands which were in line with bourgeois rationality. Hence some declined to resume their labours until they received the roughly twentyfold increase implicit in the ICU's demand for eight shillings a day. Others were inspired by the belief that they were sheltered from the wrath of landlords by the external power of the state, in the form of impending legislation or the ICU's legal victories. Thus there were labour tenants who legitimated their rejection of their status as labourers by calmly informing masters that 'they were told that the law was that they could live on the white man's farms'. But even when such resistance evidenced the internalization of certain norms of capitalist society, these challenges to private property and the wage relation were primarily those of semi-proletarianized peasants, not workers.[47]

There were a number of tenants, however, who were at least as attracted by the Union's focus on their plight as labourers. This predilection was most pronounced amongst those whose dispossession was greatest, and who were working together in comparatively large groups for cash as well as for allotments. In Umvoti, the stoppages were shaped by two almost equal forces: the appeal of time-linked, higher wages to these quasi-industrial workers on the one hand, and land-hunger and large harvests on the other. Sometimes, however, working-class interests were clearly dominant. While this was understandable amongst the displaced tenants on the diamond diggings, it was significant that farm strikes for improved pay in the Free State similarly reflected the fact that resident workers' lives revolved mainly around their status as labourers rather than as tenants. Moreover, although various demands for improved rations and shorter hours appear to have fallen on stony ground, there was at least one occasion when a wage increase was attributed to 'the ICU preaching sedition'.[48]

Amongst labour tenants of all persuasions, the most common effect of Union orations was undoubtedly 'insolence'. Indeed, one farmer informed his fellows that ICU members could be recognized even if they had successfully concealed their red tickets in roofs or cattle byres, since they immediately became 'impertinent and lazy'.[49] If this was a product of his febrile imagination, the intensification of covert and overt resistance was not. At times, when the ICU's presence further encouraged vengeful blacks to exact rough justice, crimes of protest could reach genuinely frightening or damaging proportions. After all, landlords could not afford to take lightly an increase in cattle-maiming, assaults, attempted murders and violent resistance against evictions. But much more frequently, farm workers shed no blood as they transgressed the boundaries of the harsh and barbarous domain to which landlords sought to confine them. Nonetheless, merely by attending meetings, abandoning white churches and calling on the Union for legal assistance, they aroused intense and disproportionate anger amongst many *ratlahoboros*.

As targets of much of this 'insolence', as well as leading figures in their communities, 'progressive' agriculturists were in the forefront of those attempting to contain ICU-influenced protest. In the context of their own tortuous emergence from a backward and vulnerable agrarian economy, at a time when they were increasingly involved in a generally depressed world market, many were themselves in such a precarious position that the ICU endangered their very class identities. Even the most successful farmers were plagued by meagre profit margins and lack of ready cash; even the most 'progressive' landlords accumulated capital by robbing workers of a living wage. There was no question of conceding black labourers' right to economic equality with their white counterparts: as one farmer expostulated,

> Don't we know how difficult it is even to find the money to pay our wage bill even at a shilling a day? Don't we know that

occasionally we manage to make two and a half per cent profit on a crop, and say 'Thank God we have not to pay more for our labour'?[50]

Despite being less concerned about profits than sheer survival on the land, struggling farmers could wholeheartedly agree with such sentiments. Moreover, whether 'progressive' or poor, landlords were almost invariably committed to the maintenance of white supremacy. Most were accustomed to taking the law into their own hands, and a tangled web of localized relationships bound many together. 'Moral panics', too, could provide additional ideological cement, as whites from all walks of life displaced a myriad tensions onto the ICU. Hence on numerous occasions, farmers in the countryside – regularly accompanied by their compatriots in small towns – had little difficulty in joining forces against a common, colour-defined enemy.

But incipient or actual class differentiation, as well as geographical, political and ideological schisms, could inhibit united action by the 'master race'. In Standerton in the Transvaal, a good third of landlords were newly arrived settlers, and struggling agriculturists were finding it almost impossible to compete with wealthier men in obtaining either tenants or hired hands. Since impoverished farmers here had concerns closer to their hearts than combating a workers' organization, the farmers' association found it difficult to draw an audience to discuss anti-ICU measures. As a spokesman for 'our smaller farmers' bluntly stated, they preferred to leave the Union to die a natural death, and to concentrate instead on eradicating sharecropping. An African ploughing on the halves, he claimed, '*word ryk en parmantig. Hy word dan 'n lid van die ICU en die kleiner boer bly 'n IOU*' (becomes rich and cheeky. He then becomes a member of the ICU and the smaller farmer remains an IOU). It was probably not true that sharecroppers formed the bulk of Union membership in this district, but his partly jesting argument did point to the fact that social differentiation profoundly affected patterns of opposition to the Union, as well as participation within it.[51]

Tactics, too, were affected by class differences and conjunctural circumstances. In both the Transvaal and the Free State, this was clearly apparent amongst certain 'progressive' landlords, already committed to revolutionizing the forces and relations of production, and subscribing to some of the ideas of economic liberalism. When they were pressurized by quantitative or qualitative labour shortages, as well as by strong popular support for the Union, they promoted a novel strategy of tightly controlled reform. Indeed, the more sophisticated even tried to capitalize on their own convergence with

ICU leaders under Ballinger's regime. They hoped to turn the Union into a weapon against workers, as well as against more primitive forms of capital accumulation. Not surprisingly, this option was heatedly rejected by weaker farmers. Likewise, the failure of the initiative of using written contracts to control ICU supporters was due at least as much to opposition from poorer agriculturists, antagonistic to state surveillance of their illegal relationships with labourers, as it was to black resistance.

'Progressive' landlords, however, won the day with evictions, which often accorded well with their own economic needs without conflicting with those of their struggling compatriots. During 1927 and 1928, the number of African households that suffered this fate due to their Union connections ran into the tens of thousands. While ejectments were not particularly extensive in the labour-hungry Transvaal, in the Free State meetings were sometimes interrupted by the desperate cries of those turned off farms: 'Yes, the whites do that; they chase us away. We are dying of hunger.' Here, in one district alone, thousands of blacks besieged the Branch Secretary asking where they should go, and as the Union ground to a halt in this province, there were many people 'fleeing about'. Matters were even worse in Natal. One authoritative estimate was that several thousand Africans had been given notice in 1927 due to their ICU connections. The following year, this figure was rapidly revised upwards: there were single districts where thousands of homesteads had been ordered to leave, due mainly to their refusal to supply labour.[52]

Above all else, it was evictions that broke the back of ICU-influenced protest on farms. Landlords 'smelled out' ICU members; they assaulted many of those discovered with red cards; sometimes they kept an 'ICU List' at their association's office to make their co-ordinated response more effective; often they razed offenders' huts to the ground or burnt all their contents; frequently they marked passes or tax receipts with the damning letters 'ICU'; and generally they either confiscated tenants' stock or left these households to wander aimlessly along roads as their emaciated cattle died on the wayside. Small wonder that the Union's Acting General Secretary concluded in 1929 that 'failure to procure land for people was the principal factor that led to the downfall of the organisation'.[53]

Numerous landlords did, of course, experience difficulties in enforcing their will, not least due to allegedly inadequate support from the state. At the most fundamental level, this supposed lack of assistance was because the Pact government's primary commitment was to the development of industrial not agricultural capital, and certain state apparatuses reflected the dominance of social forces opposed to the backwardness of farmers. The arm of the law, in particular, was not one on which landlords had much purchase. Few attempts had been made to impose order on the welter of legislation governing evictions, much of which was far from appropriate for capitalizing agriculturists. To make matters worse, the ICU's legal victories spurred on tenant resistance. The resultant tension was aptly captured by the Estcourt magistrate, who expressed the views of many landlords within and outside the district. He peremptorily informed his superiors that since the ICU was

> backed up by Quixotic Judges obsessed with the idea that they are the God sent Protectors of the blacks against imaginatively harsh Magistrates and oppressive farmers, the position now in the County is that farmers cannot get Natives who fail to fulfil their contracts moved off their land if the natives do not choose to move.[54]

But if the mills of the state ground slow in protecting white private property, they also ground exceedingly fine. Choleric magistrates to the contrary, reform was not even remotely on the agenda on any such issue that touched the vital interests of capital. The ruling classes were not confronting a deep-seated economic or political crisis; they were not, in the main, promoting formative action to resolve new contradictions. Indeed, even before social forces favouring recognition of black trade unions had been soundly defeated, repression was the order of the day in the sphere of enforcing evictions. Thus, in general, it was only temporarily that the ICU and some tenants managed to exploit the fact that certain state branches and functionaries were not simply the instruments of landlords.[55]

Perhaps a counter-example best illustrates the extent to which ICU-influenced tenant protest was defused by evictions backed by the power of the state. In the Dunn reserve in Natal, the anomalous appointment of John Dunn as a white chief in the nineteenth century continued to reverberate fifty years later. Although many of his 'coloured' heirs still lived in the location, they had neither freehold rights over their plots, nor access to the criminal code if they wished to eject Africans residing on their land. From at least 1920, there was continuous friction over evictions, as many 'coloured' kulaks tried to expand production on their one-hundred-acre allotments. African labour tenants and residents were justifiably angry about being removed from one of the few parts of South Africa to which they could lay claim. And in 1928, under the auspices of the ICU *yase* Natal, Champion fervently adopted their cause.[56]

He held meetings in the reserve and told Africans under notice of eviction to stay where they were, since they had greater claim to the land than the Dunns. He also threatened a test case, on the grounds that ejectment of Africans from a location was illegal. Since he was perfectly correct, this caused some concern amongst white officials. 'Coloured' plot-holders were even more perturbed, as Africans joined the Union and became ever more confident of their rights. Conflict steadily escalated, and, with Champion's continued encouragement, simmered on for over a decade. On the one hand, Africans insulted and assaulted their 'coloured' landlords, assailed their oxen, reappropriated ground, and forcibly prevented Dunn's heirs from ploughing. They also expanded their own planting to the point where it could extend over three-quarters of an allotment; they brought in cattle from adjacent reserves so that some 'coloured' farmers could barely graze their own stock; they built more huts on the plots, and even set fire to the house of one landlord. On the other hand, Dunn's descendants retaliated with assaults and with uprooting Africans' crops, with threatening to shoot both humans and herds, and finally, with court cases. These last, however, were of little avail. Since many of Dunn's heirs were too poor to afford protracted civil actions, and because their lack of individual titles meant that Africans could not even be prosecuted for trespass, ICU-arranged defences tended to be successful. Hence with much greater justification than white landlords, their 'coloured' counterparts claimed that the state was providing absolutely no assistance, and fulminated about taking matters into their own hands. Clearly, in the absence of two key factors underlying the crushing of labour tenant protest on white-owned farms − private property in land, and relatively rapid state support for enfranchized agriculturists − ICU-influenced struggles in the countryside could be both extremely acrimonious and exceptionally protracted.[57]

No Easy Struggle For Freedom

In general, however, rural protest inspired by the ICU was rapidly and decisively crushed. However much the character of Union leaders or their inexperienced supporters contributed to this, persecution by farmers and the state was of greater importance. World-wide, the power of dominant groups is such that the under-classes rarely win even individual battles. Strikes, for example, 'end disastrously for the workers mostly'. And the history of all early organizations of the labouring poor 'is a long series of defeats of the working men, interrupted by a few isolated victories'.[58]

Nonetheless, the ICU's internal flaws undoubtedly accelerated its collapse in the countryside. Indeed, since evictions and imprisonment were common experiences amongst rural blacks, peculation by leaders bulked far larger as a grievance amongst many members. For them, it was intolerable that they had been robbed by their deliverers. In the angry words of one old man, Kadalie was 'a great cheat'. When probed further on the issue, he exploded with resentment pent-up for almost sixty years. 'Hey! Look here. A great cheat. He was cheating us of our money!' To add insult to injury, leaders frequently used members' contributions for 'Bacnalian and immoral debauches'. An ex-sharecropper acidly recalled that males came to hate the well-dressed ICU organizer Jason Jingoes, because he was 'moving around "marrying" women', and 'messed around' with other men's wives.[59]

But in order to appropriate Union funds either to impress local women or to emulate the *AmaRespectables*, activists had first to persuade people to hand over their pennies. Due to the ICU's focus on mass meetings and its outlaw status – as well as to the unsophisticated nature of popular consciousness – many impatient young leaders intuitively resorted to sweeping assertions about the power of the 'I SEE YOU'. Unfortunately, this approach failed dismally in transcending a major contradiction between popular aspirations and political possibilities:

> In order to mobilise the people in . . . the countryside they had to move beyond wage demands and narrowly defined trade union concerns; in so doing, they promised more than they could deliver; thus they made the programme of the movement more fragile by adopting an immediatist popular perspective that virtually invited its own defeat.[60]

The unattainable was not within imminent reach – and by disseminating an ideology declaring it was, organizers contributed much to the Union's downfall. Ex-believers were justifiably indignant or apathetic: indeed the easy victories claimed by the ICU doubtless fuelled the political quiescence of the following decade. When an official tried to revive one Union branch, he was met by disillusioned people 'telling me that Jingoes promised them the world's things and none of his promises has ever been fulfilled, so they are no more following'. Others were 'no more following' any organization at all. Soon after the ill-fated Dundee branch had collapsed, Congressmen tried to persuade local African men to buy their blue membership cards and to subscribe money for the purchase of a farm. They were met with intense hostility. The small group of listeners bluntly informed the speakers that they had 'had enough of these meetings'. They might consider the matter if the land was first purchased by Congress, they stated, and added: 'first the Red tickets came and now the blue tickets and they do not get any satisfaction through the tickets'.[61]

The ICU's very tactics ensured that many others derived little satisfaction from their red cards. When asked how the organization he had joined had aided blacks, a Transvaal ex-labour tenant wearily replied: 'I personally saw nothing in that respect. It all ended up in speeches.' His judgement was rather too harsh when applied to the country at large, since negotiations with farmers and resort to the courts could and did help individuals. But with the notable exception of Natal, legal battles often did little to alleviate the wretched conditions of the bulk of members, who expected far more of the movement for which they were risking so much. Furthermore, to the extent that Union officials were demanding the reform or abolition of racial oppression and capitalist exploitation, their tactics jarred with their objectives. Even at a local level, there was not much effort to institutionalize members' control over leaders – and so prevent officials from scrambling into the petty bourgeoisie at the expense of the poor. Nor were there many attempts to develop concrete programmes of action, or to establish structures which could co-ordinate resistance. Hence activists frequently failed to move beyond the articulation of generalized grievances to the mobilization of supporters around particular issues. Although Ballinger often forgot that the ICU was operating in a very different context from British trade unions (which themselves had a long history of painful experiments with methods of channelling rank-and-file militancy), his assessment of the movement was not unfair. The ICU, he stated sanctimoniously, 'played quite a good bluff on the people of this country for quite a while; they carried forward their propaganda without having any real force behind them'.[62]

Today, numerous Africans recall the Union with bitterness, and state that they burnt their membership cards when they realized 'that nothing was going on'.[63] Those whose impromptu protests ensured that at least something occurred could justifiably be even more resentful. Most of the rural struggles influenced by the ICU suffered from precisely the same limitations as those fought in the absence of a formal organization. They were small-scale, transient, and scattered in time and place; Union leaders were often unaware of their existence. Since this resistance enjoyed comparatively little economic or political assistance, and often involved participants deluded about the power of red cards, it was generally relatively easily contained by landlords and the state.

According to white liberal advisors to the Union, the resounding defeat of the rural poor vindicated their counsel that 'the country native is a peaceful, contented creature . . . He should not be disturbed yet.' With a more realistic diagnosis but a remarkably similar prognosis, some left-wing analysts also interpreted the ICU's rural campaigns as fruitless. Both at the time and subsequently, the latter have argued that the vulnerable, scattered under-classes in the countryside are 'notoriously unorganisable', and that ICU leaders were doomed to failure because 'they were co-ordinating a constituency of "losers"'.[64]

The disunity and impoverishment of parochial rural Africans did indeed make successful organization in the countryside a Herculean task. And many of the Union's failings should certainly be situated in this context. In the bloody and backward South African countryside of the 1920s, the rural poor were hardly ideal candidates for disciplined and sustained militancy. Their lives were too deeply affected by the tyranny of season-bound labour on their plots, and many were also 'clinging grimly to the raft of insecure and intermittent employment in the sea of available surplus labour'.[65] Large numbers were illiterate, had narrow horizons, and had no experience of mobilizing in modern organizations to right their wrongs. Unlike industrial workers, atomized rural blacks largely lacked even the potential to generate organic intellectuals, to 'beget community, national bond and political organisation', and hence to constitute an independent social class engaged in collective struggle.[66]

Furthermore, when ICU activists provided the unifying element of external leadership, they did so in a careless, haphazard fashion. There was little attempt to understand – let alone transcend – the contradictions that plagued their rural movement: between the national and the local, between organization and spontaneity, and between discipline and democracy. Far from agonizing over the political relationship between urban workers and the rural poor, they did not even internalize an important criticism of their tactics in moving from town to countryside. In his capacity as ICU General Secretary, the Communist Party member James la Guma had argued as early as 1926:

we have adopted the wrong tactics in organising during the past, i.e. enlarging our sphere of activity in the country without having first organised the principal industrial centres to the extent required to make them the effective weapons we will have to rely upon in time of emergency.[67]

Yet to note the disabilities of the rural poor, and to recognize the deficiencies of the ICU, is not to argue that the Union was mistaken in turning to the countryside. On the contrary: the ICU's greatest achievement was to demonstrate the ability and willingness of the rural poor to ally with other popular classes in South Africa. Elsewhere, of course, the political significance of this feat was already apparent. Indeed, the Chinese Communist Party was almost simultaneously embarking on the road to acquiring a mass rural base, through which 'the proletarian revolution will obtain that chorus without which its solo song becomes a swan song in all peasant countries'.[68] In South Africa itself during the twentieth century, there were also sporadic signs that political movements accorded theoretical weight to the countryside. For the Communist Party of the later 1920s, the rural poor constituted the motive force of the revolution; for a handful of Trotskyists in the 1930s, the agrarian question was 'the axis, the alpha and omega of the revolution'; for Nelson Mandela in the 1950s, 'the problem of organisation in the countryside poses itself as one of major importance for the liberatory movement'.[69] But at a time when South Africa was an overwhelmingly agrarian country, and in a century when most black mass movements made little progress in this intractable arena, it was the ICU that put flesh on these abstract bones. For a brief period, its leaders recognized the centrality of land-hunger, forged solid links between land and liberation, concentrated on the countryside where some 85 per cent of Africans lived, and rallied rural blacks on a scale never remotely approached by any other South African movement.

They also, in however limited and rudimentary a fashion, provided an unprecedented organizational input into the countryside. By doggedly travelling to or living on farms and reserves, ICU leaders actively contested the isolation of rural blacks. They attracted thousands of dispersed Africans to their meetings, where the power and necessity of unity was palpable. They established branches in an astounding number of villages, and articulated a message with so much resonance that it was itself a mobilizing force. Significantly, too, branch activists' ideological and organizational practices were usually flexible enough to allow for considerable influence from below, yet sufficiently structured to impose some order on popular consciousness and protest. Moreover, so extensive was the range of services provided from above – agitational and educational, religious and juridical, defensive and social – that many branches became embryonic centres of dual power, and numerous blacks perceived the Union as a law-making government.

Many whites, too, were shocked by the extent to which rural Africans were mobilized, not comforted by thoughts that this was a virtually unorganizable constituency. And they were initially far from sure that their opponents faced inevitable defeat. At a time when ongoing primitive accumulation was already stoking the flames of conflict, white masters were only to conscious of the inflammability of the black populace, and the latent power of rural resistance. 'The ICU will get you' was thus a nightmare sufficiently real to white parents to be deployed as a credible scare tactic, ensuring that children hastened home before darkness enveloped the countryside.[70] Moreover, although such fears were exaggerated and overdetermined, they were not entirely unfounded. As the Union transformed hidden grievances into public aspirations, it performed the same alchemy on previously covert and individualistic challenges in the countryside. And by operating as a national organization, it gave a novel degree of unity and coherence to previously spontaneous upsurges. Consequently, the very foundations of white worlds were shaken by struggles occurring simultaneously over large parts of South Africa, infused with a radical vision of a return to the past, permeated with a spirit of peasant insurgency, or imbued with the conviction that blacks were the equals of whites.

While the dominant classes could crush this resistance in the immediate present, they could not extirpate the ICU's contributions to challenges of the future. People learnt from their protests: indeed, they learnt lessons taught only by struggle, which discloses to an oppressed group the 'magnitude of its own power, widens its horizon, enhances its abilities, clarifies its mind, forges its will'.[71] All over the countryside, men ignorant of the mechanisms maintaining their exploitation were victims of state repression, and received a baptism of fire into the connections between material deprivation and political powerlessness. Furthermore, through ICU-influenced struggles, many internalized the importance of organizing the labouring poor. Some then devoted their lives in imparting this knowledge. As an ICU assistant in a Transkeian village, Oscar Mpetha was understandably 'greatly amazed at such a big movement conducted by Africans'. And it was to this experience that he attributed his subsequent career in trade unions and Congress.[72]

As was testified by the trail of children (and cows) named 'ICU' or 'Kadalie', many ordinary rural blacks found easier ways of extending an oppositional tradition forward in time. But in their memories and their oral traditions, they kept alive a political education often painfully acquired from the ICU. The Union's grave shortcomings generated crucial insights, not the least significant of which was to distrust leaders who could not be controlled from below. Yet while many rural blacks gave short shrift to the Union's organizational deficiencies, they simultaneously applauded its ability to mesh together class and nationalist aspirations in ways which tapped the well-springs of rural radicalism. As ex-sharecropper Voetganger Manapa expressed it, 'The ICU was a man amongst men. It was not child's play . . . Had it been more strongly and better organized, we would be better off today.' Jubilee Kok, who was previously a miner living on a company-owned farm, also reflected on the present in terms of the past. He laconically encapsulated the similarities between the mass-based Union, with its message of 'freedom' for the poor and oppressed, and Congress of later days. 'What today we are to call ANC man', he stated firmly, 'in that time we called them ICU.' Even more succinct, but pregnant with meaning, was Rose Mthimunye's comment. For her, as for tens of thousands of labour tenants locked into a cruel and violent world, the ICU's penetration of the countryside meant that 'we, too, tasted freedom'.[73]

Sixty years later, the South African countryside is still a cesspit of poverty and misery, and neither the racist state nor capitalism have been overthrown. There is no quick or infallible route to liberation; there is no easy way forward for the millions scrabbling for survival on farms and in rural ghettoes. There is but the certainty that the ANC and the Communist Party have long since surpassed the organizational and theoretical capabilities of the ICU. There is the path pioneered by resilient blacks who have successfully opposed resettlement and 'retribalization'. There is also the evidence that ever more class-conscious movements are already intersecting with sustained and concerted forms of spontaneous resistance in both town and countryside.

And there is the hope derived from history. There is the memory of a political organization that received and transmitted the grievances of peasants and migrants, tenants and farm labourers; it linked their struggles, albeit tenuously and fitfully, with those of other South Africans. There is the knowledge that the downtrodden, far-flung and ignorant rural poor could combine in the ramshackle ICU. Against all odds, they dared to resist their exploitation and oppression. They struck fear into the hearts of white landlords. They challenged the world they inhabited, and sought to transform their place in it. If this was the possibility of the past, then how much greater is the promise of the future for a longer-lasting taste of freedom.

NOTES

The following abbreviations have been used in the notes:

Advertiser	*Kokstad Advertiser and East Griqualand Gazette*
A.M.	Annie Mgetyana
A.R.B.	Labour Department files
A.S.I.	African Studies Institute
Baptist	*The South African Baptist*
C.A.	Cape Archives Depot
C.G.S.	Chief of the General Staff
Chronicle	*The Harrismith Chronicle*
C.I.D.	Criminal Investigation Department
C.M.T.	Chief Magistrate of the Transkeian Territories
C.N.C.	Chief Native Commissioner
Compol	Commissioner of Police
Courant	*Ladybrand Courant and Ficksburg News*
C.P.S.A.	Church of the Province of South Africa Archives
D.C.	District Commandant
D.N.L.	Director of Native Labour
E.N.E.C.	Evidence to the Native Economic Commission
E.N.R.C.	Evidence to the Native Riots Commission
Farmer's Weekly	*The Farmer's Weekly*
F.D.	Frank Deyi
Friend	*The Friend*
Gazette	*The Greytown Gazette*
G.N.L.B.	Director of Native Labour files
H.B.	Helen Bradford
H.C.L.	Hull Central Library, England
Herald	*The Workers' Herald*
H.G.	Orange Free State Supreme Court cases
Jus.	Department of Justice files

K.C.L.	Killie Campbell Library, Durban
L.D.B.	Department of Agriculture files
Mag.	Magistrate
Mail	*Rand Daily Mail*
Mercury	*Natal Mercury*
N.A.	Natal Archives Depot
N.A.D.	Native Affairs Department
Natal Farmer	*The Natal Farmer*
N.A.U.	Natal Agricultural Union
N.C.	Native Commissioner
N.T.S.	Department of Native Affairs files
Observer	*The Middelburg Observer*
O.F.S.A.	Orange Free State Archives Depot
O.H.P.	Oral History Project
S.A.A.U.	South African Agricultural Union
S.A.P.	South African Police
S.B.A.	Standard Bank Archives, Johannesburg
S.J.	Secretary for Justice
S.N.A.	Secretary for Native Affairs
Star	*The Star*
T.A.	Transvaal Archives Depot
Territorial News	*The Territorial News*
U.C.T., M.L.	University of Cape Town, Manuscripts Library
Umteteli	*Umteteli wa Bantu*
U.W.	University of the Witwatersrand
Vaderland	*Ons Vaderland*
V.N.	Vusi Nkumane
W.B.	William Beinart
Witness	*The Natal Witness*
Worker	*The South African Worker*

PREFACE

1. J. Frederikse, *South Africa: A Different Kind of War* (Johannesburg 1986), p. 176.
2. *Ibid.*
3. One organizer expressed this as: 'The African must remake his past in order to make his future.' Clements Kadalie, in asking for more information on the Chilembwe uprising in Nyasaland, wanted it both to inspire ICU leaders, and also 'for the future history of Africa as I believe that the white men will not preserve the genuine history of the black man'. Such emphases on the racial identities of those reappropriating African resistance are not, in ex-colonies, totally misplaced. Until it is written as well as made by ordinary blacks, the history of the South African under-classes will undoubtedly remain both partial and blinkered.
4. The exchange in Ixopo between my assistant Vusi Nkumane (hereafter V.N.) and Nokwala Mthembu (hereafter N.M.) was typical. After being introduced

and spending some time in informal talk, we asked permission to start taping, and began by asking her name.

N.M. You want me to be heard all over again.
V.N. I want to know to whom I am speaking.
N.M. So that you will be in a better position to arrest me?
V.N. No, I won't do that. Why should I arrest you?
N.M. How do I know whether you want to arrest me or not?
V.N. Really, I cannot arrest you.
N.M. Naturally one says that.

Mrs Mthembu eventually became more forthcoming even on tape, although her continuing unease was manifested in such statements as: 'Here is the cock crowing. It says you should stop this thing.' The suspicion of tape-recorders common amongst rural blacks partially explains why some interviews consist merely of notes.

CHAPTER 1

1. B. Bunting, *Moses Kotane: South African Revolutionary* (London 1975), p.33. See also T.A., Department of Justice files, JUS 289, 3/1064/18, Commissioner of Police to Secretary for Justice, 15 June 1926; J. and R. Simons, *Class and Colour in South Africa 1850–1950* (London 1983), p. 268.
2. *The Natal Witness*, 26 March 1928.
3. See for example E. Roux, *Time Longer than Rope: The Black Man's Struggle for Freedom in South Africa* (Madison 1972), pp. 135–56.
4. *Friend*, 14 July 1920; C. Kadalie, *My Life and the ICU: the Autobiography of a Black Trade Unionist in South Africa* (London 1970), pp. 13–14, 42. In the early 1920s, Congress was renamed as the South African National Congress.
5. *Friend*, 14 July 1920. See also T.A., files of S.A.P., SAP Conf. 6/698/19, Inspector-in-Charge C.I.D. to Deputy Commissioner C.I.D. Pretoria, 16 July 1920.
6. *Friend*, 14 July 1920; T.A., Native Affairs Department files, NTS 7661, 23/332(1), report by S.A.P. officer on unrest in Volksrust, 17 March 1921; T.A., SAP Conf. 6/698/19, District Commandant, C.I.D., Bloemfontein, to Deputy Commisssioner, S.A.P., Bloemfontein, 21 July 1920; P. Walshe, *The Rise of African Nationalism in South Africa: the African National Congress 1912–1952* (London 1970), p. 206.
7. In 1921, there were 235,665 African mine workers, and 368,122 African farm labourers. The 71,441 'coloured' agricultural workers were overwhelmingly concentrated in the Cape, while the 19,478 Indians in the same occupation resided almost exclusively in Natal. By the mid-1920s there were over 500,000 regular black farm workers, fewer than 110,000 blacks employed in privately owned secondary industries, and an estimated 300,000 'detribalized' Africans in towns.
8. T.A., NTS 7659, 10/332(1), Mag. Kroonstad to S.N.A., 2 Aug. 1920; Mag. Kroonstad to Secretary for Justice, 26 Nov. 1920; P. Wickins, 'The Industrial and Commercial Workers' Union of Africa', Ph.D., University of Cape Town, 1973, p.147.
9. K.C.L., J. Marwick papers, MS MAR 2108.48, C. Kadalie to B. Ncwana, 20 May 1920. Over the following year, doubtless desirous of finding an alternative vehicle for his ambitions, Kadalie drew closer to the Cape Town offshoot of Garvey's American movement. This, the Universal Negro Improvement Association, was best known for its advocacy of 'Africa for the Africans'.

10. R. Bloch, 'The high cost of living: The Port Elizabeth "Disturbances" of October, 1920', *Africa Perspective*, 19, 1981, pp. 40–41, 45.

11. *Farmer's Weekly*, 7 Jan. 1920, 14 Jan. 1920, 3 Nov. 1920; T.A., NTS 7657, 3/332, Secretary of the South African Agricultural Union to Prime Minister, 25 Oct. 1920; Simons and Simons, *Class*, pp. 222–30.

12. *Cape Times*, 30 Nov. 1920. See also T.A., NTS 7659, 10/332(1), Justice of the Peace, Honey Kloof Station, to Mag. Jacobsdal, 23 Nov. 1920.

13. T.A., Labour Department files, ARB 713, L.C. 1054/25, Booklet containing the rules and objectives adopted by the I.C.U. on 24 Oct. 1921; Wickins, 'I.C.U.', p. 178. In a bizarre footnote to the history of rural organization, this reshuffling also helped redirect attention to farm workers in the northern provinces. Disillusioned with Kadalie's drive for greater political power, a coterie of his associates deserted him for Msimang. Besides some Garveyists, these included white trade unionists and social democrats who had been some of the moving spirits behind the formation of the originial I.C.U. in Cape Town. They were also men with links to The Workers' Union in Britain, where the organization of agricultural workers was proceeding apace. Channelling funds through the I.C.U.'s founding father (Albert Batty), and a South African Labour Party Member of Parliament (Walter Madeley), the Workers' Union paid Msimang to organize for its miniscule South African section. Despite this body's insistence on the importance of agricultural organization (because 'the Farm Worker is the lowest paid, works the longest hours, and has the least security for his job than any other class of worker in South Africa'), and despite the existence of a (possibly all white) Farm Workers' Branch of The Workers' Union in South Africa, Msimang appears to have concentrated on Transvaal urban blacks. He was not particularly successful, and by the beginning of 1923 his white mentors had abandoned the effort. Ironically, they concluded that there seemed no hope of organizing Africans.

14. T.A., NTS 7657, 3/332, C. Kadalie to General Smuts, 30 Jan. 1923, and undated newsclipping of interview with Minister of Mines and Industries; T.A., NTS 7659, 10/332, Report by S.A.P. officer, Wepener, 15 April 1925.

15. *Farmer's Weekly*, 29 April 1925, 19 August 1925; O.F.S.A., Orange Free State Supreme Court files, H.G. 4/1/2/230, case no. 111 of 1925, preparatory examination of A. Letetho and thirty-three others.

16. *Herald*, 2 April 1925, 15 May 1925; K.C.L., Marwick papers, KCM 8322, evidence given by the I.C.U. to the Economic and Wage Commission, 16 Sept. 1925; Wickins, 'I.C.U.', pp. 336–8.

17. *Annual Departmental Reports. South African Police. Calendar Year 1925*, U.G. 6–1927, pp. 72–3. See also K.C.L., Marwick papers, Evidence given by the I.C.U. to the Economic and Wage Commission, 16 Sept. 1925; Wickins, 'I.C.U.', p. 336. The Commissioner of Police was not entirely correct: in 1925 Kadalie spent a week addressing Ciskeian meetings held under the auspices of chiefs, and the Eastern Cape Provincial Secretary also proselytized in the Transkeian Territories. In what was probably a more reliable breakdown of membership – which possibly referred to paid-up supporters alone – the Assistant General Secretary claimed at the end of 1924 that members were distributed as follows in the I.C.U.'s thirty branches.

African	6,739	Males	10,138	Semi-skilled	3,859
'coloured'	4,995	Females	1,596	unskilled	7,778
				skilled	97
					11,734

18. B. Bozzoli, 'Capital and the State in South Africa', *Review of African Political*

Economy, 11, 1979, pp. 44–5; M. de Kock, *The Economic Development of South Africa* (London 1936), p. 82; Simons and Simons, *Class*, pp. 249, 304–5.

19. *Star*, 9 Feb. 1928, 12 Sept. 1928, 2 Nov. 1929; R. Davies, *Capital, State and White Labour in South Africa 1900–1960: an Historical Materialist Analysis of Class Formation and Class Relations* (Brighton 1979), especially pp. 180–227. Between 1915/16 and 1929/30, the number of both manufacturing establishments and labourers employed in privately owned industries almost doubled. In terms of percentage contributions to the National Income, sectoral changes were as follows:

	1911/12	1917/18	1927/28	1932/33
Agriculture	16.1	21.6	18.2	12.2
Mining	27.5	30.3	18.6	24.3
Manufacturing	6.8	9.6	13.2	13.6

20. M. Legassick, 'The Making of South African "Native Policy", 1903–1923: the Origins of Segregation', paper presented at University of London, Institute of Commonwealth Studies, 1972, p.9.

21. M. Perham, *African Apprenticeship: An Autobiographical Journey in Southern Africa, 1929* (London 1974), p. 152. See also *Report of the Native Affairs Department for the Years 1922 to 1926*, U.G. 14–1927, p. 1; J. Lewis, '"The new Unionism": Industrialization and Industrial Unions in South Africa 1925–1930' in E. Webster (ed.), *Essays in Southern African Labour History* (Johannesburg 1978), pp. 125–6.

22. Kadalie, *Life*, p. 56; Wickins, 'I.C.U.', p. 222.

23. T.A., ARB 713, L.C. 1054/25, C. Kadalie to Registrar of Trade Unions, 24 June 1924, enclosing 1924 revisions to 1921 constitution; University of Cape Town, Manuscripts Library, W. Ballinger papers, BC 347, A5.1, Constitution and Rules, 1927; P. Wickins, 'The Organization and Composition of the ICU', *South African Labour Bulletin*, 1, 6, 1974, pp. 27–34.

24. U.W., C.P.S.A., L. Forman papers, AD 1714 Mfe, B3.178, Special Congress in Kimberley, 16 Dec. 1927; U.W., C.P.S.A., A. Saffery papers, AD 1178, Part 1, B5, H. Tyamzashe, 'Summarized History of the Industrial and Commercial Workers' Union of Africa', p. 13; J. Jingoes, *A Chief is a Chief by the People: the Autobiography of Stimela Jason Jingoes* (London 1975), p. 120; T.D. Mweli Skota, *The African Yearly Register: Being an Illustrated National Bibliographical Dictionary (Who's Who) of Black Folks in Africa* (Johannesburg 1932), p. 433.

25. *Worker*, 29 April 1927; K.C.L., KCAV 151, interview with B. Mkhize by D. Collins and A. Manson, 22 Aug. 1979; T.A., JUS 289, 3/1064/18, General Secretary's Report of Inspection of Branches, 6 March 1926 (which contains a swingeing indictment of prevalent undemocratic practices); D. du Toit, *Capital and Labour in South Africa: Class Struggles in the 1970s* (London 1981), p. 109.

26. *Worker*, 6 Aug. 1926; T.A., JUS 289, 3/1064/18, General Secretary's Report of Inspection of Branches, 6 March 1926; U.W., A.S.I., O.H.P., interview with C. Kumalo by H.B. and V.N., Mooi River, 28 Nov. 1981; H. Bradford, 'Class Contradictions and Class Alliances: the Social Nature of ICU Leadership, 1924–1929' in T. Lodge (ed.), *Resistance and Ideology in Settler Societies: Southern African Studies* Vol. 4 (Johannesburg 1986), p. 50.

27. U.W., C.P.S.A., Forman papers, A. Maduna to A. Champion, 13 Oct. 1927; U.W., C.P.S.A., Saffery papers, Tyamzashe, 'History', p. 48; Kadalie, *Life*, pp. 163–4.

28. T.A., JUS 289, 3/1064/18, Divisional Officer C.I.D., Witwatersrand, to Deputy Commissioner S.A.P., Witwatersrand, 21 April 1925.

29. *Adelaide Free Press and Farmers' Friend*, 1 April 1925 (thanks to Ian Phimister for

this reference); U.W., C.P.S.A., Forman papers, B2.59, The I.C.U. Funds by G. Lenono; B2.52, fragment of a letter to the National Council, 28 Oct. 1926; Wickins, 'I.C.U.', pp. 338, 341, 388; M. Hunter, *Reaction to Conquest: Effects of Contact with Europeans on the Pondo of South Africa* (London 1936), p. 519.

30. U.W., C.P.S.A., Forman papers, B2.39, C. Kadalie to A. Champion, 22 July 1926. See also U.W., C.P.S.A., Forman papers, B2.41, C. Kadalie *et al* to Executive of Durban branch, 30 July 1926; B2.42, C. Kadalie to Comrades, July 1926; T.A., JUS 289, 3/1064/18, General Secretary's Report of Inspection of Branches, 6 March 1926; Roux, *Time*, p. 161.

31. Moving from disenchanted to untouched districts was absolutely characteristic of the I.C.U.'s expansion, and applied even within one region. Thus in Dundee, the Union originally concentrated on coal workers, and members helped foment a series of colliery strikes in mid-1927. But I.C.U. propagandists were sacked; Champion officially repudiated the strikes, and mine-worker interest in the I.C.U. declined dramatically. It was at precisely this point that local organizers turned their attention to farm labourers.

32. *Herald*, 15 Feb. 1927, 12 May 1928; U.W., C.P.S.A., Forman papers, B3.25, Financial Statement for May – December 1927; B3.65, statement by S. Dunn, 26 Nov. 1927; Wickins, 'I.C.U.', pp. 359, 388. By September 1927 there were fifty-six paid organizers and clerks in Natal, and between May and November of that year the I.C.U.'s wage and salary bill rose from two hundred to five or six hundred pounds a month.

33. *The Times*, 10 Oct. 1927.

34. With respect to the I.C.U. in particular, there are some historians who claim that the central dynamics of the movement lay in the cities, or that it reached neither farm workers nor mine migrants. Almost all accounts are silent or simply wrong on the issue of the I.C.U.'s penetration of the reserves. Thus Wickins mentions that there was only one Union branch in the Transkeian Territories: a somewhat inadequate assessment of the impact made by at least five different versions of the I.C.U. organizing in the Territories for over a decade. He also recognizes farm labourers' protest only when it parallels that of fully proletarianized urban workers: 'Cheekiness (*sic*) seems to have taken the form chiefly of a demand for higher wages . . .rural members may have been serfs, but their principal demand was for higher wages, not for commutation of labour services.' ('I.C.U.', pp. 370, 602.) This is far from the truth, and the reference to 'serfs' demanding wages also symbolizes the poverty of an approach that neglects the specificities of rural capitalization.

35. Prime examples here are Wickins, 'I.C.U.', and S. Johns, 'Trade Union, Political Pressure Group, or Mass Movement? The Industrial and Commercial Workers' Union of Africa', in R. Rotberg and A. Mazrui (eds.), *Power and Protest in Black Africa* (New York 1970).

36. du Toit, *Capital*, pp. 109–16; Johns, 'Trade Union', pp. 718–27; S. Neame, 'The I.C.U. and British Imperialism' in Institute of Commonwealth Studies, *Collected Seminar Papers on the Societies of Southern Africa in the 19th and 20th Centuries, 1969–1970*, Vol. 1, p. 146; Roux, *Time*, pp. 161–97; Simons and Simons, *Class*, pp. 356–64.

37. *Worker*, 6 Aug. 1926, 31 Dec. 1926, 7 Jan. 1927; T.A., NTS 7602, 20/328, Report of I.C.U. meeting in Middelburg, 16 Jan. 1927; archives of the International Labour Organization, Geneva, File N312/3/65/2, 1927, J. Jordan to H. Taberer, 25 Nov. 1926 (copy of material made available to author by Charles van Onselen); Simons and Simons, *Class*, p. 356; Lewis, 'Unionism', pp. 122–3.

38. *Herald*, 12 May 1928.

39. *Worker*, 31 Dec. 1926, 30 March 1928; *Herald*, 18 Jan. 1928; U.W., C.P.S.A., W.

Ballinger papers, C2.3.7, File 1, E. Lewis to Dr Keppel, 8 Aug, 1927; G. Coka, 'The Story of Gilbert Coka of the Zulu Tribe of Natal, South Africa', in M. Perham (ed.), *Ten Africans* (London 1936), pp. 297–305; Jingoes, *Chief*, pp. 120–25.

40. See H. Bradford, 'Class Contradictions', p. 51.
41. U.W., C.P.S.A., Industrial and Commercial Workers' Union Records, File 3, W. Ballinger to W. Holtby, 2 Sept. 1930.
42. *Herald*, 15 Dec. 1926; T.A., JUS 289, 3/1064/18, T. Mbeki to G. Hardy, 25 June 1926.
43. J. Sartre, quoted by D. Goldsworthy, 'Ethnicity and Leadership in Africa: the "Untypical" Case of Tom Mboya', *Journal of Modern African Studies*, 20, 1, 1982.
44. See for example R. Davies *et al*, 'Class Struggle and the Periodisation of the State in South Africa', *Review of African Political Economy*, 7, 1976, pp. 9–10; D. Kaplan, 'Class Conflict, Capital Accumulation and the State: an Historical Analysis of the State in Twentieth Century South Africa', Ph.D., University of Sussex, 1977, pp. 35–44; M. Morris, 'The Development of Capitalism in South African Agriculture: Class Struggle in the Countryside', *Economy and Society*, 5, 1976; D. O'.Meara, *Volkskapitalisme: Class, Capital and Ideology in the Development of Afrikaner Nationalism, 1934–1948* (Johannesburg 1983), pp. 22–31.
45. Davies *et al*, 'Class Struggle', pp. 9–10; Kaplan, 'Class Conflict', pp. 87, 219–24; M. Lacey, *Working for Boroko: The Origins of a Coercive Labour System in South Africa* (Johannesburg 1981), pp. 18–51; O'Meara, *Volkskapitalisme*, pp. 27–8, 258. Belinda Bozzoli, in 'Capital' and in *The Political Nature of a Ruling Class: Capital and Ideology in South Africa, 1890–1933* (London 1981), is the only analyst to argue convincingly that industrial capital was in the vanguard of national capital's struggle for hegemony.
46. K. Marx, *Capital*, Vol. 3 (New York 1972), pp. 879–80.
47. T.A., Evidence to the Native Economic Commission, K26, chief Mgizo, Nongoma, p. 1778.
48. H. Slater, 'A Fresh Look at the I.C.U.: the Case of Natal', paper presented at University of Sussex, School of Asian and African Studies, June 1971, p. 11.
49. The term 'traditionalist' is an uneasy one, for traditions were constantly changing. It has however been retained – without inverted commas in future references – to refer to those who resisted full proletarianization, defended rural resources, and drew on the past in so doing.
50. U.W., C.P.S.A., Industrial and Commercial Workers' Union Records, File 2, E. Lewis to W. Holtby, 12 Dec. 1928. See also U.W., C.P.S.A., W. Ballinger papers, File 2, E. Lewis to C. Kadalie, 10 Jan. 1927 (misdated for 1928).

CHAPTER 2

1. *Herald*, 15 Nov. 1926. *Baas* means master.
2. *Farmer's Weekly*, 31 Oct. 1928.
3. U.W., C.P.S.A., Industrial and Commercial Workers' Union Records, A 924, File 3, undated article by W. Ballinger, 'Native Workers of South Africa'.
4. V. Lenin, quoted by J. Banaji, 'Modes of Production in a Materialist Conception of History', *Capital and Class*, 3, 1977, p. 8.
5. P. Wickins, 'The Industrial and Commercial Workers' Union of Africa', Ph.D., University of Cape Town, 1973, p. 524. See also E. Hobsbawm and G. Rudé, *Captain Swing* (London 1969), p. 66, where the moderation of pre-1830

protests by English farm labourers is attributed to their being struggles by a
rural proletariat for redistribution within the capitalist system, not by a
peasantry for land.

6. U.W., A.S.I., O.H.P., interview with M. Moloko by B. Moeketsi, Mathopestad, 20 Nov. 1979 (*ratlahoboros* is an onomatopoeic word referring to gun-toting
Boers); *Report of the Natives Land Commission*, Vol. II, U.G. 22–1916, p. 29.
'Squatting' was the ideologically loaded term used by white settlers to refer to
African tenants on white-owned farms paying cash rent. Sharecropping
involved tenants who, owning all or most of the means of production except
land, handed over one-half to three-quarters of their crops to their landlords.

7. *Report of the Select Committee on the Subject of the Union Native Council Bill,
Coloured Persons' Rights Bill, Representation of Natives in Parliament Bill, and the
Natives Land (Amendment) Bill,* S.C. 10–1927, p. 121; *Report of the Department of
Lands for the Period 1st April, 1926, to 31st March 1927,* U.G. 17–1928, p. 24;
*Report of the Agricultural and Pastoral Production of the Union of South Africa,
1922–1923,* U.G. 25–1925, p. 6; *Report of the Agricultural and Pastoral Production
of the Union of South Africa, 1927–1928,* U.G. 41–1929, pp. 79–80.

8. *Farmer's Weekly,* 27 Nov. 1929, 27 Aug. 1930; *Report of the Agricultural and
Pastoral Production of the Union of South Africa, 1929–1930,* U.G. 12–1932, p. 14;
J. Grosskopf, *Rural Impoverishment and Rural Exodus* in *Report of the Carnegie
Commission: The Poor White Problem in South Africa,* Part I (Stellenbosch 1932),
pp. 93, 122; E. Sewell-Dawson, *Farm Management in South Africa* (Johannesburg 1931), p. 121. Between 1910 and 1930, the general cost of living index
rose only about 40 per cent. A morgen is just over two acres.

9. *Final Report of the Drought Investigation Commission,* U.G. 49 –1923, pp. 69–70.
While this report refers primarily to conditions in the Cape, the same process is
detailed for the Free State by T. Keegan, 'The Transformation of Agrarian
Society and Economy in Industrialising South Africa: the Orange Free State
Grain Belt in the Early Twentieth Century', Ph.D., University of London,
1981, pp. 156–68. For other references, see *Farmer's Weekly,* 2 Sept. 1925;
*Report of the Agricultural and Pastoral Production of the Union of South Africa,
1928–1929,* U.G., 35–1930, pp. 20, 31; W. Macmillan, *Complex South Africa:
an Economic Foot-note to History* (London 1930), pp. 77–8.

10. L. Flemming, *A Fool on the Veld* (Bloemfontein 1933), pp. 1–2.

11. *Farmer's Weekly,* 24 Oct. 1928; *Star,* 26 March 1929; *Report of the Economic and
Wage Commission (1925),* U.G. 14–1926, p. 75; A. Bosman, *Cattle Farming in
South Africa* (Johannesburg 1932), p. 17; Grosskopf, *Impoverishment,* p. 85.

12. *Star,* 24 June 1927, 19 July 1927, 29 Sept. 1927; *Umteteli wa Bantu,* 30 July 1927;
Farmer's Weekly, 24 Oct. 1928.

13. Interview with D. Raife by H.B., Estcourt, 1 Dec. 1981; *Drought Investigation
Commission,* p. 27; *Wage Commission,* pp. 21, 119; *Report of the Commission to
Inquire into Co-operation and Agricultural Credit,* U.G. 16–1934, p. 139; Mac-
millan, *South Africa,* pp. 73, 89.

14. *Report of the Agricultural and Pastoral Production of the Union of South Africa,
1925–1926,* U.G. 24–1928, pp. 83, 93; *Wage Commission,* p. 79; *Report of the
Native Farm Labour Committee, 1937–39,* Annexure 520–1939, pp. 22–3; M. de
Kock, *Some Aspects of the Economic and Financial Situation in South Africa* (Cape
Town n.d.), p. 60; D. Kaplan, 'Class Conflict, Capital Accumulation and the
State: an Historical Analysis of the State in Twentieth Century South Africa',
Ph.D., University of Sussex, 1977, pp. 41–2, 131, 246; M. Legassick, 'South
Africa: Capital Accumulation and Violence', *Economy and Society,* 3, 3, 1974, p.
261; S. Marks, 'Natal, the Zulu Royal Family and the Ideology of Segreg-
ation', *Journal of Southern African Studies,* 4, 2, 1978, p. 184; I. Phimister,

'Accommodating Imperialism: the Compromise of the Settler State in Southern Rhodesia, 1923–1929', *Journal of African History*, 25, 3, 1984, p. 289; C. Schumann, *Structural Changes and Business Cycles in South Africa, 1806–1936* (London 1938), p. 158.

15. *Star*, 27 May 1927, 30 May 1927, 15 July 1927, 26 Oct. 1927, 15 Aug. 1928, 6 Sept. 1929; *Mail*, 18 Sept. 1929, 16 Oct. 1929; *Witness*, 25 May 1927; *Farmer's Weekly*, 25 July 1928, 19 Sept. 1928; *Minutes of Evidence of the Eastern Transvaal Natives Land Committee*, U.G. 32–1918, p. 150; C. Dawson, *Practical Maize Production in South Africa* (Wynberg 1927), pp. 28–9; de Kock, *Aspects*, p. 13; South African Railways and Harbour Administration in collaboration with the Department of Agriculture, *Farming Opportunities in the Union of South Africa* (Cape Town 1926), pp. 8–9.

16. *Fifteenth Yearly Report of the Central Board of the Land and Agricultural Bank of South Africa for the Year Ended 31st December, 1926*, U.G. 12–1927, p. 12.

17. C. Hall, writing in 1923, quoted by Keegan, 'Transformation', p. 157.

18. *Commission into Credit*, p.154; J. Bottomley, 'The South African Rebellion of 1914: the Influence of Industrialization, Poverty and Poor Whiteism', paper presented at U.W., A.S.I., 14 June 1982, p.1; Grosskopf, *Impoverishment*, p.95; Keegan, 'Transformation', pp. 152–71; MacMillan, *South Africa*, p. 75; C. Schumann, *Die Kredietmark in Suidafrika* (Rotterdam 1928), pp. 271–5. Between 1908 and 1930, mortgage bonds on Free State farms rose from an estimated three and a half million pounds to over twenty million pounds. In 1925, fifty-nine million pounds were estimated to be outstanding on bonds throughout the country. Contrary to much received wisdom (see, for example, Kaplan, 'Class Conflict', p.209), the Land Bank played a minor role in the mortgage market in this period. By 1930, it had invested only about eleven million pounds in farm mortgages.

19. See footnote 18; also R. Davies, *Capital, State and White Labour in South Africa 1900–1960: an Historical Materialist Analysis of Class Formation and Class Relations* (Brighton 1979), p.75.

20. Grosskopf, *Impoverishment*, p.94; R. Morrell, 'Rural Transformations in the Transvaal: the Middelburg District, 1919–1930', M.A., U.W., 1983, pp.243–52.

21. *Report of Committee of Enquiry re Taxation of Incomes Derived from Farming Operations*, U.G. 3–1919, pp.4, 12; *Wage Commission*, p.75; Banaji, 'Modes', pp.21, 32; Sewell-Dawson, *Management*, p.57. To insist that a drive for profits is a distinguishing feature of capital, is not to deny that agrarian capital has assumed a variety of historical forms, often fundamentally different from those found in industry or in historical materialist texts.

22. *Report of the Agricultural and Pastoral Production of the Union of South Africa, 1924–1925*, U.G. 13–1927, pp.104, 106; *Report of Agricultural Production 1929–30*, pp. 14, 45; *Thirteenth Yearly Report of the Central Board of the Land and Agricultural Bank of South Africa for the Year Ended 31st December, 1924*, U.G. 24–1925, p.28.

23. Phimister, in 'Compromise', pp.287–93, describes similar processes in Southern Rhodesia.

24. According to a newspaper which in the 1920s was primarily concerned with matters of high finance – the *Sunday Times*, 5 June 1927 – 'successful' farmers formed 10 per cent of those engaged in rural production. In 1928, on its own admission, the S.A.A.U. represented only 10 to 20 per cent of all farmers.

25. *Ficksburg News*, 7 April 1928; *Farmer's Weekly*, 19 Sept. 1928, 3 Oct. 1928, 19 Dec. 1928; T. Keegan, 'The Dynamics of Rural Accumulation in South Africa: Comparative and Historical Perspectives', paper presented at U.W., A.S.I., 18 March 1985, pp.7–10; MacMillan, *South Africa*, pp.76–7; Transvaal Agricul-

tural Union, *Die Boere van Transvaal en hul Organisasie 1897–1957* (Pretoria n.d.). The last is a collection of life histories of numerous Transvaal farmers, and gives a good indication of rural-urban osmosis.

26. *Committee of Enquiry re Taxation*, p.12; Grosskopf, *Impoverishment*, p.123; W. MacMillan, *My South African Years: an Autobiography* (Cape Town 1975), p.134; Morrell, 'Middelburg', p.226; D. O'Meara, *Volkskapitalisme: Class, Capital and Ideology in the Development of Afrikaner Nationalism, 1934–1948* (Johannesburg 1983), p.32. The extent to which capitalist farmers were committed to developing the forces of production in a low profit sector should not be exaggerated. Understandably, many preferred to invest their returns in other arenas or in various forms of conspicuous consumption.

27. The Department of Agriculture had its origins in Milner's reconstruction period; it was markedly out of touch with small, Afrikaans-speaking farmers, and acquired in 1925 a Division of Economics and Marketing to promote the 'managerial and business aspects of farming'.

28. *Star*, 19 Dec. 1929. See also *Vaderland*, 27 Sept. 1929; *Wage Commission*, p.116.

29. F. Wilson, 'Farming, 1866–1966', in M. Wilson and L. Thompson (eds.), *The Oxford History of South Africa, II, South Africa 1870–1966* (Oxford 1971), pp.137–8. During the Pact period, state aid for export-oriented agriculture included the reduction of rail rates mainly on export traffic; a decrease in the cost of ocean transportation; the establishment of state boards to facilitate the export of fruit and dairy products; protection of the extremely backward but key export sector of sugar; advances to co-operatives to facilitate exports; and the opening of an office in London to promote South African produce. Decreased duties on farm implements and fertilizers, as well as Land Bank loans and income tax amendments giving a fillip to farm improvements, should also be placed in the broader context of enhancing export potential. The heavy dependence of industrial growth on export earnings has always been a critical constraint in the development of a national bourgeoisie in South Africa. Between 1924 and 1929, imports rose by over 25 per cent, while the national debt increased by thirty-five million pounds.

30. *Friend*, 21 Sept. 1929; *Mail*, 25 Sept. 1929, 10 Oct. 1929; *Star*, 14 May 1927, 14 Sept. 1928, 15 Dec. 1928; *Witness*, 30 May 1927; *Farmer's Weekly*, 2 May 1928, 22 Aug. 1928; T.A., files of the N.A.D., NTS 9255, 4/371, correspondence between the S.A.A.U. and the S.N.A. over the former's usually unsuccessful appeals and recommendations; S.A.A.U., S.A.A.U. Executive Committee Minute Book, July 1926–October 1928, meetings held 12 Jan. 1927, 22 Sept. 1928; S.A.A.U., Agricultural Advisory Board Minute Book, 14 July 1926–30 Nov. 1934, meetings held 15 Sept. 1926, 16 Sept. 1929. The support base of the Farmers' Party appears to have been wealthier, English-speaking farmers disillusioned with the South African Party. It was not, admittedly, only 'progressive' farmers from whom the state was 'relatively autonomous': mining and even manufacturing capitalists had reason to complain about the lack of consultation.

31. *Friend*, 21. Sept. 1927; *Mail*, 25 Sept. 1929; *Star*, 20 Sept. 1927, 2 Nov. 1927, 14 Sept. 1928, 22 Jan. 1929, 29 Oct. 1929, 22 Feb. 1930; *Vaderland*, 25 Jan. 1929; *Farmer's Weekly*, 2 May 1928, 22 Aug. 1928, 3 Oct. 1928, 24 Oct. 1928, 10 April 1929, 6 July 1929; *Land Bank Report for 1926*, p.10; T.A., NTS 8607, 35/362, minutes by Secretary for Labour, 19 Sept. 1927; S.A.A.U., S.A.A.U. Executive Committee Minute Book, July 1926–October 1928, meetings held 29 Oct. 1926, 12 Jan. 1927, 18 Jan. 1928, 22 Sept. 1928. Other sources of friction included the 1928 German trade treaty, hotly opposed by 'progressive' farmers who depended on the British market and the Imperial Preference

Scheme; the Pact government's ban on the importation of scrub Rhodesian cattle, since capitalist pastoralists feared this would intensify competition in the sphere of better quality stock; and the free importation of Mozambican oil, which aided soap manufacturers at the expense of local peanut producers.

32. These included land settlement schemes, special credit facilities which for the first time were extended to white tenants, the writing off of loans to maize co-operatives, special livestock societies to advance stock to the needy, assistance to sectors in particularly parlous states in the hope they would act as 'sponge[s] capable of absorbing the unemployed', and extension of transport facilities with the explicit aim of keeping smaller farmers on the land. See also *Commission into Credit,* pp.160–62; H. Leppan, *The Agricultural Development of Arid and Semi-Arid Regions with Special Reference to South Africa* (Pretoria 1928), p.269.

33. *Sunday Times,* 3 April 1927. See also D. Innes and M. Plaut, 'Class Struggle and the State', *Review of African Political Economy,* 11, 1979, p.60.

34. MacMillan, *Autobiography,* p.181.

35. *Report of the Orange Free State Local Natives Land Committee, U.G.* 22–1918, p.4; *Transvaal Land Committee,* p.141; *Report of the Native Affairs Commission for the Years 1925–26, U.G.* 17–1927, p.39; *Report of the Native Economic Commission 1930–1932, U.G.* 22–1932, p.10; M. Lacey, *Working for Boroko: the Origins of a Coercive Labour System in South Africa* (Johannesburg 1981), pp.25–6.

36. T.A., NTS 8616, 38/362, undated memorandum from the Native Affairs Commission to the Minister of Native Affairs detailing responses to their tour, 9 Aug. 1926–26 Nov. 1926.

37. T.A., E.N.E.C., K26, Rev. J. Dube, Durban, pp.6441, 6447. See also U.W., A.S.I., O.H.P., interview with Moloko; B. Sundkler, *Bantu Prophets in South Africa* (London 1961), p.104.

38. D. Coplan, *In Township Tonight! South Africa's Black City Music and Theatre* (Johannesburg 1985), p.73. See also *Select Committee on Native Bills,* p.85; S. Marks, 'The Ambiguities of Dependence: John L. Dube of Natal', *Journal of Southern African Studies,* 1, 2, 1975, p.177.

39. *Star,* 16 April 1927. For an indication of the specificities of Natal, and the strength of particularist loyalties, see J. Clegg, '*Ukubuyisa Isidumbu* – "Bringing Back the Body": An Examination into the Ideology of Vengeance in the Msinga and Mpofana Rural Locations, 1882–1944', in P. Bonner (ed.), *Working Papers in Southern African Studies* Vol. 2 (Johannesburg 1981); Marks, 'Natal'.

40. *Farmer's Weekly,* 30 Nov. 1927; T.A., NTS 1909, 147/278(1), N.A.D. draft report on the years 1927–32, which mentions that rent-paying tenancy, though extensive in Natal, attained much higher proportions in the Transvaal. A 1926 estimate was that nearly one-third of Africans living on Transvaal land largely occupied by whites were 'squatters'.

41. *Mail,* 21 Sept. 1927. The claim was made by E.K. du Plessis of Ventersdorp, a leading figure in the South African Maize Breeders, Growers and Judges' Association.

42. Grosskopf, *Impoverishment,* p.168. In the later 1920s, sharecropping existed on a scale large enough to perturb 'progressive' farmers in the districts of Heidelberg, Kroonstad, Krugersdorp, Lindley, Potchefstroom, Reitz, Rustenburg, Standerton and Wolmaransstad. It also continued in Natal and the Cape, although to a lesser extent.

43. U.W., A.S.I., O.H.P., interview with T. Manoto by M. Molepo, Heilbron, 26 Feb. 1980 (*derde deel* refers to sharing on the thirds).

44. *Report of the Native Affairs Department for the Years 1922 to 1926, U.G.* 14–1927, p.12; Keegan, 'Transformation', pp.259–67.

45. *Wage Commission,* p.97. See also *Native Economic Commission Report,* pp.51–7,

185–99; T.A., E.N.E.C., Duiwelskloof farming representatives, Pietersburg, pp.444–5; M. Raath, Bloemfontein, p.5248.

46. *Report of the Inter-Departmental Committee on the Labour Resources of the Union* (Pretoria 1930), p.19; N.A., correspondence of Weenen Mag. with C.N.C., Vol. 3/3/1, file on contraventions of the 1913 Land Act, minutes of meeting between Mag. and chiefs, 9 June 1933; T.A., E.N.E.C., C. Neveling, Memorandum on Native Farm Workers, p.6 (presented in Pretoria preceding his evidence, pp.8469–8515).

47. T.A., E.N.E.C., K. Rasangane, Louis Trichardt, p.182. See also *Native Economic Commission Report*, p.320; *Farming in South Africa,* 5, 54, 1930, p.256.

48. A. Kuper, *Wives for Cattle: Bridewealth and Marriage in Southern Africa* (London 1982), p.3; T.A., E.N.E.C., Dr. C. Moroka, Thaba 'Nchu, p.4881.

49. *Native Economic Commission Report*, pp.55–6; *Native Farm Labour Committee Report*, p.47; *Report of the Select Committee on Subject-Matter of Masters and Servants Law (Transvaal) Amendment Bill*, S.C. 12–1925, p.44; T.A., E.N.E.C., farmers' representatives, Vryheid, pp.1497–8; M. Hunter, *Reaction to Conquest: Effects of Contact with Europeans on the Pondo of South Africa* (London 1936), pp.511–13. Trek passes had to be obtained by tenants to leave farms with their cattle.

50. *Native Economic Commission Report*, p.56; T.A., E.N.E.C, Mag., Newcastle, pp.1198–9; U.W., A.S.I., interview with G. Skhosana by M. Ntoane, Lydenburg, 7 Sept. 1979.

51. *Committee on Masters and Servants*, pp.44–5, 52–7; T.A., E.N.E.C., farmers' representatives, Vryheid, pp.1493, 1498. There were certainly parents who sided with their children and even encouraged them to defy farmers. Some idea of the conflicting forces at work is given in M. Nkadimeng and G. Relly, 'Kas Maine: the Story of a Black South African Agriculturist' in B. Bozzoli (ed.), *Town and Countryside in the Transvaal: Capitalist Penetration and Popular Response* (Johannesburg 1983), pp.101–3.

52. *Friend*, 19 July 1927. See also *Star*, 21 Jan 1928; *Native Economic Commission Report*, pp.51–2; T.A., E.N.E.C., representatives of farm workers, Lydenburg, p.615; U.W., A.S.I., O.H.P., interview with P. Masike by M. Molepo, Viljoenskroon, 24 Feb., 1980; U.W., C.P.S.A., South African Institute of Race Relations papers, AD 843, B64.7, evidence submitted to the Native Farm Labour Committee by Frankfort farm labourers. *Môre-kom* means 'Come tomorrow'; the *somaar* (arbituary) system was called *lekelela* (helping) in Natal.

53. T.A., E.N.E.C., M. Raath, Bloemfontein, p.5247.

54. U.W., A.S.I., O.H.P., interview with R. Mapaila by M. Molepo, Acornhoek, 16 March 1983.

55. U.W., A.S.I., interview with E. Sibanyoni and R. Mthimunye by V.N., Middelburg, 4 Sept. 1979. Mike Morris argues (in 'The Development of Capitalism in South African Agriculture: Class Struggle in the Countryside', *Economy and Society*, 5, 1976) that most labour tenants in this period received over half their wages in cash or rations. His claim is based on statistics that first refer only to a few (and almost exclusively the most capitalized) regions, and secondly were computed by the Department of Agriculture, which blithely ignored the fact that contracts were honoured more in the breach than the observance. Evidence given to the Native Economic Commission paints a very different picture. It is for this reason that the Commission's *Report* stresses the large proportion of remuneration paid in the form of land, and claims that while cash wages were sometimes given, 'More frequently the tenant, or his family, must supply their cash needs during the free period' (p.52).

56. *Herald*, 31 Dec. 1928; T.A., E.N.E.C., Rev. W. Wentzel, Newcastle,

pp.1239–40; South African Institute of Race Relations, *Farm Labour in the Orange Free State: Report of an Investigation undertaken under the Auspices of the South African Institute of Race Relations, April, 1939* (Johannesburg 1939), p.15.

57. U.W., A.S.I., O.H.P., interview with Mapaila (taking 'joyini' refers to being recruited for the mines: despite the fact that contracts lasted over nine months from the mid-1920s, tenants continued to exacerbate farmers' conflicts with mine owners by 'joining up'); U.W., A.S.I., O.H.P., interview with E. Thabethe by V.N., Ledig, 23 Nov. 1979.

58. *Star*, 4 Aug. 1928, 22 Aug. 1928; *Friend*, 18 Feb. 1927; *Farmer's Weekly*, 3 July 1929; T.A., E.N.E.C., Chairman of Ngogo farmers' association, Newcastle, pp.1188, 1191; V. Ross, Kroonstad, p.4694; U.W., A.S.I., O.H.P., interview with L. Mhlongo by H.B. and V.N., Vryheid, 24 Nov. 1981. Domestic service was probably a key area of employment: in 1913 it was estimated by General Smuts that 95 per cent of Johannesburg's domestic servants had their homes on farms.

59. T.A., E.N.E.C., I. Twale, Lydenburg, p.624. For other references to slavery or serfdom, see next paragraph.

60. *Star*, 18 Dec. 1929; *Native Economic Commission Report*, p.195; T.A., E.N.E.C., representatives of farm workers, Lydenburg, pp.612–20; T.A., NTS 280, 227/53, C.N.C. to S.N.A., 9 Feb. 1928 (which contains a graphic annexure detailing labour tenant grievances in northern Natal); O.F.S.A., correspondence of Harrismith Mag., Vol. 225, File 2/2/18, T. Mdaki *et al* to S.N.A., 22 Jan. 1923; U.W., A.S.I., O.H.P., interviews with Mapaila, Moloko and Skhosana; E. Haines, 'The Economic Status of the Cape Province Farm Native', *South African Journal of Economics*, 3, 1, 1936, p.59; J. Jingoes, *A Chief is a Chief by the People: The Autobiography of Stimela Jason Jingoes* (London 1975), p.107. The Shakespearian quote comes from *The Merchant of Venice*, IV.

61. Here and elsewhere ideology refers to a relatively well-organized system of ideas, disseminated by intellectuals, materialized in practices, and related to but not reducible to class. By culture is meant expressions of material conditions of existence in beliefs, values, symbols, customs, institutions and practices. That is, culture refers to 'the common sense or way of life of a particular class, group or social category, the complex of ideologies that are actually *adopted* as moral preferences or principles of life'. (R. Johnson, 'Three Problematics: Elements of a Theory of Working-Class Culture' in J. Clarke *et al* (eds.), *Working Class Culture: Studies in History and Theory* (London 1980), p.234).

62. B. Bozzoli, *The Political Nature of a Ruling Class: Capital and Ideology in South Africa, 1890–1933* (London 1981), pp.182–9.

63. O.F.S.A., J. Hugo papers, A379, D.F. Malan, 'Die Groot Vlug'.

64. *Transvaal Land Committee*, p.153.

65. K. Marx, *Grundrisse* (Harmondsworth 1977), p.489.

66. *Farmer's Weekly*, 5 May 1920, 9 July 1920, 22 May 1929; *Natal Farmer*, 24 Aug. 1928; U.W., A.S.I., O.H.P., interview with Moloko; L. Marquard and T. Standing, *The Southern Bantu* (London 1939), p.113.

67. U.W., A.S.I., O.H.P., interview with L. Nqandela by T. Flatela, Ledig, 4 Jan. 1983 ('Ma, a person is approaching' . . . 'Oh! No, Ma, it's not a person, it's a kaffir.') See also U.W., A.S.I., O.H.P., interview with J. Motha by V.N., Middelburg, 11 Sept. 1979; Hunter, *Reaction*, pp.527, 543. Other forbidden practices included drinking white tea, or greeting a farmer whilst retaining a hat on one's head. In the 1950s in Natal, labour tenants were still being evicted for adopting a westernized appearance.

68. Hunter, *Reaction*, p.507.

69. T.A., E.N.E.C., Helpmekaar farmers' representatives, Dundee, pp.1322–3;

farmers' representatives, Vryheid, p.1505; M. Raath, Bloemfontein, p.5254; U.W., A.S.I., O.H.P., interview with M. Majola by H.B. and V.N., Mooi River, 30 Nov. 1981; E. Genovese, *Roll, Jordan, Roll: the World the Slaves Made* (New York 1976), pp.3–7; Hunter, *Reaction*, pp.510–26; V. Rosenberg, *Sunflower to the Sun* (Cape Town 1976), p.40.

70. T.A., E.N.E.C., A. Gilbertson, Potgietersrust, p.51.
71. U.W., A.S.I., D.H.P., interview with N. Makume by T. Flatela, Viljoensdrift, 10 Aug. 1982. See also T.A., E.N.E.C., Helpmekaar farmers' representatives, Dundee, p.1323; Hunter, *Reaction*, p.527.
72. T.A., E.N.E.C., F. Neethling, Potgietersrust, p.24; farmers' representatives, Dundee, p.1270; G. van Riet, Rydal Mount, pp.4960–61, 4970; O.F.S.A., Orange Free State Supreme Court cases, H.G. 4/1/2/262, Case no. 80 of 1928, *Rex* vs. J. Mofokeng; U.W., A.S.I., O.H.P., interview with Makume, 10 Aug. 1982; Marquard and Standing, *Bantu*, p.114.
73. *Wage Commission*, pp.92–3, 148, 166, 332; T.A., NTS 8607, 35/362, correspondence relating to application of Wage Board determinations to Africans; Bozzoli, *Ruling Class*, pp.182–97. In 1929, mining and seasonal agricultural labour shortages were estimated to be between eighteen and twenty-nine thousand Africans.
74. *Farmer's Weekly*, 6 April 1930 ('*Ryk*' means 'Rich'); *Natal Farmer*, 11 Oct. 1929; *Star*, 12 Sept. 1928.
75. *Farmer's Weekly*, 2 Sept. 1925. In 1931, a leading official in the Department of Agriculture went so far as to propose legalization of sharecropping, on the grounds that a few prosperous peasants would inspire the mass of farm workers to work more productively, and would allow Africans, as producers, to buy goods from industries.
76. *Natal Farmer*, 8 July 1927 (*induna* means foreman here); U.W., A.S.I., O.H.P., interview with Mhlongo; Hunter, *Reaction*, pp.514, 523–4; Marquard and Standing, *Bantu*, pp.111–2.
77. *Land Commission*, p.361; N.A., correspondence of Weenen Mag., N1/1/3, minutes of meeting with Cunu tribe, 14 May 1929; Clegg, '*Ukubuyisa*', pp.186–7.
78. *Mail*, 12 Jan. 1928; *Land Commission*, p.299; T.A., E.N.E.C., J. Yates, Middelburg, p.860; G. van Riet, Thaba 'Nchu, p.4977; W. Beinart, 'Ethnic Particularism, Worker Consciousness and Nationalism: an Individual Experience of Proletarianisation, 1930–1960', paper presented at conference, 'South Africa in the Comparative Study of Class, Race and Nationalism', New York, Sept. 1982, p.4; Hunter, *Reaction*, pp.505–6; Jingoes, *Chief*, p.66; N. Mokgatle, *The Autobiography of an Unknown South African* (London 1971), p.129.
79. *Farmer's Weekly*, 3 July 1929; T.A., E.N.E.C., farmers' representatives, Dundee, p.1293.
80. N.A., Stanger Criminal Cases, *Rex* vs. S. Kanyile, 28 July 1928.
81. T.A., E.N.E.C., chief Bogale, Rustenburg, p.1105.
82. Hunter, *Reaction*, p.506.
83. *Committee on Masters and Servants*, p.3; *Land Commission*, pp.260, 263; *Transvaal Land Committee*, p.83; T.A., E.N.E.C., J. van Rensburg, Duiwelskloof, p.381; G. Schwellnus, Lydenburg, p.804; Chief Inspector of Native Education in the Orange Free State, Bloemfontein, p.4987; Hunter, *Reaction*, pp.505–8, 522–30.
84. T.A., E.N.E.C., Rev. W. Wentzel, Newcastle, p.1242; chief Bikelabani, Vryheid, p.1523.
85. *Witness*, 17 May 1928. See also *Land Commission*, p.266; T.A., E.N.E.C., chief Manok, Lydenburg, pp.734–9; Mokgatle, *Autobiography*, p.137.
86. *Land Commission*, pp.309–10; *Sixth Census of the Population of the Union of South*

Africa, enumerated 5th May, 1936, Vol. IX, U.G. 12–1942, p. xviii; *Third Census of the Population of the Union of South Africa, enumerated 3rd May, 1921*, U.G. 37–1924, p.242; *Transvaal Land Committee*, p.126; P. Delius and S. Trapido, 'Inboekselings and Oorlams: the Creation and Transformation of a Servile Class' in Bozzoli, *Town*, pp. 75–9; Sundkler, *Prophets*, pp.33, 84–6, 104.

87. T.A., NTS 7657, 1/332, Mr Piesold of Standerton to Prime Minister, 12 April 1927. See also *Report of Native Churches Commission*, U.G. 39–1925, pp.18, 30, 32; T.A., E.N.E.C., Rev. W. Wentzel, Newcastle, p.1249; T.A., NTS 7602, 21/328, Mag., Lydenburg, to S.N.A., 5 Nov. 1924; T.A., NTS 7606, 37/328, correspondence referring to preacher Miliod Ndebele; Hunter, *Reaction*, p.543; Sundkler, *Prophets*, pp.86–90.

88. *Native Economic Commission Report*, p.56; U.W., A.S.I., O.H.P., interview with J. Lusiba by V.N., Barberton, April 1981; interview with K. Maine by C. van Onselen, Ledig, 24 Feb. 1981; interview with Sibanyoni.

89. *Farmer's Weekly*, 5 Jan. 1919, 6 April 1921, 30 Jan. 1929, 20 March 1929; *Mail*, 16 Aug. 1928; *Star*, 25 April 1929, 14 Feb. 1930; *Native Economic Commission Report*, p.186; U.W., A.S.I., O.H.P., interviews with Lusiba and K. Maine; H. Braatvedt, *Roaming Zululand with a Native Commissioner* (Pietermaritzburg 1949), p.87.

90. *Star*, 3 Dec. 1927.

91. *Farmer's Weekly*, 31 Oct. 1928, 7 Nov. 1928, 9 Jan. 1929; *Mail*, 21 Aug. 1929; U.W., A.S.I., O.H.P., interview with L. Maine by M. Nkadimeng, Ledig, 27 July 1980.

92. T.A., E.N.E.C., F. Neethling, Potgietersrust, p.23.

93. *Farmer's Weekly*, 31 Oct. 1928; *Natal Mercury*, 14 July 1927; T.A., E.N.E.C., farmers' representatives, Dundee, p.1282; L. Maling, Vryheid, pp.1589–90; U.W., A.S.I., O.H.P., interviews with Lusiba and Monoto.

94. T.A., E.N.E.C., E. Andrews, Barberton, p.516.

95. *Star*, 14 Dec. 1929. See also T.A., E.N.E.C., Duiweksloof farming representatives, Pietersburg, p.445; T. Emmett, Rustenburg, p.1068; farmers' representatives, Dundee, p.1281; Institute of Race Relations, *Farm Labour*, p.16.

96. U.W., C.P.S.A., E.N.E.C., AD 1438, Box 11, Ladybrand Mag. to Secretary of the Commission, 10 Feb. 1931.

97. N.A., Umzinto court cases, *Rex* vs. N. Makanye, 21 March 1929.

98. T.A., NTS 280, 227/53, C.N.C. to S.N.A., 9 Feb. 1928, enclosing Annexure 2, statement no. 48.

99. *Farmer's Weekly*, 9 June 1920, 28 July 1920, 12 Aug. 1925; *Vaderland*, 26 April 1927, 20 March 1928; T.A., E.N.E.C., Chairman of Ngogo farmers' association, Newcastle, p.1182.

100. *Farmer's Weekly*, 8 April 1925, 29 April 1925, 3 June 1925; *The South African Outlook*, July 1928; *Witness*, 5 Aug. 1928.

101. *Farmer's Weekly*, 7 Nov. 1928; *Native Economic Commission Report*, p.195; T.A., E.N.E.C., Mag., Pietersburg, pp.419–28; Mag., Newcastle, p.1200; M. Perham, *African Apprenticeship: an Autobiographical journey in Southern Africa, 1929* (London 1974), pp.161, 178; P. Kallaway, 'F.S. Malan, the Cape Liberal Tradition and South African Politics, 1908–1924', *Journal of African History*, 15, 1, 1974, pp.117, 120.

102. *Committee on Masters and Servants*, pp.5–6, 33–6, 44, 49; H. Bradford, 'Strikes in the Natal Midlands: Landlords, Labour Tenants and the I.C.U.', *Africa Perspective*, 22, 1983, pp.5–6.

103. *Natal Farmer*, 10 Feb. 1928; *Witness*, 26 April 1928; *Report of the Inter-Departmental Committee on the Native Pass Laws*, U.G. 41–1922, pp.7, 9, 14;

U.W., A.S.I., O.H.P., interview with K. Maine by M. Nkadimeng, Ledig, 7 Nov. 1984; T.A., E.N.E.C., Mag., Newcastle, pp.1194–9.

104.   *Annual Departmental Reports. South African Police. Calendar Year 1925*, U.G. 6–1927, p.54. *Annual Report by the Commissioner of Police for the Year ending 31st December, 1926*, U.G. 7–1928, pp.20–21; *Annual Report of the Commissioner of the South African Police for the Year 1930–31*, U.G. 35–1931, p.22; T.A., E.N.E.C., farmers' representatives, Dundee, p.1265; N.a., correspondence of Himeville Mag., subfile 15/1/5, Mag., Himeville, to C.N.C., 27 Feb. 1930. Police charges for merely arresting a deserter could reach some fifteen pounds.

105.   T.A., E.N.E.C., A. Gilbertson, Potgietersrust, p.58; M. Raath, Bloemfontein, p.5244; U.W., A.S.I., O.H.P., interview with Makume, 10 Aug. 1982.

106.   *Farmer's Weekly*, 26 May 1920, 8 May 1929; *The South African Outlook*, June 1928; *Star*, 18 Jan. 1928, 19 Dec. 1928; *Witness*, 23 March 1928; T.A., E.N.E.C., W. 'Mote, Kroonstad, p.4804.

107.   *Select Committee on Native Bills*, pp.108, 203, 208–12, 218–24.

108.   *Mail*, 29 July 1929.

109.   *Farmer's Weekly*, 27 Aug. 1930; *Farming in South Africa*, 5, 54, 1930, p.255.

110.   *Farmer's Weekly*, 19 Sept. 1928; *Native Economic Commission Report*, p.186.

111.   *Native Economic Commission Report*, pp.51, 187; *Union Statistics for Fifty Years* (Pretoria 1960), Table I–5; T.A., E.N.E.C., farmers' representatives, Dundee, p.1307; Institute of Race Relations, *Farm Labour*, p.22; Mokgatle, *Autobiography*, p.128.

112.   U.W., A.S.I., O.H.P., interview with J. Molete by M. Nkadimeng, Kroonstad, 26 Feb. 1980.

113.   N.A., C.N.C. files, CNC 22/482, N2/2/2(11), C.N.C. to S.N.A., 27 Jan. 1927; U.W., A.S.I., M. Swanson, 'Interview with A.W.G. Champion', p.53; U.W., A.S.I., O.H.P., interview with M. Mokhacane by M. Ntoane, Klerksdorp, 28 Nov. 1979, and interview with Manoto; Keegan, 'Transformation', pp.194 – 5. Between 1918 and 1930, the number of two-furrow ploughs owned by whites increased by over 50 per cent to reach an average of 1.3 per white-occupied farm. The 'pick-me-up' referred to the old '*vyf-ensewentig*' plough which had to be supported by hand during ploughing.

114.   T.A., E.N.E.C., Ladysmith chief, Ladysmith, p.2425.

115.   *Farmer's Weekly*, 5 Sept. 1928.

116.   *Government Gazette Extraordinary*, 23 July 1926; *Committee on Masters and Servants*, p.39.

117.   U.W., A.S.I., O.H.P., interview with V. Manapa by M. Ntoane, Evaton, 24 Nov. 1980. See also interviews with Makume, Manoto and Molete; S. Trapido, 'Putting a Plough to the Ground: a History of Tenant Production on the Vereeniging Estates 1896–1920', paper presented at University of London, Institute of Commonwealth Studies, 15 Oct. 1983, p.23.

118.   *Farmer's Weekly*, 13 May 1925, 2 Oct. 1929; T.A., NTS 9252, 1/371, S.N.A. to Secretary N.A.U., 9 Aug. 1928; T.A., NTS 9255, 3/371, S.N.A. to Secretary to T.A.U., 1 March 1929; Lacey, *Boroko*, pp.18–51; O'Meara, *Volkskapitalisme*, p.27.

119.   *Friend*, 13 April 1927; *The Harrismith Chronicle*, 12 Feb. 1927.

120.   *Witness*, 23 Nov. 1927.

121.   T.A., E.N.E.C., Ladysmith chief, Ladysmith, p.2419.

122.   *Land Commission*, Appendix IV, p.9; *Sixth Census of the Population*, pp.100–1.

123.   *Native Economic Commission Report*, p.193; *Select Committee on Native Bills*, p.43.

124.   *Native Economic Commission Report*, p.51. See also *Report of the Native Affairs Commission for the Years 1927–1931*, U.G. 26–1932, p.15.

125. T.A., E.N.E.C., Rev. A. Kumalo, Ixopo, p.2231.
126. *Witness*, 1 June 1927.
127. P. Mayer, *Townsmen or Tribesmen: Conservatism and the Process of Urbanization in a South African City* (Cape Town 1961), p.166. See also *Native Farm Labour Committee Report*, pp.32–3, 43; *Native Economic Commission Report*, p.56; M. Morris, 'The Development of Capitalism in South African Agriculture: Class Struggle in the Countryside', *Economy and Society*, 5, 1976, p.319; H. Robertson, 'The Economic Condition of the Rural Natives' in I. Schapera (ed.), *Western Civilisation and the Natives of South Africa* (London 1934), pp.152–3.
128. M. Hanagan, 'The Politics of Proletarianization: A Review Article', *Comparative Studies in Society and History*, 21, 1979, p.227.
129. Union of South Africa, House of Assembly Debates, 30 March 1927, p.2043. See also Bradford, 'Strikes', pp.6–7.
130. U.W., A.S.I., O.H.P., interview with Makume, 10 June 1982.
131. *Star*, 20 Sept. 1927.

CHAPTER 3

1. K. Marx, letter to P. Annekov, 28 Dec. 1846, in K. Marx and F. Engels, *Selected Works in One Volume* (London, 1977), p.668. 'Petty bourgeoisie' is used here to cover both the 'old petty bourgeoisie' (self-employed small producers) and its 'new' counterpart (see footnote 26 below and also G. Carchedi, 'On the Economic Identification of the new middle class', *Economy and Society*, 4, 1, 1976.)
2. K. Marx and F. Engels, 'Manifesto of the Communist Party' in Marx and Engels, *Selected Works*, p.44. 'Middle class' (or 'classes') is used here as a broad label for social groups – including the petty bourgeoisie – standing between the bourgeoisie and the proletariat.
3. *Third Census of the Population of the Union of South Africa, enumerated 3rd May, 1921*, U.G. 37–1924, pp.240–44; C. Bundy, *The Rise and Fall of the South African Peasantry* (London 1979), p.140; P. Walshe, *The Rise of African Nationalism in South Africa: the African National Congress 1912–1952* (London 1970), p.240. Sam Dunn and Kadalie were amongst those related to chiefs, while Henry Tyamzashe, Abe Phoofolo and Selby Msimang were included in those who were the sons of professionals. Officials possibly connected to Mfengu peasantry were Ethelbert Maliza and Absalom Geduka.
4. N.A., files of the C.N.C., CNC 39/4, N2/8/3(27), Part 1, S.N.A. to C.N.C., 25 Aug. 1928, enclosing a petition from the Dunns. Champion claimed to have enjoyed 'a European standard of living since my birth'.
5. S. Marks, *The Ambiguities of Dependence in South Africa: Class, Nationalism and the State in Twentieth-Century Natal* (Johannesburg 1986), p.57.
6. G. Coka, 'The Story of Gilbert Coka of the Zulu Tribe of Natal, South Africa' in M. Perham (ed.), *Ten Africans* (London 1936), pp.274–88. Other junior sons included Champion, Jabavu, Kadalie, Msimang and Tyamzashe.
7. Coka, 'Story', p.288. See also P. Bonner, 'The Transvaal Native Congress 1917–1920: the Radicalisation of the Black Petty Bourgeoisie on the Rand' in S. Marks and R. Rathbone (eds.), *Industrialisation and Social Change in South Africa: African Class Formation, Culture and Consciousness, 1870–1930* (London 1982), p.288.
8. *Herald*, 17 May 1927; Walshe, *Nationalism*, p.77. Amongst the branch organizers who had qualified as teachers were J. Mancoe, E. Maliza and A.

Nzula, while N. Tantsi, E. Maliza, J. Nhlapo and G. Coka had all passed Standard Eight. At least one-third of the 1927 National Council had obtained Standard Six.

9. J. Jingoes, *A Chief is a Chief by the People: the Autobiography of Stimela Jason Jingoes* (London 1975), p.74. See also A. Grundlingh, 'Die Suid-Afrikaanse Gekleurdes en die Eerste Wêreldoorlog', D. Litt. en Phil., University of South Africa, 1981, pp.207–8; C. Loram, *The Education of the South African Native* (London 1917), p.318 (the answer to the history question is the defeat of the Zulu army by the Voortrekkers in the battle of Blood River); M. Perham, *African Apprenticeship: an Autobiographical Journey in Southern Africa, 1929* (London 1974), pp.60, 79. Future ICU leaders who enlisted included Dunn, Jim London, Modiakgotla, S. Bennett Ncwana, and P. Sijadu. Kadalie went so far as to apply, but backed off when he realized how badly the Southern Rhodesian Native Regiment was equipped.

10. *Star*, 27 April 1920; E. Brookes, *Native Education in South Africa* (Pretoria 1930), p.18; M. Legassick, 'The Rise of Modern South Africa Liberalism: its Assumptions and its Social Base', paper presented at University of London, Institute of Commonwealth Studies, 1972, p.2; R. Shepherd, *Lovedale, South Africa:the Story of a Century 1841–1941* (Lovedale 1941), p.338; M. Swanson, 'Champion of Durban', paper presented at African Studies Association, Los Angeles, 18 Oct. 1968, pp.1–2. In 1927, an ICU organizer voiced the grievances of many schooled Africans when he complained that mission education was so elementary that pupils could not compete with those who had obtained better schooling elsewhere. 'Those missionaries were not concerned with the quality of education they offered to blacks', he concluded.

11. B. Hirson, 'Tuskagee, the Joint Councils, and the All African Convention', in *Collected Seminar Papers no. 26: The Societies of Southern Africa in the 19th and 20th Centuries*, Vol. 10 (London 1981), pp.69–70; T. Davenport, *The Beginnings of Urban Segregation in South Africa: the Natives (Urban Areas) Act of 1923 and its Background* (Grahamstown 1971), p.16.

12. This was the notorious 'Stallard doctrine', quoted by Davenport, *Segregation*, p.13.

13. *Chronicle*, 23 Oct. 1926. See also M. Lacey, *Working for Boroko: The Origins of a Coercive Labour System in South Africa* (Johannesburg 1981), pp.59–119.

14. *Report of the Native Affairs Commission for the Year 1922*, U.G. 36–1923, p.11; *Report of the Native Affairs Commission for the Years 1925–26*, U.G. 17–1927, p.72; T.A., Native Affairs Department files, NTS 7665, 46/332, E.N.R.C., p.372; N.A., CNC 39/4, Box 42, N2/8/3(27), Part II, minutes of meeting with members of the Dunn family, 14 Sept. 1931; Lacey, *Boroko*, p.387.

15. *Mercury*, 14 Sept. 1927. See also *Statistics of Production (Twelfth Industrial Census, 1928)*, U.G. 51–1928, p.xiii; A. Dodd, *Native Vocational Training: a Study of Conditions in South Africa, 1652–1936* (Lovedale 1938), especially pp.38, 106. Amongst other bootmakers active in ICU branches were Stephen Nkosi of Vryheid and Abel Dilape of Bloemfontein. Of the eight African bootmakers in Kroonstad in 1931, five were working full-time and two on a piece-work basis for whites.

16. T.A., E.N.E.C., K26, C. Mbolekwe, Pretoria, p.8518. Branch ICU leaders who were butchers included Phileon Hlope and Mishanka Maseko of Bethal, who were harassed for not having a licence as soon as their ICU involvement became known.

17. *Census of 1921*, p.244; O.F.S.A., correspondence of Parys Town Clerk, MP 1/1/7, minutes of Town Council meeting 26 Jan. 1928; Bonner, 'Congress', pp.286–7; J. Mancoe, *First Edition of the Bloemfontein Bantu and Coloured People's*

Directory (Bloemfontein 1934), pp.76, 103.

18. *Star*, 24 May 1927; O.F.S.A., Orange Free State Supreme Court cases, H.G. 4/1/2/253, case no. 101 of 1927, J. Mogorosi vs. *Rex*.

19. *Herald*, 15 Dec. 1926, 15 June 1927; A.S.I., O.H.P., interview with E. Ngcobo by H.B. and V.N., Bulwer, 3 Dec. 1981; P. Wickins, 'The Industrial and Commercial Workers' Union of Africa', Ph.D., University of Cape Town, 1973, p.272.

20. N.A., Kranskop Criminal Records 1890–1948, case no. 158 of 1928, *Rex* vs. J. Nel *et al*.

21. C. Kadalie, *My Life and the I.C.U.: The Autobiography of a Black Trade Unionist in South Africa* (London 1970), pp.69–70.

22. *Herald*, 15 May 1926; R. Cohen, 'Albert Nzula: the Road from Rouxville to Russia', in B. Bozzoli (ed.), *Labour, Townships and Protest: Studies in the Social History of the Witwatersrand* (Johannesburg 1978), p.328; Kadalie, *Life*, pp.88, 222.

23. T.A., E.N.E.C., Rev. J. Dube, Durban, p.6262.

24. *Report of the Interdepartmental Committee on Native Education 1935–1936*, U.G. 29–1936, pp.16, 40, 109; *Report of the Native Economic Commission 1930–1932*, U.G. 22–1932, pp.217–8; D. Jabavu, *The Segregation Fallacy and Other Papers* (Lovedale 1928), p.73; R. Peteni, *Towards Tomorrow: the Story of the African Teachers' Association of South Africa* (Morges 1979), pp.22, 51–3, 83; K. Marx, quoted by H. Draper, *Karl Marx's Theory of Revolution*, Vol. II (New York 1978), p.513. Jason Jingoes preferred underground mine work to that of a clerk because the pay was better.

25. *Province of Natal: Report of the Superintendent of Education for the Year 1927*, N.P. 4–1928, p.41; U.W., A.S.I., M. Swanson, 'Interview with A.W.G. Champion', pp.16–31; Jingoes, *Chief*, p.98.

26. U.W., A.S.I., O.H.P., interview with C. Kumalo by H.B. and V.N., Mooi River, 28 Nov. 1981; D. Jabavu, *The Black Problem: Papers and Addresses on Various Native Problems* (Lovedale 1920), pp.83, 95; Kadalie, *Life*, p.37; R. Davies, *Capital, State and White Labour in South Africa 1900–1960: an Historical Materialist Analysis of Class Formation and Class Relations* (Brighton 1979), Appendix I. Davies defines the white new petty bourgeoisie as wage-earners who were supervisors, were based in the state's repressive or ideological apparatuses, or occupied 'intellectual' positions in circulation or service sectors. It was no coincidence that Wellington Buthelezi organized in the Transkei in the later 1920s around the problems of the black teacher 'handicapped by a syllabus . . . If you dared to peep through you get a clap . . .if he dare to teach [the child] further than the syllabus he is expelled.'

27. Loram, *Education*, p.149.

28. U.W., C.P.S.A., E.N.E.C., AD 1438, undated statement made by the Kranskop Mag., p.15. See also *Census of 1921*, p.244; *Report of the Interdepartmental Committee on the Native Pass Laws*, U.G. 41–1922, p.5; Peteni, *Tomorrow*, pp.19–20.

29. H. Tyamzashe, 'Why have you Educated Me?' in D. Perrot and F. Wilson (eds.), *Outlook on a Century: South Africa 1870–1970* (Lovedale 1973), pp.210–11.

30. U.W., C.P.S.A., A. Saffery papers, AD 1178, Part I, B5, H. Tyamzashe, 'Summarised History of the Industrial and Commercial Workers' Union of Africa', p.7; Kadalie, *Life*, p.78.

31. Draper, *Karl Marx's Theory*, p.545. Thousands of Africans were being churned out of Standard Six each year, and the number of secondary school pupils – miniscule though it was – doubled between 1924 and 1930.

32. *Vaderland*, 23 Dec. 1927; Jingoes, *Chief*, pp.58–9, 66–9.

33. Kadalie, *Life*, pp.33–7, 220; E. Roux, *S.P. Bunting: a Political Biography* (Cape Town 1944), p.70.
34. O.F.S.A., correspondence of Bloemfontein Town Clerk, MBL 4/8/1/81, minutes of Municipal Wages Committee, 22 Feb. 1926; O.F.S.A., H.G. 4/1/2/240, case no. 124 of 1926, *Rex* vs. S. Elias; U.W., C.P.S.A., W. Ballinger papers, A410, C2.3.7, file 3, P. Seme to A. Champion, 9 Nov. 1928; Wickins, 'I.C.U.', pp.87, 497, 667.
35. J. Ngubane, *An African Explains Apartheid* (London 1963), p.87. Similar sentiments are expressed by G. Gerhart, *Black Power in South Africa* (Berkeley 1978), p.48.
36. University of Cape Town, Manuscripts Library, W. Ballinger Papers, BC 347, A5.II.I, manifesto by C. Kadalie, 9 July 1928.
37. Kadalie, *Life*, pp.60, 73; Walshe, *Nationalism*, pp.71, 104; Wickins, 'I.C.U.', p.241.
38. *Courant*, 16 Sept. 1926.
39. Jabavu, *Problem*, p.19. See also *Committee on Pass Laws*, p.4; *Report of the Native Affairs Commission for the Year 1923*, U.G. 47–1923, p.28; U.W., C.P.S.A., L. Forman papers, AD 1714 Mfe, B3.102, J. Kunene to A. Champion, 24 Sept. 1927; Kadalie, *Life*, pp.91, 146. The 1927 Native Administration Act gave legislative force to the administrative practice of limiting exemption certificates.
40. U.W., A.S.I., Swanson, 'Interview', pp.71–2. See also *Report of Native Churches Commission*, U.G. 39–1925, p.18; Jabavu, *Segregation*, p.82.
41. O.F.S.A., correspondence of Brandfort Town Clerk, MBR 9/5/4, *Ds.* J. Strydom (Mission Secretary of the Free State Nederduitsch Gereformeerde Kerk) to Stadsklerk Brandfort, 10 July 1926.
42. Mancoe, *Directory*, pp.11, 102. See also N.A., *Notule van die Vyf-en-Vyftigste Algemene Vergadering van die Nederduitsch Ger. Kerk van Natal*, April 1928, pp.57–8; D. Jabavu, 'Christianity and the Bantu' in M. Stauffer (ed.), *Thinking with Africa: Chapters by a Group of Nationals Interpreting the Christian Movement* (London 1928), p.121.
43. O.F.S.A., correspondence of Lindley Town Clerk, LLI 2/1, N9/10/2, B. Moshanyana to Lindley Mag., 26 April 1928; M. Hunter, *Reaction to Conquest: Effects of Contact with Europeans on the Pondo of South Africa* (London 1936), p.543; B. Sundkler, *Bantu Prophets in South Africa* (London 1961), p.89.
44. A. Gramsci, *Selections from Prison Notebooks* (London 1978), pp.19–20; Jingoes, *Chief*, p.92. See also G. Pirio, 'The Role of Garveyism in the Making of the Southern African Working Classes and Namibian Nationalism', paper presented at conference, 'South Africa in the Comparative Study of Class, Race and Nationalism', New York, Sept. 1982, pp.3–9.
45. *Star*, 12 May 1927; J. Langley, *Pan-Africanism and Nationalism in West Africa, 1900–1945* (Oxford 1973), pp.107, 110.
46. T.A., Department of Police files, SAP Conf. 6/698/19, prospectus of '"The Black Man" Company Ltd'; Pirio, 'Garveyism', pp.1, 11–20.
47. F. Johnstone, 'The I.W.A. on the Rand: Socialist Organising among Black Workers on the Rand, 1917–1918' in Bozzoli, *Labour*, pp.255, 265.
48. *Ibid*, p.263; *The South African Worker*, 23 July 1926; Roux, *Bunting*, pp.69–75. I.C.U. leaders who were at some time in the later 1920s C.P. members included R. de Norman, J. Gomas, E. Khaile, J.la Guma, J. Nkosi and A. Nzula. In 1926, de Norman and Mbeki renounced Party membership in order to remain on the National Council.
49. Tyamzashe, 'Educated', p.210.
50. Coka, 'Story', pp.284–7; P. Cook, *The Transvaal Native Teacher: a Socio-Educational Survey* (Pretoria 1939), p.68; Peteni, *Tomorrow*, p.71.
51. Coka, 'Story', pp.286–7, also p.275; Z. Matthews, 'The Tribal Spirit among

Educated South Africans', *Man*, 26, 1935.

52. Kadalie, *Life*, p.78; I. Schapera, 'The Teacher and His Community' in H. Dumbrell (ed.), *Letters to African Teachers* (London 1935), p.26. For comparative material, see Gramsci, *Prison Notebooks,* p.14, and E. Hobsbawm and J. Scott, 'Political Shoemakers', *Past and Present*, 89, 1980. In the Transvaal and the Free State, most African schools were on farms.

53. *Chronicle*, 6 Nov. 1926; N.A., correspondence in CNC 56/5, N2/2/2(X), relating to Ngcobo; O.F.S.A., correspondence of Harrismith Mag., Vol. 255, S.N.A. to Harrismith Mag., 27 July 1922; T.A., NTS 7606, 49/328, C.N.C. to S.N.A., 8 Nov. 1929, enclosing a translation of '*Igazi ne Zinyembezi*'; Jingoes, *Chief*, pp.83–4; Kadalie, *Life*, pp.34–7; Wickins, 'I.C.U.', p.409.

54. Gramsci, *Prison Notebooks*, p.15.

55. U.W., A.S.I., O.H.P., interview with Kumalo. See also *Native Economic Commission Report*, p.100.

56. *Herald*, 12 Jan. 1927; *Star*, 7 Oct. 1927; N.A., Kranskop Criminal Records 1890–1948, Case no. 158 of 1928, *Rex* vs. J. Nel *et al*, enclosing *Rex* vs. Z. Gwaza; O.F.S.A., H.G. 4/1/2/253, Case no. 101 of 1927, J. Mogorosi vs. *Rex*; T.A., NTS 7665, 46/332, E.N.R.C., pp.337–8, 446; U.W., C.P.S.A., Forman papers, B2.59, 'The I.C.U. Funds' by G. Lenono.

57. U.W., C.P.S.A., W. Ballinger papers, A410, C2.3.7, file 4, B. Gwabini to W. Ciume, 30 Jan. 1929.

58. T.A., NTS 1872, 39/278(1), copy of *Udibi lwase Afrika*, 1,1, February 1928; U.W., C.P.S.A., Forman papers, B3.131, R. Tshabalala to all Provincial and Branch Secretaries, 27 Oct. 1927.

59. *Herald*, 15 Aug. 1927, 15 Oct. 1927.

60. U.W., A.S.I., O.H.P., interview with K. Maine by T. Couzens, M. Nkadimeng and G. Relly, Ledig, 2 July 1980. See also *Cape Times*, 14 July 1927; *Chronicle*, 16 Oct. 1926; *Herald*, 6 April 1927, 15 July 1927; *Friend*, 19 July 1927, 19 Aug. 1927; U.W., C.P.S.A., Ballinger papers, undated memoir by W. Ballinger on his experiences in the Union; U.W., A.S.I., O.H.P, interview with D. Makiri by M. Ntoane, Evaton, 20 Nov. 1980; Wickins, 'I.C.U.', pp.368–9.

61. *Chronicle*, 23 Oct. 1926, 6 Nov. 1926; *Vaderland*, 12 Oct. 1928; *Star*, 17 Dec. 1927; T.A., NTS 7606, 27/328, Commissioner of Police to S.N.A., 18 May 1927. Special pleading was often precipitated by intransigence on the part of white authorities. Thus Elias, rebuffed in 1926 in efforts to secure the opening of the Bloemfontein market to all Africans, retreated into putting the case for 'the respectable non-European': 'this time I am not appealing for the masses as a whole, but for a certain class of people'. Amongst the small-town members of Advisory Boards were Johannes N'Geti, a Middelburg trader, and Moshoko of Harrismith.

62. T.A., NTS 7665, 46/332, E.N.R.C., p.378.

63. *Ibid*, p.340; *Herald*, 15 Sept. 1927; *Courant*, 16 Sept. 1926; O.F.S.A., H.G. 4/1/2/263, case no. 103 of 1928, *Rex* vs. W. 'Mote.

64. *Cape Times*, 6 Aug. 1927; *Chronicle*, 15 Sept. 1928; *Herald*, 12 May 1928; T.A., NTS 7665, 46/332, E.N.R.C., pp.288, 429.

65. *Friend*, 2 Sept. 1927.

66. *Star*, 27 April 1928.

67. *Vaderland*, 12 Oct. 1928; J. Richards, 'The Workers' Herald, May 1925–December 1928', Honours essay, Department of Journalism, Rhodes University, 1979. I.C.U. pamphlets had many complicated words such as 'diabolical', and obscure metaphors such as 'sword of Damocles'. Richards estimated that 25 per cent of the English articles in *The Workers' Herald*

required a high-school education to be comprehensible, while 75 per cent needed tertiary education. This, to be sure, was a high 'fog index'.

68. *Herald*, 15 Sept. 1927; T.A., NTS 7606, 49/328, Director of Native Labour to S.N.A., 21 Oct. 1930, submitting representation by Champion.
69. U.W., C.P.S.A., Ballinger papers, file 4, L. Greene to W. Ballinger, 1 March 1929.
70. O.F.S.A., H.G. 4/1/2/263, Case no. 103 of 1928, *Rex* vs. W. 'Mote; U.W., C.P.S.A., Forman papers, B2.30, A. Ngcobo to A. Champion, 13 July 1926 (in which Ngcobo envisaged a mutual exchange of information with Durban police).
71. Perham, *Apprenticeship*, p.133.
72. Cape Archives Depot, correspondence of East London Town Clerk, 1/ELN 86, c3(1), Special Native Detective, East London, to District Commandant, 25 June 1928.
73. E. Roux, 'Agrarian Revolt in South Africa', *British Labour Monthly*, 10, 1, 1928, p.59.
74. *Herald*, 15 Nov. 1926; U.W., A.S.I., O.H.P., interview with Kumalo; interview with E. Sibanyoni and R. Mthimunye by V.N., Middelburg, 4 Sept. 1979.

CHAPTER 4

1. Although occasional references are made to events falling outside this period, the focus here is on the parent I.C.U. during its heyday rather than on its secessionary offshoots. Organization in the cities is included as a sub-theme, since many rural blacks came into contact with the I.C.U. there. The growing influence of liberals is discussed largely in Chapter 5. Since I.C.U. activities in Natal and the Orange Free State are not accorded separate treatment elsewhere, organization in these provinces is weighted more heavily. It will be indicated where this deviated from the national norm.
2. O.F.S.A., Orange Free State Supreme Court cases, H.G. 4/1/2/263, case no. 103 of 1928, *Rex* vs. W. 'Mote.
3. *Witness*, 28 June 1927; *Mail*, 11 March 1927; N.A., files of the C.N.C., Box 81, CNC 58/7/3, Vryheid Mag. to C.N.C., 15 Feb. 1928; T.A., E.N.E.C., K26, Location Superintendent, Barberton, p.532; G. Coka, 'The Story of Gilbert Coka of the Zulu Tribe of Natal, South Africa' in M. Perham (ed.), *Ten Africans* (London 1936), p.295.
4. *Mercury*, 7 Feb. 1928; *Vaderland*, 17 June 1927.
5. *Cape Times*, 13 May 1927; *Friend*, 17 March 1927; *Herald*, 12 May 1928; O.F.S.A., H.G. 4/1/2/264, case no. 121 of 1928, *Rex* vs. R. Dumah and W. 'Mote; B. Bozzoli, 'History, Experience and Culture' in B. Bozzoli (ed.), *Town and Countryside in the Transvaal: Capitalist Penetration and Popular Response* (Johannesburg 1983), p.11.
6. U.W., A.S.I., O.H.P., interview with E. Ngcobo by H.B. and V.N., Bulwer, 3 Dec. 1981.
7. U.W., A.S.I., O.H.P., interview with L. Mhlongo by H.B. and V.N., Vryheid, 24 Nov. 1981; interview with M. Buthelezi by H.B. and V.N., Bulwer, 6 July 1980.
8. See, for example, *Cape Times*, 13 May 1927; *Vaderland*, 8 July 1927; *Herald*, 12 Jan 1927; C.A., correspondence of the East London Town Clerk, 1/ELN 86, c3(1), Special Native Detective, East London, to D.C., East London, 28 May 1928, 25 June 1928; C.A., 1/ELN 87, c3(2), Detective Sergeant, East London,

to D.C., East London, 14 Jan. 1932; T.A., files of S.A.P., SAP Conf. 6/698/19, S.A.P. report of I.C.U. meeting on 14 May 1919.

9. *Cape Times*, 13 July 1927; *Herald*, 15 Dec. 1926; T.A., Department of Labour files, ARB 713, L.C.1054/25, J. la Guma to Registrar of Trade Unions, 5 Nov. 1924.

10. U.W., A.S.I., O.H.P., interview with L. Nqandela by T. Flatela, Ledig, 4 Jan. 1983; interview with J. Ntambo and L. Nhlabathi by V.N., Ledig, 23 Nov. 1979.

11. U.W., A.S.I., O.H.P., interview with L. Mathebula by H.B. and V.N., Vryheid, 25 Nov. 1981; J. Burger, *The Black Man's Burden* (London 1943), p.204; C. Kadalie, *My Life and the I.C.U.: the Autobiography of a Black Trade Unionist in South Africa* (London 1970), pp.44–5; G. Shepperson, 'Clements Kadalie and Africa', *Journal of African History*, 14, 1, 1973, pp.159–61.

12. T.A., Native Affairs Department files, NTS 7602, 20/328, report on Bloemfontein meeting, 27 March 1927; N. Mouzelis, 'Ideology and Class Politics: a Critique of Ernesto Laclau', *New Left Review*, 112, 1978. Although the I.C.U. displayed many of the 'populist' organizational and ideological traits noted by Laclau and Mouzelis, the term has been used sparingly in this book. In large part, this is because it has been used in very different ways by various academics and activists, and hence carries a host of contradictory connotations. The I.C.U. was populist in the sense of incorporating popular-democratic traditions, for example, but it was not populist in the sense of trying to suppress class differences.

13. *Herald*, 6 April 1927; *Chronicle*, 16 Oct. 1926; O.F.S.A., H.G. 4/1/2/263, case no. 103 of 1928, *Rex* vs. W. 'Mote; T.A., NTS 7665, 46/332, E.N.R.C., pp.390–1; M. Swanson (ed.), *The Views of Mahlathi: Writings of A.W.G. Champion, a black South African* (Pietermaritzburg 1982), p.xxv. Oratorical skills extended to playing on names. Thus Champion was allegedly so-called because he could defeat his enemies, while one innovative organizer explained that Clements meant 'claiming' and Kadalie meant 'I don't care'. Therefore, in his version, Kadalie was defiantly claiming freedom for Africa from her usurpers.

14. R. Isaac, quoted by P. McPhee, 'Popular Culture, Symbolism and Rural Radicalism in Nineteenth-Century France', *Journal of Peasant Studies*, 5, 2, 1978, p.244.

15. *Herald*, 15 June 1927; U.W., C.P.S.A., L. Forman papers, AD 1714 Mfe, B3.165, statement by S. Dunn, 26 Nov. 1927; F. Johnstone, 'The I.W.A. on the Rand: Socialist Organising among Black Workers on the Rand, 1917–1918' in B. Bozzoli (ed.), *Labour, Townships and Protest: Studies in the Social History of the Witwatersrand* (Johannesburg 1978), p.253. Organizers often set their own enrolment fees: two shillings and sixpence was a common figure, perhaps because this was the Congress fee. Collections were also taken at meetings for various purposes, including officials' travelling expenses.

16. U.W., C.P.S.A., Forman papers, B3.143, Statement on Head Office Income and Expenditure for 1927; U.W., C.P.S.A., W. Ballinger papers, A410, C2.3.7, undated memoir by W. Ballinger on his experiences in the Union. Branches could unconstitutionally hold on to enrolment and subscription fees: in 1927, Durban passed on less than a quarter of its total income. Even here, subscriptions paid were less than a fifth of those owed.

17. Quotations (in sequence) are from *Herald*, 15 June 1927 ('WAKE UP AFRICA! COME BACK AFRICA!'); *Star*, 13 April 1928; *Mail*, 5 Dec. 1928; T.A., NTS 7602, 20/328, report on meeting in Middelburg township, 16 Jan. 1927.

18. E. Hobsbawm, *The Age of Revolution 1789–1848* (New York 1962), p.168.

19. A. Gramsci, *Selections from Prison Notebooks* (London 1978), p.238.

20. T. Nairn, *The Break-Up of Britain: Crisis and Neo-Nationalism* (London 1977), pp.343–4.

21. The terms used here are derived from Gramsci's analysis of hegemonic ideologies. The actual quotes are from B. Bozzoli, *The Political Nature of a Ruling Class: Capital and Ideology in South Africa 1890–1933* (London 1981), p.18, and C. Mouffe, 'Hegemony and Ideology in Gramsci' in C. Mouffe (ed.), *Gramsci and Marxist Theory* (London 1979), p.195. See also Gramsci, *Selections*, and G. Rudé, *Ideology and Popular Protest* (New York 1980).

22. *Herald*, 15 Dec. 1926; U.W., A.S.I., O.H.P., interview with C. Kumalo by H.B. and V.N., Mooi River, 28 Nov. 1981; Coka, 'Story', p.297. Kumalo claimed the Estcourt office was open from seven in the morning to nine at night on weekdays, and from eight to one on Saturdays. Champion somewhat wearily stated that as soon as he arrived in Durban, 'my office was full of natives complaining'.

23. P. Mayer, 'The Origin and Decline of Two Rural Resistance Ideologies' in P. Mayer (ed.), *Black Villagers in an Industrial Society: Anthropological Perspectives on Labour Migration in South Africa* (Cape Town 1980), pp.41–6. In 1930, the Native Commissioner for Sekhukhuneland claimed Sepedi speakers flocking from the farms to the reserve wished to turn the clock back by more than a century, and to return to the period when their paramountcy was at the height of its powers. 'They say "Let us go back to the day of Thulare." . . . It means "Let us go back to our old customs and let us be free from every one; let us go back to the good old times."'

24. E. Laclau, *Politics and Ideology in Marxist Theory: Capitalism – Fascism – Populism* (London 1979), p.157.

25. *Mercury*, 12 July 1927.

26. *Cape Times*, 13 May 1927; *Friend*, 31 May 1928; *Herald*, 28 April 1926; *Courant*, 20 Oct. 1927; U.W., A.S.I., O.H.P., interview with Nqandela; U.W., C.P.S.A., Forman papers, B3.165, statement by S. Dunn, 26 Nov. 1927; T.A., Department of Justice files, JUS 289, 3/1064/18, Divisional Officer of the C.I.D. to Deputy Commissioner of the S.A.P., Witwatersrand, 21 April 1925. In January 1928, the I.C.U. claimed 85 per cent of its members were African, 14.75 per cent were 'coloured', and 0.25 per cent were white.

27. J. Saul, 'The dialectic of Class and Tribe', *Race and Class*, 20, 4, 1979, pp.351–2, p.354.

28. *Herald*, 6 April 1927; *Report of Native Churches Commission*, U.G. 39–1925, p.6; U.W., C.P.S.A., A. Champion papers, A922, Letter Book 1925–26, A. Champion to C. Kadalie, 29 Dec. 1925; U.W., C.P.S.A., Forman papers, B3.178, minutes of Special Congress, 16 Dec. 1927; C.A., correspondence of East London Town Clerk, 1/ELN 86, c3(1), Special Native Detective, East London, to D.C., 20 Feb. 1928.

29. *Witness*, 17 May 1928. See also *Cape Times*, 14 July 1927, 8 Sept. 1927; *The Farmer's Weekly*, 7 Sept. 1927, 5 Oct. 1927; *Report of the Select Committee on the Subject of the Union Native Council Bill, Coloured Persons' Rights Bill, Representation of Natives in Parliament Bill, and the Natives Land (Amendment) Bill*, S.C. 10–1927, p.385; South African Defence Force Archives Depot, files of the C.G.S., CGS GP1 43, File 63, Lieutenant Colonel Commanding No. 3 Military District to C.G.S., 19 May 1927; T.A., correspondence in NTS 01, 13/1(1) referring to the political expediency of entertaining chief Swayimana so lavishly.

30. N.A., CNC 58/7/3, Box 81, D.C. Eshowe to Mag. Eshowe, 2 Nov. 1929; S. Marks, *The Ambiguities of Dependence in South Africa: Class, Nationalism, and the State in Twentieth-Century Natal* (Johannesburg 1986), p.6. This and following comments about Solomon draw heavily on the latter reference, and on S. Marks, 'Natal, the Zulu Royal Family and the Ideology of Segregation', *Journal of Southern African Studies*, 4,2,1977.

31. K.C.L., G. Nicholls papers, MS NIC 2.08.1, file 5, KCM 3348, G. Nicholls to J. van Zutphen, 28 May 1929.

32. *Star*, 6 May 1927; N.A., CNC 58/7/3, Box 81, Inspector, D.C. Eshowe to Deputy Commissioner, Natal S.A.P., 5 April 1928; Marks, *Ambiguities*, p.37.

33. *Ilanga lase Natal*, 12 Aug. 1927.

34. *Star*, 15 Aug. 1927, 3 Nov. 1927; N.A., CNC 58/7/4, Box 84, NI/1/3(32), Major Herbst to C. Wheelwright, 7 April 1928. Solomon's anti-I.C.U. career also included a 1928 speech to young men being trained as chiefs – an occasion which was arranged by sugar planter Heaton Nicholls. See the Conclusion for further details about Solomon's 'ambiguity'.

35. *Cape Times*, 14 July 1927; *Herald*, 15 Sept. 1927; T.A., E.N.E.C., J. Penzhorn, Rustenburg, p.1012; P. Wickins, 'The Industrial and Commercial Workers' Union of Africa', Ph.D., University of Cape Town, 1973, pp.372–3.

36. N.A., correspondence of Kranskop Mag., N1/1/3, S.A.P. officer, Kranskop, to Mag. Kranskop, 4 March 1928; U.W., C.P.S.A., Forman papers, B3.140, K. 'Mote to A. Champion, 31 Oct. 1927; B3.141, B. Gwabini to A. Champion, 31 Oct. 1927.

37. *Herald*, 14 Oct. 1926, 15 Aug. 1927 (in which Swayimana was denounced as a political 'numskull'); W. Beinart and C. Bundy, 'The Union, the Nation and the Talking Crow: the Ideology and Tactics of the Independent ICU in East London', paper presented at U.W., A.S.I., 4 March 1985, pp.15–16. The quote is from Gramsci, *Selections*, p.10.

38. Nairn, *Break-Up*, p.141. 'Imagined political community' is the phrase used to identify a nation by B. Anderson, *Imagined Communities: Reflections on the Origin and Spread of Nationalism* (London 1983), p.15. But the I.C.U. generally managed only to construct much smaller groups whose members thought they were linked by a common political aim.

39. Coka, 'Story', p.296; Kadalie, *Life*, p.96.

40. *Mercury*, 19 May 1927; Coka, 'Story', p.296; J. Guy, *The Destruction of the Zulu Kingdom: the Civil War in Zululand, 1879–1884* (Johannesburg 1982), pp.115–16. The reference to the 'famous Abaqulusi' is also a good example of local ideological struggle. The Abaqulusi Land Union had been operating in Vryheid since 1926 under the leadership of M. Maling, himself connected to the network surrounding Solomon. It united chiefs and labour tenants in northern Natal on a fairly radical programme of opposition to exploitation on farms and to the landlessness of chiefs. It was infused with royalist sentiments, with references to the Zulu Nation, and with longings for the lost land seized from the Zulu kingdom by the Boers in 1884–5. Small wonder that the I.C.U. attempted to wrest from it some of its ideological elements.

41. *Mercury*, 19 May 1927; T.A., NTS 7606, 31/328, S.A.P. report on Zastron meeting, 13 Feb. 1927; U.W., A.S.I., M. Swanson, 'Interview with A.W.G. Champion', p.182.

42. *Herald*, 6 April 1927, 15 June 1927, 30 Nov. 1928; *Mail*, 15 Jan. 1929; U.W., A.S.I., O.H.P., interview with J. Motha by V.N., Middelburg, 11 Sept. 1979; M. Lacey, *Working for Boroko: the Origins of a Coercive Labour System in South Africa* (Johannesburg 1981), p.52. A favourite proverb was 'A child who

does not cry will die in its cradle.' It is difficult to identify the Cape districts where 'tribal jealousies' were invoked, or even to decide whether this referred to the whipping up of 'coloured'/African antagonisms.

43. *Herald*, 18 March 1927; U.W., C.P.S.A., Forman papers, B.3.168, minutes of National Council meeting, 18–25 Nov. 1927; B3.178, minutes of Special Congress, 16 Dec. 1927; U.W., C.P.S.A., W. Ballinger papers, file 4, W. Ballinger to A. Brockway, 15 May 1929; Coka, 'Story', p.298; Kadalie, *Life*, p.157; J. Jingoes, *A Chief is a Chief by the People: the Autobiography of Stimela Jason Jingoes* (London 1975), pp.111–12, 120–1.

44. U.W., C.P.S.A., A. Saffrey papers, AD 1178, Part I, B5, H. Tyamzashe, 'Summarised History of the Industrial and Commercial Workers' Union of Africa', pp.14–15; Hull Central Library, England, E. Lewis letters, Part I, HCL D4 F7, E. Lewis to W. Holtby, 3 Sept. 1928 (thanks to Tim Couzens for this reference); R. Suttner, *The Freedom Charter – The People's Charter in the Nineteen-Eighties* (Cape Town 1984), pp.30–31. In 1922, Sidney Bunting of the C.P. argued that only a black organization led by blacks could reach the rural proletariat and the peasantry. Despite the opposition of most organizers, the machinations of Kadalie and his coterie of white supporters led to the arrival of William Ballinger as an Advisor to the Union. Shouts from audiences such as 'Get out! We don't want you', and antagonism from activists to their new white *baas*, left little doubt about the foolhardiness of introducing him. Ballinger himself was later to admit that the great majority of Africans perceived anything introduced by whites as anathema.

45. *Herald*, 12 Jan. 1927. See also *Herald*, 18 March 1927; *Natal Farmer*, 19 Aug. 1927; Kadalie, *Life*, pp.202, 222; J. Mancoe, *First Edition of the Bloemfontein Bantu and Coloured People's Directory* (Bloemfontein 1934), p.102.

46. Coka, 'Story', pp.295–6.

47. U.W., A.S.I., O.H.P., interview with P. Masike by M. Molepo, Viljoenskroon, 24 Feb. 1980; interview with T. Mdhlalose by H.B. and V.N., Vryheid, 25 Nov. 1981.

48. *Herald*, 12 May 1928; A. Myburgh, *The Tribes of Barberton District* (Pretoria 1949), p.110. Chief Dhlamini, who appeared at the I.C.U.'s 1927 conference, had been sent by his Richmond followers, all of whom were based on private farms. Other Natal chiefs who supported the Union included Kopolo of Umzinto, and Jana Ntuli ka-'Mcobela of Mapumulo, both of whom led followings based entirely on private land, Crown land or mission reserves. For further details about Transvaal and Transkeian chiefs who supported the movement, see Chapters 5 and 7.

49. *Herald*, 15 July 1927; *Witness*, 6 July 1927; U.W., C.P.S.A., W. Ballinger papers, undated memoir by W. Ballinger on his experiences in the Union.

50. U.W., A.S.I., O.H.P., interview with Ngcobo. See Chapter 6 for a similar message in Umvoti, and for Weenen and Estcourt, see H. Bradford, 'Strikes in the Natal Midlands: Landlords, Labour Tenants and the I.C.U.', *Africa Perspective*, 22, 1983. In *Black Power in South Africa* (Berkeley 1978), Gail Gerhart similarly argues that Africanism was closely associated with peasant aspirations. For further treatment of the 'magical' powers of I.C.U. tickets, see Chapter 7.

51. *Mercury*, 11 April 1927; Coka, 'Story', p.295; S. Marks, *Reluctant Rebellion: the 1906–1908 Disturbances in Natal* (Oxford 1970), pp.144–68.

52. N.A., CNC 22/135, N2/10/3(25), Melmoth Mag. to C.N.C., 25 July 1927.

53. N.A., CNC 22/135, N2/10/3(25), Melmoth Mag. to C.N.C., 7 Jan 1928. The above two paragraphs are constructed from correspondence in this file, as well as that in T.A., NTS 3216, 409/307; T.A., E.N.E.C., evidence given by

various witnesses, Melmoth, pp.1848–1969.

54. T.A., JUS 437, 4/366/27, Estcourt Mag. to S.J., 2 April 1928; Nairn, *Break-Up*, p.349; M. Swanson, 'Champion of Durban', paper presented at African Studies Association, Los Angeles, 18 Oct. 1968, pp.8–9.

55. *Herald*, 6 April 1927, 15 Sept. 1927; *Witness*, 9 Sept. 1927; U.W., A.S.I., O.H.P., interview with N. Mthembu by H.B. and V.N., Ixopo, 5 July 1980; U.W., C.P.S.A., Forman papers, B3.70, unsigned letter to A. Champion, 25 Aug. 1927 (internal evidence reveals Mcunu as the author).

56. T.A., NTS 1702, 45/276(1), Post Commander, S.A.P., Moguntia, to D.C., Ixopo, 5 July 1928.

57. U.W., A.S.I., O.H.P., interview with I. Dinkebogile by T. Phiri, Phokeng, 28 July 1981; interview with I. Mathuloe by T. Phiri, Phokeng, 13 May 1981. For further references to pigs, see Chapter 7.

58. O.F.S.A., Correspondence of Harrismith Mag., N2/2/3, P. Lamula to Harrismith Mag., 7 Oct. 1929; T.A., NTS 7657, 3/332, C. Kadalie to General Smuts, 30 Jan. 1923; T.A., JUS 289, 3/1064/18, Commissioner of Police to S.J., 15 June 1926; U.W., A.S.I., O.H.P., interview with Ngcobo; J. Jingoes, *Chief*, pp.107–10, 116–17.

59. *Mercury*, 23 Aug. 1927; N.A., Kranskop Criminal Records 1890–1948, Case no. 158 of 1928, *Rex* vs. J. Nel *et al*, enclosing *Rex* vs. Z. Gwaza; U.W., C.P.S.A., Forman papers, B3. 74, Eshowe Branch Secretary to A. Champion, 30 Aug. 1927; U.W., A.S.I., O.H.P., interview with Kumalo.

60. N.A., CNC 2/73/59, Box 82, N1/1/3(10), Estcourt Mag. to C.N.C., 3 Sept. 1928; U.W., A.S.I., O.H.P., interview with Mdhlalose.

61. N.A.U., Executive Committee Minute Book, meeting on 2 June 1927 (when a Dundee farmer complained of regular I.C.U. meetings being held on holdings in his district); U.W., A.S.I., O.H.P., interview with A. Mokale by T. Flatela, Evaton, 2 April 1982, and interview with Kumalo. After his car had broken down in early 1928, Solomon ka Dinizulu was given an unwelcome reminder of the extent to which I.C.U. activists were operating on the farm themselves. After retiring to sleep on a remote Babanango holding, he and his retinue were rudely disturbed by the owner, who thought they were I.C.U. representatives.

62. *Star*, 14 Sept. 1928. See also Chapter 6.

63. N.A., correspondence in CNC 56/5, N2/2/2(X), especially C.N.C. to S.N.A., 10 March 1927, enclosing correspondence by Abel Ngcobo; CNC 36/7, Box 40, N2/2/2(28), statement by M. Goba to Ndwedwe Mag., 1 June 1927; U.W., A.S.I., O.H.P., interview with Ngcobo; Jingoes, *Chief*, p.123.

64. *Mercury*, 14 July 1927; U.W., A.S.I., O.H.P., interview with Kumalo; Marks, *Ambiguities*, p.100. Areas in Natal where the I.C.U. established an informal presence in reserves included Empangeni, Melmoth, Mtunzini, Ndwedwe, Nkandla and Nqutu, while there were branches in Eshowe and Mapumulo. In the Free State, Witzieshoek was serviced by the Harrismith branch, and there was also a short-lived branch in Thaba 'Nchu. For the Transvaal and Cape, see Chapters 5 and 7.

65. *Cape Times*, 13 May 1927; N.A., CNC 57/27, N1/1/3(43), statement by M. Kumalo, 4 July 1929; N.A., correspondence of Kranskop Mag., N1/1/3, S.A.P. officer, Kranskop, to Mag. Kranskop, 4 March 1928. An ex-Vryheid teacher claimed that meetings in this village were attended by Africans living up to one hundred kilometres away, because the I.C.U. sent emissaries to chiefs asking for people to attend on a particular date.

66. T.A., NTS 1702, 45/276(1), Post Commander S.A.P., Moguntia, to D.C., Ixopo, 5 July 1928.

67. T.A., NTS 1702, 45/276(1), Major Herbst to Governor-General, 26 Sept. 1927; T.A., NTS 7606, 49/328, C.N.C. to S.N.A., 8 Nov. 1929, enclosing translation of '*Igazi ne Zinyembezi*'; Kadalie, *Life*, pp.145, 204. Natal's C.N.C. advised magistrates to block penetration of the reserves because 'bodies such as the ICU which purport to be trade unions can only legitimately concern themselves with natives in employment in urban or industrial areas . . . permission for their officials to hold meetings in the Reserves can therefore legitimately be refused'. Despite the barriers it faced, the Union had an impact in Basutoland, Bechuanaland, Nyasaland, Portuguese East Africa, both Rhodesias and South West Africa. Perhaps the worst victimization was experienced by Isa Lawrence, sentenced to three years imprisonment for importing into Nyasaland six copies of the Garveyist *Negro World*, and two of *The Workers' Herald*.

68. *Courant*, 20 Oct. 1927; *Star*, 24 Oct. 1927; U.W., C.P.S.A., Forman papers, B3.74, Eshowe Branch Secretary to A. Champion, 30 Aug. 1927. Butha-Buthe, Leribe, Mafeteng and Maseru were amongst the four to seven towns allegedly blessed with I.C.U. branches, which were probably established with help from the Basutoland Progressive Association.

69. N.A., correspondence of Richmond Mag., N1/1/3/8, Richmond Mag. to C.N.C., 26 Jan. 1929, enclosing statements taken at a meeting on 23 Jan. 1929. Correspondence in this file details the course of the conflict between ardent I.C.U member Phillip Ngcongo, a teacher and lay-preacher who held I.C.U. meetings at his home, and acting chief Nxamalala Mkhize, whose succession to the post in 1926 had been hotly contested. In 1927, Nxamalala imposed a one-pound levy on all girls, to be collected from their fathers if they had no lovers.

70. T.A., NTS 1702, 45/276(1), Post Commander S.A.P., Moguntia, to D.C., Ixopo, 5 July 1928.

71. U.W., A.S.I., O.H.P., interview with Ngcobo.

72. This estimate was for December 1927 and is fairly reliable, given that it was made by Detective Sergeant Arnold and confirmed by Dunn.

73. *Herald*, 18 March 1927.

74. T.A., NTS 7606, 27/328, Acting Commissioner S.A.P. to S.N.A., 14 Jan. 1927. See also *Chronicle*, 16 Oct. 1926; *Mercury*, 22 July 1927; *Star*, 13 June 1927, 8 Oct. 1928; *Witness*, 13 May 1927.

75. Nairn, *Break-Up*, p.357.

76. *Herald*, 28 April 1926, 12 Jan. 1927. For overseas consumption in late 1927, Kadalie claimed that 'We are utterly opposed to nationalism. Our goal is international Socialism.' Bill Andrews was a C.P. member who continued to assist the I.C.U., while ex-C.P. member C. Glass – who resigned in 1924 because the Party was 'running after the Natives who could not possibly appreciate the noble ideals of Communism' – became the I.C.U.'s auditor from 1927. By mid-1928 the I.C.U. and C.P. were holding joint demonstrations in Cape Town, and Kadalie had addressed a C.P. meeting. By 1929, even Champion was hosting C.P. leaders like Wolton on an I.C.U. platform.

77. Wickins, 'I.C.U.', p.252. See also *ibid*, p.518; *Star*, 22 July 1927, 22 Feb. 1928, 25 Feb. 1928. Wainer had an inglorious end: questions were raised about him in Parliament, and the Prime Minister rapidly persuaded him to direct his idealism elsewhere. The I.C.U.'s preamble contains many echoes of that of the famous American 'Wobblies' (Industrial Workers of the World).

78. *Courant*, 16 Sept. 1926.

79. O.F.S.A., correspondence of Bloemfontein Town Clerk, MBL 4/6/1/46, Town Clerk, Kroonstad, to Town Clerk, Bloemfontein, 11 June 1927,

enclosing poster. See also *Chronicle*, 15 Sept. 1928; *Courant*, 17 Feb. 1927, 20 Oct. 1927; *Star*, 31 May 1927, 24 June 1927, 31 June 1927, 7 May 1928, 8 Oct. 1928; *Vaderland*, 17 June 1927.

80. *Star*, 13 June 1927, 22 July 1927. In mid-1927, Dube was railing against the I.C.U.'s wage demands: 'Are any of their leaders engaged in business employing a number of people for farming and paying 8 shillings a day to their workers? How about that for the men of Groutville, Amanzimtoti and Ifafa! Are they prepared to pay their employees that wage? How long can they raise cane at a profit if they pay such wages?'

81. *Mail*, 17 Dec. 1927; T.A., JUS 289, 3/1064/18, Secretary, Office of the High Commissioner, London, to Commissioner of Police, 15 July 1926, enclosing T. Mbeki to 'Comrade', 23 June 1926; B. Bunting, *Moses Kotane* (London 1975), pp.29, 39, 65; J. and R. Simons, *Class and Colour in South Africa 1850–1950* (London 1983), p.355.

82. *Courant*, 17 Feb. 1927; *Star*, 9 July 1928; S. Johns, 'Trade Union, Political Pressure Group, or Mass Movement? The Industrial and Commercial Workers' Union of Africa' in R. Rotberg and A. Mazrui (eds.), *Protest and Power in Black Africa* (New York 1970), p.695.

83. *Herald*, 15 Oct. 1925, 12 May 1928; *Star*, 7 May 1928; Coka, 'Story', p.296; Jingoes, *Chief*, pp.100–1.

84. Bunting, *Kotane*, p.51. See also *Chronicle*, 16 Oct. 1926, *Courant*, 16 Sept. 1926; *Herald*, 12 Jan. 1927; U.W., A.S.I., O.H.P., interview with J. Molete by M. Nkadimeng, Kroonstad, 26 Feb. 1980.

85. *Star*, 21 April 1928, 27 April 1928; K.C.L., KCAV 151, interview with B. Mkhize by D. Collins and A. Manson, Durban, 22 Aug. 1979; U.W., C.P.S.A., Forman papers, B2.59, 'The I.C.U. Funds' by G. Lenono; B4.31, Investigation and Report: Natal Provincial and Durban Office of the I.C.U.; Coka, 'Story', pp.302–4; L. Witz, 'Support or Control: The Children of the Garment Workers' Union, 1928–1948', paper presented at U.W., History M.A. seminar, 23 June 1983, pp.9–10.

86. *South African Communists Speak* (London 1981), pp.93–4.

87. Johns, 'Trade Union', p.695.

88. *Friend*, 6 July 1927; *Herald*, 15 June 1926, 12 May 1928; *Witness*, 20 Aug. 1927; T.A., NTS 7606, 31/328, S.A.P. report of I.C.U. meeting in Lindley, 10 April 1927 ('Take your goods and leave Ferreira' was a well-known Afrikaans song, which probably had its origins in the evictions of white tenants); Jingoes, *Chief*, p.101.

89. *Star*, 22 July 1927; *Vaderland*, 14 April 1927; U.W., A.S.I., O.H.P., interview with Kumalo, and interview with T. Manoto by M. Molepo, Heilbron, 26 Feb. 1980.

90. *Friend*, 19 Aug. 1927. See also *Courant*, 16 Oct. 1926; *Friend*, 19 April 1928, 19 July 1928; *Star*, 22 Nov. 1927.

91. *Courant*, 20 Oct. 1927. Binda's use of Afrikaans was unusual: although it was better understood than English by most Free State audiences, it also identified activists too closely with 'Boers'. See also *Farmer's Weekly*, 31 Aug. 1927; *Natal Farmer*, 30 Sept. 1927; *Star*, 5 Aug. 1927, 2 Sept. 1927; U.W., C.P.S.A., Forman papers, B3.134, Acting National Secretary to Secretary of the South African Agricultural Union, 28 Oct. 1927. Champion confirmed in 1928 that this letter had actually been sent.

92. T.A., E.N.E.C., G. Schwellnus, Lydenburg, p.799. Throughout South Africa, the imposition of a uniform contract was a central element in farmers' response to the I.C.U. A typical liberal argument in favour of this tactic was given in an editorial in the *Witness*, 18 Aug. 1927: 'If work is to be done

satisfactorily and without I.C.U. interruptions it is necessary that . . . when differences arise there should be some means of ensuring that they can be amicably adjusted without sudden strikes on the one side or ejectments on the other.' There was a dispute within the I.C.U. about the advisability of advocating written contracts – some argued that labourers under them were in the same position as convicts – but a motion in favour of this tactic was passed at the April 1928 conference.

93.   *Mercury*, 19 Nov. 1927; *Star*, 18 Feb. 1928.
94.   See pp.81–5, 120–21.
95.   *Courant*, 26 Sept 1926; *Observer*, 7 May 1926; *Star*, 8 Aug. 1927, 21 Oct. 1927, 10 March 1928, 1 June 1928, 28 June 1928; O.F.S.A., H.G. 4/1/2/263, case no. 103 of 1928, *Rex* vs. W. 'Mote.
96.   *Chronicle*, 16 Oct. 1926, 2 July 1927; *Courant*, 16 Sept. 1926; *Friend*, 28 Nov. 1927; *Mail*, 8 July 1927; *Natal Farmer*, 8 April 1927; *Star*, 13 June 1927, 9 April 1928, 23 April 1928, 7 May 1928, 28 June 1928, 25 Sept. 1928, 13 Sept. 1929; *Vaderland*, 29 July 1927, 12 Oct. 1928; O.F.S.A., H.G. 4/1/2/240, case no. 124 of 1926, *Rex* vs. S. Elias.
97.   M. Legassick, 'Liberalism, Social Control and Liberation in South Africa', unpublished paper, 1975, pp.7–8.
98.   F. Engels and K. Marx, quoted by H. Draper, *Karl Marx's Theory of Revolution*, Vol. 2 (New York 1978), p.307.
99.   This was largely due to the specificities of South Africa's capitalist development: a late-industrializing country, with the foreign exchange for this momentous task derived largely from mining and agriculture, themselves critically dependent on a cheap, highly repressed labour force. But what was true of the 1920s should not uncritically be applied to the present.
100. *Star*, 29 June 1927; T.A., JUS 289, 3/1064/18, Divisional Inspector C.I.D. to Deputy Commissioner S.A.P., Witwatersrand, 21 April 1925; N.A., *Notule van die Vyf-en-Vyftigste Algemene Vergadering van die Nederduitsch Ger. Kerk van Natal*, April 1928, pp.165–7.
101. *Friend*, 12 May 1927. See also *Friend*, 19 July 1927; E. Genovese, *Roll, Jordan, Roll: The World the Slaves Made* (New York 1976), pp.165–7.
102. *Natal Farmer*, 13 May 1927.
103. *Star*, 9 Aug. 1927 and T.A., NTS 7606, 27/328, Compol to S.N.A., 18 May 1927. See also *Courant*, 16 Sept. 1926; *Friend*, 19 Aug. 1927; *Herald*, 18 March 1927; *Mail*, 5 Dec. 1928; *Witness*, 6 July 1927, 31 Aug. 1927.
104. *Friend*, 6 June 1927; *Herald*, 6 April 1927, 15 Sept. 1927; U.W., C.P.S.A., Forman papers, B3.83, A. Champion to W. 'Mote, 12 Sept. 1927; L. Barnes, *Caliban in Africa: an Impression of Colour-Madness* (London 1930), p.99. Church services could even be part of I.C.U. meetings.
105. D. Coplan, *In Township Tonight! South Africa's Black City Music and Theatre* (Johannesburg 1985), p.46.
106. *Vaderland*, 23 Dec. 1927. See also *Herald*, 6 April 1927, *Mercury*, 12 July 1927; Coka, 'Story', p.296; Coplan, *Township*, p.46; Kadalie, *Life*, p.89; M. Hunter, *Reaction to Conquest: Effects of Contact with Europeans on the Pondo of South Africa* (London 1936), p.573.
107. *Observer*, 9 July 1926; *Star*, 7 May 1928; Coplan, *Township*, pp.121, 134.
108. *Herald*, 18 March 1927; *Star*, 5 July 1927; N.A., Durban C Court Criminal Records, 1920–1951, Inspector of Police vs. A. Champion, 23 Feb. 1926; Kadalie, *Life*, p.221.
109. *Star*, 7 May 1928; T.A., NTS 7606, 49/328, C.N.C. to S.N.A., 8 Nov. 1929, enclosing translation of *Igazi ne Zinyembezi*; U.W., A.S.I., O.H.P., interview with P. Masike by M. Molepo, Viljoenskroon, 24 Feb. 1980; R.

Hill, "'Africa for the Africans": Marcus Garvey, the UNIA, and the Struggle of African Nationalism in South Africa in the Nineteen-Twenties', paper presented at conference, 'South Africa in the Comparative Study of Class, Race and Nationalism', New York, Sept 1982, pp.1, 43; Kadalie, *Life*, p.66. See also Chapter 7.

110. *Friend*, 19 July 1927; *Herald*, 15 Nov. 1926, 6 April 1927; *Mail*, 20 Jan. 1928; U.W., A.S.I., O.H.P., interview with Ngcobo; T.A., NTS 7665, 46/332, E.N.R.C., pp.29–34: M. Perham, *African Apprenticeship: an Autobiographical Journey in Southern Africa, 1929* (London 1974), p.132. Badges were obtained from England and kept running out, which perhaps explains why some informants recall them as white, or wore instead 'pins' with 'I.C.U.' inscribed on them, or 'artificial flowers . . . painted in Kadalie's colours'. The uniform used in Bulwer is redolent of that of the *abaqhafi*, a Zulu-speaking migrant-based group that emerged in the 1920s, and distinguished itself from both traditionalists and *AmaRespectables* through dress. This characteristically included black or multicoloured mufflers or handkerchiefs knotted around necks, and cowboy hats, and 'showed very clearly the influence of the American Wild West'. But *Amalaita* gangs also often wore special hats and coloured handkerchiefs used as scarves. Ngcobo himself commented that the cap was like that used by the police, and that the uniform reminded him of the Salvation Army!

111. T. Couzens, *The New African: A Study of the Life and Work of H.I.E. Dhlomo* (Johannesburg 1985), p.277. See Chapter 7 for further discussion of American liberators and the I.C.U.

112. O.F.S.A, correspondence of Bloemfontein Town Clerk, MBL 4/8/1/81, minutes of meeting of Municipal Native Wages Committee, 24 Feb. 1926; O.F.S.A., H.G. 4/1/2/240, Case 124 of 1926, *Rex* vs. S. Elias.

113. *Star*, 15 June 1927; O.F.S.A., correspondence of Bloemfontein Town Clerk, MBL 4/8/1/81, minutes of meeting of Municipal Native Wages Committee, 22 Feb. 1926; O.F.S.A., correspondence of Frankfort Town Clerk, MFR, Minute Book of the Town Council, meeting held 27 June 1927. Champion too made a point of including uneducated Africans on all his deputations, to the distress of a municipal official who witnessed a crippled worker crawl on all fours into his office.

114. *Friend*, 28 June 1926; *The South African Worker*, 8 July 1927; T.A., NTS 7606, 27/328, Compol to S.N.A., 10 March 1927, 19 May 1927. 'Mote had demanded at least four shillings and sixpence for farm workers at a January meeting in Frankfort, and two weeks previously had spoken in a neighbouring village urging eight shillings a day for all blacks. The three shillings and sixpence demand harked back to I.C.U. recommendations in Bloemfontein in 1926.

115. *Friend*, 19 July 1927; *Star*, 28 June 1927, 18 July 1927; O.F.S.A., correspondence of Frankfort Town Clerk, Frankfort Munisipaliteit, Notule Komitee Vergaderings 1924–1931, vergadering van die Finans en Algemene Doeleindes Komitee, 18 July 1927.

116. *Friend*, 18 July 1927, 8 Aug. 1927, 23 Aug. 1927; K.C.L., N.A.U. Letter Book, letters to affiliates, 15 July 1927, 23 July 1927. In late 1928, Champion claimed to have been turned away at the last moment from farmers' meetings in Bloemfontein, Pietermaritzburg and Pretoria. Chiefs, Advisory Boards and direct meetings between officials, landlords and workers were all used to frustrate I.C.U. attempts to win recognition. 'Mote was so infuriated by this that he offered the Kroonstad Town Council five hundred pounds if they would only discuss residents' refusal to pay rates.

117.   P. Anderson, 'The Limits and Possibilities of Trade Union Action' in T. Clarke and L. Clements (eds.), *Trade Unions Under Capitalism* (Glasgow 1978), p.335. See also *Chronicle*, 16 Oct. 1926; *Star*, 18 April 1927, 22 July 1927; T.A., NTS 4408, 352/313, Sergeant S.A.P., Klerksdorp, to D.C., S.A.P., Potchefstroom, 16 July 1928.

118.   *Natal Farmer*, 13 May 1927. See also *Chronicle*, 7 July 1928; *Herald*, 15 Dec. 1926; *Mail*, 6 July 1927; *Star*, 9 April 1928; O.F.S.A., H.G. 4/1/2/240, case no. 124 of 1926, *Rex* vs. S. Elias.

119.   *Mail*, 6 Jan 1928; *Mercury*, 22 July 1927; *Star*, 9 April 1928; N.A., Bergville Preparatory Examinations 1922–1931, preparatory examination of J. Motoung and E. Tshabalala, 2 May 1928.

120.   T.A., NTS 7606, 31/328, S.A.P. report of Zastron meeting, 13 Feb. 1927.

121.   *Farmer's Weekly*, 27 July 1927; *Mercury*, 22 July 1927; *Star*, 13 June 1927; *Graaff-Reinet Advertiser*, 24 June 1927; T.A., NTS 7606, 27/328, Acting Commissioner S.A.P. to S.N.A., 14 Jan 1927, enclosing reports of I.C.U. meetings; O.F.S.A., H.G. 4/1/2/263, case no. 103 of 1928, *Rex* vs. W. 'Mote; U.W., C.P.S.A., Forman papers, B3.165, statement by S. Dunn, 26 Nov. 1927.

122.   Engels, quoted by Draper, *Revolution*, p.515.

123.   *Witness*, 6 July 1927. See also T.A., NTS 7606, 27/328, Acting Commissioner, S.A.P., to S.N.A., 14 Jan 1927, enclosing reports of I.C.U. meetings. 'Platskiet politiek' – politics based on shooting people down – was the accusation levelled at General Smuts by Hertzog.

124.   O.F.S.A., H.G. 4/1/2/240, case no. 124 of 1926, *Rex* vs. S. Elias; U.W., A.S.I., Swanson, 'Interview', pp.86–7.

125.   *Herald*, 27 March 1926, 6 April 1927, 30 Nov. 1928; T.A., NTS 7602, 20/328, report on meeting in Middelburg, 16 Jan. 1927; Engels, quoted by Draper, *Revolution*, p.525. According to Dunn in 1927, strikes were the ultimate weapon but would be misconstrued by Africans, 75 per cent of whom were illiterate.

126.   U.W., A.S.I., Swanson, 'Interview', p.50.

127.   *Vaderland*, 8 July 1927.

128.   *Courant*, 20 Oct. 1927; *Herald*, 28 April 1926, 17 May 1927; *Star*, 5 July 1927; T.A., NTS 7665, 46/332, E.N.R.C., pp. 335–6; T.A., NTS 7602, 20/328, report on meeting in Middelburg, 16 Jan. 1927; Swanson, 'Champion', p.5.

129.   *Star*, 16 Nov. 1928; U.W., C.P.S.A., Forman papers, B3.76, A. Champion to I. Ndaba, 9 Dec. 1927; U.W., C.P.S.A., W. Ballinger papers, file 4, undated letter from W. Ballinger to H. Pim on the Durban riots; U.W., A.S.I., O.H.P., interview with Kumalo.

130.   *Mercury*, 14 Sept. 1927; *Natal Farmer*, 12 Aug. 1927, 19 Aug. 1927; *Witness*, 19 Aug. 1927; T.A., NTS 7606, 37/328, Bergville Mag. to C.N.C., 21 March 1928.

131.   H. Wolpe, 'Towards an Analysis of the South African State', *International Journal of the Sociology of Law*, 8, 1980, p.419. See also arguments in Chapter 2. Organizers repeatedly informed audiences that while justice might not be obtained from magistrates, it was to be found in the Supreme Court.

132.   *Witness*, 19 Aug. 1927; Jingoes, *Chief*, p.111; Wickins, 'I.C.U.', pp.346–9.

133.   *Natal Farmer*, 24 June 1927, 12 Aug. 1927; *Star*, 17 Aug. 1927; N.A., correspondence of Weenen Mag. with Commissioners, 7/7/6, Weenen Mag. to S.J., 31 Aug. 1927; T.A., JUS 437, 4/366/27, Head Constable Ladysmith to District Constable Dundee, 12 Jan. 1928; U.W., C.P.S.A., Forman papers, B4.7, Ratcliffe to A. Champion, 30 Jan. 1928; B4.30, C. Cowley to General Secretary, 20 March 1928.

134. *Friend*, 6 March 1928; *Star*, 11 Jan. 1928, 15 March 1928, 23 Oct. 1928; *Vaderland*, 30 Sept. 1927; O.F.S.A, MFR Minute Book of the Frankfort Town Council, meeting 13 June 1927; Jingoes, *Chief*, p.105. Towns where visitors' or lodgers' permits were refused included Bethulie, Brandfort, Koffiefontein, Memel, Parys, Senekal, Schweitzer-Reneke and Springfontein. Towns where meetings were at least initially forbidden included Durban, Frankfort, Kestell, Koffiefontein, Springfontein, Standerton and Witbank.

135. N.A., correspondence of Umzinto Mag., A. Mncadi to Prime Minister, 24 March 1927.

136. K.C.L., interview with Mkhize. For the popularity of legal tactics elsewhere, see *Courant*, 16 Sept. 1926; *Herald*, 18 March 1927; *Star*, 5 Aug. 1927, 7 May 1928.

137. F. Engels, quoted by I. Cummins, *Marx, Engels and National Movements* (London 1980), p.97. See also B. Fine *et al* (eds.), *Capitalism and the Rule of Law: from Deviancy Theory to Marxism* (London 1979), pp.39–40; Genovese, *Roll, Jordan, Roll*, p.115.

138. *Herald*, 18 March 1927; U.W., A.S.I., O.H.P., interview with Kumalo; Jingoes, *Chief*, p.99. A common variation on the I.C.U.'s name was 'I See You, white man'. For criticisms of legal activities replacing other forms of struggle, see for example D. du Toit, *Capital and Labour in South Africa: Class Struggles in the 1970s* (London 1981), p.109.

139. *Star*, 8 Oct. 1928, 16 Oct. 1928; Kadalie, *Life*, p.93.

140. Engels, quoted by Draper, *Revolution*, p.118. See also Chapters 6 and 8.

141. *Ilanga lase Natal*, 12 Aug. 1927; *Mercury*, 26 April 1927; *Witness*, 30 July 1927. See also Chapters 5 and 6.

142. Gramsci, *Selections*, p.263. For Dumah's address, see *Chronicle*, 7 July 1928.

143. *Star*, 21 April 1927; B. Santos, 'Popular justice, dual power and Socialist Strategy' in Fine *et al*, *Capitalism*, p.162.

144. *Herald*, 18 March 1927; *Star*, 20 Jan. 1928; N.A., Durban C Court Criminal Records, 1910–1951, Inspector of Police vs. A. Champion, 23 Feb. 1926; U.W., C.P.S.A., Forman papers, B3.132, A. Batty to A. Champion, 27 Oct. 1927; B4.19, W. 'Mote to A. Champion, 29 Feb. 1928. Depending on local circumstances, the Advisory Boards were either boycotted or captured.

145. P. la Hausse, 'The Struggle for the City: Alcohol, the Ematsheni and Popular Culture in Durban, 1902–1936', M.A., University of Cape Town, 1984, p.184. This instance of militia formation – as in East London, where the Union's 'army' wore football jerseys – occurred in a secessionary I.C.U. movement.

146. Jingoes, *Chief*, pp.111–13; I. Schapera, 'Law and Justice' in I. Schapera (ed.), *The Bantu-Speaking Tribes of South Africa: an Ethnographical Survey* (London 1937), pp.212–7. In East London, organizers of the Independent I.C.U. were later to complain about the amount of work involved in settling marital disputes.

147. *Cape Times*, 4 July 1930; U.W., C.P.S.A., Forman papers, B3.168, Minutes of National Council meeting, 18–25 Nov. 1927; U.W., C.P.S.A., Saffery papers, Tyamzashe, 'History', p.45; Jingoes, *Chief*, p.113; P. Wickins, 'The Organization and Composition of the I.C.U.', *South African Labour Bulletin*, 1, 6, 1974, pp.30–34.

148. U.W., C.P.S.A., Forman papers, B3.56, W. ka Jonga to A. Champion, 18 Aug. 1927; B3.57, A. Champion to W. ka Jonga, 19 Aug. 1927; B3.132, A. Batty to A. Champion, 27 Oct. 1927; B3.165, statement by S. Dunn, 26 Nov. 1927.

149. O.F.S.A., MBL 4/7/1/56, Minutes of Native Affairs Committee meeting, 7

Oct. 1926; T.A., JUS 289, 3/1064/18, General Secretary's Report of Inspection of Branches, 6 March 1926; U.W., C.P.S.A, Forman papers, B4.4, National Council meeting 8 Jan. 1928.

150. O.F.S.A., H.G. 4/1/2/240, case no. 124 of 1926, *Rex* vs. S. Elias; U.W., A.S.I., O.H.P., interview with Kumalo.

151. *Herald*, 15 Nov. 1926; *Star*, 9 Aug. 1927; U.W, A.S.I., O.H.P., interview with Kumalo; U.W., C.P.S.A., Saffery papers, Tyamzashe, 'History', p.8; Coka, 'Story', p.306; Coplan, *Township*, pp.134, 142; Kadalie, *Life*, pp.80, 85; R. Phillips, *The Bantu are Coming: Phases of South Africa's Race Problems* (London 1930), photograph facing p.49.

152. N.A., Durban C Court Criminal Records, 1910–1951, Inspector of Police vs. A. Champion, 23 Feb. 1926; Kadalie, *Life*, p.95. Many in the audience were small-traders, dressmakers, washerwomen and shoemakers. A similar petty bourgeois composition probably characterized gatherings at choir concerts in Bloemfontein in 1926, where on one occasion the Branch Secretary led the *Coup-de-Grâce* to victory over the I.C.U. Shellers, thereby winning a silver cup for his choir's rendition of *The Sea Has Its Pearls*.

153. Coplan, *Township*, p.135.

154. *Star*, 29 April 1927; Coplan, *Township*, pp.65–7, 129. The 'new African' idea had its origin in Garveyism, and was used by organizers to distinguish themselves either from blacks in the time of 'savagery', or from moderates who wanted no part of mass protest.

155. *Herald*, 12 Jan. 1927; U.W., A.S.I., O.H.P., interview with Kumalo; personal communication from Philip Bonner, who interviewed Jubilee Kok about the appearance of an I.C.U. brass band in Pilgrims Rest; Coplan, *Township*, p.133.

156. University of Cape Town, Manuscripts Library, W. Ballinger papers, BC 347, C. Kadalie to Executives and Members of the I.C.U., 13 March 1929; U.W., A.S.I., Swanson, 'Interview', p.46; Shepperson, 'Clements Kadalie', p.160.

157. Gramsci, *Selections*, p.10.

158. *Ibid.*, p.377.

CHAPTER 5

1. T.A., Native Affairs Department files, NTS 7081, 1/323, J. Ntshona to General Hertzog, date-stamped 21 Jan. 1925.

2. T.A., E.N.E.C., J. Penzhorn, Rustenburg, p.1000.

3. *Agricultural Census, 1918: Statistics of Agricultural and Pastoral Production*, U.G. 53–1919, p.12; *Agricultural Census No. 4, 1921: Statistics of Agricultural and Pastoral Production*, U.G. 44–1922, p.18; *Report on the Agricultural and Pastoral Production of the Union of South Africa, 1922–1923*, U.G. 25–1925, p.6; *Report of the Agricultural and Pastoral Production of the Union of South Africa, 1929–1930*, U.G. 12–1932, pp.14, 45, 94; *Minutes of Evidence of the Eastern Transvaal Natives Land Committee*, U.G. 32–1918, p.168; *Report of the Economic and Wage Commission (1925)*, U.G. 14–1926, p.16; *Report of the Native Economic Commission 1930–1932*, U.G. 22–1932, p.197; T.A., NTS 8599, 13/362, Klerk van die Volksraad to Secretary to the Prime Minister, 22 April 1921.

4. *Majority Report of the Eastern Transvaal Natives Land Committee*, U.G. 31–1918, p.5; see also *Transvaal Land Committee*, p.176.

5. T.A., E.N.E.C, Archdeacon Hill, Johannesburg, p.7576; see also pp.7574–5.

6. U.W., A.S.I., O.H.P., interview with E. Thabethe by V.N., Ledig, 23 Nov. 1979.

7. T.A., NTS 7661, 23/332(2), Sub-Native Commissioner, Pokwani, to S.N.A., 16 Jan. 1925; H. Macmillan, 'A Nation Divided? The Swazi in Swaziland and the Transvaal, 1865–1984', in L. Vail (ed.), *The Political Economy of Ethnicity in Southern Africa in the Nineteenth and Twentieth Centuries* (forthcoming).
8. *Star*, 21 May 1927; T.A., E.N.E.C., chief Kgologkwe, Lydenburg, p.756; T.A., NTS 7204, 17/326, N.C., Barberton, to S.N.A., 4 Jan. 1927, enclosing a letter from a White River farmer.
9. T.A., NTS 7661, 23/332(1), Sergeant, S.A.P., Volksrust, to D.C., S.A.P., Heidelberg, 14 March 1921; T.A., NTS 7661, 23/332(2), Minister of Justice to Minister of Native Affairs, enclosing a letter from a Zoutpansberg farmer, 1 April 1925; and J. le Roux to Rustenburg Mag., 7 Dec. 1925.
10. For Middelburg and the T.N.C., see correspondence in NTS files mentioned in footnote 9; also T.A., NTS 7084, 7/323, correspondence relating to Waterberg farm 'Canton'.
11. *Herald*, 6 April 1927; P. Wickins, 'The Industrial and Commercial Workers' Union of Africa', Ph.D., University of Cape Town, 1973, pp.597–9.
12. *Vaderland*, 14 Oct. 1927; *Mail*, 5 May 1928; T.A., NTS 7606, 33/328, undated report by Second Sergeant, Barberton, to Public Prosecutor, for the case *Rex vs. D. Labase*; T.A., NTS 7606, 38/328, correspondence relating to the conviction and deportation of Abdul Mahomed.
13. *Herald*, 15 June 1926; *Observer*, 23 April 1926, 14 May 1926; T.A., correspondence of Middelburg Town Clerk, MMG 4/1/20, Town Clerk to Director of Education, 29 April 1926; MMG 1/1/17, Town Council meeting, 18 Oct. 1926 (thanks to Rob Morrell for these Middelburg references).
14. *Observer*, 16 July 1926; *Herald*, 31 Dec. 1928.
15. *Umteteli wa Bantu*, 15 Nov. 1924; *Herald*, 14 Oct. 1926, 18 March 1927, 6 April 1927, 15 June 1927; T.A., JUS 289, 3/1064/18, Divisional Officer of the C.I.D., Witwatersrand, to Deputy Commissioner of S.A.P., Witwatersrand, 25 April 1925.
16. *Herald*, 15 June 1927.
17. *Herald*, 12 May 1928; T.A., NTS 7606, 38/328, correspondence relating to the conviction and deportation of Abdul Mahomed.
18. *Herald*, 17 May 1927.
19. *Ibid*; P. Walshe, *The Rise of African Nationalism in South Africa: The African National Congress 1912–1952* (London 1970), p.211.
20. *Herald*, 6 April 1927, 12 May 1928; Macmillan, 'Divided Nation?'. Amongst the Swazi chiefs who supported the Union were Mhlaba Hlatshwayo of Piet Retief, Dantyi Nkosi of Nelspruit, Msogwaba Nkosi of Nelspruit, and Hoyi Ngomane of Barberton.
21. *Mail*, 22 April 1927, 13 May 1927; *Star*, 30 Jan. 1928, 29 March 1929; *Land and Agricultural Bank of South Africa: Report for the Year ended 31st December, 1917*, U.G. 28–1918, p.12; South African Defence Force Archives Depot, Chief of General Staff files, CGS 67 IL 45, Lieutenant J. Measroch to Colonel Nussey, 21 March 1928, enclosing a list of I.C.U. supporters amongst chiefs and headmen in Piet Retief; U.W., A.S.I., O.H.P., interview with T. Mashile by P. Bonner and M. Molepo, Pilgrims Rest, 10 Aug. 1984.
22. T.A., NTS 1702, 45/276(1), Medical Superintendent Leper Institution, Pretoria, to Secretary for Public Health, 12 Dec. 1927; U.W., A.S.I. O.H.P., interview with J. Lusiba by V.N., Barberton, April 1981; interview with chief L. Mogane *et al* by P. Bonner, A. Mabin, M. Molepo and J. Kok, Hlabekisa, 22 Feb. 1985.
23. *Herald*, 12 May 1928; T.A., NTS 3534, 566/308, Branch Secretary Barberton to Native Affairs Department, 20 Jan 1928; T.A., NTS 7602, 20/328, report of

meeting in Middelburg, 16 Jan. 1927; Archives of the International Labour Organization, Geneva, File XT 1/1/1, 1927 notes by H. Butler on his trip to South Africa.

24.   *Star*, 30 April 1927, 21 July 1928; *Vaderland*, 28 Feb. 1928; T.A., E.N.E.C., J. Yates, Middelburg, pp.836–7, 854; representatives of Middelburg township, Middelburg, p.940; U.W., A.S.I., O.H.P., interview with E. Sibanyoni and R. Mthimunye by V.N., Middelburg, 4 Sept. 1979.

25.   *Observer*, 30 July 1926; *Vaderland*, 9 Aug. 1927; T.A., E.N.E.C., Middelburg Town Clerk, Middelburg, p.877; U.W., A.S.I., O.H.P., interview with J. Motha by V.N., Middelburg, 11 Sept. 1979.

26.   *Herald*, 14 Aug. 1926. See also *Observer*, 9 July 1926; R. Morrell, '"Pipping a little game in the bud": Pixley Isaka ka Seme, Land Purchase and Rural Differentiation in the Eastern Transvaal', unpublished paper, 1986, p.21.

27.   V.I. Lenin, 'What is to be Done?' in T. Clarke and L. Clements (eds.), *Trade Unions Under Capitalism* (Glasgow 1978), p.68. See also T.A., NTS 7602, 20/328, Newcastle Mag. to C.N.C., 23 March 1926; C. Kadalie, *My Life and the I.C.U.: the Autobiography of a Black Trade Unionist in South Africa* (London 1970), pp.39–40. There were many versions of the 'pavement tale'. Kadalie's written one was that in an incident witnessed by Batty, he was pushed off the sidewalk by a constable. He made so bold as to lay a charge, and was subsequently drawn into Batty's political and trade union activities. In the 1920s, 'pavement campaigns' were also popular in Natal and the Free State.

28.   T.A., correspondence of Middelburg Town Clerk, MMG 4/1/20, Location Superintendent to Town Clerk, 6 July 1925 (misdated for 1926); T.A., NTS 4291, 140/313, notes on interview between J. Mabatho and S.N.A., 13 July 1918; U.W., A.S.I., O.H.P., interview with Sibanyoni and Mthimunye.

29.   T.A., MMG 4/1/20, Town Clerk to Director of Education, 29 April 1926; T.A., E.N.E.C., J. Yates, Middelburg, pp.824–5; representatives of Middelburg location, Middelburg, p.940; T.A., NTS 7602, 20/338, report on meeting in Middelburg, 16 Jan. 1927; T.A., NTS 7661, 23/332(2), Detached Clerk, Pokwani, to S.N.A., 6 Nov. 1924; U.W., A.S.I., O.H.P., interviews with Motha, and with Sibanyoni and Mthimunye; interview with Sibanyoni and Mthimunye by V.N., Middelburg, 19 Oct. 1979.

30.   *Star*, 5 July 1927; *Vaderland*, 16 March 1928; T.A., NTS 7606, 33/328, N.C. Barberton to S.N.A., 2 Sept. 1927; U.W., C.P.S.A., South African Institute of Race Relations papers, AD 843, B53.7, interview with J. Neethling by Senator Rheinallt-Jones, Feb. 1941.

31.   *Star*, 19 April 1929; T.A., E.N.E.C., P. Bosman and J. Williams, Middelburg, p.948 (where they complained that the intolerable treatment of Bethal recruited workers made it impossible for farmers in adjacent districts to obtain labour).

32.   T.A., correspondence in GNLB 1933/13/154, especially J. Smalberger to Minister of Native Affairs, 13 Nov. 1926.

33.   *Herald*, 12 Jan. 1927; *Star*, 4 April 1928; T.A., GNLB 1933/13/154, note attached to letter from N.C., Bethal, to D.N.L., 17 Nov. 1925. The surname 'Rand' suggests prior experience on the Witwatersrand.

34.   *Mail*, 6 Jan 1928. Included amongst Gafenowitz's labourers were men recruited from the Cape, Bechuanaland and Natal.

35.   Details of this incident are drawn from *Mail*, 5 Jan. 1928, 6 Jan. 1928, 12 Jan. 1928, 4 April 1928; and *Star*, 5 Jan. 1928, 6 Jan. 1928, 11 Jan. 1928, 4 April 1928.

36.   *Mail*, 6 Jan. 1928; *Star*, 4 April 1928.

37.   J. Clarke, S. Hall, T. Jefferson and B. Roberts, 'Subcultures, Cultures and

Class' in S. Hall and T. Jefferson (eds.), *Resistance through Rituals: Youth Subcultures in post-war Britain* (London 1982), pp.71–2.

38. *Farmer's Weekly*, 1 Jan 1919, 28 Sept. 1927, 5 Oct. 1927; *Vaderland*, 3 June 1927, 24 June 1927, 16 March 1928, 2 July 1929; U.W., C.P.S.A., Middelburg District Farmers' Union papers, A 1382, meeting 21 July 1926.

39. Clarke *et al*, 'Subcultures', p.74. See also *Star*, 3 March 1928; *Farmer's Weekly*, 24 Aug. 1927; U.W., A.S.I., O.H.P., interview with J. Ntambo and L. Nhlabathi by V.N., Ledig, 23 Nov. 1979.

40. *Vaderland*, 6 Sept. 1927, 27 Sept. 1927; T.A., E.N.E.C., Major Hunt, Lydenburg, p.716.

41. *Vaderland*, 3 Feb. 1928, 6 March 1928; T.A., correspondence in GNLB 1933/13/35, especially P. Oliphant to Theron and Co., 9 Feb. 1928; T.A., correspondence in NTS 7664, 40/332, especially statement by Dingley, March 1928; T.A., correspondence in NTS 7665, 42/332; T.A., NTS 280, 227/53, C.N.C. to S.N.A., 9 Feb. 1928. The other Ngotshe estate involved was that where Mtateni Ndwandwe worked (see p.521). This incident occurred just after the lynch attempt in Greytown – see Chapter 6 – which undoubtedly increased tension amongst whites.

42. T.A., NTS 7664, 40/332, D.C., S.A.P., Ermelo to D.C., S.A.P., Pretoria, 8 March 1928; T.A., NTS 7665, 42/332, Major Herbst to Imperial Secretary, Cape Town, 8 March 1928; S. Hall *et al*, *Policing the Crisis: Mugging, the State, and Law and Order* (London 1982), pp.17–19.

43. *Vaderland*, 23 Dec. 1927.

44. U.W., C.P.S.A., W. Ballinger papers, A410, C2.3.7, file 4, W. Ballinger to F. Brockway, 15 May 1929. I have called members of this group 'liberals', although this is a somewhat inadequate term to encompass the self-confessed 'definitely negrophile' Winifred Holtby, who saw Africans as 'a gay, smiling people'; the conservative, anti-Communist Lewis, who adhered to liberal segregationism; and the accountant Howard Pim, committed to *laissez-faire* free enterprise. However the concept is given much the same elasticity by Martin Legassick in 'The Rise of Modern South African Liberalism: its Assumptions and its Social Base', paper presented at University of London, Institute of Commonwealth Studies, March 1972.

45. H.C.L., E. Lewis letters, Part I, HCL D4 F7, E. Lewis to W. Holtby, 27 July 1926, E. Lewis to W. Holtby, 26 April 1927; letters of A. Creech Jones, Part II, HCL D2 11/50, A. Creech Jones to C. Kadalie, 15 Sept. 1927; letters from A. Creech Jones, HCL D4 F6, A. Creech Jones to C. Kadalie, 16 Oct 1928; Kadalie, *Life*, pp.129, 138, 140, 157.

46. *Herald*, 18 Jan. 1928; U.W., C.P.S.A., L. Forman papers, AD 1714 Mfe, B3.180, Circular: Reorganization of the ICU; B3.187, Report to the National Council by the General Secretary; G. Coka, 'The Story of Gilbert Coka of the Zulu Tribe of Natal, South Africa' in M. Perham (ed.), *Ten Africans* (London 1936), pp.298–9.

47. *Star*, 8 Oct. 1928. See also *Friend*, 23 Feb. 1928; *The South African Worker*, 22 Aug. 1928; U.W., C.P.S.A., Forman papers, B3.168, minutes of the National Council Meeting, 18–25 Nov. 1927; B4.4, fragment of a Report, 8 Jan. 1928.

48. *Star*, 10 Feb. 1927, 23 Oct. 1928; T. Clynick, 'The Lichtenburg Alluvial Diamond Diggers, 1926–1929', paper presented at U.W., History Workshop, Feb. 1984, pp.8–9; E. Hobsbawm, *Primitive Rebels: Studies in Archaic Forms of Social Movement in the 19th and 20th Centuries* (Manchester 1971), p.79.

49. *Mail*, 8 May 1928; *Star*, 26 Sept. 1928; U.C.T., M.L., W. Ballinger papers, BC 347, A.5. VIII, Financial Statements 1 Nov. 1928–30 April 1929; A.5.XII.1, Weekly News Letter, 19 Oct. 1928; J. Wells, '"The Day the Town Stood

Still": Women in Resistance in Potchefstroom 1912–1930' in B. Bozzoli (ed.), *Town and Countryside in the Transvaal: Capitalist Penetration and Popular Response* (Johannesburg 1983), p.283.

50.   *Mail*, 28 Nov. 1928; U.W., A.S.I., O.H.P., interview with I. Mathuloe by T. Phiri, Phokeng, 13 May 1981; J. Jingoes, *A Chief is a Chief by the People: the Autobiography of Stimela Jason Jingoes* (London 1975), pp.114–16.

51.   *Mail*, 14 March 1927, 1 April 1927; Clynick, 'Diggers', pp.4, 13, 15; U.W., A.S.I., O.H.P., interview with K. Maine by C. van Onselen, Ledig, 24 Feb. 1981. Maine was partly referring to earlier digging experiences on a different field, but his remarks typified the way of life of Lichtenburg farmer-diggers and their tenants.

52.   *Star*, 15 Feb. 1927, 16 Jan. 1928; T.A., JUS 421, 3/978/26, Meeting held in S.A.P. station, 20 June 1928; U.W., C.P.S.A., Forman papers, B3.141, B. Gwabini to A. Champion, 31 Oct. 1927; B3.145, C. Modiakgotla to A. Champion, 1 Nov. 1927; B3.179, Delegates to National Conference, 16 Dec. 1927; T. Clynick, 'The 1928 Alluvial Diamond Workers' Strike: a Preliminary Account of Capital, the State and Labour in the South Western Transvaal', paper presented at U.W., M.A. History seminar, 20 Sept. 1983, p.25.

53.   *Friend*, 30 Jan. 1928; *Star*, 9 April 1928; T.A., JUS 421, 3/978/6, meeting held in S.A.P. station, 20 June 1928; Clynick, 'Diggers', pp.8–19; J. Grosskopf, *Rural Impoverishment and Rural Exodus* in *Report of the Carnegie Commission: the Poor White Problem in South Africa*, Part I (Stellenbosch 1932), p.153.

54.   *Mail*, 19 June 1928, 20 June 1928; *Star*, 19 June 1928, 20 June 1928; T.A., JUS 421, 3/978/6, meeting held in S.A.P. station, 20 June 1928.

55.   T.A., JUS 421, 3/978/6, meeting held in S.A.P. station, 20 June 1928.

56.   *Star*, 21 June 1928; U.W., A.S.I., O.H.P., interview with Maine, 24 Feb. 1981; Clynick, 'Diggers', p.23.

57.   *Mail*, 21 June 1928; *Star*, 22 June 1928, 25 June 1928, 9 July 1928.

58.   Quotes (in sequence) are from U.W., C.P.S.A., W. Ballinger papers, file 3, E. Lewis to Prime Minister, 15 Oct., 1928; U.W., C.P.S.A., Forman papers, B4.63, R. de Norman to A. Champion, 26 June 1928; V. Brittain, *Testament of Friendship: the Story of Winifred Holtby* (London 1941), p.209. Fortunately, there were limits to the types of enterprises in which Ballinger's supporters involved themselves to keep their man in the country. Winifred Holtby, who 'made love to an old very rich man of 74 trying to interest him in the natives and give me some money', ultimately decided that 'at 74, even for Ballinger and the I.C.U., I fear I cannot!'

59.   *Star*, 19 Oct. 1928; H.C.L., E. Lewis letters, Part I, HCL D4 F7, E. Lewis to W. Holtby, 25 July 1928; T.A., NTS 7606, 40/328, Secretary for the Interior to S.N,A,, 30 May 1928; T.A., JUS 289, 3/1064/18, article by E. Roux on the I.C.U. sent to South African authorities by the London High Commissioner.

60.   U.C.T., M.L., W. Ballinger papers, A.5.III.3, minutes of meeting of National Council, 28 Feb. 1929; A.5.XII.1, Weekly News Letter, 21 Nov. 1928; U.W., C.P.S.A., Industrial and Commercial Workers' Union Records, A924, W. Ballinger to W. Holtby, 14 Aug. 1928, A. Creech Jones to W. Holtby, 10 Sept. 1928; U.W., C.P.S.A, W. Ballinger papers, file 3, E. Lewis to Prime Minister, 15 Oct. 1928; file 4, W. Ballinger to F. Brockway, 15 May 1929; file 4, Report by W. Ballinger, July 1928 to June 1929; W. Macmillan, *My South African Years: an Autobiography* (Cape Town 1975), p.159; R. Phillips, *The Bantu are Coming: Phases of South Africa's Race Problem* (London 1930), pp.148–50. Ballinger's policy on leaders was so well known by October 1928 that the Bloemfontein Location Superintendent wrote to him suggesting that, especially if the ICU intended to negotiate with farmers, Elias should be replaced

by the Assistant Branch Secretary who had a 'deep sense of courtesy to all authorities'.

61. *Herald*, 31 Dec. 1928; *Star*, 20 Sept. 1928.
62. *Natal Farmer*, 11 Nov. 1927; *Star*, 25 July 1927, 13 Sept. 1928, 21 March 1929.
63. *Star*, 5 Aug. 1927, 29 Sept. 1928, 22 Oct. 1928; *Report of the Native Farm Labour Committee, 1937–1939*, Annexure 520–1939, p.32; T.A., E.N.E.C., Dr. P. Seme, Johannesburg, p.7424.
64. *Herald*, 31 Dec. 1928; *Star*, 22 Oct. 1928; U.W., C.P.S.A., W. Ballinger papers, file 3, W. Gillespie to W. Ballinger, 3 Oct. 1928; E. Brookes to W. Ballinger, 17 Oct. 1928.
65. *Star*, 22 Oct. 1928; T.A., E.N.E.C., W. Ballinger, Johannesburg, p.8223; H.C.L., letters from W. Ballinger, HCL D4 F10, W. Ballinger to W. Holtby, 28 Dec. 1932.
66. *Star*, 22 Oct. 1928.
67. *Star*, 12 Oct. 1928; T.A., NTS 2127, 232/280, Secretary of the South African Trade Union Congress to Prime Minister and Minister of Native Affairs, 19 Oct. 1928; Additional N.C., Pretoria, to S.N.A., 2 Jan. 1929; Director of Veterinary Services to Secretary for Agriculture, 2 May 1930.
68. T.A., Department of Labour files, ARB 713, L.C. 1054/25, Secretary for Labour to General Secretary I.C.U., 8 Aug. 1924.
69. T.A., NTS 8607, 35/362, Conference between Native Affairs Department, Native Affairs Commission, Department of Labour and Wage Board, on Regulation of Native Labour in Industry, 25–27 Oct. 1927; R. Hyman, *Industrial Relations: A Marxist Introduction* (London 1979), p.89. The Director of Native Labour largely agreed with the Secretary for Labour, although he hedged his bets by suggesting that Africans should be represented by the Native Affairs Department in wage negotiations, so that the I.C.U. was not encouraged.
70. *Star*, 2 Nov. 1928; N.A., correspondence of Dundee Mag., 1/DUN, 6/1/2/1, Union Circular 30/1927, 1 July 1927, 'Native Administration: Interference'; T.A., NTS 8607, 35/362, Conference between Native Affairs Department, Native Affairs Commission, Department of Labour and Wage Board on Regulation of Native Labour in Industry, 25–27 Oct. 1927.
71. *Star*, 6 Oct. 1928, 9 Oct. 1928, 12 Oct. 1928; T.A., NTS 2127, 232/280, Secretary of South African Trade Union Congress to Prime Minister and Minister of Native Affairs, 19 Oct. 1928.
72. *Star*, 16 Oct. 1928; *Vaderland*, 12 Oct. 1928; V.I. Lenin, 'On Strikes' in Clarke and Clements, *Trade Unions*, p.61.
73. *Star*, 11 Oct. 1928, 12 Oct. 1928, 16 Oct. 1928, 18 Oct. 1928, 25 Oct. 1928; U.C.T., M.L., W. Ballinger papers, A.5.XII.1, A. Phoofolo to Editor of Weekly News Letter, 26 Nov. 1928; U.W., C.P.S.A., Industrial and Commercial Workers' Union Records, file 3, W. Ballinger, 'Native Workers of South Africa'.
74. *Mail*, 3 Nov. 1928; *Star*, 7 Nov. 1928; Kadalie, *Life*, p.180.
75. *Mail*, 30 Oct. 1928; U.W., C.P.S.A., Industrial and Commercial Workers' Union Records, file 1, E. Lewis to Dr. Henderson, 28 Oct. 1928; U.W., C.P.S.A., W. Ballinger papers, file 3, E. Lewis to Prime Minister, 15 Oct. 1928; E. Lewis to C. Kadalie, 17 Oct. 1928; copy of letter from two members of the Joint Council to General Hertzog, 19 Oct. 1928.
76. U.C.T., M.L., W. Ballinger papers, A.1.IX, C. Kadalie to Executives and Members of the I.C.U., 13 March 1929; U.W., C.P.S.A., A. Saffery papers, AD 1178, Part 1, B5, H. Tyamzashe, 'Summarised History of the Industrial and Commercial Workers' Union of Africa', pp.52–3; Jingoes, *Chief*, p.127; S.

Johns, 'Trade Union, Political Pressure Group or Mass Movement? The Industrial and Commercial Workers' Union of Africa' in R. Rotberg and A. Mazrui (eds.), *Protest and Power in Black Africa* (New York 1970), pp.742–3.

77. T.A., NTS 7204, 17/326, undated S.A.P. report on I.I.C.U. meeting in Zebedelia location, 23 Aug. 1929; U.C.T., M.L., W. Ballinger papers, A.5.V, Advisory and Financial Secretary to A. Phoofolo, 3 Sept. 1929; U.W., C.P.S.A., Saffery papers, Tyamzashe, 'History', pp.29–30. Mbeki's jail experience probably contributed to his becoming a police informer in 1930; by 1932 he was back organizing for the I.I.C.U.

78. U.C.T., M.L., A.5.XII.1, Weekly News Letter, 21 Nov. 1928, Weekly News Letter, 5 Dec. 1928.

79. *Farmer's Weekly*, 28 Nov. 1928; *Friend*, 22 June 1928; *Mail*, 7 May 1929, 10 Oct. 1929; *Star*, 4 Sept 1927, 29 Nov. 1927, 3 April 1928, 24 Sept. 1929; *Vaderland*, 19 April 1929, 10 May 1929.

80. *Star*, 23 April 1928; *Vaderland*, 12 June 1928; T.A., NTS 7204, 17/326, Sub-N.C. Nylstroom to N.C. Nylstroom, 26 Feb. 1919.

81. *Farmer's Weekly*, 5 Oct. 1927, 9 Sept. 1928, 24 Oct. 1928, 4 June 1930; *Star*, 2 Oct. 1928.

82. *Farmer's Weekly*, 6 Feb. 1929; *Friend*, 22 June 1928; *Star*, 16 Feb. 1928, 30 June 1928, 26 Feb. 1929, 16 March 1929, 28 March 1929; Transvaal Agricultural Union, *Die Boere van Transvaal en hul Organisasie 1897–1957* (Pretoria n.d.), p.45.

83. *Farmer's Weekly*, 29 May 1929; *Mail*, 19 Feb. 1929, 8 March 1929, 18 June 1929; *Vaderland*, 5 April 1929; T.A., NTS 7084, 7/323, correspondence relating to Waterberg farm 'Canton'.

84. *Mail*, 7 May 1929; U.W., C.P.S.A., W. Ballinger papers, file 4, W. Ballinger to W. Holtby, 4 Aug. 1929.

85. *Farmer's Weekly*, 8 Aug. 1928; *Mail*, 13 Aug. 1929; *Star*, 1 July 1929.

86. *Farmer's Weekly*, 24 July 1929; *Report of the Natives Land Commission*, Vol. II, U.G. 22–1916, pp.345–6; *Report of the Select Committee on the Subject of the Union Native Council Bill, Coloured Persons Rights Bill, Representation of Natives in Parliament Bill, and the Natives Land (Amendment) Bill*, S.C. 10–1927, pp.203, 210; E. Sewell-Dawson, *Farm Management in South Africa* (Johannesburg 1931), pp.176, 186.

87. *Vaderland*, 9 July 1929. Ballinger had quickly absorbed the ideas of his liberal mentors on labour tenancy, and the September 1929 issue of the *Herald* proclaimed that 'a squatter is to us the greatest evil ever known and the greatest drawback in all Bantu efforts towards self-betterment . . . a squatter is a slave-monger who sells the labour of his children free that he may procure for his livestock grazing ground. The stock he is so solicitous about is of the scrub kind and usually of no market value . . . if our people would place value on their stock not in terms of their ancestors' conception of it but according to current market values . . . much development . . . would result.'

88. *Star*, 29 June 1929; *Vaderland*, 9 July 1929.

89. *Farmer's Weekly*, 28 Aug. 1929, 25 Sept. 1929; *Mail*, 18 June 1929; *Star*, 7 May 1929, 23 July 1929, 31 July 1929; T.A., E.N.E.C., W. Ballinger, Johannesburg, p.8223; South African Agricultural Union, Agricultural Advisory Board Minute Book, 14 July 1926–30 Nov. 1934, meeting on 19 Jan. 1928.

90. *Star*, 20 Aug. 1929. See also *Farmer's Weekly*, 24 July 1929; *Star*, 31 July 1929.

91. *Farmer's Weekly*, 19 Sept. 1928, 2 Oct. 1929; *Mail*, 19 Aug. 1929; *Star*, 12 Aug. 1929; U.W., C.P.S.A., W. Ballinger papers, file 4, W. Ballinger to W. Holtby, 4 Aug. 1929.

92. *Farmer's Weekly*, 18 July 1928, 1 Jan. 1930; *Mail*, 10 Oct. 1929; *Vaderland*, 10

May 1929, 31 May 1929, 13 Sept. 1929.

93. *Farmer's Weekly*, 2 Oct. 1929; *Mail*, 12 Sept. 1929; *Star*, 11 Sept. 1929; *Vaderland*, 13 Sept. 1929, 17 Sept. 1929.

94. U.W., C.P.S.A, Industrial and Commercial Workers' Union Records, File 4, W. Ballinger, 'The Industrial and Commercial Workers' Union of Africa', Feb. 1933.

95. H.C.L., E. Lewis letters, Part II, D4 F7, E. Lewis to W. Holtby, 26 Nov. 1930; U.W., C.P.S.A., Industrial and Commercial Workers' Union Records, file 3, W. Ballinger, 'Native Workers of South Africa'; U.W., C.P.S.A., W. Ballinger papers, file 4, W. Ballinger to F. Brockway, 15 May 1929.

96. K. Marx, *Capital*, vol. 1 (London 1959), p.737.

97. U.W., A.S.I., O.H.P., interview with J. Ntambo and L. Nhlabathi by V.N., Ledig, 23 Nov. 1979.

98. E. Lewis, *Wild Deer* (Johannesburg 1984), pp.xvi–xvii.

99. *Vaderland*, 23 March 1928.

CHAPTER 6

1. *Mercury*, 2 March 1928; *Star*, 3 March 1928; T.A., Department of Justice files, JUS 437, 4/366/27, D.C., S.A.P., Pietermaritzburg, to Deputy Commissioner, S.A.P., Pietermaritzburg, 2 March 1928.

2. *The South African Worker*, 10 June 1927; *Annual Report by the Commissioner of Police for the Year Ending 31st December, 1927*, U.G. 40–1928, p.21; T.A., Native Affairs Department files, NTS 7606, 27/328, Captain Adj. Els of Heilbron Command to Officer in Command, Bloemfontein, 10 May 1927, and Parys Mag. to S.N.A., 14 May 1927; U.W., A.S.I., O.H.P., interview with M. Mafumane by V.N., Koppies, 14 April 1980.

3. Orange Free State Archives Depot, Orange Free State Supreme Court Cases, H.G. 4/1/2/264, case no. 121 of 1928, *Rex* vs. R. Dumah and W. 'Mote.

4. *Mercury*, 22 Sept. 1927; *Mail*, 15 Sept. 1927; N.A., files of the C.N.C., CNC 2/73/59, Box 82, N1/1/3(10), Estcourt Mag. to C.N.C., 3 Sept. 1928; T.A., JUS 437, 4/366/27, comments of Minister of Justice written on a letter from A. Champion to Minister of Justice, 12 Sept. 1927.

5. T.A., JUS 437, 4/366/27, Officer of S.A.P., Kranskop, to Deputy Commissioner, S.A.P., Pietermaritzburg, 3 March 1928; S. Marks, *Reluctant Rebellion: the 1906–1908 Disturbances in Natal* (Oxford 1970), pp.200–10.

6. *uMgungundlovu*, 'the gathering place of the royal elephant', was the name of Dingane's main homestead, the political centre of the Zulu kingdom. After this was destroyed by the Voortrekkers, Zulu-speakers gave the capital city of Natal the same name. They also aptly called Greytown, effectively the capital of the countryside and situated in a region where struggles between black and white tended to be particularly intense, 'little *uMgungundlovu*'.

7. *Herald*, 6 April 1927; *Minutes of Evidence of the Natal Natives Land Committee*, U.G. 35–1918, p.142.

8. *Natal Native Commission 1881–2: Evidence Taken by the Sub-Commission for Umvoti County* (Pietermaritzburg 1882), p.23; S. Ford, *Talks with Natal Farmers* (Pietermaritzburg 1909), p.39; Marks, *Rebellion*, p.201.

9. *Report of the Natives Land Commission*, Vol. II, U.G. 22–1916, pp.544–8.

10. *Ibid*, pp.546–7; T.A., NTS 3238, 736/307, J. Heraughty and H. Marlin to S.N.A., 9 Aug. 1937; U.W., A.S.I., O.H.P., interview with M. Majola by H.B. and V.N., Mooi River, 30 Nov. 1981.

11. *Colony of Natal, Native Affairs Commission 1906–7. Evidence* (Pietermaritzburg

1907), pp.34–5, 530; U.W., A.S.I., O.H.P., interview with J. Dhlomo by H.B. and V.N., Greytown, 2 July 1980, and interview with Majola.

12. S.B.A., 1/1/220, Joint General Manager of Standard Bank to Manager Greytown branch, 17 July 1925.

13. S.B.A., 1/1/220, Inspection Reports on Greytown branch, 1914–28 (see in particular Inspection Reports of 31 Oct. 1919 and 14 Dec. 1916). It was precisely because land was overvalued that the giant British-owned Forestal Land, Timber and Railways Company, and its subsidiary the Natal Tanning Extract Company, bought wattle farms in northern Natal and Piet Retief rather than in Umvoti during the boom.

14. S.B.A., 1/1/220, Inspection Reports on Greytown Branch, 1920–26; U.W., A.S.I., O.H.P., interview with J. Dladla by H.B. and V.N., Greytown, 3 July 1980; P. Havemann, *My Mother – A Voortrekker*, (n.d., no place of publication), p.14.

15. *Star*, 27 March 1929; S.B.A., 1/1/220, Inspection Reports on Greytown branch, 1914–28. See p.209 for the role of James Martens in combating the I.C.U.

16. *Farmer's Weekly*, 23 May 1928, 3 Oct. 1928, 28 Nov. 1928; S.B.A., 1/1/220, Inspection Reports on Greytown branch, 1920–28; The Board of Trade and Industries, 'The Wattle Growing and Tanning Extract Industries', *The South African Journal of Industries*, 7, 9, 1924, pp.586–91; A. Hicks, *The Story of Forestal* (London 1956), pp.23, 42; N. Hurwitz, *Agriculture in Natal 1860–1950* (Cape Town 1957), p.59.

17. *Gazette*, 7 Dec. 1928; *Report on the Agricultural and Pastoral Production of the Union of South Africa, 1922–1923*, U.G. 25–1925, p.35; *Report of the Agricultural and Pastoral Production of the Union of South Africa, 1925–26*, U.G. 24–1928, p.106; *Report of the Agricultural and Pastoral Production of the Union of South Africa, 1928–1929*, U.G. 35–1930, p.39; *Report of the Agricultural and Pastoral Production of the Union of South Africa, 1929–1930*, U.G. 12–1932, pp.17, 48; Weenen County (Estcourt) Farmers' Association minutes, Estcourt, Presidential Report, 17 Nov. 1926.

18. T.A., NTS 3235, 700/307, C.N.C. to S.N.A., 4 Feb. 1930.

19. *Mercury*, 29 Oct. 1927; *Star*, 31 June 1927; *Witness*, 7 March 1928; *Report of the Native Economic Commission 1930–1932*, U.G. 22–1932, p.193; J. Grosskopf, *Rural Impoverishment and Rural Exodus* in *Report of the Carnegie Commission: The Poor White Problem in South Africa*, Part I (Stellenbosch 1932), p.47. Correspondence in N.A., CNC 22/97, Box 123, N2/9/6(11) gives a good indication of the changed uses to which 'labour farms' were being put by wattle companies and 'progressive' farmers.

20. T.A., JUS 429, 1/667/27, Annual Report for Umvoti by Mag., 1927; T.A., JUS 440, 1/82/28, Annual Report for Umvoti by Mag., 1928; T.A., NTS 8588, 2/362, C.N.C. to S.N.A., 15 April 1925; Umvoti Agricultural Society minutes, Greytown, meeting 2 Dec. 1928; Ford, *Talks*, pp.31–66.

21. *Natal Farmer*, 14 May 1926; *Witness*, 21 May 1927; N.A., correspondence of New Hanover Mag., N1/5/6, Annual Report for the district of New Hanover for the year 1930; T.A., E.N.E.C., K26, representative of Kambula farmers' association, Vryheid, p.1550; Dr G. Park Ross, Durban, pp.6101–2.

22. *Gazette*, 1 March 1929; *Report of the Agricultural and Pastoral Production of the Union of South Africa, 1924–1925*, U.G. 13–1927, p.167; *Report of Agricultural Production, 1929–1930*, p.95; S.B.A., 1/1/220, Inspection Report on Greytown branch, 28 Feb. 1930; T. Sim, *Tree Planting in South Africa, including the Union of South Africa, Southern Rhodesia, and Portuguese East Africa* (Pietermaritzburg 1927), pp.197, 203.

23. J. Clegg, '*Ukubuyisa Isidumbu* – "Bringing Back the Body": An Examination

into the Ideology of Vengeance in the Msinga and Mpofana Rural Locations, 1882–1944' in P. Bonner (ed.), *Working Papers in Southern African Studies*, Vol. 2 (Johannesburg 1981), pp.186–7. For Cunu labourers applying this concept in Umvoti, see T.A., NTS 290, 322/53, proceedings of inquiry into conduct of chief Mkwenyana, 22 Feb. 1932.

24. These had been operating in Umvoti from at least the early twentieth century.

25. *Cape Times,* 11 May 1927; *Natal Farmer,* 20 May 1927; *Star,* 7 June 1927; N.A., *Notule van die Vyf-en-Vyftigste Algemene Vergadering van die Nederduitsch Ger. Kerk van Natal,* April 1928, p.57; U.W., A.S.I., O.H.P., interview with Dhlomo. Unfortunately, little is known about Gwaza's background, and the fact that he was also repeatedly referred to as Magwaza confuses the matter. When charged in court, his name was given as above, and he was said to be a Bomvu commoner under chief Makasana. There was however a Reverend Magwaza in Greytown, who, according to an I.C.U. official in early April 1927, was eager to meet Union organizers. And although informants do not recall Gwaza as a minister, his separatist leanings, together with his desire to unite Zulu-speakers, were clearly manifested. Probably, too, he was the same man as the 'Zebulon Magwaza', who, together with the 1927–28 Kranskop Branch Secretary, was a leading I.C.U. *yase* Natal figure in the Durban riots of 1929. At that time Magwaza was praised as a man 'who saw Usuthu and Mandlakazi, and on consulting the bible saw inscribed therein three letters "I.C.U."'. In local Umvoti terms, this could be translated as the I.C.U. uniting traditional enemies: the Bomvu and Bambatha's people.

26. N.A., Kranskop Criminal Records, 1890–1948, case no. 158 of 1928, *Rex* vs. J. Nel *et al*, enclosing *Rex* vs. Z. Gwaza, 15 Nov. 1927; Marks, *Rebellion*, p.222; J. Stuart, *A History of the Zulu Rebellion, 1906, and of Dinizulu's Arrest, Trial and Expatriation* (London 1913), pp.159, 170.

27. *Die Natal Afrikaner,* 24 April 1927; *Star,* 7 June 1927; N.A., Kranskop Criminal Records, 1890–1948, case no. 158 of 1928, *Rex* vs. J. Nel *et al*, enclosing *Rex* vs. Z. Gwaza, 15 Nov. 1927; U.W., C.P.S.A., L. Forman papers, AD 1714 Mfc, B4.31, Investigation and Report: Natal Provincial and Durban Offices of the I.C.U.

28. *Sixth Census of the Population of the Union of South Africa. Enumerated 5th May, 1936,* Vol. IX, U.G. 12–1942, p.99; N.A., correspondence of Umvoti Mag., 2/3/2, Umvoti Mag. to C.N.C., 25 Aug. 1928; U.W., A.S.I., O.H.P., interview with Dladla; H.B., notes of interview with L. Ngubane by H.B. and V.N., Greytown, 3 July 1980.

29. *Mail,* 10 May 1927; T.A., JUS 429, 1/667/27, Annual Report for Umvoti by Mag., 1927; H. Bradford, 'Strikes in the Natal Midlands: Landlords, Labour Tenants and the I.C.U.', *Africa Perspective,* 22, 1983.

30. I have discovered no press reports indicating that Gwaza spoke about wages, and in his subsequent founding of the Northern Trade Native Union (*sic*), he indicated interest in the ending, not the reform, of wage labour. Numerous informants vigorously denied that the local I.C.U. spoke of eight shillings a day, although Dhlomo believed they mentioned whites underpaying blacks.

31. Union of South Africa, House of Assembly Debates, 19 May 1927, W. Deane, Cols. 3888, 3923.

32. T.A., JUS 429, 1/667/27, Annual Report for Umvoti by Mag., 1927; T.A., JUS 440, 1/82/28, Annual Report for Umvoti by Mag., 1928. It is tempting to speculate that many of these Mpondo and Basotho men were alienated from the Greytown branch by its emphasis on Zulu nationalism.

33. *Mercury,* 23 April 1927, 9 May 1927; N.A., correspondence of Umvoti Mag., N2/3/2, Umvoti Mag. to C.N.C., 25 Aug. 1928, and J. Sandstrom to Native

Commissioner, Greytown, 22 May 1930; T.A., NTS 263, 133/53, C.N.C. to
S.N.A., 14 June 1924; U.W., A.S.I., O.H.P., interview with Dhlomo; Marks,
Rebellion, p.146.

34. *Mercury*, 5 Aug. 1927; T.A., NTS 3235, 700/307, C.N.C. to S.N.A., 29 Feb.
1928. A farmer in an adjacent district told the Weenen magistrate in 1927 how
difficult it was to deal with recalcitrant tenants on 'labour farms': 'I am
carrying on a dairy farm here which keeps me tied down very much and these
natives know how difficult it is for me to get away and take advantage of the
fact.' In the main, both Zondi and Cunu commoners in the thornveld
supported relatives of chiefs who had been deposed for their involvement in
Bambatha's rebellion, rather than the loyalist state-appointees nominated as
their rulers. Although Cunu men had not actually joined the Zondi rebels, they
also refused to participate in quelling the 1906 uprising.

35. *Natal Farmer*, 20 May 1927; T.A., Smuts papers, Vol. 39, No. 135 (new vol.
no. 223), General Smuts to Dr A. Edington, 18 May 1927 (thanks to Jeremy
Krikler for this reference).

36. Farmers both reaped their bumper maize crop and paid off many of their
liabilities with wattle bark proceeds. It is unclear how those affected by the
strikes obtained their labour: wealthier farmers may well have recruited
workers from farther afield, while some strikers were possibly forced back to
work by various threats.

37. T.A., JUS 429, 1/667/27, Annual Report for Umvoti by Mag., 1927. See also
Mercury, 19 May 1927; N.A., *Notule van Vergadering van die N.G.K. Kerk van
Natal*, April 1928, p.57; T.A., JUS 440, 1/82/28, Annual Report for Umvoti
by Mag., 1928.

38. Umvoti Agricultural Society minutes, meeting 28 Feb. 1925; H.B., notes on
interview with Ngubane; U.W., A.S.I., O.H.P., interview with E. Zondi by
V.N. and H.B., Greytown, 3 July 1980. August Kohrs, a leading wool farmer
heavily involved in the Anti-I.C.U. (see p.209), widely advertized his method
of controlling African servants: to strip them to the waist and give them 'a
good hiding'. Louis Nourse, referred to below, justified his physical abuse of
servants by claiming 'otherwise they will do as they like and become top dog'.

39. N.A., Greytown Criminal Records, 1915–39, *Rex* vs. N. Magutshwa and V.
Zakwe; N.A., Kranskop Criminal Records, 1890–1948, preparatory examination of M. Cele, 1 Dec. 1927.

40. N.A., CNC 63/2/52, Box 89, N1/9/2(4), N.C. Weenen to C.N.C., 9 Jan.
1935; T.A., NTS 290, 322/53, Lieutenant S.A.P., Pietermaritzburg, to Deputy
Commissioner, S.A.P., Pietermaritzburg, 11 Aug. 1931, and proceedings of
inquiry into conduct of chief Mkwenyana, 22 Feb. 1932. Another indication of
the emergence of youthful subcultures in Umvoti were *'iminjonjo'* beer parties
which, to the distress of the magistrate, were not being held at the homesteads
of responsible men.

41. N.A., Greytown Criminal Record Book, 1927; U.W., A.S.I., O.H.P.,
interview with Dladla. Eileen Krige's statement in *The Social System of the
Zulus* (Pietermaritzburg 1981), p.126, that 'no Zulu man will discuss anything
of importance with a woman', was certainly substantiated at the above-
mentioned meeting on the thornveld farm. Gwaza and Makanya addressed the
gathering in a venue from which women were excluded, and left in the car the
two females with whom they had been travelling.

42. *Witness*, 6 July 1927.

43. *Report of the Native Farm Labour Committee, 1937–1939*, Annexure 520–1939,
p.56; H. Bradford, 'The Industrial and Commercial Workers' Union in the
Natal Countryside: Class Struggle on the Land', Hons., University of Cape

Town, 1980, pp.62–4.
44. *Witness*, 6 July 1927; N.A., CNC 120/3, Box 123, N3/13/4(X), C.N.C. to S.N.A., 30 Dec. 1927. Some Umvoti landlords were possibly also concerned about arguments propagated by both the press and South African Party Parliamentarians that victimization of trade union members, simply for possession of a red ticket, was undesirable under a Labour Party coalition government.
45. T.A., correspondence in NTS 3238, 736/307, relating to opposition from officials and farmers to the I.C.U.'s buying of Lonsdale; U.W., A.S.I., O.H.P., interview with Dhlomo and interview with J. Mchunu by H.B. and V.N., Mooi River, 1 Dec. 1981; U.W., C.P.S.A., Forman papers, B3.154, C. Martens to A. Champion, 10 Nov. 1927, and B3.162, C.N.C. to A. Champion, 17 Nov. 1927; G. Coka, 'The Story of Gilbert Coka of the Zulu Tribe of Natal, South Africa' in M. Perham (ed.), *Ten Africans* (London 1936), p.299.
46. T.A., NTS 9252, 1/371, C.N.C. to S.N.A., 27 June 1928; U.W., A.S.I., O.H.P., interview with Majola.
47. *Gazette*, 16 March 1928; *Witness*, 14 May 1927, 6 July 1927.
48. *Farmer's Weekly*, 2 May 1928; *Witness*, 30 May 1927.
49. *Gazette*, 16 March 1928; *Die Natal Afrikaner*, 17 May 1927; N.A., Greytown Criminal Record Book, 1927; T.A., NTS 9252, 1/371, C.N.C. to S.N.A., 27 June 1928; U.W., A.S.I., O.H.P., interview with E. Zondi by H.B. and V.N., Greytown, 3 July 1980.
50. *Witness*, 6 July 1927.
51. N.A., Greytown Criminal Records, 1915–39, M. Mcunu vs. *Rex*, 31 Oct. 1927.
52. *Farmer's Weekly*, 28 Nov. 1928; *Mercury*, 12 March 1928; T.A., JUS 429, 1/667/27, Annual Report for Umvoti by Mag., 1927; Bradford, 'Strikes', pp.19–22.
53. *Mercury*, 2 March 1928, 3 March 1928, 13 April 1928; *Star*, 17 April 1928; *Herald*, 17 March 1928; Marks, *Rebellion*, p.309.
54. A considerable number of those who participated in the raids and/or the Anti-I.C.U. meetings had fought for king and country in battles ranging from those of 1879 and 1906 to those of 1914–18. This military background, together with ongoing involvement in the Umvoti Mounted Rifles, was apparent in their march down the streets of Greytown, and their raising of the South African war-cry outside the Pietermaritzburg office. Boer traditions were in evidence in the calls for laagering, while more than one spectator referred to the raiders as 'the Greytown commando'.
55. *Star*, 23 March 1928; *Witness*, 6 March 1928; T.A., correspondence in JUS 437, 4/366/27 relating to the raids.
56. Defence Force Archives Depot, Pretoria, Chief of General Staff files, CGS 67, 1G 45, C. Wheelwright (C.N.C.) to Major Herbst (S.N.A.), 11 Jan 1928. For other references to 'May' and Armageddon, see *Star*, 9 Aug. 1927, and T.A., NTS 7606, 37/328, C.N.C. to S.N.A., 24 March 1928, enclosing statement by Ndhlovu, 21 March 1928. Wheelwright had been sufficiently perturbed in May 1927 to send a confidential letter to Herbst about his fears of an impending insurrection. Almost certainly, Dunn's information was largely fabricated. Parts of his statement were blatant lies: it is for example inconceivable that the entire National Council discussed and agreed on this plan.
57. Defence Force Archives, CGS 67, 1G 45, C. Wheelwright to Major Herbst, 11 Jan. 1928, and Major Herbst to General Brink, 30 Jan. 1928; T.A., JUS 437, 4/366/27, Deputy Commissioner, Natal Division of S.A.P., to Commiss-

ioner, S.A.P., Pretoria, 26 Feb. 1928, and Minister of Defence to Prime Minister, 5 March 1928.

58.   T.A., JUS 437, 4/366/27, Estcourt Mag. to Secretary for Justice, 2 April 1928.

59.   *Gazette*, 16 March 1928; personal communication from M. Hawthorne, daughter of Cyril Browning; *Braby's Natal Directory, 1928* (Durban n.d.).

60.   This is subject to the qualification that only about a third of the men involved in the raids were ever charged, and that poorer whites were more obvious targets for exemplary punishment than their wealthier compatriots.

61.   *Mercury*, 28 March 1928; *Land Commission*, pp.544–9; N.A., correspondence in CNC 22/97, Box 123, N2/9/6(11), which gives an indication of the location of the farms on which many raiders lived; N.A., Kranskop Criminal Records 1890–1948, Case no. 158 of 1928, *Rex* vs. J. Nel *et al*; N.A., correspondence of Greytown magistrate, N4/5/3/8, application for loan by T.J. Hansmeyer, 24 Nov. 1935; N.A., Greytown Criminal Record Book, 1927; S.B.A., 1/1/220, Inspection Reports of Greytown branch, 1913–28; T.A., NTS 3241, 774/307, Director of Agriculture to S.N.A., 12 Dec. 1929; *Braby's Directory, 1928*. Klipnek means Stony Ridge.

62.   The South African Party's majority in the 1924 elections was cut in Umvoti from 329 (in 1921) to 111.

63.   *Gazette*, 16 March 1928.

64.   *Mercury*, 14 March 1928; T.A., NTS 8588, 2/362, Confidential Circular from Department of Justice to all Natal Magistrates, 15 Dec. 1927; N.A.U. Executive Committee minutes, Pietermaritzburg, meetings on 15 June 1928, 28 Sept. 1928.

65.   *Herald*, 12 May 1928; *Witness*, 25 June 1928; T.A., JUS 437, 4/366/27, S.A.P. Officer, Kranskop, to Deputy Commissioner, S.A.P., Pietermaritzburg, 3 March 1928; T.A., NTS 7606, 49/328, C.N.C. to S.N.A., 8 Nov. 1929, enclosing translation of *Igazi ne Zinyembezi*; C. Kadalie, *My Life and the I.C.U.: the Autobiography of a Black Trade Unionist in South Africa* (London 1970), p.159.

66.   *Farmer's Weekly*, 9 May 1928; *Witness*, 25 June 1928; Umvoti Agricultural Society minutes, meeting on 19 Jan. 1928.

67.   *Gazette*, 11 May 1928, 5 Oct. 1928; N.A., correspondence of Greytown Mag., N2/3/2, Rev. Sandstrom to Greytown Mag., 13 May 1931; T.A., NTS 5407, 118/313G, Greytown Mag. to C.N.C., 28 Nov. 1928, and C.N.C. to S.N.A., 30 Nov. 1928. *Utshwala* was a grain-based drink of low alcoholic content.

CHAPTER 7

1.   E. Hobsbawm, *Primitive Rebels: Studies in Archaic Forms of Social Movement in the 19th and 20th Centuries* (Manchester 1971), pp.58, 90. See also M. Barkun, *Disaster and the Millennium* (New Haven 1974) and N. Cohn, *The Pursuit of the Millennium: Revolutionary Millenarians and Mystical Anarchists of the Middle Ages* (London 1978). The definition of millenarian movements used here is that of Cohn's (p.13): they are movements whose followers perceive their salvation as collective, terrestrial, imminent, total and miraculous (although not necessarily occurring through divine intervention).

2.   C. Bundy, *The Rise and Fall of the South African Peasantry* (London 1979), p.123.

3.   General Smuts, in Foreword to M. Hunter, *Reaction to Conquest: Effects of Contact with Europeans on the Pondo of South Africa* (London 1936), p.viii. See also *ibid*, p.349; W. Beinart, *The Political Economy of Pondoland 1860–1930* (Johannesburg 1982), p.161.

4.   C.A., correspondence of Bizana Mag., 1/BIZ 6/21, 2/27/5/1, Rev. Brailsford

to Bizana Mag., 14 Aug. 1933; T.A., Native Affairs Department files, NTS 1767, 57/276, C.M.T. to S.N.A., 3 Sept. 1929; T.A., NTS 8491, 24/360, C.M.T. to S.N.A., 30 Nov. 1926; Beinart, *Pondoland*, pp.157, 173; Hunter, *Reaction*, p.3.

5.   For such an interpretation of the I.C.U. in Pondoland, see Hunter, *Reaction*, p.571.

6.   T.A., NTS 1681, 2/276, Inspector-in-Charge, C.I.D., to Deputy Commissioner, C.I.D., 11 Oct. 1920; R. Hill, '"Africa for the Africans": Marcus Garvey, the UNIA, and the Struggle of African Nationalism in South Africa in the Nineteen-Twenties', paper presented at conference 'South Africa in the Comparative Study of Class, Race and Nationalism', New York, Sept. 1982, pp.40A–B.

7.   E. Smith, *Aggrey of Africa: A Study in Black and White* (New York 1930), pp.180–81; Hill, 'Marcus Garvey', pp.29, 39–40D.

8.   C.A., 1/BIZ 6/61, R. Saunders to Bizana Mag., 11 May 1925; G. Coka, 'The Story of Gilbert Coka of the Zulu Tribe of Natal, South Africa' in M. Perham (ed.), *Ten Africans* (London 1936), pp.277–8; Hill, 'Marcus Garvey', pp.48, 59–60, 62, 77.

9.   *Advertiser*, 30 Sept. 1927. See also *Umteteli*, 8 Oct. 1927; T.A., NTS 1681, 2/276(1), copy of *Negro World*, 3 May 1924; B. Edgar, 'Garveyism in Africa: Dr. Wellington and the American Movement in the Transkei', *Ufahamu*, 6, 3, 1976, pp.38–9. An extraordinary array of movements in Africa invoked American liberators in the 1920s. In the Congo they were expected to sail up the river to usher in freedom; in Northern Rhodesia they would arrive bearing motor-bikes. In Nyasaland they would fly over killing whites with bombs; in Southern Rhodesia only baptism would save blacks from American bullets, and in South West Africa some thought American soldiers would issue from the ground.

10. T.A., NTS 7660, 22/332, Deputy Commissioner, Divisional C.I. Officer, Witwatersrand, to Deputy Commissioner, Witwatersrand, 12 July 1930; Edgar, 'Dr. Wellington', pp.32 – 41. Another attempt to organize an 'American movement' was made by African agents of Abraham le Fleur, who had for decades been attempting to win back Griqua land by capitalizing on African discontent. le Fleur himself never went beyond preaching 'Africa for Coloured Races'. But by early 1926 his African sub-leaders were declaring in Matatiele that Americans were coming to help chief le Fleur; that after victory there would be no more taxes, passes or dipping; and that 'a certain kind of thing would come from Heaven, chase away the Europeans and also the Natives who did not belong to le Fleur'.

11. *Territorial News*, 6 June 1929; *Star*, 22 Dec. 1927; C.A., correspondence of East London Town Clerk, 1/ELN 87, c3(2), Special Native Detective, East London, to D.C., East London, 23 July 1930. The attraction of planes filled with Americans only increased when an unimaginative Defence Force tried to intimidate Wellingtonites with demonstrations of government planes. The belief that these were being flown by Garvey's liberators was so widespread that a loyalist chief nearly murdered a luckless white pilot who crash-landed.

12. *The Daily Dispatch*, 6 April 1927; C.A., correspondence of Mount Frere Mag., 1/MFE 8/1/14, 2/12/4, Sergeant, S.A.P., Mount Frere, to D.C., S.A.P., Kokstad, 19 Dec. 1927; C.A., correspondence of Qumbu Mag., 1/QBU 7/1/9, 2/17, Qumbu Mag. to C.M.T., 1 April 1927; W. Beinart, '*Amafelan-dawonye* (The Diehards): Rural Popular Protest and Women's Movements in Herschel District, South Africa, in the 1920s', paper presented at U.W., History Workshop, Feb. 1984, pp.17–33; Edgar, 'Dr. Wellington', pp.42–7; B. Edgar, 'Garveyism in Africa: Dr Wellington and the "American Movement"

in the Transkei, 1925–40' in *Collected Seminar Papers no. 20: The Societies of Southern Africa in the 19th and 20th Centuries,* Vol. 6 (London 1974), p.109.

13. Beinart, '*Amafelandawonye*', pp.32–6, 44–5; W. Beinart and C. Bundy, 'State Intervention and Rural Resistance: The Transkei, 1900–1965' in M. Klein (ed.), *Peasants in Africa: Historical and Contemporary Perspectives* (Beverly Hills 1980), p.292; Beinart, *Pondoland*, pp.157–9; Hunter, *Reaction*, p.571. These contradictions amongst *Ama Melika* believers – and the I.C.U.'s role – have not been recognized by some historians, including Hill, 'Marcus Garvey'.

14. T.A., NTS 4408, 352/313, Location Superintendent Randfontein to Chief Sanitary Inspector, Krugersdorp, 14 Nov. 1927; interview with Gqambuleni *et al* by W.B. and F.D., Lusikisiki, 25 March 1977 (thanks to William Beinart for access to this and other interviews).

15. *Cape Times*, 8 Sept. 1927; *The Natal Farmer*, 1 July 1927; *The Times*, 10 Oct. 1927; N.A., files of the Chief Native Commissioner, CNC 58/7/3, Box 81, Inspector, D.C., Eshowe, to Deputy Commissioner, S.A.P., 5 April 1928; Beinart, *Pondoland*, p.143; Coka, 'Story', p.295.

16. *Herald*, 12 Jan. 1927; interview with J. Mvunelo by W.B., Lusikisiki, 13 March 1977; U.W., C.P.S.A., Forman papers, B3.119, A. Champion to T. Lujiza, 12 Oct. 1927.

17. C.A., 1/BIZ 6/50, N1/1/2, C.M.T. to Bizana Mag., 11 Dec. 1925; C.A., 1/BIZ 6/70, Bizana Mag. to C.M.T., 23 Sept. 1926; C.A., correspondence of Ngqeleni Mag., 1/NQL 19, N1/15/6, Acting Mag. to S.N.A., 20 Sept 1926; T.A., E.N.E.C., K26, calculation by F. Lucas regarding take-home pay of cane labourers, p.1821; Beinart, *Pondoland*, pp.102–3; P. Guénault and J. Reedman, 'Taxation' in E. Hellman (ed.), *Handbook on Race Relations in South Africa* (New York 1949), p.296.

18. *Territorial News*, 10 Nov. 1927; T.A., NTS 7206, 42/326, Tsomo Mag. to C.M.T., 12 Jan. 1925; T.A., correspondence in NTS 8491, 24/360, including telegram W. Stuart to 'Natives', Pretoria, 1 July 1927; Beinart, *Pondoland*, pp.118–20, 155–6.

19. *Star*, 2 Feb. 1927; *Umteteli*, 30 July 1927, 21 April 1928; T.A., files of Department of Agriculture, LDB 978, R 1074/21, meteorological observations referring to Transkeian Territories, July to December 1927; C.A., correspondence of Lusikisiki Mag., 1/LSK 35, 2/2/2, minutes of quarterly meeting, 4 Oct. 1927; Beinart, *Pondoland*, pp.50, 52, 79, 100, 102, 151.

20. *Advertiser*, 23 Sept. 1927; *Herald*, 15 Sept. 1927; T.A., NTS 7665, 46/332, statement made by Detective Sergeant Arnold during consultation in office of C.N.C., 7 Sept. 1929; U.W., C.P.S.A, Forman papers, B3.119, A. Champion to T. Lujiza, 12 Oct. 1927.

21. *Advertiser*, 28 Oct. 1927, 4 Nov. 1927; *Natal Mercury*, 20 Jan. 1928; U.W., A.S.I., O.H.P., interview with L. Mdingi by H.B., Bizana, 17 May 1984.

22. C.A., correspondence of Kentani Mag., 1/KNT 40, 12, T. Lujiza to Kentani Mag., 30 Aug. 1927; C.A., 1/LSK 38, 2/9/2, Lusikisiki Mag. to C.M.T., 28 Nov. 1932; interview with S. Mbunquka by H.B., Bizana, 18 May 1984; interview with E. Pato by H.B., Bizana, 19 May 1984; U.W., A.S.I., O.H.P., interview with L. Mdingi by W.B. and H.B., Bizana, 2 April 1984, and interview with Mdingi, 17 May 1984.

23. Interview with Pato; U.W., A.S.I., O.H.P., interview with Mdingi, 2 April 1984; interview with B. Mgetyana by H.B. and A.M., Bizana, 20 May 1984, and interview with Z. Sincuba by H.B. and A.M., Bizana, 18 May 1984; Hunter, *Reaction*, pp.344–8.

24. Interview with Pato; interview with A. Soji by W.B. and F.D., Lusikisiki, 23 March 1977.

25. Interview with Soji; U.W., A.S.I., O.H.P., interview with Mgetyana and interview with J. Nomsuka by H.B. and A.M., Bizana, 20 May 1984; Beinart, *Pondoland*, p.157.
26. N.A., CNC 348, 1/29/7, statement made by Rev. E. Koti before Harding Mag., 12 Jan. 1928 (thanks to William Beinart and Bob Edgar for access to copies of documents in this box); U.W., A.S.I., O.H.P., interview with Nomsuka. Mdodana's American training was financed by the Foreign Mission Board of the Baptists Association (Philadelphia).
27. U.W., A.S.I., O.H.P., interview with Nomsuka; Hunter, *Reaction*, pp.294–303. *Imithi* means medicines.
28. Hunter, *Reaction*, p.319.
29. Orange Free State Archives Depot, Orange Free State Supreme Court cases, H.G. 4/1/2/240, case no. 124 of 1926, *Rex* vs. S. Elias; Hunter, *Reaction*, p.275, 492. At various times, I.C.U. leaders thought Kadalie and Champion had been charmed or bewitched by enemies; and a Natal Branch Secretary was believed to have died from sorcery. During the Second World War, a Xhosa-speaking rural cultivator vividly articulated the belief that *impundulu* could be used in conjunction with modern military might. He wondered 'why the white people were dragging the war out so long, when all they had to do was to engage a woman who 'kept' a lightning bird, and then, together, they could wipe out large crowds in no time'.
30. A. Berglund, *Zulu Thought Patterns and Symbolism* (Uppsala 1976), pp.52, 180, 192, 310–11, 341; E. Krige, *The Social System of the Zulus* (Pietermaritzburg 1981), pp.311–19; O. Raum, *The Social Functions of Avoidance and Taboos among the Zulu* (Berlin 1973), pp.218, 236; R. Sayce, 'Lightning Charms from Natal', *Man*, 26 April 1926, pp.69–70.
31. Hunter, *Reaction*, p.317.
32. Personal communication from William Beinart about lard on insteps; interview with J. Dhlomo by H.B., Pretoria, 17 Aug. 1984; W. Hammond-Tooke, *Bhaca Society* (Cape Town 1962), p.271; Hunter, *Reaction*, p.298.
33. This was a common trend way beyond South African borders, but for references to Mpondo uses of protective charms drawn from unclean, vile objects, see Hunter, *Reaction*, pp.290–92, and for such uses by Zulu-speakers see Berglund, *Symbolism*, pp.290–91. Amongst the southern Nguni, the power of lard was also related to the notion that pigs were the only animals that could not be killed by snakes.
34. *Umteteli*, 30 June 1928; M. Harris, *Cows, Pigs, Wars and Witches: the Riddles of Culture* (New York 1974), pp.36–43; R. Plant, *The Zulu in Three Tenses: Being a Forecast of the Zulu's Future in the Light of his Past and his Present* (Pietermaritzburg 1905). The Mpondo word for 'pig' originated with Khoi (who were linked by earlier trade); this should perhaps form part of the explanation for why the Mpondo considered pigs less unclean than did Zulu-speakers, who were introduced to pigs by whites.
35. *Territorial News*, 5 Jan. 1928; Hunter, *Reaction*, pp.46, 71; B. Sundkler, *Bantu Prophets in South Africa* (London 1961), pp.215–19.
36. Beinart, *Pondoland*, pp.157–8; Hunter, *Reaction*, p.275.
37. C.A., files of Native Affairs Department, correspondence in NA 707 B2926, relating to swine-slaughter in the Transkei; Edgar, 'Dr. Wellington', p.42; S. Marks, *Reluctant Rebellion: the 1906–8 Disturbances in Natal* (Oxford 1970), pp.165–6.
38. C.A., 1/QBU 7/1/9, Qumbu Mag. to C.M.T., 1 Sept. 1927, 26 Sept. 1927; T.A., NTS 7604, 26/328(1), Flagstaff Mag. to C.M.T., 27 Aug. 1927; U.W., A.S.I., O.H.P., interview with A. Cwele and P. Jali by H.B. and A.M.,

Bizana, 18 May 1984. State officials thought that the Kokstad/Umzimkulu killings were inspired by le Fleur's agents, who may well have been amongst those urging hog-slaughter at this time.

39. Some Wellingtonites not only preached the same message, but also catered for the specific needs of 'school people' by exhorting them to paint their houses black and abandon needles, which symbolized lightning.

40. T.A., NTS 7604, 26/328(1), Mount Ayliff Mag. to C.M.T., 19 Sept. 1927; interview with Mvunelo; interview with Soji.

41. U.W., A.S.I., O.H.P., interview with Mdingi, 2 April 1984.

42. See, for example, A. Lee, 'Ngoja and Six Theories of Witchcraft Eradication', *Ufahamu*, 6, 3, 1976, and M. Marwick, 'Another Modern Anti-Witchcraft Movement in East Central Africa', *Africa* 20, 1950, pp.100–108.

43. Interview with Pato; U.W., A.S.I., O.H.P., interview with E. Hlangabezo by H.B. and A.M., Bizana, 20 May 1984, and interview with Mdingi, 17 May 1984.

44. *Advertiser*, 23 Sept. 1927, 7 Oct. 1927; *Mail*, 10 Dec. 1927; *Territorial News*, 27 Oct. 1927; N.A., CNC 348, 1/29/7, Detective Head Constable, S.A.P., Harding, to Deputy Commissioner, S.A.P., Pietermaritzburg, 15 Dec. 1927, and statement by M. Dhlamini, 11 Jan. 1928; T.A., correspondence in NTS 7604, 26/328(1), especially Deputy Commissioner, S.A.P., Transkei, to Commissioner, S.A.P., 22 Sept. 1927; Marks, *Rebellion*, p.154. Some Wellingtonites were also setting the cataclysm for Christmas Day.

45. C.A., 1/BIZ 6/65, N1/9/3, telegram Tembu to Bizana Mag., 13 Dec. 1927; Bizana Mag. to Tembu, 14 Dec. 1927; Tembu to Bizana Mag., 28 Dec. 1927; statement by Constable B. Sontsele, 6 Jan. 1928; U.W., A.S.I., O.H.P., interview with Nomsuka; U.W., C.P.S.A., Forman papers, B3.25, Financial Statement for May to December 1927.

46. *Baptist*, 25 Dec. 1927; U.W., A.S.I., O.H.P., interview with Mgetyana and interview with Cwele and Jali; Hobsbawm, *Rebels*, pp.89–90. The notion that 'the I.C.U. would inherit the earth' is very reminiscent of the last line of the Union's national anthem, which, as '*I.C.U. Uligqibe Lonke*' – 'the I.C.U. has conquered/spread all over the country' – was certainly being sung in Lusikisiki by 1928.

47. *Territorial News*, 27 Oct. 1927; *Umteteli*, 1 Oct. 1927, 17 Dec. 1927; interview with Pato; U.W., A.S.I., O.H.P., interview with Mgetyana. Ironically, the claim which Mgetyana recollected about I.C.U. shops was partially fulfilled: the first African-owned store in Bizana was established by the ex-I.C.U. Treasurer with ill-gotten wealth from his Union days.

48. C.A., 1/BIZ 6/65, N1/9/3, Bizana Mag. to C.M.T., 11 Oct. 1928; U.W., A.S.I., O.H.P., interview with Mdingi, 2 April 1984.

49. T.A., NTS 7605, 26/328(2), Sergeant S.A.P., Lusikisiki, to D.C., S.A.P., Kokstad, 31 May 1928; interview with Pato; U.W., A.S.I., O.H.P., interview with Mgetyana.

50. T.A., NTS 7604, 26/328(1), Flagstaff Mag. to C.M.T., 27 Aug. 1927; Mount Ayliff Mag. to C.M.T., 19 Sept. 1927; interview with Soji; U.W., A.S.I., O.H.P., interviews with Mgetyana, Nomsuka and Sincuba.

51. U.W., A.S.I., O.H.P., interview with Mdingi, 17 May 1984. See also *Baptist*, 25 Dec. 1927; N.A., CNC 348, 1/29/7, statement by Rev. Koti, 12 Jan. 1928; interview with Soji; U.W., A.S.I., O.H.P., interviews with Mgetyana and Nomsuka; interview with W. Mbelo and R. Mdibe by H.B. and Leonard Mdingi, Bizana, 20 May 1984; Hunter, *Reaction*, p.571.

52. Hobsbawm, *Rebels*, p.71. Perhaps the best-known association between stock-killing and the perfect age in South Africa was the 1856–7 Xhosa cattle-killing, inspired by the prophetess Nonquase. I.C.U. activists in Pondoland at

this time were in fact repeatedly referred to by opponents as the 'new Nonquases'.

53. C.A., 1/BIZ, 6/70, Bizana Mag. to C.M.T., 23 Sept. 1926; U.W., A.S.I., O.H.P., interview with Hlangabezo; Hunter, *Reaction*, pp.305, 310.

54. Interview with Gqambuleni *et al*; U.W., A.S.I., O.H.P., interview with Cwele and Jali.

55. N.A., CNC 348, 1/29/7, statement by Constable M. Lubelo; interview with Gqambuleni *et al*; U.W., A.S.I., O.H.P., interview with Mdingi, 17 May 1984; Hunter, *Reaction*, p.302.

56. *Transkeian Territories General Council: Proceedings and Reports of Select Committees at the Session of 1930* (King William's Town 1930), p.83; U.W., A.S.I., O.H.P., interview with Hlangabezo. In *Pigs for the Ancestors: Ritual in the Ecology of a New Guinea People* (New Haven 1967), Roy Rappoport explores similar economic reasons for hogs' prominence in periodic ritual slaughters. Although accuracy was doubtless not the first concern of those who enumerated pigs, their numbers were both large and probably rapidly increasing. In 1927, some 70,000 hogs – 40 per cent of all those in the Transkeian Territories – were counted in Pondoland. Between 1923 and 1927, they allegedly increased by a startling 100 per cent in Bizana alone. Nonetheless, such economic pressures were relieved by hog-slaughtering on a mass scale only because pigs already symbolized so much.

57. *Mail*, 10 Dec. 1927; *Report of the Agricultural and Pastoral Production of the Union of South Africa, 1926–1927*, U.G. 37–1928, p.51; *Report of the Agricultural and Pastoral Production of the Union of South Africa, 1927–1928*, U.G. 41–1929, p.56; C.A., 1/LSK 35, 2/2/2, minutes of quarterly meeting, 4 Oct. 1927; interview with Mvunelo; U.W., A.S.I., O.H.P., interviews with Mgetyana and Nomsuka; Hunter, *Reaction*, p.572. Neither stock-killing nor beliefs associating the I.C.U. with planes were confined to the Transkeian Territories in this period. In the Free State, 'Mote cannily swam with the tide in early 1928 when he encouraged a Frankfort audience to get rid of white fowl and white cattle – but to sell them to whites rather than to slaughter them. By the end of the year, blacks in Odendaalsrus thought that Kadalie was present in every plane that flew over.

Apart from the Transkei, it appears to have been only in Natal that the I.C.U. was associated with pig-killing. According to an Eston farmer, in December 1929 – when tensions were running extremely high due to the beer boycotts and raids in Durban – 'two kaffir girls . . . preached to the Natives that they should kill all their pigs . . . They said that if they did not destroy them the lightning would come and it would strike the pig and the pig would run about with fire in its mouth and burn all the kraals. The emissaries were really sent by the I.C.U. . . . that statement was made to me by Natives . . . The girls went about with a crow which was supposed to speak and warn the people . . . and the result was that there was not a pig in the district.' If there was indeed I.C.U. involvement in this slaughter, it is tempting to speculate about the activities of Women's Auxiliary members in this period. Bertha Mkhize, for example, had been organizing in Bizana, and was a leading figure in the Durban beer boycotts.

58. Interview with S. Mbunquka by H.B., Bizana, 18 May 1984, and interviews with Mvunelo and Soji; U.W., A.S.I., O.H.P., interviews with Hlangabezo, Mdingi (2 April 1984), Mgetyana, Mbelo and Mdibe, and Nomsuka; Hunter, *Reaction*, p.572.

59. *Baptist*, 25 Dec. 1927; *Transkeian Council Proceedings, 1930*, p.83; U.W., A.S.I., O.H.P., interviews with Hlangabezo and Mdingi (2 April 1984).

60. *Transkeian Council Proceedings, 1930*, p.83; N.A., CNC 348, 1/29/7, Detective Head Constable, S.A.P., Harding, to Deputy Commissioner, S.A.P., Pieter-maritzburg, 15 Dec. 1927; interview with Soji; U.W., A.S.I., O.H.P., interviews with Hlangabezo, Nomsuka and Sincuba.

61. U.W., C.P.S.A., Forman papers, B3.143, statement showing Branch Trans-fers and Requisitions for Year ended 31 Dec. 1927; interview with Mbunquka; U.W., A.S.I., O.H.P., interviews with Mgetyana and Sincuba.

62. *Herald*, 18 March 1927; U.W., A.S.I., O.H.P., interview with Nomsuka; interview with Cwele and Jali; Hunter, *Reaction*, p.297; H. Ngubane, *Body and Mind in Zulu Medicine: an Ethnography of Health and Disease in Nyuswa-Zulu Thought and Practice* (London 1977), pp.115, 126–32.

63. Interview with Soji; U.W., A.S.I., O.H.P., interview with Mgetyana. In 1927, the Secretary of the Natal Agricultural Union complained that I.C.U. activists were issuing red tickets to members, 'which tickets were said to protect the Natives from magisterial and police interference'. At the same meeting, a landlord said an African had shown him the I.C.U. card 'and stated that he possessed with it all the privileges of the white man'. The attraction the Union had for lepers, and the taking of red cards to hospitals, also epitomizes widespread hopes that the I.C.U. ticket was a new form of *imithi*.

64. Interview with Soji; interview with L. Xoko by H.B. and A.M., Bizana, 19 May 1984; U.W., A.S.I., O.H.P., interview with Mdingi, 17 May 1984.

65. *Star*, 22 Dec. 1927; interview with Mbunquka; U.W., A.S.I., O.H.P., interview with Mdingi, 17 May 1984.

66. N.A., CNC 348, 1/29/7, statement by M. Jali, 9 Feb. 1928; statement by chief Jali, 9 Feb. 1928.

67. *Ibid.*, also statements by C. Vezi, 8 Feb. 1928 and by H. Basterman, 13 Feb. 1928; T.A., NTS 7604, 26/328(1), Mount Ayliff Mag. to C.M.T., 19 Sept. 1927; interview with Soji; U.W., A.S.I., O.H.P., interviews with Mgetyana, Nomsuka and Sincuba. Mdodana was perhaps one of the few organizers who could truthfully add to his claim that 'this I.C.U. was from overseas in America' the boast that the States was where he had been educated.

68. U.W., A.S.I., O.H.P., interview with Mbelo and Mdibe; see also interviews with Mgetyana and Nomsuka. The undertones of the song are interesting: Damoyi was possibly himself 'coloured', while it was common knowledge that 'the Mpondo' despised 'the Shangaans'. It also provides a contrast to the Wellingtonites' Africanism. One of the reasons for Kadalie's opposition to Champion's association with Buthelezi was that while the I.C.U. sought 'to unite together both white, black and brown, and form one organization, Buthelezi had no time to organize Indians or Coloured people.'

69. N.A., CNC 348, 1/29/7, statement by Rev. E. Koti, 12 Jan. 1928; interview with Mvunelo, and interview with Xoko; Beinart, *Pondoland*, p.139.

70. *Star*, 22 Dec. 1927; *Umteteli*, 17 Dec. 1927; C.A., 1/LSK 35, 2/2/2, minutes of quarterly meeting, 4 Oct. 1927; interviews with Pato and with Soji; Beinart, *Pondoland*, pp.141–3. See footnote 52 for Nonquase's role in the nineteenth century.

71. *Witness*, 10 Dec. 1927.

72. C.A., 1/BIZ 6/65, N1/9/3, Bizana Mag. to Tembu, 9 Jan. 1928; Bizana Mag. to C.M.T., 4 Aug. 1928; Sergeant, S.A.P., Flagstaff, to Officer Commanding C.I.D., Umtata, 16 Jan. 1929; Post Commander, S.A.P., Bizana, to Bizana Mag., 12 Feb. 1929; U.W., A.S.I., O.H.P., interviews with Mgetyana and Sincuba.

73. In Port St John's, for example, an 'ordinary blanketed man' held I.C.U. meetings at his homestead in the late 1920s. Some years after Union activities

had ebbed in his district, he became a member of a Wellingtonite church. His home became the centre of both a school and of the sect, whose fifty-odd adherents were by 1939 all still claiming membership of the I.C.U. On the outbreak of the Second World War, his aspirations for a changed world readily found a new outlet. He travelled round the district preaching 'that when the Germans came the natives would pay no taxes': 'that all the white people are going to leave this country', and that Hitler's government would be 'a very good one'. (See correspondence in T.A., NTS 1681, 2/276(2).)

74. *Report of Agricultural Production, 1926–1927*, p.40; *Report of Agricultural Production, 1927–1928*, p.44; C.A., 1/KNT 40, 12, Sergeant, S.A.P., Bizana, to D.C., S.A.P., Kokstad, 19 March 1930; T.A., NTS 7605, 26/328(2), statement by E. Mgani, 31 Jan. 1929; U.W., A.S.I., O.H.P., interviews with Mdingi (17 May 1984), Mgetyana and Nomsuka.

75. T. Nairn, *The Break-Up of Britain: Crisis and Neo-Nationalism* (London 1981), p.340.

76. *Ibid.*

77. *Territorial News*, 18 Oct. 1928, 6 Dec. 1928; *Umteteli*, 15 Dec. 1928; C.A., 1/ELN 86, c3(1), Special Native Detective, East London, to D.C., S.A.P., East London, 20 Feb. 1928, 14 May 1928, 28 May 1928, 20 Nov. 1928, 4 Nov. 1929; C.A., 1/ELN 87, c3(2), Special Native Detective, East London, to D.C., S.A.P., East London, 25 June 1930, 16 July 1930, 12 Jan. 1931; C.A., 1/KNT 40, 12, Report by Detective Sergeant, S.A.P., Kentani, 5 Feb. 1930; Deputy Commissioner, S.A.P., Transkei, to C.M.T., 15 Feb. 1930; Detective Sergeant, S.A.P., Kentani, to D.C., S.A.P., Kokstad, 19 March 1930; C.A., 1/MFE 8/1/14, 2/12/7, L. Faro *et al* to Kokstad Mag., 26 March 1928; Mount Frere Mag. to Kokstad Mag., 2 April 1928; C.A., 1/QBU 7/1/8, 2/17/1, Qumbu Mag. to C.M.T., 4 Aug. 1928; T.A., NTS 7214, 56/326, Report by Detective Sergeant Arnold on I.C.U. *yase* Natal, 6 Sept. 1929; T.A., NTS 7215, 62/326(2), correspondence relating to the formation of Mabodla's Independent Industrial and Commercial National Union of the Transkei; T.A., NTS 7645, 48/331, Deputy Commissioner, S.A.P., Transkei, to Commissioner, S.A.P., 17 April 1928; C. Kadalie, *My Life and the I.C.U.: the Autobiography of a Black Trade Unionist in South Africa* (London 1970), p.203.

78. U.W., A.S.I., O.H.P., interview with O. Mpetha by H.B., Cape Town, 21 Sept. 1983.

79. C.A., 1/KNT 40, 12, undated report by Constable, S.A.P., Kentani, on (Independent) I.C.U. meeting, 15 March 1930; T.A., NTS 7660, 22/332, Deputy Commissioner, Divisional C.I. Officer, Witwatersrand, to Deputy Commissioner, Witwatersrand, 12 June 1930.

80. T.A., NTS 7605, 26/328(2), Sergeant, S.A.P., Lusikisiki, to D.C., S.A.P., Kokstad, 31 May 1928. Although all four organizers were drawn from the Transkei, they probably represented the parent body rather than any offshoots. An I.C.U. presence was still apparent in some Lusikisiki locations in 1929; it is unclear what form this took.

81. *Umteteli*, 14 April 1928; C.A., 1/KNT 40, 12, Deputy Commissioner, S.A.P., Transkei, to C.M.T., 15 Feb. 1930, enclosing report of I.I.C.U. meeting in Kentani, 30 Jan. 1930; T.A., NTS 3519, 353/308, Kentani Mag. to C.M.T., 9 July 1925; T.A., NTS 7660, 22/332, Sergeant, S.A.P., Umtata, to Officer Commanding Police Mobile Troop, 2 Jan. 1921; T.A., NTS 7603, 9/378, undated (1925) address to General Hertzog by Gaikas and Gcalekas of Kentani.

82. C.A., 1/ELN 86, c3(1), Special Native Detective, East London, to D.C., S.A.P., East London, 4 Nov. 1929; C.A., correspondence in 1/KNT 40, 12, relating to I.I.C.U. meetings in Kentani, January to April 1930, especially

report by Detective Sergeant and Native Detective Constable, 6 Feb. 1930; report by Native Detective Constable, 8 Feb. 1930; report by Detective Sergeant and Native Detective Constable, 25 March 1930; T.A., NTS 7660, 22/332, Deputy Commissioner, Divisional C.I. Officer, Witwatersrand, to Deputy Commissioner, Witwatersrand, 12 June 1930.

83. C.A., 1/ELN 87, c3(1), Special Native Detective, East London to D.C., S.A.P., East London, 7 June 1930, 16 July 1930, 22 Sept. 1930, 10 Nov. 1930, 17 Nov. 1930 (report on I.C.U. meeting), 17 Nov. 1930 (report on I.I.C.U. meeting), 29 Dec. 1930, 5 Jan. 1931, 12 Jan 1931; W. Beinart and C. Bundy, 'The Union, the Nation and the Talking Crow: the Ideology and Tactics of the Independent ICU in East London', paper presented at U.W., A.S.I., 4 March 1985, pp.43–8.

84. C.A., 1/ELN 87, c3(1), Inspector, D.C., S.A.P., East London, to East London Mag., 14 June 1932.

85. C.A., correspondence of Nqamakwe Mag., 1/NKE 58, N1/9/3, Mount Frere Mag. to Nqamakwe Mag., 28 July 1927; statement by R. Zazele, 16 June 1928; Acting Nqamakwe Mag. to C.M.T., 8 May 1930; Senior Clerk of Nqamakwe Mag. to Minister of Native Affairs, 22 July 1932; T.A., NTS 7660, 22/332, Deputy Commissioner, Divisional C.I. Officer, Witwatersrand, to Deputy Commissioner, Witwatersrand, 12 June 1930. As in Nqamakwe, Wellington-ite and I.C.U. offshoots were sometimes amicably intertwined – exchanging ideas, merging with or succeeding one another. On other occasions, they competed so viciously for the same 'school' constituency that violent clashes culminated in at least one death.

86. C.A., 1/NKE 58, N1/9/3, Senior Clerk of Nqamakwe Mag. to Minister of Native Affairs, 22 July 1932, enclosing Annexure H; Nqamakwe Mag. to Deputy Commissioner, S.A.P., Umtata, 13 Aug. 1934.

CHAPTER 8

1. L. Barnes, *Caliban in Africa: an Impression of Colour-Madness* (London 1930), p.102.

2. T.A., Native Affairs Department files, NTS 7606, 49/328, booklet *'Dingis-wayo'* produced by the I.C.U. *yase* Natal.

3. P. la Hausse, 'The Struggle for the City: Alcohol, the Ematsheni and Popular Culture in Durban, 1902–1936', paper presented at U.W, History Workshop Conference, Feb. 1984, p.7. The following abridged account of the Natal beer boycotts is also derived from H. Bradford, '"We are now the men": Women's Beer Protests in the Natal Countryside, 1929' in B. Bozzoli (ed.), *Class, Community and Conflict* (Johannesburg 1987), pp.292–323.

4. T.A., NTS 7054, 110/332, A. Champion to C.N.C., 14 Oct. 1929.

5. These were Dundee, Estcourt, Glencoe, Howick, Ladysmith, Newcastle, Pinetown, Vryheid and Weenen.

6. T.A., NTS 7054, 110/322, D.C., S.A.P., Dundee, to Deputy Commissioner, S.A.P., Pietermaritzburg, 25 Sept. 1929.

7. G. Coka, 'The Story of Gilbert Coka of the Zulu Tribe of Natal, South Africa' in M. Perham (ed.), *Ten Africans* (London 1936), pp.311–12.

8. There were numerous other reasons why men were largely absent from or antagonistic to the rural protests. Apart from the fact that they were not directly affected by the new legislative restrictions on brewing, white employers or more coercive state measures were far more immediate targets. In addition, shebeens were not always the answer for tired workers, whose

living-quarters were sometimes physically separated from those of female beer-sellers, and who had limited time, money and transport facilities on hand. If the price of a beer in a canteen enabled men to escape the stifling confines of domestic life, evade the police and prisons of settler society, and relax after work into masculine activities, then it was a price many were only too willing to pay.

9. *Star*, 26 Sept. 1929.
10. *Ibid.*
11. N.A., correspondence of Weenen Mag., 2/3/4, minutes of meeting between Weenen N.C. and female deputation, 6 Sept. 1929.
12. T.A., NTS 7606, 49/328, C.N.C. to S.N.A., 8 Nov. 1929, enclosing translation of *Igazi ne Zinyembezi* (the 'woman in the man' was Ma-Dhlamini); U.W., A.S.I., O.H.P., interview with C. Kumalo by H.B. and V.N., Mooi River, 28 Nov. 1981.
13. The acts of *bricolage* involved in creating new identities were sometimes extremely innovative. Male officers of the Union's 'Unity League' signalled their status and repudiated their humiliating daily lives with glorious uniforms. On one occasion, a man studded the standard red tunic of the League with 'soda bottle tops, and he wore a sun helmet on the top of which was perched the brass knob from a bedstead. Folded around his waist was a leopard skin, which signalled his rank.' When combined with the symbols of chieftaincy and the trappings of British imperialists, objects which domestic servants were forced to fetch or polish each day clearly acquired new and more challenging meanings.
14. M. Perham, *African Apprenticeship: an Autobiographical Journey in Southern Africa, 1929* (London 1974), pp.196–200. See also *Mercury*, 2 Dec. 1929; U.W., A.S.I., M. Swanson, 'Interview with A.W.G. Champion', pp.88–9; C. van Onselen, *Studies in the Social and Economic History of the Witwatersrand 1886–1914*, Vol. 2, *New Nineveh* (Johannesburg 1982), p.59. Perham referred to the imitation of the 'Tommies' as a 'priceless burlesque': a comic dance-form called '*ukukomika*' had in fact developed amongst Zulu migrants by this time. This was also evident at a public display of dancing organized by Champion in December 1929, although for the benefit of whites, the military '*ukukomika*' was replaced by one which satirized tennis playing.
15. T.A., NTS 7606, 49/328, D.C., S.A.P., Durban, to Deputy Commissioner, S.A.P., Pietermaritzburg, 16 June 1930.
16. In 1927, Solomon's personal secretary was in touch with and allegedly supportive of the Vryheid Branch Secretary. And in 1928, police desperately tried to establish whether a secret meeting between Solomon and Kadalie had occurred. A spy at I.C.U. headquarters had revealed the latter's intention of offering Solomon a cut of Union contributions in exchange for his support.
17. *The Natal Advertiser*, 6 Sept. 1930; N.A., correspondence in CNC 58/7/3, Box 81, especially C.N.C. to S.N.A., 9 Aug. 1930; Detective Sergeant Arnold to Officer in Charge, C.I.D., 16 Sept. 1930; and minutes of an interview with chief Solomon by C.N.C., 22 Oct. 1930; S. Marks, *The Ambiguities of Dependence in South Africa: Class, Nationalism, and the State in Twentieth-Century Natal* (Johannesburg 1986), pp.87–91. A month previously, Solomon had declared to the Governor General that he alone was King, not only of Zululand but also of all South Africa.
18. T.A., NTS 7606, 49/328, Detective Sergeant Arnold to Officer in Charge, C.I.D., Durban, 2 June 1930; Commissioner of Police to Minister of Justice, 19 Sept. 1930; Acting S.N.A. to C.N.C., 20 Sept. 1930. See also correspondence in N.A., CNC 58/7/3, Box 81, for comments about the dangers of

allowing the association between Champion, chiefs and 'tribal' workers. Officially, the reason for cutting Solomon's salary was his insolence before the Governor General months earlier. While Champion was allowed to enter the districts of Dundee, Newcastle and Utrecht, black men here were never enamoured with the I.C.U. *yase* Natal. On also learning that a white Newcastle farmer had recently killed an African minister, Champion steered clear of Natal almost throughout his banishment.

19.   In essence, these were based on the dual premises that the ecological crisis in the reserves had to be tackled, and that the subsistence base of location inhabitants should be reduced to the point where they moved into non-agricultural villages serving as labour reservoirs for decentralized industries. Although it was still a year before the proclamation of 'betterment areas' became legally possible, Bergville officials had already begun to inaugurate the projects to which Vilikazi was referring.

20.   T.A., NTS 7665, 40/332, Sub-Inspector, C.I.D., Durban, to Deputy Commissioner, S.A.P., Pietermaritzburg, 10 March 1937; Lieutenant Sergeant, S.A.P., Oliviershoek, to D.C., S.A.P., Dundee, 16 April 1938.

21.   T. Lodge, *Black Politics in South Africa since 1945* (Johannesburg 1983), p.25. As regards the parent I.C.U., a mass meeting of farm labourers was held in Heilbron in 1930 in order to form an agricultural section of the I.C.U. But little is known of the extent to which this fulfilled its aims of seeking–'by constitutional means'–better wages, enforcement of written contracts, and schooling for children. There were still, however, extant branches in Bloemfontein, Heilbron, Kroonstad, Parys and Paul Roux in 1933. In the same year there was one branch in the Cape (East London), possibly one in Natal (Ladysmith), and nine in the Transvaal (Barberton, Carolina, Ermelo, Heidelberg, Johannesburg, Makwassie, Piet Retief, Pretoria and Schweizer-Reneke.) Most, if not all, were effectively run as independent units. It is unlikely, for example, that Jason Jingoes maintained financial or organizational links with the nominal headquarters during the latter half of the 1930s, as he continued to use the I.C.U.'s name to mobilize blacks in the south-western Transvaal. Apart from the parent body, there were in 1933 at least seven other offshoots which incorporated 'I.C.U.' into their titles.

22.   The 1926 Natives Land Amendment Bill was eventually passed a decade later. Lydenburg was the only district in which Chapter Four of the Native Trust and Land Act (as it was now named) was implemented. From December 1937, all labour tenants here were legally obliged to work nearly seven months a year, and all 'squatters' had to be licensed. The licence fees – which would almost inevitably have been passed on to tenants – increased annually (until 'squatting' was putatively abolished thirty years later). The application of the Act resulted in mass black demonstrations in Lydenburg, demands for trek passes, and numerous desertions. Chapter Four was consequently suspended for years, and the local magistrate speculated that the establishment of the United I.C.U.'s Lydenburg branch was inspired by the notoriety which the district had acquired.

23.   T.A., NTS 351, 241/55, R. Malatji to Minister of Native Affairs, 13 Sept. 1945; T.A., NTS 7202, 3/326, N.C. Sekhukhuneland to S.N.A., 17 April 1944. The following account of the tenants' struggle is derived from correspondence in the latter file. If the apartheid regime survives – and if it maintains its existing obstructive rulings about consulting archival material – the year 2003 is the next time this file can be consulted. So the events are described in some detail.

24.   There were other traces of the I.C.U. in the eastern Transvaal in the 1950s. In

1951, one J. Mazibuko, who termed himself an I.C.U. leader at Waterval-Boven, appealed to be allowed to make a living by showing movies, and promised not to organize. And in 1953, there was evidence of I.C.U. activities in Komatipoort location, where there were plans to open an I.C.U. club.

25. T.A., correspondence in NTS 7602, 20/328, especially S.A.P. report on meetings in Port Elizabeth, 4 Dec. 1934, and C.N.C. to S.N.A., 16 June 1942; U.W., C.P.S.A., Industrial and Commercial Workers' Union Records, A924, File 4, W. Ballinger, 'The Industrial and Commercial Workers' Union of Africa'.

26. A. Gramsci, *Selections from the Prison Notebooks of Antonio Gramsci* (London 1978), p.198.

27. *Ibid.*

28. *Herald*, 12 Jan. 1927. See also *Herald*, 27 March 1926, 15 July 1927, for references to urban 'coloured' membership. There had been friction between African and 'coloured' leaders since at least 1926, based on political and regional differences as well as racial prejudice.

29. *Friend*, 19 Aug. 1927; *Ladybrand Courant and Ficksburg News*, 20 Oct. 1926, 24 Nov. 1927; *Star*, 22 Feb. 1928; O.F.S.A, Orange Free State Supreme Court cases, H.G. 4/1/2/263, Case no. 103 of 1928, *Rex* vs. W. 'Mote; U.W., C.P.S.A., A. Saffery papers, AD1178, Part I, B5, H. Tyamzashe, 'Summarised History of the Industrial and Commercial Workers' Union of Africa', p.8.

30. *Herald*, 15 July 1927; *Star*, 25 March 1927, 18 Jan. 1928; T.A., Department of Justice files, JUS 289, 3/1064/18, Commissioner of Police to Secretary for Justice, 15 June 1926; U.W., C.P.S.A., L. Forman papers, AD1714 Mfe, B2.31, R. de Norman to A. Champion, 15 July 1926; C. Kadalie, *My Life and the I.C.U.: the Autobiography of a Black Trade Unionist in South Africa* (London 1970), pp.90, 97–8, 119, 144; K. Luckhardt and B. Wall, *Organize . . .or Starve! The History of the South African Congress of Trade Unions* (London 1980), p.53. Charles Kumalo's perception of Indians was probably fairly common amongst Natal Africans in the 1920s. When asked if the Indian man who rented them offices in Estcourt had joined the I.C.U., he exclaimed: 'Oh, that one was a white – he was Naidoo. He was just like a white man.'

31. This remark is taken from a biographical manuscript on H. Basner by M. Basner, and was made after 'Mote's experience of militant female protest in Kroonstad. Other instances of urban, I.C.U.-influenced resistance amongst women occurred in eastern Transvaal villages as well as in East London. In the countryside, females could also display greater defiance than men, precisely because of their different economic and political situations. Since farm women were generally neither full-time workers nor subject to passes, they were, according to Jacob Motha, 'always ready to challenge [Boers'] authority, because they would not be arrested as we men would be'.

32. U.W., A.S.I., O.H.P., interview with E. Sibanyoni and R. Mthimunye by V.N., Middelburg, 19 Oct. 1979; interview with E. Mekgwe by M. Nkotsoe, Phokeng, 2 March 1982.

33. See for example L. Marquard and T. Standing, *The Southern Bantu* (London 1939), pp.66, 78.

34. *The Friend*, 4 Feb. 1928, 11 April 1928; U.C.T., M.L., W. Ballinger papers, BC 347, A5.XII.I, Weekly News Letter, 5 Dec. 1928. Similar sentiments were expressed in 1929 by *The Natal Farmer*, which urged landlords to counter the I.C.U. by encouraging their labourers to join mission churches, 'which uphold the precept of "Servants, obey your masters"'.

35. *Herald*, 15 July 1927; U.W., A.S.I., Swanson, 'Interview', p.53; U.W., A.S.I.,

O.H.P., interview with V. Manapa by M. Ntoane, Evaton, 24 Nov. 1980.

36. U.W., A.S.I., O.H.P., interview with K. Maine by T. Couzens, M. Nkadimeng and G. Relly, Ledig, 2 July 1980; interview with K. Maine by C. van Onselen, Ledig, 24 Feb. 1981.

37. *Herald*, 15 June 1927; U.W., A.S.I., O.H.P., interview with N. Makume by T. Flatela, Viljoensdrift, 10 June 1982; interview with J. Molete by M. Nkadimeng, Kroonstad, 26 Feb. 1980. See also U.W., A.S.I., O.H.P., interview with T. Manoto by M. Molepo, Heilbron, 26 Feb. 1980. Another sharecropper, Voetganger Manapa, only attended one Heilbron meeting, and threw his red ticket away fairly promptly, because 'Boers searched people's houses for cards.'

38. *Witness*, 6 Dec. 1927; T.A., correspondence in NTS 8628, 48/362, especially Agerende Adjunk-Kommissaris, S.A.P., to Kommissaris, S.A.P. 23 Sept. 1927, and Estcourt Mag. to Secretary for Justice, 24 Sept. 1927; Ixopo Agricultural Society minutes, meeting on 10 June 1927. Eviction was illegal if tenants were residing on ground which was in the course of alienation from the state to a landlord. If they had lived on the same holding prior to the passage of the 1913 Land Act, civil proceedings were necessary to secure their legal ejectment.

39. *Mercury*, 29 Aug. 1927; *Star*, 29 June 1927; U.W., A.S.I., Swanson, 'Interview', p.76.

40. *Witness*, 5 Aug. 1927. The speaker was the Weenen Member of Parliament and landlord, Major Richards.

41. See for example H. Alavi, 'Peasantry and Revolution', *The Socialist Register*, 1965, pp.348–75; H. Alavi, 'Peasant Classes and Primordial Loyalties', *Journal of Peasant Studies*, 1, 1973–4, pp.24–9; E. Wolf, 'On Peasant Rebellions' in T. Shanin (ed.), *Peasants and Peasant Societies* (Harmondsworth 1979), p.269.

42. See for example R. Hilton, 'Peasant Societies, Peasant Movements and Feudalism in Medieval Europe' in H. Landsberger (ed.), *Rural Protest: Peasant Movements and Social Change* (London 1974), p.70; E. Wolf, *Peasant Wars of the Twentieth Century* (London 1973), p.202.

43. U.W., C.P.S.A., Forman papers, B3.123, A. Bennett to A. Champion, 19 Oct. 1927.

44. *Mercury*, 25 May 1927, 28 Oct. 1927; *The Farmer's Weekly*, 17 Aug. 1927, 5 Oct. 1927; N.A., files of the C.N.C., CNC 22/135, N2/10/3(25), Melmoth Mag. to C.N.C., 4 Aug. 1927; U.W., A.S.I., O.H.P., interview with L. Nqandela by T. Flatela, Ledig, 4 Jan. 1983.

45. T.A., E.N.E.C., K26, T. Tembe, Newcastle, p.1275. The Young Turks of the I.C.U. were in this sense precursors of the A.N.C.'s Youth League, the Soweto generation, and the young township 'comrades' of the 1980s.

46. Coka, 'Story', p.295; H. Bradford, 'Strikes in the Natal Midlands: Landlords, Labour Tenants and the I.C.U.', *Africa Perspective*, 22, 1983, pp.7–12; K. Marx, quoted by H. Draper, *Karl Marx's Theory of Revolution*, Vol. II (New York 1978), p.352.

47. Bradford, 'Strikes', p.7.

48. *Star*, 29 June 1927; *Natal Farmer*, 12 Aug. 1927, 27 April 1928.

49. *Star*, 26 July 1927.

50. *Natal Farmer*, 4 Feb. 1927.

51. *Vaderland*, 20 Sept. 1927; *Vaderland*, 7 Oct. 1927, 16 July 1929.

52. *Herald*, 12 May 1928; *Farmer's Weekly*, 22 Aug. 1928; *Witness*, 25 April 1928; O.F.S.A., H.G.4/1/2/263, case no. 103 of 1928, *Rex* vs. W. 'Mote.

53. Killie Campbell Library, Durban, Richmond Agricultural Society, minutes of Annual General Meetings, 1922–31, KCM 3365, meeting 21 May 1927; U.W.,

C.P.S.A., W. Ballinger papers, file 4, Administrative Report by Acting General Secretary, 20 June 1929; undated memoir by W. Ballinger on his experiences in the Union; Kadalie, *Life*, p.159. Stock could be legally confiscated either because tenants were indebted to landlords, or because East Coast Fever restrictions barred the movement of cattle to another district, whereafter farmers appropriated the stock to cover grazing and dipping fees.

54. T.A., JUS 437, 4/366/27, Estcourt Mag. to Secretary for Justice, 2 April 1928.

55. In December 1927, 'confidential instructions' were sent to all Natal magistrates informing them of the best way of enforcing evictions. By mid-1928, policemen had been instructed that they could not, as the Estcourt magistrate claimed, assume 'the powers of a Superior Appeal Court'. And in 1929, the Native Service Contract Registration Bill was introduced, partly in response to the problems associated with evictions experienced by farmers in the I.C.U.'s heyday.

56. *Natal Regional Survey Additional Report No. 4: The Dunn Reserve* (Pietermaritzburg 1953), pp.1–15. Champion's ardour was probably influenced by the fact that he was not only related to some of the tenants under threat of eviction, but also harboured grievances against Sam Dunn, who held a plot in this reserve. Dunn's conviction for peculation earlier that year had contributed to suspicions that Champion was guilty of the same offence, which in turn, when Champion was suspended pending investigation of his financial management, had facilitated the formation of the I.C.U. *yase* Natal.

57. This paragraph is a summary of evidence in five bulky files in N.A., CNC 39/4, N2/8/3(27), Parts I-V. The fire-arms used by the 'coloured' landlords were possibly obtained from Sam Dunn, who by late 1928 was gun-running from Portuguese East Africa to Zululand, and claiming that the weapons he sold came from America. Legislative intervention in 1935 did grant to each genuine descendant of John Dunn the right to a one hundred acre allotment which, while not freehold, would no longer be administered as part of the reserve. But due to the state's 'inability or reluctance' to survey the plots for sixteen years (*Natal Survey*, p.27), bitter struggles continued until at least 1940, still peripherally influenced by Champion.

58. F. Engels, 'Labour Movements' in T. Clarke and L. Clements (eds.), *Trade Unions under Capitalism* (Glasgow 1978), pp.34–5.

59. U.W., A.S.I., O.II.P., interview with I. Dinkebogile by T. Phiri, Phokeng, 13 May 1981; interview with M. Molohlanyi by M. Nkadimeng, Wolmaransstad, 19 April 1984, and 28 June 1985; U.W., C.P.S.A., W. Ballinger papers, file 4, W. Ballinger to F. Brockway, 15 May 1929. By the 1940s, one of the songs sung during *ndlamu* dancing in Natal referred indirectly to this treachery by educated I.C.U. leaders: 'The clerk embezzled our money/ Do you know this clerk/ He embezzled our money'.

60. W. Beinart and C. Bundy, 'The Union, the Nation and the Talking Crow: the Ideology and Tactics of the Independent ICU in East London', paper presented at U.W., A.S.I., 4 March 1985, p.52.

61. N.A., CNC 64/2, N1/9/3(X), District Commander, Wasbank, to D.C., S.A.P., Dundee, 9 July 1928; U.W., C.P.S.A., W. Ballinger papers, file 6, H. Maleke to W. Ballinger, 11 March 1931. Charles Kumalo claimed that the following song was sung at Estcourt I.C.U. concerts, but given both its mournful content and the different locale to which it refers, it almost certainly emerged after the collapse of the Union:

> We come from Mooi River, from Mooi River
> From the roots of Kadalie,
> There is no help in this world.

62. T.A., E.N.E.C., W. Ballinger, Johannesburg, p.8207; U.W., A.S.I., O.H.P., interview with J. Ntambo and L. Nhlabathi by V.N., Ledig, 23 Nov. 1979.
63. U.W., A.S.I., O.H.P., interview with Ntambo and Nhlabathi.
64. U.W., C.P.S.A., Industrial and Commercial Workers' Union Records, File 2, E. Lewis to W. Holtby, 12 Dec. 1928; Barnes, *Caliban*, p.99; P. Bonner, 'The Decline and Fall of the ICU – a Case of Self-Destruction?' in E. Webster (ed.), *Essays in Southern African Labour History* (Johannesburg 1978), pp.114, 116–17.
65. E. Hobsbawm and G. Rudé, *Captain Swing* (New York 1975), p.293.
66. This is a paraphrase of the famous comment by Marx, who argued that 'In so far as there is merely a local interconnection among these small-holding peasants, and the identity of their interests begets no community, no national bond and no political organization among them, they do not form a class.'
67. T.A., JUS 289, 3/1064/18, General Secretary's Report of Inspection of Branches, 6 March 1926.
68. K. Marx, quoted by Draper, *Karl Marx's Theory*, p.391.
69. C. Bundy, 'Land and Liberation: The South African National Liberation Movements and the Agrarian Question, 1920s–1960s', *Review of African Political Economy*, 29, 1984, pp.20, 27.
70. T. Couzens, *The New African: A Study of the Life and Work of H.I.E. Dhlomo* (Johannesburg 1986), p.277.
71. V. Lenin, 'Lecture on the 1905 Revolution' in H. Selsam, D. Goldway and H. Martel (eds.), *Dynamics of Social Change: A Reader in Marxist Social Science* (New York 1983), p.184.
72. U.W., A.S.I., O.H.P., interview with O. Mpetha by H.B., Cape Town, 21 Sept. 1983.
73. U.W., A.S.I., O.H.P., interview with J. Kok by P. Bonner and A. Mabin, Pilgrims Rest, 9 Aug. 1984; interview with Manapa; interview with Sibanyoni and Mthimunye.

BIBLIOGRAPHY

This bibliography has been divided into:

I.   MANUSCRIPT SOURCES

    A.   OFFICIAL

        1. Union of South Africa, held at Transvaal Archives Depot
        2. Union of South Africa, held at South African Defence Force Archives Depot
        3. Cape Archives Depot (Cape Town)
        4. Natal Archives Depot (Pietermaritzburg)
        5. Orange Free State Archives Depot (Bloemfontein)
        6. Transvaal Archives Depot (Pretoria)

    B.   UNOFFICIAL

        1. At Archives
        2. Private Papers

II.   PRINTED PRIMARY SOURCES

    A.   OFFICIAL RECORDS
    B.   NEWSPAPERS AND PERIODICALS

III. SECONDARY SOURCES

    A.   SELECT BOOKS
    B.   SELECT ARTICLES AND PUBLISHED THESES
    C.   SELECT UNPUBLISHED ARTICLES AND THESES

IV. INTERVIEWS CITED IN TEXT

    A.   Those where tapes and transcripts are in possession of Oral History Project, African Studies Institute, University of the Witwatersrand
    B-G. Those where tapes and/or transcripts are located elsewhere.

I.   MANUSCRIPT SOURCES

    A.   OFFICIAL

       1.   Union of South Africa, held at Transvaal Archives Depot (hereafter T.A.)
          (i)   Commissioner of South African Police
               SAP Conf. 1/2/48–1/2/54, Confidential Reports, 1917–26
          (ii)   Director of Native Labour
               GNLB, Correspondence, 1918–28
          (iii)   Secretary for Agriculture
               LDB, Correspondence, 1925–39
          (iv)   Secretary for Justice
               JUS, Correspondence, 1918–51
          (v)   Secretary for Labour
               ARB 713, L.C. 1054/25, Correspondence relating to I.C.U., 1921–30
          (vi)   Secretary for Native Affairs
               NTS, Correspondence, 1917–53

       2.   Union of South Africa, held at South African Defence Force Archives
          (i)   Chief of General Staff
               CGS GPI 63–67, Correspondence, 1920–30
          (ii)   Secretary for Defence
               DC, Correspondence, 1919–31

       3.   Cape Archives Depot
          (i)   Chief Magistrate of the Transkeian Territories CMT, Correspondence, 1916–47
          (ii)   Native Affairs papers
               NA 706–707, Correspondence, 1906
          (iii)   Adelaide Magistrate
               1/ADE, Correspondence, 1925–36
          (iv)   Bizana Magistrate
               1/BIZ, Correspondence and court records, 1918–33
          (v)   East London Town Clerk
               1/ELN 86–87, Correspondence, 1920–33
          (vi)   Flagstaff Magistrate
               1/FSF, Correspondence, 1928–34
          (vii)   Kentani Magistrate
               1/KNT 40, 124, Correspondence, 1927–30
          (viii) Libode Magistrate
               1/LBO, Correspondence, 1928–36

(ix)   Lusikisiki Magistrate
1/LSK, Correspondence and court records, 1923–38

(x)   Mount Frere Magistrate
1/MFE, Correspondence, 1927–8

(xi)   Ngqeleni Magistrate
1/NGL 14–19, Correspondence, 1925–36

(xii)   Nqamakwe Magistrate
1/NKE 58, Correspondence, 1927–39

(xiii)   Port St Johns Magistrate
1/PSJ 53, Correspondence, 1929–36

(xiv)   Qumbu Magistrate
1/QBU, Correspondence, 1926–8

(xv)   Tsolo Magistrate
1/TSO, Correspondence, 1926–30

4.   Natal Archives Depot
(i)   Chief Native Commissioner,
CNC, Boxes 1–125, Correspondence, 1915–42

(ii)   Babanango Magistrate
Correspondence, 1914–30

(iii)   Bergville Magistrate
Correspondence and Preparatory Examinations, 1922–31

(iv)   Camperdown Magistrate
Correspondence, 1927–30

(v)   Dundee Magistrate
Correspondence, 1926–30; Dundee Town Council Minutes, 1926–30

(vi)   Durban Magistrate
Correspondence, 1929; Criminal Records, 1910–51

(vii)   Estcourt Magistrate
Correspondence, 1925–31; Criminal Records, 1910–42; Criminal Record Book, 1927–8

(viii)   Greytown Magistrate
Correspondence, 1925–34; Criminal Records, 1915–39; Criminal Record Book, 1927–8; Preliminary Examinations, 1923–50

(ix)   Himeville Magistrate
Correspondence, 1918–33

(x)   Ixopo Magistrate
Correspondence and Criminal Records, 1915–33

(xi)   Kranskop Magistrate
Correspondence and Criminal Records, 1890–1940

(xii)   Louwsburg Magistrate
Criminal Records, 1910–64

(xiii) Mapumulo Magistrate
        Correspondence, 1925–9
(xiv)   New Hanover Magistrate
        Correspondence, 1925–34
(xv)   Paulpietersburg Magistrate
        Criminal Records, 1904–54
(xvi)   Port Shepstone Magistrate
        Correspondence, 1930
(xvii) Richmond Magistrate
        Correspondence and Preparatory Examinations, 1926–40
(xviii) Stanger Magistrate
        Criminal Records, 1928–30
(xix)   Umzinto Magistrate
        Correspondence and Criminal Records, 1923–37
(xx)   Vryheid Magistrate
        Correspondence, 1925, and Vryheid Town Clerk
        Minute Book, 1927–30
(xxi)   Weenen Magistrate
        Correspondence, 1921–30, and Criminal Record Book,
        1926–8

5.   Orange Free State Archives Depot (hereafter O.F.S.A.)
     (i)   Bethlehem
             LBM, Correspondence of Magistrate, 1926–30; MBM,
             Correspondence of Town Clerk, 1923–31
     (ii)   Bethulie
             MB, Correspondence of Town Clerk, 1926–32
     (iii)   Bloemfontein
             MBL, Correspondence of Town Clerk, 1925–32, and
             Town Council Minutes, 1925–30
     (iv)   Boshof
             LBO, Correspondence of Magistrate, 1924–30
     (v)   Brandfort
             MBR, Correspondence of Town Clerk, 1927–33
     (vi)   Clocolan
             MCL, Correspondence of Town Clerk, 1926–8
     (vii)   Fouriesburg
             LFB, Correspondence of Magistrate, 1926
     (viii) Frankfort
             MFR, Correspondence of Town Clerk, 1924–32, espe-
             cially Town Council Minute Book, *Notule Komiteever-*
             gaderings
     (ix)   Harrismith
             LH, Correspondence of Magistrate, 1926–30, and
             MH, Correspondence of Town Clerk, 1923–34

(x)   Jagersfontein
      LJA, Correspondence of Magistrate, 1928
(xi) Koffiefontein
      MKF, Correspondence of Town Clerk, 1927–9
(xii) Kroonstad
      MKR, Correspondence of Town Clerk, especially
      Native Affairs Committee Minutes, 1923–31
(xiii) Lindley
      LLI, Correspondence of Magistrate, 1925–39
(xiv) Memel
      LVR, Correspondence of Vrede Magistrate, 1928
(xv) Parys
      LP, Correspondence of Magistrate, 1925–30, and MP,
      Correspondence of Town Clerk, 1923–31
(xvi) Petrus Steyn
      LPS, Correspondence of Magistrate, 1928–30
(xvii) Thaba 'Nchu
      LTN, Correspondence of Magistrate, 1928–30
(xviii) Ventersburg
      MV, Correspondence of Town Clerk, 1927
(xix) Vrede
      MVR, Correspondence of Town Clerk, 1925–30
(xx) Orange Free State Supreme Court Cases, H.G. 4/1/2/
      230–4/1/2/276, 1926–30

6.   T.A.
     (i)   Bethal
           Correspondence of Magistrate, 1927–31
     (ii) Lydenburg
           Correspondence of Magistrate, 1920–28
     (iii) Middelburg
           MMG, Correspondence of Town Clerk, 1925–30
     (iv) Pretoria
           Correspondence of Town Clerk, 1926–8

B.   UNOFFICIAL

1.   At Archives
     (i)   Hull Central Library, England, W. Holtby papers, D2
           11/50, D4 (F4–F23), D6
     (ii) International Labour Organization, Geneva, File N312/
           3/65/2, 1927, and File XT 1/1/1
     (iii) Killie Campbell Library, Durban
           (a) Besters Farmers' Association Minutes, 1925–38,
               KCM 33680

(b) Donnybrook Farmers' Association Minutes, 1925–38, KCM 43086

(c) Eshowe Co-operative Timber and Sugar Company, Minute Book of Board of Directors, 1924–9, KCM 30623

(d) J. Marwick papers, KCM MS MAR 2.08.48

(e) Mooi River Farmers' Association Minute Book, 1929–38, KCM 30625

(f) H. Nicholls papers, KCM MS NIC 2.08.1

(g) Paddock and Plains Farmers' Association Minute Book, 1923–32, KCM 30889

(h) Richmond Agricultural Society, Minutes of Annual General Meetings, 1922–31, KCM 33651

(i) Umvoti Agricultural Society Minutes, 1925–36, KCM 33660

(j) Upper Umzimkulu Farmers' Association Minutes, 1926–46, KCM 30886

(iv) O.F.S.A., J. Hugo papers, A379

(v) Standard Bank Archives Depot, 1/1/220, Inspection Reports on Greytown Branch, 1902–28

(vi) T.A., Evidence to the Native Economic Commission, K26

(vii) University of Cape Town, Manuscripts Library, W. Ballinger papers, BC347

(viii) University of the Witwatersrand, Church of the Province of South Africa Archives Depot

(a) A. Champion papers, A922

(b) Evidence to the Native Economic Commission, AD1438

(c) L. Forman papers, AD1714 Mfe

(d) Industrial and Commercial Workers' Union Records, A924

(e) Middelburg District Farmers' Union papers, A1382

(f) A. Saffery papers, AD1178, Part I

(g) South African Institute of Race Relations papers, AD843

(h) W. Ballinger papers, A410, C2.3.7

2. Private Papers

(i) Estcourt Farmers' Association, Weenen County (Estcourt) Farmers' Association Minutes, 1926–8

(ii) A. Farleigh, Ixopo, Ixopo Agricultural Society Minutes, 1926–9

(iii)   Natal Agricultural Union, Pietermaritzburg, Natal Agricultural Union Executive Committee Meetings, 1926–30

(iv)   South African Agricultural Union, Pretoria, South African Agricultural Union Executive Committee Minute Book, July 1926–October 1928; South African Agricultural Union Agricultural Advisory Board Minute Book, 14 July 1926 to 30 November 1934

II.   PRINTED PRIMARY SOURCES

A.   OFFICIAL RECORDS

Annual Reports of the Commissioner of Police, 1919–30
Annual Reports of the Agricultural and Pastoral Production of the Union of South Africa, 1918–30
Annual Reports of the Department of Lands, 1922–31
Annual Reports of the Department of Native Affairs, 1913–36
Annual Reports of the Land and Agricultural Bank of South Africa, 1917–29
Annual Reports of the Native Affairs Commission, 1921–31
Colony of Natal: Natal Native Commission 1881–2. Evidence Taken by the Sub-Committee for Umvoti County (Pietermaritzburg 1882)
Colony of Natal: Native Affairs Commission 1906–1907. Evidence (Pietermaritzburg 1907)
Final Report of the Drought Investigation Commission, October 1923, U.G. 49–1923
First Report of the Select Committee on Native Affairs, S.C.3–1923
Government Gazette Extraordinary, 23 July 1926
Index to Natal Tribes Register (Pietermaritzburg 1926)
Majority Report of the Eastern Transvaal Natives Land Committee, 1918, U.G. 31–1918
Minutes of Evidence of the Eastern Transvaal Natives Land Committee, U.G. 32–1918
Minutes of Evidence of the Natal Natives Land Committee, U.G. 35–1918
Province of Natal: Report of the Superintendent of Education for the Year 1927, N.P.4, 1928
Report of Committee of Enquiry re Taxation of Incomes derived from Farming Operations, U.G. 3–1919
Report of Native Churches Commission, U.G. 39–1925
Report of the Commission to Inquire into Co-operation and Agricultural Credit, U.G. 16–1934

Report of the Economic and Wage Commission (1925), U.G. 14–1926

Report of the Inter-Departmental Committee on the Labour Resources of the Union (Pretoria 1930), chaired by J. Holloway

Report of the Inter-Departmental Committee on Native Education 1935–1936, U.G. 29–1936

Report of the Inter-Departmental Committee on the Native Pass Laws, 1920, U.G. 41–1922

Report of the Native Economic Commission 1930–1932, U.G. 22–1932

Report of the Native Farm Labour Committee, 1937–1939, Annexure 520–1939

Report of the Natives Land Commission (Beaumont Commission), Vol. II, U.G. 22–1916

Report of the Orange Free State Local Natives Land Committee, U.G. 22–1918

Report of the Select Committee on Subject-Matter of Masters and Servants Law (Transvaal) Amendment Bill, S.C.12–1925

Report of the Select Committee on the Subject of the Union Native Council Bill, Coloured Persons Rights Bill, Representation of Natives in Parliament Bill, and the Natives Land (Amendment) Bill, S.C.10–1927

Sixth Census of the Population of the Union of South Africa, Enumerated 5th May, 1936, Vol. I, U.G. 21–1938; Vol. IX, U.G. 12–1942; *Supplement* to Vol. IX, U.G. 50–1938

Statistics of Production (Twelfth Industrial Census, 1928), U.G. 51–1928

Third Census of the Population of the Union of South Africa, Enumerated 3rd May, 1921, U.G. 37–1924

*Transkeian Territories General Council: Proceedings and Reports of Select Committees at the Session of 1930 (*King William's Town 1930)

Union of South Africa, House of Assembly Debates, 1927–30

Union Statistics for Fifty Years (Pretoria 1960)

B.   NEWSPAPERS AND PERIODICALS

Adelaide Free Press and Farmers' Friend, 1925

Cape Times, 1927–8

Die Natal Afrikaner, 1926–9

Farming in South Africa, 1926–30

Ficksburg News, 1926–30

Imvo Zabantsundu Bomzantsi Afrika, 1924–9

Ladybrand Courant and Ficksburg News, 1926–30
Natal Mercury, 1927–30
Ons Vaderland, 1927–30
Rand Daily Mail, 1926–30
Sunday Times, 1927–9
The Farmer's Weekly, 1919–30
The Friend, 1927–30
The Greytown Gazette, 1927–30
The Harrismith Chronicle, 1926–30
The Kokstad Advertiser and East Griqualand Gazette, 1927–30
The Middelburg Observer, 1926–27
The Natal Advertiser, 1927–30
The Natal Farmer, 1927–30
The Natal Witness, 1927–9
The South African Outlook, 1924–30
The South African Worker, 1926–30
The Star, 1927–30
The Territorial News, 1927–30
The Times, 1927
The Workers' Herald, 1924–9
Umteteli wa Bantu, 1927–30

III.   SECONDARY SOURCES

A.   SELECT BOOKS

Beinart, W. *The Political Economy of Pondoland 1860–1930* (Johannesburg 1982)

Bozzoli, B. *The Political Nature of a Ruling Class: Capital and Ideology in South Africa, 1890–1933* (London 1981)

Bundy, C. *The Rise and Fall of the South African Peasantry* (London 1979)

Clarke, T. and Clements, L. *Trade Unions under Capitalism* (Glasgow 1977)

Coplan, D. *In Township Tonight! South Africa's Black City Music and Theatre* (Johannesburg 1985)

Dawson, C. *Practical Maize Production in South Africa* (Wynberg 1927)

Draper, H. *Karl Marx's Theory of Revolution,* Vol. II, *The Politics of Social Classes* (New York 1978)

Gramsci, A. *Selections from the Prison Notebooks of Antonio Gramsci* (London 1978)

Grosskopf, J. *Rural Impoverishment and Rural Exodus* in *Report of* the Carnegie Commission: the Poor White Problem in South Africa, Part I (Stellenbosch 1932)

Hall, S., Critcher, C., Jefferson, T., Clarke, J. and Roberts, B. Policing the Crisis: Mugging, the State, and Law and Order (London 1982)

Hobsbawm, E. Primitive Rebels: Studies in Archaic Forms of Social Movement in the 19th and 20th Centuries (Manchester 1971)

Hobsbawm, E., and Rudé, G. Captain Swing (New York 1975)

Hunter, M. Reaction to Conquest: Effects of Contact with Europeans on the Pondo of South Africa (London 1936)

Jingoes, J. A Chief is a Chief by the People: the Autobiography of Stimela Jason Jingoes (London 1975)

Kadalie, C. My Life and the I.C.U.: the Autobiography of a Black Trade Unionist in South Africa (London 1970)

Laclau, E. Politics and Ideology in Marxist Theory: Capitalism–Fascism–Populism (London 1979)

Leppan, H. The Agricultural Development of Arid and Semi-Arid Regions with Special Reference to South Africa (Pretoria 1928)

Macmillan, W. Complex South Africa: an Economic Foot-note to History (London 1930)

Mancoe, J. First Edition of the Bloemfontein Bantu and Coloured People's Directory (Bloemfontein 1934)

Marks, S. Reluctant Rebellion: the 1906–8 Disturbances in Natal (Oxford 1970)

Marks, S. The Ambiguities of Dependence in South Africa: Class, Nationalism, and the State in Twentieth-Century Natal (Johannesburg 1986)

Marx, K. and Engels, F. Selected Works in One Volume (London 1977)

Nairn, T. The Break-Up of Britain: Crisis and Neo-Nationalism (London 1981)

O'Meara, D. Volkskapitalisme: Class, Capital and Ideology in the Development of Afrikaner Nationalism 1934–1948 (Johannesburg 1983)

van Onselen, C. Studies in the Social and Economic History of the Witwatersrand 1886–1914, Vol. 2, New Nineveh (Johannesburg 1982)

Perham, M. African Apprenticeship: an Autobiographical Journey in Southern Africa, 1929 (London 1974)

Poulantzas, N. State, Power, and Socialism (London 1978)

Roux, E. Time Longer than Rope: the Black Man's Struggle for Freedom in South Africa (Madison 1972)

Rudé, G. Ideology and Popular Protest (London 1980)

Sewell-Dawson, E. *Farm Management in South Africa* (Johannesburg 1931)

Simons, J. and R. *Class and Colour in South Africa 1850–1950* (London 1983)

Sundkler, B. *Bantu Prophets in South Africa* (London 1961)

Walshe, P. *The Rise of African Nationalism in South Africa: the African National Congress 1912–1952* (London 1970)

B.   SELECT ARTICLES AND PUBLISHED THESES

Banaji, J. 'Modes of Production in a Materialist Conception of History', *Capital and Class*, 3, 1977

Bonner, P. 'The Decline and Fall of the ICU – a Case of Self-Destruction?' in Webster, E. (ed.), *Essays in Southern African Labour History* (Johannesburg 1978)

Bonner, P. 'The Transvaal Native Congress, 1917–1920: the Radicalisation of the Black Petty Bourgeoisie on the Rand' in Marks, S. and Rathbone, R. (eds.), *Industrialisation and Social Change in South Africa: African Class Formation, Culture and Consciousness, 1870–1930* (Harlow 1982)

Bradford, H. 'Strikes in the Natal Midlands: Landlords, Labour Tenants and the I.C.U.', *Africa Perspective*, 22, 1983

Clegg, J. '*Ukubuyisa Isidumbu*– "Bringing Back the Body"': an Examination into the Ideology of Vengeance in the Msinga and Mpofana Rural Locations, 1882–1944' in Bonner, P. (ed.), *Working Papers in Southern African Studies*, Vol. 2 (Johannesburg 1981)

Coka, G. 'The Story of Gilbert Coka of the Zulu Tribe of Natal, South Africa' in Perham, M. (ed.), *Ten Africans* (London 1936)

Davies, R., Kaplan, D., Morris, M. and O'Meara, D. 'Class Struggle and the Periodisation of the State in South Africa', *Review of African Political Economy*, 7, 1976

Edgar, B. 'Garveyism in Africa: Dr. Wellington and the American Movement in the Transkei', *Ufahamu*, 6, 3, 1976

Johns, S. 'Trade Union, Political Pressure Group, or Mass Movement? The Industrial and Commercial Workers' Union of Africa' in Rotberg, R. and Mazrui, A. (eds.), *Protest and Power in Black Africa* (New York 1970)

Marks, S. 'Natal, the Zulu Royal Family and the Ideology of Segregation', *Journal of Southern African Studies*, 4, 2, 1978

Mayer, P. 'The Origin and Decline of Two Rural Resistance Ideologies' in Mayer, P. (ed.), *Black Villagers in an Industrial Society: Anthropological Perspectives on Labour Migration in South*

Africa (Cape Town 1980)

Morris, M. 'The Development of Capitalism in South African Agriculture: Class Struggle in the Countryside', *Economy and Society*, 5, 1976

Saul, J. 'The Dialectic of Class and Tribe', *Race and Class*, 20, 4, 1974

Wickins, P. 'The Industrial and Commercial Workers' Union of Africa', Ph.D., University of Cape Town, 1973, published as *The Industrial and Commercial Workers' Union of Africa* (Cape Town 1978)

C.   SELECT UNPUBLISHED ARTICLES AND THESES

Beinart, W. '*Amafelandawonye* (The Diehards): Rural Popular Protest and Women's Movements in Herschel District, South Africa', paper presented at University of the Witwatersrand, History Workshop, Feb. 1984

Beinart, W. 'Ethnic Particularism, Worker Consciousness and Nationalism: an Individual Experience of Proletarianisation, 1930–1960', paper presented at conference 'South Africa in the Comparative Study of Class, Race and Nationalism', New York, Sept. 1982

Beinart, W. and Bundy, C. 'The Union, the Nation and the Talking Crow: the Ideology and Tactics of the Independent ICU in East London', paper presented at University of the Witwatersrand, African Studies Institute, 4 March 1985

Hill, R. '"Africa for the Africans": Marcus Garvey, the UNIA, and the Struggle of African Nationalism in South Africa in the Nineteen-Twenties', paper presented at conference 'South Africa in the Comparative Study of Class, Race and Nationalism', New York, Sept. 1982

Hirson, B. 'The Bloemfontein Riots, 1925: A Study in Community Culture and Class Consciousness', paper presented at University of London, Institute of Commonwealth Studies, 13 May 1983

Keegan, T. 'The Transformation of Agrarian Society and Economy in Industrialising South Africa: the Orange Free State Grain Belt in the Early Twentieth Century', Ph.D., University of London, 1981

la Hausse, P. 'The Struggle for the City: Alcohol, the Ematsheni and Popular Culture in Durban, 1902–1936', paper presented at University of the Witwatersrand, History Workshop, Feb. 1984

Legassick, M. 'The Rise of Modern South African Liberalism: its Assumptions and its Social Base', paper presented at University of London, Institute of Commonwealth Studies, 1972

Slater, H. 'A Fresh Look at the I.C.U.: the Case of Natal', paper presented at University of Sussex, School of Asian and African Studies, June 1971

Swanson, M. 'Champion of Durban', paper presented at African Studies Association, Los Angeles, 18 Oct. 1968

Tyamzashe, H. 'Summarised History of the Industrial and Commercial Workers' Union of Africa' in University of the Witwatersrand, Church of the Province of South Africa Archives, A. Saffery papers, AD1178, Part I, B5

IV.   INTERVIEWS CITED IN TEXT

A.   INTERVIEWS WHERE TAPES AND TRANSCRIPTS ARE IN POSSESSION OF ORAL HISTORY PROJECT, AFRICAN STUDIES INSTITUTE, UNIVERSITY OF THE WITWATERSRAND

Bogopane, T.   by T. Phiri, Phokeng, 11 Sept. 1981
Cwele, A. and Jali. P. by H. Bradford and A. Mgetyana, Bizana, 18 May 1984
Dhlomo, J.   by H. Bradford and V. Nkumane, Greytown, 2 July 1980
Dinkebogile, I.   by T. Phiri, Phokeng, 28 July 1981
Hlangabezo, E.   by H. Bradford and A. Mgetyana, Bizana, 20 May 1984
Kok, J.   by P. Bonner and A. Mabin, Pilgrims Rest, 9 Aug. 1984
Kumalo, C.   by H. Bradford and V. Nkumane, Mooi River, 28 Nov. 1981
Lusiba, J.   by V. Nkumane, Barberton, April 1981
Mafumane, M.   by V. Nkumane, Koppies, 14 April 1980
Maine, K.   by T. Couzens, M. Nkadimeng and G. Relly, 2 July 1980
Maine, K.   by C. van Onselen, Ledig, 24 Feb. 1981
Maine, K.   by M. Nkadimeng, Ledig, 7 Nov. 1984
Maine, L.   by M. Nkadimeng, Ledig, 27 July 1980
Majola, M.   by H. Bradford and V. Nkumane, Mooi River, 30 Nov. 1981
Makiri, D.   by M. Ntoane, Evaton, 20 Nov. 1980

Makume, N.   by T. Flatela, Viljoensdrift, 10 June 1982
Makume, N.   by T. Flatela, Viljoensdrift, 10 Aug. 1982

Manapa, V.   by M. Ntoane, Evaton, 24 Nov. 1980
Manoto, T.   by M. Molepo, Heilbron, 26 Feb. 1980
Mapaila, R.   by M. Molepo, Acornhoek, 16 March 1983

Mashile, T.   by P. Bonner and M. Molepo, Pilgrims Rest, 10 Aug. 1984

Masike, P.   by M. Molepo, Viljoenskroon, 24 Feb. 1980

Mathebula, L.   by H. Bradford and V. Nkumane, Vryheid, 25 Nov. 1981

Mathuloe, I.   by T. Phiri, Phokeng, 13 May 1981
Mbelo, W. and   by H. Bradford and L. Mdingi, Bizana,
Mdibe, R.   20 May 1984
Mchunu, J.   by H. Bradford and V. Nkumane, Mooi River, 1 Dec. 1981

Mdhlalose, T.   by H. Bradford and V. Nkumane, Vryheid, 25 Nov. 1981

Mdingi, L.   by H. Bradford and W. Beinart, Bizana, 2 April 1984

Mdingi, L.   by H. Bradford, Bizana, 17 May 1984
Mekgwe, E.   by M. Nkotsoe, Phokeng, 2 March 1982
Mgetyana, B.   by H. Bradford and A. Mgetyana, Bizana, 20 May 1984

Mhlongo, L.   by H. Bradford and V. Nkumane, Vryheid, 24 Nov. 1981

Mogane, L. and   by P. Bonner, J. Kok, A. Mabin and M.
E., Silwane, J.   Molepo, Hlabekisa, 22 Feb. 1985
and Malele, A.
Mokale, A.   by T. Flatela, Evaton, 2 April 1982
Mokhacane, M.   by M. Ntoane, Klerksdorp, 28 Nov. 1979

Molete, J.   by M. Nkadimeng, Kroonstad, 26 Feb. 1980

Molohlanyi, M.   by M. Nkadimeng, Wolmaransstad, 19 April 1984

Molohlanyi, M.   by M. Nkadimeng, Wolmaransstad, 28 June 1985

Moloko, M.   by B. Moeketsi, Mathopestad, 20 Nov. 1979

Motha, J.   by V. Nkumane, Middelburg, 11 Sept. 1979

Mpetha, O.	by H. Bradford, Cape Town, 21 Sept. 1983
Mthembu, N.	by H. Bradford and V. Nkumane, Ixopo, 5 July 1980
Ngcamu, N. and Zuma, D.	by H. Bradford and V. Nkumane, Richmond, 9 July 1980
Ngcobo, E.	by H. Bradford and V. Nkumane, Bulwer, 3 December 1981
Nomsuka, J.	by H. Bradford and A. Mgetyana, Bizana, 20 May, 1984
Nqandela, L.	by T. Flatela, Ledig, 4 Jan. 1983
Ntambo, J. and Nhlabathi, L.	by V. Nkumane, Ledig, 23 Nov. 1979
Sibanyoni, E. and Mthimunye, R.	by V. Nkumane, Middelburg, 4 Sept. 1979
Sibanyoni, E. and Mthimunye, R.	by V. Nkumane, Middelburg, 19 Oct. 1979
Sincuba, Z.	by H. Bradford and A. Mgetyana, Bizana, 18 May 1984
Skhosana, G.	by M. Ntoane, Lydenburg, 7 Sept. 1979
Thabethe, E.	by V. Nkumane, Ledig, 23 Nov. 1979
Zondi, E.	by H. Bradford, and V. Nkumane, Greytown, 3 July 1980

B. TAPED INTERVIEWS WHERE ONLY TRANSCRIPTS ARE IN POSSESSION OF AFRICAN STUDIES INSTITUTE

Champion, A.	by M. Swanson, place and date unknown (but probably Durban, mid-1970s)

C. INTERVIEWS WHERE ONLY TAPES ARE IN POSSESSION OF KILLIE CAMPBELL LIBRARY, DURBAN

Mkhize, B.	by D. Collins and A. Manson, Durban, 22 Aug. 1979

D. INTERVIEWS WHERE TAPES AND TRANSCRIPTS ARE IN POSSESSION OF WILLIAM BEINART

Gqambuleni, Gqude and others	by W. Beinart and F. Deyi, Lusikisiki, 25 March 1977
Mvunelo, J.	by W. Beinart, Lusikisiki, 13 March 1977

Soji, A.   by W. Beinart and F. Deyi, Lusikisiki,
                            23 March 1977

E.   INTERVIEWS WHERE TAPES AND TRANSCRIPTS ARE IN
      MY POSSESSION

Raife, D.   by H. Bradford, Estcourt, 1 Dec. 1981

F.   INTERVIEWS WHERE TAPES ARE IN POSSESSION OF
      SOUTH AFRICAN SECURITY POLICE AND NOTES TAKEN
      DURING INTERVIEWS ARE IN MINE

Buthelezi, M.   by H. Bradford and V. Nkumane,
                            Bulwer, 6 July 1980
Ngubane, L.   by H. Bradford and V. Nkumane,
                            Greytown, 3 July 1980

G.   UNTAPED INTERVIEWS WHERE NOTES ARE IN MY POSS-
      ESSION

Dhlomo, J.   by H. Bradford, Pretoria, 17 August
                            1984
Mbunquka, S.   by H. Bradford, Bizana, 18 May 1984
Pato, E.   by H. Bradford, Bizana, 19 May 1984
Xoko, L.   by H. Bradford and A. Mgetyana,
                            Bizana, 19 May 1984

INDEX

abaphakathi, 113, 125, 143, 199, 261
Adelaide, 8, 11
Advisory Boards, 83, 149, 299n61; collaboration and, 129, 150; reform and, 67; resistance to, 139, 311n144
aeroplanes, 329n57; Garveyism and, 215, 216, 217, 226; millenarianism and, 229, 231, 234, 235, 236; witchcraft and, 228
African Methodist Episcopal Church, 76
African National Congress: ICU and, 16, 64, 266; ideology, 3, 17, 72, 81, 83, 115; post-1930, ix, xi, 254, 273, 277, 278; structure and administration, 4, 76, 93, 125. *See also* Natal Native Congress; South African Native National Congress; Transvaal Native Congress
African nationalism: churches and, 76, 123, 125; class and, 17, 81, 82, 141, 254, 259, 277; growth of, 76–7; material base of, 94, 100, 143, 239–40, 256–7; middle class and, 2, 15, 75–6, 94, 239; socialism and, 114, 115–16, 118; varieties of, 93–4, 96, 101, 102–3, 113, 116, 126, 152, 174, 237, 321n25, 321n32, 330n68
African Workers' Club, 81, 141, 196
African Workers' Co-operative Society, 81, 82, 117–18
Africanism, 101, 106, 113, 195, 242; Wellington movement and, 217, 330n68
Afrikaner nationalism, 8, 31–2, 77, 122, 180–1
agriculture
  banks and, 26, 27, 190–1, 192, 207
  capitalism and, 60, 146–7, 170, 197; constraints on development of, 24–9, 32–3, 55, 60, 190–2; primitive nature of, 16, 22, 29, 37, 38, 39–41, 42, 51, 119, 122, 183, 268; productive forces, 25, 26, 31, 32, 41, 44, 55, 57, 169, 176, 178, 193, 194, 288n26, 294n113; profits, 26, 29, 31, 175, 191, 269
  Cape Province, 25, 29, 31, 33, 56, 164
  depression, 25–6, 29, 165, 192, 194
  international markets, 25–6, 61, 192, 288n29, 288n31
  manufacturing and, 31, 32, 40, 45, 59–60, 192, 270, 292n75
  merchant capital and, 25, 26, 31, 33, 157, 175, 191, 207
  mining capital and, 33, 192, 207
  Natal, 29, 35–6, 39–40, 59, 203, 265
  Orange Free State, 29, 36, 39–40, 56, 289n42
  state and, 8, 23, 31, 32, 33, 175, 270, 288n27, 288n29, 288n32
  Transvaal, 29, 35, 36, 39–40, 145–8, 163–4, 165, 175, 177, 179, 270, 289n40, 289n42. *See also* cattle; crops; drought; farmers; labour tenants; peasants; sheep; wattle industry; and *see individual districts*

Amaci, 229, 232, 233
AmaRespectables, 65, 83, 162, 273; collaboration, 97, 98, 150; lower middle class and, 74, 75, 76; under-class mobilization opposed by, 16, 86
American blacks: admiration for, 127, 142, 214, 337n57; as liberators, 19, 158, 212, 215–17, 219, 222, 226–30 *passim*, 239, 242, 244, 325n9, 325n10; South Africans seen as, 126, 142, 218, 228, 236, 237
ANC, *see* African National Congress
Anti-ICU, 209, 210, 211
apartheid, ix, 58, 255
Arnold, Detective Sergeant R., 83–4

Ballinger, William, 102, 167, 173, 174, 304n44; deputations and, 129, 169, 170, 177, 178, 180; dominant class support for, 167–8, 181, 183, 184, 262; farmers' opposition to, 170, 176, 179, 181; *re* ICU, 182, 274
Bambatha, 189, 196, 209; rebellion, 106, 189, 195–6, 198, 200, 226, 238, 253; Umvoti, echoes of rebellion in, 186, 188, 195, 196, 205, 207
banks, 26, 27, 190–1, 192, 207, 209
Bantu Men's Social Centre, 66, 83
Barberton: land question, 146, 147, 151–2, 153; repression, 149; resistance, 151, 155–6; under-class mobilization, 93, 151, 334n21
Basutoland, 110; under-class mobilization, 3, 99, 111, 306n67, 306n68; workers from, 157, 188, 193
Batty, Albert, 118, 121, 282n13
Bedford, 8, 11
beer, 6, 40; boycotts, 212, 247–51, 332n8; drinks, 46, 47, 110, 322n40; under-class mobilization and, 102, 108–9, 196, 254
Bergville, 187–8, 254, 334n19
Bethal, 161, 183; agrarian economy, 31, 146, 156, 157, 183; under-class mobilization, 73, 151, 158
Bizana, 225, 232, 239; conditions deteriorating, 221, 239; millenarianism, 215, 222, 229, 230, 233, 236, 240; organizational methods, 223, 235, 237; repression, 110, 238; separatist churches, 215, 223, 230, 237
Bloemfontein: farmers, 6, 129; middle class, 68, 73; resistance, 3, 6, 128, 131, 224; under-class mobilization, 3, 140, 142, 312n152, 334n21
Bloemhof, 163
Bomvu, 198, 321n25
boycotts, 2; of Advisory Boards, 311n144; of beer halls, 19, 212, 247–51
bridewealth, 35, 37, 57, 100, 140, 190
Britain, 13, 102, 215; Afrikaner nationalism and, 8, 31, 77; imperialism and, 207, 217; liberalism and, 122, 162; middle class and, 64, 66; trade unions in, 162, 163, 274, 282n13; trade with South Africa, 68, 192, 288n31

Bulwer, 89–90, 108, 127, 309n110
Bunga, 220
Buthelezi, Wellington, 217, 218, 226, 227, 330n68

Caluza, Alphabet, 96
Campbell, William, 98, 99
Cape Agricultural Union, 31
Cape Province: agrarian economy, 25, 29, 31, 33, 56, 164; ICU and, *see under* ICU; ICWU in, 4–5, 6
Cape Town, 2, 3, 306n76
capitalism, 230; accumulation and, 44, 184; defined, 16; development of, 25, 60, 127, 183, 308n99; racial oppression and, 9, 116, 118, 122–3; wages and, 34, 268. *See also* agriculture; primitive accumulation
Carolina, 145, 146, 160, 334n21
Cathcart, 8
cattle, 52, 103, 169, 214, 277
  as bridewealth, 35, 37
  confiscation, 52, 193, 205, 270, 337n53
  farming, 21–2, 190, 191, 209
  importance of, 37, 38
  killing, 230, 233, 329n57
  resistance and, 37–8, 104, 177, 197; to dipping, 156, 183, 220; maiming, 2, 50, 207, 268; theft, 51, 53
  'squeezing' of labour tenants and, 56, 146, 190, 193, 249, 265
Cetshwayo, 35, 97, 101, 103, 195
Champion, A.W.G., 129, 309n116; background, 67, 68, 71, 76, 295n4, 337n56; black perceptions of, xi, 92, 117, 301n13; as Durban leader, 10, 12, 139, 162, 221, 240, 252, 333n14; ethnicity and, 83, 101, 142; ICU leaders' relationship with, 132, 211, 327n29; land question and, 104, 106, 162, 204; litigation and, 133, 134, 137, 262, 271–2; as middle-class leader, 15, 81–2, 85, 121, 141, 284n31; post-1930 career, 253, 254, 334n18, 337n57
chiefs: collaboration, 3, 48, 75, 97, 98, 99, 112, 198, 238, 255; ICU as substitute for, 136, 139; labour tenants and, 48, 97, 202; land and, 48, 101, 103, 112, 147, 198; paramount, 14, 187, 220, 238, 240; proletarianization, 103, 147; repression of dissent, 48, 97, 98, 99, 150, 238; reserve-dwellers and, 35, 48, 111, 214, 215, 241, 271; under-class mobilization supported by, 97, 99, 101, 103, 109–10, 151–2, 154, 223, 229, 231, 240, 252, 282n17, 304n48, 305n65, 313n20
children: of labour tenants, 37–44 *passim*, 46, 50, 57, 121, 146, 190; mobilization of, 187, 234, 237; resistance and, 176, 277; women and, 37, 90, 250
Christiana, 163
Christianity, 48–9, 63, 76, 113, 123–5, 217, 242. *See also* churches
Christmas Day, 5, 153, 229, 236, 239, 328n44
churches, 21
  mission, 65, 89, 200, 234, 237, 261–2, 335n34
  separatist: millenarianism and, 76, 215, 230; nationalism and, 76, 123, 195; rural blacks and, 49, 61, 195, 214, 215; under-class organization and, 89, 124–5, 139, 217, 237, 244. *See also* Christianity
Ciskei, 216, 240, 282n17
'civilized labour' policy, 9, 67
class: nationalism and, 17, 81, 82, 141, 254, 259, 277
Coka, Gilbert, 64–5, 78, 79, 95
collaboration: Advisory Boards and, 129, 150, 309n116; *AmaRespectables* and, 97, 98, 150; black intellectuals and, 76, 84, 208, 318n77; chiefs and, 3, 48, 75, 97, 98, 99, 112, 198, 238, 255; headmen and, 112; labour tenant elders and, 38, 50
'coloured' people, xii; Africanism and, 96, 330n68; as farm workers, 43, 260, 281n7; mobilization of,

2, 3, 259–60, 282n17, 302n26; political activists from, 70, 96; nationalism and, 96, 118, 237, 330n68; under-class mobilization opposed by, 96, 271–2
Communism, 82, 115, 128; fears re, 158, 168, 179, 181, 210. *See also* Russian Revolution
Communist Party of South Africa, 15, 85, 86, 115, 168, 278; ICU, conflict with, 14, 128, 164; liberals and, 14, 262; programme and tactics, 78, 114, 116, 117, 118, 306n76; rural emphasis, 1–2, 12, 276
Congress, *see* African National Congress
consciousness: Africanist (*see also* Africanism), 35, 44, 76, 104, 149, 152, 241, 244–5, 304n44, 304n50; ambiguities of, 16, 61, 199; attitudes to law, 136, 137–8, 145, 201, 206, 238, 263; beliefs in magic, 91–2, 217, 224–8, 232, 235, 238, 243–5, 267, 327n29; ethnic, 35, 46–8, 79, 83, 96–7, 100–1, 102, 157–8, 242, 252, 303n40; labour tenant, 45–8, 61, 178, 194–5, 199, 216; parochial, 19, 100, 241, 256, 257, 259; traditionalist, 35, 46, 95–106 *passim*, 194, 214, 230, 232, 241–5 *passim*, 250–2, 253, 257, 261, 267
contracts: labour tenants and, 37, 41, 128, 169, 178, 179, 307n92; recruited farm workers and, 3, 129; repression of dissent and, 121, 134, 211, 264, 270
courts of law, 52, 139; farmers' conflicts with, 53, 54, 134, 200, 205–6, 209, 270–1; under-class victories in, 135–6, 137, 164, 196, 205–6, 262, 264, 272. *See also* Supreme Courts
Cowley, Cecil, 134, 136
CP, *see* Communist Party of South Africa
crops: cotton, 29, 52, 107, 147; fruit, 147; peanuts, 29, 176, 288n31; tobacco, 147, 153, 179. *See also* maize; sugar industry
Cunu, 194, 201, 202, 206
curfew, 108, 240–1

Damoyi, W., 221, 237
De Aar, 82
Deane, William, 197–8
'Dem Darkies', 68, 252
depressions: *1920–22*, 8, 29, 67, 192, 242; *1929–31*, 243, 249. *See also* agriculture
Dhlomo, Jacob, xii, 190, 194, 198
diamond-diggings, 164–7, 182, 262, 268
Dingane, 96, 159, 319n6
Dinizulu, 226, 227, 253
Dippa, James, 11, 70
Dladla, Jumaima, 191, 197, 202
dock workers, 2, 4, 5, 216, 247
domestic servants, 38, 73, 142, 155, 251, 291n58
Doyle, Major, 176, 178, 181
droughts, 24–5, 29, 33, 109, 179, 207, 220–1; resistance and, 25, 164, 210–11, 220–1, 239, 257
'dual revolution', 94, 113, 143, 256
Dube, John, 34, 70, 98, 307n80
Duff, John, 175, 176, 178, 179, 181
Dumah, Robert, 102, 138
Dundee, 132, 248, 250, 273–4, 284n31, 305n61
Dunn, Sam, 96, 100, 195, 310n125; background, 67, 73, 295n3, 296n9; militarism and, 208, 337n57
Dunn's reserve, 137, 271–2, 337n57
Durban: black culture, 126, 141, 142, 251–2; Garveyists, 215, 216; ICU provincial headquarters, 93, 229, 301n16; resistance, 19, 83, 132, 247, 248, 251–2; rural blacks and, 21, 105; under-class mobilization, 12, 82, 92, 105, 117–18, 136, 139, 253, 302n22

East Griqualand, 50–1, 223; millenarianism, 217, 226, 227, 229, 231; under-class mobilization, 221, 240
East London: strikes, 242, 256; under-class mobiliz-

ation, 124, 174, 243, 255, 311*n*145, 311*n*146, 334*n*21
education, 91; middle class and, 65–6; under-class organization and, 117, 139, 168, 230. *See also* schools; teachers
Elias, Simon, 73, 124, 129, 130, 133, 299*n*61
Elliotdale, 240
Emfundisweni, 216, 219
Empangeni, 68, 305*n*64
Ermelo, 145, 146, 334*n*21
Estcourt: argrarian economy, 192, 249; land question, 34, 106, 187; repression, 187, 204, 207, 208, 264, 271; resistance, 197, 249, 263; under-class mobilization, 11, 95, 108, 109, 134, 142, 302*n*22, 335*n*30
ethnicity: ambiguities of, 258; Christianity and, 113, 242; consciousness of, 35, 46–8, 79, 83, 96–7, 100–1, 102, 157–8, 242, 252, 303*n*40; ideological appeals to, 100–1, 112–13, 195–6, 242, 252, 253, 260, 261, 303*n*40; 321*n*25, 321*n*32; material base of, 96; whites and, 180, 209; Zulu-speakers and, 96–101 *passim*, 195, 196, 252, 253, 260, 265
evictions, 3, 265
    farmers and, 145, 169, 192–3; repression of dissent, 11, 20, 61, 150, 155, 159, 164, 168, 202–4, 211, 248, 270
    ideological opposition to, 108, 119, 120, 204
    prevalence of, 17, 57, 105, 147, 195, 265, 272–3
    resistance to, 81, 135, 204–9 *passim*, 254–5, 263, 271–2
    state and, 205–10 *passim*, 271, 336*n*38, 337*n*55

'faction fights'. 46, 157, 189, 202, 250
farm workers (*see also* labour tenants), 4, 146, 281*n*7
    'coloured' people as, 43, 260, 281*n*7
    casual, 36, 147, 176, 189, 198, 264
    contracts, 3, 134, 179, 264, 270
    as ICU members, 6, 8, 11, 13, 93, 97, 171, 176
    ICU unattractive to some, 84, 99, 198, 218, 264
    ideological perceptions of, 12–13, 15, 100, 119–21, 180, 274–5
    Indian people as, 189, 191, 281*n*7
    mobilization of, 4, 6, 11, 14, 86, 89, 100, 103, 107–9, 138, 161, 172, 196, 265, 305*n*61
    political activists from, 73
    recruited for capitalist farmers, 36, 134, 146, 147, 156, 157, 169, 193
    resistance, 2, 13, 18, 158, 171, 176, 177, 264; of recruited workers, 47, 157–8, 198, 264; work stoppages, 167, 172–3, 182–3, 197–8
    skilled/supervisory, 43, 46, 47, 48, 54, 157, 160; farmers' need for, 44, 171, 173, 177–8, 179–80, 184
    wages, 3, 6, 100, 189, 220, 268–9
    white people as, 55, 157, 160
farmers:
    ICU, responses from: alliances formed against, 6, 204–5, 262, 266, 335*n*34; court action, 134, 150, 151, 205–6, 211, 270; evictions, 11, 20, 61, 150, 155, 159, 164, 168, 202–4, 211, 248, 270; fears, 5, 6, 97, 134, 156, 158–60, 164, 177, 187, 205, 238, 276–7; meetings, 129, 186, 210, 269; organizations to oppose, 159–60, 209; repression, effect of, 272; support, 96, 260; violence, 107–8, 135, 158, 179, 186–7, 207, 209–10, 211, 270
    labour control, 40, 41, 55, 150, 151, 156
    labour shortages, 44, 68, 157, 177, 292*n*73, 314*n*31; concessions due to, 18, 168–9, 179, 180, 184, 264, 269
    proletarianization and, 17, 60
    racism and, 41–3, 129, 181, 182, 201, 291*n*67
    segregation and, 58, 180, 181
    white wage-earners and, 55, 157, 160, 210

    See also agriculture; evictions; 'progressive' farmers; repression; struggling farmers
Farmers' Party, 32, 176, 180, 288*n*30
Faro, Louis, 240
Fingoland, 223, 244
Flagstaff, 221, 223, 226, 229, 231, 233
forced resettlement, ix, x, 254, 255, 278
forests, 92, 233, 234, 236, 237
fowl, 38, 225, 226, 229, 232, 329*n*57
franchise: Africans' loss of, 75; Africans with, 64, 74; Africans without, 63, 65, 94; demands for, 115, 118, 122, 123
Frankfort, 128, 311*n*134, 329*n*57

Gafenowitz, Sam, 156, 157, 158, 183
Gaika, 242
Garvey, Marcus, 5, 141, 244
Garveyism, 77–8, 93–4, 126–7, 143, 214–15, 222, 306*n*67, 312*n*154
Gcaleka, 242, 244
Gillespie, W., 169, 171
goats, 38, 249, 265
gold, *see* mining capital
government, *see* Pact government
Graaf-Reinet, 25
Grasfontein, 164, 165, 166
Greytown, 78, 196, 212, 319*n*6; repression, 186, 199, 204, 207, 209, 210, 211. *See also* Umvoti
Gumbs, J.G., 73, 126
Gwaza, Zabuloni, 186, 195, 206, 207, 321*n*25, 322*n*41

Harding, 223; millenarianism, 229, 231–8 *passim*
Harrismith, 80, 305*n*64
Havemann, Daniel, 191
Havemann, Paul, 191, 209
headmen, 99–100; collaboration, 112; under-class mobilization supported by, 109, 151, 152, 196, 221, 223, 231, 236, 238
Heidelberg, 145, 146, 334*n*21
Heilbron, 187, 334*n*21
Hertzog, General, 174, 208, 217; reform and, 168; repression and, 58, 62, 172, 173; white supremacy and, 101, 174
Hintsa, 96, 243
historiography, 13–17, 280*n*3, 284*n*34
Hlubi, 108, 187, 218
Holtby, Winifred, 20, 184, 315*n*44, 316*n*58
horses, 38, 89, 90, 146, 215, 236

ICU (Industrial and Commercial Workers' Union of Africa):
    African National Congress and, 16, 64, 266
    badges, 127, 187, 309*n*110
    Communist Party of South Africa, relationship with, 114, 116, 117; co-operative, 1, 12, 15, 78, 115, 275, 298*n*48, 306*n*76; conflictual, 14, 15, 128, 162, 164, 168
    concerts, 108, 124, 126, 140–2, 251–2, 312*n*152
    conferences, 9, 10, 15, 83, 102, 119, 123, 140, 151, 162, 168, 169, 182
    constitution, 3, 6, 114, 134, 140, 162, 306*n*76
    demise, 85, 167, 174–5, 182, 183, 239, 243, 270, 272, 273
    democracy, lack of, 10–11, 14, 15, 86–7, 88, 92, 120, 274
    discontinuities, 2, 9, 12–13, 15, 19, 161, 167, 174, 246
    dual power and, 137–40, 231, 238, 239, 276
    early history, 2–8
    farmers and, *see under* farmers
    finances, 6, 9, 12, 93, 164, 167, 204, 239, 284*n*32, 301*n*15, 301*n*16
    ideology, *see* ICU ideology

as intermediary, 132–3, 136–7, 259
leadership, *see* ICU leaders
liberals' relationship with, 184; ambiguities of, 83, 85–6, 181; collaborative, 14, 18, 85, 102, 120, 162, 169, 178, 182; conflictual, 20, 102, 168, 173–4, 274–5, 304*n*44; dominant class support for, 167–8, 169–70
membership cards as talismans, 93, 104–5, 127, 152–3, 155, 161, 218, 219, 228–35 *passim*, 238, 267, 274, 330*n*63
membership figures, 2, 112, 117, 148–9, 177, 196, 234, 260, 270, 282*n*17, 302*n*26
mission churches and, 89, 200, 234, 237, 261–2, 335*n*34
Natal Agricultural Union and, 59, 129, 202
organization, limitations of, 131–3, 143, 156, 247, 256, 274, 277
recognition desired, 162, 171–2
recognition granted, 128, 168–70, 171, 173, 177–82
recognition refused, 128, 129–30, 172, 179, 309*n*116
regional organization (*see also individual districts*): in Basutoland, 99, 111; in Cape, 3, 5, 6, 8, 9, 11, 12, 69–70, 82, 99, 101, 107, 125, 142, 149, 260, 265; in Ciskei, 282*n*17; in East Griqualand, 221, 227, 231; in Natal, 12, 18–19, 69, 89, 96, 97, 98, 100, 104, 105, 111, 112, 127, 130, 132–6 *passim*, 140, 149, 162–3, 185, 187, 218, 222, 259–62 *passim*, 265, 270, 274, 284*n*31, 305*n*64; in Orange Free State, 6, 12, 15, 83, 93, 96, 101, 102, 108, 113, 114, 115, 120, 124, 126, 135, 138–9, 140, 162, 186, 260, 262, 265, 270, 305*n*64; in Pondoland, 19, 219–41 *passim*, 244, 259; in southern Africa, 110, 306*n*67; in Swaziland, 102–3, 152, 160; in Transkeian Territories, 19, 110, 240, 241, 244–5, 261, 282*n*17; in Transvaal, 12, 14, 18, 69, 83, 84, 88, 93, 99, 101, 103, 104, 107, 108, 109, 111, 126, 136, 138, 148–85 *passim*, 270
resistance and, *see* ICU-influenced resistance
rural recruiting drives, 99–100, 106–8, 152, 164, 196, 276, 305*n*61; in reserves, 109–12, 155, 176, 198, 219, 221, 222, 305*n*64
secession from, 163, 174, 246, 256–7. *See also* ICU *yase* Natal; Independent ICU of the Transkei; Independent Independent ICU; Transkeian ICU; United ICU
separatist churches and, 89, 124–5, 139, 237
segregation and, 9, 82
South African Agricultural Union and, 121
state and, *see under* state response to ICU
structure and administration, 9–11, 69, 88–9, 93, 95, 101–2, 108, 132–3, 139–42, 162–3
support for, *see* ICU support-base
tactics, 3, 83–4, 85, 127, 131, 168, 180, 274, 275; deputations, 128–30, 169–70, 171, 177, 178, 204, 309*n*113; litigation, 108, 111, 121, 132–8, 162, 164, 196, 205–6, 209, 231, 262, 271, 272, 274
trade unionism and, 2, 9, 15; desire for, 20, 161, 162, 163, 168; difficulties of, 2, 22, 163, 172, 174, 181–2, 183
Transvaal Agricultural Union and, 62, 175, 176, 179, 180–2, 183, 184, 264
Transvaal Native Congress and, 150, 151, 152, 164
under-classes shape, 18, 19, 93, 94–5, 100, 104–5, 106, 107, 108, 111, 143, 152, 155, 161, 166, 196, 197, 232–3, 239, 256–8, 259, 261
Universal Negro Improvement Association and, 77, 281*n*9
unpopular, *see* ICU's unpopularity
victories, 32, 72, 83, 112, 151, 156, 167, 241,
275–6; legal, 111, 135, 136, 137, 164, 196, 205–6, 209, 262, 264
vigilantes and, 136, 166, 186–8, 207, 209–10, 211
Wellington movement and, 218, 332*n*85
white wage-earners and, 114, 116, 118, 260
See also African Workers' Club; African Workers' Co-operative Society; Workers' Halls; *Workers' Herald*
ICU ideology: Africanism and, 84, 101, 106, 113, 149, 195; Christianity and, 76, 101, 113, 123–5, 143, 195, 230, 258, 308*n*104; elitism and, 69–70, 83–5, 90, 132, 133, 141, 299*n*61, 310*n*125; ethnicity and, 100–1, 112–13, 195–6, 260, 261, 303*n*40; Garveyism and, 77–8, 93–4, 126–7, 143, 222, 312*n*154; hegemony and, 94, 138, 143–4, 259, 276; land question and, 16, 18, 39, 82–3, 103–7, 108, 112, 113, 119, 123, 127, 130, 131, 151, 152, 153, 155, 162, 168, 174, 175, 187, 188, 195, 204, 258; liberalism and, 83, 113, 119–23, 128, 178; militarism and, 19, 82, 124, 127, 130, 131, 132, 139, 142, 152–3, 207–8, 224, 227; millenarianism and, 19, 76, 124, 153, 197, 212, 214, 218–19, 222, 226–8, 229, 230; moderation of, 18, 133, 161, 163; nationalism and, 15, 17, 59, 77, 81, 82, 84, 91, 93–4, 96, 100, 101, 102–3, 112–13, 114, 115–16, 118, 122, 123, 125, 126, 141, 143, 167, 174, 237, 240, 256–7, 259, 306*n*76, 321*n*25, 321*n*32, 330*n*68; passes and, 81, 83, 115, 122, 124, 130, 131, 164, 167, 174, 175; petty bourgeois concerns and, 82–3, 117; socialism and, 113–18, 141, 143, 150, 306*n*76; strikes, support for in, 14, 99, 128, 129, 130, 131, 140, 157, 166–7, 172, 173, 224; strikes, opposition to in, 14, 140, 166, 168, 284*n*31, 310*n*125; taxation and, 115, 130, 131, 231, 238; traditionalism and, 96–7, 101–3, 112–13, 143, 239; under-class focus in, 12–13, 88, 93, 94, 115, 118, 126, 138, 141, 142, 154–5, 167, 263; wages and, 6, 14, 69, 81, 113, 115, 118–22 *passim*, 130, 157, 161, 163, 176, 230, 238, 241
ICU-influenced resistance:
on African-owned farms, 164
characteristics of, 2, 3, 16, 17, 22, 156, 257, 259, 264, 274
chiefs and, 18, 151
diamond-diggers and, 165–7, 182, 268
farm workers and, 2, 13, 18, 157–8, 171, 176, 177; work stoppages, 167, 172–3, 182–3, 197–8
labour tenants and, 18, 19, 137, 138, 151, 155, 156, 164, 201, 264, 265; anti-evictions, 204–9 *passim*, 271; refusals to work, 105, 197, 198–9, 200, 209, 210, 266, 267, 268, 270
mission reserve dwellers and, 80, 109
reserve-dwellers and, 137, 176, 179, 198, 231, 235, 238
rural Africans and, 151, 154, 155–6
sharecroppers and, 262
'squatters' and, 263
tenants and, 81, 137, 204, 205, 271–2
urban blacks and, 4–5, 6, 25, 69, 80, 81, 115, 128, 137, 138–9, 154–5, 173, 331*n*144, 335*n*31
women and, 69, 80, 260, 335*n*31
youths and, 176, 200, 201
ICU leaders: as Advisory Board members, 83, 149, 299*n*61; background in elite, 63–4, 65, 67, 70 (*see also* mine clerks; teachers); class character, 15–16, 79, 81, 87; Congressmen different from, 16, 64, 72, 81, 115; corruption, 163, 164, 168, 273; differentiation, 10–11, 14–15, 69–70, 86, 149–50, 211, 222–3, 257; peculation, 11, 73, 82, 85, 97, 117, 163, 164, 168, 208, 239, 256, 273, 328*n*47, 337*n*56, 337*n*59; proletarianization of, 16, 63, 67–9, 71–4, 80–1; self-appointed, 111, 196, 219, 236–7; separatist churches and, 76, 223, 224, 321*n*25; shop-stewards as, 10, 78, 107, 108, 111,

222; victimization of, 75, 107–8, 110, 114, 135, 137, 149–50, 170, 175, 179, 183, 186, 187, 207, 211, 221–2, 238–9, 253, 296n16, 306n67
ICU support-base: *abaphakathi*, 113, 261; chiefs, 97, 99, 101, 103, 109–10, 151–2, 154, 223, 229, 231, 240, 282n17; children, 187, 234; Christians, 89, 123, 125, 143, 200, 237, 261; 'coloured' people, 2, 259–60, 282n17, 302n26; diamond-diggers, 165, 167; domestic servants, 142; farm workers, 6, 8, 11, 13, 86, 89, 93, 100, 103, 109, 138, 161, 171, 176; foreign blacks, 99, 111, 306n67; headmen, 109, 151, 152, 196, 221, 223, 231, 236, 238; Indian people, 204, 260; labour tenants, 9, 22, 39, 91, 95, 108, 109, 129, 136, 150, 152, 153–4, 157, 169, 175–6, 183, 201, 204, 259, 264–5, 270, 278; middle class, 9, 15, 16, 62, 63, 74, 77, 78–81, 86, 117, 142, 154–5, 219, 231, 237, 246, 261; migrant labourers, 157, 231; mine workers, 140, 216, 218; policemen, 85, 248; reserve-dwellers, 80, 109, 111, 112, 176, 179, 198, 221, 223, 229, 231, 234–5, 236, 272; rural Africans, 2, 12–13, 16, 89, 104–5, 110, 112, 127, 136–7, 139, 151, 169, 183, 196, 204, 246; sharecroppers, 269; traditionalists, 19, 103, 218, 227, 232, 237, 239, 261; urban blacks, 2, 6, 8, 12, 25, 69, 72, 81, 92, 105, 115, 117, 136, 137, 139, 141, 142, 168, 173, 302n22, 312n152; whites, 14, 84, 85–6, 78, 96, 114, 162, 182, 260, 306n76, 306n77; women, 19, 89, 110, 139, 142, 153, 154, 229, 233–4; youths, 88, 112, 200, 201, 223, 266
ICU's unpopularity: among Advisory Board members, 150; *AmaRespectables*, 86, 97, 98, 150; chiefs, 48, 97–9, 109, 111, 112, 150, 198, 202, 238; 'coloured' people, 96, 260; Congressmen, 98, 150, 307n80; elders, 202, 266; farm workers, 84, 198, 218, 264; headmen, 112; Indian people, 260; labour tenants, 105, 163, 248, 274; migrant labourers, 198, 218, 264; reserve-dwellers, 153, 241; rural Africans, 99, 273–4; 'school people', 237, 239, 263; sharecroppers, 120, 163, 262–3, 273, 336n37; traditionalists, 19, 95–7, 163, 241, 244, 261; urban blacks, 164; women, 11, 19, 90–1, 202, 260–1
ICU *yase* Natal, 240, 252–3, 254, 260; beer boycotts and, 247, 248, 250; black opposition to, 211–12, 248, 334n18; formation of, 101, 337n57
ICWU (Industrial and Commercial Coloured and Native Workers' (Amalgamated) Union of Africa), 3–6, 96
ideology: African National Congress, 3, 17, 72, 81, 83, 115; defined, 303n40; 'derived' and 'inherent' ideas meshed in, 94, 127, 143, 153–5, 230, 243, 259. *See also* ICU ideology
Idutywa, 240
igoso, 46, 47, 202
IICU, *see* Independent ICU
impundulu, *see* lightning
Independent ICU, 174, 240, 242, 243, 244
Independent ICU of the Transkei, 240
Independent Independent ICU, 255
Industrial Conciliation Act (1925), 9, 162, 171, 172
Indian people, 237; Africans and, 260, 330n68, 335n30; as property owners, 72, 204, 260; as workers, 189, 191, 281n7
Industrial Workers of Africa, 78, 92
industry, *see* manufacturing
Inkatha ka Zulu, 98
intellectuals, 79, 80, 275. *See also* middle class
IWA, *see* Industrial Workers of Africa
Ixopo, 60, 106

Jabavu, Alexander, 11, 67, 86, 295n6
Jagersfontein, 186
Jingoes, Jason: background, 46, 66, 71, 73, 77,

297n24; as political activist, 135, 137, 163, 164; post-1930, 334n31; unpopularity, 273
Johannesburg, 66, 72, 161, 184, 221, 334n21; ICU head office, 12, 132, 136, 141, 142, 168; resistance, 137, 173; rural blacks and, 40, 177, 243
Joint Councils, 66–7, 167, 174

Kadalie, Clements, 200, 337n61; avoids confrontation, 132, 211; background, 71, 73, 79, 154, 295n3, 295n6, 296n9; charisma, 91–2; elitism, 69–70, 85, 90; ICU before 1926 and, 3, 4–5, 6, 11, 91, 96, 314n27; ICU meetings and, 101, 114, 119–20, 126, 164, 165, 217, 235; IICU and, 174; Independent IICU and, 255–6; land question and, 106, 153, 155; liberals and, 20, 102, 162, 173; militarism and, 130, 132; as National Secretary, 12, 14, 163; nationalism and, 142, 152, 174, 260, 280n3, 306n76, 330n68; perceived as liberator, 25, 62, 91, 105, 137, 155, 172, 183, 237, 244, 277, 301n13, 329n57; unpopularity of, 117, 182, 256, 273; victimization of, 75, 137, 175; whites' perceptions of, 159, 166, 181
Kalkfontein, 254–5
Kemp, General: as Minister of Agriculture, 31, 172, 173
Kentani, 240, 242, 243, 244
King William's Town, 8, 256
Kinross, 151, 156, 157
Klerksdorp, 164
Kokozela, Joe, 178
Kopolo, chief, 109, 110
Kranskop, 85, 195, 209; chiefs, 97, 99, 109–10; repression, 97, 207, 210, 211; resistance, 200, 201
Kroonstad, 91, 334n21
 repression, 187
 resistance: female, 69, 260, 335n31; over rates, 69, 81, 115, 163, 309n116; rural, 4
Kumalo, Charles, xii, 11, 81, 95, 108, 119, 250, 335n30

la Guma, James, 275, 298n48
Labase, Donald, 149
labour, migrant, *see* migrant labour
labour, non-migrant, *see* domestic servants; dock workers; farm workers; manufacturing; white wage-earners
labour control, *see under* farmers; legislation; passes; taxes; violence
'labour farms': labour tenant advantages on, 189–90; 'progressive' farmers and, 55–6, 169, 171, 191, 193; resistance on, 199, 265, 322n34
Labour Party, 8, 9, 67, 120, 173, 175, 210, 282n13
labour shortages, 44, 58; farmers and, 44, 68, 157, 177, 292n73, 314n31; farmers' concessions due to, 18, 168–9, 179, 180, 184, 264, 269; mining capital and, 166, 177, 292n73
labour tenants: children, 37–46 *passim*, 50, 57, 121, 146, 190; chiefs and, 48, 97, 202; Christianity and, 21, 49, 195; conditions, 21–2, 36–41, 45, 61, 95, 169, 189; contracts, 37, 41, 56, 121, 128, 169, 178, 179, 211, 307n92; division of labour, 37, 38; passes and, 38, 40, 41, 52, 55, 150, 151; relations of exploitation, 22, 37–41, 51, 53, 56, 60; resistance, *see* labour tenants' resistance; 'squeezing' of, 9, 55–8, 60, 62, 145, 146, 153, 189, 190, 192–3, 249, 265, 334n22; stock, 38, 40, 55, 56, 190 (*see also* cattle; fowl; goats; horses; sheep); subcultures, 40, 42, 45–8, 61, 109, 194–5, 199; urban links, 21, 40, 165, 177, 189, 195, 291n58; wages, 40, 41, 146, 169, 190, 193, 200, 290n55; women, 37–41 *passim*, 44, 45–6, 146, 155, 194, 200, 201, 250, 255
labour tenants' resistance, 19, 137, 138, 264, 265; anti-evictions, 204, 205, 206, 207, 209, 271–2;

anti-passes, 54, 151; day-to-day, 37, 40, 43, 49–52, 54, 189; 'insubordination', 18, 155, 156, 164, 201, 206, 207, 267, 272; refusal to work, 54, 105, 197, 198–9, 200, 209, 210, 266, 267, 268, 270; by women, 202, 335n31; by youths, 38, 50, 54, 57, 61, 201
Lady Frere, 240
Ladysmith, 132, 332n5, 334n21
land: African-owned, 59, 64, 67, 68, 89, 103, 107, 109, 164; company-owned, 23, 35, 152, 175, 278; Crown, 23, 57, 103, 148, 152, 263; dispossession of Africans, 2, 23, 34, 35, 56–7, 61, 67, 105, 106, 107, 146, 152, 183, 193, 257 (*see also* evictions; labour tenants; proletarianization); mortgaging of, 26–7, 39, 83, 190, 191, 287n18; values, 23–4, 55, 56, 57, 190
Land Amendment Bill (Natives, 1926), 34, 57–8, 59, 61–2, 138, 334n22
Land Bank, 33,, 287n18
land hunger: black, 34, 35, 37, 46, 49, 62, 101, 148, 189, 194, 199, 265, 268, 276; white, 23, 24
land question: Congress and, 151; 'derived' solutions to, 82–3, 104, 105; farmers and, 59; ICU and, *see under* ICU ideology; IICU and, 174; importance of, 16, 34, 81, 168, 276; 'inherent' solutions to, 4, 34, 51, 104, 105, 113, 152, 199, 252
landlords, *see* farmers
Langalibalele, 108, 187
le Fleur, Abraham, 325n10, 327n38
legislation, 165; labour control and, 9, 32, 52, 53–4, 120, 138, 162, 171, 172, 173, 200, 202, 203, 264, 337n55; land dispossession and, 23, 35; middle class affected by, 67, 75, 298n39; political dissent curbed by, 114, 149, 169, 175, 253; urban control and, 67, 75, 247, 248. *See also individual Acts*
leprosy, 152, 219
Lewis, Ethelreda, 20, 161, 173, 182, 184, 315n44
liberalism, 83, 113, 121–3; ambiguities of, 258; economic, 44–5, 53, 60, 119, 120–1, 143, 169, 178, 180, 181, 183, 269, 307n92; middle class and, 66, 74; state and, 58, 135
liberals, 315n44; ICU and, *see under* ICU; middle class and, 74, 122; reform and, 9, 120, 121, 161–2, 181, 184, 307n92, 318n87; rural organization opposed by, 20, 162, 173, 184, 274–5. *See also* Ballinger; Holtby; Lewis
Lichtenburg, 164, 167, 174, 182
lightning, 224–9 *passim*, 235, 327n29
Lindley, 43, 76
Liquor Act (1928), 247, 248
locations, *see* reserves
London, Jim, 80, 296n9
Lonsdale, 189, 204
Lovedale, 65, 66, 72
Lusiba, July, 50, 51, 152
Lusikisiki, 218, 223; millenarianism, 227, 230, 232–3, 236; resistance to taxes, 231, 235; under-class organization, 219, 221, 238, 240, 241, 328n46, 331n80
Lydenburg, 146, 147, 149, 159; resistance, 156, 254–5, 334n22

Mabilu, S., 254, 255
Mabodla, Elias, 240, 242, 244
Madeley, Walter, 173, 210, 282n13
Madoda Azibozo, *see* Jabuvu, Alexander
Maduna, Alex, 73
Mafeking, 165
magic, 91–2, 217, 238, 243, 267. *See also* witchcraft
Mahomed, Abdul, 149
Maine, Kas, 50, 51, 165, 262
maize, 193, 232; harvests, 220–1, 239; labour

demands, 157, 168–9, 177, 194, 197; price, 29, 62; profitability, 26, 61, 175; 'progressive' farmers and, 128, 156, 175; resistance and, 197–8, 200, 265; as staple, 190, 194, 197, 220–1; tenants and, 56, 146, 153
Majola, Moses, 43, 190, 204
Makanya, Ignatius, 195, 204, 322n40
Makatshwa's Choir, 141, 142
Makume, Ndie, 43, 62, 263
Makwassie, 139, 164, 334n21
Malatji, Robert, 254, 255
Malaza, Joseph, 73, 151, 161, 163, 183
Manapa, Voetganger, 58, 277
Mancoe, John, 162, 295n8
Mandela, Nelson, xi, 276
manufacturing, 9, 41, 184, 192, 285n45; agriculture and, 31, 32, 45, 59–60, 270, 288n31, 292n75; growth, 8, 60, 171, 219, 282n19; labour, 9, 40, 44, 45, 59, 281n7
Maqolo, Edward, 239, 244
Marico, 181
Martens, James, 192, 209, 211
Masabalala, Samuel, 5, 6
Masike, Phillip, 39, 103
Masters and Servants Acts, 52, 53–4, 138, 173, 200, 202, 203, 264
Mathuloe, Israel, 107, 164
Maxexe, Charlotte, 4
Mazibuko, Lot, 168, 169, 170, 178
Mbeki, Thomas, 73, 90–1; Communist Party and, 78, 116, 298n48; corruption, 163, 174, 318n77; meetings and, 91, 92, 102, 126, 153; in Middelburg, 149, 153, 154, 155
Mcunu, Nathaniel, 106
Mdhlalose, Trifinah, 103, 108
Mdingi, Leonard, xii, 227, 228, 230, 233
Mdletye, Enoch, 221–2, 230
Mdodana, Reverend Filbert, 223–4, 229, 230, 238–9, 240, 327n26, 330n68
Melmoth, 105
Memel, 187
merchant capital, 64; agriculture and, 25, 26, 31, 33, 157, 175, 191, 207; peasants and, 40, 221, 234; reform and, 66; resistance and, 5, 176–7, 179, 215, 230, 236, 242
Mfengu, 84, 218, 264
Mgetyana, Bertie, 223, 229, 235, 238
Middelburg: agrarian economy, 146, 147, 148, 153; repression, 149, 150, 159; under-class mobilization, 153–5, 175
middle classes: alliance with under-classes, 9, 15, 16, 62, 63, 66, 74, 78–81, 86, 117, 142, 154–5, 219, 231, 237, 246, 247, 261; defined, 295n2; elitism, 65–6, 69–70, 81–5, 86, 132, 133, 141, 237–8, 263, 299n61, 310n125; Garveyism and, 77, 214, 215; nationalism and, 2, 15, 75–6, 94, 239; pressures on, 9, 64–5, 66, 70, 74–5, 78–9; proletarianization and, 16, 63, 67–9, 71–4, 80–1; reform and, 66–7; segregation and, 9, 82; separatist churches and, 76; Wellington movement and, 217–18, 243. *See also AmaRespectables*; mine clerks; petty bourgeoisie; teachers; traders
migrant labour, 58, 213, 214; agriculture and, 36, 134, 146, 147, 156, 157, 169, 193; chiefs and, 3, 48; families of, 79, 249; opposition to, 3, 115, 242; reasons for, 219, 230, 242; resistance, 47, 157–8, 198, 218, 247, 248, 250–2; rural links of, 5, 19, 59, 221, 229. *See also* dock workers; mine workers; reserves
millenarianism, 197, 243, 259; abnormal conditions and, 153, 214, 221; American liberators and, 19, 212, 215–19, 222, 226–30, 236–7, 242, 244; Christianity and, 76, 124; movements and, 213, 231, 239, 241, 258, 324n1, 325n9, 325n10; rituals

and, 231–5, 238, 329n57. *See also* Christmas Day; Wellington movement
mine clerks, 70, 76, 79, 216
mine workers, 203, 221; black, 85, 122, 215, 281n7; exploitation as perceived by intellectuals, 14, 76, 78, 79, 117, 118, 141, 242; Mozambican, 9, 177; organization desired, 3, 14, 218, 264, 284n31; political activists from 46, 73, 78; Rand Revolt, 8, 67, 168; state and, 58, 166; tenants and, 40, 177, 291n57; white, 8, 186
mining capital, 64, 96, 113, 238; agriculture and, 33, 152, 192, 207; Chamber of Mines, 76, 167–8, 174, 184; chiefs and, 3, 99; labour shortages and, 166, 177, 292n73; reform and, 66, 167–8, 174, 184; state and, 44, 58, 165, 166, 184
mission churches, *see under* churches
mission reserves, 64, 67, 103, 106, 111, 194, 261; under-class mobilization in, 80, 109, 155
Mkhize, Bertha, 10, 110, 117, 136
Modiakgotla, Conan Doyle, 64, 68, 165, 166, 167, 296n9
Mogaecho, James, 68
Mogorosi, Johannes, 81
Mokgatle, Naboth, 46, 48
Mooi River, 207, 337n61
'moral panic', 158, 159, 183, 269
Moroe, Ishmael, 172, 178
Moroka, 101
Moshoeshoe, 96, 101
Moshoko, Josiah, 80
'Mote, Keable, 127–8, 260; background, 70, 131; conservatism, 133, 163, 166, 167; meetings and, 67, 77, 89, 92, 111, 113, 124, 165, 329n57; victimization, 75, 166, 187
Motha, Jacob, 42, 153, 155
Mount Ayliff, 227, 231
Mount Fletcher, 240
Mount Frere, 240–1
Mozambican labourers, 9, 44, 177
Mpande, 96
Mpanza valley, 195, 209
Mpetha, Oscar, 240, 277
Mpondo, 110, 213–41 *passim*, 257. *See also* Pondoland
Mqayi, Dorrington, 242
Msane, Herbert, 78
Msimang, H. Selby, 3, 4, 6, 67, 282n13, 295n6
Mtamo, chief, 99, 109–10
Mthembu, Nokwala, 106, 280n4
Mthimunye, Rose, 152, 155, 278
music, 142, 258, 312n155. *See also* songs
Mvunelo, James, 219, 227, 233

Natel: agrarian economy, 29, 34–6, 39–40, 59, 203, 215, 225, 265; ICU (*see also* ICU yase Natal), *see under* ICU
Natal Agricultural Union, 32, 58, 205, 211; ICU and, 59, 129, 202
Natal Native Congress, 215, 252
Nationalist Party, 159, 168, 181, 205, 210, 255; constituency of, 8, 41–2, 67, 180, 210
Native Adminstration Act (1927), 75, 114, 149, 169, 175, 298n39
Native Advisory Boards, *see* Advisory Boards
Native Affairs Department, *see* state
Native Service Contract Registration Bill (1929), 337n55
Natives Land Act (1913), 23, 35
Natives Land Amendment Bill, *see* Land Amendment Bill
Natives Urban Areas Act (1923), 67
NAU, see Natal Agricultural Union
Ndebele, 153, 157
Nelspruit, 146, 147, 151, 152, 153

Newcastle, 247
Ngcobo, Abel, 80
Ngcobo, Elijah, x–xi, 89, 104, 108, 112
Ngcobo, James, 69, 85, 110, 211
Ngomane, Hoyi, 103
Ngotshe, 52, 150, 315n41
Ngqeleni, 240
Nguni, 225, 226, 235, 243
Nhlabathi, Lucas, 91, 183
Nhlapo, Jacob, 79
Nkandla, 92, 305n64
Nkosi, Diniso, 151, 152
Nkosi Sikelel' iAfrika, 125, 137, 151, 154, 328n46
Nkumane, Vusi, x, xii
Nobulongwe, chief, 223, 229, 233
Nomsuka, Lenze, 223, 224, 229
Nonquase, 238, 328n52
Nourse, Louis, 201, 202
Nqamakwe, 240, 244
Nqandela, Lucas, 42, 91, 96, 266
Nqutu, 305n64
Ntsikana, 242
Nxumalo, Norman, 152
Nyasaland, 3, 96, 280n3, 306n67
Nylstroom, 176, 177, 178, 179, 180
Nzula, Albert, 70, 295n8, 298n48

Onderstepoort Laboratory, 171, 172–3, 182
Ons Vaderland, 159, 180
Orange Free State: agrarian economy, 29, 36, 39–40, 56, 289n42; ICU in, *see under* ICU; ICWU in, 3, 4, 5

Pact government, 8–9, 210; middle class and, 9, 62, 72, 74, 75; 'progressive' farmers and, 32–3, 53, 58, 270; wages and, 32, 68, 72
Pan-Africanism, 78, 126, 142, 149
paramount chiefs, *see under* chiefs
Parys, 68, 186–7, 311n134, 334n21
passes:
  exemption from, 65, 67. 73, 75
  labour control and, 40, 41, 48, 52, 55, 75, 150, 151, 164, 171, 180
  opposition to: ideological, 3, 81, 83, 115, 122, 124, 130, 131, 164, 167, 174, 175; legal, 135, 137, 138, 161; under-class, 2, 54, 80, 148, 150, 151, 153, 156, 164, 176, 183
  reform and, 53, 135
  repression and, 75, 110, 135, 149, 150, 159, 270, 311n134
  'specials', 55, 150, 151
  trek, 38, 155, 180, 290n49, 334n22
paternalism, 43–4, 263
peasants, 2, 13, 180, 213, 276; consciousness, 105, 194, 223, 241, 244, 267, 338n66; merchant capital and, 40, 221, 234; pressures on, 60, 61, 194; struggles of, 22, 80, 188, 242. *See also* Pondoland; sharecroppers; 'squatters'
petty bourgeoisie: 'new' sector, 70–2; self-employed, 63, 67–9, 70, 72, 75; use of term, 15–16, 63, 295n1; white, 68, 71. *See also* middle classes
Phoofolo, Abe, 163, 172, 295n3
Pietersburg, 164
Pietermaritzburg, 132, 207, 211
Piet Retief, 146, 152, 160, 320n13, 334n21
pigs, 38, 107, 119, 225, 234, 327n33, 327n34; killing of, 212, 218, 225–33 *passim*, 237, 238, 241, 329n56, 329n57; lard, 225–33 *passim*
Pilgrims Rest, 146, 152
ploughs, 57, 178, 221, 294n113
police, *see under* state
political economy, 8–9, 94, 96, 256–7. *See also*

agriculture; capitalism; manufacturing; merchant capital; mining capital; state
Pondoland: chiefs, 14, 220, 223, 229, 231, 238, 240, 241; middle class, 219, 231, 237–8; migrant labour, 193, 198, 213, 214, 218, 222; millenarianism, 215, 218, 221, 226–39 *passim*; political economy, 213–14, 219–21, 231, 239; separatist churches, 214, 215, 223, 230, 231, 237; taxation, 219–20, 231, 235, 238; under-class mobilization, 219, 221–4, 229, 234–5, 237
'poor whites', 27, 31, 57, 60, 179, 181; competition with blacks, 9, 68, 72; state and, 8, 33, 165
Port Elizabeth, 5, 8
Port St Johns, 221, 230, 240, 330*n*73
Potchefstroom, 164
Pretoria, 176, 183
primitive accumulation, 26, 59, 119, 193; resistance and, 22, 266, 276. *See also* land; proletarianization
productive forces, *see under* agriculture
'progressive' farmers, 190–1; alliances with chiefs, 97, 98–9; characteristics, 29, 31, 33, 59–60, 175, 265, 287*n*24; ICU leaders and, 18, 119, 120–1, 184, 307*n*92; ICU not recognized by, 180, 181–2, 309*n*116; ICU opposed by, 6, 22, 97, 98–9, 121, 209–10, 259, 268–9, 270; ICU recognized by, 128–9, 169–70, 177–81, 183–4, 269–70; labour and, 36, 39, 43–4, 146–7, 156–7, 177–8, 189, 193; 'labour farms' and, 55–6, 169, 171, 191, 193; labour tenants and, 51–2, 55–6, 60, 178; reform and, 43, 44–5, 59, 269–70; state and, conflicts between, 32–3, 58–9, 60, 158, 200, 203, 205–7, 208–9, 210, 288*n*30, 288*n*31; struggling farmers, alliances with, 209–10, 269; struggling farmers, conflicts with, 18, 32–3, 121, 129, 170, 179, 269, 270. *See also* liberalism; paternalism; sheep; sugar industry; wattle industry
proletarianization: acceptance of, 113; chiefs and, 103, 147; farmers and, 17, 60; middle class and, 16, 63, 67–9, 71–4, 80–1; as process, 16, 59, 61; resistance and, 17, 60, 61, 118, 201; struggle against, 12, 16, 17, 35, 61, 148, 188, 199, 242, 243, 245; tenants and, 60, 146, 147, 189. *See also* primitive accumulation
protest, *see* resistance

Qulusi, 100
Qumbu, 240

Raath, Marthinus, 39, 55
racism, 70, 102, 260, 335*n*28; towards 'coloured' people, 96, 260, 330*n*68; farmers and, 41–3, 129, 181, 182, 201, 291*n*67; towards Indian people, 330*n*68
Ramonti, Theo, 149
Rand, *see* Witwatersrand
Rand, Isaac, 157, 158
recruited workers, *see* farm workers, migrant labour
reform: liberals and, 9, 120, 121, 161–2, 181, 184, 307*n*92, 318*n*87; middle class as object of, 66–7; 'progressive' farmers and, 43, 44–5, 59, 128–9, 169–70, 177–81, 183–4, 269–70; state and, 9, 32, 53, 67, 68, 72, 168; trade unions and, 162, 170, 171–2, 179, 181, 271, 303*n*44; wages and, 8–9, 32, 44–5, 68, 128, 166, 168, 173, 179
Reitz, 79, 186
rent-paying tenants, *see* 'squatters'
repression: by farmers, day-to-day, 21, 40, 49; via courts, 52, 54, 107, 121, 193, 202, 264; by state, 217, 250, 253, 255. *See also* state response to ICU; *see under* farmers; reserves; violence; and *see under individual districts*
reserves, 96; chiefs and, 35, 48, 111, 214, 215, 241, 271; conditions, 34, 59, 61, 147–8, 195; farm

workers and, 46, 61, 176, 193, 203; ICWU and, 3; repression in, 110–11, 212, 217, 221–2, 238–9, 253, 306*n*67; under-class mobilization in, 107–12 *passim*, 155, 174, 176, 198, 217–18, 219, 221–3, 240–4, 254, 305*n*64. *See also* Dunn's reserve; migrant labour; mission reserves; Transkeian Territories; Sekhukhuneland, Umvoti; Witzieshoek
resident workers, *see* labour tenants
resistance: ambiguous trajectories of, 16, 61, 199, 267–8; anti-dipping, 156; anti-eviction, 81, 135, 204–9 *passim*, 254–5, 263, 271–2; anti-mission churches, 49, 155, 195, 200, 212, 230; anti-passes, 2, 54, 80, 135, 137, 138, 148, 150, 151, 153, 156, 161, 164, 176; anti-proletarianization, 12, 16, 17, 35, 61, 80, 105, 148, 188, 199, 242, 243, 245, 334*n*22; anti-taxes, 25, 156, 189, 198, 200, 226, 231, 235, 238; anti-traders, 176–7, 179, 230, 242; cattle-maiming, 2, 50, 207, 268; crops and, 262; day-to-day, 37, 49–52, 177, 200, 202, 212, 335*n*31; droughts and, 25, 164, 210–11, 220–1, 239, 257; 'insolence', 156, 164, 199–200, 268; land and, 4, 37, 80, 112, 137, 138, 148, 199, 267, 303*n*40; political, other, 80, 151, 154–5, 206, 240–1; primitive accumulation and, 22, 266, 276; proletarianization and, 17, 60, 61, 118, 201, 266; rural Africans and, 1, 275; theft, 51, 53, 112, 148, 177; urban, 2–3, 4, 5, 6, 69, 80, 81, 115, 128, 137, 154–5, 173, 242, 247, 248, 250, 252, 256, 335*n*31; violence and, 5, 47, 148, 151, 157–8, 177, 201, 208, 247, 250, 253, 266, 272; wages and, 4–5, 6, 40, 80, 115, 128, 146, 155, 157–8, 165–7, 171, 176–7, 197–8, 199, 209, 242, 268. *See also* Bambatha; boycotts; ICU; millenarianism; riots; strikes; work stoppages
Rhodesia, 79, 110, 157, 306*n*67
Riotous Assemblies Act, 253
riots, 2, 5, 6, 128, 157–8
rumours, 62, 105, 106, 137, 160, 187, 237
rural Africans, 4
    attitudes to organizing held by: black intellectuals, 1, 3–4, 15, 276, 284*n*31; liberals, 20, 162, 173, 184, 274–5; socialists, 1–2, 276, 282*n*13
    intellectuals and, 79, 80, 275
    resistance inhibited, 1, 275
    separatist churches and, 49, 195, 214, 215
    urban areas, links with, 5, 19, 21, 40, 59, 105, 165, 177, 189, 191, 195, 221, 229, 243, 291*n*58
    see also farm workers; reserves
Russian Revolution: impact on dominant classes, 1, 33, 97, 181, 205; impact on under-classes, 5, 115

SAAU, *see* South African Agricultural Union
schools: 'American', 217, 244, 331*n*73; farm, 43, 49, 299*n*52; mission, 65–6. *See also* education; Lovedale
Schweizer-Reneke, 334
segregation, 9, 22, 242; farmers and, 58, 180, 181; middle class and, 9, 82; 'retribalization' and, 48, 97, 211, 253
Sekhukhuneland, 255, 302*n*23
separatist churches, *see under* churches
Settlers, 176, 179
Shaka, 96, 253
sharecroppers, 43, 50, 83, 265, 289*n*42, 292*n*75; defined, 286*n*6; pressures on, 23, 36, 57, 58, 62, 263; resistance, 36, 262; struggling farmers and, 269; under-class mobilization supported by some, 262, 269; under-class mobilization opposed by some, 120, 163, 262–3
sheep, 6; labour tenants 'squeezed' by increase of, 18–19, 145, 146, 153, 192–3, 265; peasants and,

38, 56, 221, 242; profitability of, 26, 29, 57, 192; resistance and, 50, 51
Sibanyoni, Esther, 40, 50, 153, 261
social democrats, 114, 162, 260, 282*n*13
socialism, 78, 113–18, 141, 143, 306*n*76
Soji, Alexander, 227, 238
Solomon ka Dinizulu: ambiguous alliances of, 98–9, 252–3, 303*n*34, 333*n*16, 333*n*17; paramountcy and, 97–8, 252; under-classes and, 98, 100, 105, 112
songs, 312*n*152, 337*n*59, 337*n*61; protest and, 35, 125–6, 141, 237, 250, 252, 328*n*46; *The Red Flag*, 126, 141, 154; *see also Nkosi Sikel' iAfrika*
South African Agricultural Union, 5, 75, 121, 287*n*21
South African Labour Party, *see* Labour Party
South African Native National Congress, 3. *See also* African National Congress
South African Party, 8, 31, 67, 180, 205, 210, 323*n*44
South West Africa, 110, 306*n*67, 325*n*9
spontaneity: leadership in relation to, 131, 212, 239, 258, 275, 277; resistance and, 200, 264
Springbok Flats, 175, 176, 177, 180, 181
'squatters', 35–6, 148, 191, 263, 265, 289*n*40; defined, 286*n*6; pressures on, 23, 58, 64, 105, 145, 147, 155, 177, 188–9, 193; resistance, 188–9, 194, 254–5, 263, 334*n*22
Standerton: agrarian economy, 146, 269; under-class mobilization in, 91, 148, 161, 183, 311*n*134
Stanger, 132
state, 8, 83–4, 99; agriculture and, 8, 23, 31, 32, 33, 175, 270, 288*n*27, 288*n*29, 288*n*31, 288*n*32; Defence Force, 97, 129, 325*n*11; defined, 138; Department of Agriculture and functionaries, 31, 45, 172, 173, 288*n*27; Department of Labour and functionaries, 168, 171–2, 173; Department of Native Affairs and functionaries, 9, 53, 58, 99, 160, 167–8, 172, 186–7, 192, 199, 205, 317*n*69; farmers' conflicts with, 53–5, 134, 200, 203, 205–8, 270–1; ICU and, *see* state responses to ICU; manufacturing and, 8, 171, 219, 270; mining capital and, 44, 58, 165, 166, 184; 'poor whites' and, 8, 33, 165; 'progressive' farmers' conflicts with, 32–3, 58–9, 60, 158, 200, 203, 205–7, 208–9, 210, 288*n*31; reform and, 9, 53, 67, 68, 72, 241; repression and, 52, 54, 107, 121, 193, 202, 217, 250, 253, 255, 264; reserves and, 110–11, 221–2, 238–9, 253, 254, 255, 306*n*67, 334*n*19; vigilantes and, 166, 186–8, 207–10; white wage-earners and, 8–9, 54, 172. *See also* chiefs; courts of law; Hertzog; legislation; Pact government; segregation
state response to ICU: ambiguities of, 171–2, 207–8, 264, 271; concessionary, 32, 85, 135–6, 151, 153, 166, 168, 171–2, 184, 208, 209, 271; repressive, 199, 205, 208, 221, 306*n*67; via law, 75, 110–11, 114, 131, 135, 137, 138, 149, 150, 159, 173, 200, 201, 205, 206, 210, 222, 238–9, 263, 270, 311*n*134; violent, 6, 131, 151, 172, 207
strikes, 2, 272; black opposition to, 14, 50, 140, 157, 166, 173, 198, 284*n*31, 310*n*125; diamond-diggers', 165–7; farm, 62, 148, 157, 160, 167, 172–3, 197–9, 201, 268; ideological support for, 4, 5, 14, 99, 128, 129, 130, 131, 140, 157, 166–7, 172, 173, 224, 241, 242, 256; urban, 4, 5, 8, 242, 256. *See also* work stoppages
struggling farmers, 27, 36, 41; ICU and, concessions to, 168–9, 170; ICU and, violence against, 179, 209–10; 'progressive' farmers, conflicts with, 18,, 32–3, 121, 129, 170, 179, 269, 270; state and, 8, 33
sugar industry, 29, 57, 192, 208, 288*n*29, ICU and,

84, 98–9, 134, 218; middle class and, 16, 67, 271, 307*n*80; workers, 47, 189, 220
Supreme Courts: farmers' conflicts with, 53, 203, 205; under-class victories in, 111, 135, 206, 262, 310*n*131
Swazi, 151, 152, 160, 313*n*20
Swaziland, 102, 152, 159, 160

Tabankulu, 240
TAU, *see* Transvaal Agricultural Union
taxes, 140; ideological opposition to, 115, 130, 131, 215, 219, 242; labour control and, 41, 159, 219, 242, 270; poll, 43, 189, 197, 200, 220, 221; resistance to, 25, 156, 189, 198, 200, 226, 231, 235, 238
teachers, 64, 66, 154; political activists from, 11, 65, 70, 71, 78–9, 149, 219, 221, 306*n*69; pressures on, 70–2, 75, 297*n*16; training college, 216, 217
tenants, *see* labour tenants, sharecroppers, 'squatters'
Thabu 'Nchu, 305*n*64
Thibedi, William, 78
TNC, *see* Transvaal Native Congress
tractors, 26, 32, 44, 169, 176, 178, 193, 194
traders: African, 16, 68–9, 149, 217, 299*n*61. *See also* merchant capital
trade unions, 134, 306*n*67; black, 3, 4–5, 6; British, 102, 162, 163, 274, 282*n*13; difficulties in countryside, 2, 22, 163, 172, 174, 179, 181–2, 183; Indian, 260; reform and, 162, 170, 171–2, 179, 181, 271, 303*n*44; white, 5, 9, 72, 114, 116, 117–18, 168, 282*n*13
traditionalists, 18, 19, 112–13, 220; consciousness, 35, 46, 95–106 *passim*, 194, 214, 230, 232, 241–5 *passim*, 250–2, 253, 257, 261, 267; defined, 285*n*49; ideological appeals to, 101–3, 239, 242, 243, 261, 303*n*40; modernizers opposed by, 95–7, 163, 241, 244, 261; unity with other social groups, 19, 103, 218, 227, 232, 237, 239, 242–3, 253, 261
Transkeian ICU, 240–1, 244
Transkeian Territories, 246; conditions in, 14, 34, 228, 241, 242; ICU *yase* Natal in, 240; IICU in, 240, 242–3, 244; IICU of the Transkei in, 240; Transkeian ICU in, 240–1, 244; Wellingtonites in, 244. *See also* East Griqualand; Fingoland; Pondoland; and *see individual districts*
Transvaal: agrarian economy, 29, 35, 36, 39–40, 145–8, 163–4, 165, 175, 177, 179, 270, 289*n*40, 289*n*42; ICU and, *see under* ICU; political economy, 18, 184
Transvaal Agricultural Union, 32; ICU and, 62, 175, 179, 180–2, 183, 184, 266; state and, 58, 181
Transvaal Native Congress, 4, 148, 154; ICU and, 150, 151, 152, 164
Tsolo, 240
Tyamzashe, Henry, 72, 82, 295*n*3, 295*n*6

Umtata, 215, 240
Umvoti, 18–19; alliances against ICU, 204–5, 209, 210, 211; labour tenants, 'squeezing' of, 189, 190, 192–3, 194; 'progressive' farmers, 188, 190; repression, non-violent, 203–4, 205, 206, 210, 211; reserves, 188, 189, 193, 194, 195, 198, 204; resistance, 188–9, 193, 194, 197–202, 204–6, 207, 209, 212; state's relationship with 'progressive' farmers, 199, 200, 203, 205–7, 208–9, 210; vigilantes, 185–6, 188, 207, 209–10
United ICU, 254–5, 334*n*22
Unity League, 139, 333*n*13
Universal Negro Improvement Association, 77, 215, 281*n*9. *See also* Garveyism
Upington, 69
upper middle class, *see AmaRespectables*

urban areas: anti-pass resistance, 2, 80; anti-rates resistance, 69, 81, 115; boycotts, 139, 212, 247–8, 250–2, 331*n*44; legislative controls, 67, 75, 247, 248; resistance, general, 25, 137, 154–5, 173, 335*n*31; riots, 2, 5, 6; rural areas, links with, 5, 19, 21, 40, 59, 105, 165, 177, 189, 191, 195, 221, 229, 243, 291*n*58; strikes, 2, 4, 5, 242, 256. *See also* manufacturing; mining capital; *see under* ICU; and *see individual cities*

Ventersburg, 184
vigilantes: black, 139, 311*n*145; white, 135, 159, 160, 166, 186–8, 207–10, 211, 250
Vilikazi, Nkonke, 254
violence; beer boycotts and, 247, 250, 253; farm workers subjected to, 42, 55, 73, 128, 136, 156, 157, 158, 200–1, 211, 270, 322*n*38; farm workers' resistance and, 5, 47, 50, 148, 157–8, 177, 201, 266, 268, 272; farmers' use against dissenters, 97, 108, 179, 186–7, 207, 209–10, 211, 270; fears *re,* 41–2, 62, 132, 160, 207–8, 212, 238, 323*n*56; ideology and, 19, 103, 127, 130, 131, 152–3, 243, 250–2; liberation expected through, 105, 183, 197, 216, 245; rural Africans and, 151; state and, 5, 8, 131, 215, 217, 255. *See also* riots; vigilantes
Volksrust, 146, 150, 168–70, 183
vote, *see* franchise
Vrede, 21, 187
Vryheid, 105, 108, 305*n*65; agrarian economy, 64, 95; ethnicity, 100, 103, 333*n*16; resistance, 132, 303*n*40, 332*n*5

Wage Act (1925), 32, 120
Wage Board, 9, 80, 128
wage earners, *see* white wage-earners
wages: capitalism and, 16, 34, 268; 'civilized', 9, 68, 72; farm workers', 6, 100, 189, 220, 268–9; farm workers' resistance and, 40, 146, 157–8, 171, 176–7, 197–8, 199, 209, 268; ideology and, 3, 14, 69, 81, 113, 118–22 *passim,* 130, 163, 176, 230, 238, 241, 242; increases expected, 161, 197; labour tenants', 40, 41, 146, 169, 190, 193, 200, 290*n*55; land and, 16, 37, 61, 146, 199, 267–8; minimum demanded for farm workers, 3, 6, 120, 128, 157, 169, 178, 309*n*114; reform and, 8–9, 44–5, 128, 166, 168, 173, 179; under-class resistance over, 4–5, 6, 80, 115, 128, 155, 165–7, 242
Wainer, John, 114
Wakkerstroom, 146, 150, 156, 159
Waterberg: agrarian economy, 175–8; reform, 177, 179–80, 181, 183; resistance, 148, 176, 177, 179, 182
wattle industry: boom, 18, 29, 152, 192, 209, 210; companies, 107, 193, 320*n*13; depression, 190, 191, 207; labour tenants 'squeezed' by, 57, 192–3
Weenen, 201; beer boycott, 247, 250; 'labour farms', 189; repression, 207, 208; strikes, 62, 197, 199; traditionalists, 46, 47, 96, 202
Wellington movement: Africanism and, 217, 330*n*68; ICU and, 332*n*85; millenarianism and, 217, 239, 244, 325*n*11, 331*n*73; pigs and, 218, 226;

supporters, 217–18, 241, 243, 244, 328*n*39. *See also* Buthelezi, Wellington
Wepener, 6
white population: ICU, membership or support from, 14, 78, 84, 85–6, 96, 114, 162, 182, 260, 306*n*76, 306*n*77. *See also* farmers; liberals; mining capital; racism; state; trade unions; white wage-earners; women
White River, 148, 149, 159
white wage-earners, 175; farmers and, 55, 157, 160, 210; ICU and, 114, 116, 118, 260; state and, 8–9, 54, 172
Willowvale, 240
Winburg, 162
witchcraft: beliefs in, 224, 225, 226, 228, 232, 235, 243, 244, 245, 327*n*29; diviners, 101, 222, 232. *See also* lightning; magic; pigs
Witwatersrand, 40, 64, 78, 139, 148, 184, 191, 218
Witzieshoek, 39, 305*n*64
women, 113, 164, 273; beer boycotts and, 247–50; discrimination against, 83, 90, 110, 249, 322*n*41; limited mobilization of, 19, 90, 91, 110, 202, 260–1, 282*n*17; mobilization of, 89, 113, 125, 139, 142, 154, 229, 234; mobilization prevented by men, 4, 90, 237; organizations of, 4, 69, 76, 247, 250, 260; reserve-dwellers, 213, 219, 225, 233–4; resistance, 4, 11, 80, 176, 202, 240, 260, 355*n*31; tenants, 37, 44, 45–6, 200, 201, 250, 255; traditionalism and, 45–6, 96, 250, 261; white, 43, 44, 102, 150, 159; work-load, 38, 40, 41, 90, 146, 155, 194
work stoppages, 2, 197–8, 266, 267–8, 270, 271
workers, *see* domestic servants; dock workers; farm workers; manufacturing; mine workers; white wage-earners
Workers' Halls, 141, 142, 162, 251, 252
Workers' Herald, The, 21, 72, 219, 260, 306*n*67; language and, 96–7, 299*n*67; nationalism and, 82, 93, 126
World War, First, 2, 71, 147, 190, 323*n*54; impact on blacks, 66, 77, 214, 217, 251, 252
World War, Second, 256, 331*n*73

Xhosa people, 84, 242, 243

young people: elders, conflicts with, 38, 50, 266; labourers from, 36, 38–9, 48, 190, 193; political activism, 64, 88, 94, 112, 131, 223, 266, 273, 336*n*45; resistance, 38, 50, 54, 57, 61, 176, 180, 200, 201; subcultures, 46, 47, 202, 322*n*40

Zebedelia, 174
Zondi, 188, 322*n*34
Zulu kingdom, 35, 97, 100, 103
Zulu people, 84, 90, 157–8, 222; ethnicity, 97, 98, 100–1, 195, 196, 260, 303*n*40; lightning and, 224–5; pigs and, 225, 232
Zululand, 191; royal family, 98, 226, 227; under-class mobilization, 68, 84, 91, 101, 105, 111, 134, 305*n*64